MW00988942

LEWIS SPERRY CHAFER

♦

SYSTEMATIC THEOLOGY
VOLUME TWO

Abridged Edition

LEWIS SPERRY CHAFER SYSTEMATIC THEOLOGY VOLUME TWO

◆

Abridged Edition

John F. Walvoord, *Editor*
Donald K. Campbell,
Roy B. Zuck,
Consulting Editors

VICTOR BOOKS®
A DIVISION OF SCRIPTURE PRESS PUBLICATIONS INC.
USA CANADA ENGLAND

2 3 4 5 6 7 8 9 10 Printing/Year 94 93 92

Recommended Dewey Decimal Classification: 230
Suggested Subject Headings: BIBLE, THEOLOGY, CHRISTIAN DOCTRINE
Library of Congress Catalog Card Number: 88-60202
ISBN: 0-89693-567-1

For information, address Victor Books,
P.O. Box 1825, Wheaton, Illinois 60189.

VICTOR BOOKS
A division of Scripture Press
Wheaton, Illinois 60187

Part Five

SOTERIOLOGY

DIVINE ELECTION

THE SAVING WORK OF THE TRIUNE GOD

THE ETERNAL SECURITY OF THE BELIEVER

Part Six
ECCLESIOLOGY

THE CHURCH AS AN ORGANISM

THE ORGANIZED CHURCH

THE BELIEVER'S RULE OF LIFE

Part Seven
ESCHATOLOGY

GENERAL FEATURES OF ESCHATOLOGY

MAJOR HIGHWAYS OF PROPHECY

PART • FIVE

SOTERIOLOGY

CHAPTER · 1

INTRODUCTION TO SOTERIOLOGY

Soteriology is that division of systematic theology which deals with the doctrine of salvation. The word "salvation" is the translation of the Greek word *soteria* which is derived from the word *soter* meaning "savior." The word "salvation" communicates the thought of deliverance, safety, preservation, soundness, restoration, and healing. In theology, however, its major use is to denote a work of God on behalf of men, and as such it is a major doctrine of the Bible which includes redemption, reconciliation, propitiation, conviction, repentance, faith, regeneration, forgiveness, justification, sanctification, preservation, and glorification. On the one hand salvation is described as a work of God rescuing man from his lost estate. On the other hand salvation describes the estate of a man who has been saved and who is vitally renewed and made a partaker of the inheritance of the saints. Accordingly Gospel preaching may on the one hand warn the wicked to flee from the wrath to come, or it may attempt to win them by contemplation of those benefits which God's infinite grace provides.

The need of salvation has already been considered in anthropology and hamartiology which described man's present fallen estate. According to Scripture man is doomed because of his fallen nature and because of his participation in Adam's original sin. Salvation therefore gives freedom from the curse of the Law (Gal. 3:13), from wrath (John 3:36; 1 Thes. 5:9), from death (2 Cor. 7:10), and from destruction (2 Thes. 1:9).

In the Old Testament the doctrine of salvation is taught but not with the same clarity as in the New Testament. According to John 1:17, "The Law was given through Moses; grace and truth came through Jesus Christ." The fact that God can provide salvation, however, is clearly taught in the Old Testament as stated in Jonah 2:9, "Salvation comes from the LORD," which may be considered the theme of the entire Bible.

In the progressive revelation of the Old Testament, however, it was not made entirely clear that the coming Messiah would die on a cross for an individual's sins though the concept of substitution and sacrifice permeates the Old Testament. In many cases in the Old Testament, salvation consisted of physical deliverance from one's enemies, and in the Psalms physical deliverance is mentioned more often than spiritual deliverance.

Frequently salvation is linked to the future restoration of Israel and their possession of their land, and spiritual salvation is linked with physical deliverance as in Deuteronomy 30:5-6, "He will bring you to the land that belonged to your fathers, and you will take possession of it. He will make you more prosperous and numerous than your fathers. The LORD your God will circumcise your hearts and the hearts of your descendants, so that you may love Him with all your heart and with all your soul, and live."

This concept is repeated many times in the Old Testament as in Jeremiah 31:33-34, " 'This is the covenant I will make with the house of Israel after that time,' declares the LORD. 'I will put My law in their minds and write it on their hearts. I will be their God, and they will be My people. No longer will a man teach his neighbor, or a man his brother, saying, "Know the Lord," because they will all know Me, from the least of them to the greatest,' declares the LORD." In Ezekiel 36:24-28 the emphasis is on the spiritual change which will take place when Israel is restored. "For I will take you out of the nations; I will gather you from all the countries and bring you back into your own land. I will sprinkle clean water on you, and you will be clean; I will cleanse you from all your impurities and from all your idols. I will give you a new heart and put a new spirit in you; I will remove from you your heart of stone and give you a heart of flesh. And I will put My Spirit in you and move you to follow My decrees and be careful to keep My laws. You will live in the land I gave your forefathers; you will be My people, and I will be your God."

The same thought is summarized in Romans 11:26-27, "And so all Israel will be saved, as it is written: 'The Deliverer will come from Zion; He will turn godlessness away from Jacob. And this is My covenant with them when I take away their sins.' "

The particular promise of salvation is first revealed in God's judgment pronounced on the devil as the serpent in Genesis 3:15, "And I will put enmity between you and the woman, and between your offspring and hers; He will crush your head, and you will strike His heel."

In 12:3 the particular blessing of God and provision for Adam and Eve is a part of the Abrahamic Covenant in which God told Abram, "All peoples on earth will be blessed through you."

God's promise of a redeemer is said to come first through Isaac, not Ishmael (26:2-5), and then through Jacob, not Esau (28:13-15). The promise of salvation through the Messiah does not assure that every individual Israelite will be saved, for this is promised only to a remnant (Rom. 9:27). The statement that "all Israel will be saved" (11:26) refers to their physical deliverance at the second coming of Christ in which saved Israelites will be allowed to enter the millennial kingdom, and unsaved Israelites will be purged out (Ezek. 20:33-38). Similarly only saved Gentiles will be allowed to enter the millennial kingdom (Matt. 25:31-46).

Though not entirely clear in the Old Testament revelation, most expositors recognize that Old Testament saints were born again through faith in the salvation God would supply to the extent that it was revealed to them. Old Testament saints, however, did not experience what Christians do in the present age, namely, being baptized, indwelt, and sealed by the Holy Spirit, things true for every believer beginning at the Day of Pentecost.

In its broadest significance the doctrine of salvation includes every divine undertaking for the believer from his deliverance out of a lost estate to his final presentation in glory when he will be conformed to the image of Christ.

Since the divine objective is so inclusive, the theme of salvation may be considered under three categories: (1) The believer was saved the moment he believed (Luke 7:50; Acts 16:30-31; 1 Cor. 1:18; 2 Cor. 2:15; Eph. 2:8-9; 2 Tim. 1:9). He is completely delivered from his lost estate, cleansed, forgiven, justified, born of God, clothed in the merit of Christ, free from all condemnation, and saved forevermore. (2) The believer is presently being saved from the dominion of sin (Rom. 6:1-14; 8:2; 2 Cor. 3:18; Gal. 2:20; 4:19; Phil. 1:19; 2:12; 2 Thes. 2:13). In this present tense of salvation the believer is divinely preserved and sanctified. (3) The believer is yet to be saved from the presence of sin when he will be presented faultless in God's glory (Rom. 13:11; 1 Thes. 5:8; Heb. 1:14; 9:28; 1 Peter 1:3-5; 1 John 3:1-3). Other passages include all three tenses of salvation (1 Cor. 1:30; Eph. 5:25-27; Phil. 1:6; 1 Thes. 1:9-10; Titus 2:11-13).

In salvation a person contributes nothing except that he puts his faith in Christ. The entire work of salvation is impossible unless a person believes. This salvation may be viewed from two angles.

(1) What may be termed the legal aspect of salvation involves satisfying those unyielding and infinitely holy demands of divine righteousness and divine government which are outraged by sin in its every form. No man can save himself or accomplish the change in his situation by human action. The penalty for man's sinful condition requires so great a judgment that only God could provide it in the substitutionary death of His Son who paid the entire price for sin.

(2) What may be termed the practical aspect of salvation involves all that enters into the estate of a saved person. No one could forgive his own sin, impart eternal life to himself, clothe himself in the righteousness of God, or write his name in heaven. The concept that salvation comes from the Lord is stated in Jonah 2:9 and is repeated in various ways throughout Scripture. The Scriptures reveal that God desired the salvation of sinners so much that He was willing for His own Son to die on the cross for their sin.

In providing salvation for man God reveals His greatest of all motives, His love for lost humanity. Though salvation is most important to the individual, it is infinitely more important to God as it is the expression of His infinite love.

In addition to revealing God's love, three other divine motives in the salvation of the lost are disclosed.

(1) It is written, "For it is by grace you have been saved, through faith—and this not from yourselves, it is the gift of God—not by works, so that no one can boast. For we are God's workmanship, created in Christ Jesus to do good works, which God prepared in advance for us to do" (Eph. 2:8-10). Salvation is the divine undertaking on the basis of pure grace in which no human works or merit may enter. Though salvation is to result in good works, it is never by means of good works.

(2) God is motivated in His salvation of men by the advantage which their salvation will be to them as John 3:36 states, "Whoever believes in the Son has eternal life, but whoever rejects the Son will

not see life, for God's wrath remains on him." The twofold benefit believers in Christ enjoy—that they will not perish and that they receive everlasting life—reveals the extensive character of divine salvation.

(3) Salvation reveals the grace of God. It is God's purpose that believers saved by grace should exhibit His grace throughout eternity as stated in Ephesians 2:7, "In order that in the coming ages He might show the incomparable riches of His grace, expressed in His kindness to us in Christ Jesus." Though angels had seen evidence of the infinity of God's attributes, they were not able to experience His grace. It is a part of the marvel of a Christian saved by grace because he will be the exhibition of divine grace in heaven and throughout eternity to come.

God's purpose that through salvation believers should be made perfect is revealed in many passages (Rom. 8:29; 1 Cor. 15:49; Phil. 3:21; Col. 1:27; 1 John 3:2). Since the most important aspect of biblical proclamation is the way of salvation, those who expound the Scriptures and preach the Word of God should emphasize what the Bible itself teaches, namely, that salvation comes from God through His grace and love. This reveals the character of God in relation to the unsaved as well as the saved. Those who preach the Gospel should emphasize that the plan of salvation is addressed to the unsaved. God has left Christians in the world as a main source of testimony to a lost world concerning salvation in Christ.

There is no greater sin than to misguide a lost soul so that he misses the way of life. As a medical doctor by error could terminate human life, a doctor of souls deals with the greater problem of man's eternal destiny. Presenting God's plan of salvation is a great privilege, and the responsibility to preach this Gospel to every creature is commanded.

The study of soteriology may be pursued under the following main divisions: (1) the Saviour, (2) divine election including the question of for whom Christ died, (3) the saving work of the Triune God, (4) eternal security of the believer including deliverance from the reigning power of sin, and (5) the terms of salvation.

THE SAVIOUR

CHAPTER · 2

THE PERSON OF THE SAVIOUR

The foundation of soteriology is the fact that there is only one Saviour and the only One who in every respect is qualified to save. This involves a twofold declaration: (1) the truth of the person of the Saviour which is properly considered in Trinitarianism and (2) the declaration of the work of Christ on the cross as the ground of salvation. Soteriology is the cornerstone of systematic theology, for it includes the revelation of the extent of salvation for lost humanity and the completeness of the work of Christ on the cross.

In relating the total revelation of Scripture concerning the Saviour, in addition to what has already been considered under Trinitarianism, four important aspects of Christ's person are revealed: (1) Christ's seven positions, (2) His offices, (3) His sonships, and (4) the hypostatic union.

CHRIST'S SEVEN POSITIONS

The spiritual progress of a Christian may be measured by the growth he makes in "the grace and knowledge of our Lord and Saviour Jesus Christ" (2 Peter 3:18). In John 16:14 it is declared that the Holy Spirit will be sent to "bring glory to Me by taking from what is Mine and making it known to you." This includes knowledge of Christ's seven positions.

1. Preincarnate. The preincarnate Christ possessed all the glory and attributes of God. This is revealed in many major passages (Isa. 7:14; 9:6-7; Micah 5:2; Luke 1:30-35; John 1:1-2, 14; Phil. 2:6-8; Col. 1:13-17; 1 Tim. 3:16).

In John 1:1-2 it is revealed, "In the beginning was the Word, and the Word was with God, and the Word was God. He was with God in the beginning." In verse 14 it is added, "The Word became flesh and lived for a while among us. We have seen His glory, the glory of the One and only Son, who came from the Father, full of grace and truth." Though Christ never referred to Himself as the *Logos,* in using this expression the Holy Spirit referred to Christ not only as a rational Person but also as the "Word" or declaration of what God is. Though the Old Testament revealed God in many ways, Christ in His person and work revealed God in a way that could never have been revealed otherwise. Though the attributes of God in themselves are unsearchable and beyond comprehension, Christ has revealed those attributes in ways that mankind can understand. Through Christ one can know the character of God and the infinite attributes He possesses.

Three important truths are revealed by John in his Gospel concerning the *Logos:* (1) Jesus Christ was one with God, and as God He is from eternity (vv. 1-2); (2) Christ became flesh (v. 14); and (3) He ever manifests the attributes of the first Person (v. 18). As such, Christ in His person is revealed to be the adorable, almighty, all-wise, eternal Person who came into the world to be the Saviour of men.

2. INCARNATE. The incarnate Christ, combining in His person undiminished Deity and perfect humanity, is a revelation of the infinite attributes of God as well as humanity in perfection. Though Christ possessed all the attributes of Deity, He added the quality of being man which He, as the second Person of the Godhead, possesses in contrast to the Father and the Spirit. Christ as incarnate continuously reveals both the characteristics of the infinite God and of the perfect Man.

3. IN DEATH. Christ in His death revealed God as He could not be revealed by any other means. The death of Christ revealed the love of God, the righteousness of God, the wisdom of God, and God's method of making possible the redemption of mankind.

4. IN RESURRECTION. The resurrected Christ also revealed the power of God in that Christ achieved His own resurrection, and He also revealed God's plans for the glorification of humanity. Christ in His resurrection achieved a state of revelation beyond anything man could have contemplated about God. In His second coming, Christ will reveal God as "the blessed and only Ruler, the King of kings and

Lord of lords, who alone is immortal and who lives in unapproachable light, whom no one has seen or can see. To Him be honor and might forever" (1 Tim. 6:15-16). The resurrection of Christ was His stepping-stone to returning to glory and being exalted above all.

5. In ascension and headship. Christ has ascended to heaven and is seated on His Father's throne, ministering as Head over all things to the church, and serving as the believers' High Priest, Advocate, and Intercessor (Heb. 7:25). Though Christ is bodily in heaven carrying on His present work, in His deity He is omnipresent, indwelling every believer and present with Christians in every situation. In heaven Christ is glorified as illustrated in His appearance to the Apostle John in Revelation 1:13-18. John fell at the glorified Saviour's feet as one who was dead. In contemplating Christ in His present work Christians should realize that Christ is now the glorified One whom they will see when He returns.

6. The Rapture. Christ's return is anticipated in many Scripture passages as a glorious appearing. To the church He will appear at the Rapture of the church when Christians will see Him as He is (Titus 2:13; 1 John 3:2). To the world He will appear at His second coming to the earth to set up His kingdom, a frequent subject of prophecy in both the Old and New Testaments (Isa. 63:1-6; Dan. 7:13-14; Matt. 24:27-31; Acts 15:16-18; 2 Thes. 1:7-10; Rev. 19:11-16). His return as King of kings is in sharp contrast to His lowly birth in Bethlehem.

7. The Second Coming. Beginning with His second coming Christ will reign forever. He will be King over the earth during the millennial kingdom and then will continue to be in authority in the new heavens and the new earth. In the sense of His political reign during the Millenium He will turn over the kingdom to God the Father once He has destroyed all opposing forces (1 Cor. 15:24-28). In other passages His reign is pictured as everlasting on the throne of His father David (Isa. 9:6-7; Ezek. 37:21-25; Dan. 7:13-14; Luke 1:31-33; Rev. 11:15). A Christian by faith accepts all that Jesus Christ is in time and eternity.

CHRIST'S OFFICES

The title "Christ" in the New Testament as well as the title "Messiah" in the Old Testament imply a threefold official responsibility, that of Prophet, Priest, and King. Each of these offices is involved in the extensive ministry of Christ.

1. Prophet. As the greatest of the prophets, Jesus is the channel of divine revelation in His person and work as well as in His teaching ministry on earth. In contrast to the work of a priest who represents man to God, the prophet presents God's message to man. The work of Christ as a Prophet refers to His major work of preaching the Gospel and illustrating the truth in His person and work.

Distinction may be observed between a prophetic office in the Old Testament and in the New Testament. In the Old Testament a prophet was a reformer or patriot who delivered God's message to the people and at the same time challenged them to serve the Lord. In the New Testament a prophet was a deliverer of the Lord's message as illustrated in the ministry of John the Baptist of whom Christ said, "A prophet? Yes, I tell you, and more than a prophet. This is the one about whom it is written: 'I will send My messenger ahead of You, who will prepare Your way before You' " (Matt. 11:9-10). John the Baptist introduced Christ, "Look, the Lamb of God, who takes away the sin of the world!" (John 1:29) John the Baptist fulfilled in some sense the prophetic office in both the Old Testament and the New Testament, and he was the first prophet to appear in the 400 years since the Book of Malachi was written.

In the Old Testament a prophet was called a "man of God" (2 Kings 1:9), and a "seer" (17:13). As a man of God a prophet was distinguished by his holy life and evident walking with God. As a seer a prophet saw beyond what the natural mind and eyes of man could see. As a prophet he delivered God's message and uttered what he had seen whether the message applied to the present or the future.

Prophets as well as the people in general were charged with the responsibility of keeping the commands of Scripture. In Deuteronomy 4:2 the people of Israel were warned, "Do not add to what I command you and do not subtract from it, but keep the commands of the Lord your God that I give you." Instruction was also given to kings who had reigned in Israel though no king reigned until 500 years after Moses: "When he takes the throne of his kingdom, he is to write for himself on a scroll a copy of this Law, taken from that of the priests, who are Levites. It is to be with him, and he is to read it all the days of his life so that he may learn to revere the Lord his God and follow carefully all the words of this Law and these decrees" (17:18-19). If a matter in the Word of God was not clear the king was to present his problem to the priests and the priests would serve as the king's judges (vv. 8-10).

The Levites were to take custody of the Scriptures and keep them with the ark of the covenant of the Lord (31:26). In contrast to this, however, a prophet of God was responsible for delivering the Word of God to the people orally. All these elements involved in the prophetic office are fulfilled completely in Christ. He is the greatest of the prophets as predicted by Moses (18:15, 18-19).

In the New Testament, prophets were usually involved in a ministry of forthtelling rather than a ministry of foretelling though the latter was sometimes involved. The prophetic office was one of the gifts given to the early church along with other gifts as itemized in Ephesians 4:11, "It was He who gave some to be apostles, some to be prophets, some to be evangelists, and some to be pastors and teachers." Though other gifts are mentioned, a prophet had a special obligation to deliver his message exactly as God had given it to him whether for the purpose of "strengthening, encouragement," or "comfort" (1 Cor. 14:3). The New Testament itself provides written revelation beyond that of either the oral or written ministry of the Old Testament prophets. Prophets, considered second in importance to the apostles, performed a special ministry in the New Testament church before the writing of the New Testament was completed. In Christ was fulfilled all that was possibly involved in the work of a prophet, and Christ claimed this designation for Himself (Matt. 13:57). Those who listened to Him testified to the fact that He was the Prophet who would come (John 6:14).

The prophetic ministry of Christ may be divided into three time periods: (1) Christ in His preincarnate ministry was involved in the revelation of God given in the Old Testament whether as the Angel of *Yahweh* or by other means. (2) The incarnate ministry of Christ provided additional revelation through Christ in His prophetic office. This extensive revelation through Christ is described in 1 Timothy 3:16, "He appeared in a body, was vindicated by the Spirit, was seen by angels, was preached among the nations, was believed on in the world, was taken up in glory." The fact that "He appeared in a body" indicates that, though Christ possesses all God's infinite qualities, He revealed Himself to man in human bodily form. As a man, Christ could thus manifest God to man in human terms.

The words "vindicated by the Spirit" mean that Christ manifested in His human life the perfections of His being. According to John

3:34 the Spirit was given to Him "without limit."

In Christ's incarnation He was "seen by angels." The angelic hosts observed the eternal Son of God with wonder and adoration as He was manifested in his humanity. Christ's being "preached among the nations" refers to the fact that His message went beyond Israel to the world as a whole, which is behind Christ's command to preach the Gospel to every creature. The affirmation that He "was believed on in the world" refers to the fact that though many in Israel rejected Him others did put their faith in Him. The final step was His ascension in which He was "taken up to glory" after He had completed His earthly ministry.

In His incarnate ministry Christ fulfilled the role of a prophet in both foretelling and forthtelling. In His three and one half years of public ministry, of which only a small portion has been preserved in Scripture, Christ delivered God's message to that generation. The Gospels contain major discourses of Christ such as the Sermon on the Mount (Matt. 5–7), His discourse on the seven mysteries revealing the course of the present age (Matt. 13), His answer to the disciples' questions concerning the end of the age (Matt. 24–25), and the Upper Room Discourse (John 13–17) in which Christ revealed the major features of the present age following His return to heaven.

In the Sermon on the Mount Christ stated the ethical principles of the kingdom He was bringing. The Jews had overemphasized the political results of their deliverance from their oppressors but had neglected the spiritual aspects of the kingdom. Though some aspects of the ethical rule of the kingdom will not be fulfilled until the millennial reign of Christ, other aspects of the Sermon on the Mount have present application and many of the truths are abiding since they come from the nature of God. The Sermon on the Mount was not intended, however, to be a declaration of the way of salvation but rather a statement of the ethical principles God expects man to obey.

In Matthew 13 Christ outlined what may be expected between the first and the second comings of Christ, a revelation not given in the Old Testament. The nature of this period was hidden from the Old Testament prophets who viewed the first and second comings of Christ as if they were the same event, and no one in the Old Testament or in the period of the Gospels seems to have comprehended that the First Coming would relate to His sufferings and death and the Second Coming to His glorious reign. After Christ's death and resurrection it became clear that there was a time period between the First and Second Comings, but even then there was little comprehension. Right up to the time of Christ's ascension the disciples were questioning how long this period would be (Acts 1:6-8). Not until Jesus' words in John 14:1-3 was it evident that the coming of Christ for His own in the Rapture of the church will be a separate act of God before the great events that lead up to the Second Coming.

In Matthew 24:1–25:46 Christ answered the questions of the disciples which had arisen concerning Christ's prophecy that the temple would be completely destroyed. The time of this destruction is discussed in Luke 21:7-24. In Matthew 24:3-31 Christ answered the questions related to the end of the age and the Second Coming itself. In this passage general signs are given in verses 3-14. The specific sign of the Second Coming is the Great Tribulation described in verses 15-29 and the Second Coming itself is described in verses 30-31. In 24:32–25:30 Jesus spoke in parables to reveal the practical application of this truth to those who were expecting the second coming of Christ. In many respects, though this passage does not refer to the Rapture, similar applications can be made to those who are waiting for the Rapture. In 25:31-46 Christ gives them more than they ask for in describing His throne in the millennial kingdom and the judgment of the Gentiles in which He separates the sheep from the goats, the saved from the unsaved, in preparation for the millennial reign of Christ. Matthew 24–25 is not dealing with the Church Age which specifically is from Pentecost to the Rapture, but rather with the whole interadvent period from Christ's first coming to His second coming.

In John 13–17, referred to as the Upper Room Discourse, Christ on the night before His crucifixion revealed to His disciples some of the distinctive things that will be true of the present age. In this discourse Christ anticipated the dramatic change that would take place on the Day of Pentecost in the distinctive work of the Spirit and the fulfillment of the purpose of God to call out from Jew and Gentile alike those who would be saved in the present age.

The discourses of Christ were delivered to His generation and yet are distinctly different in their subject matter. Each of them to some extent is prophetic of the future but deals with different subjects in relation to God's program for the world.

Besides being a Forthteller, Christ was also a Foreteller. Much of His messages dealt with the future. Included in His predictions were the immediate actions of individuals, His death, His resurrection, and His ascension. Included also were predictions of the advent of the Spirit (John 14:26; Acts 1:5), the nature of the work of the Spirit in the present age, the distinction of the present age from what precedes it and what follows it, the distinctive character of the church and its Rapture, His second coming preceded by the Great Tribulation, and the judgments on Israel and the Gentiles as well as the introduction of His kingdom's glorious reign. Christ also indicated the future state of both the saved and the unsaved.

Revealed in the New Testament also is the present ministry of Christ in heaven as the believer's High Priest, Advocate, and Intercessor. His messages to the seven churches of Asia (Rev. 2–3) were His final word recorded in Scripture to the churches of the present age. In every respect He fulfilled Moses' prophecy (Deut. 18:15) that a prophet greater than Moses would succeed him.

Christ also fulfilled the office of a prophet in foretelling the future. His discourses had present application but also predicted a future course of events that only God could know. No other prophet in Scripture covers as many subjects as did Christ, and He merits the designation as the greatest of the prophets.

The ministry of Christ continued after He went to heaven. The messages to the seven churches of Revelation 2–3 were a revelation from Christ after His ascension. Revealed also is the continued message of Christ from heaven that He would come again (22:12, 20). Christ continues to reveal prophetic truth through the work of the Holy Spirit in helping believers understand the content of biblical revelation.

2. Priest. Christ fulfilled completely the office of priest. This is foreshadowed in the Old Testament types and is taught in considerable detail in the Epistle to the Hebrews. Christ fulfilled the Aaronic priesthood as one who offered gifts and sacrifices and interceded for the Lord's people. Also His priesthood is compared to that of Melchizedek. Melchizedek was the historical character to whom Abraham paid tithes (7:1). Melchizedek's genealogy is not revealed in Scripture, and his right to priesthood came from direct divine appointment (v. 3). Because Christ fulfilled what was involved in the priesthood of Melchizedek, Christ is presented in Hebrews as greater than Aaron and the Aaronic priesthood (vv. 5-28).

Christ's role as High Priest on behalf of believers in the present age was confirmed at the baptism of Christ when God the Father affirmed that Jesus Christ is His appointed Son (Matt. 3:13-17). At that time Christ also was identified as the promised Son of God and High Priest when the Holy Spirit descended on Him as a dove.

Because Christ was of the tribe of Judah, which was not the priestly tribe, it was necessary for Him to have a special divine appointment similar to that of Melchizedek in order for Him to minister as a High Priest both in offering His sacrifice on the cross and in interceding for the saints from His throne in heaven. Many Scriptures testify that Christ offered Himself as the sacrificial Lamb (Eph. 5:2; Titus 2:14; Heb. 9:14; 10:12). In Hebrews Christ is contrasted, however, to the Aaronic priesthood in that He did not have to offer a sacrifice for His own sins (Lev. 16:6; Heb. 9:7). Also God the Father offered His Son as a sacrifice as anticipated typically in Abraham's offering of Isaac (Gen. 22:1-13), and as confirmed by many Scriptures (Isa. 53:6-10; John 3:16; Rom. 8:32; 2 Cor. 9:15). Christ is also said to have been offered by the eternal Spirit (Heb. 9:14).

The evidence that Christ follows the order of Melchizedek in His priesthood is supported first by the nature of His person. In the Melchizedek priesthood the typological anticipation is revealed in that Melchizedek was a king-priest. As the King-Priest, Christ heads the church which is a holy and royal priesthood (1 Peter 2:5, 9). While Israel had a priesthood in the Aaronic priesthood, the church is a priesthood with every believer a priest. The work of Christ as the believer's Priest is revealed in Hebrews 4:14-16. The fact that the church is a priesthood over which Christ is the High Priest is an encouragement for believers to pray in the name of Christ, and believers can go to the throne of grace in boldness (vv. 14-16).

The present priesthood of the church is contrasted to the Aaronic priesthood and also to the form of priesthood that existed before the Mosaic Law. In the early history of the human race the head of each family operated as a family priest (Gen. 8:20; 26:25; 31:54). When the Mosaic Law was introduced this arrangement was changed and the Aaronic priesthood was substituted. In the present Church Age a further change has been made in that the entire church is constituted of a kingdom of priests (Rev. 1:6). An individual believer by his new birth is entitled to the office of priesthood just as the Aaronic priests were entitled to priesthood by their birth in that family.

As priests, Christians in the present age offer a fourfold sacrifice: (1) their own bodies (Rom. 12:1; Phil. 2:17; 2 Tim. 4:6; James 1:27; 1 John 3:16); (2) praise to God (Heb. 13:15); (3) the sacrifice of good works (v. 16); and (4) sharing gifts of money and service to others (Rom. 12:13; Gal. 6:6, 10; Titus 3:14; Heb. 13:2, 16). In addition to offering these gifts that characterize the priesthood, believers in Christ can be intercessors in their prayer lives (Col. 4:12; 1 Tim. 2:1).

Christ received the priestly office by divine appointment (Heb. 5:5-6, 10). This is also confirmed in the discussion of Christ's being in the order of Melchizedek (6:20). In contrast to the Aaronic priesthood Christ has an eternal priesthood. Like Melchizedek, He did not derive His priesthood from His lineage, and like Melchizedek, there were no descending priests who succeeded Christ. This is stated in Psalm 110:4, "The LORD has sworn and will not change His mind: 'You are a priest forever, in the order of Melchizedek.' " The eternal character of Christ's priesthood is also supported by Hebrews 7:20-28 which points out that He has an unchangeable priesthood and has no successors. The reason for this, of course, is that priests in the Aaronic priesthood were subject to death in keeping with the destiny of all human beings who are mortal. In His resurrection Christ continues His high priestly work (vv. 1-3, 25).

3. KING. Christ also fulfilled the office of King as predicted in the Davidic Covenant. "The LORD declares to you that the LORD Himself will establish a house for you: When your days are over and you rest with your fathers, I will raise up your offspring to succeed you, who will come from your own body, and I will establish his kingdom. He is the one who will build a house for My name, and I will establish the throne of his kingdom forever" (2 Sam. 7:11-13).

The fact that the Messiah would be a King in David's line is taught in many Scriptures. Isaiah 9:6-7 reveals, "For to us a Child is born, to us a Son is given, and the government will be on His shoulders. And He will be called Wonderful Counselor, Mighty God, Everlasting Father, Prince of Peace. Of the increase of His government and peace there will be no end. He will reign on David's throne and over his kingdom, establishing and upholding it with justice and righteousness from that time on and forever. The zeal of the LORD Almighty will accomplish this."

To Mary the prediction was given that her Son would reign forever over Jacob. "You will be with Child and give birth to a Son, and you are to give Him the name Jesus. He will be great and will be called the Son of the Most High. The Lord God will give Him the throne of His father David, and He will reign over the house of Jacob forever; His kingdom will never end" (Luke 1:31-33). In Matthew 2:2 He is spoken of as "King of the Jews." He claimed to be King (27:11). He was recognized as King by some of the Jews (John 12:13). When He died on the cross He died as the King of Israel (Matt. 27:37). He will come again not only as the King of Israel but as Lord of all kings (Rev. 19:16). Recognition of Christ's three offices of Prophet, Priest, and King are integral to Christian theology and faith and describe not only His person but also His work in the past, present, and future.

THE SONSHIPS OF CHRIST

In Scripture Christ is presented as having four sonships while He was on earth.

1. Son of God. Christ is presented in Scripture as the Son of God. The meaning of this title has been debated in theology, and various attempts have been made to explain it.

Some believe that He became the Son of God by virtue of His incarnation in which Deity and humanity were united in one Person. This implies that He was not the Son of God before the Incarnation. Another view is that He became the Son of God by baptism, because at His baptism the Father declared, "This is My Son, whom I love; with Him I am well pleased" (Matt. 3:17). This point of view, however, has no support in Scripture.

Still another theory is that He became a Son by means of His resurrection. According to Romans 1:4 Christ "through the Spirit of holiness was declared with power to be the Son of God by His resurrection from the dead: Jesus Christ our Lord." This passage, however, declares that the resurrection of Christ confirmed that He is the Son of God. Added evidence for this point of view is found in Acts 13:32-33 which quotes Psalm 2:7, "We tell you the good news: What God promised our fathers He has fulfilled for us, their children, by raising up Jesus. As it is written in the second Psalm, 'You are My Son; today I have become Your Father.' " The reference to "raising up Jesus" does not refer to the Resurrection but to the fact that Jesus Christ was given by God to the world in His incarnation.

This concept is separated from Christ's resurrection which is mentioned in the next verse. The promise of Psalm 16:10 that Christ would not remain in the grave is quoted in Acts 13:35. The view that Christ became the Son of God by His resurrection wrongly suggests that Christ would not be the Son of God before His resurrection.

According to some, Christ is the Son of God only in the sense that He has that title or official position. This is contradicted by evidence that He is the Son of God in a more real sense.

Still another theory is that He became the Son of God at the exaltation to the right hand of God, a view based on Hebrews 1:3. Like other views, this is refuted by the fact that Christ was the Son of God before His exaltation, and instead was exalted because He is the Son of God.

Another view is that the sonship of Christ was by covenant relationship, but this view too lacks scriptural support and does not explain the biblical references to Christ as the Son of God.

The only view fully sustained by the Scriptures is the fact that the sonship of Christ is eternal. God was eternally His Father and Christ was eternally the Son. This relationship goes back to the relationship of the Trinity in which the Father is the first Person and Jesus Christ is the second Person. This is sometimes referred to as eternal generation. If this terminology is used it is clear that it is not generation in the ordinary sense because Christ's generation is unique and eternal and there never was a time when He was not the Son. The fact that Christ as the Son of God shared the life of Deity with God the Father, however, indicates a relationship that could be described by sonship.

In presenting the concept of Christ as the Son of God the Scriptures do not refer to Him as becoming the Son of God in time. Instead, they refer to Him as the eternal Son of God (Isa. 9:6; John 3:16-17; Gal. 4:4). This is also supported by Psalm 2:7, "I will proclaim the decree of the Lord: He said to Me, 'You are My Son; today I have become Your Father.' " Inasmuch as a decree of God is eternal and God declared Him to be the Son of God, it may be concluded that He was eternally begotten and was eternally the Son.

The eternal sonship of Christ is in harmony with many of the great creeds of the church and is supported by many Scriptures (Matt. 16:13-16; 26:63-64; Luke 2:11, 26, 38; John 1:49; 3:16, 18, 35-36; 11:27; Acts 9:20; Heb. 1:2, 8; 1 John 2:23; 5:9-12). In addressing God, Christ as the eternal Son addressed Him as Father. When speaking from His humanity Christ referred to the Father as His God (John 20:17).

The doctrine of Christ as the Son of God is supported by statements that refer to Christ as the Firstborn (Rom. 8:29; Col. 1:15, 18; Heb. 1:6; Rev. 1:5), that is, as the Heir of all creation because of His resurrection.

Also reference to Christ in His deity is found in the term "only begotten" (Gr., *monogenes*), which is used five times in the KJV (John 1:14, 18; 3:16, 18; 1 John 4:9). The NIV translates the word as "one and only Son." The Greek word, however, does mean "only begotten." The thought is that Christ is the Son of God in a sense that no one else is. This is illustrated in Isaac being called the only son of Abraham (Heb. 11:17) even though Ishmael was born earlier (Gen. 16:15-16; cf. other instances of *monogenes,* Luke 7:12; 8:42). As the only begotten Son of God Christ possesses an eternal relationship to the Father.

2. SON OF MAN. Christ is also called the Son of man about 80 times in the New Testament (e.g., Matt. 8:20; 9:6; 11:19; 12:8). In other instances He is called the Son of David (9:27; 12:23). Another title given to Jesus is the Son of Mary (13:55). Of great significance is the fact that even a Canaanite would apply the term "Son of David" to Him (15:22).

The term "Son of man" is used often in the Gospels because the unique and new factor in the person of Christ was His humanity. He is also called "the last Adam" (1 Cor. 15:45), referring to the fact that He represented the human race in what He did. The title "Son of David" refers to His fulfillment of the Davidic Covenant as the promised Descendant of David who would sit on the throne. In general Christ's first coming fulfilled all that He as the God-Man could do including His prophetic ministry (Matt. 11:19; Luke 19:10), His death and resurrection (Matt. 12:40; 20:18-19; 26:2), and His second coming (24:37-44; Luke 12:40).

The term "Son of man" is also found frequently in prophetic portions of the Old Testament. In Ezekiel alone God addressed Christ by this designation about 90 times. The concept of a man in heaven is also seen in Ezekiel 1:5, 26. The concept of a coming man blessed by God is prominent in the Old Testament (Gen. 1:26; 3:15; 12:2-3; Pss. 8:4; 80:17; Isa. 7:14; 9:6-7; Zech. 13:7). Though conservative theology tends to emphasize the deity of Christ, failure to declare His true humanity is just as destructive to Christian doctrine as denying His deity.

3. Son of David. As the Son of David, Christ is the One prophesied to reign on the throne of David forever (2 Sam. 7:11-13; Matt. 1:1, 6, 20; 9:27; 12:23; 15:22; 20:30-31; 21:9). In a similar way the title occurs in the other Gospels and throughout the New Testament. Christ is seen as the Descendant of David in Revelation 3:7; 5:5; and 22:16. The fact that Christ is called the Son of David shows that part of God's purpose was for Christ to fulfill the promise to David that a Descendant of his would sit on his throne forever.

4. Son of Abraham. The Son of Abraham is another title given to Christ. Just as the term Son of David links Christ to the promise given to David, so the term Son of Abraham relates Christ to the promises given to Abraham (Matt. 1:1; Luke 3:23-34; 19:9). The promise given to Abraham extending to the whole human race (Gen. 12:3) indicates the wide extent of Christ's ministry as the Son of Abraham and forms the basis for the Gospel going throughout the entire earth (Matt. 28:18-20).

THE HYPOSTATIC UNION

The uniqueness of the person of Christ, including all that is God and all that is man apart from sin, is at the heart of all of His work as the Incarnate Son of God. In understanding the Scriptures relating to the Incarnate Christ the interpreter must be constantly diligent on the one hand not to neglect the evidence of His deity and on the other hand not to neglect the essential character of His humanity. It is difficult in some of the acts of Christ to detect how the two natures combine in their activity. Since the hypostatic union was considered at length in theology proper, it is only necessary here to say that the two natures constitute the one and only theanthropic Person, and no one before or after Christ will ever have these characteristics. In attempting to understand what Christ accomplished in His incarnation, knowledge of the person of Christ and the hypostatic union of the two natures is essential to all He did in His life, death, and resurrection.

CHAPTER · 3

INTRODUCTION TO THE SUFFERINGS OF CHRIST

In approaching the subject of the sufferings of Christ, one is impressed that he is standing on holy ground much as Moses did in the presence of the burning bush (Ex. 3:1-6). Though divine revelation has attempted to reveal the infinite truth involved in Christ's sufferings, anyone approaching the subject is soon impressed with human limitations. How can anyone really understand the infinite love of God which motivated the Father to give His Son and the infinite love of Christ which made Him willing to suffer even to the extent of dying on the cross?

Probably no other subject is as essential to the theology and revelation of biblical truth as the fact that Christ suffered and died for the sins of the world. In His sufferings Christ supremely revealed the infinite love of God, the commitment of God to infinite righteousness, and the desire of God to make fallen humanity savable. It was not only a man who suffered, but God was in Christ when the blood of Christ was shed on the cross (Acts 20:28).

In studying this subject one marvels not only at the love of God but also at His omniscience in which He knew fully what would eventuate if God created the world and man in it. If there had been any other way to accomplish God's purpose He would not have required His Son to die on the cross. The fact that He was motivated to offer Christ and that it was absolutely necessary to accomplish salvation reveals God's attributes of love, righteousness, omnipotence, and divine goodness.

The sufferings of Christ may be considered under two headings: (1) the sufferings of Christ in life, and (2) His sufferings in His death. The theological importance of His sufferings in death outweighs the sufferings in His life.

SUFFERINGS IN LIFE

The sufferings of Christ in His life are in keeping with the requirement that the Passover lambs be without blemish, being kept for four days to demonstrate their perfection. In His sufferings in life Christ manifested all the perfection of God's holiness.

The life sufferings of Christ can be classified under three subdivisions: (1) sufferings due to His character, (2) sufferings due to His compassion, and (3) sufferings due to His anticipation of the supreme ordeal of His sacrificial death. His sufferings in life were the proper background for the finished work which He accomplished in dying on the cross.

1. Suffering due to character. Many of Christ's sufferings were due to His holy character in which He was tested beyond what man is normally tested. If Lot was vexed by the wickedness of those in Sodom (2 Peter 2:7-8), how much more must the spotless Son of God have been distressed by living in a world that is so full of the moral darkness and corruption of fallen man. Christ suffered because He is infinitely holy and pure. To live in such an impure world must have been a constant distress to Him. In it all Christ, who knew no sin, was made sin for mankind (2 Cor. 5:21). Because of Christ's holy character there was constant tension between His life and that of the world. Apart from His holiness and deity, He would not have been tested by Satan and hated by the world (Matt. 4:1-10; Mark 1:12-13; Luke 4:1-13; John 15:18-20). His sufferings in the hours preceding His crucifixion no doubt were a part of His substitutionary sacrifice, but apart from His actual death and shedding of blood, there would have been no final answer to the problem of redemption from sin. Isaiah 53:3-11 includes Christ's sufferings leading up to the cross with His actual death on behalf of sinners.

2. Suffering due to compassion. Some of Christ's sufferings were due to His compassion. The psalmist describes the compassion of God. "As a father has compassion on his children, so the Lord has compassion on those who fear Him" (Ps. 103:13).

The miracles of Christ served the double purpose of revealing the compassion of God and the deity of Christ. The Gospels connect His healing ministry with Isaiah 53. "When evening came, many who were demon-possessed were brought to Him, and He drove out the spirits with a word and healed all the sick. This was to fulfill what was spoken through the Prophet Isaiah: 'He took up our infirmities and carried our diseases' " (Matt. 8:16-17). His sufferings in life paved the way to understanding the infinite love of God which would have its final display in the death of Christ.

3. Suffering due to anticipation. Some of Christ's sufferings were due to His anticipation of what the cross would mean to Him. Before His death Christ indicated that He was contemplating the infinite cost of His death on the cross (Matt. 16:21; 17:12, 22-23; Mark 9:30-32; Luke 9:31, 44; John 12:27). In the institution of the Lord's Supper, the sufferings at Gethsemane, and His prayer for the will of God, it is clear that Christ understood fully what would eventuate in His death. In His baptism by John the Baptist, Christ anticipated that His ultimate end would be to suffer and die for the sins of the world. Christ had no need for forgiveness of sin or repentance as baptism sometimes signifies, but it did identify Him with the will of God which would lead to the cross.

The baptism of Christ must be contrasted to John the Baptist's baptizing others who came with repentance, and to the later baptism of Christians in the church today. Each has a distinct character. Though the rite of baptism is commanded, Christians are not baptized because Christ was baptized or because John the Baptist baptized. Christians are baptized because they belong to the body of Christ formed by the baptism of the Holy Spirit which places them in Christ and thereby separates them from the world.

A distinction is sometimes made between active obedience and passive obedience. In reference to Christ, active obedience is illustrated in His perfect life in which He kept every divine requirement perfectly. Passive obedience means that He submitted to the ultimate suffering on the cross. He not only did no wrong but He also perfectly fulfilled every right action. Though Christ presented His own infinitely perfect character to God, He bore the penalty of the sins of the whole world. Salvation is based on the blood of the cross and not on the blood of circumcision or even the sweatdrops of blood which He shed in the garden. Only in His death could He provide redemption, reconciliation, and propitiation.

SUFFERINGS IN DEATH

The centrality of the Cross is acknowledged by all who accept the Bible as the inspired Word of God. To the world the Cross is foolishness (1 Cor. 1:18-19). If in fact Christ did not accomplish redemption for the entire race and did not bear the sins of the whole world, the death of Christ was indeed useless and without result. If the death of Christ accomplished what the Bible said it did, namely, to permit God to be just and at the same time to justify the ungodly who believe, then the Cross is of infinite worth (Rom. 3:26; 4:5; 1 Cor. 1:23-24). To Paul the Cross was supreme, not only in salvation but in his whole relationship to God in contrast to his relationship to the world. Paul stated at the close of his Epistle to the Galatians, "May I never boast except in the cross of our Lord Jesus Christ, through which the world has been crucified to me, and I to the world" (Gal. 6:14). The Cross demonstrated the enormity of the sin of the world and at the same time should stand between the world and its charms and the Christian and his commitment to God. The significance of Christ's suffering in death is essential to the integrity of Christian theology. If the meaning of the Cross as revealed in Scripture is rejected, the whole structure of Christian doctrine falls. Not only is the death of Christ a supreme truth from history, but also it is involved in the life to come. Twenty-four elders standing before the throne will sing a new song, "You are worthy to take the scroll and to open its seals, because You were slain, and with Your blood You purchased men for God from every tribe and language and people and nation. You have made them to be a kingdom and priests to serve our God, and they will reign on the earth" (Rev. 5:9-10). In response the countless number of angels and saints, and all creatures end with the song, "Worthy is the Lamb, who was slain, to receive power and wealth and wisdom and strength and honor and glory and praise! . . . To Him who sits on the throne and to the Lamb be praise and honor and glory and power, forever and ever!" (vv. 12-13)

In connection with the death of Christ certain truths need to be emphasized.

1. The Crucifixion is to be contrasted to the Cross. In itself the crucifixion of Christ, the execution of the Holy Son of God, was the greatest crime man could perform. On the other hand the Crucifixion itself and Christ's dying on the cross is the basis for a Christian's hope of redemption. Though unbelievers may misrepresent the truth as if God the Father was heartless in requiring the death of His Son, the crucifixion of Christ was an act not only of God the Father but also of the Son in which Both for Their infinite

love of the world made possible the redemption that could not be bought in any other way. Though the natural mind with its blindness to spiritual truth may center on the brutality and injustice of the death of Christ, for the believer in Christ the fact that He died is the supreme revelation of His holiness, love, and compassion toward lost humanity.

Though Christ on the cross was faced with the unbelief of the crowd, the Jewish rulers, and those who were crucified with Him, His sorrowing disciples and the one thief on the cross who appealed to Christ to remember him illustrate the wide separation between unbelief and faith in what Christ was accomplishing on the cross. What His disciples saw was beyond their understanding and belief at the time. It seemed to contradict what they had been taught in the Old Testament as well as in the public teaching of Christ. It was not until later that they realized the necessity of Christ's death and His resurrection. In the modern world the cross of Christ also separates those of faith and those of unbelief. It is difficult to comprehend how Christ's death on the one hand was predetermined by God as illustrated in Psalm 22 and Isaiah 53 and at the same time was the act of wicked men who nailed Him to the cross. In his sermon on the Day of Pentecost Peter referred to the crime of the cross. "This Man was handed over to you by God's set purpose and foreknowledge; and you, with the help of wicked men, put Him to death by nailing Him to the cross" (Acts 2:23). On the other hand, Peter said that Christ's resurrection demonstrated the approval of God and the power of Christ over death and the finished work that He accomplished in dying. "But God raised Him from the dead, freeing Him from the agony of death, because it was impossible for death to keep its hold on Him" (v. 24). The transforming power of Christ's death is revealed not as a human tragedy but as divine reconciliation of man to God. The death and resurrection of Christ are counterparts of one divine undertaking in which man has no part.

2. Who put Christ to death? In Scripture both human and divine responsibility were involved in Christ's death. In all, eight individuals or groups are accountable. Four of these are named in Acts 4:27-28, "Indeed Herod and Pontius Pilate met together with the Gentiles and the people of Israel in this city to conspire against Your holy Servant Jesus, whom You anointed. They did what Your power and will had decided beforehand should happen." The fifth responsible individual was Satan, which is brought out in the predic-

tion that Christ would bruise the serpent's head, but in turn His heel would be bruised (Gen. 3:15). The Cross was the ultimate in the mighty conflict waged between Christ and the powers of darkness (cf. John 12:31; 14:30; 16:11; Col. 2:14-15).

The remaining three who are said to be accountable for Christ's death are the Father, the Son, and the Holy Spirit. In the death of Christ God Himself provided the Lamb (Gen. 22:8). As Christ indicated on the cross, there is a sense in which God the Father forsook Christ the Son as He became a sin offering (Ps. 22:1; Matt. 27:46; Mark 15:34). Many other Scriptures indicate that the death of Christ was at the hands of God the Father (Ps. 69:20; Isa. 53:10; John 1:29; 3:16; Acts 2:23; 4:28; Rom. 8:32).

Just as Isaac did not resist his father who was about to sacrifice him on Mount Moriah, so Christ was silent (Isa. 53:7) and asserted that He laid down His life willingly (John 10:15, 17-18). When His work as a sacrifice was complete, Christ commended His spirit to God (Luke 23:46). In His death He gave Himself for the church (Eph. 5:25). Paul stated that Christ gave Himself for Paul (Gal. 2:20). One of the purposes of His death was to redeem us from all sin (Titus 2:14). His purpose in His death was to provide a ransom for many (Matt. 20:28) and to lay down His life for us (1 John 3:16). In His death Christ fulfilled the will of God (Heb. 10:7). The sanctifying power of the death of Christ in the life of the Christian is revealed in 9:14.

3. Suffering from men and the Father. What Christ suffered at the hands of men should be distinguished from what He suffered at the hands of His Father. As illustrated in the death of Christ and the two thieves, human hands might inflict physical suffering and death on one who is crucified, but only God could make Christ a sin offering and place on Him the sins of the world (Isa. 53:6; 2 Cor. 5:21). It was not by human power that the sins of the world were laid on Christ. Even Pilate who gave the order that Christ should be crucified had no authority to make Christ the Sin-Bearer. Though Christ died at the hands of men, He suffered as a sacrifice for sin to the Father. How inscrutable is the fact that God loved the world so much that He was willing to sacrifice His Son and Christ was willing to be that sacrifice.

4. Value of suffering. The value of Christ's sufferings to the Father is also indicated in Scripture. Though difficult to understand, in the death of Christ the problem of the conflict between the love

of God and the justice of God is resolved. Having died on the cross and paid the penalty for sin, God is now free to love and to save those who are unlovely sinners. The grace of God is far beyond the power of men to comprehend. The fact that God can love freely in grace what is unlovely and sinful is beyond human comprehension. The church in the ages to come will manifest the marvel of this grace of God (Eph. 2:7).

5. Wisdom and power of God. The sacrifice of God in Christ on the cross demonstrates both the wisdom and the power of God. In the sacrifice of Christ God is enabled to extend grace on behalf of the lost. His wisdom is demonstrated in the plan of salvation which is utterly beyond human invention to create. The power and wisdom of God is supremely revealed in the fact that "He who did not spare His own Son, but gave Him up for us all—how will He not also, along with Him, graciously give us all things?" (Rom. 8:32) The crucifixion of Christ required the unified action of all three Persons of the Godhead though only Christ could suffer and die on the cross. The Father gave the Son and the Son was offered by the eternal Spirit (John 3:16; Heb. 9:14).

The Father gave the Son, sent the Son, loved the Son, and glorified the Son, and He was Himself glorified by the Son (John 3:16-17, 35; 14:13; Acts 3:13). Though the role of each Member of the Trinity in the death of Christ is different, it is clear that all Persons of the Trinity were involved. The death of Christ involved the Father giving the Son, the Son died, and the Spirit applies the value of that death to those who believe.

6. Two major features. Two major features of soteriology are (1) the finished work of the Saviour on the cross, and (2) the application of that work to those who believe. Both of these factors have been determined from the dateless past and determined by God before the foundation of the world (Eph. 1:4; Rev. 13:8). Also believers in Christ are foreordained to walk in good works (Eph. 2:10). Essential elements of the eternal counsels of God in respect to the church involved the foreordained Saviour, a foreordained salvation, and a foreordained service.

On the cross Christ provided for all men, but the application of what He accomplished is only to those who believe. The unsaved are asked to believe that God has graciously provided a sacrifice in Christ, which is sufficient for a holy God to receive a sinful soul. God has been propitiated, that is, His justice has been completely satisfied, and He is now able to receive the sinner who trusts in Christ to restore in him a measure of holiness even in this world, and ultimately to present him perfect in heaven.

CHAPTER · 4

THINGS ACCOMPLISHED BY CHRIST IN HIS SUFFERINGS AND DEATH

The theme of the sufferings of Christ in death is the ground of all right doctrine and cannot be overestimated as an important central fact in biblical theology. His sufferings and death were a major purpose of His becoming Incarnate. When Pilate said, "You are a King, then!" Jesus replied, "You are right in saying I am a King. In fact, for this reason I was born, and for this I came into the world, to testify to the truth. Everyone on the side of truth listens to Me" (John 18:37). Earlier Christ had said, "For the Son of man came to seek and to save what was lost" (Luke 19:10).

The revelation in Scripture of the meaning of Christ's sufferings may be divided into 14 topics: (1) a substitution for sinners, (2) Christ the end of the Law principle on behalf of those who are saved, (3) a redemption toward sin, (4) a reconciliation toward man, (5) a propitiation toward God, (6) judgment of the sin nature, (7) the ground of a believer's forgiveness and cleansing, (8) the ground for the deferring of righteous, divine judgments, (9) the taking away of precross sins once covered by sacrifices, (10) the national salvation of Israel, (11) the millennial and eternal blessings on the Gentiles, (12) the spoiling of principalities and powers, (13) the ground of peace, and (14) the purification of things in heaven.

A SUBSTITUTION FOR SINNERS

Christ's sacrifice for sinners involves the doctrine of substitution, that is, Christ's dying for sinners and in their place. The doctrine of substitution may be considered under five aspects: (1) the words that imply substitution, (2) vicarious suffering in general, (3) mediation,

(4) substitution with respect to the judgment of sin, and (5) substitution in the realms of divine perfection.

1. The words that imply substitution. Two Greek prepositions are involved in the aspect of this theme, *anti* and *hyper.* In general *anti* presents the concept of substitution. This word means substitution on a human plane in several passages (Matt. 5:38; 17:27; Luke 11:11; John 1:16; Rom. 12:17; 1 Thes. 5:15; Heb. 12:2, 16; 1 Peter 3:9). For instance in Matthew 5:38 Christ said, "You have heard that it was said, 'Eye for [*anti*] eye, and tooth for [*anti*] tooth.' " In this instance the blinding of one eye is demanded as a substitute for another person's blinded eye and the extraction of a tooth is required as a substitute for another person's tooth. In Matthew 17:27 Christ said in regard to the tax money being required, "But so that we may not offend them, go to the lake and throw out your line. Take the first fish you catch; open its mouth and you will find a four-drachma coin. Take it and give it to them for [*anti*] My tax and yours." The coin was a substitute for their obligation to pay a tax.

Reference is made to the death of Christ as a substitute for sinners in Matthew 20:28 and Mark 10:45. Both passages refer to Christ's giving His life "a ransom for [*anti*] many." As the coin was a substitute for the obligation of tax, so Christ's death was a substitution for the sins of believers.

The word *hyper* is a very common word in the New Testament and does not always refer to substitution. But many times it is used to refer to the substitution of Christ (Luke 22:19; John 6:51; 10:15; 15:13; Rom. 5:8; 8:32; 2 Cor. 5:14; Gal. 3:13; 1 Tim. 2:6; Titus 2:14; Phile. 13; Heb. 2:9; 1 Peter 2:21; 3:18). The first reference, Luke 22:19, is typical, "And He took bread, gave thanks, and broke it, and gave it to them, saying, 'This is My body given for [*hyper*] you; do this in remembrance of Me.' " Christ's sacrifice, referred to as the giving of His body, was an act of substitution for the sinner. John 10:15 is another example: "Just as the Father knows Me and I know the Father—and I lay down My life for [*hyper*] the sheep." Here Christ said He would lay down His life for the sheep, that is, for mankind. The death of Christ reveals both the justice and mercy of God, justice in that Christ had to die for our sins and mercy in that God has provided a substitute for sinners.

2. Vicarious suffering in general. The fact that Christ died makes clear that this was the only way by which an infinite God could on the one hand save the sinner and on the other hand do this

in perfect justice. Sometimes theologians distinguish between personal and vicarious satisfaction to God for sin. When a sinner bears his own penalty and dies without salvation, his sufferings are a personal satisfaction for God. When a believer accepts the vicarious death of Christ as a work on behalf of his salvation, the satisfaction is vicarious in that God has provided another to take the sinner's place. When a lost person dies, he is judged according to his works in contrast to a Christian who is regarded as being justified by faith.

Because God had foreknown and predetermined that Christ would die on the cross for the sins of mankind, God was free from the beginning in exercising His love toward objects of His affection even though they were sinners. Calvary was the necessary basis for the grace and love of God throughout eternity past as well as in eternity future. Whatever God does in grace, He is free to do because of the Cross. In ages to come He will display His grace by means of that salvation which He has achieved (Eph. 2:7).

3. Mediation. Job eloquently expressed the need for a mediator between God and man, "He is not a man like me that I might answer Him, that we might confront each other in court. If only there were someone to arbitrate between us, to lay his hand upon us both, someone to remove God's rod from me, so that His terror would frighten me no more. Then I would speak up without fear of Him, but as it now stands with me, I cannot" (Job 9:32-35). What Job indicated, as absolutely necessary in his case, pointed to the same conclusion regarding a Christian's salvation. Christ is the Mediator between God and man (1 Tim. 2:5) to reconcile man to God. In this role as Mediator is combined His work as Prophet and Priest. In His work as Prophet He represented God to man, and in His work as Priest He represented man to God, offering Himself as a sacrifice for sin.

4. Substitution in respect to the judgment of sin. The many passages that support the doctrine of substitution have done more to engender trust in God for the pardon of sin than all the ethical teachings of Christ and His life-example combined. Probably more has been written on the theme of Christ's death than any other subject relating to Christ in the Bible. The biblical assertions are clear and convincing. "Christ died for our sins according to the Scriptures" (1 Cor. 15:3). "He Himself bore our sins in His body on the tree" (1 Peter 2:24). "God made Him who had no sin to be sin for us" (2 Cor. 5:21). "Christ redeemed us from the curse of the Law

by becoming a curse for us" (Gal. 3:13). "For there is one God and one Mediator between God and men, the Man Christ Jesus, who gave Himself as a ransom for all men" (1 Tim. 2:5-6). These passages are so clear that objections to these declarations can only be justified if the Bible itself is wrong. The truth is self-justifying, and it is difficult indeed to argue against something that always produces the blessings it offers.

An extended classification of the passages that bear what was accomplished by Christ in His death is found in *The Doctrine of Holy Scripture Respecting the Atonement*, by T.J. Crawford (London: Blackwood and Sons, 1871). The following is an adaptation of this material based on the *King James Version:*

> 1. Passages that speak of Christ (a) as dying for sinners (Matt. 20:28; Luke 22:19-20; John 6:51; 10:11, 15, 18; 15:12-13; Rom. 5:6-8; 8:32; 2 Cor. 5:14-15, 21; Gal. 2:20; 3:13; Eph. 5:2, 25; 1 Thes. 5:9-10; 1 Tim. 2:5-6; Titus 2:13-14; Heb. 2:9; 1 Peter 3:18; 1 John 3:16), (b) as suffering for sins (Isa. 53:5, 8; Rom. 4:25; 8:3; 1 Cor. 15:3; Gal. 1:4; Heb. 10:12; 1 Peter 3:18), (c) as bearing our sins (Isa. 53:6, 11-12; Heb. 9:28; 1 Peter 2:24), and (d) as being "made sin" and "made a curse for us" (2 Cor. 5:21; Gal. 3:13).
>
> 2. Passages that ascribe to the death of Christ (a) the removal and remission of sins, and deliverance from their penal consequences (Matt. 26:28; Luke 24:46-47; John 1:29; 3:14-17; Acts 10:43; 13:38-39; Eph. 1:6-7; Col. 1:13-14; 1 Thes. 5:9-10; Heb. 9:26; 1 John 1:7; Rev. 1:5-6), (b) justification (Isa. 53:11; Rom. 3:24-26; 5:8-9), (c) redemption (Matt. 20:28; Acts 20:28; Rom. 3:23-24; 1 Cor. 6:20; Eph. 1:7; Col. 1:14; Heb. 9:12; 1 Peter 1:18-19; Rev. 5:9), and (d) reconciliation (Rom. 5:10-11; 2 Cor. 5:18-19; Eph. 2:16; Col. 1:21-22).
>
> 3. Passages in which the Lord Jesus Christ is represented (a) as a Propitiation for sin (Rom. 3:25; Heb. 2:17; 1 John 2:2; 4:10), (b) as a Priest (Ps. 110:4; Heb. 2:17; 3:1; 4:14; 7:22, 26; 10:21), and (c) as a Representative (Rom. 5:12, 18-19; 1 Cor. 15:20-22, 45-49; Heb. 5:1).
>
> 4. Passages that present the sufferings of Christ as "sacrificial" (John 1:29; 1 Cor. 5:7; Eph. 5:2; Heb. 9:22-28; 10:11-14; Rev. 7:14-15).
>
> 5. Passages that connect our Lord's sufferings with His interces-

sion (Phil. 2:8-10; 1 Tim. 2:5-6; 1 John 2:1-2; Rev. 5:6).

6. Passages that represent the mediation of Christ (a) as procuring the gracious influence of the Holy Spirit (John 7:39; 14:16-17, 26; 15:26; 16:7; Acts 2:33; Gal. 3:13-14; Titus 3:5-6), (b) as conferring all Christian graces which are fruits of the Spirit (John 1:16; 15:4-5; 1 Cor. 1:4-7, 30; Eph. 1:3-4; 2:10; 4:7; Col. 2:9-10), (c) as delivering man from the dominion of Satan (John 12:31-32; Col. 2:15; Heb. 2:14-15; 1 John 3:8), and (d) as obtaining eternal life for believers (John 3:14-15; 5:24; 6:40, 47, 51; 10:27-28; 14:2-3; 17:1-2; Rom. 5:20-21; 6:23; 2 Tim. 2:10; Heb. 5:9; 9:15; 1 Peter 5:10; 1 John 5:11; Jude 21).

7. Passages that indicate the state of the Saviour's mind in anticipating and enduring His sufferings (Matt. 26:36-44; 27:46; Luke 12:50; John 10:17-18; 12:27).

8. Passages that speak of the mediation of Christ in relation (a) to the free call and offer of the Gospel (John 14:6; Acts 4:12; 1 Cor. 3:11; 1 Tim. 2:5), and (b) to the necessity of faith in order to obtain the blessings of the Gospel (John 1:12; 3:18, 36; 6:35; Acts 13:38-39; 16:31; Rom. 1:16; 3:28; 5:12; 10:4; Gal. 5:6; Eph. 2:8-9).

9. Passages that speak of the mediatorial work and sufferings of Christ in relation to (a) His covenant with the Father (John 6:38-40, 51), and (b) His union with believers (15:4; Rom. 6:5; 2 Cor. 4:10; Gal. 2:20; Eph. 2:5-6; Phil. 3:10; Col. 2:12; 3:3).

10. Passages that speak of the death of Christ (a) as a manifestation of the love of God (John 3:16; Rom. 5:8; 8:32; 1 John 4:9-10), (b) as furnishing an example of patience and resignation (Luke 9:23-24; Heb. 12:1-3; 1 Peter 2:20-21) and (c) as designed to promote the believer's sanctification (John 17:19; 2 Cor. 5:15; Gal. 1:4; Eph. 5:25-27; Titus 2:14; Heb. 10:10; 13:12; 1 Peter 2:24).

Many passages referring to Christ's death seem to indicate that His main purpose for coming was to be a sacrifice for sinners. Some claim that leaving heaven, deprivation, and hardship of life were vicarious in character. No doubt others were benefited, but His life as such was not a sacrifice for sin. Only by dying on the cross did Christ provide a sacrifice sufficient to satisfy both the love and righteousness of God.

All objections to the scriptural doctrine of substitution in Christ's death try to escape the difficulty that if Christ did not die for the sins of all, then His death was unjust because He Himself was sinless. The fact that Christ could not avoid the cross, even though this was His prayer, supports the conclusion that the death of Christ on the cross was the only way by which He could die for the sins of the whole race. His death was forensic in that His sacrifice was infinite in value and sufficient for the sins of the entire race. The tragedy continues that mankind apart from salvation goes into eternal punishment not because it is inevitable, but because unbelievers have rejected what God in His love has provided.

In conclusion it may be observed that Christ in His sufferings and death bore more than the penalty of sin. As the many Scriptures already cited indicate, Christ identified with the sinner by taking on Himself both the sin and its penalty. In suffering for man's sin, however, Christ did not injure His own holy character; He had to be a perfect sacrifice in order to take the sinner's place. Though the death of Christ remains to limited human minds an inscrutable mystery as to what was consummated when the infinite God accomplished His greatest undertaking, it is possible for man in his limitations to accept by faith what God has provided in the death of Christ.

5. Substitution in the realms of divine perfection. Salvation of a lost soul involves much more than removal or subtraction of sin from the sinner which forgiveness achieves. Also much is added including eternal life as the gift of God (Rom. 6:23) and the righteousness of God imputed to those who believe (5:17). These two features of salvation—eternal life and the gift of righteousness—unite in the one great fact of the believer's union with Christ: "You are in Me, and I am in you" (John 14:20). The first clause, "You are in Me," reveals that all spiritual blessing is secured by the Christian's position in Christ (cf. Eph. 1:3). The expression, "I am in you," which refers to the indwelling of Christ, is made possible by the fact that every Christian has eternal life as stated in 1 John 5:11-12, "And this is the testimony: God has given us eternal life, and this life is in His Son. He who has the Son has life; he who does not have the Son of God does not have life."

In a believer's identification with Christ He is given to the believer and the believer is given by the Father to Christ (John 17:2, 6, 9, 11-12, 24). A believer's position in Christ could only be secured through what was provided for the believer's righteousness in the substitution of Christ on the cross.

A believer's position in Christ is accomplished by the baptism of the Spirit (1 Cor. 12:13). The ritual of water baptism is best understood depicting this work of the Spirit as His taking a believer at the moment of salvation out of Adam and placing him in Christ.

While Christ was on earth, He prophesied that He would baptize with the Holy Spirit (Matt. 3:11; Mark 1:8; Luke 3:16; John 1:33; Acts 1:5).

In Acts and the Epistles of Paul, the baptism of the Holy Spirit is said to place believers into Christ's body, the church (Rom. 6:3; 1 Cor. 12:13; Gal. 3:27). To be placed in Christ by the baptism of the Spirit is to take the believer out of Adam and place him in Christ, the last Adam. This tremendous fact indicates the new position a believer has in Christ and the body of Christ, and his new relationship to Christ as the Head of the new creation.

In Leviticus 1:1–7:38 the five principal offerings are enumerated which were celebrated under the Mosaic Law. The sin offering (4:1-35) is viewed as a satisfaction to God for the sins of the people. The trespass offering (5:1–6:7) also dealt with the need for cleansing from sin. The sin and trespass offerings had in mind the necessity of forgiveness for the sinner which Christ's death provided for on the cross.

In contrast to the sin and trespass offerings, which were regarded as nonsweet savor offerings, three other offerings represent the positive side of the death of Christ, that is, the righteousness which His death bestowed on the sinner. The burnt offering (1:1-17) represented the righteousness Christ achieved for man in His sacrifice for sin. This offering depicted justification by faith or the bestowal of righteousness.

In like manner the meal offering (2:1-11) referred to the moral perfection that is in Christ, the God-Man, in His life on earth and in His death on the cross. This is the ground for justification.

The peace offering (3:1-17) pictured the peace provided by the death of Christ. The sinner is estranged from God and requires reconciliation. Christ in His death on the cross established peace with God for believing sinners.

The various offerings provided in the Mosaic Law for an Israelite typologically looked forward to fulfillment in Christ. They anticipated the coming of Christ and His sacrifice.

It should be emphasized, as affirmed in Romans 3:21-31, that the salvation God provides through Jesus Christ is not an arbitrary act of God, but is in keeping with the justice and righteousness of God in that Jesus Christ, God's Son, has offered Himself as a sacrifice for the sins of the whole world. This makes not only forgiveness of sins possible but also the imputation of righteousness to every believer.

THE DEATH OF CHRIST AS THE END OF THE LAW PRINCIPLE FOR THOSE WHO ARE SAVED

In the Old Testament the Mosaic Law was not intended as a way of salvation. Those who were saved were obligated to keep the Law as a basis for fellowship with God. The Mosaic Law was a meritorious system in which God promised blessing for those who kept the Law and punishment for those who broke it. As such, the Law of Moses was the rule for an Israelite's conduct for almost 1,500 years beginning with the giving of the Law at Mount Sinai. Its force ended at the Cross of Christ, which introduced and made possible the present age of grace. The Law was a conditional agreement, for its blessings were conditioned on human faithfulness. This is brought out clearly in Deuteronomy 28. "If you fully obey the LORD your God and carefully follow all His commands I give you today, the LORD your God will set you high above all the nations on earth. All these blessings will come upon you and accompany you if you obey the LORD your God" (vv. 1-2). Moses outlined the character of these blessings in verses 3-14.

If the Israelites disobeyed the Law, God promised that He would curse them. "However, if you do not obey the LORD your God and do not carefully follow all His commands and decrees I am giving you today, all these curses will come upon you and overtake you: You will be cursed in the city and cursed in the country. Your basket and your kneading trough will be cursed. The fruit of your womb will be cursed, and the crops of your land, and the calves of your herds, and the lambs of your flocks. You will be cursed when you come in and cursed when you go out" (vv. 15-19). The rest of chapter 28 describes in detail how God would discipline and punish the Israelites including driving them out of the land if they failed to keep His Law.

The Law was a schoolmaster or "child governor" which was designed to point Israelites to Christ. This is revealed especially in Galatians 3:21-25, "Is the Law, therefore, opposed to the promises of

God? Absolutely not! For if a Law had been given that could impart life, then righteousness would certainly have come by the Law. But the Scripture declares that the whole world is a prisoner of sin, so that what was promised, being given through faith in Jesus Christ, might be given to those who believe. Before this faith came, we were held prisoners by the Law, locked up until faith should be revealed. So the Law was put in charge to lead us to Christ that we might be justified by faith. Now that faith has come, we are no longer under the supervision of the Law."

The Law in itself did not offer or promise salvation for those who observed the Law. It was designed to make clear that salvation is only by grace in every dispensation, and that man is hopelessly sinful and can be saved only by the grace of God. As such, the Mosaic Law was a preparation for the people of Israel to make them understand that when Jesus Christ came He introduced additional revelation that made clear that salvation is not by the Law but by grace.

The New Testament clearly teaches that Christ is the end of the Law for righteousness. "Christ is the end of the Law so that there may be righteousness for everyone who believes" (Rom. 10:4). Paul stated that Christian Gentiles, who had not followed the Mosaic Law, attained righteousness by faith while Israel, following the righteousness provided in the Mosaic Law, did not obtain righteousness because of their incomplete obedience (Rom. 2). Abraham, to whom God promised that he would be the source of blessing to the whole world (Gen. 12:3), was counted righteous because he believed in God (15:6; Rom. 4:3, 9). It was possible even under the Law for one who trusted God to have righteousness imputed to him. As David was quoted in verses 7-8, "Blessed are they whose transgressions are forgiven, whose sins are covered. Blessed is the man whose sin the Lord will never count against him."

Because all religions outside of Christianity are based on a legal principle by which individuals are trying to secure favor with God by works, it is also natural that Israel would have difficulty in understanding salvation by faith and by the grace of God alone. The message of justification by faith is the central feature of the Gospel. "I am not ashamed of the Gospel, because it is the power of God for the salvation of everyone who believes: first for the Jew, then for the Gentile. For in the Gospel a righteousness from God is revealed, a righteousness that is by faith from first to last, just as it is written: 'The righteous will live by faith' " (1:16-17). The same thought is stated in 3:21-24, "But now a righteousness from God, apart from Law, has been made known, to which the Law and the Prophets testify. This righteousness from God comes through faith in Jesus Christ to all who believe. There is no difference, for all have sinned and fall short of the glory of God, and are justified freely by His grace through the redemption that came by Christ Jesus." Righteousness by faith is further described in Romans 4, which relates the principle of justification to Abraham: "What then shall we say that Abraham, our forefather, discovered in this matter? If, in fact, Abraham was justified by works, he had something to boast about—but not before God. What does the Scripture say? 'Abraham believed God, and it was credited to him as righteousness' " (vv. 1-3).

In summarizing this truth Paul stated, "But the Scripture declares that the whole world is a prisoner of sin, so that what was promised, being given through faith in Jesus Christ, might be given to those who believe" (Gal. 3:22).

In contrast to Israelites under the Mosaic Law, believers in the present age maintain fellowship with God by the grace principle. Their good works are not itemized as a means of gaining favor with God, but are an evidence in the human heart of the love of God that is engendered in the believer when he realizes that he has been saved completely by the grace of God. Works never provided salvation as Romans 11:6-7 makes clear: "And if by grace, then it is no longer by works; if it were, grace would no longer be grace. What then? What Israel sought so earnestly it did not obtain, but the elect did."

In the Jerusalem Council in Acts 15, Gentile Christians were not obligated to keep the Law, even the law of circumcision. "Now then, why do you try to test God by putting on the necks of the disciples a yoke that neither we nor our fathers have been able to bear?" (v. 10)

In addition to the definition of the Gospel in Romans 1:16-17 Paul said in 3:21-22, "But now a righteousness from God, apart from the Law, has been made known, to which the Law and the Prophets testify. This righteousness from God comes through faith in Jesus Christ to all who believe. There is no difference."

The entire section of Romans 1:18–3:20 records the universality of sin with the prospect that by the grace of God sinners under condemnation can be saved.

Other passages which clarify this issue are found frequently in Scripture (Rom. 3:31; 4:5, 11, 13-16, 23-24; 5:19; 2 Cor. 5:21; Gal.

3:8; 4:19-31; 5:1).

In summary it can be restated that in the three sweet savor offerings, Christ established the righteous ground on which God can freely justify even the ungodly who believe. In the nonsweet savor offerings, there is ground in the death of Christ for justifying the sinner by declaring him righteous in the presence of the holy God.

A REDEMPTION TOWARD SIN

Three great doctrinal words need to be considered in connection with the death of Christ, namely, redemption, reconciliation, and propitiation. These doctrines define Christ's death as it relates to forgiveness, regeneration, justification, and sanctification with each of these doctrines contributing an important aspect to the doctrine as a whole.

In redemption the work of Christ on the cross paid in full the price of releasing the sinner from the bondage and judgment of his sins. When on the cross Jesus said, "It is finished" (John 19:30), He referred to the fact that His death had fully paid all that God demanded for the forgiveness of sinners.

Redemption is the sinward aspect of Christ's work on the cross and has to do with the payment of the price of the sins of the whole world. Redemption is an act of God by which He Himself pays as a ransom the price of human sin, which price the outraged holiness and government of God requires. This contrasts with reconciliation, which pertains to the solution of the problem of the sinful state of the sinner, and with propitiation, which relates to the fact that God has been offended by sin. Redemption offers the sinner release from sin and from the situation of being a bondservant to sin. Redemption results in liberation because the price has been paid to free the sinner from his sin.

In the Old Testament, redemption pertains mostly to Israel as a redeemed people. The Book of Exodus speaks of Israel's redemption from Egypt. And Boaz, the husband of Ruth, typologically pictured Christ, the Kinsman-Redeemer, when he secured Ruth for his wife (Ruth 4:1-12).

In the New Testament various Greek words are translated "redeemed" or "redemption." The basic Greek word is *agorazo,* which means to purchase in the market (*agora*). The concept here is that an unsaved person is a bondslave to sin because he was "sold as a slave to sin" (Rom. 7:14). Before being saved a person is dominated by Satan (1 Cor. 12:2; Eph. 2:2); and is "condemned" (John 3:18; Gal. 3:10). Christ in His death paid the ransom price for the sinner's redemption (Matt. 20:28).

A second Greek word used for redemption is *exagorazo,* which means to purchase "out" of the market (the preposition *ek* means "out of"). This has the added thought of not only being redeemed but also removing the one redeemed from the marketplace and not leaving him up for sale (Gal. 3:13; 4:5).

A third word *lytroo,* means to loose or set free from bondage (Luke 24:21; Titus 2:14; 1 Peter 1:18). The noun *apolytrosis* is derived from *lytroo.* This is translated "redemption" (Luke 21:28; Rom. 3:24; 8:23; 1 Cor. 1:30; Eph. 1:7, 14; 4:30; Col. 1:14; Heb. 9:15, "ransom").

Christ in His death on the cross went into the marketplace and bought the unsaved who are regarded as slaves. His death made it possible for Him to take them out of the marketplace and not subject them to further resale, and to set them free from the bondage and judgment of sin.

The doctrine of redemption is typologically anticipated in Exodus 21:1-6 and Deuteronomy 15:16-17. In this situation a slave is set free by his master so that he could leave his master if he wished. But sometimes a slave volunteered to stay with his master. By having his ear pierced he indicated that he wanted to serve his master for the rest of his life. In a similar way Christians, having been set free by the redemption that is in Christ, should fulfill the exhortation of Romans 12:1-2, offering their bodies as living sacrifices, voluntarily yielding themselves to the will of God. In like manner Christ made Himself submissive to God the Father (Heb. 2:5-7).

The doctrine of redemption depicts the full payment for all sin accomplished by the death of Christ so that one who formerly was a slave to sin and subject to the righteous judgment of God is set free to serve the Lord voluntarily in a gracious relationship.

A RECONCILIATION TOWARD MAN

In Scripture, reconciliation is the manward aspect of Christ's work on the cross. It is strictly a New Testament doctrine. In ordinary human relations, reconciliation is usually viewed as each of two parties conceding something to bring about harmony in their relationship. In the Bible reconciliation is the work of Christ on the cross which completely changes man in his relationship to God by removing all grounds for condemnation. The central idea is that man is completely changed. In the Old Testament, though some English translations such as the KJV use the word "reconciliation," a better translation is "making an atonement for sin" (Lev. 6:30; 8:15; 16:20; 1 Sam. 29:4; 2 Chron. 29:24; Ezek. 45:15, 17, 20; Dan. 9:24). Though different Hebrew words are used, none of them connotes precisely the doctrine of reconciliation as taught in the New Testament. They view sin as being covered or they refer to that for which atonement has been made.

In the New Testament, reconciliation of members of the human race is mentioned in Matthew 5:24 which uses the Greek word *diallassomai.* This word is used only here of human relations and is never used of reconciliation of man to God.

Katallasso, which speaks of man as in relation to God is used five times (Rom. 5:10 [twice]; 2 Cor. 5:18-20). The key verse is Romans 5:10, "For if, when we were God's enemies, we were reconciled to Him through the death of His Son, how much more, having been reconciled, shall we be saved through His life!" The noun form (*katallage*) is also found three times (Rom. 11:15; 2 Cor. 5:18-19). A more intensive verb, *apokatallasso,* appears three times (Eph. 2:16; Col. 1:20-21). All these passages speak of man being reconciled to God rather than God being reconciled to man.

Man is changed by God rather than God being changed in His relation to man. Reconciliation involves the fact that man is a new creature, he has been justified by faith, and now is seen in Christ. Just as redemption is toward sin, reconciliation is toward man, and propitiation is toward God.

In 2 Corinthians 5:19-20 the world is said to be reconciled to God. This means that the world has been changed in its relationship to God because of the death of Christ. This change makes the world savable. As the passage makes clear in its exhortation to preach the Gospel of reconciliation, the completion of reconciliation of man to God is accomplished immediately when a man accepts Christ as his Saviour. The concept of being reconciled to God is difficult for man to comprehend, for all non-Christian religions have the idea that man must somehow make peace with God through his human works. This of course is denied in the New Testament which makes the work of Christ the only possible basis by which a sinner can be reconciled to God. Reconciliation becomes effective for the individual Christian at the moment he trusts Christ as his Saviour. By this means a person is made a new creature in Christ and is acceptable to God.

A PROPITIATION TOWARD GOD

Propitiation refers to the value of Christ's death as a satisfaction of God's righteousness and a vindication of His righteousness in saving sinners. Propitiation in the New Testament is revealed in various words that stem from the same Greek word (*hilasmos,* 1 John 2:2; 4:10); the place of propitiation (*hilasterion,* Rom. 3:25, KJV; Heb. 9:5, "atonement cover," or "mercy seat," KJV); to be merciful or forgiving (*hileos,* 8:12, "forgive," "merciful," KJV); and to be merciful or propitiated (*hilaskomai,* Luke 18:13, "have mercy," "be merciful," KJV).

In each case propitiation has in view the effect of the death of Christ on a righteous God, and the truth that the death of Christ satisfied God completely as far as His righteous demands are concerned. In 1 John 2:2, Christ "is the atoning sacrifice [propitiation] for our sins, not only for ours but also for the sins of the whole world." The same thought is embodied in 4:10, "This is love: not that we loved God, but that He loved us and sent His Son as an atoning sacrifice [a propitiation] for our sins."

In the holy of holies in the tabernacle was a mercy seat, which contained tablets of the Law. On the Day of Atonement the mercy seat was sprinkled with the blood of sacrifice, thus changing the place that demanded the righteousness of the Law to a mercy seat or a place of propitiation. This is the thought in Hebrews 9:5, "Above the ark were the cherubim of the Glory, overshadowing the atonement [the place of propitiation]." Christ is presented as the place of propitiation in Romans 3:25, "God presented Him as a sacrifice of atonement [a mercy seat, or a place of propitiation], through faith in His blood." Christ is to a believer what the mercy seat, or place of propitiation, was for Israel in the Old Testament.

Another reference to propitiation is found in Hebrews 8:12, "For I will forgive [will be propitiated in regard to] their wickedness and will remember their sins no more." God's forgiveness is conditioned on the fact that He has been propitiated or satisfied by the death of the sacrifice.

In the story of the Pharisee and the tax collector, "The tax collector stood at a distance. He would not even look up to heaven, but beat his breast and said, 'God, have mercy on me [be propitiated in regard to me], a sinner' " (Luke 18:13). Christians can expect God to have mercy on them because He has been propitiated or satisfied by the death of Christ.

It is not necessary for a sinner to beg God for mercy, but he should recognize that God is propitiated by the death of Christ and is "faithful and just and will forgive" (1 John 1:9). God is ready to receive a person who comes in genuine confession of sin.

As is true in other aspects of the death of Christ, propitiation has a relation to the world in that the world is rendered savable by faith in Christ and His death. Individuals who have put their trust in Christ have a relationship to the Lord that is based on God being propitiated.

This is illustrated in the familiar story of the Prodigal Son (Luke 15:11-32). When the wayward son returned to his father, the son was received with open arms even before he confessed his sins. A sinner placing his faith in God for salvation, or a Christian coming in confession is assured that God's arms are open to welcome them because Christ's death on the cross is the ground of God being propitious both to the unsaved world and toward Christians. The Scriptures are clear, however, that though God has been propitiated, a person who does not receive Christ by faith as his Saviour and God is just as lost as if Christ had not died. The tragedy of eternal punishment is that the finished work of Christ on the cross was sufficient for all but is applied only to those who believe.

THE JUDGMENT OF THE SIN NATURE

The Scriptures distinguish individual or personal sins from sin as a nature. In 1 John 1:8 the statement is made, "If we claim to be without sin, we deceive ourselves and the truth is not in us." Here sin, used in the singular, refers to the sin nature. In verses 9-10, however, the acts of sin are mentioned, as indicated by the plural, "If we confess our sins, He is faithful and just and will forgive us our sins and purify us from all unrighteousness. If we claim we have not sinned, we make Him out to be a liar and His Word has no place in our lives." Christians sin because they have sin natures. The death of Christ, just as it deals with personal sins, also is God's remedy for the sin nature. For instance 1 Corinthians 15:3 states, "Christ died for our sins according to the Scriptures," but Romans 6:10 (KJV) states that "He died unto sin once." The same verse in the NIV reads, "The death He died, He died to sin once for all; but the life He lives, He lives to God." He died for the sins of the world, but He also died in respect to the sin nature.

The relationship of the death of Christ to the sin nature, however, does not eradicate or change the sin nature as such. It transforms a believer into a new creation, which includes a divine nature that longs to obey God.

The secret of victory over the sin nature is not its eradication but the presence of the indwelling Holy Spirit who can enable the divine nature to fulfill its longing to walk in the will of God. The Christian remains in a sinful world, possesses a sin nature or "the flesh," and contends with the devil. These problems are not removed, but there is added to the Christian's experience the possibility of being filled with the Spirit and not fulfilling the lusts of the sin nature.

This is confirmed by the fact that when Christ died, He gained victory over Satan. According to John 16:11, "The prince of this world now stands condemned." Though Satan has been condemned, his final disposition awaits a future judgment from God. In like manner a Christian retains his sin nature that awaits a future removal at the time of his death or the Rapture.

In God's plan for the sanctification of the believer, provision has been made for a sinner to conquer the desires of the flesh (the sin nature) and live a holy life in the will of God.

The central passage bearing on the judgment of the sin nature is Romans 6:1–8:13. In contrast to the earlier chapters of Romans which relate to sin and salvation, these chapters discuss the Christian's sanctification and victory over sin. The problem is what the Christian is able to do about his sin nature. In the opening verses of this passage, Paul stated, "What shall we say, then? Shall we go on sinning so that grace may increase? By no means! We died to sin; how can we live in it any longer?" (6:1-2) As Paul then explained, whatever Christ did becomes true of the Christian as well because he has been baptized into Christ. In Christ the Christian dies, in Christ the Christian is buried, and in Christ the Christian is raised from the dead. This is a picture of new life in Christ, made possible because the believer is identified with Christ in His death and resurrection.

Since this is true, there should be a corresponding change in the life of a Christian as Paul stated, "If we have been united with Him in His death, we will certainly also be united with Him in His resurrection. For we know that our old self was crucified with Him so that the body of sin might be rendered powerless, that we should no longer be slaves to sin—because anyone who has died has been freed from sin. Now if we died with Christ, we believe that we will also live with Him. For we know that since Christ was raised from the dead, He cannot die again; death no longer has mastery over Him. The death He died, He died to sin once for all; but the life He lives, He lives to God" (vv. 5-10). Because Christ died once for all and believers died in Him, Paul exhorted them, "In the same way, count yourselves dead to sin but alive to God in Christ Jesus. Therefore do not let sin reign in your mortal body so that you obey its evil desires" (vv. 11-12).

Paul then affirmed that through the death of Christ a believer, who once was a slave to sin and living in accord with the desires of the sin nature, is now made new in Christ. He has died with Christ and was raised again and is able now by the power of the Spirit to refuse to let the sin nature reign. Paul concluded, "For sin shall not be your master, because you are not under Law, but under grace" (v. 14).

In verse 6 Paul referred to "our old self" which is translated in the KJV as "our old man" (cf. Eph. 4:22; Col. 3:9). Many take the expression "old man" to be equivalent to the sin nature, but they may not be identical. Though a Christian died with Christ and has been raised with Christ, he still has an active sin nature, and the sin nature has been judged but not eradicated. The "old self" (also called the "old man") may be different from "the flesh" (KJV) or "sinful nature" (Gal. 5:16-21).

"The old self" or "the old man" may refer to the manner of life a Christian had before he was saved. The manner of life could be viewed as dead with Christ and the new life may be considered as raised with Christ. Though the old nature cannot be reckoned as dead in the sense of being nonexistent, the old life can be left behind when a Christian begins to serve the Lord. At the same time it is true that when Christ died, He robbed the sin nature of its authority to enslave unbelievers and sets those who put their trust in

Christ free from sin and death.

Though interpreters sometimes disagree, the baptism in Romans 6:3 probably refers to the baptism of the Spirit by which the believer is placed in Christ. This supports the fact that in Christ he died and was raised from the dead. Spiritual baptism therefore refers to the initiation of the believer into Christ but not the process of death and resurrection as is commonly taught.

Romans 6:1–8:13 includes the following truths: (1) Christ died in respect to sin so that a believer would not continue in sin (6:12). (2) A merit system of human works and effort to establish a relationship with Christ is denied, for a person is saved by grace and by faith. In 7:7-25 Paul spoke of his own struggles and the conflict of the new nature with the old nature with victory possible only through Jesus Christ. (3) The believer can lead a triumphant life, with victory over sin, as the will of God is fulfilled in him (8:1-13). Deliverance is by the power of the Spirit of life in Christ (v. 2). The new nature, ineffective by itself in opposing the old nature, is enabled by Christ and the Holy Spirit to have victory. The righteousness of God is fulfilled in Christians who do not walk after the old nature but according to the Holy Spirit (vv. 1-6).

It may be concluded that in Christ's death He secured a judgment against the sin nature on the basis of which the Holy Spirit can righteously deliver believers from the power of that nature and will deliver all those who do not live according to the sinful nature but according to the Spirit (v. 4).

THE GROUND OF THE BELIEVER'S FORGIVENESS AND CLEANSING

Sin can be cured only by the blood of Christ. In the case of the unsaved, they are forgiven judicially and are justified by faith. After justification, when a Christian sins, restoration is needed between himself as a child of God and his Heavenly Father. This restoration is obtained only by confession of sin. All forgiveness and justification depends on the blood of Christ and the act of Christ in dying for the sinner on the cross of Calvary.

A major discussion of a believer's forgiveness and cleansing is found in 1 John 1:1–2:2. In contrast to an unsaved person who is forgiven when he believes in Christ, a Christian is forgiven in the family relationship with his Heavenly Father when he confesses his sin. The effect of a Christian's sinning without confession of sin is spiritual darkness. The cure is confession of sin which makes possible his walking in the light, that is, the light of God's revelation. Walking in the light is not a matter of attaining sinless perfection but of living within the moral guidelines revealed in the Word of God. This involves a willingness to confess every sin immediately as soon as it is recognized to be sin. Such confession brings a Christian into moral agreement with God and makes possible his fellowship with God. In his continued walk in the light of God's revelation the blood of Christ continually cleanses believers from all sin.

The central truths relating to this declaration are introduced in 1:5-7, "This is the message we have heard from Him and declare to you: God is light; in Him there is no darkness at all. If we claim to have fellowship with Him yet walk in the darkness, we lie and do not live by the truth. But if we walk in the light, as He is in the light, we have fellowship with one another, and the blood of Jesus, His Son, purifies us from all sin."

This passage plainly affirms that since no Christian is perfect he needs constant cleansing to walk in the light of God's will. As John stated, "If we claim to be without sin, we deceive ourselves and the truth is not in us. If we confess our sins, he is faithful and just and will forgive us our sins and purify us from all unrighteousness. If we claim we have not sinned, we make Him out to be a liar and His Word has no place in our lives" (vv. 8-10). This passage, addressed to Christians, sets forth the fact that no one is without a sin nature nor is anyone without acts of sin. When acts of sin become known to a believer, he is called on to confess this to God immediately. He is then promised continued fellowship with Christ and cleansing by His blood.

A sinning Christian who claims to be without sin may deceive himself, but he does not deceive others. In addition he must disregard God and the plain revelation of Scripture concerning sin. A life of fellowship with God requires constant confession of known sin and walking in the will of God as far as the individual knows God's perfect will.

Another aspect of this truth is brought out in 2:1-2, "My dear children, I write this to you so that you will not sin. But if anybody does sin, we have One who speaks to the Father in our defense—Jesus Christ, the Righteous One. He is the atoning sacrifice for our sins, and not only for ours but also for the sins of the whole world." John's purpose in revealing this truth was to prevent sin, but he recognized that in spite of a Christian's effort to be perfect, he will fall short and sin. In that case the believer needs an advocate. Jesus Christ presents His righteous work of dying on the cross as an atoning sacrifice for the Christian's sins. This should encourage a Christian both to walk in the light of God's will and also to confess any sins that occur, being assured that Christ is already interceding for him at the right hand of God and is pleading the sufficiency of His finished work on the cross. This is the work of Christ in propitiation previously discussed, which is the ground of a Christian's confidence.

THE GROUND FOR DEFERRING RIGHTEOUS DIVINE JUDGMENTS

The preceding discussion of the seven objectives accomplished by Christ in His sufferings and death have to do with this work of Christ as it relates to Christians.

Another aspect of the death of Christ relates to the unsaved world. In the history of man righteous judgments against him are often deferred. In addition to forgiving and making a Christian righteous, God is free to defer holy judgments which otherwise would fall immediately on every unsaved person. Deferred judgments are not an abandonment or renunciation of God's righteousness. The day of divine wrath cannot be escaped except by one coming to Christ and trusting in His redeeming blood. The Bible does reveal God's patience toward sinners and His long-suffering in waiting for them to come to Himself (Rom. 9:22; 1 Peter 3:20; 2 Peter 3:9, 15). The Bible reveals the certainty of judgment on all those who take advantage of divine patience because God is ever holy in character and righteous in His actions, whether in His long-suffering or His judgments (Matt. 24:48-51; Rom. 2:4-5).

THE TAKING AWAY OF PRECROSS SIN ONCE COVERED BY SACRIFICE

In the Old Testament those who were saved were temporarily covered by offering the sacrifices in anticipation of the complete sacrifice for sin which Christ would offer on the cross. The Hebrew word *kaphar* is frequently used in the Old Testament in regard to the atonement for sin and related doctrines. The Old Testament sacrifices were a temporary covering for sin as implied in *kaphar,* with all such sacrifices being temporary in value and looking forward to the final act of Christ on the cross which would provide a sacrifice for sin forever.

As stated in Hebrews 10:1-5, "The law is only a shadow of the good things that are coming—not the realities themselves. For this reason it can never, by the same sacrifices repeated endlessly year after year, make perfect those who draw near to worship. If it could, would they not have stopped being offered? For the worshipers would have been cleansed once for all, and would no longer have felt guilty for their sins. But those sacrifices are an annual reminder of sins because it is impossible for the blood of bulls and goats to take away sins. Therefore, when Christ came into the world, He said: 'Sacrifice and offering You did not desire, but a body You prepared for Me.' " Christ became incarnate in order to fulfill by the offering of His body on the cross what was revealed by types in the Old Testament.

The temporary nature of forgiveness in the Old Testament is stated in Romans 3:25-26, "God presented Him as a sacrifice of atonement, through faith in His blood. He did this to demonstrate His justice, because in His forbearance He had left the sins committed beforehand unpunished—He did it to demonstrate His justice at the present time, so as to be just and the One who justifies the man who has faith in Jesus." The Old Testament saints were forgiven, as it were, by credit as they looked forward to the final payment by Christ on Calvary.

In Hebrews 10 the contrast between the relationship of Old Testament saints to those in the church today confirms the temporary nature of Old Testament sacrifices and the permanence of Christ's finished work on the cross. Christ is the Mediator of the New Covenant in His death on the cross (Heb. 9:15). As provided in this covenant, grace is extended to those who put their trust in Christ.

THE NATIONAL SALVATION OF ISRAEL

The Scriptures reveal that individual Israelites need to be saved from sin and delivered from condemnation just as unsaved Gentiles need salvation. This was true in the Old Testament and also in the present age (Rom. 3:9). In the present age God is calling both Jews and Gentiles to put their trust in Christ.

In the light of God's present work of salvation for Israel the question is raised whether the covenants of God with Israel in the Old Testament are abrogated. The answer is clearly given in Romans 11, that their covenants (except for the Mosaic Covenant) are irrevocable. The question is posed whether God has rejected His people (v. 1). As Paul pointed out, God has not rejected His people Israel; in the present age He is saving individual Israelites such as Paul. In every age godly Israelites have been saved, even in the time of Elijah (vv. 2-4) when Israel as a whole was apostate. Most Israelites, however, in the present age have not come to Christ and are to a limited extent blind to the truth of the Gospel (v. 25). In the present age Gentiles have been grafted into the olive tree, which represents the place of God's blessing and grace (v. 17). He predicts, however, that in the future Israel will be grafted in again and become a primary recipient of the grace of God.

When the Rapture occurs, Israel's present blindness will be lifted and many will come to the Lord. Then "all Israel" will be "saved" (v. 26), that is, she will be delivered from her persecutors for "the Deliverer will come from Zion; He will turn godlessness away from Jacob. And this is My covenant with them when I take away their sins" (vv. 26-27).

Paul stated that the great covenant promises of the Old Testament are not revoked: "For God's gifts and His call are irrevocable" (v. 29). God's gracious purpose for Israel is future and many individual Jews will be saved. The nation will be restored and regathered to her Promised Land (Gen. 13:15; Isa. 66:22; Jer. 31:36). In the millennial kingdom the Davidic throne will be restored (2 Sam. 7:16; Jer. 33:15, 17, 21; Dan. 7:14). At the beginning of the Millennium Israelites who are unsaved will be purged out (Ezek. 20:37-38) and the saved will be rescued from their persecutors.

At the time of Christ's second coming when righteous Israel will be regathered and brought into the land (Jer. 23:5-8), the sins of the godly remnant will be forgiven, and they will continue to experience the grace of God in the millennial kingdom. The death of Christ made possible the grace of God for Israel as well as for the church. Many other Scriptures confirm the future restoration of Israel (Isa. 11:10; 35:10; 40:1-2, 11; 54:5, 8, 17; Ezek. 34:11-14; Rom. 11:13-

26). The death of Christ makes it possible for God to save individual Israelites graciously and to restore and bless the nation Israel in fulfillment of her covenants.

MILLENNIAL AND ETERNAL BLESSINGS ON THE GENTILES

The grace of God made possible by the death of Christ is sufficient not only for Jews but also for Gentiles. Some Gentiles are saved in the present age, but even in the millennial kingdom where Israel is in prominence, Gentiles will share the millennial earth with Israel. The godly remnant of Gentiles at the Second Coming are "the sheep," who will have eternal life and enter the kingdom (Matt. 25:31-46). References to the blessings of Gentiles are revealed in many passages (Isa. 60:3; 62:2). The saved among the Gentiles are also seen in the new earth in eternity (Rev. 21:24). Eternal mercies to Gentiles as well as to Israel stem from the sacrifice of Christ on the cross.

THE SPOILING OF RULERS AND AUTHORITIES IN HEAVEN AND IN EARTH

The Scriptures refer frequently to powers represented by earthly rulers as well as extramundane authorities. In some instances the same word (*arche*) is used to refer to political powers on earth (Rom. 13:1; Titus 3:1) as well as the power of Satan (Eph. 1:21; 3:10; 6:12; Col. 1:16; 2:10, 15). The same word (*exousia*) is used for the power of Satan (Acts 26:18), and the power or authority of God is found in many passages (Matt. 9:6, 8; 10:1; 28:18; Mark 2:10; 3:15; 6:7; Luke 4:6, 32; 5:24; 10:19; 12:5; John 1:12; 10:18; 17:2; 19:11; Acts 1:7; 8:19; Rom. 9:21; 13:1; 2 Cor. 13:10; Eph. 1:21; Col. 2:10, 15).

Because Satan is referred to as the prince of this world who has power over the political rulers (Matt. 9:34; 12:24; John 12:31; 14:30; Eph. 2:2), both political governments on earth and the powers of Satan in the demon world are sometimes comingled and are both regarded as evil. On the other hand Christians are urged to abide by the government of civil rulers (Rom. 13:1; Titus 3:1) unless this requires them to transgress the law of God. In contrast to both political powers on earth and extramundane powers in heaven,

Christ is supreme with all things under His authority (Col. 2:10-15). This indicates that Christ is the final power over both political rulers and the demon world. Though some fallen angels were immediately bound after their first transgression (Jude 6) the Scriptures indicate that Satan and the demon world have great power.

The fallen angels are created beings (Col. 1:16), and their abode though above the sphere of humanity (Heb. 2:9) is lower than the throne of God where Christ is now seated (Eph. 1:21; Heb. 10:12). The fallen angels who are free exercise their power in maintaining an invisible war against the saints and the holy angels (Eph. 6:12). Satan as "the ruler of the kingdom of the air" (2:2) leads the fallen angels in their opposition to God (Matt. 25:41; Rev. 12:7-9). Though busy against the works of God in the present age, Satan and the fallen angels will be thrown out of heaven in the future (v. 9), will be confined for a thousand years during the millennial kingdom (20:1-3) but will finally be cast into the "lake of fire" (v. 10, KJV) or "lake of burning sulfur" which was "prepared for the devil and his angels" (Matt. 25:41). The future judgment of Satan was predicted by God Himself but is not yet executed (Gen. 3:15; cf. Isa. 14:12; Ezek. 28:16-19).

The combat between Christ and Satan, which was waged on Calvary's hill when Christ died, is beyond comprehension by finite minds. The Scriptures reveal that Satan exercised his utmost power which led to the death of Christ. This striking of the heel of the Saviour also resulted in Satan's head being crushed, that is, Satan's power was destroyed (Gen. 3:15).

On the divine side, the death of Christ was determined by His Father (John 3:16; Rom. 3:25; 8:32), by Christ Himself as a sacrifice (John 10:18; Gal. 2:20), and through the work of the eternal Spirit (Heb. 9:14).

In His death, however, Christ overcame Satan (John 12:31; 16:11). Christ clearly won a victory over Satan on the cross (Col. 2:14-15). In offering salvation to man, Christ fulfilled what was anticipated in Isaiah 61:1 where He is said to have provided freedom for those who were captives. This is in contrast to Satan who "would not let his captives go home" (14:17).

The world of the unsaved is under six unalterable indictments recorded in Ephesians 2:11-12, "Therefore, remember that formerly you who are Gentiles by birth and called 'uncircumcised' by those who call themselves 'the circumcision' (that done in the body by the hands of men)—remember that at that time you were separate from Christ, excluded from citizenship in Israel and foreigners to the covenants of the promise, without hope and without God in the world." The world, without hope apart from Christ, is offered the wonderful hope of eternal salvation through faith in Him.

THE GROUND OF PEACE

Because of the death of Christ, it is possible for a sinner through faith in Christ to have peace with God as stated in Romans 5:1, "Therefore, since we have been justified through faith, we have peace with God through our Lord Jesus Christ" (cf. Eph. 2:13-14).

In the present age it is also true that there is peace between Jews and Gentiles who have been brought together in the body of Christ (vv. 11-12). It is also possible for Christians to experience the peace of God (Phil. 4:6-7).

In the future Millennium, peace will be brought to the nations of the world (Col. 1:20). This peace will follow the judgments of God at the Second Coming (Isa. 63:1-6; Ps. 2:1-3, 8-9; Matt. 25:31-46). Ultimately, having established peace, Christ will deliver the kingdom up to the Father (1 Cor. 15:27-28).

THE PURIFICATION OF THINGS IN HEAVEN

Because of the original sin of Satan and the fallen angels and the added pollution of the world resulting from the human race falling into sin, it is necessary for things both in heaven and earth to be purified. Sin has brought the entire creation into bondage (Rom. 8:20-23). Heavenly things also have to be purified with sacrifices, but only Christ was able to do this cleansing of heaven (Heb. 9:23-28). The same thought is expressed in verses 11-12. Inasmuch as Satan has been permitted to accuse brethren in heaven, it follows that in a sense heaven itself has been introduced to sin (Rev. 12:10). Christ, having shed His own blood on earth, is prepared to enter into heaven as a holy place and by His sacrifice bring sinners who are saved with Him. In extending the purification of things on earth to things in heaven through the cleansing blood of Christ, the Bible does not teach universalism, or that all men will be saved. The

Scriptures are clear that those who reject Christ do not receive the benefits of His death on the cross.

CHAPTER · 5

THE SUFFERINGS AND DEATH OF CHRIST IN TYPES

In systematic theologies typology is a neglected subject and is rarely mentioned. The Scriptures are clear, however, that God intended some events, objects, and persons to be types in the sense that a type is a divinely purposed anticipation which illustrates its antitype. Though some have gone to extremes by trying to find types in every situation, the Scriptures are relatively conservative, but those designated as types in the New Testament indicate that all types are not expressly mentioned.

Three major factors exhibit the unity between the two Testaments: type and antitype, prophecy and fulfillment, and continuity in the progress of narration and doctrine. These factors run from one text to the other and are like woven threads combining them into one fabric.

Two Greek words are used to represent types in the New Testament, *typos* and *hypodeigma. Typos* is variously translated in the KJV and other English translations, but the thought is that of an example (1 Cor. 10:11; Phil. 3:17; 1 Peter 5:3) or a model (1 Thes. 1:7; 2 Thes. 3:9). The word *deigma* means a specimen, and when combined with *hypo* it means "example" (John 13:15; Heb. 4:11; James 5:10). Both words clearly illustrate that types are an example or model for truth.

Types can be classified as persons (Rom. 5:14; Adam, Melchizedek, Abraham, Sarah, Ishmael, Isaac, Moses, Joshua, David, Solomon, etc.); events (1 Cor. 10:11; the preservation of Noah and his sons in the ark, redemption from Egypt, the Passover memorial, the Exodus, the passing through the Red Sea, the giving of manna, the water drawn from the rock, the serpent lifted up, and many sacrifices); things (Heb. 10:20; cf. the tabernacle, the laver, the sacrificial lamb, the Jordan River); a city (Rev. 11:8); and institutions (Heb. 9:11; the Sabbath, sacrifices, the priesthood); and ceremonials (1 Cor. 5:7).

It is important to distinguish types from allegories or analogies. Obviously any type identified in the New Testament should be considered a biblical type, but there are other types not specifically mentioned. In referring to the many historical acts of Israel when they committed sin, Paul stated, "These things happened to them as examples and were written down as warnings for us, on whom the fulfillment of the ages has come" (1 Cor. 10:11). The events he itemized are considered examples though they are not formally identified or defined. For example Joseph is no doubt a type of Christ, even though he is not directly so specified in the New Testament. A true type is a prophecy of its antitype and has been designed by God to have an antitype. Of all the antitypes Christ is the outstanding One and the supreme Object of both Old and New Testament typology.

THE GENERAL SACRIFICES OF THE OLD TESTAMENT

Abel's offering (Gen. 4:4) indicates that divine instruction on the importance and value of blood sacrifices had been given to the first of the human race as they emerged in the Garden of Eden. By his sacrifice Abel obtained witness that he was righteous (Heb. 11:4; cf. 9:22).

Noah's altar and sacrifice (Gen. 8:20-22) also indicate that the revelation had been given about the necessity of blood sacrifice. As Exodus 20:24-26 makes clear, it is not the altar which is important but the sacrifice on the altar even though specific instructions are given on the construction of an altar. All sacrifices of the Old Testament which anticipate the death of Christ are types.

PRESCRIBED SACRIFICES OF THE OLD TESTAMENT

1. The Paschal lamb. The Paschal lamb, offered on the night of the Passover, is an obvious type of the Lord Jesus in His death. Since the blood of the lamb blotted out sin, partaking of the roasted lamb speaks of divine fellowship. The Paschal lamb had six essential re-

quirements: it was to be without blemish; it was to be tested; it was to be slain; its blood was to be applied; its blood was a perfect propitiation against divine judgment; the lamb was to be partaken of as food. Christ fulfilled these types when He as the antitype became the Lamb of God which takes away the sin of the world (see John 1:29).

2. Five types of Christ. The five offerings in Leviticus 1:1–7:38 are types of Christ. The sweet savor offerings—the burnt offering, the meal offering, and the peace offering—speak of Christ and His death on the cross as representing obedience to God. The sin offering and the trespass offering, referred to as nonsweet savor sacrifices, represent Christ's bearing the sin of the whole world as a substitute for mankind. In the sweet savor offerings the obedience of Christ is considered as righteousness, and on this basis God can justify sinners. In the nonsweet savor offerings the death of Christ is anticipated as judgment on sin.

3. Two birds (Lev. 14:1-7). These were to be sacrificed in connection with the cleansing of leprosy. The first bird slain speaks of Christ "delivered over to death for our sins," and the second bird which was released represents Christ "raised to life for our justification" (Rom. 4:25).

4. The Day of Atonement. This clearly represents Christ in His death on the cross. On that occasion the bullock was offered as a sacrifice for the high priest (Lev. 16:3-4). The two goats were offered as a sacrifice for the Children of Israel (vv. 5, 7-10). The goat that was killed was a sacrifice for sin. The goat that was allowed to escape represented Christ taking away our sins.

5. The red heifer (Num. 19:1-22). This is a type of the cleansing of the believer as stated in 1 John 1:7-9. The ashes of the red heifer were used as a ceremonial cleansing from defilement. When the red heifer was offered, the sin of defilement was confessed, and cleansing resulted.

The central features of this ordinance included the provision of an animal without blemish, the slaying of the animal, the consuming of the entire animal by fire, the use of the ashes from the fire for cleansing, the mingling of the ashes with water, and the application of water and ashes for the cleansing from defilement. This pictures the cleansing of defilement in a believer's life by the blood of Christ, which is applied to the believer in response to confession of sin (1 John 1:9).

MISCELLANEOUS TYPES OF CHRIST'S DEATH

1. God supplied coats of skin for Adam and Eve (Gen. 3:21). Obviously blood was shed to secure the skins, and the covering represents God's covering of man's sin. In a sense the offering of these skins introduced the whole matter of animal sacrifice which prompted Abel to offer a suitable sacrifice.

2. Noah's ark (Gen. 6:14–8:19). The ark has many suggestions of vital truth. The safety of those in the ark seems to be a definite foreview of the safety of those who are in Christ Jesus. Pitch was used to cover the ark and by it the waters of judgment were resisted. The Hebrew word for pitch (*kapher*), mentioned in 6:14, is the same word used for atonement more than 60 times in the Old Testament (e.g., Ex. 29:36-37; 30:10, 15-16; 32:30). Just as pitch kept out the waters of judgment from the ark, so the atonement of Christ preserves the believer from judgment.

3. The bread and wine in the hands of Melchizedek (Gen. 14:17-24). These suggest two important truths, namely, that Abraham represented a Christian under grace and not a Jew under the Law (John 8:56). Partaking of the bread and wine on Abraham's part may not have been completely understood by either Melchizedek or Abraham, but it anticipated the death of Christ represented in the Lord's Supper.

4. The offering of Isaac (Gen. 22:1-14). This is obviously a type of Christ and Abraham appears as a type of the Father offering His Son. Though Abraham was spared the ordeal of sacrificing his son by offering a substitute, according to Romans 8:32 God the Father "did not spare His own Son, but gave Him up for us all." In this sacrifice Isaac was a type of the Son who was willing and obedient to death. The ram in the thicket is the type of a sacrifice offered as a substitute.

5. Joseph (Gen. 37:2–50:26). Joseph is an obvious type of Christ though he is never so identified in the New Testament. Joseph's being placed in a pit is a type of the death of Christ, and his being lifted out is a type of Christ's resurrection. Like Christ, Joseph was loved by his father and hated by his brothers. He later rescued his people in a time of famine, after he had taken a Gentile wife, who is typical of the church.

6. Manna. Just as the manna came from heaven to give life to Israel, so Christ is the Bread which came down from heaven and

gives life to the world (John 6:30-59).

7. THE SMITTEN ROCK (EX. 17:5-7; NUM. 20:7-13). This represents Christ, as stated in 1 Corinthians 10:4. By His death the water of life was released and He was smitten only once. Moses was judged severely for smiting the rock twice, thus in a sense spoiling the type. The death of Christ is infinitely sufficient and admits no reenactment because He died once to sin.

8. THE TABERNACLE (EX. 25:1–40:38). This is one of the most extensive illustrations of typology in the Old Testament. The tabernacle itself is a type of Christ as the only way to God. The ark of the covenant sprinkled with blood is the place of propitiation. The showbread is another type of Christ as the Bread of Life given for the world; silver speaks of redemption. The altar of bronze represents the judgments against sin which Christ bore in His death. The lampstand is a type of Christ, the Light of the world. The golden altar is that aspect of Christ's death which was a sweet incense to God. The laver of bronze foreshadowed the cleansing of the believer priest through the blood of Christ (1 John 1:7, 9).

THE DEATH OF CHRIST ACCORDING TO VARIOUS SCRIPTURES

Only a brief outline of this extensive revelation can be provided here. The death of Christ is a major theme of the Bible with important revelation in both the Old and New Testaments.

1. ACCORDING TO GENESIS. Genesis 3:15 is a preview of the death of Christ, in which He triumphed over Satan and the fallen angels.

2. ACCORDING TO OLD TESTAMENT PROPHECY. The death of Christ was prophesied in Psalms 22:2-21; 40:6-7; and Isaiah 52:13–53:12.

3. ACCORDING TO THE GOSPELS. The death of Christ was portrayed in all four Gospels and anticipated in His frequent predictions of it.

4. ACCORDING TO ROMANS, 1 AND 2 CORINTHIANS, AND GALATIANS. The death of Christ is a major theme of Romans, 1 and 2 Corinthians, and Galatians, and is prominent in all four epistles (Rom. 3:22-26; 4:25; 5:7-10; 6:1-15; 14:9, 15; 1 Cor. 1:18–2:8; 15:3; 2 Cor. 5:14-21; Gal. 1:4; 2:20; 3:10-13; 6:14).

5. According to Ephesians, Philippians, and Colossians. The death of Christ in Ephesians, Philippians, and Colossians is also presented as a vital truth (Eph. 5:25-27; Phil. 2:5-8; Col. 1:14, 20).

6. According to Hebrews. The death of Christ is a major theme of Hebrews especially as fulfilling the typology of the Old Testament. Hebrews reveals more on the death of Christ than any other New Testament book (Heb. 1:3; 2:9; 5:1-10; 7:25-27; 9:12-18; 10:1-21; 12:2, 24; 13:10-13). The Book of Leviticus contributes more on the death of Christ than any other book in the Old Testament.

7. According to other New Testament books. The death of Christ is frequently mentioned in other books of the New Testament (Acts 17:3; 1 Thes. 4:14; 5:10; 1 Peter 1:18-21; 2:21; 3:18; 4:1; 1 John 2:2; Rev. 5:6, 9, 12; 13:8).

CHAPTER · 6

BIBLICAL TERMINOLOGY RELATED TO CHRIST'S SUFFERINGS AND DEATH

In biblical theology and translations of the Bible into English, certain specific words are employed by the authors. These terms in some cases are biblical and in other cases are established by theological usage. At least 13 important terms are used that relate to Christ's suffering and death.

ATONEMENT

In theology as well as in the Old Testament KJV the word "atonement" is used to express the entire work of Christ on the cross. The almost universal use of the word for this purpose gives it authoritative acceptance even though the term itself is not entirely accurate in this reference. The etymology of the word suggests at-one-ment, but actually its use in Scripture does not refer to this concept.

The word "atonement" is not used in the KJV in any New Testament passage, but it is found frequently in the Old Testament where it translates either *kaphar* or *kippurim.* In about 70 instances in the Old Testament it is a translation of *kaphar* and is translated "make an atonement" (e.g., Ex. 29:36-37; 30:10, 15-16; 32:30). The noun *kippurim* is found only 8 times and means "a covering" (e.g., Ex. 29:36; 30:10, 16; Lev. 23:27-28; 25:9; Num. 5:8; 29:11). In all these passages the concept is that the sacrifices of the Old Testament were temporary coverings of sin in anticipation of the final sacrifice of Christ on the cross. Through the sacrifice of Christ on the cross, the concept of covering is no longer accurate, and the New Testament uses other terms. While the Old Testament sacrifices provided temporary covering from divine judgment, the death of Christ takes away the sin of the world (John 1:29; 1 John 3:5).

EXPIATION

Expiation is the act of bearing a penalty for sin. Though not a biblical word, the concept is supported in the act of redemption (Rom. 3:23-25). When Christ died, He died in the place of mankind and in His offering paid the demands of justice.

FORGIVENESS AND REMISSION

The death of Christ made possible divine forgiveness of sins because Christ provided expiation for the sins of the world (Eph. 1:7; Col. 1:14).

GUILT

In the Old and New Testaments guilt means offending God's moral character and will. In this respect all persons are guilty before God (1 Cor. 11:27; James 2:10).

The guilt of the whole world was transferred to Christ in His substitutionary death on the cross (2 Cor. 5:18-21; 1 John 2:2). In His act of dying Christ made it possible for those who are guilty to be forgiven and have no further obligation to the matter of justice.

JUSTIFICATION

The doctrine of justification is repeatedly mentioned in both the Old and New Testaments. When a person places his trust in Christ, he is said to be justified (Rom. 3:26; 4:25; 5:16, 18). The question of Job, "How then can a man be righteous before God? How can one born of woman be pure?" (Job 25:4; cf. 9:2) is answered fully in the New Testament (Rom. 2:13; 3:24, 28, 30; 4:2, 5; 5:1, 9; 8:30, 33; 1 Cor. 6:11; Gal. 2:16-17; 3:11, 24; Titus 3:7). To be justified means to be legally declared as righteous. Being in Christ, a believer partakes of His righteous work on the cross which not only forgives but also adds the legal judgment that the believer is righteous before God.

JUSTICE

Justice is a synonym of righteousness. God is said to be just (not merciful) when He justifies the ungodly (Rom. 3:26; 4:5).

JUDGMENT

The penalty of sin is clearly said to be that of judgment and, apart from the death of Christ, everyone would pay the full price for his sins. This penalty for sin was borne by Christ on the cross, and those who believe in Him have the penalty of sin removed (1 Peter 3:18).

PROPITIATION

As previously discussed, propitiation is the Godward effect of the value of the Cross. Since Christ has died, God is propitious (1 John 2:2). This truth is the heart of the Gospel which is to be believed.

RECONCILIATION

As previously discussed, reconciliation represents the manward effect of the value of the Cross and indicates that man in the sight of God is completely changed and is made a new creature in Christ. Though reconciled to God, man is still a sinner by nature and by acts but is reconciled because of the death of Christ for his sins (2 Cor. 5:17-21).

REDEMPTION AND RANSOM

These two terms are practically the same in meaning and indicate the payment of the price for freeing Christians from the slavery of sin, delivering them from this bondage, and setting them free. The price has been completely paid for the sinner's redemption by

Christ's death on the cross (Matt. 20:28; Mark 10:45; Gal. 3:13; 1 Tim. 2:6; Titus 2:14; 1 Peter 1:18-19).

SACRIFICE

Though this term often means to relinquish what one may hold in his possession, its doctrinal meaning is that of an offering to God. The sacrifices of the Old Testament under the Mosaic Law anticipated the one final and perfect sacrifice which Christ became for lost men (Heb. 9:26; 10:12).

SATISFACTION

The doctrine of satisfaction is a synonym of propitiation. It means that God, as an infinitely righteous Person, must demand satisfaction for sin. In Christ's death on the cross a complete satisfaction or propitiation was made by the death of Christ, and God now can accept sinners who deserve judgment as if they were perfect.

VICARIOUS AND SUBSTITUTIONARY

The words "vicarious" and "substitutionary" are identical in meaning and refer to the suffering of one in place of another in the sense that by that suffering on the part of one, the other is wholly relieved. A vicar is an authorized or accepted substitute in office or service and is not merely someone who provides a benefit in general. Christ died that men might not be required to bear their burden of condemnation. This is the central truth of the Gospel, and to reject it is to reject the heart of Christian faith.

CHAPTER · 7

THEORIES TRUE AND FALSE ON THE VALUE OF CHRIST'S DEATH

No doctrine is more essential to Christian theology than the fact of Christ's death and its value to God, man, and angels.

PRELIMINARY CONSIDERATIONS

1. General facts revealed. General facts about the value of Christ's death are revealed in Scripture. Before man sinned, he was in harmony with God, and Adam and Eve had unbroken communion with God. When Adam and Eve sinned, however, God was compelled to drive them from the Garden and to deal with them and all mankind on the basis of forgiveness which can be provided only through the shedding of blood. The value of Christ's death therefore becomes an essential factor of Christian faith and hope.

As redemption was applied to Israel in the Old Testament under her covenants, she was restored to fellowship with God and enjoyed communion with Him and a life of tranquility on the earth.

Because of the death of Christ, Christians also have a right relationship to God. The death of Christ makes possible their spiritual possessions, their position in Christ, their eternal life, and their future hope. Three features stand out: God is man's Saviour, God originated the plan by which man may be saved, and God determined the terms on which man may be saved. These basic truths constitute a starting point for the study of the complex problem of the various theories men have formed in respect to the death of Christ.

As Christ is the center of Christian theology, so redemption is the center of God's work for man. Because of this it is natural in systematic theology to give attention to the doctrine of the value of Christ's death. Those who do not accept the complete authority of Scripture and who seek to escape the biblical revelation of salvation may support theories that are not completely in harmony with the Bible.

2. Uniqueness of death. The death of Christ is a unique act in the history of the world and is without parallel. In His death Christ offered no resistance, and He died voluntarily. Christ stated, "No one takes it from Me, but I lay it down of My own accord. I have authority to lay it down and authority to take it up again. This command I received from My Father" (John 10:18). The reason Christ was willing to die was that it was the Father's will (Isa. 53:6, 10). Man with his limitations can only partially understand this central fact of Christian faith though its character is obvious.

3. Extent. The extent of the value of Christ's death makes it clear that it is more than a ransom or redemption. His death is also the ground of imputed righteousness and justification as well as the basis for forgiveness. The death of Christ also made possible man's walking with divine enablement by the indwelling Holy Spirit and by the truth of Scripture. The death of Christ resulted in much more than forgiveness of sin.

4. Three directions. The death of Christ involves three directional relationships: redemption toward sin, reconciliation toward man, and propitiation toward God. In this plan of God, He Himself provides and receives a ransom, or redemption toward sin; He originates, provides, and acknowledges His own Son as the One who bears away sin, thus providing reconciliation. This results in God being propitiated. Though natural man unaided by spiritual enlightenment has great difficulty understanding the idea of Christ as a Substitute and as the One who satisfies a righteous God, this is the teaching of Scripture.

5. Divine satisfaction is not salvation. Divine satisfaction or propitiation through Christ's death is concerned with more than personal salvation. What was provided in the death of Christ is God's provision that salvation can come only when a believer appropriates by faith what Christ has done for him, but Christ's death provided much more than propitiation—it establishes a whole new relationship with God which enables Him to deal with the believer as an object of grace in time and in eternity.

6. Type and antitype. As previously discussed, the doctrine of types and antitypes relates to the death of Christ. In His death

Christ fulfilled the anticipation of all the Old Testament sacrifices, including the sacrifice of Isaac by Abraham which was prevented by God's intervention, and all other types and antitypes.

7. Theories subject to question. Theological theories are always subject to question and correction as they are compared to what the Bible actually teaches. Though theology is by its nature an induction, and any induction is no better than the facts that support it, students of theology should challenge each theory for its respective support in Scripture.

HISTORICAL RECORD

The history of the church provides a record of the struggle of theologians to understand the death of Christ properly. Various views of the value of Christ's death may be divided into three time periods: (1) from the beginning of Christian theology to Anselm (c. 1100); (2) Anselm to Grotius (c. 1600); and (3) from Grotius to the present time.

1. From the beginning to Anselm. The first thousand years of Christian theology were built on the early church accepting in simplicity that Christ died for the sins of the world. The comprehension of the early church, however, was not entirely accurate as some taught that Christ paid the ransom to Satan when He died on the cross. Though it is true that Christ in His death on the cross accomplished the judgment of Satan (John 12:31; 16:11; Col. 2:14-15), Satan, rather than receiving a ransom for sin, was defeated at the cross. Satan had no right to such a payment, and it is far better to consider the doctrine of propitiation as teaching that when Christ died He was satisfying not an obligation to Satan but the requirements of the righteousness of God. Some godly men did oppose the concept of a payment to Satan and accepted the scriptural view that God accepted the value of Christ's death because it was in keeping with His moral government of the universe and because it made possible man's salvation and sanctification.

2. From Anselm to Grotius. In the 500 years from Anselm to Grotius the writing of Anselm in his *Cur Deus Homo,* "Why the God Man," helped to teach the doctrine of divine propitiation. But some failed to comprehend the full-orbed work of Christ on the cross as it related to other aspects of the plan of God for salvation and there

was diversity in doctrine as it related to the death of Christ.

In this period there also was discussion on the question of whether Christ actually bore the total penalty of sin on the cross, or whether He died in a forensic sense, that is, His death was universal in its value and was applicable to all men even though some would be unsaved. The concept that Christ became actually the one who sinned when He died on the cross was inaccurate, because if Christ were actually the sinner, then His death would not be adequate for all men. Because He was God His death was forensic, that is, sufficient for all even though it was not applied to all.

Another problem that occupies theologians is the question whether divine freedom is curtailed by the fact that God requires justice. This is answered by attention to the larger problem of things that God cannot do, such as the fact that God could not sin, God could not lie, God could not do something that is foolish. Such limitation, however, is actually a strength rather than a weakness just as a Christian who is guided by Christian principles is not thereby limited but is actually able to fulfill to a larger degree what he ought to be.

Socinianism attempted to teach that Christ's death was universal, that is, that all men were saved by His death. This again is not what the Bible teaches because what Christ accomplished on the cross does not become applicable to an individual until he is born again.

The answer of limited atonement, often attributed to Calvin, that Christ died only for the elect, has the difficulty of not being what the Scriptures teach. Whether it was Christ's purpose to die for the elect only or for all men, the fact is that His death was forensic, that is, sufficient for all.

3. FROM GROTIUS TO THE PRESENT. From Grotius (1583-1645) to the present time there has been little advance of his so-called governmental theory of the value of Christ's death. Like many other theories it is short of what the Bible actually teaches and is not superior to the view of Anselm that the death of Christ satisfied God, a view which has become the predominant view of orthodoxy since the Protestant Reformation.

THEORIES IN GENERAL

With the foregoing survey of various approaches to the death of Christ, attention will now be given to some of the more important theories that have evolved in the history of the church. In these theories the question was raised whether the work of Christ was an answer primarily to the demands of Satan. Did the work of Christ affect only man? Was the death of Christ primarily a moral influence? Did the death of Christ relate to both God and man, but to man primarily or to God primarily?

In addition to these various approaches modern liberal theology has advanced universalism, the view that all men will eventually be saved. Others have suggested conditional immortality, the concept that only the righteous will be resurrected. Others hold that God is generous and forgives sin without respect to Christ's death. Some theories suggest that the death of Christ was unnecessary because God could sovereignly forgive. A study of these various opinions will help one to appreciate the proper Christian doctrine.

1. Christ was a martyr. The theory that Christ was a martyr is built on the concept that the death of Christ was to be an encouragement to man in his limitations, because dying as a martyr would ultimately confirm His other doctrines and demonstrate His sincerity. This view is deficient in explaining how the Bible refers to the death of Christ as absolutely necessary. "From that time on Jesus began to explain to His disciples that He must go to Jerusalem and suffer many things at the hands of the elders, chief priests, and teachers of the Law, and that He must be killed and on the third day be raised to life" (Matt. 16:21). Christ described His death as something that He "must" do. From the nature of the doctrine of sin and the righteousness of God, it is clear that His death, viewed simply as that of a martyr, does not have the power to achieve what the Scriptures refer to as salvation.

2. Christ died to stimulate morality. The moral influence theory that Christ died to stimulate morality, often attributed to Faustus Socinus (1539-1604), likewise comes far short of what the Bible teaches. Man, who is dead in trespasses and sins and under divine judgment from God, needs more than simply moral influence. Unitarians, who approach the death of Christ from a view similar to the moral influence theory, also fail to account for the Scriptures. Unitarians and Socinians do not accept the Bible as the inerrant Word of God and tend to ignore passages that would contradict their theories. Though it is true that Christ's death has a moral effect on the lives of those who are saved (2 Cor. 5:15), obviously more than a moral influence was required to bring men into harmony with God.

Christ did not die merely to show sympathy for men or to become a companion to those who die. He died that men might not die. He does not merely hold their hands while they suffer the judgment of their sins. Instead He died that they might never be required to bear the judgment of their sins.

3. Christ identified with men. The identification theory holds that Christ so identified Himself with men that He was able to represent them before God, confess their sins, and repent on their behalf. Though this has an element of substitution, the essential element of expiation is not sufficiently expressed in this view. The idea that God can justify man simply because He is God and acts sovereignly does not account for how this can be related to His attribute of righteousness.

4. The governmental theory. In the governmental theory Hugo Grotius, mentioned earlier, recognized the need of an objective work of Christ with respect to God. Compared to the concept that God is satisfied by the death of Christ, as advanced by Anselm, it becomes obvious that the point of view of Grotius is inferior. Grotius attempted to answer the point of view of Unitarians and Socinians by teaching the objective value of Christ's death and yet he avoided some of the rational criticism made against the doctrine of satisfaction. He suggested that the death of Christ was necessary for God's government of the world. This was refuted by others, especially by those who followed Calvin.

These two systems of interpretation of Grotius and Anselm agree that the death of Christ and the shedding of His blood play a large part in the salvation of men. But the proper doctrine of satisfaction holds that a penal substitution is involved which has the objective purpose of providing a just and righteous ground for God to forgive the sins of those for whom Christ died (cf. Rom. 3:26).

The governmental theory of Grotius, however, held that the death of Christ was vicarious but did not have a bearing on the punishment that would otherwise be due mankind. Grotius objected to the concept of imputation, the view that human sin was imputed to Christ or that the righteousness of God is imputed to those who believe. He objected to the doctrine of satisfaction that states Christ died for all men. For he held that then it would follow that all men were saved. This, however, is expressly denied in the Scriptures that affirm that some men are lost in spite of the death of Christ. The concept that because God is love He obviously would save people without necessity for judgment on sin in the form of satisfaction is not supported by Scripture. God is righteous in His judgments even though He is a God of love.

Grotius and those who followed him distinguished between what was governmental and what was personal in God in respect to judgment of sin. They held that God could not judge sin on a personal basis or as that which outrages His holiness since He is love and so He must judge sin on grounds that are corrective or governmental in relation to man. No penalty would fall on either the substitute or the penitent sinner because he is forgiven by an act of divine compassion.

The contest between Grotius and the orthodox view is a contrast between penitence and forgiveness without respect to other values found in Christ's death. Basically the Grotian view was in harmony with Arminianism, whereas the satisfaction theory is more in harmony with Calvinism.

In the nineteenth century John Miley, professor of systematic theology at Drew Theological Seminary in New Jersey, presented a spirited support of the governmental theory (John Miley, *Systematic Theology*, New York: Hunt and Eaton, 1894, II, pp. 176-84).

Three objections can be made to the governmental theory: (a) It is a hypothesis based on human reason and makes no avowed induction of the Scriptures while contending that the Scriptures can be made to harmonize with it. (b) The view attempts an impossible distinction between the sufferings of Christ as sacrificial and the sufferings of Christ as penal. The illustrations used by Miley are not an actual parallel to the sacrifice of Christ and fail to recognize the distinction between divine and human government. (c) The view restricts the scope of the value of Christ's death to forgiveness of sins of the unsaved on the assumption that fallen man needs only forgiveness. The fact that Christ's death relates not only to sin but also to the sin nature and the matter of imputed righteousness and eternal life is not adequately included.

5. The doctrine of satisfaction. This doctrine holds that Christ met the righteous demands of God against sin. This view has been held by many who are orthodox and who approach the Scriptures with a moderate Calvinistic view.

The doctrine of satisfaction falls into two general classifications or schools of interpretation—the absolute and the moderate. By the term "absolute" reference is made to a school of theologians who teach that if Christ rendered satisfaction to God for the sins of a person that person would thereby be one of the elect and must of necessity be saved because the penalty no longer exists since it was borne by Christ as his substitute.

The "moderate" interpretation of the satisfaction view of Christ's death contends that on the authority of Scripture, Christ died for the whole world but that no one benefits from Christ's death until he believes. This is illustrated for instance in Ephesians 2:1-2 when the Ephesian Christians are addressed, "As for you, you were dead in your transgressions and sins, in which you used to live when you followed the ways of this world and of the ruler of the kingdom of the air, the spirit who is now at work in those who are disobedient." The Ephesian Christians before they were saved were just as dead in trespasses and sins as any other unsaved person. The truth of this point of view will be brought out in later discussion of this doctrine.

A proper view of the value of Christ's death must include the great doctrines of redemption, reconciliation, propitiation, justification, eternal life, being baptized into the body of Christ, and other truths. A proper view will account for the forgiveness of the personal sins committed by Christians as well as the correction of the broad effects of the death of Christ even on heaven itself.

Views other than the satisfaction theory dishonor God by assuming that He can disregard His own holiness by an attitude of leniency toward sin, a view that would deny the Word of God and make the death of Christ a foolish act.

CONCLUSION

The problem with all views on the value of Christ's death except the view of satisfaction is that they have a weak view of sin, a limited comprehension of the extent of salvation provided in Christ, and in one sense or another suggest that Christ's death was not an actual substitution. To deny the satisfaction theory is in effect to deny that man is as desperately sinful as the Bible presents. For a comprehensive summary of this see Benjamin B. Warfield, *Studies in Theology* (New York: Oxford University Press, 1932, pp. 289-97).

CHAPTER • 8

THE RESURRECTION OF JESUS CHRIST

IMPORTANT DEMARCATIONS BETWEEN THE OLD AND NEW COVENANTS

The resurrection of Jesus Christ is one of the important demarcations separating the Old and New Covenants. The important events indicating a change in dispensations begin with the death of Christ, a significant event relative to the salvation of believers but also marking a decisive step in the redemptive process.

1. Before the death of Christ individuals were saved and forgiven, as it were, on credit; sin was not brought into proper judgment before God until the death of Christ. This is stated in Romans 3:25-26, "God presented Him as a sacrifice of atonement, through faith in His blood. He did this to demonstrate His justice, because in His forbearance He had left the sins committed beforehand unpunished—He did it to demonstrate His justice at the present time, so as to be just and the One who justifies the one who has faith in Jesus."

Though Old Testament saints were saved and forgiven, their situation differed from that of believers in the present age. Old Testament believers had their sins covered, that is, temporarily forgiven, while awaiting the final answer in the death of Christ. The sacrifices and offerings they prepared could not finally take away sin. As stated in Hebrews 10:4: "It is impossible for the blood of bulls and goats to take away sins." For this reason, "Christ was sacrificed once to take away the sins of many people" (9:28). The sins were not actually taken away until Christ died (John 1:29; Rom. 3:25). When Christ died the sins of believers were paid for with finality so that believers have no condemnation and are forgiven all their sins (Rom. 8:1; Col. 2:13). The Law made no one perfect but "by one sacrifice He has made perfect forever those who are being made holy" (Heb. 10:14). Accordingly, the death of Christ is an important reminder that something new has been brought in.

2. Along with the death of Christ, the resurrection of Christ is an important demarcation between the old order and the new. Though the covenant of grace extends throughout all dispensations, it is not correct to ignore the progress of revelation and the progress of the work of God as embodied in the death and resurrection of Christ.

3. In addition to the death and resurrection of Christ, the fact that Christ ascended into heaven and is carrying on His present ministry as High Priest on the throne of God also marks an important change from the Old Testament order in which earthly priests interceded for the people of Israel.

4. Since the coming of the Holy Spirit on the Day of Pentecost, every believer is indwelt by the Holy Spirit and baptized into the body of Christ. This is another important demarcation which separates the old from the new and introduces a new dispensation in which spiritual truths are introduced characterizing the new age of grace. The new creation, composed of both Jews and Gentiles, stands in contrast to what was true in the Old Testament and provides a base for the present ministries of the Holy Spirit.

5. The introduction of a new program featuring Jews and Gentiles in one body in the church through the baptism of the Spirit also provides a line of demarcation that ends the special Jewish character of the Mosaic Law. As Scripture reveals, many of the glorious prospects of the earthly kingdom detailed in Old Testament prophecy are not being fulfilled in the present age but await a future dispensation after the present age has run its course and the second coming of Christ has occurred.

6. The important events marking the introduction of the new age also make clear that what is now being fulfilled was not a part of Old Testament prophecy and is not a fulfillment of what God promised Israel concerning the future earthly kingdom. The attempt to spiritualize Old Testament prophecy as given to Israel, and to consider them fulfilled in the present age is an unjustified method of interpretation that ignores the important events marking the introduction of a new age.

7. A study of the resurrection of Christ should be seen in its twofold revelation, first as anticipated in the Old Testament and then as fulfilled and applied in the New Testament.

THE OLD TESTAMENT DOCTRINE OF THE RESURRECTION OF CHRIST

The Old Testament provides many revelations concerning Jesus Christ, including His birth, His life, His ministry, His death, His resurrection, and His ultimate glorious reign in a kingdom on earth. Though it was not commonly understood by those living in the Old Testament period that the Messiah, when He came, would die and need to be resurrected, the Scriptures are clear that this is what was to be fulfilled. This is indicated first of all in the types relating to the resurrection of Christ.

1. Four typical foreshadowings of Christ's resurrection are found in the Old Testament. In Genesis 14, Abram was revealed to have attacked the kings who had seized Sodom and Gomorrah and had carried off Lot as a captive. Assembling 318 trained men in his own household, Abram attacked by night the kings who had conquered Sodom and Gomorrah and routed them, pursuing them as far as Hobah, north of Damascus (vv. 14-15). He was able to recover all the goods that they had plundered, especially his nephew Lot and his possessions (v. 16). When Abram returned from this successful battle, "Melchizedek king of Salem brought out bread and wine. He was priest of God Most High, and he blessed Abram, saying, 'Blessed be Abram by God Most High, Creator of heaven and earth and blessed be God Most High, who delivered your enemies into your hand.' Then Abram gave him a tenth of everything" (vv. 18-20).

In contrast to the Aaronic priesthood, Christ is introduced in Hebrews as in Psalm 110:4, "A Priest forever, in the order of Melchizedek" (cf. Heb. 5:6). This truth is further discussed in Hebrews 7 where it is pointed out in relation to Melchizedek, that he was "without father or mother, without genealogy, without beginning of days or end of life, like the Son of God he remains a priest forever" (v. 3).

Melchizedek undoubtedly was born like all other human beings and undoubtedly died. But his claim to priesthood was not based on genealogy but by the direct appointment of God. Because the Melchizedekian priesthood does not end, so Christ is a Priest forever fulfilling the type of Melchizedek.

Another type of Christ is seen in the two birds mentioned in Leviticus 14:4-7. In this passage two birds are used in sacrifice, with one being killed and the other being set free. As such, they are types of Christ in His death and in His resurrection.

In connection with the ceremony of cleansing of diseased people God said, "The priest is to go outside the camp and examine him. If the person has been healed of his infectious skin disease, the priest shall order that two live clean birds and some cedar wood, scarlet yarn, and hyssop be brought for the one to be cleansed. Then the priest shall order that one of the birds be killed over fresh water in a clay pot. He is then to take the live bird and dip it, together with the cedar wood, the scarlet yarn and the hyssop, into the blood of the bird that was killed over the fresh water. Seven times he shall sprinkle the one to be cleansed of the infectious disease and pronounce him clean. Then he is to release the live bird in the open fields" (vv. 3-7).

This type is fulfilled in the fact that Christ died and then rose from the dead.

A third type of Christ is revealed in connection with the firstfruits (23:10-11). In connection with the feasts of Jehovah itemized in Leviticus 23, God declared, "The LORD said to Moses, 'Speak to the Israelites and say to them: "When you enter the land I am going to give you and reap its harvest, bring to the priest a sheaf of the first grain you harvest. He is to wave the sheaf before the LORD so it will be accepted on your behalf; the priest is to wave it on the day after the Sabbath' " (vv. 9-11). As the first sheaf of grain representing the harvest was waved before God, so Christ is declared to be the first-fruits in His resurrection (1 Cor. 15:23). Some believe the people who are raised at the time of the resurrection of Christ were such a token sheaf of the harvest to come, as the sheaf was composed of several stocks (Matt. 27:52-53). The sheaf of grain waved before the priest therefore became a type of the resurrection of Christ.

Another type of the resurrection of Christ is found in Aaron's rod that budded (Num. 17:8). The Scriptures record, in connection with the presentation of Aaron's rod to the leaders of Israel who were grumbling, "So Moses spoke to the Israelites, and their leaders gave him twelve staffs, one for the leader of each of their ancestral tribes, and Aaron's staff was among them. Moses placed the staffs before the LORD in the Tent of Testimony. The next day Moses entered the Tent of the Testimony and saw that Aaron's staff, which represented the house of Levi, had not only sprouted but had budded, blossomed and produced almonds. Then Moses brought out all the staffs from the LORD's presence to all the Israelites. They looked at them and each man took his own staff" (vv. 6-9). Aaron's rod that budded was distinguished from the other rods and became a type of the resurrection of Christ in which His dead body was restored to life.

2. Three principal Old Testament prophecies refer to the fact that Christ was to rise from the dead. In connection with David's hope of resurrection, he wrote, "Therefore my heart is glad and my tongue rejoices; my body also will rest secure, because You will not abandon me to the grave, nor will You let Your Holy One see decay" (Ps. 16:9-10). Though it was initially an expression of David's hope of resurrection, the prophecy goes beyond that of David in that it predicts that the body will not decay in the tomb, and this is related to the "Holy One," which refers to Christ. The fact that Christ's resurrection was the fulfillment of this passage was confirmed elsewhere in Scripture by Peter and Paul (Acts 2:24-31; 13:34-37). The important fact that distinguished the resurrection of Christ from all other resurrections is that Christ's body did not see corruption. Though His body was in the grave it was not allowed to decay. It is in keeping with this that Paul states to Timothy, that Christ "alone is immortal" (1 Tim. 6:16).

A second important passage dealing with the death and resurrection of Christ is Psalm 22:22-31. The opening of this psalm contains some of the very words which Christ spoke on the cross, "My God, My God, why have You forsaken Me?" (v. 1) After describing the death of Christ in detail (vv. 2-21), the psalmist, anticipating what would be true of Christ declares, "I will declare Your name to My brothers; in the congregation I will praise You." This declaration refers to the postresurrection ministry of Christ. The close of Psalm 22 also pictures universal dominion of the Lord (vv. 27-31).

A third important passage referring to the resurrection of Christ is found in Psalm 118:22-24, "The stone the builders rejected has become the capstone; the Lord has done this, and it is marvelous in our eyes. This is the day the Lord has made; let us rejoice and be glad in it."

In the New Testament in Acts 4:10-11, this passage is quoted as evidence of the resurrection of Christ: "Then know this, you and everyone else in Israel: It is by the name of Jesus Christ of Nazareth, whom you crucified but whom God raised from the dead, that this man stands before you completely healed. He is 'the stone you builders rejected, which has become the capstone.' " The stone which the builders rejected, referring to the rejection of Christ, was now to be made the prominent capstone.

Though the resurrection of Christ preeminently shows Christ as the Head of the church and the new creation, it is also true that His resurrection made possible His sitting on the Davidic throne in the future millennial kingdom (2:23-31). His reign will go on forever because Christ is a resurrected being and will have no successors.

THE NEW TESTAMENT DOCTRINE OF THE RESURRECTION OF CHRIST

The New Testament doctrine of Christ's resurrection will be considered under seven divisions: (1) Christ's own predictions of His resurrection; (2) His resurrection is subject to valid proof; (3) His resurrection was a bodily resurrection; (4) His resurrection resulted in a new order of beings; (5) seven reasons for His resurrection; (6) His resurrection as the present standard of divine power; and (7) the Lord's Day as a commemoration of His resurrection.

1. Christ's own predictions of His resurrection. It is remarkable that the disciples did not understand or believe that Christ would die and be resurrected even though it was the subject of many Scriptures (Matt. 16:21; 17:23; 20:17-19; 26:12, 28, 31; Mark 9:30-32; 14:8, 24, 27; Luke 9:22, 44-45; 18:31-34; 22:20; John 2:19-21; 10:17-18; 12:7).

Though many questions have been raised concerning the inability of the disciples to understand these plain prophecies concerning the death and resurrection of Christ, it should be remembered that they approached the subject of Christ's ministry on earth from the standpoint of the Old Testament. According to their belief, the Old Testament taught that when Christ came He would bring in a kingdom of righteousness and would conquer the world. They expected to have prominent places in Christ's kingdom. Accordingly, it became increasingly difficult for them to understand the opposition to Christ and the lack of evidence that He was progressing to the point where all would acknowledge Him as their King. What they did not understand was that the prophecies of His death and resurrection related to His first coming and His prophecies of His glorious return to the earth and the setting up of His kingdom related to His second coming and that there would be an age in between. There is no evidence that anyone understood this truth until it actually began to be fulfilled after Christ returned to heaven on the Day of Ascension.

Accordingly, the death and resurrection of Christ was totally foreign to their understanding of the process by which Christ would bring in His kingdom. They felt they had misunderstood His predictions. Also, they did not remember the precise words of Christ relative to His predictions about His death and resurrection.

In the second chapter of John, when Christ predicted that the temple could be raised in three days, the disciples did not understand that He was referring to His body and its resurrection. John 2:22, however, records, "After He was raised from the dead, His disciples recalled what He had said. Then they believed the Scripture and the words that Jesus had spoken." When Christ prophesied His death and resurrection in Luke 18:31-33, the Scriptures record, "The disciples did not understand any of this. Its meaning was hidden from them, and they did not know what He was talking about" (v. 34).

By contrast, it is remarkable that the enemies of Christ remembered His predictions, and so they requested that the tomb be sealed to prevent anyone from stealing the body of Jesus. All this did, of course, was to confirm the fact of His resurrection when it actually took place.

The Scriptures also make clear that Christ was in the grave for three days. This fact supports the prophecy of Psalm 16:10 that His body would not "see decay." It was traditionally believed that after three days the body would begin to decay. This is brought out in the miracle of Lazarus' resuscitation; they affirmed that his body had been in the grave four days (John 11:17). Christ purposely did not come to Bethany during the three-day period because He wanted to make clear that this was an unusual resuscitation (vv. 6, 17). In contrast to that of Lazarus, however, it was important that Jesus' body not see decay. The resurrection of Christ, accordingly, is in direct literal fulfillment of the psalmist's prophecy of His resurrection.

2. The Resurrection is subject to valid proof. The certainty that Christ rose from the dead as stated in Scripture has long been recognized as one of the most important evidences for the Christian faith. If Christ did not rise, the whole edifice of Christian theology tumbles and is without adequate foundation. If Christ did rise from the dead, that fact supports and sustains the major doctrines of the Christian faith. Both friend and foe recognize the importance of the resurrection of Christ and the evidence supporting it.

One of the foremost evidences for the resurrection of Christ is the empty tomb. As the Scriptures bear witness, the enemies of Christ did all they could to assure that the body of Christ would never leave the tomb. They sealed it with the Roman seal, and they protected it by soldiers who were assigned to guard the tomb. In spite of this protection, the stone was rolled away from the tomb and the tomb was found to be empty. The testimony of the angelic messengers that the tomb was empty and Christ was risen (Matt. 28:5-7; Luke 24:4-7) is supported by the fact that the apostles and others, as they examined the tomb, found the body of Christ no longer there (John 20:3-9).

Certain collateral evidence also is provided in the tomb, supporting the certainty of the bodily resurrection of Christ. In His death He was bound with linen cloth saturated in ointment (19:40) that in the course of several days would cause this cloth to become dry and hard and form a casement for the body. If the body had been stolen or taken in any physical way, the graveclothes would have disappeared with the body. Instead of that, the disciples found in the empty tomb the strips of linen cloth that had surrounded the body of Christ as well as the napkin that was over His face (Luke 24:12; John 20:6-7). It is possible that Christ's resurrection body slipped out of the graveclothes, leaving it in the form of a body. This would have demonstrated that the body was resurrected, not stolen.

Significantly, on the Day of Pentecost 3,000 Jews believed that Christ was resurrected. In the interim between the death of Christ and Pentecost, as the word went out that the tomb was empty, no doubt many of the Jews inspected the tomb for themselves and saw the eloquent evidence that Christ was raised. There is no valid explanation of the empty tomb apart from the facts of Scripture that He was raised from the dead.

A second important line of evidence is the physical appearance of Christ to the disciples. His first appearance was to Mary Magdalene who came back to the tomb the second time after announcing that the tomb was empty (vv. 10-18). He also appeared to the women who were hurrying to announce the empty tomb to the disciples (Matt. 28:8-10). Christ also appeared to Peter on the afternoon of His resurrection (Luke 24:34; 1 Cor. 15:5). Christ appeared to the disciples as they walked toward Emmaus on the Resurrection Day and revealed Himself to them (Mark 16:12-13; Luke 24:13-35). Later that evening Christ appeared to the disciples as they were discussing His appearances (Mark 16:14; Luke 24:36-43; John 20:19-23). Other appearances followed.

His sixth appearance was to the 11 disciples a week later, and this time Thomas was present (vv. 26-29). The seventh appearance was to seven disciples on the Sea of Galilee (21:1-23). According to 1 Corinthians 15:6, His eighth appearance was to the 500 and is offered by Paul as a certain proof of His resurrection. Christ also appeared to His brother James in His ninth appearance (v. 7). His tenth appearance was to 11 disciples (Matt. 28:16-20). His eleventh appearance occurred on the day of His ascension at the Mount of Olives (Luke 24:44-53; Acts 1:8-9). Later appearances were supernatural: to Stephen (7:55-56), Paul (9:3-6; cf. 22:6-11; 26:13-18), and to Paul in Arabia (Gal. 1:12, 17). A further appearance was to Paul (Acts 22:17-21; cf. 9:26-30; Gal. 1:18). A final appearance of Christ to Paul occurred when Paul was in prison in Caesarea (Acts 23:11). Jesus' final supernatural appearance was to the Apostle John (Rev. 1:12-20). The many appearances of Christ constitute solid evidence that Christ actually rose from the dead.

The appearances were not only a factual matter, but also brought about the transformation of the disciples who had been in fear and in sorrow and disappointment in the days between Christ's death and resurrection. There is no evidence that they were gullible or looking for any kind of fragile evidence that Christ was raised. Rather, it took solid evidence for them to be convinced. Christ appeared to them and could be handled (John 20:27) to be sure that it was not a ghost. The change in the disciples was an absolute one where, from grief and disappointment and disillusionment they suddenly were joyous, fearless, even willing to die for the fact that Christ died on the cross and rose again. They experienced not only the normal psychological change that would be brought about by such evidence, but also the supernatural power of the Holy Spirit, as fulfilled in Acts 2 and later incidents in the Book of Acts.

Historically, the fact of the Christian church remains a solid monument to the resurrection of Christ. It would have been impossible to build a following to Jesus Christ if the death of Christ and His resurrection had not been assured historical facts. The church has been a dynamic force in the world ever since, with millions of people examining the evidence and coming to the conclusion that Jesus Christ is indeed all He claimed to be, the Son of God, the risen Saviour and the Lord of the universe. This constitutes additional evidence for the resurrection of Christ.

There also exists an evident congruity between the fact of the Resurrection and all we know of Christ. If Christ is indeed what the Scriptures present, the virgin-born Son of God who performed the supernatural miracles including resurrection from the dead, it is understandable that this same Person would have the omnipotence of God and would be able to raise Himself as Christ Himself claimed (John 10:18). No event in the ancient world has more sustaining evidence than the facts of Scripture that Christ died and that He rose again.

3. THE RESURRECTION OF CHRIST WAS AN ACTUAL BODILY RESURRECTION. As is always the case when Scripture revelation is given, attempts have been made to weaken the truth and rob it of its essential character. The Resurrection has sometimes been interpreted to be simply a revival of the ideas of Christ or the hope of Christ or the hope of God's ultimate victory. But these approaches to the resurrection of Christ leave unanswered the solid proof that it was a historic event, that Christ died, that His body had been placed in the tomb and was actually raised from the dead in a new glorified body suited for heaven. The factual resurrection of Christ is important to the believers' hopes that those who die in Christ or who are awaiting His coming at the Rapture of the church will receive new physical bodies suited for heaven and for everlasting worship and service in the presence of the Saviour.

4. THE RESURRECTION OF CHRIST ALSO INTRODUCES A NEW ORDER OF BEING, THOUGH THERE HAVE BEEN RESTORATIONS TO LIFE FREQUENTLY THROUGHOUT SCRIPTURE. These restorations imply that death again overtook the body at a later time. The resurrection of Christ, however, is the first of a new order of beings who receive bodies that will never be destroyed. The resurrection of Christ introduced immortality, a body that is without death (1 Tim. 6:16; 2 Tim. 1:10). As stated in verse 10, "It has now been revealed through the appearing of our Saviour, Christ Jesus, who has destroyed death and has brought life and immortality to light through the Gospel."

5. AT LEAST SEVEN REASONS MAY BE ADVANCED FOR THE RESURRECTION OF CHRIST: (a) Christ arose because of who He is; (b) Christ arose that He might fulfill the Davidic Covenant; (c) Christ arose that He might be the source of resurrection life; (d) Christ arose that He might become the source of resurrection power; (e) Christ arose to be Head over all things to the church; (f) Christ arose on account of justification being accomplished; and (g) Christ arose to be the firstfruits.

a. CHRIST AROSE BECAUSE OF WHO HE IS. According to Acts 2:24, "God raised Him from the dead, freeing Him from the agony of death, because it is impossible for death to keep its hold on Him." It is inconceivable that Jesus Christ who is the eternal God having become incarnate could remain physically dead. Peter then quoted Psalm 16:8-11, pointing out that it was only to be expected that Jesus Christ would not remain in the grave but would rise from the dead and be filled with life (Acts 2:25-28). John 5:26 states, "For as the Father has life in Himself, so He has granted the Son to have life in Himself." This life referred not simply to His human nature but also to the eternal life which was in Christ from eternity past. Being the person He is, it was impossible for the grave to hold Him.

b. CHRIST ROSE TO FULFILL THE DAVIDIC COVENANT. The Davidic Covenant predicted that David's throne and kingdom would continue forever (2 Sam. 7). This of course would be difficult for earthly kings who lived and died. It required a resurrected person, such as Christ, who had immortality to occupy this throne in perpetuity. The truth of the everlasting character of the Davidic kingdom is stated beautifully in Psalm 89:20-37. Because of His resurrection, Christ is qualified to fulfill the Davidic Covenant and to sit on the throne of David forever. Other Scriptures support this view of the perpetuity of the reign of Christ (Isa. 9:6-7; Luke 1:31-33; Acts 2:25-31; 15:16-18).

c. CHRIST BECAME THE SOURCE OF RESURRECTION LIFE. It would be impossible for a dead savior to impart life to those who put their trust in him. It was God's purpose that through Christ that life would be given to His sheep (John 10:10-11). It is also true that those who believe in Christ receive eternal life. As stated in 1 John 5:11-12, "And this is the testimony: God has given us eternal life, and this life is in His Son. He who has the Son has life; he who does not have the Son of God does not have life." A future fellowship with God in time and eternity also speaks of having the life of Christ in us (Eph. 2:6; Col. 3:1-4).

d. CHRIST AROSE TO BE THE SOURCE OF RESURRECTION POWER. In contrast to the Old Testament standard, which refers to the deliverance of the Children of Israel from Egypt, a Christian has a new standard in the resurrection of Christ. This power is referred to in Ephesians 1:19-21, "and His incomparably great power for us who believe. That power is like the working of His mighty strength, which He exerted in Christ when He raised Him from the dead and seated Him at His right hand in the heavenly realms, far above all rule and authority, power and dominion, and every title that can be given, not only in the present age but also in the one to come."

e. CHRIST ROSE FROM THE DEAD TO BE HEAD OVER ALL THINGS TO THE CHURCH. It is obvious that the new creation of Jew and Gentile to form the body of Christ could be accomplished only by resurrection power. In the nature of resurrection it replaces death with life, the old creation with the new creation. This is stated in 2 Corinthians 5:17, "Therefore, if anyone is in Christ, he is a new creation; the old has gone, the new has come!" The church is an outstanding illustration of the infinite power of Christ released through His resurrection making possible the church and forming a new creation with Christ as its head.

f. CHRIST ROSE ON ACCOUNT OF OUR JUSTIFICATION BEING ACCOMPLISHED. In His resurrection from the dead, Christ indicated that our justification had been completed, as stated in Romans 4:25, "He was delivered over to death for our sins and was raised to life for our justification." The thought was not that His life constituted our justification, but rather that He was able to be raised from the dead because in His death He had provided sufficient grounds for God justly to declare a sinner righteous. This is stated in 3:24, "And are justified freely by His grace through the redemption that came by Christ Jesus." Being justified, we are assured of deliverance from the wrath of God, "Since we have now been justified by His blood, how much more shall we be saved from God's wrath through Him!" (5:9)

g. CHRIST WAS RAISED TO BE THE FIRSTFRUITS FROM THE DEAD. The concept of being the firstfruits or the token of a future harvest is sometimes used of Israel (Jer. 2:3), sometimes of the Spirit's blessing on a Christian (Rom. 8:23), of the first believers in any given locality (16:5; 1 Cor. 16:15), of the saints of the present age (James 1:18), of the 144,000 (Rev. 14:4), and of Christ also in His resurrection. As stated in 1 Corinthians 15:20-23, "But Christ has indeed been raised from the dead, the firstfruits of those who have fallen asleep. For since death came through a man, the resurrection of the dead comes also through a man. For as in Adam all die, so in Christ all will be made alive. But each in his own turn: Christ, the firstfruits; then, when He comes, those who belong to Him. Then the end will come, when He hands over the kingdom to God the Father after He has destroyed all dominions, authority and power." As the firstfruits, Christ represents the saints in heaven and assures them of their ultimate presence in the glory of the Father, Christ being the firstfruits, and others will follow in the spiritual harvest that will come.

6. THE RESURRECTION OF CHRIST IS THE PRESENT STANDARD OF

DIVINE POWER. As mentioned previously, the resurrection of Christ is the standard of power for the present age. In the Old Testament, Israel's deliverance from Egypt demonstrated that God was the God of power who could deliver them (Ex. 20:2). In the prophetic future when Israel is regathered in the millennial kingdom, this will be their new standard of power (Jer. 23:7-8). For the present age, however, the believer in his conflict with evil and Satan can be assured of the power of God. As stated in Ephesians 1:19, Christ manifests this power first in the fact that He Himself was raised from the dead. No other one had the power to lay down his life and take it again as Christ affirmed (John 10:18). It was the power of God that raised Christ, as repeatedly stated in Scripture. This included Christ's own power, the power of God the Father, and the power of the Holy Spirit.

The power manifested in Jesus' resurrection is further illustrated in the ascension of Christ. Ephesians 1:20 speaks of the power "exerted in Christ when He raised Him from the dead and seated Him at His right hand in the heavenly realms."

In addition to these evidences, Scripture states, "And God placed all things under His feet and appointed Him to be Head over everything for the church, which is His body, the fullness of Him who fills everything in every way" (vv. 22-23). Placing "all things under His feet" refers to putting down His enemies and the power of this world. In addition to this, He is given the added role of being Head over the church, which is His body. He is the Director of the church as the Head of the body, and is the Bestower of gifts on the church by the Spirit (1 Cor. 12:7-11). Like branches drawing their life and fruitfulness from the vine, so the church draws its vitality and life and fruitfulness from Christ.

7. THE RESURRECTION OF CHRIST MADE POSSIBLE THE CELEBRATING OF THE FIRST DAY OF THE WEEK AS THE LORD'S DAY. In the Old Testament the Sabbath was observed in commemoration and as a day of rest. In the New Testament Christians commemorate the first day of the week as the day of Christ's resurrection with all that this means theologically and spiritually.

Though the Scriptures record that God rested on the seventh day from His Creation (Gen. 2:2), there is no record of regulations given to man concerning the Sabbath until the Mosaic Covenant was given. Under the Mosaic Covenant, Israel was to observe the seventh day as a day of rest (Ex. 20:8-11).

In the New Testament, however, no instruction is given to the church concerning observing the Sabbath. Instead the custom was to meet on the first day of the week in commemoration of the resurrection of Christ and to worship and serve God in a special way on that day. Though the provision continues to be one day in seven as set aside for God, no regulation concerning rest or inactivity is revealed in Scripture concerning the first day of the week.

The first day of the week is observed by the New Testament church in commemoration of the fact that in the death and resurrection of Christ, He provided the foundation for the church as a new creation composed of the church as the body of Christ and Christ as the Head.

Important events form a background for observing the first day of the week. According to Scripture, Christ rose from the dead on the first day of the week (Matt. 28:1). On that first day He also met His disciples (John 20:19) and enjoyed the new fellowship that came after His resurrection. On the first day of the week He gave the disciples special instructions concerning their walk with the Lord (Luke 24:36-49). On the first day of the week Christ breathed the Holy Spirit into the disciples (John 20:22). On the first day of the week He also ascended to heaven (Acts 2:1-4). On the first day of the week it was customary for believers to gather to break bread (20:6-7), and to bring their offerings as God had prospered them (1 Cor. 16:2). Though no command is found in the New Testament relative to observing the first day of the week, it is obvious that God had blessed the early church, as well as the church in subsequent centuries, which has observed this day as a special day of recognition of the resurrection of Christ.

It is not too much to say that the doctrine of Christ's resurrection is one of the most important doctrines of Scripture. Without the resurrection of Christ there would be no anchor for the Christian faith, no assurance of His deity, and no support for the concept that He died on the cross for our sins efficaciously. The resurrection of Christ is also the basis of the hope of believers for their resurrection, as argued by Paul in 1 Corinthians 15. The doctrine of resurrection is also our assurance that our present body, so inadequate and so mortal, will be replaced by a body that is suitable for the eternal worship and service of God in glory.

DIVINE ELECTION

CHAPTER • 9

THE FACT OF DIVINE ELECTION

In view of the extended discussion of divine decrees already treated in biblical theism, only a limited discussion on the doctrine of election is necessary in connection with the subject of salvation.

Many students of Scripture find difficulty in accepting the doctrine of divine election. This is because divine election and the human experience of choice are difficult to harmonize.

In the universe there are things which God obviously determines, such as Creation, one star differing from another, men being born in various races with differing advantages, great variety in human civilizations, and differences in natural gifts. Though divine election seems to be an arbitrary work of God, it must be considered in light of the fact of God's universal love revealed in sending His Son (John 3:16). Much that cannot be entirely understood by human intelligence can nonetheless be accepted by faith. The ultimate question is, What does the Bible teach? Obviously the Bible does not teach what would contradict divine justice, divine love, or divine goodness. Christians have little difficulty in seeing the infinite blessing of measureless possessions and positions in Christ and the wonder of their being the objects of His grace. Difficulties do arise when contemplating God in His relationship to the unsaved world which never avails itself of the grace of God.

Obviously God chose the saved before they chose Him (John 15:16). One who is saved can to some extent understand sovereign grace, election, God's calling, His redemption, and His regeneration. Christians can also experience God's divine preservation and the hope of being presented faultless before the glory of God in the future. To attain these ends God has employed means such as the sacrifice of His only begotten Son. It is not enough that sin should be declared sinful. Its curse must be borne by the Lamb of God, the will of man must be moved to take the step of faith, regeneration must be wrought by the Spirit, and every spiritual heavenly blessing must be secured by union with Christ. In human experience, man is conscious only of his power to choose or reject salvation in Christ with the realization that he is saved or lost according to his belief or disbelief in Christ as Saviour.

Much in the doctrine of divine election transcends the limitations of finite understanding, but it is obvious that both God and man have the power of choice and that God's will is infinitely greater than human will. Accordingly in the study of the doctrine of divine election, the human mind must submit to divine revelation which should be accepted by faith even though it may not be entirely understood.

The treatment of divine election falls into two major parts, the fact of divine election treated here and the order of elective decrees discussed in the next chapter.

The study of divine election may be subdivided into four features: (a) the terms used, (b) a clear revelation, (c) essential truths embraced, and (d) the objections to the doctrine.

THE TERMS USED

1. Election. In biblical usage the word "election" designates a sovereign, divine purpose so formulated as to be independent of human merit, consent, or cooperation. This entire doctrine is in harmony with the truth of God's sovereignty observed in His creation in which both variety and selection are everywhere present. The term is used of Israel (Isa. 65:9, 22), of the church (Rom. 8:33; Col. 3:12; 2 Tim. 2:10; 1 Thes. 1:4; 1 Peter 5:13), and of Christ (Isa. 42:1; 1 Peter 2:6).

2. Chosen. As seen in the preceding discussion, the word "chosen" is a synonym for the word "election." Those elected of God are chosen by Him from all eternity, and the same term is applied to Israel (Isa. 44:1), the church (Eph. 1:4; 2 Thes. 2:13; 1 Peter 2:9), and the apostles (John 6:70; 13:18; Acts 1:2).

3. Drawn. God draws those who are to be saved. "But I, when I am lifted up from the earth, will draw all men to Myself" (John 12:32). In 6:44 a similar revelation is given: "No one can come to

Me unless the Father who sent Me draws him, and I will raise him up at the last day."

4. Called. The calling of God is a divine activity in which unsaved men are drawn to God. The calling of God, though mentioned in many passages, is linked in Romans 8:30 to predestination, justification, and glorification: "And those He predestined, He also called; those He called, He also justified; those He justified, He also glorified."

5. Divine purpose. Election is according to divine purpose (Eph. 1:9; 3:11). It should be obvious that divine purpose and divine activity involve the same works of God.

6. Foreknowledge. Foreknowledge is another term indicating that God knows beforehand what is going to happen. It is used of Israel (Rom. 11:2) and the church (8:29).

7. Foreordination and predestination. These words are practically synonymous and declare the truth that God determines what shall come to pass before it happens. God's foreordination and predestination precede all history. As foreknowledge recognizes the certainty of future events, foreordination and predestination make those events sure. Events are not predestined because they are foreknown but rather they are foreknown because they are predestined. The two divine activities of foreseeing and foreordaining naturally function together and are dependent since either one is impossible without the other.

SCRIPTURAL REVELATION

Though the facts of divine election may be difficult to understand, the doctrine stands on specific revelation of Scripture. This is not to say it is free from complexity or that it is capable of complete human comprehension.

It should be obvious to anyone who believes in the infinity of God's attributes that God could not be unaware of what is going to happen in the universe inasmuch as He willed to bring the universe into being in the first place. If God did not know and to some extent control the future, He would not be God. If one considered for a moment the possibility of God being a fiendish despot, the great contrast can immediately be seen between fatalism, which has no purpose in certainty, and divine election, which is in keeping with the purposes of God. Man exercises free will to some extent but only in the sense that he has choices. He cannot will to be a creature other than himself, and he cannot necessarily change his circumstances.

To some extent God's election is governed by the same problems. God is not free to elect what contradicts His love or righteousness or what is foolish and not good in its ultimate end. The Bible reveals that God is supreme in authority and is sovereign in creation. God willed that men should have a sphere of freedom within His larger purposes but that this freedom is limited to certain choices.

God made an unconditional covenant with Abraham in which he made certain promises. Yet those promises depended somewhat on man fulfilling what God anticipated man would do, including the ultimate repentance and return to God of the godly remnant of Israel in the period before His second coming.

The fact that God elects to do things that perhaps man would not choose is obvious. As Luke 4:25-27 illustrates, there were many widows in Israel, but Elisha was sent to only one widow whom he sustained in a time of famine. Many lepers were in Israel, but God chose to cleanse Naaman the Syrian. The choice of Mary to be the mother of Christ (1:28) was not a human decision. In choosing the apostles, man's choice probably would have been different. Even Pharaoh is declared to have been chosen for a demonstration of divine power (Rom. 9:17). Another illustration is that of Cyrus, whom God predicted by name before he appeared on the pages of history to fulfill a special role in relation to Israel (Isa. 45:1-4).

In other instances, as when for example God chose Jacob and rejected Esau, sovereign choice was indicated. The question remains as to how divine election can be justified in view of man's moral choices.

Though it is difficult for man to conceive of divine election as being other than an arbitrary act of God, it should be clear from Scripture that God in eternity past chose a perfect plan. He is omniscient and knew all possible plans. Because He is infinitely good, He must choose the best of all possible plans. Giving man choices, God knew that he would choose the wrong path. God knew not only those who would respond to the revelation of God but also those who would not respond. In adopting any plan that involved freedom of choice God automatically chose the results even though to some extent people are free to choose one way or the other so far as their own experience is concerned. It was impossible for God to give angels or men choices without the certainty that some would choose the wrong way. In choosing that plan, God knew who these would be and yet they are entirely responsible for their choices. Election is that aspect of the divine decree that relates to those who are chosen.

ESSENTIAL TRUTHS EMBRACED

1. God by His election has chosen some but not all to salvation. The fact of divine election is clearly stated in the Word of God. The fact that man can only partially understand it does not change the certainty of the truth. These Scriptures are clear in this teaching (Rom. 9:23; 16:13; Eph. 1:4-5; 2 Thes. 2:13; 1 Peter 1:2). In the very act of divine election or choosing some are obviously not elected or chosen. If there had been a better plan by which more could have been elected, God would have chosen that plan. But in the nature of human choices, some were elected and some were not.

2. Divine election was accomplished in eternity past. God elected some to salvation before He even created the world. As stated in Ephesians 1:4, "For He chose us in Him before the Creation of the world to be holy and blameless in His sight." God's foreknowledge extends to all events (Acts 15:18; 2 Tim. 1:9) and not simply to election.

The concept that election takes place in time does not take into consideration that the Bible declares it to be eternal (2 Thes. 2:13-14).

3. Election does not merely rest on foreknowledge. There is an obvious distinction between foreknowledge and foreordination or predestination. As previously explained, God has knowledge of all possible plans, and chose the best plan. Having chosen that plan, He has foreknowledge. Accordingly foreknowledge, foreordination, and predestination cannot be placed in sequence, but all were included in the original decree. God could not foreknow as certain something that had not been foreordained, and He could not know that it was foreordained until He chose the plan. The passages that deal with foreknowledge and predestination indicate that they extend to the same truths, but the temporal order is not indicated when the verses are properly translated (Acts 2:23; Rom. 8:29; 1 Peter 1:2). It is also true that man is saved not by good works but according to God's

grace (Rom. 11:5-6).

An illustration of divine choice is God's choosing Jacob instead of Esau, which occurred before either one of them had done any good or bad works (9:10-13). In a similar way election from eternity past occurred before man was created.

4. Divine election is immutable. That is, it cannot change in the history of the human race. God does not adjust Himself to the will of man, and in fact He knew all that man would do even before He created him. Human language cannot express a more positive assertion than what appears in 8:30, "And those He predestined, He also called; those He called, He also justified; those He justified, He also glorified."

5. Election in relation to Christ's mediation. The question is sometimes raised as to whether Christ died for men because of their election to salvation or whether they are elect because Christ died for them. This question is not a matter of chronology, but rather what is logical and what is cause and effect in the mind of God. This will be discussed in the next chapter.

In keeping with His plan God was impelled to give His Son for the world (John 3:16). The death of Christ on the cross was necessary because God had elected some to salvation. From the standpoint of chronology, however, the decision relating to election and the decision relating to Christ's death on the cross are both eternal. Though they are in keeping with each other, there is not a cause and effect relationship.

The problems of understanding election and other difficult doctrines is mentioned in Romans 11:34, "Who has known the mind of the Lord? Or who has been His counselor?" The doctrine of election is not without its difficulties as is normal when a finite person tries to understand what is infinite. What man cannot understand he can believe on the basis of the infallible Word of God.

OBJECTIONS TO THE DOCTRINE OF ELECTION

Objections to the doctrine of election naturally arise from man's reasoning on this problem. Some suggest that election makes God unjust. The problem, of course, is that God is not obligated to save anyone except as a satisfaction of His love. No person merits salvation, and the fact that some are saved and some are not saved is no objection to election. God is also said to be partial in selecting some and not others without a suitable basis. A similar objection, of course, could be made of God's selection of nations such as Israel and of individuals such as Abraham and Cyrus. In connection with the fall of angels, God chose not to save any of those who sinned.

Some object to the doctrine of election on the basis that God is arbitrary. The Bible does indicate that God is sovereign, but in exercising His judgments He is guided by His wise and sovereign will in ways that are inscrutable to man. The Scriptures do not picture God as a fatalistic, arbitrary chooser, but rather One who makes all His choices in keeping with His infinite attributes.

Another objection is that electing some to salvation and not others leads to immorality on the part of man. On the contrary the Scriptures reveal that those who are saved have a compelling reason for yielding their lives to Christ in appreciation for their gracious regeneration and sanctification.

Others say the doctrine of election leads to human pride. However, God does not choose those elected because they are better than others; He chose the elect in the freedom of grace. The doctrine of election is also opposed on the ground that it hinders evangelism and reaching out to the world with the Gospel. This is a faulty conclusion because no one knows who is elected and who is not elected, and it is God's plan that everyone, whether elect or not elect, should hear the Gospel. Election is opposed by some because they hold to a decree of reprobation as the alternative to election. But while all events occur within the permissive will of God a person is unsaved because of his self-chosen rebellion. His punishment is the natural consequence.

CHAPTER • 10

THE ORDER OF ELECTIVE DECREES

In chapter 14 of volume one the doctrine of the decree of God was presented, and for this reason only a brief study of elective decrees is necessary in relation to soteriology.

In discussing the order of elective decrees theologians seek to distinguish the causal from the effective aspects of the decrees. Actually, because God's decree is eternal, establishing the order of elective decrees is only for human understanding of the problem of their relation to each other.

The various lapsarian views, which relate to mankind's fall into sin, are motivated by the question of how election relates to Creation, the Fall, and the provision of salvation. In general four views have been set forth.

SUPRALAPSARIANISM

This view is advanced by followers of John Calvin who emphasize the sovereignty of God and divine election. The order of elective decrees defended by supralapsarians is as follows: (1) decree to elect some to be saved and to reprobate all others; (2) decree to create men both elect and nonelect; (3) decree to permit the Fall; (4) decree to provide salvation for the elect; (5) decree to apply salvation to the elect.

Objections to this view are advanced by moderate Calvinists because, logically, man must be created before God can elect people for their respective destinations. The Scriptures picture those who are elect as chosen out of the mass of humanity (John 15:19). Also, when election is indicated, it relates to men chosen for salvation including justification and sanctification (Eph. 1:4-6; 1 Peter 1:2). Man has already fallen before election takes place. Even the ungodly are judged as such after Creation (Jude 4). It would be impossible therefore for God before the decree either to select the elect or pass by the nonelect.

INFRALAPSARIANISM

The view advanced by those who are more moderate Calvinists includes the decrees in the following order: (1) decree to create all men; (2) decree to permit the Fall; (3) decree to provide salvation for man; (4) decree to elect those who do believe and leave condemned all who do not believe; (5) decree to apply salvation to those who believe.

This order commends itself as being related to the logical order of events. It is similar to sublapsarianism.

SUBLAPSARIANISM

The order set forth by sublapsarians varies only slightly from that advanced by infralapsarians. This view is as follows: (1) decree to create all men; (2) decree to permit the Fall; (3) decree to elect those who do believe and leave condemned those who do not believe; (4) decree to provide salvation for men; (5) decree to apply salvation to those who believe.

Sublapsarianism is similar to infralapsarianism in that the decree to elect comes immediately after the Fall and before the decree to provide salvation. However, infralapsarianism places the decree to provide salvation before the decree of election, whereas the sublapsarian view reverses them.

ARMINIAN VIEW OF LAPSARIANISM

The Arminian view is similar to the infralapsarian view, but election is made dependent on foreseen human virtue, faith, and obedience. The proper infralapsarian view makes election more of a sovereign choice and without any foreseen human merit.

As previously discussed, Arminians tend to ignore the fact that the decree of God is eternal. Any attempt to set forth a logical order ignores the fact that the decree of God is one act which covers all events rather than a series of decrees.

Preferable is the point of view that the original decree of God including all events took into consideration the varied motives, creatures, natural laws, and the intervention of God in human history. God decreed what was perfect, just, and good. The plan adopted in the decree of God made all events certain even though the decree provided that some events should result from the choice of angels and men. It is difficult for human minds to understand the chronology of events that succeed each other or the factor of cause and effect. It is also difficult for finite man to comprehend the eternal decision of God in which all events are rendered certain even though they occur in chronological order. Calvinists contend that divine election is the sovereign choice of God which expresses His grace apart from any form of human works. The Arminian school, by making election to be no more than foreknowledge of human merit, tends to make man's election a choice made by himself by his faith and obedience. The intrusion of human reason into the views of both Calvinists and Arminians is the real source of the difficulty.

CHAPTER • 11

FOR WHOM DID CHRIST DIE?

The question of the purpose of Christ's death is often related to the so-called five points of Calvinism: (1) total depravity, (2) unconditional election, (3) limited atonement, (4) irresistible grace, (5) perseverance or eternal security of the saved.

These five points often are referred to as TULIP, which is an acronym based on the initial letter of each of the five points. Strict Calvinists hold that Christ died only for the elect (limited atonement), whereas moderate Calvinists hold that Christ died for the whole world (unlimited atonement). Since capable orthodox theologians hold each view, it is not a question of orthodoxy versus nonorthodoxy. Ultimately the question is what the Bible teaches.

The so-called TULIP was an outgrowth of the Synod of Dort (1618-19) which affirmed limited atonement in opposition to the teachings of Jacob Arminius (1560-1609). The Synod of Dort took the position that when an unsaved man, who was elect, comes to faith in Christ, he experiences irresistible grace which causes him to be regenerated. Then, because he is regenerated, he comes to faith in Christ. Moderate Calvinists feel that this position is in error because it confuses what is called prevenient grace with regeneration. The proper order should be that an unsaved person is graciously enabled by God to believe, and then, as a result of believing, he is regenerated. The Synod of Dort changed that order and viewed regeneration as preceding faith. This reduced the human response to the Gospel to a minimum and affirmed that salvation even to the point of a person's willingness to believe is all the work of God. The Scriptures, however, do not use the adjectives irresistible or efficacious, in relation to grace, nor do they use the word "sufficient," which is often used by Arminians. Though it is true as Christ stated,

"No one can come to Me unless the Father who sent Me draws him" (John 6:44), the Scriptures constantly refer to salvation as involving man's faith.

CLASSIFICATION OF VIEWS

Limited redemptionists are divided into two general groups, and unlimited redemptionists are also divided into two general groups making four divisions in all in regard to this question.

1. The extreme limited redemptionists. These are sometimes identified with a strict form of Calvinism which includes the supralapsarian view of the decrees. It makes the decree of divine election precede all other aspects of the decree. Those who hold this view say that the Gospel is to be proclaimed to some but not to all mankind.

2. Moderate Calvinists who are limited redemptionists. Some more moderate Calvinists hold the position of infralapsarianism that God's decree to create logically precedes His decree to permit the Fall. They differ from the extreme limited redemptionists in that they emphasize that while Christ died for the elect, His death was forensic, that is, sufficient for all. They could conceivably offer the Gospel to any human being.

3. Moderate Calvinists who are unlimited redemptionists. These people accept the four points of Calvinism with the exception of limited atonement. This form of Calvinism is characteristic of many Bible teachers and is often the point of view of Baptist churches. Advocates of this view hold that Christ in His death provided redemption for all mankind thereby rendering every man savable. They agree with Calvin that only the elect will be saved but hold that the issue in dealing with the unsaved is a question whether they will place their faith in Christ as stated in John 3:18, "Whoever believes in Him is not condemned, but whoever does not believe stands condemned already because he has not believed in the name of God's one and only Son." Though it is true that the death of Christ in itself saved no one, it is also true that His death makes possible the salvation of anyone.

4. The Arminians. The Arminian point of view is that Christ died for all and that He provided not only common grace but also sufficient grace for all unsaved to believe if they will. According to this view, men are subject to divine judgment because of their willful

rejection of Christ's salvation.

TWO SCHOOLS OF MODERATE CALVINISTS CONTRASTED

(1) The two schools of moderate Calvinists—views two and three above—have the common belief that not everyone will be saved and they reject universalism or restitutionism. (2) They both hold that the death of Christ is suitable in the sense that it answers the need of every fallen man and renders him savable. (3) They both hold that people can be saved by no means other than the death and resurrection of Christ. (4) The Gospel should be preached to all. (5) Faith must be wrought in the unsaved by the Holy Spirit. (6) Only the elect will be saved. (7) Whatever Christ did on the cross for the elect or nonelect is not applied until a person believes. (8) The death of Christ provides salvation for all men, but one view emphasizes the purpose of God to save only the elect whereas the other view affirms that it was the purpose of God to provide salvation for all.

On the cross Christ secured not only forgiveness through His death but also the right to bestow eternal life, justification, and a believer's position in Christ. Also some aspects of sanctification are made possible by Christ's death.

Because Christ died for the lost, God is free to express divine benevolence toward those who are saved by not only giving them forgiveness but also a place in the family and household of God, adoption, heavenly citizenship, access to God, and freedom under grace from the merit system of the Law.

Clarity is given to the situation when it is realized that the elect before they believe are just as lost as the nonelect. Any view on the extent of Christ's death must respect the doctrine of election which indicates that all who are predestined for salvation are ultimately glorified (Rom. 8:30).

As will be seen in the study of unlimited redemption, this doctrine is supported by many other aspects of divine revelation: (1) dispensational aspects of the problem, (2) three doctrinal words, (3) the necessity of faith, (4) universal Gospel preaching, (5) the question of whether God is defeated if men for whom Christ died are lost, (6) the nature of substitution, and (7) the testimony of the Scriptures.

DISPENSATIONAL ASPECTS OF THE PROBLEM

Because the dispensations in Scripture deal with rules of life rather than ways of salvation, dispensationalism has only an oblique relationship to the question of unlimited atonement.

In dispensationalism Israel is regarded as an elect nation and is therefore subject to future restoration as a nation. The elect in Israel and the church will be saved and glorified (Rom. 8:30).

National election should not be confused with individual election (9:4-13). Individual Israelites were not saved by the fact that they were part of the elect nation. They needed individual salvation just as any Gentile did. Even in the prophetic future many Israelites will be rejected (Ezek. 20:33-44; Dan. 12:1-3). It is true, however, that God is gracious in recognizing that a remnant of Israel will be saved and will have a part in His eschatological purposes (Rom. 11:5, 27). Israel's national salvation will ultimately be realized when the godly Israelite remnant will have her sins taken away (Jer. 31:34). Even in the present age individual Israelites can be saved by faith in Christ though Gentiles are predominantly being blessed in the present age (Acts 15:14). Israel's future restoration is promised (Amos 9:11-15; Acts 15:16-17). In the Mosaic dispensation the Law was not a way of salvation, though it is probable that those who were saved sought to keep the Law. Salvation is always by faith and through grace.

THREE DOCTRINAL WORDS

As previously considered, redemption, reconciliation, and propitiation summarize the work of the death of Christ. These great realities, redemption from sin, reconciliation to God, and the death of Christ as a propitiation or satisfaction to God, apply to all who believe. Other great words are used in regard to salvation such as forgiveness, regeneration, justification, and sanctification, and all who experience one experience the others. (For further discussion see chap. 4.)

THE NECESSITY OF FAITH

Though some oppose unlimited redemption on the ground that if Christ died for all then all are saved, the Scriptures are clear that salvation was *provided* for all but is *applied* only to those who believe when they believe. So even an elect person before he comes to faith may manifest all the depravity of an unsaved person. An elect person is not saved or regenerated until the moment of faith. In their spiritual condition before salvation the elect and nonelect are indistinguishable. Inasmuch as even the elect are not saved until they believe, it should be clear that the death of Christ is provisional for all but effective only in those who believe.

UNIVERSAL GOSPEL PREACHING

In preaching the Gospel should those who believe in the doctrine of election avoid offering salvation to all? In Scripture God discloses nothing whereby the elect can be distinguished from the nonelect as both classes are unregenerate. Since a preacher of the Gospel cannot know who in his audience is elect, he is free to offer salvation to all without creating a problem for the nonelect. Even some elect persons may resist the claims of the Gospel until the day of their death. Because the Bible affirms that Christ died for all, all can be offered the Gospel without anyone attempting to determine whether they are elect or nonelect.

IS GOD DEFEATED IF MEN ARE LOST?

This question relates to the larger question as to whether any sin or defiance of God means that God is defeated. Actually the total process of people being saved or unsaved brings glory to God because it manifests His infinite attributes. There is no defeat for God because His purposes are being perfectly fulfilled even by the judgment on the lost in which His holiness and righteousness are revealed. Rejecting Christ and His redemption, as every unbeliever does, is anticipated in the plan of God, though at the same time it is not according to the wishes of God who is benevolent in His relationship to all mankind. As stated in 2 Peter 3:9, "The Lord is not slow in keeping His promise, as some understand slowness. He is patient with you, not wanting anyone to perish, but everyone to come to repentance."

Three major passages are often quoted in support of limited

atonement.

In John 8:24 Christ said, "I told you that you would die in your sins; if you do not believe that I am the One I claim to be, you will indeed die in your sins." It should be noted that the unsaved are not said to be unregenerate because Christ did not die for them but because they did not believe. Any other point of view would contradict not only unlimited atonement but also limited atonement for in both cases it is clear that the application is delayed until the time of belief even for the elect.

Another passage used to support limited atonement is Ephesians 5:6, "Let no one deceive you with empty words, for because of such things God's wrath comes on those who are disobedient." The words "those who are disobedient" do not refer simply to the nonelect but to the fact that even elect people were disobedient before salvation. Again it is proved that the value of Christ's death is applied to the elect not at the cross but when they believe.

Revelation 20:12 states, "The dead were judged according to what they had done as recorded in the books." These are unsaved people whose names are not in the Book of Life (v. 15). Because they are not saved, they pay the price of divine judgment for their sins for which Christ died but for which they never claimed salvation by faith in Christ. Their failure to believe in Christ leaves them at the final judgment in the same position as if Christ had not died.

The view that all men are saved by Christ's death for them is not supported in Scripture, for both the lost and the elect are equally regarded as unregenerate and unsaved until the individuals involved place their trust in Christ. The sin of unbelief is the greatest of all sins, but it leaves untouched the sins for which Christ died because His redemption is never applied. Though the sin of unbelief was included in the sins for which Christ died, when one fails to put his trust in Christ the sacrifice of Christ is seen as a work of God which is not applied to the individual believer in his unbelief.

THE NATURE OF SUBSTITUTION

As previously discussed, the Scriptures teach that Christ was the believer's Substitute when He died on the cross. Though He died for the unsaved as well as the saved, in both cases His substitutionary work is not applicable to the individual until he believes. In the nature of Christ's work it is perfect in character and is sufficient for all men, but His redemption and substitutionary work is applied only when one believes. This belief is not a good work which God recognizes as justifying salvation. Belief simply claims by faith what God alone can do. Faith makes possible the application of the death of Christ to the individual who believes.

THE TESTIMONY OF THE SCRIPTURES

In addition to the Scriptures already cited, other passages are important in upholding unlimited atonement.

1. Some passages advanced by those who hold to limited atonement virtually do not support that view. In John 10:15 Christ said, "I lay down My life for the sheep." The statement that Christ laid down His life for the sheep is said to exclude those who are not His sheep.

In 15:13 Christ said, "Greater love has no one than this, that one lay down his life for his friends." The argument here also is that Christ is said to have died only for His friends and not for the whole world.

In 17:2, 6, 9, 20, and 24 Christ referred to the fact that those who will be saved have been given to Him by the Father. The argument here is similar to previous verses that inasmuch as Christ singled out the saved, He was stating that His death was only for the elect.

In Romans 4:25 Paul stated, "He was delivered over to death for our sins and was raised to life for our justification." The use of the word "our" is taken by some to limit the death of Christ to the elect.

In Ephesians 1:3-7 an extended revelation is given on God's great purpose of saving all who have been predestined to salvation. In the verses that follow, promises are applied to those who are chosen for salvation.

In 5:25-27 a comprehensive view is given of the church for which Christ "gave Himself up" (v. 25).

No one disagrees that Christ in His death provided for the elect. The question is whether He limited His death to that purpose. In addressing Christians Paul could obviously say that Christ died for them, but this does not settle the question as to whether He died for others as well. At best it is an argument from silence, and the issue has to be settled by other references where the Bible explicitly refers to the death of Christ as providing salvation for the whole world.

Various Scriptures say explicitly that Christ died for the lost. For example Luke 19:10 affirms, "For the Son of man came to seek and to save what was lost." This verse does not include an express statement that the death of Christ is limited in its provision to the elect. Any passage that states that Christ died for the elect is not decisive in itself. When Paul wrote in Galatians 2:20, "I live by faith in the Son of God, who loved *me* and gave Himself for *me*" (italics added), he obviously was not claiming that he is the only one who is saved. In John 11:51-52 John wrote of Caiaphas, "He did not say this on his own, but as high priest that year he prophesied that Jesus would die for the Jewish nation, and not only for that nation but also for the scattered children of God, to bring them together and make them one." Obviously Christ did not die only for the Jewish nation as some might suggest. The same thought is expressed in Isaiah 53:8 where Christ is said to have been "stricken" "for the transgression of My people." The issue has to be settled by the total revelation of Scripture and not by isolated texts.

2. Many passages affirm that Christ's death was for the whole world. These passages require explanation on the part of those who hold to limited atonement. In Isaiah 53:6 the prophet wrote, "We all, like sheep, have gone astray, each of us has turned to his own way; and the Lord has laid on Him the iniquity of us all." The use of the word "all" can in some instances in Scripture be limited, but the fact that it is repeatedly used in connection with the death of Christ makes unlimited redemption plausible.

In the familiar passage of John 3:16-20 limited exegesis is illustrated when some try to refer this only to the elect, "For God so loved the world that He gave His one and only Son, that whoever believes in Him shall not perish but have eternal life. For God did not send His Son into the world to condemn the world, but to save the world through Him. Whoever believes in Him is not condemned, but whoever does not believe stands condemned already because he has not believed in the name of God's one and only Son. This is the verdict: Light has come into the world, but men loved darkness instead of light because their deeds were evil. Everyone who does evil hates the light, and will not come into the light for fear that his deeds will be exposed." In this passage the Greek word *kosmos* is used to refer to the organized world. To limit the "world" in verse 16 to the elect is to contradict what the passage says. It is obvious from verse 17 that God did not send His Son to the elect but to the entire world. Verse 19 declares that "light has come into the world," and that this light is rejected by people who love darkness. Here the word "world" clearly refers to the entire creation including the non-elect. In the light of the context, an important element in exegesis, the word "world" in verse 16 is universal.

In 2 Corinthians 5:19 Paul stated that "God was reconciling the world to Himself in Christ, not counting men's sins against them. And He has committed to us the message of reconciliation." Those who would hold to limited atonement must understand the word *kosmos* here to include only the elect. But this is not supported by the passage itself. The believer is to declare to everyone that Christ has reconciled the world. To limit this declaration to the elect is to make the passage say what it does not say.

Hebrews 2:9 also reveals that the death of Christ was for everyone. "But we see Jesus, who was made a little lower than the angels, now crowned with glory and honor because He suffered death, so that by the grace of God He might taste death for everyone." Only by reading into the passage what it does not say can the term "everyone" be made to mean "all the elect."

In 1 John 2:2 the point is made that Christ is not only the sacrifice for the sins of those who are saved but also for the sins of the world. "He is the atoning sacrifice for our sins, and not only for ours but also for the sins of the whole world." It would be impossible to make it any clearer that the death of Christ provided for the entire world. Interpreting the word "world" as referring only to the elect must ignore many passages in the Bible where the word "world" is used in a universal sense (John 15:18-19; 17:16; 1 John 5:19).

3. Many passages are all inclusive in scope. Romans 5:6 states that "Christ died for the ungodly." This is illustrated in 2 Corinthians 5:14, "For Christ's love compels us, because we are convinced that One died for all, and therefore all died." In the verse that follows Paul contrasted the fact that Christ died for all to the more limited scope of those who live, "And He died for all, that those who live should no longer live for themselves but for Him who died for them and was raised again" (v. 15). In 1 Timothy 2:6 the statement is made that Christ "gave Himself as a ransom for all men." First Timothy 4:10 has a similar statement: "We have put our hope in the living God, who is the Saviour of all men, and especially of those who believe." Here the distinction is made between the

entire world of people for which Christ died and those who believe and receive salvation. In Titus 2:11 the statement is made that "salvation has appeared to all men."

4. WHOSOEVER. The word "whosoever" is used about 110 times in the New Testament with the obvious inference that it is universal in its application. In regard to the death of Christ as providing salvation, the word "whosoever" is used in John 3:16 (KJV) in the statement, "whosoever believeth in Him should not perish." A similar statement is made in Acts 10:43, "All the prophets testify about Him that everyone who believes in Him receives forgiveness of sins through His name." Even in the final invitation to the unsaved to come to Christ, Revelation 22:17 states, "The Spirit and the bride say, 'Come!' And let him who hears say, 'Come!' Whoever is thirsty, let him come; and whoever wishes, let him take the free gift of the water of life." All the passages that state that Christ died for the elect are not decisive in themselves, but even one statement in Scripture that Christ died for all should be sufficient to support the doctrine of unlimited atonement.

5. SECOND PETER 2:1-2. A passage that makes especially clear that Christ died for the ungodly is 2 Peter 2:1-2 where the false prophets who are condemned are said to have been bought or redeemed by Christ. "But there were also false prophets among the people, just as there will be false teachers among you. They will secretly introduce destructive heresies, even denying the sovereign Lord who bought them—bringing swift destruction on themselves." *Agorazo*, the primary word for redemption, is translated by the verb "bought." Those who adopt limited atonement must say dogmatically that this word is not used in a redemptive sense, but if *agorazo* is not used in the redemptive sense then in what sense is it used? In what sense could Christ have died and bought the unsaved? In view of the fact that this is the standard word for redemption, it would seem to be a direct affirmation that Christ died not simply for the elect but for all the ungodly. Those who hold to unlimited redemption do not question that Christ died for the elect or even that He has a love for the elect which is somewhat different from His love for the world though His love for unsaved man is infinite.

The argument of Romans 5:8-10 is that if Christ died for sinners, how much more would those who have been justified by faith be saved from God's wrath. Romans 5:10 concludes, "For if, when we were God's enemies, we were reconciled to Him through the death of His Son, how much more, having been reconciled, shall we be saved through His life!" Here again it is expressly declared that God's enemies were reconciled by the death of Christ. If this is true for the unsaved, how much more is the hope of those who are saved and have been justified and promised glorification.

While godly men will continue to differ on this subject, what appears from the study of the writings of those who hold to limited atonement is that they arrive at this conclusion rationally from the doctrine of election. In the process they ignore or misrepresent what the Scriptures state. The point of view that says that Christ died for all but that the value of His death is applied only to those who believe is what the Scriptures teach in the many passages that have been cited.

THE SAVING WORK OF THE TRIUNE GOD

CHAPTER • 12

THE FINISHED WORK OF CHRIST

The saving work of the Triune God may be discussed in seven divisions: (1) the finished work of Christ, (2) the convicting work of the Spirit, (3) the riches of divine grace, (4) the doctrine of security, (5) deliverance from the reigning power of sin, (6) deliverance from human limitations, and (7) the believer as presented faultless in glory.

Though the preceding discussion has referred to the death of Christ many times, further consideration is necessary to clarify an issue that has often been confused in the history of doctrine, namely, that salvation is a work of God for man, not a work of man for God.

Many Scriptures assert that "salvation comes from the LORD" (Jonah 2:9). In various ways salvation is spoken of at least 150 times in the Old and New Testaments (e.g., Ps. 3:8; Jer. 3:23; Acts 4:12; Rom. 1:16).

Because in all heathen religions salvation is by works, it is not surprising that this concept has influenced the Christian doctrine of salvation. The Bible clearly indicates that a person who is saved will produce good works, but the good works are the product of salvation not the cause of it.

When Christ said on the cross, "It is finished" (John 19:30), He was signifying that the way of salvation was fully supported by His death on the cross, and what remained was to apply this finished work to those who believe. As previously discussed, Christ in His death on the cross provided redemption, reconciliation, and propitiation. It is clear from such passages as Ephesians 2:8-9 that salvation is not by works even though believers having been saved, then produce good works (v. 10). As men in their limited understanding tend toward legalism and seek to find some ground by which God can accept them on the basis of their own works, the Word of God clarifies the fact that the work of Christ on the cross is finished. Christians participate in this finished work when they put their trust in Christ.

Since Christ's work is finished, it should be clear that salvation is not a work of man for God. When a person comes to Christ, he is acknowledging that he cannot save himself but has now recognized the work of salvation God has wrought for him and which he accepts as God's gift. Salvation originates in God's purposes, not in man's, and is forever delivered from any legalistic approach that would elevate human works as a ground for salvation.

The supremacy of Christ in every respect is brought out in Colossians 1:15-18. This supremacy includes the fact that all creation is under Him and that He participated in the Creation of the universe. Of supreme importance is the fact that Christ is Head of the church on whom He is going to bestow "the riches of His glorious inheritance in the saints" (Eph. 1:18).

The finished work of Christ makes it possible for God in infinite righteousness to save the sinner who is guilty of infinite sin, and He is able to justify the ungodly because Christ in His finished work paid the price for man's redemption on Calvary.

CHAPTER • 13

THE CONVICTING WORK OF THE SPIRIT

In accomplishing the salvation of an individual two factors are involved: (1) a righteous dealing with the problem of sin which Christ accomplished as the Lamb of God who takes away the sin of the world; (2) faith in the heart of man in what God has promised and provided in Christ in His plan of salvation. The inner work of God in the heart of one who comes to faith in Christ is inscrutable, but Scripture portrays it as including both the action of man who wills to believe and the action of God who by grace enables the person to believe.

When Christ's death is considered an unlimited redemption, it enables the person who is attempting to lead souls to Christ to offer salvation to everyone, even though he knows that only the elect will respond. There must be a corresponding work of God as He calls, draws, and enlightens the unsaved person, making possible his intelligent reception of Christ.

It is dangerous for an evangelist to adopt superficial means to encourage more decisions for Christ. Though it is necessary to present the Gospel in attractive form and in clarity by the power of the Spirit, the Scriptures indicate that all who are justified will be called, and all who are justified will be glorified. The paradox of the combined action of the human will and the will of God in the salvation of an individual believer cannot be completely understood, but it remains true that everyone who sincerely wants to believe is enabled to put his trust in Christ.

In connection with the convicting work of the Spirit it is necessary to examine three areas: (1) the need of the Spirit's work, (2) the fact of the Spirit's work, and (3) the result of the Spirit's work.

THE NEED OF THE SPIRIT'S WORK

In order for an unsaved man to come to faith in Christ it is necessary that he be the object of the convicting work of the Holy Spirit. Man in his natural mind cannot comprehend the mystery of the death of Christ for the sins of the whole world and how this truth applies to him personally. In the Upper Room Discourse of Christ it is recorded in John 16:8-11 that the Spirit of God would reveal to the unsaved their need of salvation and God's remedy for it. "When He comes, He will convict the world of guilt in regard to sin and righteousness and judgment: in regard to sin, because men do not believe in Me; in regard to righteousness, because I am going to the Father, where you can see Me no longer; and in regard to judgment, because the prince of this world now stands condemned."

As these verses indicate, the Holy Spirit will first make an unsaved person realize the fact of his guilt and sinfulness before God and the fact that God has a plan by which he can be saved and declared righteous. Further, it will be revealed that the one sin that stands between the unsaved and salvation is the sin of unbelief, "Because men do not believe in Me" (v. 9). The Spirit of God will also reveal God's infinite righteousness and the fact that God can bestow righteousness on a believer in Christ. Because Christ was going to the Father, He no longer would be personally present to reveal the righteousness of God in His life and words. So the Holy Spirit will need to impress on the unsaved person the fact that God is righteous and that the unsaved person when he puts his trust in the Saviour can receive the righteousness from God which has been provided in Christ. Also revealed to some extent is the fact that judgment took place on the cross. In Christ's act of dying He secured victory over Satan, "The prince of this world" (v. 11). Because of Christ's death, Satan now stands condemned, but the execution of his judgment will not take place until later in God's prophetic program.

Other Scriptures reveal the same truth and expound on it in more detail. Romans 3:10-18 makes clear that all have sinned and come short of the glory of God and that none are righteous and therefore all need salvation. Unregenerate man is without any ground for favor with God and in fact will not seek after God unless the Holy Spirit works on him. All the human race is under sin (v. 9) and all are hopelessly lost unless they are saved by Christ. And yet Christ is seeking sinners: "For the Son of man came to seek and to save what was lost" (Luke 19:10).

First Corinthians 2:14 reveals that the "natural" man (the unsaved person) does not have the capacity to receive truth about God for it seems to be foolishness to him. Only as the heart of unsaved man is enlightened by the Spirit in the convicting work which Christ prophesied can an unsaved person understand the terms of the Gospel. It cannot be overemphasized that man naturally does not subject himself to the law of God, and he has rejected God and turned to vain and empty religious beliefs that are contrary to Scripture.

According to 2 Corinthians 4:3-4 the Gospel is hidden. "And even if our Gospel is veiled, it is veiled to those who are perishing. The god of this age has blinded the minds of unbelievers, so that they cannot see the light of the Gospel of the glory of Christ, who is the image of God."

The natural sinfulness of man makes clear that without the work of God in grace a person would never come to the knowledge of Christ even though human response is required before salvation can be effected. In addition to man's natural blindness there is the activity of Satan who attempts to keep people from the truth and to obscure the preaching of the Gospel (v. 4). In Ephesians 4:18 this natural darkness is described. "They are darkened in their understanding and separated from the life of God because of the ignorance that is in them due to the hardening of their hearts."

The work of the Holy Spirit in relation to man's salvation is frequently mentioned in Scripture as in Colossians 1:13 where a saved person is said to have been rescued "from the dominion of darkness and brought . . . into the kingdom of the Son." Ephesians 4:18 also refers to natural blindness and insensitivity to spiritual truth. In 2:1-5 the believer is declared to be made "alive with Christ" even though Paul wrote to them, "As for you, you were dead in your transgressions and sins" (v. 1).

Many other passages state the necessity for the radical change of being born again in order to be saved. In John 3:3, Nicodemus was informed that "unless a man is born again, he cannot see the kingdom of God." Similar Scriptures include 6:44; 14:6; Acts 4:12; and Hebrews 7:25.

A key passage to understand is Ephesians 2:8-9, "For it is by grace you have been saved, through faith—and this not from yourselves, it is the gift of God—not by works, so that no one can boast." Those holding to limited atonement try to gather from this verse that even faith is the gift of God and that faith must be preceded by regeneration in order for a man to believe. A correct understanding of this verse, however, is that the whole plan of salvation is the gift of God. "Faith" is in the feminine gender, but the word "this" is neuter, indicating the whole work of salvation is in view. It is through grace, that is, by divine enablement that a person believes and is offered salvation. Through faith God's gift of salvation is received. Salvation is not dependent on human works (v. 9); the believer is God's new creation.

THE FACT OF THE SPIRIT'S WORK

In the Upper Room where Christ was speaking of the present age, He gave a new revelation concerning the work of the Holy Spirit in the hearts of unregenerate men. This is not equivalent to regeneration but relates to the general field of common grace. It is the enlightenment of an unsaved man by the Spirit which enables him to know the facts concerning the way of salvation.

Christ said, "But I tell you the truth: It is for your good that I am going away. Unless I go away, the Counselor will not come to you; but if I go, I will send Him to you. When He comes, He will convict the world of guilt in regard to sin and righteousness and judgment: in regard to sin, because men do not believe in Me; in regard to righteousness, because I am going to the Father, where you can see Me no longer, and in regard to judgment, because the prince of this world now stands condemned" (John 16:7-11).

This ministry of the Holy Spirit attends the preaching of the Gospel and necessarily extends to those who have not heard the plan of salvation. In this passage Christ predicted that when He would ascend to heaven the Holy Spirit would come, and one of His ministries would be to "reprove the world of sin, and of righteousness, and of judgment" (KJV) or "convict the world of guilt in regard to sin and righteousness and judgment" (v. 8).

The word "convict" (*elegcho*) refers to an unbeliever coming to the knowledge of his sin, of righteousness, and judgment. The barrier between the unbeliever and salvation is lack of faith in Christ. The supreme sin is the sin of unbelief. Other sins can be forgiven.

The Spirit of God also convicts the unsaved person of the fact that the righteousness of God has been demonstrated by Christ on earth. Now with His departure to the Father the Holy Spirit takes up this revelation. Judgment is also revealed by the fact that "the prince of this world now stands condemned" (v. 11). Though Satan is allowed freedom in the present world, the truth is that he stands condemned, and it is only a matter of time until he is judged along with all others who do not trust in Christ. An unbeliever may not completely understand all of this, but these are the three areas in which he needs illumination.

1. Of guilt. The expression "convict the world of guilt" (v. 8) has in view the revelation of Christ's finished work of redemption on the cross, and the issue now is not how bad a sinner is but whether he has put his trust in Christ as his Saviour. The general opinion that the Spirit enlightens the mind in respect to all the sins the individual has committed is not the main point though this may be true to some extent. The purpose of the work of the Spirit is not to create shame or remorse, but rather to illumine a person about the necessity of trusting Christ in view of the sins he has committed. The fact that unbelief is the sole cause for a person to be lost is stated plainly in 3:18, "Whoever believes in Him is not condemned, but whoever does not believe stands condemned already because he has not believed in the name of God's one and only Son." Apart from this convicting work of the Spirit no preacher, however eloquent, will be able to win a lost soul to Christ. This emphasizes the necessity of prayer on the part of Christians for those who do not believe that their eyes may be opened to the Gospel.

2. Of righteousness. The word "righteousness" in 16:8, 10 probably includes several concepts. This righteousness is related to the fact that Christ would ascend into heaven and no longer be present on the earth. In other words while on earth He demonstrated the righteousness of God for all to see. But now with Christ in heaven the Holy Spirit will teach the unsaved the righteousness of God and with it the fact that in the Gospel God is offering His righteousness to sinful men who put their trust in Christ. The unbeliever must understand that it is not a question of his working for salvation (Rom. 4:5), but that he needs the righteousness of God, which is available to those who put their trust in Christ. This concept would not be understood by an unsaved person apart from the work of the Spirit.

The fact that the righteousness of God and God's way of salvation are included in the illumination of unsaved people by the Spirit indicates also that a preacher of the Gospel should emphasize on the one hand the righteousness of God and on the other hand that imputed righteousness is available to all who believe. The unsaved are not given salvation because they do good works such as believing in Christ or because they are sorry for their sins and resolve to do better. The issue is simply the question of whether they by faith accept the wonderful salvation God is ready to give without consideration of the individual's merit.

3. Of judgment. The reference to "judgment" and the statement that "the prince of this world now stands condemned" refers to the effect of the Cross on Satan. From one point of view crucifying Christ was the supreme achievement of Satan and a revelation of his utter wickedness. On the other hand because Christ died, Satan stands condemned. Christ's death demonstrates the superior power of God which will be seen when Satan is cast into the lake of fire. Even an unsaved person may comprehend to some extent that the battle with sin and evil in the world is ultimately a victory for God and not Satan, and the person who identifies himself with Christ through faith partakes in that victory.

According to Isaiah 61:1-2 unsaved people are captives and prisoners who need to be released by the death of Christ. "The Spirit of the Sovereign Lord is on me, because the Lord has anointed me to preach good news to the poor. He has sent me to bind up the brokenhearted, to proclaim freedom for the captives, and release for the prisoners, to proclaim the year of the Lord's favor and the day of vengeance of our God, to comfort all who mourn."

In the synagogue at Nazareth Christ read this quotation from Isaiah and stated, "Today this Scripture is fulfilled in your hearing" (Luke 4:21). In Colossians 2:14-15 Christ is said to have victory over those under satanic influence, and in His death He triumphed over them. The transition from being under the power of Satan to being under the power of grace is mentioned in 1:13, "For He has rescued us from the dominion of darkness and brought us into the kingdom of the Son He loves."

The revelation given in John 16:7-11 is of tremendous significance in that it defines the area of truth relating to salvation and the truth as it should be preached to the unsaved world. The work of the Spirit in the unsaved, however, is not equivalent to regeneration nor does it include the larger ministries of the Spirit such as regeneration, indwelling, baptism, or sealing. These are elements that become effective when the unbeliever is saved, but before his salvation an unbeliever by the gracious intervention of God needs illumination regarding the nature of salvation and the necessity of faith.

THE RESULTS OF THE SPIRIT'S WORK

Before an unbelieving individual can be saved the supernatural work of the Spirit is required to enlighten him and make clear to him the terms of the Gospel which are stated emphatically in Ephesians 2:8, "For it is by grace you have been saved, through faith—and this not from yourselves, it is the gift of God." This verse is interpreted by those who hold to limited atonement as indicating that faith is a gift of God, but this is an inaccurate exegesis of this verse. The point in the verse is that salvation is by grace in its totality. The use of "this" (*touto,* neuter gender) makes it plain that it is not related to faith (*pisteos*), which is in feminine gender. The word "this" refers to the whole work of salvation as coming from God, not any particular part of it. Though it is true that faith on the part of an unsaved person would be impossible apart from divine help, it nevertheless is a human decision, however difficult it may be to separate the human work from the divine work. The problem with making faith a particular gift from God is that it removes from man any responsibility to believe and leaves it entirely in the hands of God. If this were true it would be useless to exhort men to believe inasmuch as they could not do so.

As far as man's experience in salvation is concerned, when he places his faith in Christ he is conscious of making a human choice even though he may or may not be conscious at the same moment of the Spirit of God working. Though the Bible upholds clearly the doctrine of the sovereignty of God, it also upholds the responsibility of man. This is in keeping with John 6:39-40, 45 where Christ stated that none who are given Him will be lost, and that everyone who believes on Christ will have everlasting life. Though it is true that "no one can come to Me unless the Father who sent Me draws him" (v. 44), it is still true that man needs to believe in order to have salvation.

The difficult question of the relationship of the supernatural to the natural in men's faith is not unlocked in Scripture and remains a paradox, but both are true. God works and man believes. The convicting work of the Spirit in itself does not assure salvation. All of these truths emphasize the truth that it is important to preach the Bible. "Consequently, faith comes from hearing the message, and the message is heard through the word of Christ" (Rom. 10:17).

CHAPTER • 14

THE RICHES OF DIVINE GRACE

THE NECESSITY OF DIVINE GRACE

In attempting to understand the limitless character of grace a clear distinction should be made between what God has divinely undertaken by way of preparation for the salvation of the soul and the act of salvation itself. Included in the sphere of preparation are such achievements as the finished work of Christ, the enlightening work of the Spirit, and all other influences that provide the righteous ground on which a lost soul may be saved. To satisfy the divine demands for a righteous solution to the problem of the unsaved, a perfect redemption, reconciliation, and propitiation are required on the divine side. On the human side there is need for man to decide to believe; this is the human act for which God provides enablement.

Another distinction needs to be observed between the work of God in the immediate salvation of an individual and those responsibilities and activities that belong to the Christian life and service. A Christian's works that follow salvation (Eph. 2:10) should not be confused with the conditions of salvation. It is in this regard that Arminianism falls short because on the one hand it makes salvation entirely a decision of man and on the other hand it views salvation as conditional and something that can be lost because it depends on the works of man.

No one would deny that a holy life is proper for a Christian in view of the fact that he is a child of God and a member of Christ's body. In Hebrews 6:9 mention is made of the "things that accompany salvation." A Christian who is born again may be expected to have a change in life, and from human observation unless there is some change there is ground for question of his salvation. On the part of God, however, no confirming works are needed as He knows the heart and can distinguish between what is true and what is not true about the believer's standing with Himself.

Because salvation is by grace, no one is partly saved and partly lost. An individual may be cultured, refined, educated, moral, and religious but still be lacking salvation as was the case of Nicodemus in John 3. A believer must be born again by the grace of God in order to qualify for God's eternal salvation.

In preaching to the public, distinction must be made between what is addressed to the unsaved and what is addressed to the saved. To the unsaved God makes no appeal in regard to his manner of life; nor is improvement or reformation required. What God requires of an unsaved person is to hear and believe the Gospel. After he believes and becomes a Christian, then the exhortations of Scripture for a God-honoring life are to be heeded.

In the later discussion of "the riches of grace" the infinite care of God for the sinner in his salvation prompted by God's infinite love will be considered. The extent of the riches of the grace of God make plain that only by God's saving of souls can His infinite love for the world be satisfied. Though salvation is wonderful in its effect and expectation on the part of man, it is also a matter of infinite satisfaction to God.

On the basis of the work of Christ on the cross God is now free to pour on the sinner who comes to Him in faith the measureless riches of the grace of God. A Christian is to manifest the grace of God not only in this life but also in the life to come. In Ephesians 2:7 this future hope is prophesied "in order that in the coming ages He might show the incomparable riches of His grace, expressed in His kindness to us in Christ Jesus." Though the angels can observe the grace of God, they can see it only in sinners who are saved by grace. Those who are saved by grace will be a constant revelation throughout eternity of the extent of God's grace which brought them into their perfect estate in heaven.

In introducing the riches of divine grace, it may be restated that saving grace is what God accomplished on the ground of Christ's death in response to an individual's faith in Christ. To be considered are three aspects of divine grace: (1) the estate of the lost, (2) the essential character of God's undertaking, and (3) the riches of divine grace.

THE ESTATE OF THE LOST

In the New Testament two widely different concepts are indicated by the word "lost." An object may be lost in the sense that it needs to be found. But this does not change the structure or the character of the lost object. It is lost only in the sense that it is not in the right place. Israel is referred to as "the lost sheep of Israel," in that Israel had wandered from her covenants. Though individual Israelites were saved, the entire nation was lost in the sense of not being true to her covenants in the Old Testament.

In a similar way a Christian out of fellowship with God is in a sense misplaced even though he has eternal life, imputed righteousness, and union with God. The Parables of the Lost Sheep, the Lost Coin, and the Lost Son, in Luke 15 all lead to the same conclusion that the sheep, the coin, and the son needed to be restored to their proper place.

Far more than the concept of being merely displaced is the truth that a person is lost because he is not saved.

1. The lost have no realities. The lost soul has attained none of the eternal realities that make a Christian what he is. The lost condition of those who have not come to Christ is described in Ephesians 2:12, "Remember that at that time you were separate from Christ, excluded from citizenship in Israel, and foreigners to the covenants of the promise, without hope and without God in the world."

2. Sinful, fallen nature. Individuals are lost because they are born with a fallen, sinful nature. Before they ever commit sin itself they are lost because their nature is sinful. They inherited a sin nature from the original sin of Adam. In receiving Christ as Saviour a Christian is delivered from the bondage of his sin nature and receives all the abundant work of God related to his salvation.

In addition to being lost because of their sin nature people are also lost because of their personal sins, which are the normal fruit of the sin nature. Changing his manner of life, however, does not cause a person to be saved as this does not solve the basic problem of his sin nature. The problem of the sin nature can only be solved by the grace of God acting on the ground of the death of Christ in saving an individual soul.

3. God declares men sinful. Men are also lost because of the decree of God which declares that all human beings apart from the

grace of God are sinful and "Jews and Gentiles alike are all under sin" (Rom. 3:9). Many other Scriptures reinforce the concept that all men are condemned as sinners such as the statement in Galatians 3:22, "But the Scripture declares that the whole world is a prisoner of sin, so that what was promised, being given through faith in Jesus Christ, might be given to those who believe."

4. MEN ARE ALSO LOST BECAUSE THEY ARE UNDER THE POWER OF SATAN. Men are blinded to the facts of saving grace as stated in 2 Corinthians 4:3-4, "And even if our Gospel is veiled, it is veiled to those who are perishing. The god of this age has blinded the minds of unbelievers, so that they cannot see the light of the Gospel of the glory of Christ, who is the image of God." In Ephesians 2:1-3 men are described as under the domination "of the ruler of the kingdom of the air, the spirit who is now in those who are disobedient" (v. 2). By contrast in Philippians 2:13 a Christian experiences God's direction, "For it is God who works in you to will and to act according to His good purpose." In Colossians 1:13 it is revealed that an unbeliever is under "the dominion of darkness." In 1 John 5:19 the statement is made that "the whole world is under the control of the evil one."

Though unsaved men are under such tremendous pressure from Satan to disregard the truth of God, the superior power of God in giving salvation to lost souls is revealed and the great task of removing man from condemnation (John 3:18), from death (2 Cor. 7:10), from the curse of the Law (Gal. 3:13), from wrath (John 3:36; 1 Thes. 5:9), and from destruction (2 Thes. 1:9) demonstrates the tremendous extent of salvation and gives perspective on the greatness of God's undertakings.

THE ESSENTIAL CHARACTER OF GOD'S UNDERTAKING IN GRACE

Before dealing with the extent of the riches of God's grace certain important facts relating to God's salvation and the riches of His grace are indicated.

1. THE RICHES OF GOD'S GRACE ARE NOT FULLY EXPERIENCED. This is not to imply that the riches are not real but rather to point out they do not fully manifest their reality to man in his limited understanding of God's work. Like the doctrine of justification, it is

not essentially experiential but rests wholly on the promise of God.

2. THE RICHES OF GOD'S GRACE ARE NOT PROGRESSIVE. Though there is a process in the divine undertaking in grace, when a person is saved he has inherited all the riches of grace that will be subsequently experienced. Just as a child is a son at birth but does not manifest his characteristics as an adult, so a Christian, who is saved by the grace of God, only understands partially the riches of divine grace.

3. THE RICHES OF DIVINE GRACE ARE NOT RELATED TO HUMAN MERIT. God has been freed to bestow grace on those who do not deserve it because of the fact that Christ has died for their sins, and in His obedience has won not only forgiveness but also justification. This can be claimed by faith when a person believes in Christ.

4. THE RICHES OF DIVINE GRACE ARE ETERNAL IN THEIR CHARACTER. Though a man's experience subsequent to salvation may be uneven and limited, the riches of God's grace continue forever just as the gift of eternal life.

5. THE RICHES OF GOD'S GRACE ARE KNOWN ONLY BY REVELATION. Though theologians can attempt to speculate and itemize the character of God's grace, the full extent of grace can only be comprehended in accepting what God's Word reveals.

6. THE RICHES OF GOD'S GRACE ARE WROUGHT BY GOD ALONE. They are a work of God for man rather than a work of man for God. This is obvious in the fact that no one can save himself, establish peace with God, transfer himself out of the power of darkness into the kingdom of the Son of God's love, become a citizen of heaven, or write down his name in heaven, for God alone is able to save.

7. THE RICHES OF GOD'S GRACE ARE NOT WROUGHT BY MAN. As a corollary to the previous fact that grace is wrought by God alone, it may be concluded that grace is not a result of man's effort. No man even with great intellectual ability could possibly devise anything as extensive as the riches of God's grace. Though man will continue to experience it in time and eternity, he will never fully comprehend all that enters into the grace of God.

THE RICHES OF DIVINE GRACE

The Scriptures reveal 33 stupendous works of God which together comprise the salvation of the soul. They are wrought by God instantaneously, are grounded on the merit of Christ, and are eternal. Accordingly each member of the human family is either perfectly saved or entirely lost. All 33 elements comprise the riches of grace which a Christian receives in salvation.

1. THE WORK OF GRACE IS A PART OF THE ETERNAL PLAN OF GOD. In eternity past God determined that He would provide grace for a fallen race even before man was created. As stated in Romans 8:29-30, those who were predestined for salvation are carried through the various steps of being called and justified, and then ultimately will be glorified.

Five terms in the New Testament are used in reference to the sovereign purpose of God in salvation: foreknown, predestinated, elected, chosen, and called.

Believers in Christ are foreknown as believers from eternity past. The doctrine of divine foreknowledge is properly restricted to what God will bring to pass and is coextensive with all that occurs. God, having decreed the future in all its detail, knows what will happen because He has decreed it. Because both are eternal, it is not a question of one being before the other. But logically foreknowledge must follow divine decision. The foreknowledge of God is mentioned in several passages (Acts 2:23; Rom. 8:29; 11:2; 1 Peter 1:2).

Predestination is another aspect of God's eternal plan which is mentioned several times in Scripture (Acts 17:26; Rom. 8:29-30; Eph. 1:5, 11; 2:10). Predestination is part of God's eternal decree, and God foreknows because He has predestined. In various passages predestination may be before or after foreknowledge, but this does not determine priority (Acts 2:23; Rom. 8:29; 1 Peter 1:2). Every believer is both predestined and foreknown by God and will certainly fulfill the realization of all of God's riches of grace.

Election is also a part of the eternal plan of God. Christ is referred to as the elect Servant of *Yahweh* (Isa. 42:1). In the Great Tribulation some will be saved who have been elected (Matt. 24:22, 24, 31; Mark 13:20, 22, 27). Christians are declared to be the elect of God (Rom. 8:33; Col. 3:12; 2 Tim. 2:10; Titus 1:1; 1 Peter 1:2; 2 John 1, 13). Christ is said to be the precious Cornerstone (1 Peter 2:4-8) who was "chosen by God" (v. 4). The central thought in all who are elected is that they have been chosen by God from eternity past.

Along with foreknowledge, predestination, and election is the concept of being chosen. This is mentioned in many passages (Mark 13:20; John 13:18; 15:16, 19; 1 Cor. 1:27-28; Eph. 1:4; James 2:5).

Like other expressions related to God's eternal plan, those who are chosen to salvation were selected in eternity past.

Still another designation is being called of God. Though the Gospel as it is preached is a general call to faith in God, the Bible uses the same expression for an effectual call, God's work in effectively bringing souls to salvation. A clear reference to God's effective call is in Romans 8:30, "And those He predestined, He also called; those He called, He also justified; those He justified, He also glorified." Another reference is found in 1 Thessalonians 5:24, "The One who calls you is faithful and He will do it." These many references to the eternal plan of God indicate that salvation for sinners is not an afterthought in God's creation but was fully in view when God decreed all future events including Creation.

2. Redeemed. The doctrine of redemption is another wonderful aspect of a Christian's salvation. This doctrine has a threefold classification: (1) It is universal in character in the sense that God has provided through His redemption a sufficient ground for righteousness on which God may save those who are lost. (2) Redemption indicates not only that God has purchased the unsaved individual, who formerly was a slave to Satan, but also that God sets him free as an act of divine grace. (3) There is a redemption of the body of believers which is yet future. This is the outworking of redemption in resurrection.

3. Reconciled. When a person is saved, he is reconciled to God. As previously discussed, reconciliation is the act of God in changing a believer so that he is acceptable to God in terms of righteousness. Though the world provisionally was reconciled (2 Cor. 5:19), the reconciliation of the individual occurs when he is saved (vv. 20-21). To be reconciled to God an individual has to come to God on the ground of the merit of Christ in recognition of his blessed position in Christ and as the recipient of God's marvelous grace.

4. Related through propitiation. Propitiation, meaning that God is satisfied by the death of Christ, is another wonderful provision for the believer when he puts his trust in Christ. God has been rendered free to act for sinners by the death of His Son because the sin problem has been perfectly solved by Christ in His death on the cross. The responsibility of each individual is to trust in Christ and accept what God has provided. In coming to God a Christian can be assured that God is satisfied (1 John 2:2). Christians in confession of sin can come to God in confidence that He will forgive.

5. Forgiven all sins. At the time of his salvation a Christian is forgiven all his sins. As stated in Colossians 2:13, "God made you alive with Christ. He forgave us all our sins." The forgiveness of sins is a frequent subject of Scripture (Eph. 1:7; 4:32; Col. 1:14; 3:13). As brought out in Romans 8:33-34, God has justified a believer and declared him righteous, and no one can properly condemn him. Romans 8 begins with "no condemnation" and ends with "no separation."

A distinction can be observed between the judicial forgiveness given a believer at the time of salvation and the repeated forgiveness a Christian experiences within the family of God as he falls short of what he ought to be and do. Because a Christian is justified, he is declared righteous and therefore he is forgiven all his sins. When a Christian sins he can, by confession, come back into fellowship with God. Forgiveness in 1 John 1:9 is forgiveness within the family relationship, forgiveness between a child and his Heavenly Father. No more sacrifices are needed as was true in the Old Testament; the death of Christ is the one sacrifice for sin and on this basis a Christian can be forgiven.

6. Joined to Christ. A Christian is vitally joined to Christ for the judgment of his sin nature. The fact that a believer is eternally connected to Christ as the head is connected to the body makes possible a new life in Christ. This is revealed in Romans 6:1-10 which speaks of the believer's union with Christ, which is symbolized by baptism. In this relationship he is united to Christ in His death and His resurrection. The believer should reckon his old self crucified and without power to take away his freedom in Christ.

7. Freed from the Law. At the time of his salvation a Christian is freed from the Law. Whether the Law refers to the Mosaic Law or to God's moral law in general, a Christian in salvation is forever freed from the need of justifying himself before God by good works. Though good works are expected of a believer, they are not the ground of his salvation which is entirely on the grace principle. Though there can be some application of the Law of Moses to a Christian's rule of life, actually the New Testament is a complete revelation of what a Christian ought to be and do, and the death of Christ has freed us from the Law (John 1:17; Acts 15:24-29; Rom. 6:14; 7:2-6; 2 Cor. 3:6-11; Gal. 5:18). Being "free from the law of sin and death" (Rom. 8:2), or dead to the law (7:4), or "no longer under the supervision of the Law" (Gal. 3:25) describe a position in

grace before God whose blessings are rich and full.

8. A CHILD OF GOD. At the time of his salvation a believer becomes a child of God, having been born again by the regenerating power of the Holy Spirit. In this new relationship God, the first Person, becomes his Father, and he has a new relationship to Christ and the Holy Spirit.

Various terms are used in the New Testament to identify this new birth. Being "born again" (John 3:3) indicates that new life has come into the saved individual. This new life comes from God and not by any earthly process (John 3:6; cf. 1:12-13; 1 Peter 1:23).

The term "regeneration" conveys the same idea as new birth (Titus 3:5, KJV). In addition to giving life there is a cleansing of the old person in salvation.

Another expression is that of being "made alive with Christ" (Eph. 2:5). What was spiritually dead is now spiritually alive (cf. Col. 2:13).

The title "sons of God" or "children of God" is used in many passages (2 Cor. 6:18; Gal. 3:26; 1 John 3:2). Having received eternal life from God believers are sons or children of God not merely by title but by actual generation.

A believer is also a new creation (2 Cor. 5:17). As such, the mighty creative power of God is manifested in the believer in making him into a new creature.

9. ADOPTED. At the time of his salvation a Christian is adopted (Eph. 1:4-5). Ordinarily adoption is a means whereby an outsider becomes a member of a family. It is a legal way to create the father-and-son relationship. Divine adoption follows this pattern of human adoption in which a father recognizes a son's relationship to him.

Divine adoption, whether referring to Israel's kinship to God (Rom. 9:4) or to the redemption or resurrection of the believer's body (8:23), is primarily a divine act by which one who is already a child of God by actual birth through the Spirit of God is placed in the position of being an adult son in his relationship to God.

At salvation a person is given immediate spiritual sonship and adoption even though he is immature spiritually. In the case of a Christian the adoption is in relationship to being a son in the father's household. In the realm of divine adoption, every child born of God is adopted at the moment he is born again. His position before God is that of a mature, responsible son.

10. ACCEPTABLE. Every Christian is made acceptable to God by

Jesus Christ. As such a Christian can offer "spiritual sacrifices acceptable to God through Jesus Christ" (1 Peter 2:5). This is because of "His glorious grace, which He has freely given us in the One He loves" (Eph. 1:6).

As one accepted by God, a believer has been declared righteous as indicated in the doctrine of justification. Two major realities constitute a Christian: imparted eternal life (John 20:31), and imputed righteousness (2 Cor. 5:21). The Gospel of John emphasizes eternal life, and the Epistle to the Romans stresses imputed righteousness. Eternal life is bestowed in the regeneration of the believer and in his new birth. Imputed righteousness is based on the truth that the believer is in Christ as stated in John 14:20, "You are in Me, and I am in you."

A Christian is also sanctified positionally, that is, he is seen in Christ and therefore is set apart as holy to God. Even the Corinthians in spite of their sins were declared to be "sanctified" (1 Cor. 6:11). Many references to sanctification in Christ and especially the use of the word "saint" refer to the believer's position in Christ. There is correspondingly the continued work of sanctification (John 17:17; Eph. 5:26). Ultimately in heaven believers will have perfect sanctification and be perfected forever (Heb. 10:14). In view of all that God has done in salvation, the believer is accepted by God. In addition the believer is "qualified . . . to share in the inheritance of the saints in the kingdom of light" (Col. 1:12).

11. A BELIEVER IS JUSTIFIED BY FAITH. As previously discussed, justification is more than forgiveness; it is a declaration that a believer is righteous. Though a person is not perfect at the time of his salvation, nevertheless he is legally declared justified or righteous because he is in Christ (Rom. 5:1).

12. BROUGHT NEAR. A Christian at the time of his salvation is "brought near through the blood of Christ" (Eph. 2:13). This new established relationship pictures a Christian in nearness to God. In keeping with this fact Christians are encouraged, "Let us draw near to God with a sincere heart in full assurance of faith, having our hearts sprinkled to cleanse us from a guilty conscience and having our bodies washed with pure water" (Heb. 10:22).

13. DELIVERED FROM DARKNESS. A person is delivered from the dominion of darkness at the time of his salvation (Col. 1:13). Before his salvation he is under the power of Satan, is blinded to the Gospel, and is living in spiritual darkness. When he is saved, a

person is delivered from this and is brought into a proper relationship to God even though the spiritual warfare continues, as mentioned in Ephesians 6:10-18.

14. Translated into the kingdom. Having been delivered from Satan, the Christian at the time of his salvation is translated into "the kingdom of the Son He loves" (Col. 1:13). Reference to this aspect of salvation is also found in 1 Thessalonians 2:12 and 2 Peter 1:11.

15. Placed on the Rock. A Christian is placed on the Rock, Christ Jesus, at the time of his salvation. In keeping with this, his house will be built on a rock, as taught in Matthew 7:24-27; that is, his life is secure in Christ. Christ is the foundation of the Christian's life (1 Cor. 3:10). Though the superstructure of his life is to be tested by fire (vv. 11-15), the foundation is sure, and every Christian will receive some reward (4:5). By contrast those who are not Christians are building on the sand which will give way when the time of testing comes.

16. Gift to Christ from God. Every Christian is a gift to Christ from God the Father. This is referred to frequently especially in Jesus' prayer in John 17 (vv. 6-9, 11-12, 24). In 18:9 Christ declared, "I have not lost one of those You gave Me." Though a believer is a gift from God the Father to Christ, there is also a sense in which Christ, having died to save them, can give them to the Father.

17. Spiritually circumcised. New believers in Christ are considered spiritually circumcised (Col. 2:11), though formerly they were considered uncircumcised (Eph. 2:11). Since circumcision was the rite by which an Israelite separated himself from the world and related himself to God, so a Christian at his salvation is separated from the world and is joined to Christ.

18. Partaker of priesthood. A Christian is made partaker of a holy and royal priesthood at the time of his salvation and declared to be "a holy priesthood" (1 Peter 2:5) and "a royal priesthood" (v. 9). Because Christ is both King and Priest, a believer in Christ likewise is a member of the royal family and his priesthood is a royal priesthood. In keeping with this Christians can pray to Christ as their High Priest and will share in His earthly reign in the millennial kingdom (2 Tim. 2:12). Though Israel had a priesthood in the tribe of Levi, every Christian is a priest and is related to Christ his High Priest who intercedes for him in heaven.

19. Chosen. The church is constituted "a chosen people, a royal priesthood, a holy nation, a people belonging to God" (1 Peter 2:9). In the present age the church includes both Jews and Gentiles who are recipients of all the wonderful works that God accomplishes at the moment of salvation. As Israel was the chosen people in the Old Testament, the church, composed of both believing Jews and Gentiles, is a chosen people in the present age. They are a royal priesthood in that they are identified with Christ who is their High Priest and King. They are a nation in a sense that they are a separate, distinct group among all the peoples of the earth. They are a "people belonging to God" in the sense that they are citizens of heaven, perfected in Christ, and appointed to live in His power to the glory of God. These truths make a large contribution to the doctrine of the riches of divine grace.

20. Heavenly citizen. A Christian at the time of his salvation becomes a heavenly citizen as stated in Philippians 3:20, "But our citizenship is in heaven. And we eagerly await a Saviour from there, the Lord Jesus Christ." Israel had a special citizenship while on earth, but in the Old Testament Gentiles were strangers as far as Israel was concerned. In the present age both Jews and Gentiles can become members of the church, the body of Christ, and are given an exalted heavenly citizenship. Christ said to the 72 followers when they returned from their mission, "Do not rejoice that the spirits submit to you, but rejoice that your names are written in heaven" (Luke 10:20). Because Christians are citizens of heaven and are "aliens and strangers on earth" (Heb. 11:13)—an expression which is applied to the church in 1 Peter 2:11—they are "Christ's ambassadors" while they are on earth (2 Cor. 5:20). Accordingly a Christian on earth is a witness, a stranger, a pilgrim, and an ambassador for the present, but Christians will enjoy heavenly citizenship forever.

21. Member of God's household. When individuals are saved they become "members of God's household" (Eph. 2:19). Paul referred to Christians as "the family of believers" (Gal. 6:10). This relationship continues forever in contrast to earthly family relations which cease at death.

As members of the family of God, Christians have a variety of responsibilities as stated in 2 Timothy 2:20-21, "In a large house there are articles not only of gold and silver, but also of wood and clay; some are for noble purposes and some for ignoble. If a man cleanses himself from the latter, he will be an instrument for noble purposes, made holy, useful to the Master and prepared to do any good work." A Christian's citizenship and membership in the family of God is another evidence of his high position in Christ.

22. FELLOWSHIP WITH SAINTS. At the time of salvation Christians have entrance into a wonderful fellowship with other saints. This is true because of the unity of the church made possible by the baptism of the Holy Spirit. This was the objective of Christ's prayer when He prayed for the unity of believers, "I will remain in the world no longer, but they are still in the world, and I am coming to You. Holy Father, protect them by the power of Your name—the name You gave Me—so that they may be one as We are One" (John 17:11). In verses 21-23 Christ prayed that believers in Him would be united with one another as Christ is one with God the Father, "Father, just as You are in Me and I am in You. May they also be in Us so that the world may believe that You have sent Me. I have given them the glory that You gave Me, that they may be one as We are One: I in them and You in Me. May they be brought to complete unity to let the world know that You sent Me and have loved them even as You have loved Me."

In the light of the fact that this unity is something God brings about, believers are never exhorted to attempt a unity by organization. Rather they are instructed to keep the unity which God by His Spirit has created (Eph. 4:3-5). The fellowship of saints on earth will be transcended by a greater fellowship in heaven.

23. HEAVENLY CITIZENS. Christians become a part of a heavenly association. Because they are in Christ, and Christ is in them, they are partners with Christ in His life (Col. 1:27). Christ is referred to as "your life" (3:4). Christians partake of eternal life which is in Christ (1 John 5:11-12), a truth mentioned many times in the New Testament. Christians also have a heavenly association with Christ because of their incomparable position in which they are raised with Christ and are joined to Him as He is seated at the right hand of God. Though a Christian is on earth, his position is in Christ in heaven.

Christians are also partners with Christ in service. This is possible because they are united with Christ (1 Cor. 1:9). Therefore they should not be yoked with unbelievers (2 Cor. 6:14). As partners with Christ, Christians are admonished by Paul, "Stand firm. Let nothing move you. Always give yourselves fully to the work of the Lord, because you know that your labor in the Lord is not in vain"

(1 Cor. 15:58). Christians are united with Christ in ministry (3:9), as "fellow workers" with God (2 Cor. 6:1); they are "servants of God" (v. 4) and "ministers of a new covenant" (3:6). Christians also have the experience of suffering with Christ and are promised that if they endure suffering they "will also reign with Him" (2 Tim. 2:12; Phil. 1:29). Peter referred to suffering with Christ (1 Peter 4:12-14). Paul rejoiced in his sufferings (Col. 1:24) and indicated "that our present sufferings are not worth comparing with the glory that will be revealed in us" (Rom. 8:18). In writing to the Thessalonians Paul spoke of suffering saints (1 Thes. 2:14) and asserted, "We sent Timothy . . . to strengthen and encourage you in your faith, so that no one would be unsettled by these trials" (3:2-3).

Though a Christian may suffer because of his identification with Christ, the fellowship of suffering which is closest to the heart of God is to share His burden for lost souls. This is a natural response but is also generated in the heart by the Holy Spirit and is an outgrowth of love as a fruit of the Spirit (Gal. 5:22) and is a work of God in us (Rom. 5:5). Paul spoke of his own sorrow for his unsaved Jewish brothers (9:1-3).

Christians are also partners with Christ in prayer and are exhorted to pray in the name of Christ. Through prayer in the name of Christ they will be able to accomplish greater things than Christ could have accomplished if He had remained on earth (John 14:12-14). Christ performed many wonderful miracles on earth, but He operated in only one place at a time. Believers in Christ may be scattered over the world, each with a direct connection with Christ on His throne and with their ministry can accomplish more than Christ could have accomplished if He had remained on earth after His resurrection.

Christians are also partners with Christ in betrothal as His bride (2 Cor. 11:2; Eph. 5:25-27). When Christ comes for the church in the Rapture, He will come as the Bridegroom claiming His bride.

Christians are also partners in Christ in their expectation of the "blessed hope" (Titus 2:13). This will be part of Christ's triumph which He is anticipating in the end time (Heb. 10:13).

24. Access to God. Christians have access to God because they are saved. This access is into His grace (Rom. 5:2). They are saved by grace (Eph. 2:8) but also stand in grace (Rom. 5:2). In that position they are to "grow in the grace and knowledge of our Lord and Saviour Jesus Christ" (2 Peter 3:18). Because of His access to Christ, a Christian has access to the Father (Eph. 2:18). As this

verse indicates, a believer has access through Christ by the Holy Spirit to the Father. Through the work of the Holy Spirit, a Christian is able to understand truth (1 Cor. 2:10), enjoy the fellowship of the Holy Spirit (2 Cor. 13:14), and partake of the Holy Spirit (1 Cor. 12:13). Access to the Father assures the believer's relationship to Christ and the Holy Spirit.

Having access to God gives a Christian reassurance and enables him to "approach the throne of grace with confidence" (Heb. 4:16), and to "have confidence to enter the most holy place by the blood of Jesus, by a new and living way opened for us through the curtain, that is, His body" (10:19-20). The amazing work of grace gives a Christian immediate access to the Almighty God and to His throne.

25. God's abounding grace. When an individual is saved he comes under the relationship of God's abounding grace. As stated in Romans 5:18-20, "Consequently, just as the result of one trespass was condemnation for all men, so also the result of one act of righteousness was justification that brings life for all men. For just as through the disobedience of the one man the many were made sinners, so also through the obedience of the one man the many will be made righteous. The Law was added so that the trespass might increase. But where sin increased, grace increased all the more."

As objects of God's love (John 3:16; Rom. 5:8; 1 John 3:16) Christians are assured of continuing grace. This is evident in God's salvation (Eph. 2:7-9), in His safekeeping (Rom. 5:2), in His service (John 17:18), and His grace is measured only by the infinite gift of Christ (Eph. 4:7). In addition the Christian comes under the divine instruction of grace (Titus 2:12-13). Christians also become objects of displaying the power of God as stated in Ephesians 1:19: "For it is God who works in you to will and to act according to His good purpose" (Phil. 2:13).

A Christian is also an object of God's faithfulness (Phil. 1:6; 1 Thes. 5:24; Heb. 13:5), and an object and recipient of God's peace. He has peace with God at salvation (Rom. 5:1), and also receives the experience of peace which Christ bestows (John 14:27; Gal. 5:22; Col. 3:15). In their trials Christians are the objects of God's consolation as stated in 2 Thessalonians 2:16-17, "May our Lord Jesus Christ Himself and God our Father, who loved us and by His grace gave us eternal encouragement and good hope, encourage your hearts and strengthen you in every good deed and word." In addition to all these aspects of divine grace Christians are also the objects of the intercession of the Holy Spirit (Rom. 8:26) and are ceaselessly the objects of Christ's intercession from His heavenly throne (Heb. 7:25). Because Christ left earth and returned to heaven, He is able to make intercession for believers in God's presence (Rom. 8:34; Heb. 9:24).

26. An inheritance in Christ. Because he is born into God's family, a Christian receives the inheritance of one who is in Christ. As stated in Ephesians 1:18, "I pray also that the eyes of your heart may be enlightened in order that you may know the hope to which He has called you, the riches of His glorious inheritance in the saints." In heaven the Christian will be glorified (John 17:22; Rom. 8:30; Col. 3:4). As such he will be the object of praise to God when he stands glorified in heaven (Eph. 1:6).

27. Inheritance in heaven. In addition to the inheritance a believer has in Christ, he also receives "an inheritance that can never perish, spoil, or fade—kept in heaven for you" (1 Peter 1:4). What a Christian now possesses even on earth "is a deposit guaranteeing our inheritance until the redemption of those who are God's possession" (Eph. 1:14). Christians will receive "an inheritance from the Lord as a reward" (Col. 3:24). Hebrews 9:15 adds, "For this reason Christ is the Mediator of a New Covenant, that those who are called may receive the promised eternal inheritance."

28. Light. The believer becomes a light that shines in a dark world according to Ephesians 5:8-9, "For you were once in darkness, but now you are light in the Lord. Live as children of light (for the fruit of the light consists in all goodness, righteousness, and truth)." This is in keeping with the fact that "God is light" and that "in Him there is no darkness at all" (1 John 1:5). Because a believer is "light in the Lord" (Eph. 5:8), he should walk in the light (1 John 1:5-7). This light is God's Word as stated in Psalm 119:105, "Your Word is a lamp to my feet and a light for my path." To walk in the light is to be living in the knowledge of God's written revelation of His will. A Christian does not become light in the Lord by his own effort; rather by the grace of God he is transformed. The secret of walking in the light is to follow the revelation of God's Word which casts light on one's conduct, and to let the indwelling presence of God manifest itself in his life.

29. United to Trinity. A believer in Christ is vitally united to the Father, the Son, and the Holy Spirit. Because he is saved, a person is in God the Father (1 Thes. 1:1), the Father is in the

believer (Eph. 4:6), the believer is in the Son (Rom. 8:1), the Son is in the believer (John 14:20), the believer is in the Spirit (Rom. 8:9), and the Spirit is in the believer (1 Cor. 2:12). This relationship of being vitally united to the Father, the Son, and the Holy Spirit was never realized by saints in the Old Testament. It was provided for believers beginning with the Day of Pentecost (Acts 2) and is the privilege of every believer in Christ. Because a believer is in God, he is also vitally related to all his fellow believers (John 17:21).

The Scriptures offer seven figures that describe the relationship a believer has in God. A believer is a member of Christ's body (1 Cor. 12:13). The believer is related to Christ as a branch is related to a vine (John 15:5). The believer is related to Christ as a stone is related to the building of which Christ is the Chief Cornerstone (Eph. 2:19-22). The believer is in Christ as a sheep is a member of his flock (John 10:27-29). The believer is a part of that company that forms the bride of Christ (Eph. 5:25-27). The believer is a priest in a kingdom of priests over which Christ is the High Priest forever (1 Peter 2:5, 9). The believer is also a part of the new creation over which Christ as the last Adam is the Head (2 Cor. 5:17). In John 14:20 the promise is given that God the Father and God the Son will indwell the believer. In this relationship the believer is in Christ, Christ is in the Father, and Christ is in the believer. These marvelous truths are true for the Christian in the present age and should be contrasted to the more limited blessings of those in the Old Testament.

30. Blessed with the deposit of the Holy Spirit. A believer in Christ is blessed with the deposit of the Holy Spirit in his heart (2 Cor. 1:22; Eph. 1:14). Indwelling the Christian, the Holy Spirit is called the firstfruits of the coming harvest (Rom. 8:23). A Christian is born of the Spirit (John 3:6), baptized by the Spirit (1 Cor. 12:13), and indwelt and anointed by the Spirit (John 7:39; Rom. 5:5; 8:9; 2 Cor. 1:21; Eph. 4:30). The Holy Spirit's indwelling seals the security of his salvation. A believer who is indwelt by the Spirit may also be filled by the Spirit (Eph. 5:18), a ministry of the Spirit which releases His power and effectiveness.

31. Glorification. Believers in Christ are assured glorification, which is part of the promise of God in saving one who trusts in Christ. In contemplating his future glory Paul wrote, "I consider that our present sufferings are not worth comparing with the glory that will be revealed in us" (Rom. 8:18). Christians in heaven will appear

with Christ in His glory (Col. 3:4). The certainty of their being glorified is revealed in Romans 8:30, which states that those predestined, called, and justified will also be glorified.

32. Complete. A Christian is complete in Christ as stated in Colossians 2:9-10, "For in Christ all the fullness of the Deity lives in bodily form, and you have been given fullness in Christ, who is the Head over every power and authority." Because of a Christian's vital union with Christ, he partakes of all that Christ is, and he is viewed by God the Father as one who is perfected in his position in Christ. Though a Christian has many great privileges in the present life, these will be eclipsed by the glory that will be experienced by Christians when they stand complete in heaven.

33. Possessing every spiritual blessing. A Christian is even now possessed of every spiritual blessing as stated in Ephesians 1:3, "Praise be to the God and Father of our Lord Jesus Christ, who has blessed us in the heavenly realms with every spiritual blessing in Christ." The riches of grace contemplated in the preceding 32 facts are all included in "every spiritual blessing" which a believer has in Christ. All the possessions which together measure the riches of divine grace are traced to the believer's place in Christ.

As all these blessings indicate, salvation is a work of God for man, not a work of man for God. What a Christian experiences is what God's love has prompted Him to do for those who had no merit before Him but who are now recognized in the merit of His Son because of their faith in Christ. The truth of the riches of divine grace are almost overwhelming, and it is difficult to give it proper recognition. Those who preach the Gospel, however, must make clear how abundant are the riches believers have in Christ when they place their faith in Him and how blessed is their eternal estate.

THE ETERNAL SECURITY OF THE BELIEVER

CHAPTER • 15

INTRODUCTION TO THE DOCTRINE OF SECURITY

The doctrine of the eternal security of a believer, called the perseverance of the saints by earlier theologians, holds that no individual once saved will ever be lost. This is affirmed by many Scriptures such as John 5:24, "I tell you the truth, whoever hears My word and believes Him who sent Me has eternal life and will not be condemned; he has crossed over from death to life." What is affirmed here is that the one who is saved receives eternal life and has the promise that in the future he will not be condemned because he has crossed over from spiritual death to spiritual life. Eternal life by its very nature cannot be terminated.

The doctrine of security is one of five points commonly related to the Calvinistic system of theology, but its proof rests on a scriptural foundation. It is true that some Christians who claim to have salvation do not bear the fruit or evidence of it. Under superficial examination some Scriptures seem to contradict the concept of eternal security. On the other hand the many Scriptures that affirm the believer's eternal security are so clear that their testimony outweighs any objections that may be raised. Generally speaking those who hold to a Calvinistic system of theology hold to eternal security or perseverance of the saints, and those who hold to an Arminian system of theology generally affirm that a saved person can be lost.

No doubt some who profess salvation have never been saved. That such people should fall away is to be expected. On the other hand the extensive character of the salvation of a believer in Christ is such that it is an irreversible work of God which cannot be changed by human decision or failure.

The concept of eternal security builds on other doctrines such as the doctrine of depravity. Because man is depraved, he cannot be saved except by divine grace. Only God can make salvation possible and actual. The fact of sovereign and eternal election makes it impossible for an elect person once saved to lose his salvation.

If salvation is something that man does for himself, obviously it could be lost. If salvation is an act of God, then it is a work that man cannot undo. This is brought out in passages such as Romans 8:30, "And those He predestined, He also called; those He called, He also justified; those He justified, He also glorified." All who are predestined to salvation will be justified, and all who are justified will be glorified. Their salvation is thus secure.

In the history of the church some have accepted the doctrine of eternal security while others have accepted the possibility that some believers may fall from salvation. In the Lutheran Church, for example, some believe that a saved person can be lost while others believe in eternal security. Historically Lutherans define regeneration as something that happens when an infant is baptized. At the same time they hold that regeneration is not equal to salvation. Ultimately the question has to be decided as to what the Scriptures teach, and obviously the Scriptures do not teach both views.

In the following discussion it will be pointed out that the truth of eternal security is inherent in the nature of salvation itself. If salvation is no more than a detached coin which one holds in his hand and which he has only by virtue of a feeble human grasp, it might easily be lost. On the other hand if salvation is the creation of a new being composed of unchangeable and imperishable elements that depend on the perfect and immutable merit of the Son of God, then there can be no failure.

Actually there is no proper ground for drawing a distinction between salvation and safekeeping though for practical purposes such a distinction may be established. The fact is that God's salvation is eternal by its very nature. Even though human experience can vacillate, eternal security means that no soul once saved has ever been lost. Doubts about security can be traced to failure to comprehend the reality that God accomplishes salvation by His sovereign grace.

THE ARMINIAN VIEW OF SECURITY

Three major systems of theology have characterized the history of the doctrine of salvation: Socinianism, Arminianism, and Calvinism.

Socinianism is usually attributed to those who are liberal in theology and who pay little attention to what the Scriptures teach. It is the forerunner of modern liberalism. Arminianism is more biblical and orthodox in its treatment of Scripture. It avoids the rationalism of Socinianism but falls short of the declarations of Calvinism.

In using the terms Arminianism and Calvinism, there is no intent to magnify human points of view but rather simply to give titles to two approaches to the doctrine of salvation. From a practical as well as a theological standpoint it is most important to establish whether the salvation of a believer continues forever or whether it can be interrupted by human failure. Partly the issue is whether the saving work of Christ on the cross includes the safekeeping of the one who has put his trust in Him or whether it does not. The question is whether a Christian can be condemned. According to Romans 8:1, "There is now no condemnation for those who are in Christ Jesus."

The importance of determining the truth in this doctrine is evident. If there is no sufficient ground for the removal of condemnation and no sufficient ground for the impartation of eternal life and imputing of the merit of Christ, then salvation is nullified. Accordingly while godly men hold differences of opinion on this subject, the importance of the conclusions cannot be overestimated.

In attempting to understand the Arminian point of view three considerations are necessary: (1) the Arminian view of the major soteriological doctrines; (2) the Arminian emphasis on human experience and reason; and (3) the Arminian appeal to the Scriptures.

THE ARMINIAN VIEW OF MAJOR SOTERIOLOGICAL DOCTRINES

In previous discussion the Arminian view of the value of Christ's death was considered. Here the particular aspect of Arminian theology relating to soteriology will be considered under seven headings: (1) the Arminian view of original sin, (2) the Arminian view of universal efficacious calling, (3) the Arminian view of divine decrees, (4) the Arminian view of the Fall, (5) the Arminian view of omniscience, (6) the Arminian view of divine sovereignty, and (7) the Arminian view of sovereign grace.

1. The Arminian view of original sin. Though Arminian theologians accept the concept of human depravity, they couple this

with a doctrine of common grace that all men are given sufficient grace to believe. Calvinists believe that common grace means that all men are influenced to some extent by the Holy Spirit, but no Scripture suggests that all men have the ability to receive Christ as Saviour. Though God's work in enlightening the unsaved is inscrutable, the Scriptures on the one hand affirm that God must act in efficacious grace and on the other hand that man must believe. The Scriptures also affirm that the convicting work of the Spirit (John 16:8-11) attends the preaching of the Gospel and makes the Gospel understandable to an unsaved person. This paves the way for grace to enable a person to believe.

2. The Arminian view of universal efficacious calling. The Bible clearly states that there is a work of grace which is efficacious in enabling an individual to believe, and in every case where a person believes this work of God is present. This is illustrated in Romans 8:28-30, which states all who are foreknown are effectively called and all who are called are justified and all who are justified are glorified.

The Arminian view is that God gives everyone the ability to accept Christ and therefore the moment of salvation involves only man's making a decision. However, that all men are in a fallen state even when convicted by the Holy Spirit is a clear teaching of Scripture (Rom. 3:11; 1 Cor. 2:14; 2 Cor. 4:3-4; Eph. 2:1-9). In providing salvation God must do a work of grace over and beyond the limits of ordinary, common grace and beyond the convicting work of the Spirit. The Bible affirms that God must do this work of grace in an unsaved person before he can be saved and it also teaches that the individual must make a decision. The Bible never attempts to remove the tension between the will of God and the will of man in this matter. Nor does the Bible solve the problem by exalting the human will so that a work of efficacious grace is unnecessary. In salvation God enables a person to understand and also gives him the will to believe (Phil. 2:13).

3. The Arminian view of divine decrees. As discussed earlier, God's eternal decree includes all events of every classification including the acts of people who make choices and who will to believe or not to believe. Arminians tend to question such a viewpoint of the will of God though some who are conservative acknowledge that God foreknows all future events.

The issue is, Did God have a plan in eternity past which He is executing in time? Socinianism, a forerunner of Arminianism, held that future events depend on secondary causes such as the human will. On the other hand Calvinists maintain that God has not only ordained whatever comes to pass but is also executing the same through His providence. Arminians have not been willing to go as far as Socinians who deny the foreknowledge of God. On the other hand they tend to qualify the concept of God's unconditional authority to act, His power to achieve, His purposes and His ability to govern in all that comes to pass. The Arminian view of foreknowledge is that God knew in advance those who would choose Christ as their Saviour, but Arminians tend to deny that any efficacious work of God provides enablement to the act of faith.

4. The Arminian view of the Fall. The Fall of Adam into sin, which plunged the whole human race into sin, has been discussed previously. Though Arminians do not reject the depravity of Adam, they hold that the difficulty of man's sinful condition is overcome by the bestowal of common grace. In Arminianism when an individual receives common grace he is different, and is free to act for or against God's will.

Calvinists on the other hand maintain that people are wholly unable to deliver themselves or to take one step in the direction of their own salvation, that men have no claim on God for salvation because of any merit, and that the salvation of men is a divine undertaking built on the righteous ground of Christ's sacrifice on the cross. The cross has made it possible for the holy God to be free to save meritless men, and it has given Him the righteous freedom by which He can keep them saved forever. Arminians tend to solve the problem of man's need of deliverance from sin by making it almost totally man's decision.

5. The Arminian view of omniscience. Arminians hold that God can only foreknow because He has the ability to foresee what man will do. They point to Peter's words in 1 Peter 1:18-20, "For you know that it was not with perishable things such as silver or gold that you were redeemed from the empty way of life handed down to you from your forefathers, but with the precious blood of Christ, a Lamb without blemish or defect. He was chosen before the Creation of the world, but was revealed in these last times for your sake." Though the death of Christ hinged on Pilate's giving the command that He be crucified and though from a human point of view Pilate was free to do as he pleased, God knew with certainty what would

happen, and it was part of His foreknowledge.

It is true that God knew all possible plans and all possible alternatives, but having decided on a plan which covered every detail in the universe, events were made certain by the divine decree of God including knowledge of what man would do and what God would do. This is brought out in Acts 2:23, "This Man was handed over to you by God's set purpose and foreknowledge; and you, with the help of wicked men, put Him to death by nailing Him to the cross."

6. The Arminian view of divine sovereignty. Arminian theologians accept the concept of divine sovereignty in that God is the supreme Ruler of the universe. They tend to qualify this divine sovereignty by saying that God adjusts His foreknowledge to include men's actions that are contrary to His will. Arminians distinguish God's antecedent will from His consequent will. The former moves Him to save all men, but the latter is conditioned by the conduct of men. Therefore the antecedent will of God is restricted by human action. This tends to make man the decisive factor and to cause God to adjust to what man will decide to do. As in other areas Arminians tend to resolve the apparent conflict between God's sovereignty and man's will by referring ultimate decisions to man rather than to God.

7. The Arminian view of sovereign grace. Calvinists and Arminians agree that grace is bestowed on a person who believes. Arminians believe that this grace is sufficient for all men to be saved, whereas the Calvinists hold that only those who receive efficacious grace can be saved. Though the Bible does not explain it, the Scriptures recognize that the grace God bestows is a sovereign grace, and in the case of those who are saved it is efficacious. Arminians, however, tend to make efficacious grace available to all.

Within the limits of man's comprehension, resolving the problem of God's efficacious grace and man's responsibility cannot finally be settled. But in keeping with Scripture the emphasis should be on the sovereignty of God rather than on the sovereignty of man.

THE ARMINIAN EMPHASIS ON HUMAN EXPERIENCE AND REASON

One of the problems in Arminian theology is the concept that the eternal security of the believer depends on man's compliance with the will of God and man's continued faith. As in the matter of salvation, so in the matter of security Arminians tend to make man responsible. Demas is cited as an illustration of one who was once saved and then lost (2 Tim. 4:10). Likewise, Judas Iscariot, who seemed to be one with the disciples through three years of their following Christ, in the end is called "the one doomed to destruction" (John 17:12). However, neither Demas or Judas was saved in the first place.

A partial answer to the problem of whether one who is saved can remain saved is found in God's provision for sinning Christians to be restored to fellowship. As previously discussed, Christ provided a propitiation for sin in His death on the cross. This makes it possible for a sinning Christian to be restored to fellowship and at the same time makes clear that, having been born again, he will never lose his relationship to God.

The promises given to those who put their trust in Christ do not depend for their fulfillment on continued acts of righteousness on the part of a saved person. Instead they rest in the finished and complete work of Christ. This is brought out in many Scriptures. For example, according to 3:18, salvation depends entirely on one's act of faith in Christ. In 5:24 the one who believes is said to be saved now but promised no future condemnation, "I tell you the truth, whoever hears My word and believes Him who sent Me has eternal life and will not be condemned; he has crossed over from death to life." A similar truth is revealed in Romans 8:1, "Therefore, there is now no condemnation for those who are in Christ Jesus." According to verse 34 nothing will cause a Christian's condemnation, "Who is he that condemns? Christ Jesus, who died—more than that, who was raised to life—is at the right hand of God and is also interceding for us."

True, God chastens and disciplines a sinning Christian and offers the remedy of self-judgment as stated in 1 Corinthians 11:31-32, "But if we judged ourselves, we would not come under judgment. When we are judged by the Lord, we are being disciplined so that we will not be condemned with the world." Though Christians not living in the will of God receive His discipline, no threat of loss of salvation is mentioned in Scripture. No Christian lives perfectly. Therefore if sin in his life would cause him to lose his salvation, no one could have assurance of salvation at any moment in his life. This is not what Scripture teaches.

Arminians charge that if one has eternal security it would encourage a Christian to continue in sin. This is without foundation. As previously indicated, Christians are not free to go on sinning because God can bring discipline in their lives even to the point of taking away their physical lives, as apparently was true of some in Corinth (1 Cor. 11:31-32).

There is no record in the Bible of a person who was born again being lost. If this were possible there would be no way for such an individual to be restored. This is because the Bible is silent on how a person once saved and then lost could be saved again. Salvation by its very nature is a work of grace which God accomplished for those who are saved and not a work by which a Christian can elevate himself spiritually into experiencing salvation.

THE ARMINIAN APPEAL TO THE SCRIPTURES

Those who approach salvation from the Arminian point of view often quote Scriptures in support of their point of view. These Scriptures, however, are carefully selected to teach what the Arminians think they teach, and at the same time the Scriptures that contradict this view are often avoided. In every case the Scriptures cited that allegedly deny the possibility of eternal security are misapplied.

1. SOME SCRIPTURES ARE DISPENSATIONALLY MISAPPLIED. One of these is Matthew 24:13, "But he who stands firm to the end will be saved." The context here is the coming Great Tribulation and the salvation mentioned is not salvation of the soul but salvation from physical death. The fact is that many who are saved will be killed before the end of the Tribulation period and many who are lost will also continue to the end of that period. This passage is simply a promise that those who survive to the end of the Tribulation will be delivered.

Matthew 18:23-35 is sometimes offered as another evidence of one who is lost who was formerly saved. Jesus referred here to a servant who was forgiven a large sum by his master and then would not forgive another person who owed him a small sum. When his master heard this, he called in the wicked servant and turned him over to the jailers until he paid his debt. This parable speaks of forgiving others and to the fact that God will discipline one who does not forgive. It does not relate to salvation from sin.

Various warning passages addressed to Israel are also offered as proof of lack of security such as Ezekiel 33:7-8 and Psalm 51:11.

However, these passages are not addressed to Christians in the present age who are saved.

2. False teachers. Some passages relate to false teachers who depart from the faith in the period before the second coming of Christ. One such instance is 1 Timothy 4:1-2, "The Spirit clearly says that in later times some will abandon the faith and follow deceiving spirits and things taught by demons. Such teachings come through hypocritical liars, whose consciences have been seared as with a hot iron." Those mentioned here are teachers who make a superficial commitment to the Christian faith which they later abandon and contradict in their teachings. They were never saved in the first place. A more graphic picture of these false teachers is found in 2 Peter 2:1-22, where they are clearly identified as those who never knew salvation. False teachers are also mentioned in Jude 4 who are described as "godless men" who "deny Jesus Christ our only Sovereign and Lord." These also were never believers.

3. Affirmation or public confession. A mere affirmation or public confession is sometimes observable in people who are not really saved. In Luke 11:24-26 for instance Christ used the illustration of one who was demon possessed. After the demons left the man, he apparently had an improvement in his moral life. In the last stage the demons returned and he was worse than ever. This and other similar passages refer to profession without reality and not to a loss of salvation.

In Matthew 13:1-8 the different receptions given the Gospel do not deal with the subject of eternal security but rather with how the Gospel is received. The falling of the seed by the wayside or in stony places obviously refers to the rejection of the Gospel. The seed that falls in good ground but is choked by weeds could conceivably refer to one who is saved but who does not bear the full fruit of his salvation. By contrast the seed that falls on good ground illustrates the one who is saved and whose life is transformed. The question of security is not an issue in this passage.

In 1 Corinthians 15:2 the Apostle Paul addressed the Corinthian church, "By this Gospel you are saved, if you hold firmly to the word I preached to you. Otherwise, you have believed in vain." In other words if they received the Gospel superficially without real faith, their faith was in vain. But if they securely put their trust in Christ, then they were saved. Though the Corinthians fell far short in their personal lives, the apostle was not implying that some of the Corinthian believers were lost for lack of faith but rather that the faith of some Corinthians had never been sufficient for salvation (cf. 2 Cor. 13:5). Even the sinning Corinthians are referred to as "those sanctified in Christ Jesus and called to be holy" (1 Cor. 1:2).

In a similar way Hebrews 3:6, 14 affirm the necessity of faith that is held firmly. In both verses the thought is that salvation is secured if one's faith is genuine rather than a mere profession. Likewise 1 John 2:19 indicates that some who made outward profession did not remain within the Christian church because they did not have true faith.

4. TRUE SALVATION IS DEMONSTRATED BY FRUITS. This is true, so far as man's observation can judge. God knows the heart and knows those who are truly saved and those who are not. However, it is proper for a believer to seek to determine the salvation of another Christian by whether faith is manifested in his life. In either case there is no question about one who is genuinely saved being lost. A similar thought is advanced in James 2:17-18, 24, 26 which suggests that faith without works is dead, that is, it is not true faith. James' point is that true faith will produce true works whereas false faith will not.

In Christ's discussion with His disciples the night before His crucifixion, He described in John 15 the necessity of abiding in Christ to bear fruit. In verse 6 He said, "If anyone does not remain in Me, he is like a branch that is thrown away and withers; such branches are picked up, thrown into the fire and burned." The point is that a person who is saved cannot have a superficial and temporary connection to Christ. As such, it would only result in dead works. A Christian who abides in Christ, that is, has a vital, living connection to Christ the Vine, will bear fruit. A contrast can be observed in this passage between union and communion. Union makes possible eternal life. Communion makes possible abundant fruit. The passage is not dealing with the matter of salvation but rather the matter of communion and fruitfulness.

The Apostle Peter addressed the problem of assurance of eternal salvation in 2 Peter 1:10-11, "Therefore, my brothers, be all the more eager to make your calling and election sure. For if you do these things, you will never fall, and you will receive a rich welcome into the eternal kingdom of our Lord and Saviour Jesus Christ." From a human standpoint a person makes his election sure by making his faith in Christ certain. From God's point of view, He knows those who are saved and those who are not. If a person is sure of placing unquestioned faith in Christ, then based on the promises of God's Word he has assurance of heaven. The Scriptures give Christians repeated warnings of the necessity of being sure that their faith in Christ is real (Matt. 7:15-20; 2 Tim. 2:12).

5. Warnings to Jews. A number of passages are warnings to the Jews as a people. The Olivet Discourse (Matt. 24–25) was delivered to Christ's disciples and contains instructions about serving Him faithfully until He comes again.

In Hebrews 6:4-9 Jews who profess salvation in Christ are urged to see that they do not depart from the truth. Many interpreters take this passage as referring to outer profession of faith in Christ without actually trusting Him and being saved. The passage is not a warning to Christians to secure their salvation, but rather is addressed to those who profess faith without reality. For if they turn from their profession in Christ, they will be lost.

In a similar way 10:26-29 is best interpreted as a warning to those who hear the Gospel that they not deliberately turn away from it. Those who turn away from the truth about Christ have "only a fearful expectation of judgment and of raging fire that will consume the enemies of God" (v. 27). Many other warnings are given in Hebrews relative to the danger of profession without real faith (2:3; 3:6, 14; 6:3-4, 6; 10:26, 38; 12:25).

6. Warnings to all. Some warnings are given to all men about the danger of turning away from the Gospel. This is illustrated in Revelation 22:19, "And if anyone takes words away from this book of prophecy, God will take away from him his share in the tree of life and in the Holy City, which are described in this book." The point is that if there is no salvation in Christ there is no salvation at all.

7. Gentiles as a group may be broken off corporately. This could happen just as Israel was broken off as a nation. In Paul's illustration of the olive tree (Rom. 11:13-24) he pointed out that just as Israel in the present age is temporarily cut off from the place of blessing (i.e., the natural branches are cut off from the olive tree) so the church corporately, which is receiving the blessing of God, having been grafted into the olive tree, is in danger of being cut off or set aside as a group. The issue in either case is not of personal salvation but of corporate relationship to God. Prophecy foretells that Gentiles will be removed from their special place of blessing at the time of the Rapture of the church and that in the Millennium

Israel will be grafted in as a favored people once again.

8. Believers may lose their rewards and be disapproved of God without losing their salvation. In Colossians 1:21-23 Paul stated, "Once you were alienated from God and were enemies in your minds because of your evil behavior. But now He has reconciled you by Christ's physical body through death to present you holy in His sight, without blemish and free from accusation—if you continue in your faith, established and firm, not moved from the hope held out in the Gospel. This is the Gospel that you heard and that has been proclaimed to every creature under heaven, and of which I, Paul, have become a servant." The point here is that if they were firmly rooted in Christ by faith they would have the prospect of being presented to God as "holy . . . without blemish, and free from accusation" (v. 22). The issue is that by the reality of their faith in Christ they can be assured of their salvation which leads to the certain prospect of their being presented completely sanctified in the presence of God in heaven.

In 1 Corinthians 9:27 Paul viewed the Christian life as a race in which it is possible to "be disqualified for the prize." The issue here is reward for service, not the danger of losing salvation. In a similar way believers are exhorted to lead a life that is approved by God (2 Tim. 2:15). Other references to rewards for faithful service are also mentioned in 1 Corinthians 3:12-15 and 2 Corinthians 5:9-10.

9. Believers may experience loss of fellowship without losing their salvation. In the conversation Christ had with Peter about washing his feet, Christ said, "Unless I wash you, you have no part with Me" (John 13:8). In verse 10 Jesus contrasted bathing with washing the feet. Since Peter had bathed before he came to the Passover feast, only his feet needed to be washed because they had been defiled by walking through the streets of Jerusalem. Likewise a Christian who has fallen into sin does not need to be saved again but needs to be cleansed in order to have his fellowship with God restored.

10. Christians may fall from grace. A familiar text often quoted by Arminians is Galatians 5:4, "You who are trying to be justified by Law have been alienated from Christ; you have fallen away from grace." The context is not talking about salvation but the rule of life of a Christian as being a gracious rule of life. A person who is saved may fall from grace as a rule of life and turn to legalism. This turning is referred to here as falling from grace. The issue of

salvation, however, is not in the passage; the verse does not refer to the question of security.

11. MISCELLANEOUS PASSAGES. Other passages are also often cited such as 1 Timothy 5:8, 12; 6:10; 2 Timothy 2:18; and Revelation 21:8, 27. These verses may be understood in the light of Philippians 2:12 where believers are exhorted, "Continue to work out your salvation with fear and trembling." Works are the working out of one's salvation but not a working for one's salvation. Expressions requiring obedience with respect to the Gospel such as Acts 5:32; 17:30; and Hebrews 5:8-9 refer not to works but to the obedience to God's command to believe in Christ.

Properly understood, eternal security is not called in question by human experience or verses of Scripture taken out of context. Ultimately the question is, Who does the saving? If man saves himself, he can lose his salvation. If it is a work of God, man is secure in the salvation God provides.

CHAPTER • 16

THE CALVINISTIC DOCTRINE OF SECURITY

The terms "Arminian" or "Calvinistic" are unsatisfactory because they relate doctrine to human interpreters who obviously are not infallible. Because Arminianism generally exalts human responsibility in one's decision to receive Christ as opposed to Calvinism which exalts God's sovereignty and grace, the two views tend to be set over against each other on the question of the Christian's eternal security. Ultimately the question is not who holds the doctrines, but what do the Scriptures actually state?

Though the discussion could consider many Scriptures, 12 reasons, each one complete and conclusive in itself, are given as evidence for eternal security. In general, the New Testament presents the Father as purposing, calling, justifying, and glorifying those who believe on Christ; the Son is presented as becoming Incarnate that He might be a Kinsman-Redeemer, as dying a substitutionary and efficacious death, as rising from the dead to be the living Saviour as Advocate, Intercessor, and as Head over all things to the church; and the Holy Spirit is presented as administering and executing the purpose of the Father and the redemption the Son has wrought. It is reasonable then that all three Persons of the Godhead should have Their individual share in bringing to fruition what God has determined for the Christian's salvation.

THE REASONS WHICH DEPEND ON GOD THE FATHER

Four reasons for security which are accomplished by God the Father are (1) the sovereign purpose of God, (2) the Father's infinite power, (3) the infinite love of God, and (4) the influence on the Father of the prayer of His Son.

1. God's sovereign purpose. The sovereign purpose of God is to provide eternal salvation for those who believe. A major theme of Scripture from Genesis to Revelation is God's purpose to save by grace those who believe apart from any worthiness on their part. The Scriptures make clear that those with many sins in their background may nevertheless come to Christ and receive eternal salvation. Even Christians, whose lives are not all they should be, are assured of their eternal salvation. Obviously the sovereign purpose of God to achieve by grace the salvation of believers cannot be defeated. Everyone who is chosen will be glorified, as stated in Romans 8:28-30. According to Ephesians 1:11-12 those who are predestined to salvation will receive salvation. It is inconceivable that anything God undertakes will not be fulfilled.

The Scriptures often present God's purpose in the form of promises. Such promises must certainly be fulfilled. This is emphasized in Paul's statements in Romans, "It was not through Law that Abraham and his offspring received the promise that he would be heir of the world, but through the righteousness that comes by faith. For if those who live by Law are heirs, faith has no value and the promise is worthless. . . . Therefore, the promise comes by faith, so that it may be by grace and may be guaranteed to all Abraham's offspring—not only to those who are of the Law but also to those who are of the faith of Abraham. He is the father of us all. . . . Yet he did not waver through unbelief regarding the promise of God, but was strengthened in his faith and gave glory to God, being fully persuaded that God had power to do what He had promised. This is why 'it was credited to him as righteousness.' The words 'it was credited to him' were written not for him alone, but also for us, to whom God will credit righteousness—for us who believe in Him who raised Jesus our Lord from the dead" (Rom. 4:13-14, 16, 20-24).

Confirmation of the fulfillment of God's promise is also found in other passages (Gal. 3:17-19, 22, 29; 4:21-23, 28). Though Abraham was obviously saved and looked forward to being in the New Jerusalem (Heb. 11:10), the promises given to a believer in the present age are more explicit because of the fuller revelation in the New Testament. Believers are promised that God "is able to keep [them] from falling and to present [them] before His glorious presence without fault and with great joy" (Jude 24). Because believers are baptized into Christ and are said to be in Christ (Eph. 1:6-7),

God's promises in grace are declared to be sure (Rom. 4:16).

The unconditional covenant of promise is a repeated theme in the New Testament as previously noted in many passages (John 3:16; 5:24; 6:37; 10:28; Rom. 8:30). It is impossible for God's promise and sovereign purpose to fall short of fulfillment.

2. The Father's infinite power. This power is set free in grace by the death of Christ. Because of this, God, who is infinitely righteous, can offer eternal salvation to one who has sinned and who will continue to be imperfect. It would be most arbitrary if God had not provided completely for His gracious dealings with them through the death of Christ. The human mind naturally tends to be legalistic and responds to the almost universal point of view in pagan religions that an individual must work to be acceptable before God. It is difficult for men to comprehend that God's salvation is purely and wholly on the basis of grace. The most godly person and the most ungodly person before they are saved are equally saved by their acceptance of Christ as Saviour. Because of the propitiation or satisfaction of God's righteousness by the death of Christ, God is now set free to save the ungodly and to apply His infinite power to His eternal salvation.

The Scriptures frequently speak of God's ability to save as in John 10:29, "My Father, who has given them to Me, is greater than all; no one can snatch them out of My Father's hand." In Romans 4:21 Abraham's unwavering faith is mentioned, "Being fully persuaded that God had power to do what He had promised." A similar thought is presented in 8:31, 38-39. Paul affirmed God's infinite power to do more than believers can possibly anticipate in prayer (Eph. 3:20). The remarkable transformation from their present sinful bodies to glorious bodies without sin will be accomplished by God's power (Phil. 3:21). Paul was fully persuaded that what God had promised regarding his eternal salvation would be fully performed (2 Tim. 1:12). The present intercession of Christ is seen as a means of continuing the salvation of believers (Heb. 7:25).

As mentioned before in Jude 24, the power of God is sufficient to keep believers from falling from their present salvation and to present them perfect in His presence in glory. The power of God, according to Ephesians 1:19-21, is the same power that raised Christ from the dead. If salvation depends on a Christian's faithfulness, no one would be saved. If one's salvation depends on God's infinite power released through the death of Christ to offer grace to the sinner, then his eternal salvation is assured.

3. THE INFINITE LOVE OF GOD. God's love supports the doctrine of eternal security. According to Ephesians 1:4-5, "In love He predestined us to be adopted as His sons through Jesus Christ, in accordance with His pleasure and will." To allow one who was once saved to become lost would be to negate the sovereignty, the purpose, and the love of God. As the Scriptures make clear, God was acting in love when He gave His Son to die for sinners (Rom. 5:7-10). If God could provide Christ for individuals when they were yet in their sins, so much more will believers be kept saved (vv. 9-10). The fact that they are indwelt by God Himself and given eternal life is another token of God's continued purpose (Col. 1:27).

4. THE INFLUENCE OF THE PRAYER OF GOD'S SON ON THE FATHER. This prayer as recorded in John 17 supports the concept of eternal salvation. Though the possibility and probability of the disciples' sinning is taken into full consideration, Christ nevertheless prayed for them as those who were given to Him (vv. 2, 6, 9, 11-12, 24). Added to His disciples were those who would believe throughout the present age (v. 20). Christ's prayer for those who were given to Him was that they might be one in the same sense that Christ and the Father are One (v. 11). Just as the Trinity cannot be severed, so believers cannot be severed from God. Even Arminians would hesitate to assert that Christ's prayer would not be answered.

THE REASONS THAT DEPEND ON GOD THE SON

The four reasons for a Christian's security which depend on God the Son are summarized in Romans 8:33-34, "Who will bring any charge against those whom God has chosen? It is God who justifies. Who is he that condemns? Christ Jesus, who died—more than that, who was raised to life—is at the right hand of God and is also interceding for us."

The scriptural teaching on justification by faith makes clear that God has declared righteous everyone who has put his trust in Christ (cf. 3:26; 8:30). The believer's justification is secured on the ground of the imputed merit of the Son of God, and it is legally his because he is in Christ Jesus. No one could ever be justified before God by his worthiness. An earthly father may correct his erring son without disrupting either the sonship or the family standing.

In like manner God as Father maintains the perfect standing of the believer's complete and eternal justification even though it is necessary for Him to correct His child. The truth therefore stands that God, having justified the ungodly (4:5), will not contradict Himself by charging them with evil, for this would reverse their justification.

The question which draws "Who is he that condemns?" (8:34) is answered by four facts about the work of Christ. Throughout the New Testament the question whether a believer is unconditionally saved forever through the provisions of God's infinite grace is answered in the affirmative. These are the words of God and not the words of a man alone. It is as if the divine Author anticipated the doubt and confusion that would arise and with that in view raised these momentous questions.

The four answers to the question, "Who is he that condemns?" name the reasons for a believer's security: (1) Christ has died, (2) Christ has risen, (3) Christ is the Advocate for believers, and (4) Christ is the Christian's Intercessor.

1. Christ has died. In His death Christ has provided complete salvation. The broad statement, "There is now no condemnation for those who are in Christ Jesus" (v. 1), is the result of Christ's dying for the sins of the whole world. Because Christ died, the Father is free to forgive righteously the sins of those who put their trust in Him because God the Father has been satisfied or propitiated by the death of Christ (1 John 2:2). Though God reserves the right to correct and chasten His children, He has never questioned the fact of the believer's state as His children as those who have been born again into His family. So if one denies eternal security he must either deny the death of Christ as sufficient for dealing with sin or deny that the believer may be disowned by the very sins Christ bore. There is no possibility of intermediate ground. Either the believer must be condemned for every sin or his sins in no way are a ground for judgment. A believer's security is secured by the death of Christ.

2. Christ is risen. The glorious truth of the resurrection of Christ provides two conclusive reasons for the security of the child of God: (a) the believer has partaken of resurrection life of the Son of God, and (b) the believer is a part of the new creation over which the resurrected Christ is the all-sufficient Head. If a believer partakes of resurrection life, it should be clear that this cannot be lost anymore than God can lose His life.

In Colossians Paul stressed that a Christian is already in the sphere of resurrection because he is in the resurrected Christ as stated in Colossians 2:12, "Having been buried with Him in baptism and raised with Him through your faith in the power of God, who raised Him from the dead." This is reaffirmed in 3:1, "Since, then, you have been raised with Christ, set your hearts on things above, where Christ is seated at the right hand of God." The spiritual resurrection of Christians even while they are living in this world is real because it involves bestowal of eternal life. Because a Christian is identified with Christ in His resurrection, he is seated with Christ as stated in Ephesians 2:6, "And God raised us up with Christ and seated us with Him in the heavenly realms in Christ Jesus." This refers to the fact that believers have received eternal life and that believers are so identified with Christ that what Christ did becomes theirs.

In Colossians 3:1-4 Paul wrote that the believer's identification with Christ in His resurrection makes it possible for them to live in the realm of heavenly things instead of earthly things. "Since, then, you have been raised with Christ, set your hearts on things above, where Christ is seated at the right hand of God. Set your minds on things above, not on earthly things. For you died, and your life is now hidden with Christ in God. When Christ, who is your life, appears, then you also will appear with Him in glory."

The concept advanced by Arminians that a Christian can lose eternal life has no basis in any Scripture. Since it is eternal and everlasting it cannot be lost. The bestowal of righteousness and eternal life is never based on a believer's merit but on the merit he has because of his relationship to Jesus Christ. If a Christian can be lost, then the very nature of eternal life has to be denied.

3. Christ is the Advocate for believers. As the Interceding One (Rom. 8:34), Christ in heaven is carrying on His ministry as High Priest and as the Intercessor for all those who trust Him as Saviour. Though there are losses of infinite proportion to a Christian who is not living in the will of God, the Scriptures never suggest that a Christian because of his sin loses his salvation in Christ. The 33 divine undertakings which constitute the salvation of an individual as previously mentioned include the wonderful fact that all sin is forgiven whether past, present, or future. Therefore in eternity no sin whether committed before or after a Christian's faith in Christ could ever be charged against a Christian once he stands in heaven perfect and complete in Christ. A Christian's security does not depend on his own merit or faithfulness but on God's own faithfulness

to His promises.

In 1 John 1:1–2:2 the promise of eternal life is made to those who are born of God (cf. John 1:12-13), but they have an Advocate who is their Representative in glory to reaffirm that complete propitiation or satisfaction of God's righteous demands has been made. On this basis the matter of a Christian's fellowship with God is discussed. No warning is given that a Christian who sins will lose his salvation but rather Christians are instructed, when they do sin, to avail themselves of forgiveness by confession (1 John 1:9). Though legal forgiveness is assured because of his justification, the issue in 1 John is the relationship of a child of God to his Heavenly Father. In this family relationship any sin that is not confessed constitutes a barrier to God's full blessing on the Christian. If a believer is to enjoy all that God intends for his spiritual life on earth, he needs to confess known sin and to continue walking in fellowship with God.

The charge of Arminians that those who hold to eternal security are guilty of antinomianism has been fully refuted by Charles Hodge:

> Antinomianism has never had any hold in the churches of the Reformation. There is no logical connection between the neglect of moral duties, and the system which teaches that Christ is a Saviour as well from the power as from the penalty of sin; that faith is the act by which the soul receives and rests on Him for sanctification as well as for justification; and that such is the nature of the union with Christ by faith and indwelling of the Spirit, that no one is, or can be partaker of the benefit of His death, who is not also partaker of the power of His life; which holds to the divine authority of the Scripture which declares that without holiness no man shall see the Lord (Heb. 12:14); and which, in the language of the great advocate of salvation by grace, warns all who call themselves Christians: "Be not deceived: neither fornicators, nor idolaters, nor adulterers, nor effeminate, nor abusers of themselves with mankind, nor thieves, nor covetous, nor drunkards, nor revilers, nor extortioners shall inherit the kingdom of God" (1 Cor. 6:9-10). It is not the system which regards sin as so great an evil that it requires the blood of the Son of God for its expiation, and the Law as so immutable that it requires the perfect righteousness of Christ for the sinner's justification, which leads to loose views of moral obligation; these are reached by the system which teaches that the demands of the Law

> have been lowered, that they can be more than met by the imperfect obedience of fallen men, and that sin can be pardoned by priestly intervention. This is what logic and history alike teach (*Systematic Theology*, vol. 3: New York: Charles Scribner's Sons, 1892, p. 241).

Instead of encouraging Christians to sin, the truth of eternal security is rather an exhortation to make their lives conform to the holiness of God in keeping with the doctrine of justification. First John affirms the truth of eternal security and argues that this provides a sufficient incentive for Christians to walk in fellowship with the Lord.

While paternal discipline may be exercised by the Father in correcting an erring child of God (Heb. 12:3-15), he is not condemned.

4. Christ is the Christian's Intercessor. In His advocacy Christ represents the believer as a lawyer would represent his client in court. In His intercession Christ deals with the weaknesses and frailties of a Christian. Though the Bible does not refer specifically to Christ as the believer's Intercessor in heaven, several passages reveal the nature and content of His intercession.

The High Priestly Prayer of Christ in John 17 is a revelation of the extent of Christ's intercession in which He prays for His own and asks that God keep them from the sin of the world.

In Romans 8:34 intercession is especially mentioned in the context of Christ's being at the right hand of God as the risen Saviour. The Scriptures affirm that there is no condemnation for the child of God because of Christ's faithful intercession.

Christ affirmed that He was interceding for Peter because of Satan's intent "to sift [him] as wheat" (Luke 22:31). Christ prayed for Peter that his faith would not fail and that he would be able to strengthen his brethren in the faith. From this instance it is clear that Christ prays for others who are in similar situations. A believer, who has sinned against God, needs restoration but not salvation which he already possesses.

Hebrews 7:23-25 points to Christ's intercession as being able to save completely those who put their trust in Christ. "Now there were many of those priests, since death prevented them from continuing in office; but because Jesus lives forever, He has a permanent priesthood. Therefore He is able to save completely those who come to God through Him, because He always lives to intercede for them."

This passage is an amazing revelation that Christ is unceasing in His intercession. Because of the infinity of God, Christ can give His full attention to each believer as if this is the only need in the world, and Christ engages in ceaseless intercession on behalf of His own. When a Christian prays, he joins a prayer meeting in heaven which has already started. Because of this it is possible for a Christian to be miraculously kept from sin even though experience points to the fact that no one is perfect.

Christ is the everlasting Priest who does not have to be succeeded by other priests as were the priests of Aaron who died. In His resurrection life Christ can intercede forever. The intercession of Christ is more than the exercise of prayer as it results in Christ's guiding the believer away from the snares and pitfalls of Satan so that he can experience the sustaining power of God in each hour of trial. David expressed this emphatically in Psalm 23:1 when he stated, "The Lord is my Shepherd, I shall lack nothing."

The four reasons for a believer's security which depend on Christ the Son of God include His substitutionary death by which He frees the Father to undertake eternal blessings for those who believe; His resurrection by which Christ provides Christians with imperishable resurrection life; His advocacy by which He meets the condemning effect of the believer's sin; and His intercession by which He engages the infinite power of God on behalf of those who believe. Each of these four facts is sufficient to achieve eternal security and together they make it impossible for one who was once saved to be lost. As pointed out previously, the reason a Christian is eternally secure is not that he is sufficient in himself, but his sufficiency lies in the finished and complete work of Christ on the cross and the continued work of Christ on behalf of the believer.

RESPONSIBILITIES BELONGING TO GOD THE HOLY SPIRIT

The nature of the work of the Holy Spirit in relation to the salvation of the child of God makes clear that his salvation is secure forever once it is received. Four distinctive achievements are wrought by the Holy Spirit: (1) the Holy Spirit regenerates, (2) the Holy Spirit indwells, (3) the Holy Spirit baptizes, and (4) the Holy Spirit seals.

1. The Holy Spirit regenerates. When an individual comes to Christ in faith the Bible declares that he is born again (John 3:3) or

reborn. As stated in Titus 3:5, "He saved us, not because of righteous things we had done, but because of His mercy. He saved us through the washing of rebirth and renewal by the Holy Spirit." The extensive nature of this transformation from one who is spiritually dead to one who is spiritually alive makes the believer a new creature as stated in 2 Corinthians 5:17, "Therefore, if anyone is in Christ, he is a new creation; the old has gone, the new has come!" In addition to being reborn and becoming a new creation in Christ a believer is said to be "raised with Christ" (Col. 3:1).

In each case it is a work of God which reaches to infinity. One who has received eternal life, been resurrected with Christ, and who has been made a new creature has so dramatically changed that there is no possibility of him returning to his former lost estate. Salvation is clearly a work of God (Eph. 2:10) and, because the believer is a new creature in Christ the rite of circumcision given to Israel is no longer necessary (Gal. 6:15). Once it is understood that salvation is the work of God in all of its aspects, not a work of man, and is accomplished apart from all human merit, it leaves the Arminian with no sufficient ground for the claim that these are all temporary and transitory acts of God.

2. The Holy Spirit indwells a Christian. In the Old Testament there were occasional sovereign indwellings of the Holy Spirit of certain individuals who were set apart for some particular work or service, but everyone who was born again in the Old Testament did not experience the indwelling of God. As Christ expressed it in John 14:16-17, "I will ask the Father, and He will give you another Counselor to be with you forever—the Spirit of Truth. The world cannot accept Him, because it neither sees Him nor knows Him. But you know Him, for He lives with you and will be in you." The new work of the Holy Spirit of indwelling every believer began on the Day of Pentecost. In the present age if one is not indwelt by the Spirit, he is not saved (Rom. 8:9). In 1 John 2:27 the indwelling of the Holy Spirit is related to "anointing" as a permanent possession of the believer.

3. The Holy Spirit baptizes every believer (1 Cor. 12:13). Just as the Holy Spirit indwells and regenerates every believer so He baptizes every believer into the body of Christ. This is true for all Christians. As the text indicates, the baptizing of the Holy Spirit is a new undertaking which did not occur before the Day of Pentecost because it is related to the special character of the church as the

body of Christ into which the believer is baptized. Unlike other works of the Spirit which may be seen either in the past or the future, the baptism of the Spirit is a work peculiar to the present age. Having been placed in Christ, however, the believer is forever safe and secure as there is no way by which anyone can undo this one-time act of God.

As in the case of other works of the Spirit, so the immeasurable grace which is manifested in placing the believer in Christ in spite of lack of merit confirms what has been previously indicated as the eternal security of the believer. Though God may discipline a justified one who is in Christ, because God has justified or declared righteous the believer, He cannot consistently charge His own with sin as God Himself is the Defender of the believer's eternal security (Rom. 8:33). As stated before, a Christian is not saved because of any merit of good works, nor can he be lost by the demerit of any of his works that are not good.

4. THE HOLY SPIRIT SEALS EVERY BELIEVER UNTIL THE TIME OF HIS RESURRECTION OR TRANSLATION (2 COR. 1:21-22; EPH. 1:13-14; 4:30). A seal represents ownership and security. The Holy Spirit Himself is the Seal. Everyone who is indwelt therefore is sealed. As such he has been sealed in anticipation of the completion of his salvation in glory and is rendered secure until that time. The presence of the Holy Spirit in the believer as a seal is also the firstfruits of the harvest that will be complete when believers in Christ are gathered in heaven (Rom. 8:23). Once the seal is given, it is God's sign of security and ownership until the day of the believer's resurrection (Eph. 4:30).

Having considered the 12 reasons why a believer is safe in his salvation, it should be clear that salvation rests not on human merit but on God's grace, that the only requirement is faith in Christ. The truth of a believer's security rests on the fact that salvation is a work of God for man and not a work of man for God.

CHAPTER • 17

THE CONSUMMATING SCRIPTURE

The Epistle of Paul to the Romans is a summary of the theology of the New Testament and is especially appropriate in its revelation of God's complete plan of salvation which includes the concept of eternal security. The Epistle to the Romans may be divided into three parts, (1) salvation, chapters 1–8; (2) dispensational truth, chapters 9–11; and (3) exhortation, chapters 12–16.

The first section, chapters 1–8, may also be subdivided into three parts. In the introduction the Apostle Paul declared that man was lost and under the universal condemnation of sin. In presenting God's remedy, salvation, three aspects are discussed: (1) salvation for the unregenerate person which is consummated in justification (3:21–5:21); (2) salvation for the believer from the power over sin unto sanctification (6:1–7:25); and (3) security for those who are saved (8:1-39). In Romans 8 the doctrine of the believer's security is presented in a clear and convincing statement. The extensive treatment of the doctrine of salvation in the Epistle to the Romans is brought to its completion in chapter 8 which answers questions concerning the extent of salvation and the security of that salvation.

The chapter begins with the broad statement, "Therefore, there is now no condemnation for those who are in Christ Jesus" (v. 1). Paul affirmed that God "condemned sin in sinful man, in order that the righteous requirements of the Law might be fully met in us, who do not live according to the sinful nature but according to the Spirit" (vv. 3-4). It should be obvious that a Christian's life is never perfect and cannot meet the requirements of the Law. It is by grace that a Christian is declared to have met the requirements of the Law. Christians are characterized by their testimony as those "who do not live according to the sinful nature but according to the Spirit"

(v. 4). The cause-and-effect relationship should be clearly established. A Christian's walk in the will of God is possible because of the fact that he is already justified. It is never a means to becoming justified. In Romans 8 the apostle offers seven proofs of the truthfulness of God's eternal salvation.

DELIVERED FROM THE LAW

In verse 2 Paul stated that "the law of the Spirit of life set me free from the Law of sin and death." Paul went on to state that this was possible only because of what Christ had done on his behalf. In this context the Law stands as representative of the merit system taught to a limited extent in the Old Testament. Some of the blessings of the Law were conditioned on the obedience of the individual. In Christ the Law principle is done away as having nothing to contribute to the outworking of the principle of grace (Rom. 4:4-5; 11:6; Gal. 5:4). Paul pointed out that the Law was a means by which God made sin known to His people. He prepared them to understand the grace of God which, though demanding a supernatural life (cf. John 13:34; 2 Cor. 10:3-5; Eph. 4:30), provided such a glorious salvation through Christ entirely apart from the merit of the person receiving it. Though a believer may often fail in conflict with the world, the flesh, and the devil, this does not alter the work of God for the believer who is in Christ. Arminianism tends to equate the imperfect daily life of a believer as ground for being lost. The New Testament teaches that those who believe are saved from the merit system by having all its demands satisfied in Christ, and thus the believer endures forever.

THE FACT OF THE PRESENCE OF THE DIVINE NATURE IN THE BELIEVER

At the time of regeneration a believer in Christ receives eternal life and with that eternal life a divine nature that corresponds to it. As stated in 2 Peter 1:3-4, "His divine power has given us everything we need for life and godliness through our knowledge of Him who called us by His own glory and goodness. Through these He has given us His very great and precious promises, so that through them you may participate in the divine nature and escape the corruption in the world caused by evil desires." To receive eternal life is to partake of the divine nature of the One who imparts the life. Christians have the old nature or the flesh and therefore are exhorted to "live by the Spirit, and you will not gratify the desires of the sinful nature" (Gal. 5:16). The fact that a Christian struggles with the old nature makes it evident that a Christian himself does not have the power to fulfill the desires of the new nature as Paul stated, "For I have the desire to do what is good, but I cannot carry it out" (Rom. 7:18).

In the battle between the old nature and the new nature the secret of victory is to draw on the power of the indwelling Holy Spirit. A person who does that is not walking in the sin nature but in the Spirit as stated in 8:9, "You, however, are controlled not by the sinful nature but by the Spirit, if the Spirit of God lives in you." Paul went on to say, "And if anyone does not have the Spirit of Christ, he does not belong to Christ. But if Christ is in you, your body is dead because of sin, yet your spirit is alive because of righteousness. And if the Spirit of Him who raised Jesus from the dead is living in you, He who raised Christ from the dead will also give life to your mortal bodies through His Spirit, who lives in you" (vv. 9-11). Once received, the new nature in the believer cannot be eradicated. The fact that God is the believer's Father cannot be reversed. The presence of the divine nature indicates a permanent relationship to God. The indwelling Holy Spirit, who is the Seal until the day of resurrection or redemption (Eph. 4:30), is evidence that the Christian is secure in his salvation until the work of salvation is complete and the body of the Christian is changed into a body of resurrection.

THE CHRISTIAN, A SON AND HEIR OF GOD

Because of the transformation caused by regeneration in which the Spirit of God makes a believer into a new creation, he is also a son and heir of God because he has partaken of the life of God as stated in Romans 8:14-17, "Because those who are led by the Spirit of God are sons of God. For you did not receive a spirit that makes you a slave again to fear, but you received the Spirit of sonship. And by Him we cry, '*Abba,* Father.' The Spirit Himself testifies with our spirit that we are God's children. Now if we are children, then we are heirs—heirs of God and coheirs with Christ, if indeed we share in His sufferings in order that we may also share in His glory."

Paul in writing to Timothy stated, "Nevertheless, God's solid foundation stands firm, sealed with this inscription: 'The Lord knows those who are His' " (2 Tim. 2:19).

Those who appear to be saved but actually turn out to be lost depart from Christian fellowship because they were never saved in the first place. As John stated it, "They went out from us, but they did not really belong to us. For if they had belonged to us, they would have remained with us; but their going showed that none of them belonged to us" (1 John 2:19). Though God may chastise an erring child as He did the sons of David (cf. 2 Sam. 7:14; Ps. 89:30-33), the chastisement of the child of God has for its supreme purpose not that of voiding his salvation but "that we will not be condemned with the world" (1 Cor. 11:32).

John also stated, "No one who is born of God will continue to sin, because God's seed remains in him; he cannot go on sinning, because he has been born of God" (1 John 3:9). The security of the believer is found in the fact that "God's seed remains in him," and this fact makes it impossible for him to practice sin like a person who is not saved. This passage does not teach that a Christian never sins but that there is something in him that restrains him from continuing in a pattern of sin in his life.

As "heirs of God and coheirs with Christ" (Rom. 8:17), a Christian is assured of his eternal inheritance. In John 17:24 Christ stated, "Father, I want those You have given Me to be with Me where I am, and to see My glory, the glory You have given Me because You loved Me before the Creation of the world." It should be obvious that any request made by the Son to the Father will be fulfilled. All who are given to Christ will ultimately stand in heaven as trophies of His grace. Those who belong to Christ also belong to the Father. As Christ said, "All I have is Yours, and all You have is Mine" (v. 10). And as Paul wrote, "You are of Christ, and Christ is of God" (1 Cor. 3:23). A Christian is assured that he is now a son of God and a coheir with Christ and forever will be.

THE DIVINE PURPOSE

The divine purpose of God as stated in Romans 8:28-30 is that believers should be conformed to the likeness of His Son: "And we know that in all things God works for the good of those who love Him, who have been called according to His purpose. For those God foreknew He also predestined to be conformed to the likeness of His Son, that He might be the Firstborn among many brothers. And those He predestined, He also called; those He called, He also justified; those He justified, He also glorified."

It should be obvious that the purposes of God will be fulfilled. This is confirmed in Ephesians. "For He chose us in Him before the Creation of the world to be holy and blameless in His sight" (1:4). The purpose of God to adopt believers as sons through Christ Jesus is stated in these words, "In love He predestined us to be adopted as His sons through Jesus Christ, in accordance with His pleasure and will" (vv. 4-5). The passage continues, "In Him we have redemption through His blood, the forgiveness of sins, in accordance with the riches of God's grace that He lavished on us with all wisdom and understanding" (vv. 7-8). In verse 11 Paul wrote, "In Him we were also chosen, having been predestined according to the plan of Him who works out everything in conformity with the purpose of His will." The passage concludes with the expression that believers "might be for the praise of His glory" (v. 12).

From these verses it is clear that God has a purpose involved in the salvation of the individual beginning with predestination and ending with glorification. It is not simply His wish but also His sovereign will, and these statements support the concept of eternal security. If God should lose one soul predestined to salvation, it would reflect on His veracity and sovereignty.

THE EXECUTION OF THE DIVINE PURPOSE

According to Romans 8:30-33 the execution of the divine purpose includes the acts of predestination, calling, justifying, and glorifying. The passage indicates that all who are predestined are carried through the process to glorification. It is impossible for a person to be saved without also being predestinated and called. And if he is predestinated and called, he also will be justified and glorified. The passage includes that this is all accomplished by grace. Having not spared His Son (v. 32) God is now able to deliver all who come to Him, and those who are elect cannot be charged with sin because God justifies (v. 33).

All who believe Scripture and the sovereignty of God recognize that God operates with absolute certainty in many realms of His vast creation. Inasmuch as God has demonstrated His sovereignty in other fields, it is reasonable to conclude that His sovereignty will be manifested in the salvation of believers. By His sovereign act God justifies believers and in the process places them in Christ where they are free from condemnation forever. The result is stated in verse 1, "Therefore, there is now no condemnation for those who are in Christ Jesus."

CHRIST'S OWN ACHIEVEMENT

In previous discussion on the fourfold work of Christ on behalf of believers, it was seen that the salvation God extends is based on Christ's death on the cross, and on His resurrection, advocacy, and intercession in heaven. Any one of these four achievements of the Son of God is sufficient to answer any contention that believers once saved can be lost as the work of Christ in salvation is a work of God, sovereignly determined by the will of God.

THE INCOMPETENCY OF CELESTIAL AND MUNDANE THINGS

Though a Christian encounters many problems in the world, the statements in verses 35-39 make clear that nothing can separate a believer from the love of God: "Who shall separate us from the love of Christ? Shall trouble or hardship or persecution or famine or nakedness or danger or sword? As it is written: 'For Your sake we face death all day long; we are considered as sheep to be slaughtered.' No, in all these things we are more than conquerors through Him who loved us. For I am convinced that neither death nor life, neither angels nor demons, neither the present nor the future, nor any powers, neither height nor depth, nor anything else in all creation, will be able to separate us from the love of God that is in Christ Jesus our Lord."

The eternal security of the believer is not only assured on the basis of the work of God for him, but this passage clearly states that no other force outside of God whether in heaven or in earth can separate a believer from the love of God, and with that is the assurance that the believer will never be separated from God in time or eternity. Paul stated his own personal faith in 2 Timothy 1:12, "I am not ashamed, because I know whom I have believed, and am convinced that He is able to guard what I have entrusted to Him for that day." As stated before, the issue is whether God is able to save eternally because salvation is a work of God for man, not a work of man for God.

It may be concluded that God's salvation is never offered except as an eternal salvation, and no soul once saved can be lost. Paul stated again his conviction of the certainty of God's salvation in Philippians 1:6, "Being confident of this, that He who began a good work in you will carry it on to completion until the day of Christ Jesus." Peter introduced his epistle in a similar way. "Praise be to the God and Father of our Lord Jesus Christ! In His great mercy He has given us new birth into a living hope through the resurrection of Jesus Christ from the dead, and into an inheritance that can never perish, spoil, or fade—kept in heaven for you, who through faith are shielded by God's power until the coming of the salvation that is ready to be revealed in the last time" (1 Peter 1:3-5).

CHAPTER • 18

DELIVERANCE FROM THE REIGNING POWER OF SIN AND HUMAN LIMITATIONS

DELIVERANCE FROM THE POWER OF SIN

A major aspect of God's plan of salvation is the deliverance God provides from the power of sin. Scripture clearly contemplates the fact that in saving individuals God is fully aware that they will fall short of perfection in their lives. So that believers may have victory over sin, God has provided abundantly for them by changing them into new creations each with a new nature, by indwelling them with the Holy Spirit, providing them the infinite truth of God's inspired Word, supporting them by the advocacy and intercession of Christ in heaven, and providing fellowship for them with others who have received Christ as their Saviour.

As previously considered, a Christian faces three opposing forces which are sources of evil—the world, the flesh, and the devil. In his unregenerate state he was part of this and did not sense any opposing force. Once a person is saved, however, he soon discovers that he has enemies and that the world, the sin nature, and the devil are all against him. God's deliverance from these entities may be summarized here.

1. THE WORLD. The world system or the *kosmos* is the vast system over which Satan is the prince (John 12:31; 14:30; 16:11). When an individual is saved through faith he is delivered out of this world (15:19; Col. 1:13; 1 John 5:19) even though he is still in the world. God's provision for Christians in their spiritual lives makes it possible for them to live without these forces overcoming them as stated in 1 John 5:4-5, "For everyone born of God overcomes the world. This is the victory that has overcome the world, even our faith. Who is it that overcomes the world? Only he who believes that Jesus is the

Son of God." While in conflict with worldly powers Christians can be sustained by God's provision in grace.

2. THE FLESH OR THE OLD SIN NATURE. This is likewise a problem for regenerated individuals. As previously brought out, though a believer has a sin nature, he also has a new nature which longs after the things of God. Though the new nature in itself cannot secure victory over the sin nature, it is possible by the power of the Spirit for a Christian to avoid fulfilling the desires of the sin nature (Gal. 5:16). The death of Christ provides a believer with the basis for victory over the old sin nature (Rom. 6:1-10; 8:3). Though a Christian's victory is necessarily incomplete until he is glorified in heaven, God has undertaken in sovereign grace to save the one who puts his trust in Christ. Once one is regenerated God guarantees that he will never come into condemnation (John 5:24).

3. THE DEVIL. Satan or the devil is also opposed to the Christian's desire to serve God and to lead a holy life. Christians who attempt to be what God wants them to be soon discover they have an enemy of great power, but they are also introduced to the fact that God has made available a power greater than that of Satan.

Paul spoke of the battle with the world and the devil in Ephesians 6:12, "For our struggle is not against flesh and blood, but against the rulers, against the authorities, against the powers of this dark world and against the spiritual forces of evil in the heavenly realms." Satan, however, has been judged and condemned (John 16:11) by the death of Christ on the cross, and in the same act Christ triumphed over the forces of evil (Col. 2:14-15). Satan today is like a criminal who has been sentenced to die but awaits the day of his execution.

A Christian who avails himself of God's provision for him is able to stand against Satan (Eph. 6:10-11). Christ is greater and more powerful than Satan (1 John 4:4). A Christian is empowered of God to resist Satan (1 Peter 5:8-9). As in the original act of God's salvation for the believer, so the continued deliverance from sin's power is a part of God's plan by which every believer will be brought ultimately to perfect holiness in the presence of God in heaven.

SALVATION FROM HUMAN LIMITATIONS

Not only is a Christian delivered from the world, the sin nature, and the devil, but also he is delivered by the grace of God from his own human limitations. A Christian endeavoring to lead a Christian life soon discovers that just as his salvation had to be a work of God so his deliverance from evil as a Christian has to be a work of God. The experience of Christians gaining victory over the forces of evil is stated in Titus 2:11-14, "For the grace of God that brings salvation has appeared to all men. It teaches us to say 'No' to ungodliness and worldly passions, and to live self-controlled, upright, and godly lives in this present age, while we wait for the blessed hope—the glorious appearing of our great God and Saviour, Jesus Christ, who gave Himself for us to redeem us from all wickedness and to purify for Himself a people that are His very own, eager to do what is good." Also it is important to take into consideration the extensive body of truth which reveals God's ministry to a Christian who desires to be God-honoring in his life and service.

1. The Spirit produces Christian character. Though a believer before his salvation did not have a righteous character, once he is saved he is able by the grace of God to manifest the fruit of the Spirit, which is "love, joy, peace, patience, kindness, goodness, faithfulness, gentleness, and self-control" (Gal. 5:22-23). A Christian, even though he has tremendous spiritual enemies, is able by the grace of God to manifest the fruit of the Spirit and to demonstrate the dramatic change in his character accomplished by the new creation.

2. Empowered for service. The Holy Spirit also empowers a Christian for service for God in the present world. The Spirit of God gives to every Christian spiritual gifts or special abilities to serve Him in various capacities. An extended list of these gifts is given in several passages of Scripture (Rom. 12:3-8; 1 Cor. 12:4-11; Eph. 4:11; 1 Peter 4:10-11).

In addition to providing these Spirit-empowered gifts the Spirit teaches the Word of God to believers (John 16:12-15; 1 Cor. 2:9–3:1; 1 John 2:27). The Holy Spirit also inspires the believer to express praise and thanksgiving (Eph. 5:19-20), He leads the child of God (Rom. 8:14; Gal. 5:18), He confirms to believers that they are God's children (Rom. 8:16), and He makes intercession for the Christian (vv. 26-27).

This brief treatment of the work of the Spirit reveals that the child of God is empowered to attain a holy character in service, and this accompanies the divine purpose in delivering the saved one from weakness and limitations.

CHAPTER • 19

THE BELIEVER PRESENTED FAULTLESS

Believers in Christ are promised ultimate perfection at the time of their presentation in glory. Paul wrote, "To Him who is able to keep you from falling and to present you before His glorious presence without fault and with great joy" (Jude 24). God promised that believers are kept from falling or "stumbling" (NASB). When presented in God's presence the church shall be a great joy to the Lord.

The same concept is declared in Ephesians 5:25-27, "Husbands, love your wives, just as Christ loved the church and gave Himself up for her to make her holy, cleansing her by the washing with water through the Word, and to present her to Himself as a radiant church, without stain or wrinkle or any other blemish, but holy and blameless."

In the present experience of the believer there is need for a constant sanctifying process to purge away imperfections. God has promised to do this. At the end of this process when a believer is presented faultless in heaven, he will have no trace of sin, age, or limitations that characterize his life on earth. From beginning to end this is a work of God for the believer rather than a work of the believer for God. The perfections that will characterize the believer in heaven which are anticipated in this life and in the prophecies of the future include the fulfillment of all that a believer yearns for in this life.

HEAVENLY CITIZENSHIP

A believer's citizenship in heaven begins at the moment of his salvation. Paul stated, "Consequently, you are no longer foreigners and aliens, but fellow citizens with God's people and members of God's household" (Eph. 2:19). Though Christians have right and title to this citizenship now, the full measure of its privilege will not be realized until they get to heaven.

A NEW FRATERNITY

In their heavenly citizenship Christians are associated with God's people and members of God's household as stated in verse 19. At their new birth Christians are baptized into the body of Christ and accordingly have fellowship with all others who have put their trust in Christ. As sons of God they also have kinship with the saints of all ages and in some respects even to the holy angels. Though these ties are not fully manifested in this life, Christians can anticipate the larger, joyous experience which awaits them in heaven.

A RENEWED BODY

When a believer is resurrected or raptured, he can anticipate a renewed body as Paul expressed in Philippians 3:20-21, "But our citizenship is in heaven. And we eagerly await a Saviour from there, the Lord Jesus Christ, who, by the power that enables Him to bring everything under His control, will transform our lowly bodies so that they will be like His glorious body." A similar truth is found in 1 Corinthians 15:42-57 and Ephesians 5:27. Believers, in their present bodies, have the threefold problem of possessing a sin nature, of being perishable as they grow older, and of being mortal. Immediately on resurrection or translation a believer will have a new body with no trace of sin, a body that is imperishable and that will last forever, and a body with freedom from mortality. Believers in heaven will have no more tears, sorrow, or pain and will never know weariness or the limitation of this life again (Rev. 21:4-5).

FREEDOM FROM THE SIN NATURE

As stated above, part of the plan of God at the time of resurrection or translation is the eradication of the sin nature. Though believers are rescued to some extent from their estate of sin at the time of their new birth, the flesh or the old nature is still there and will not be eradicated until death or the Rapture. Believers will never experience in heaven the temptations of this life or the limitations and frailties of their present bodies.

TO BE LIKE CHRIST

Much is indicated in the simple phrase "like Him" (1 John 3:2). Though believers will not be omnipotent, omnipresent, or omniscient, they will have the same eternal life that is in Christ, the same sinless character, and the same quality of being everlasting. As stated in 1 Corinthians 15:49, "As we have borne the likeness of the earthly man, so shall we bear the likeness of the man from heaven." Whatever God does He does to perfection, and the Christian when fully perfected in heaven will be an everlasting token of the grace of God.

TO SHARE IN CHRIST'S GLORY

In Christ's High Priestly Prayer in John 17:24, He said, "Father, I want those You have given Me to be with Me where I am, and to see My glory, the glory You have given Me because You loved Me before the Creation of the world." In verse 22 Christ also said, "I have given them the glory that You gave Me, that they may be one as We are One." A similar truth is stated by Paul, "And we, who with unveiled faces all reflect the Lord's glory, are being transformed into His likeness with ever-increasing glory, which comes from the Lord, who is the Spirit" (2 Cor. 3:18). It is also true that "our light and momentary troubles are achieving for us an eternal glory that far outweighs them all" (4:17).

In Hebrews 2:10 added revelation is given concerning this, "In bringing many sons to glory, it was fitting that God, for whom and through whom everything exists, should make the author of their salvation perfect through suffering." The Apostle Peter added, "And the God of all grace, who called you to His eternal glory in Christ, after you have suffered a little while, will Himself restore you and make you strong, firm, and steadfast" (1 Peter 5:10). Paul also wrote that the believers' sufferings in the present time are small in comparison to the glory they will have (Rom. 8:18; 2 Tim. 2:12).

From these many passages it is revealed that Christians in this world to some extent can manifest the glory of God as they manifest God's perfections through the Holy Spirit working in and through them. However, the perfect revelation awaits their arrival in heaven. Though Christians have the responsibility to avail themselves of God's power and deliverance in grace, their efforts will always be short of the perfection they will realize in heaven.

In reviewing what has been presented concerning God's wonderful plan of salvation for the believer, it is clear that salvation is a work of God based on the finished work of Christ, the present work of the Holy Spirit in revealing truth, the process of sanctification which is realized by the Christian in this life, the keeping work of God in which He protects us, and consummated in the work when God presents believers perfect and complete in heaven. In every step it is God and His power and grace that accomplishes these things, and a Christian can rest in the fact that God will be faithful in performing what He has promised to do. A Christian in heaven will have no ground for his own boasting, but instead he will be a manifestation of the wonderful salvation of God through grace in Christ Jesus.

The prayer of the Apostle Paul to this end in Ephesians 1:17-21 provides a summary of this great truth, "I keep asking that the God of our Lord Jesus Christ, the glorious Father, may give you the Spirit of wisdom and revelation, so that you may know Him better. I pray also that the eyes of your heart may be enlightened in order that you may know the hope to which He has called you, the riches of His glorious inheritance in the saints, and His incomparably great power for us who believe. That power is like the working of His mighty strength, which He exerted in Christ when He raised Him from the dead and seated Him at His right hand in the heavenly realms, far above all rule and authority, power and dominion, and every title that can be given, not only in the present age but also in the one to come."

CHAPTER • 20

THE TERMS OF SALVATION

Few doctrines of the Bible are more important than the subject of the terms of salvation. As provided in Scripture, many exhortations like the one to the Philippian jailer simply say, "Believe in the Lord Jesus, and you will be saved—you and your household" (Acts 16:31). Though it is common in evangelism to make appeals to "give your heart to Christ" or "invite Christ into your heart," it is questionable whether an unbeliever is able to do this until he believes.

In making faith the sole condition for receiving salvation, it should be understood that it is not simply mental assent that is called for or a superficial agreement with the facts. In view of the fact that man's personality includes intellect, sensibility, and will, when a person accepts Christ as his Saviour, his acceptance is an act of the mind, the emotions, and the moral will.

Included in the concept of faith is the thought of repenting. Peter stated in his sermon at Pentecost, "Repent and be baptized, every one of you, in the name of Jesus Christ so that your sins may be forgiven. And you will receive the gift of the Holy Spirit" (2:38). Because those to whom he was speaking had previously rejected Christ, he asked them to repent or to change their minds regarding Christ and place their faith in Him. This repentance is an aspect of faith. Repentance as an act of sorrow, however, is not involved nor can unbelievers be challenged effectively to change their lives before salvation.

The all-important command is to believe in Christ. Normally this includes a reversal of any previous acts of unbelief, and it includes recognizing Jesus Christ as God. Experientially many Christians do not submit to Christ as Lord of their lives until sometime after their personal salvation, though in the nature of their faith in Christ they had to accept Him as God. Accordingly all appeals to change of life and change of attitudes apart from faith in Christ are not accurate Gospel presentations. In Peter's case he also asked them to be baptized, that is, to make a public confession of their faith in Christ through the ritual of water baptism. In many other passages baptism is not mentioned, but obviously baptism is public evidence of one's faith in Christ. On the Day of Pentecost the 3,000 who were saved were then baptized. Water baptism, however, was not essential to their salvation but was a confirmation of their act of faith. Obviously the thief on the cross, who accepted Christ, had no opportunity for the ritual of baptism and yet was assured that he would meet Christ in paradise.

In presenting the terms of salvation one should make it clear that salvation is entirely by grace and not a reward for the good work of faith or the good moral work of resolutions to change lives. Salvation is entirely a work of God given in response to the act of faith in Christ. Salvation is totally undeserved and is God's promised response to anyone who places his faith in Christ. It is only too obvious both in Scripture and in life that superficial acceptance of Christ is not enough. The act of trusting God has to be a work of the human will as well as the work of the grace of God. The nature of faith or belief in Christ can be further distinguished from erroneous concepts of the terms of salvation.

REPENT AND BELIEVE

The common use of repentance as a way of salvation following the example of Peter (Acts 2:38) needs to be studied to define its particular meaning: (1) the meaning of the word, (2) the relationship of repentance to believing, (3) the relationship of repentance to covenant people, (4) the absence of the demand for repentance from salvation Scriptures, and (5) the significance of repentance in specific passages.

1. THE MEANING OF THE WORD. "Repentance" is a translation of *metanoia* which means "a change of mind." The idea of sorrow or anguish for sin is not in the word "repentance" though sorrow and anguish may accompany faith. In 2 Corinthians 7:10 the statement is made, "Godly sorrow brings repentance that leads to salvation and leaves no regret, but worldly sorrow brings death." It is true that in

some cases people who have lived wickedly will be brought to Christ partly through sorrow for these sins. However, sorrow in itself does not bring salvation as illustrated in the case of Judas Iscariot. Sorrow is a regret but not necessarily a change of mind and a decision to trust Christ. The son, mentioned by Christ in Matthew 21:28-29, first said, "I will not," but later he repented and changed his mind. This is a true example of the precise meaning of the word. The New Testament call to repentance is not an urge to self-condemnation but is a call to a change of mind which promotes a change being pursued. This word applies especially to those who had previously rejected Christ.

2. The relationship of repentance to believing. Repentance is not an added feature to believing but is involved in the act of believing in Christ. If a person has previously rejected Christ, he is urged to change his mind or to believe, and therefore repentance becomes a synonym for faith. Repentance, however, should be seen not as an added requirement for salvation but rather as an aspect of true faith.

Though anguish of a soul before faith in Christ is sometimes experienced, such emotion cannot itself be the way of salvation. Unbelievers are not encouraged to look inwardly at themselves to see if there is sorrow for sin; instead they are exhorted to look to Christ. Salvation can be conditioned only on faith, not on feelings. People who are led by this error to measure the validity of their salvation by the intensity of anguish which precedes or accompanies it are clouding the real issue of simple faith in Christ. God is not made propitious by human tears but by the death of Christ. Having died, Christ can now offer the good news that people can be saved by simply believing.

Repentance for sin focuses on sinful acts which are not the basic problem for a person who is unsaved. His sin nature is the major problem and he needs a new nature in order to be saved. This can be received only by faith.

3. The relationship of repentance to covenant people. Whether referring to Israel or the church, it should be recognized that those who are included are people to whom God has made promises. If a Christian is saved by faith and becomes a part of the family of God, he is not called on to place his confidence in anything other than the fact that he has put his trust in Christ. David, who was already saved, had to come to God in confession in order to

have his joy restored (Ps. 51:12). Once an individual enters into a covenant relationship through salvation, the appeal is then to confess and to maintain a walk of fellowship with the Lord by the grace of God.

4. The absence of the demand for repentance from salvation Scriptures. Approximately 150 New Testament passages condition salvation on believing, and an additional 35 passages condition salvation on faith. In most of these passages nothing is added by way of additional requirements. For example in dealing with the Philippian jailer Paul stated that the jailer's salvation depended on the simple act of believing in Jesus Christ.

5. The significance of repentance in specific passages. The word "repentance" is often used as a synonym for believing (Acts 17:30; Rom. 2:4; 2 Tim. 2:25; 2 Peter 3:9). Repentance is sometimes addressed to those who are already Christians and are covenant people. Their problem is not lack of faith but lack of complete change of mind in regard to their sin. In some passages the change of mind is the main thought (Acts 8:22; 11:18; Heb. 6:1, 6; 12:17; Rev. 9:20). Three passages relate to Israel as a covenant people and have in mind her earlier rejection of Christ, and therefore an appeal was given for a change of mind (Acts 2:38; 3:19; 5:31).

In Luke 24:47 the statement is made, "And repentance and forgiveness of sins will be preached in His name to all nations, beginning at Jerusalem." The use of repentance is in relationship to Israel which is primarily in view in this passage. These were Israelites who had been confronted with the facts about Christ but had not put their trust in Him. So, they needed not only to believe but also to change their minds from unbelief.

In Acts 11:18 in connection with the conversion of Cornelius the statement is made, "So then, God has granted even the Gentiles repentance unto life." Here repentance is used as a synonym for belief because in all cases a person who believes is changing an earlier attitude of unbelief. Paul also stated, "I have declared to both Jews and Greeks that they must turn to God in repentance and have faith in our Lord Jesus" (20:21). In this passage repentance again is made a synonym of faith as it requires a change of mind concerning trusting Christ.

A similar statement is found in 26:20, "I preached that they should repent and turn to God and prove their repentance by their deeds." Repentance and faith came first; then after salvation they were able to turn to God and do works that proved they had a genuine change of mind. First Thessalonians 1:9 refers to the faith of the Thessalonians, "They tell how you turned to God from idols to serve the living and true God." The very act of turning to Christ was an act of turning from idols and having a change of mind regarding the object of their faith.

In this discussion it has been brought out that repentance is not a good work on which to base salvation but is rather intrinsic in any act of true faith as it involves an act of the will which has not been previously exercised in regard to trusting Jesus Christ.

BELIEVE AND CONFESS CHRIST

It is customary in public evangelism to require public confession of Christ. Obviously this is a natural result of the transformation that takes place when a person trusts in Christ as his Saviour. Such public confession, however, should not be made a condition of salvation.

1. Scriptures bearing on confession of Christ. In Matthew 10:32 Christ said, "Whoever acknowledges Me before men, I will also acknowledge him before My Father in heaven. But whoever disowns Me before men, I will disown him before My Father in heaven." This passage was addressed to Jesus' 12 disciples, and it was related to their preaching. It concerned their identification with Christ. If they freely identified themselves with Christ on earth, they would be identified with Him in heaven. A denial of Christ on earth carries with it the implication that they were not saved in the first place. Outer confession of Christ is as natural for a believer in Christ as breathing is to a newborn baby, and in both cases it is an evidence of life.

The truth is stated in Romans 10:9-10, "If you confess with your mouth, 'Jesus is Lord,' and believe in your heart that God raised Him from the dead, you will be saved. For it is with your heart that you believe and are justified, and it is with your mouth that you confess and are saved." Here the idea of confession is a confirmation of the faith in their hearts, but confession should not be added as a necessary requirement for salvation. The verses which follow make this clear, "As the Scripture says, 'Everyone who trusts in Him will never be put to shame.' For there is no difference between Jew and Gentile—the same Lord is Lord of all and richly blesses all who call on

Him, for, 'Everyone who calls on the name of the Lord will be saved' " (vv. 11-13). In this passage believing in Christ is related to confession, and justification is related to the initial act of faith, but confession confirms the matter to all who observe. However, again this passage refers to trusting Christ (v. 11) and calling on Him (vv. 12-13). Though many outward signs may be evident in the case of a believer in Christ, the central fact remains that faith is what saves him.

2. CONVINCING REASONS ARE GIVEN IN THE SCRIPTURE FOR NOT MAKING PUBLIC CONFESSION ESSENTIAL TO SALVATION.

a. MAKES SCRIPTURE A LIAR. To claim that a public confession of Christ as Saviour is required in addition to believing on Christ is to contend that 150 passages in which believing alone appears are incomplete and to that extent misleading.

b. DISCREDITS PRIVATE SALVATION. To require a public confession of Christ as a prerequisite to salvation by grace is to discredit the salvation of the innumerable company who have been saved under circumstances which made public action impossible or unnecessary. While confession, like breathing, is a natural sign of life, God looks at the heart rather than to external manifestations and knows whether one has really trusted Him. It is a Christian's privilege and duty to confess Christ publicly, but it is not a condition of salvation by grace for then works would intrude where only a work of God reigns.

BELIEVE AND BE BAPTIZED

As previously mentioned, in Peter's sermon at Pentecost, he included baptism along with belief as a way of salvation (Acts 2:38). It should be remembered that as baptism is mentioned in Scripture, sometimes it refers to real baptism, that is, the baptism of the Holy Spirit which occurs at the moment of faith and in other cases to the ritual of water baptism. It is possible to take this verse in either sense. If it refers to real baptism, then Peter was saying that if the Jews believed and had this belief confirmed by being baptized into the body of Christ, they would be saved. Or if it refers to water baptism then Peter was saying that that ritual was an outward confirmation of their faith. In any case immediately afterward, Peter baptized 3,000 (v. 41), who were by this token publicly aligning themselves with Christ and indicating that they were leaving their former

Jewish confidence in the Law.

For Jews to confess Christ publicly was a real problem because they often lost their families, their employment, and their wealth. For their faith to be confirmed by water baptism in this case made clear that they were genuinely saved. In any event ritual baptism does not save, and the reference to baptism in verse 38 does not suggest that water baptism was a requirement for salvation. The many instances in which faith is mentioned as a condition of salvation without reference to baptism should make this clear. Even Peter himself later said that forgiveness of sins is based on faith alone (10:43; 13:38-39).

In Acts 19 some Jews in Ephesus had been baptized by John the Baptist but had not put their trust in Christ. When they were informed that it was necessary for them to believe in Christ, the Scriptures recorded, "On hearing this, they were baptized into the name of the Lord Jesus" (v. 5). This again makes clear that water baptism in itself does not save but is a token or evidence that a person has put his trust in Christ.

BELIEVE AND SURRENDER TO GOD

In presenting the Gospel it is a subtle temptation to urge people not only to believe but also to surrender to God because of course this is the ultimate objective of their salvation. However, in explaining the terms of salvation this brings in a confusing human work as essential to salvation which the Bible does not confirm. Evidence that surrender to God is not part of the act of salvation may be approached under three aspects: (1) the incapacity of the unsaved, (2) what is involved in salvation, and (3) the preacher's responsibility.

1. THE INCAPACITY OF THE UNSAVED. The Arminian belief that through the reception of common grace anyone is competent to accept Christ as Saviour is a rather mild assumption as compared to the idea that an unregenerate person is able to dedicate his life to God. The fact is that unbelievers are dead and unable to respond unless the Holy Spirit enables them. Accordingly the unsaved can receive the convicting work of the Spirit by which the terms of the Gospel are made known to them and may receive grace to put their trust in Christ. To add to this, however, the concept of surrendering their lives to the Lord is asking them to do something they are ill

prepared to do at the time of initial salvation. Though it is clear that grace is necessary for belief (Eph. 2:8), to add the additional requirement of surrendering to God as a condition to salvation is unreasonable and contrary to Scripture.

Once a person is saved the appeal can be made to him to yield his life to Christ, but this should not be made a part of the process of the new birth.

2. What is involved in salvation. The most subtle form of meritorious works is often found in the practice of urging unbelievers to accept the lordship of Christ. Trusting in Christ for salvation means accepting Him as God, but the added step of yielding to Him as Lord is usually postponed until later.

An extreme case of dedication to God is involved in the death of a martyr. It is true that a Christian who has put his trust in Christ should be willing to die for Christ's sake, and in the course of human history millions have died. To make this a condition of salvation, however, is to put a stricture on the Gospel which is not natural to its offer in grace. Certainly one cannot identify Christians simply on the issue of whether they are willing to die for Christ. It is possible that those who have been born again and genuinely desire to serve the Lord have not reached that stage of spiritual maturity where they are willing to become martyrs.

Being spiritually dead an unregenerate person has no ability to desire the things of God (1 Cor. 2:14) or to anticipate what his outlook on life will be after he is saved. In presenting the Gospel the emphasis should be on appealing to the unsaved to exercise faith for salvation rather than to confuse the issue by raising problems of dedication to God.

3. The preacher's responsibility. The preacher is responsible to present the terms of salvation. Those who have this responsibility should first recognize that God uses a clear presentation which can be the basis for the convicting work of the Spirit. The Gospel must be presented as God's way of salvation and faith as the way by which this salvation can come to an individual. The issue in salvation itself is not a question of morality but a question of where the individual puts his faith. Once a Christian has accepted Christ as Saviour, then he is in a position to consider the larger sphere of what he should do for God in view of what God has done for him.

In discussing the way of salvation with unsaved people it is important that there be clarity in presenting the single issue of whether they will trust in Christ for salvation. All other issues are foreign at this point. The Holy Spirit will use a clear presentation of the grace of God that prompts salvation based on the finished work of Christ. This is the area the Holy Spirit can reveal to an unsaved person in preparation for faith.

BELIEVE AND CONFESS SIN OR MAKE RESTITUTION

In 1 John 1:9 confession is exhorted, "If we confess our sins, He is faithful and just and will forgive us our sins and purify us from all unrighteousness." In the context it is clear that John is addressing children of God or those who have been born again, and he is dealing with the relationship of a child of God to his Heavenly Father. If a child of God sins, it is most important that he confess his sin and be restored to fellowship with the Father.

The concept that confession of sin is necessary for salvation is again a mixing of grace and works. A person is not saved by confessing his sins as illustrated in the case of Judas Iscariot. No doubt there are many others who are free to acknowledge that they are sinners but in that acknowledgment they do not exercise faith in Christ. Confession of sin properly understood in Scripture has to do with a Christian's walk with the Lord after he is saved but not with the act of salvation itself.

Unsaved man is given to legalism and the concept that somehow he could gain favor with God by doing certain things is natural. But this is false and characterizes all false religions of the world. By contrast, the Scriptures make clear that salvation is not by works even though in saving a person God prepares him for good works (Eph. 2:8-10).

Christ did not die for those who were good and needed only a little help to be saved. Rather according to Romans 4:5, "However, to the man who does not work but trusts God who justifies the wicked, his faith is credited as righteousness."

Romans 5:6-10 clearly presents the fact that Christ died for the ungodly and that the unsaved by faith are justified by the blood of Christ and reconciled to God through the death of His Son. Having come to Christ as Saviour and receiving salvation, the result is that a Christian will experience God's continued work of salvation in his life (v. 10).

BELIEVE AND IMPLORE GOD TO SAVE

Another misconception is that people are saved by praying.

1. Seek Him. In Isaiah 55:6 God invited His covenant people Israel to seek Him, "Seek the Lord while He may be found; call on Him while He is near." In the present age, however, the Gospel of grace is being offered in a situation where people are not in relationship to God and do not seek Him. This is affirmed in Romans 3:11, "There is no one who understands, no one who seeks God." In the present age God is seeking out sinners. Christ Himself said that He had come to seek out sinners and save them (Luke 19:10). The unsaved are blinded to the truth of the Gospel (John 3:3; 2 Cor. 3:4). Only when the Spirit of God gives light in the form of conviction concerning the Gospel is the will of man enabled to believe (Eph. 2:8). While this may involve to some extent a movement in the heart of an unsaved person to seek the Lord, it obviously is not a universal invitation nor universally realized.

2. Believe and pray. Frequently an unbeliever is told to pray to seek salvation. It may be proper for one who is putting his trust in Christ to come to the Lord in his new faith and pray concerning his need and for the outworking of his salvation, but salvation is not given in answer to prayer because God has already promised to save everyone who comes to Him in faith. An unsaved person does not need to plead with God to be merciful and kind or to persuade God to be good. God has already manifested these attributes in offering salvation by grace in the first place.

The prayer of the publican in Luke 18:13 is often cited, "But the tax collector stood at a distance. He would not even look up to heaven, but beat his breast and said, 'God, have mercy on me, a sinner.' " In the plea to God to be merciful the publican was actually asking God to be propitiated toward him. At that time the publican was not aware of the fact that God would be completely propitiated by the death of Christ. In referring to this instance, however, Christ pointed out that the publican arrived at the proper approach to God. The issue was whether God was propitiated, which has now been revealed to have been accomplished by the death of Christ. God is merciful because He is a propitiated God. On the other hand the Pharisee was much farther from God than the publican because he based his hope for reception by God on his own works rather than on the propitiation of God.

In summarizing human terms related to salvation several factors may be restated.

First, every feature of man's salvation including his ultimately being presented in glory is a work of God so supernatural that only God can bring it about. The successive steps include election in eternity past, the sacrifice of the Saviour, the enlightenment by the Holy Spirit, the saving work of God and its manifold achievements, the keeping work of the Father, the Son, and the Spirit, the delivering work of the Spirit, the empowering work of the Spirit, and the final perfecting and presenting in glory. This itemization of what God accomplishes for the person who believes should make it clear that salvation is a work of God that no man can earn or receive apart from God's grace.

Second, it has been asserted that the primary divine purpose of saving a soul is the satisfying of the infinite divine love for that soul in the exercise of sovereign grace. The slightest human work of merit cannot be allowed to intrude on this great divine undertaking as men are clearly saved apart from every form of human worthiness.

Third, in about 150 passages the New Testament declares directly without complication that people are saved on the sole principle of faith. It has been shown that this is not a matter of faith and repenting, of faith and confessing Christ, of faith and being baptized, of faith and surrender to God, of faith and confessing sin, or of faith and pleading with God for salvation, but it is believing in God and in Christ alone. Such belief is apart from human works (Rom. 4:5; Eph. 2:9). It is a definite turning away from former unbelief by turning to God (1 Thes. 1:9). The word of Paul to the Philippian jailer echoes through the centuries as the essence of the condition of salvation, "Believe in the Lord Jesus, and you will be saved" (Acts 16:31).

Perhaps no verse of Scripture more accurately portrays the wonder of God's salvation than John 3:16, "For God so loved the world that He gave His one and only Son, that whoever believes in Him shall not perish but have eternal life." In this one text is marshaled the wonderful fact that "God so loved the world" even though the world was sinful and contrary to the holiness of God. This verse states that God "gave His one and only Son." In these few words the immeasurable sacrifice of the Son in dying on the cross is expressed. The third major element is stated in the words "that whoever believes in Him," which asserts that salvation is through Christ alone and is secured by faith alone uncomplicated by any work of merit. In this verse also the expression "shall not perish" contrasts the state of the saved with the state of the lost. Finally the verse promises "but have eternal life." Here the ultimate goal of salvation is to give the believer, unworthy as he is, the same kind of life that characterizes God's everlasting life.

In this incomparable text at least nine great doctrines of soteriology are included: infinite love, infinite sacrifice for the sinner, sovereign election, sovereign grace, unlimited redemption, salvation a work of God, salvation from perdition, eternal security, and salvation by grace through faith alone.

PART • SIX

ECCLESIOLOGY

CHAPTER • 21

INTRODUCTION TO ECCLESIOLOGY

Ecclesiology is that branch of theology that deals with the doctrine of the church, the term coming from the Greek *ekklesia*, meaning "assembly." In the history of Greece the assembly of citizens to consider legislation in a Greek town was called *ekklesia*, meaning an assembly of people gathered in one place. It is used in this sense of the assembly of the Jews in the desert. In the New Testament it is also used of congregations of Christians in a given locality and is used in this sense at least 100 times (e.g., Acts 9:31; 14:23; 15:41; Rom. 16:1; 1 Cor. 1:2; Gal. 1:2; 1 Thes. 1:1). In some instances, however, it is used of the church or the body of believers regardless of geographic location (Matt. 16:18; Eph. 1:22; 3:10; 5:23-25, 27; Col. 1:18).

Because the Greek translation of the Old Testament (LXX) uses *ekklesia* for assemblies in the Old Testament, some have argued from this that the church is also in the Old Testament. An examination of all instances of the various Hebrew words translated *ekklesia* demonstrates that the word is never used in the Old Testament in a religious sense and used only of a geographic assembly of people whether or not it has religious connotation. Accordingly the concept that all the saints of the Old Testament form a church as well as the saints of the New Testament is not based on Scripture and tends to ignore the distinct sense in which *ekklesia* is used in the New Testament in reference to those who are the saints from the Day of Pentecost until the Rapture. Introducing the doctrine of the church in the Old Testament has led to the conclusion that Israel and the church are to be identified as one entity and the concept that the church includes the saved of all ages. A careful reading of the New Testament, however, reveals that *ekklesia*, though it refers to local assemblies which were churches, is also used in a purely religious sense of *all* those who were united by faith in Christ in the period beginning with the Day of Pentecost.

The Apostle Paul was given the great responsibility of receiving and declaring two separate revelations. First, Paul was given a clear revelation of the Gospel of grace, the good news that through the death and resurrection of Christ a perfect and eternal salvation into a heavenly state is provided to both Jews and Gentiles on the sole condition of saving faith in the Lord Jesus Christ. Paul referred to this in Galatians 1:11-12, "I want you to know, brothers, that the Gospel I preached is not something that man made up. I did not receive it from any man, nor was I taught it; rather, I received it by revelation from Jesus Christ."

The importance of this Gospel revealed to Paul was reflected in the warnings of judgment that would fall on those who misstate this truth as he wrote in verses 8-9, "But even if we or an angel from heaven should preach a gospel other than the one we preached to you, let him be eternally condemned! As we have already said, so now I say again: If anybody is preaching to you a gospel other than what you accepted, let him be eternally condemned!" Though this truth was obscured in some periods of church history, in the Protestant Reformation it was reclaimed and became the central doctrine of Protestant theology.

Second, the revelation was given Paul concerning the unique divine purpose in the present age that Jews and Gentiles should partake equally of the Gospel and be heirs of Christ as stated by Paul in Ephesians 3:1-6, "For this reason I, Paul, the prisoner of Christ Jesus for the sake of you Gentiles—Surely you have heard about the administration of God's grace that was given to me for you, that is, the mystery made known to me by revelation, as I have already written briefly. In reading this, then, you will be able to understand my insight into the mystery of Christ, which was not made known to men in other generations as it has now been revealed by the Spirit to God's holy apostles and prophets. This mystery is that through the Gospel the Gentiles are heirs together with Israel, members together of one body, and sharers together in the promise in Christ Jesus."

The Old Testament made clear that Gentiles were to be saved but the mystery element was that Jew and Gentile would be one in the church, the body of Christ formed by the baptism of the Holy Spirit (1 Cor. 12:12-13). In this union the earthly distinction of Jew and

Gentile disappeared (Eph. 2:14-15; Col. 3:10-11). Accordingly in Paul's writings in the New Testament the doctrine, position, walk, and destiny of the church is revealed.

In approaching the doctrine of ecclesiology in the New Testament certain major facts and distinctions must be observed.

THE FOUR MAJOR CLASSES OF RATIONAL BEINGS IN THE UNIVERSE

From Scripture, four classes of moral and rational beings are disclosed: the angels, the Gentiles, the Jews, and Christians. Each of these four classes has its own theology and program in the past, present, and future.

1. Angels. The angels are created beings (Ps. 148:2-5; Col. 1:16); their abode is in heaven (Matt. 24:36); their activity is both on earth and in heaven (Ps. 103:20; Luke 15:10; Heb. 1:14); and their destiny is the celestial city (12:22; Rev. 21:12). Angels do not change their essential situation though some of them fell into sin and became the demon world under Satan's direction. Each of the angels was the immediate object of God's creation, they are not increased in number, and they neither propagate nor do they die. Though fallen angels are subject to eternal punishment (Matt. 25:41), they are still classed as angels.

2. Gentiles. The Gentiles are a second group of rational beings. Racially the Gentiles had their origin in Adam, and they are an extensive subject of prophecy. Except for their situation in the present age, they were subordinated to Israel. In the coming millennial kingdom they will again be subordinated to Israel (Isa. 2:4; 60:3, 5, 12; 62:2; Acts 15:17). From Adam to Christ, Gentiles were under a fivefold indictment, namely, they were "separate from Christ," "excluded from citizenship in Israel," "foreigners to the covenants of the promise," "without hope," and "without God in the world" (Eph. 2:12).

In the present age because of the death, resurrection, and ascension of Christ and the descent of the Spirit on the Day of Pentecost, Gentiles and Jews share the same Gospel (Acts 10:45; 11:17-18; 13:47-48), and from Jews and Gentiles alike God is calling an elect company (Acts 15:14). Though Gentiles do not share the prophetic promises given especially to Israel, in the present age they enjoy the riches of grace in Christ Jesus on an equal basis with Israel and are privileged to be partakers of a heavenly citizenship in glory.

Beginning with the fall of Jerusalem to Nebuchadnezzar in 605 B.C. and continuing until the second coming of Christ, a time period is designated as "the times of the Gentiles" (Luke 21:24; cf. Dan. 2:36-44). Throughout this long period Israel is not enjoying possession of her entire Promised Land, and the political restoration that characterizes Israel today is made possible by Gentile support and particularly support by the United States. At the second coming of Christ the times of the Gentiles will come to an end, Gentile nations will be judged, and the Jews will be restored to their Promised Land as revealed to Abraham (Gen. 12:1, 7; 15:18-21; Jer. 23:5-8).

In the period between the Rapture and the second coming of Christ to the earth, Jews and Gentiles will be treated as separate peoples and those among Jews and Gentiles who come to Christ will be delivered by Christ from their persecutors at His second coming (30:7-11; Ezek. 20:34-38; Matt. 25:31-46).

3. ISRAEL. Beginning with Abraham and his call to go to the Promised Land, God designated Israel as a special people. The promises given to Abraham's seed are narrowed to Isaac rather than Ishmael and to Jacob rather than Esau. Jacob was given the name Israel and the 12 sons of Jacob were called Israel. The term "Jew" is derived from Judah, the son of Jacob. Because Judah was the tribe through which Christ came, "Jews" is often used for the entire 12 tribes in both the Old Testament (Es. 3:6, 13; 8:8-9, 11, 13, 16-17, etc.) as well as in the New Testament (Matt. 2:2; 27:11, 29, 37; 28:15; Rom. 1:16; 9:24; 1 Cor. 10:32). Most of the Old Testament from Genesis 12 to Malachi 4:6 presents the history of Israel, the record of God's dealings with them, and prophecies of the future course of God's program for Israel.

The Scriptures reveal that God has selected Israel as a primary race to reveal His revelation to man through prophets and writers of Scripture, through the apostles and prophets of the New Testament, and supremely through Jesus Christ. The special purposes of God for Israel are summarized in Romans 9:4-5, "Theirs is the adoption as sons; theirs the divine glory, the covenants, the receiving of the Law, the temple worship and the promises. Theirs are the patriarchs, and from them is traced the human ancestry of Christ, who is God over all, forever praised!"

In His covenants with Israel five eternal features are dominant: a national entity (Jer. 31:36), a land in perpetuity (Gen. 13:15), an everlasting throne (2 Sam. 7:16; Ps. 89:36), a king (Jer. 23:5-6; 33:19-21), and a kingdom (Dan. 7:14). Though the Old Testament records God's disciplines and judgments on His ancient people, His ultimate purposes for them do not change. He promises Israel that she will be regathered and possess her land (Deut. 30:1-6; Jer. 23:5-8; Ezek. 37:21-25). The rightful King, Jesus Christ, the Son of David, as One who is resurrected, will occupy the Davidic throne forever (Ps. 89:34-37; Isa. 9:6-7; Jer. 33:17; Luke 1:31-33; Rev. 11:15).

Though interpreters of the Old Testament were perplexed by the dual prophecies of a suffering and a glorious reigning Messiah as referred to by Peter (1 Peter 1:10-11), in the New Testament it became clear that prophecies of His first coming to die have been fulfilled. The prophecies of His second coming to reign are still future. Though God's Son would die a sacrificial death (Pss. 22:1-21; 69:20-21), He would be resurrected and occupy David's throne forever (2 Sam. 7:16-29; Ps. 89:34-37). Though no one in the Old Testament understood the two comings of Christ, David apparently had some insight as he reasoned that if God's Son was to occupy the throne forever, He must first die and be raised from the dead and therefore freed to reign forever. This truth was featured in Peter's Pentecostal sermon (Acts 2:25-36). In His first coming Christ offered Himself to Israel as her King (Zech. 9:9; cf. Matt. 21:5). In His second coming He will return as a conquering Ruler (Rev. 19:15-16).

To avoid confusion in interpretation of Scripture, the promises given to Israel, which were repeated by Christ in His first coming, must be distinguished from the promises to the church. The church in this age is given a special place and is composed of both Jews and Gentiles. The future program for the church differs from the program for Israel as Israel's program is related primarily to the earth and to her ultimate national restoration to the Promised Land.

In His first coming Christ was rejected nationally by Israel and her leaders though many individual Israelites such as the Apostles and others put their trust in Him. Offering Himself to Israel as her Messiah, He was offering Himself in a sense as her King. Because Israel rejected this, however, the promise of the kingdom will be fulfilled at the time of His second coming. The kingdom is postponed in the same sense that the Jews, who were given the promise of the Promised Land, had their occupancy of the land postponed by their failure to trust God at Kadesh Barnea. As a result they wandered in the wilderness for 40 years until the time came for them to enter the land.

When the church is called to heaven at the time of the Rapture of the church, God will resume His program for Israel, including the time of Great Tribulation and suffering, and then will rescue the godly remnant of Israel at the time of Christ's second coming.

Prominent in prophecy is the Day of the Lord *(Yahweh)*, which will begin after the Rapture of the church. The period includes the entire time of trouble from the Rapture to the end of the thousand-year reign of Christ. As defined and used in the Old Testament, the Day of *Yahweh* is a time when God deals directly with human sin as He will do in the time of the Tribulation as well as in the millennial kingdom. Many of the promises relating to the Day of *Yahweh* will be considered later in the section on eschatology.

4. The church. Starting with the Day of Pentecost believers are placed into the church, the body of Christ, by the baptism of the Spirit. The church continues on earth until the future Rapture. The church as a body of people distinguished from both Jews and Gentiles is given the term "Christian" (Acts 11:26).

The major features of the present age are not mentioned in the Old Testament though some passages imply that there is a period of time between Christ's first and second comings (Dan. 9:26). In His earthly life Christ did not deal with the subject of the church in any detail until the Upper Room Discourse the night before His crucifixion. The apostles only slowly understood the dramatic difference between the present age and the previous dealings of God with Israel. The extensive body of Scripture of which Paul is the human author thoroughly points out that in the present age God is dealing with both Jew and Gentile on the same level of privilege. In the present age believing Jews and Gentiles are united in the church with the middle wall of partition broken down (Eph. 2:14). The New Testament records that individual Christians are indwelt by Christ who is their hope of glory (Col. 1:27). In their new standing before God they are justified and righteousness is imputed to them (Rom. 5:1). Christians are already constituted heavenly citizens (Phil. 3:20) and are viewed as raised with Christ (Col. 3:1-3), seated with Christ (Eph. 2:6), and in a sense are removed from the world as far as their position in Christ is concerned (John 17:14-16; cf. 15:18-

19).

The church is declared to be a new creation (2 Cor. 5:17; Gal. 6:15). The church is given a special responsibility as a heavenly people and Christians should adorn by Christlike living the doctrine they represent, and be witnesses to the uttermost parts of the earth. They are not striving to secure a standing with God for they are already in Christ (Eph. 1:1) and are blessed with great spiritual blessings (v. 3; Col. 2:10).

In view of their high calling believers are given the indwelling Holy Spirit to empower them to lead a Christian life and manifest the glory of God. At the time of the Rapture Christians who have died will be resurrected and living saints will be translated (1 Cor. 15:51-57; 1 Thes. 4:13-17). In glory the individuals who comprise the church will be judged and given rewards for service (1 Cor. 3:9-15; 9:24-27; 2 Cor. 5:10-11). The church is already married to Christ and is waiting as a betrothed maiden for her husband to come to claim her (2 Cor. 11:2; Eph. 5:25-27). The church having been raptured will later return with Christ in His second coming (Luke 12:35-36; Jude 14-15; Rev. 19:11-16). The church will continue to maintain its identity throughout eternity (Heb. 12:22-24; Rev. 21:1–22:5). In contrast to promises given to the Jews, Christians do not have a Promised Land (Ex. 20:12); house (Matt. 23:38; Acts 15:16); an earthly capital or city (Ps. 137:5-6; Isa. 2:1-4); an earthly throne (Luke 1:31-33); a king, though Christians may speak of Christ as "the King" (1 Tim. 1:17; 6:15); and have no altar other than the cross of Christ (Heb. 13:10-14).

THE DISPENSATIONS

A dispensation is a stage in God's progressive revelation defining a rule of life which constitutes a distinct stewardship. Dispensations are found in different time periods (Eph. 2:7; 3:5, 9; Heb. 1:2). An age differs from a dispensation in that the age is the time period and the dispensation is the stewardship that constitutes God's rule of life in that time period. The fact that there are various ages in the history of the world is recognized in the Bible (John 1:17; cf. 5:21-22; 2 Cor. 3:11; Heb. 7:11-12).

Man's relationship to God varies in different ages. In each dispensation man is tested under different rules of life and invariably fails, and he is able to be rightly related to God only by grace.

In the various dispensations certain elements remain the same such as God's holy character, basic morality, and the way of salvation. Though salvation is by faith and by grace in every age, the manner in which that faith is demonstrated in life differs.

In interpreting the dispensations it is important to distinguish their primary and secondary applications. Though some instructions pertaining to a particular dispensation are superseded by later instructions, the entire Scriptures contain truths that can be applied in a secondary way as reflecting God's holy Person and what is normative in every dispensation. Accordingly there is unity as well as diversity in the dispensations.

A clear dispensational distinction can be observed in comparing the rule of life for Christians in the present age to the rule of life for Israel under the Mosaic Law. Many of the instructions given to Israel under the Law do not apply to Christians. For example the requirement to keep the Sabbath on the seventh day is superseded by the resurrection of Christ on the first day of the week. No one believes that the instructions in the Law to kill a man for gathering sticks on the Sabbath is applicable today (Num. 15:32-36).

The Greek word *aion*, which properly means an "age" is wrongly translated in the KJV by the word "world." This is usually corrected in modern translations. Matthew 13:49 for instance refers not to "the end of the world" (KJV) but the end of an age which is actually followed by another age.

Seven dispensations are found in Scripture: (1) innocence, (2) conscience, (3) government, (4) promise, (5) law, (6) grace, and (7) millennial kingdom. However, only three dispensations, law, grace, and kingdom, are given detailed revelation.

While not everyone recognizes seven dispensations, one must recognize the concept of dispensations in the Scriptures if a normal, literal interpretation of the Bible is employed. The attempt to erase dispensational distinctions in the Scriptures can be accomplished only by interpreting the Scriptures in a nonliteral sense.

In addition to interpreting Scripture in a normal, literal sense, a second principle basic to dispensationalism is progressive revelation. This is recognized by practically all biblical scholars. A third principle is that later revelation sometimes supersedes earlier revelation. This accounts for the fact that Christians do not observe the laws given to Israel.

Because the Bible was not written before Moses, not many facts are given about the four earlier, pre-Mosaic dispensations. Attention is directed in Scripture to three major dispensations: (1) the Mosaic Law; (2) grace, the present Church Age; and (3) the future Kingdom Age. Some scholars who deny they are dispensationalists actually mean they do not accept the seven dispensations often recognized by premillennial scholars. The fact is, however, that even those who deny that they hold to dispensationalism actually are dispensationalists according to its proper definition. All expositors recognize progress in revelation and the fact that later revelation supersedes previous revelation, and if they are premillennial they will recognize a future kingdom period.

1. Innocence. The first dispensation, the dispensation of innocence, relates to the rule of life for Adam and Eve before they fell into sin (Gen. 1:26-27). The dispensation of innocence ended when they partook of the forbidden fruit (3:6). In the dispensation of innocence man was given a relatively simple rule of life. He was to subdue the earth, have dominion over animals, eat vegetables for food, care for the Garden of Eden, and be fruitful in multiplying the human race (1:28-29; 2:15).

When sin entered and Adam and Eve were driven out of the Garden, they experienced God's judgment, spiritual death, the knowledge of good and evil, loss of fellowship with God, and fear of His judgment. Once sin entered the race, however, God gave Adam and Eve the promise of a Redeemer (3:15). Coats of skin which necessarily required the killing of an animal, shedding of blood, and typically representing redemption (v. 21) were given. Though Adam and Eve eventually died physically they were allowed to live out a long life.

2. Conscience. The dispensation of conscience began in verse 7 and extended to 8:19. As a result of sin, Satan was cursed (3:14-15), and a curse was imposed on Adam and Eve (vv. 16-19). Apparently no detailed code of ethics or rule of life was given to Adam and Eve after they sinned. They were governed by their consciences. As a rule of life, however, conscience could convict but could not solve man's moral problems (John 8:9; Rom. 2:15; 1 Cor. 8:7; 1 Tim. 4:2). The sin nature, which every descendant of Adam and Eve possesses, manifested itself in Cain's murder of Abel (Gen. 4:8). A preliminary revelation of the need of a blood offering apparently was

given to Abel (v. 7). Though Cain and his descendants demonstrated man's depravity, Enoch (5:24), and Noah's family (6:8-10; Heb. 11:7), were saved by God's grace. The dispensation of conscience demonstrated that men failed under this new situation, deserved divine judgment, but could become recipients of salvation if they put their trust in God.

3. Government. The dispensation of human government began with a covenant with Noah and continued from Genesis 8:20 through 11:9. God gave Noah promises which may be referred to as the Noahic Covenant (8:20–9:17). God promised that never again would there be a universal flood (8:21; 9:11). Noah was also informed that the course of nature would continue with the various seasons (8:22). As with Adam and Eve, God told Noah and his sons to multiply their descendants (9:1). Noah was allowed dominion over animals (v. 2) and for the first time man was allowed to eat animal flesh (v. 4). An important element of the covenant with Noah was that for the first time the principle of human government was introduced in that man was given the right to kill (vv. 5-6). Like preceding dispensations this one also revealed human failure. This is seen in Noah's drunkenness (v. 21), Ham's sin (v. 22), and the period of moral religious depravity that followed (11:1-4). Human sin reached the point of rebellion against God in the building of the Tower of Babel (v. 4). As a result God judged their sin and gave them diverse languages which forced them to scatter (vv. 5-9). Even in this period, however, some were saved as illustrated in Abram and his family (vv. 10-12).

An element of continuity in the dispensations may be seen in the fact that conscience and human government have continued ever since they were introduced. Later dispensations built on this foundation in the sense that conscience and human government continued in later dispensations.

4. Promise. The dispensation of promise began in verse 10 and continued until the giving of the Law in Exodus 19:2. However, the promises continued through later dispensations. The promises given to Abraham were not applicable universally and of course were not recorded as Scripture until the time of Moses. The promises given to Abraham include what is known as the Abrahamic Covenant (Gen. 12:1-3; 13:16; 15:5; 17:6). A major portion of the Abrahamic Covenant was the promises given to Abraham's descendants that they (Israel) would become a great nation and a channel of God's special

blessings (12:2-3; 13:16; 15:5, 18-21; 17:7-8; 28:13-14; Josh. 1:2-4). The great promise of blessing to the entire earth also was prophesied as coming through Abraham, "All peoples on earth will be blessed through you" (Gen. 12:3). This was fulfilled in that the divine revelation of the Old and New Testaments was given through descendants of Abraham, except for Luke whom some consider a Gentile, and were fulfilled supremely in the coming of Jesus Christ as the Messiah and Saviour.

Important elements of the Abrahamic Covenant included the promise that Israel would be a nation forever, would inherit the Promised Land, would be blessed in many ways including spiritual blessings, and would enjoy divine protection (17:7-8; 26:2-5; 28:13-15). Israel was given a special sign of circumcision (17:13-14).

The Abrahamic Covenant is essentially a gracious covenant not conditioned on human response. It is unconditional in the sense that though its promises could be delayed in their fulfillment the ultimate fulfillment was absolutely sure. Already fulfilled in Abraham's lifetime were many spiritual blessings, including the birth of his descendants. The Abrahamic Covenant, unlike the Mosaic Covenant which followed, was declared to be an everlasting covenant and will continue to be observed in time and eternity (vv. 7, 13, 19; 1 Chron. 16:16-17; Ps. 105:10).

In spite of the many blessings involved in the Abrahamic Covenant, Abraham also failed God. Abraham imperfectly obeyed God's command to go to the land and leave his kindred (Gen. 11:31–12:1). The birth of Ishmael also resulted from Abraham's unbelief in God's promise (16:1-16). Abraham's growth in grace, however, is revealed in his willingness to sacrifice Isaac (Gen. 22).

Failure is evident in Abraham's descendants. Isaac, while obeying God by not going to Egypt, lived close to Egypt (26:6-16). Jacob failed in many ways, and as a result he had to leave home to avoid his brother's revenge. Jacob was guilty of being dishonest (27:1-29). Some believe he was also in error when he moved to Egypt to avoid the famine in the land (46:1-4).

In the Exodus from Egypt Israel's constant complaining showed lack of faith (Ex. 2:23; 4:1-10; 5:21; 14:10-12; 15:24). Some even wanted to abandon the trip to the Promised Land and go back to Egypt (14:11-12). In their journeys they murmured against Moses and Aaron (15:24; 16:2; Num. 14:2; 16:11, 41). Their lack of faith in God resulted in their failure at Kadesh Barnea (Num. 14; 32:8).

In each of the dispensations failure on the part of man is evident under the rule of life which applied but with it was the revelation of God's divine grace so that in every dispensation those who were willing to trust the Lord received a gracious salvation.

5. LAW. The dispensation of the Law began in Exodus 19:3 and extends through the whole period up to the cross of Christ.

An important fact is that the Mosaic Law was never given to the world as a whole but was directed only to Israel. There is no record of Gentiles ever being judged by its standards. The Law had three major divisions: (1) the commandments, God's moral standards for Israel (Ex. 20); (2) the judgments, the social and civil life of Israel (21:1–24:11); and (3) the ordinances, the religious life of Israel (24:12–31:18). Over 600 regulations governed Israel's life.

In the dispensation of Law there was more failure than in the previous dispensations. Israel's moral departure from God is evident in the Book of Judges, and continued throughout the reign of the Kings especially in the Divided Kingdom after the death of Solomon. During parts of that period of time the written Law was completely forgotten and ignored, and Israel gave themselves to idolatry. In the New Testament this pattern of failure persisted even up to the time of the cross of Christ.

In the Law, however, there were gracious elements as seen in the sacrificial system by which a sinning Israelite could be restored to fellowship and in the priestly system which was both gracious and legal. Civil government in this dispensation could best be defined as a theocracy in which God governed through prophets, priests, and kings in the latter part of the period. Unlike the preceding covenants the Mosaic Law was temporary and was preparatory for the coming of the Messiah of Israel (Gal. 3:24-25).

In the dispensation of Law, Israel experienced God's judgments. These included the Assyrian and Babylonian captivities and (after the close of the Mosaic dispensation) the destruction of Jerusalem in A.D. 70 and the scattering of Israel all over the world. The troubles Israel experienced under the Mosaic Covenant, however, will be exceeded by her future time of trouble in the Great Tribulation which will precede the second coming of Christ (Jer. 30:11; Dan. 12:1; Matt. 24:22).

The dispensation of the Law ended at the cross (Rom. 10:4; 2 Cor. 3:11-14; Gal. 3:19, 25). The dispensation of grace, however, did not formally begin until the Day of Pentecost with the coming of the Holy Spirit.

Unlike the preceding dispensations of conscience and human government, the Mosaic Law ended. The purpose of the Law to bring about a righteous manner of life for Israel proved instead to be an instrument of divine judgment in revealing the true character of sin. The Law could not justify (Rom. 3:20; Gal. 2:16). It failed to sanctify (Heb. 7:18-19) and could not regenerate (Gal. 3:21-22), and the Mosaic Law should settle forever the question as to whether detailed laws of conduct can bring holiness to the human race (Rom. 3:19). Instead, man's need of Christ was made more evident than ever (7:7-25; Gal. 3:21-27).

6. Grace. The present age is distinguished from former dispensations as an age of grace or the age of the church, the body of Christ. It began on the Day of Pentecost and will culminate in the Rapture of the church. Christ anticipated the future dispensation of grace in His parting message to His disciples (John 13–17).

Just as the covenant of the Law related only to Israel, so the dispensation of grace relates only to the church. The world as a whole continues under conscience and human government. In the present age salvation is more clearly defined, however, than it was in the Old Testament (Rom. 1:16; 3:22-28; 4:16; 5:15-19). The spiritual and moral standards of the dispensation of grace exceed that of any preceding period (John 13:34-35; Rom. 12:1-2; Phil. 2:5; Col. 1:10-14; 3:1; 1 Thes. 5:23).

Even under grace, however, the failure of man is evident. In spite of extensive preaching of the Gospel many still reject Christ. Even within the professing church the Scriptures predict apostasy as its final spiritual state (1 Tim. 4:1-3; 2 Tim. 3:1-13; 2 Peter 2–3; Jude).

In the present age, however, God is attaining His purpose of calling out from Jews and Gentiles a people for His name—people who are united in the church, the body of Christ.

When the Rapture occurs, the church will be lifted out of the world. Then the consummation of the times of the Gentiles as well as the final period of Israel's predicted history before the Second Coming will be fulfilled. Meanwhile the church itself will be judged at the Judgment Seat of Christ in heaven (2 Cor. 5:10-11).

In no preceding age was grace more graphically portrayed than in the present age (John 1:17). Grace is evident both in the salvation of those who put their trust in God as well as in their position or standing before God (Rom. 3:24; 5:1-2, 15-20; Gal. 1–2; Eph. 2:4-

10). For the first time a gracious rule of life is introduced (Gal. 3–5). This is not to suggest, however, that grace was absent in other dispensations. In every dispensation God manifests His grace in moving those who trust in Him.

After the Rapture the church will be judged and rewarded in heaven, but the remaining professing church, consisting of those who will be entirely apostate, will be judged by God (Rev. 17:16).

Many contrasts exist between the present age and the Mosaic dispensation. The present age deals with Gentiles and Jews alike, whereas the Mosaic dispensation dealt specifically with Israel. In the present age grace is revealed as never before in the person and work of Jesus Christ.

7. Kingdom. The dispensation of the kingdom will begin with the second coming of Christ (Matt. 24; Rev. 19). The time period between the Cross and the Day of Pentecost and the time period between the Rapture and the Second Coming do not form distinct dispensations but are transition periods from the Law to the kingdom with the present age of grace interposed.

Major prophecies dealing with the millennial kingdom are numerous (Ps. 72; Isa. 2:1-7; 11; Jer. 33:14-17; Dan. 2:44-45; 7:9-14, 18, 27; Hosea 3:4-5; Zech. 14:9; Luke 1:31-33; Rev. 19–20). Because of the special characteristics of the millennial kingdom, there will be greater manifestation of righteousness in the human race than in any other dispensation (Isa. 11:3-5). Satan will be bound and Christ will be reigning supremely and visibly in the city of Jerusalem. The human responsibility in the kingdom will be to obey the King. In contrast to the age of grace the dispensation of the kingdom will be a theocratic rule. Animal sacrifices will be resumed, not to fulfill the Law of Moses but to serve as a memorial of the death of Christ (Ezek. 40–48).

In spite of the unusual characteristics of the kingdom period, the millennial dispensation will end with failure (Isa. 65:20; Zech. 14:16-19), and there will be rebellion at the close of the dispensation when Satan will be loosed (Rev. 20:7-9). The dispensation of the kingdom ends with the destruction of the present earth and heavens and the creation of the new heavens and the new earth (Isa. 65:17; 66:22; 2 Peter 3:10) on which the New Jerusalem will rest (Rev. 21:1-4).

Though the kingdom rule will be basically legal, saving grace will be extended to those who believe and the New Covenant will be fulfilled (Jer. 31:31-34). Probably more will be saved than in any previous dispensation (Isa. 12), and there will be much better social, moral, and governmental blessings than in any previous dispensation. Israel will be regathered (11:11-12; Jer. 30:1-11; Ezek. 39:25-29), and her sins will be forgiven. Divine revelation will reach a new high, Christ will reign on His throne on earth and the knowledge of the Lord will extend around the world (Isa. 11:9; Jer. 31:34; Hab. 2:14).

The dispensation of the kingdom forever answers the question as to whether man would be evil if Satan were bound. In the seven dispensations God has tested man under every condition possible, with man failing, and God saving by grace. When the eternal estate begins God will have demonstrated man's complete need of salvation by grace and deliverance from sin which can be provided by God alone.

SCRIPTURE DOCTRINE VIEWED DISPENSATIONALLY

In the progress of doctrine from Genesis to Revelation the Bible reveals different periods of time with different stewardships which are viewed as dispensations of God's government. As the dispensations before Moses were already history when Scripture was written, the earlier dispensations are given relatively brief revelation.

In the Mosaic Law for the first time a complete religious system was provided with at least seven distinctive features: (1) an acceptable standing on the part of man before God, (2) a manner of life consistent with that standing, (3) divinely appointed service, (4) a righteous ground whereby God may graciously forgive and cleanse the erring, (5) a clear revelation of responsibilities on the human side which lead to divine forgiveness and cleansing, (6) an effective base on which God may be worshiped and petitioned in prayer, and (7) a future hope.

1. An acceptable standing on the part of man before God. From the call of Abram to the giving of the Mosaic Law, two widely different divine provisions are made for man who may by the grace of God stand in favor with God, though he is utterly fallen into sin.

a. divine grace on israel. To partake of the covenant blessings for the people of Israel an individual had to have been born physically in the line of Jacob. Paul, for instance, boasted of his Jewish lineage in Philippians 3:5, "Circumcised on the eighth day, of the people of Israel, of the tribe of Benjamin, a Hebrew of Hebrews; in regard to the Law, a Pharisee." The special blessings given to the nation of Israel are recorded in Romans 9:3-5, "For I could wish that I myself were cursed and cut off from Christ for the sake of my brothers, those of my own race, the people of Israel. Theirs is the adoption as sons; theirs the divine glory, the covenants, the receiving of the Law, the temple worship, and the promises. Theirs are the patriarchs, and from them is traced the human ancestry of Christ, who is God over all, forever praised! Amen."

Throughout its history Israel remained a redeemed nation, that is, a nation set apart especially for God. In this setting individual Jews could be saved by grace through faith in God, and other Jews, though racial descendants of Jacob, did not experience the new birth. Paul took note of this in verse 6, "It is not as though God's Word had failed. For not all who are descended from Israel are Israel." Accordingly, even in the Jewish economy national blessings need to be distinguished from the individual blessings of being saved.

As a nation, however, God gave favor to Israelites as seen in their redemption from Egypt by means of the Passover lamb, which spoke prophetically of the coming Lamb of God who would take away the sin of the world. Israel's special favor is revealed in a number of passages (Ex. 8:23; 9:6, 26; 10:23). Israel in a special sense belonged to the Lord (19:5; Deut. 4:32-40; Ps. 135:4). As a nation Israel will be preserved forever, a remarkable fact even in the present age (Gen. 17:7-8; Isa. 66:22; Jer. 31:35-37).

Individual Israelites, however, were subject to the penalty of individual judgment for failure (Deut. 28:58-62; Ezek. 20:33-44; Matt. 24:51; 25:12, 30). It is important and to be emphasized that under the Mosaic Code individual Israelites were saved by the grace of God made possible by the sacrifice of Christ.

b. DIVINE GRACE ON CHRISTIANS. In a special sense God's blessing is resting on His church in the present age as previously brought out. When Christ died Christians died (Rom. 6:1-10), and spiritually they rose in Christ's resurrection (Col. 3:1-3). As such, positionally, Christians are now seated with Christ "in the heavenly realms" (Eph. 2:6). In Christ they have a unity which is compared to the unity of the Godhead (John 17:21-23).

In all these details Christians are exalted above anything that Israel realized in the Old Testament and are the supreme revelation of what the grace of God can do with those who were once lost and dead in sin. Though grace is evident in God's dealings both with Israel and the church, in a special sense the present age is a manifestation of the grace of God, and Christians who are saved will be illustrations of the grace of God eternally (Eph. 2:7).

2. A DIVINELY SPECIFIED MANNER OF LIFE. Though prior to Moses a detailed rule of life is not revealed for preceding dispensations, in the Law God set forth more than 600 regulations governing the life of Israel from a religious standpoint. The Mosaic Law was addressed to Israel and not to the angels or the Gentiles. While Israel was under the Mosaic Law from the time of Moses to the time of Christ, the Gentile world was still under the dispensations of human government and conscience.

In Scripture three distinct and complete divine rulings govern human action. Two are addressed to Israel. One is past and is designated the Mosaic Law, and the other is future and is Israel's required conduct in the messianic kingdom which will be set up by Christ at His second coming. A third rule of life, revealed in the New Testament, is for Christians. It directs Christians to have a standard of life in keeping with their heavenly calling. Though the saved in the present age can learn much of God's moral government by reading the Old Testament, they are given a special and more detailed revelation of their relationship to Christ for the present age in the New Testament. This rule of life for Christians differs from the rule of life for Israel.

The Mosaic system was designed to govern Israel in the land and was a temporary form of divine government administered from Moses to Christ (John 1:17; Rom. 4:9-16; Gal. 3:19-25). As mentioned earlier, the Mosaic Law was divided into three divisions: (a) the commandments, which governed Israel's moral life (Ex. 20:1-17); (b) the judgments, which governed Israel's civic life (21:1–24:11); and (c) the ordinances, which governed Israel's religious life (24:12–31:18). The provisions of the Law were holy, just, and good (Rom. 7:12, 14), but they carried a penalty for disobedience (Deut. 28:58-62). Because they were not kept, Israel experienced the discipline of God in the wilderness, and in the captivities. She also is under that discipline in the present, and will be in the future.

The Law did not offer a way of salvation, and heaven was not among its rewards nor was hell among its punishments. In keeping the Law a Jew could manifest his faith in God and God's provided redemption even though he only partially understood what God was providing through Christ in the future. As a specific rule of life, the Law was terminated with the death of Christ (John 1:17; Rom. 6:14; 7:2-6; 10:4; 2 Cor. 3:6-13; Gal. 3:23-25; 5:18). The Law is declared to be "done away" (KJV) and "abolished" (KJV), or "fading away" (2 Cor. 3:11-13).

In the present age, Christians have the privileged position of their standing in the perfection of Christ (Rom. 3:22; 5:1; 8:1; 10:4; 2 Cor. 5:21; Gal. 3:22; Eph. 1:6). They are perfected forever in Christ (Heb. 10:9-14). Because of their high standing in Christ they are exhorted to live in accord with it (Rom. 12:1-2; Eph. 4:1-3; Col. 3:1-3).

In the Mosaic Law many blessings were conditioned on an individual's obedience to the Law. In some respects the Mosaic Law was a merit system as far as earthly blessings were concerned. By contrast Christians have been given the infinite blessings that are theirs in grace and are called on to walk worthy of this not to receive a reward but to be in keeping with what God has done for them.

In the future Millennium when Christ will reign on earth, a different administration will be realized. This will be distinct from the Law of Moses as well as from the present age of grace. Christ will rule as an absolute Ruler (Rev. 19:5). At the same time the kingdom will be a supreme revelation of the righteousness of God and His gracious provision for those who put their trust in Christ. Those who obey the King will be rewarded, and those who do not will be punished. The distinctions between Law, grace, and kingdom relate to their time periods of application. But it should be made clear that in each dispensation salvation is by grace and not by Law, and the differences in dispensations are according to the degree of revelation given and the responsibilities demanded of man. Because God is the same God from eternity past to eternity future, every dispensation has its witness to the holiness of God and the necessity of salvation by grace for all the human race.

It is important to understand to whom Scripture is addressed. Some portions are addressed to Jews, some to Christians, and others to the future inhabitants of the millennial kingdom. Because God does not change, many of the moral principles in one are also applicable in the next. Yet the Scriptures detail differences. Under the Law the Jews were required to observe the Sabbath on the seventh day of the week. Christians have the privilege of observing the resurrection of Christ on the first day of the week and are not under the law of the Sabbath. Sabbath-breakers could be stoned to death (Num. 15:32-36). In the present age of grace no such command is given the church regarding disobedience of God's commands. While there are similarities between the different dispensations, the contrasts should also be observed.

3. A DIVINELY APPOINTED SERVICE. A true religion requires service for God. In the case of Judaism, service consisted in the maintenance of the tabernacle and temple rituals and the giving of tithes and offerings to support the priesthood. In Christianity, service is involved in preaching the Gospel to every creature and includes the edification of the saints.

4. A RIGHTEOUS GROUND WHEREON GOD MAY GRACIOUSLY FORGIVE AND CLEANSE THE ERRING. Any religious economy must provide a ground for forgiveness and restoration of those who fail. From a biblical perspective, as all men have a fallen nature, there is no possibility of anyone continuing in right relation to God who is not constantly being renewed and restored by the gracious power of God. In Judaism God forgave sin and renewed His fellowship with Israelites on the ground of His own certainty that a sufficient sacrifice would be made in due time by Christ. In Christianity God is revealed to be propitious concerning "our sins" (1 John 2:2) based on the fact that Christ has already borne the penalty (1 Cor. 15:3). As the believers' High Priest, Christ in heaven also serves as their Advocate Intercessor who represents them when they sin (1 John 2:1).

5. A MEANS FOR SECURING DIVINE FORGIVENESS AND CLEANSING. In general in the Old Testament those seeking forgiveness would present an offering of an animal sacrifice. After the death of Christ, divine forgiveness for the believer is conditioned on confession of sin as an outward expression of inward repentance (1 John 1:9).

In the Old Testament there does not seem to be a revealed provision for Gentile needs of forgiveness and restoration. Apparently God had revealed directly to Adam and his successors that it was necessary to offer sacrifices for sin, but no written instruction was given.

Being a covenant people, Israel was instructed to bring sacrifices as the basis for divine forgiveness and as a way back into those blessings of relationships belonging to their covenants. Offering sacrifices was not a way of salvation nor a ground for entrance into the covenant. Because of their physical birth in the Jewish race, they came under the instructions God gave through Moses for a sacrificial system. Offering sacrifices was a ground for forgiveness and restoration of a covenant people. The parallel in Christianity is the fact that Christ has died and through His death a Christian may be forgiven and cleansed. This is in contrast to the continuous offering of animal sacrifices in the Old Testament.

Salvation in the Old Testament was obtained by faith in God and faith in the fact that God could forgive sins and save those who came to Him. This apparently was true for both Jews and Gentiles in the Old Testament.

6. AN EFFECTIVE BASE ON WHICH GOD MAY BE WORSHIPED AND PETITIONED IN PRAYER. Old Testament saints prayed on the basis of their covenants. Prayers recorded in the Old Testament called on God to observe and do what He promised He would do. In the New Testament the ground of prayer is the death, resurrection, and ascension of Christ, and the descent of the Holy Spirit. Christians are instructed to approach God in the name of Christ (John 14:13-14; 16:23-24). This new approach to God through prayer was instituted by Christ Himself.

7. A FUTURE HOPE. Both Judaism and Christianity have a future hope. Prophecy concerning Israel reaches into eternity and is based on the covenants and promises of God which are everlasting. Christians have a somewhat different eschatology in the more extensive revelation concerning their hope.

a. THE FUTURE OF THIS LIFE. Individual Israelites were promised that they would "live long in the land the LORD your God is giving you" (Ex. 20:12) as a reward for keeping the fifth commandment by honoring their parents. In the New Testament Christians are given the hope of the imminent coming of Christ at the Rapture to take His church from earth to heaven. Christians have no prospect of possessing a land nor promise of earthly things beyond their personal needs. In the period before the second coming of Christ Israel is commanded to watch for His coming (Matt. 24:36-51; 25:13). By contrast Christians are told to "wait for His Son from heaven" (1 Thes. 1:10). Both Jews and Christians who are saved are promised that they will spend eternity in the presence of God. The eternal hope of the Old Testament saints is stated in Hebrews 11:16, "Instead, they were longing for a better country—a heavenly one. Therefore God is not ashamed to be called their God, for He has prepared a city for them." The promise of the city referring to the

New Jerusalem should not be confused with the promise of their millennial kingdom on earth. Jews had hope of restoration to their earthly land as a nation, but beyond this there was the eternal hope of the heavenly city.

b. INTERMEDIATE STATE. In Luke 16:19-31 Christ refers to the hope of Jews who were saved. The rich man was in torment because he was lost whereas Lazarus, the beggar, was seen with Abraham. For Christians at death they "depart" and are "with Christ" (Phil. 1:23; cf. 2 Cor. 5:8).

c. RESURRECTION. The doctrine of resurrection is clearly taught in the Old Testament, as seen in Daniel 12:1-3. According to this Scripture Daniel's people will be resurrected following the Great Tribulation (11:36-45). Some believe the resurrection of the Old Testament saints will occur at the time of the Rapture. However, Daniel 12:1-3 and Isaiah 26:19 seem to place this after the Tribulation period. The faith of Israel in a future resurrection is illustrated by Martha (John 11:24; cf. Heb. 6:1-2).

The doctrine of resurrection for Christians includes two parts: (1) Believers have already been raised and seated with Christ (Eph. 2:6), and so are spiritually raised from the dead (Col. 3:1-3), and (2) should they die, their bodies will be raised at the Rapture when Christ comes for His own (1 Cor. 15:23; 1 Thes. 4:16-17).

d. ETERNAL LIFE. Though Old Testament saints had an acceptable relationship to God, they did not apparently participate in the peculiar blessings Christians inherit in the present day as stated in Colossians 3:1-3. Though Old Testament saints were born again, their status differed from that of Christians in the present age: (1) Israelites were born into covenant relations with God which in itself was a demonstration of abounding grace. (2) In the case of failure to meet the moral and spiritual obligations resting on them because of their covenant position, sacrifice was provided as a righteous basis for their restoration to covenant privileges. (3) It was possible for an individual Israelite to so fail in his conduct in neglect of sacrifices as to be disowned by God and cast out (Gen. 17:14; Deut. 28:58-61; Ezek. 3:18; Matt. 10:32-33; 24:50-51; 25:11-12, 29-30). Though a Jew's salvation did not rest on obedience to the Law, failure to obey the Law would point to the conclusion that he was not saved. (4) The national salvation and forgiveness of Israel is a future expectation and will occur when the Deliverer comes out of Zion, referring to Christ's second coming (Rom. 11:26-27). This salvation, however, is physical deliverance from her enemies rather than spiritual deliverance from the guilt of sin.

At the second coming of Christ there will be both saved and unsaved among Israel. Though all Israel will be saved, that is, delivered from her persecutors by the Second Coming, only the righteous will be allowed to enter the kingdom, and the unbelieving in Israel will be purged out (Ezek. 20:34-38).

Though an individual Jew was under the Law as a rule of life, his salvation as an individual depended on the grace of God. Like a Christian, a Jew who was saved could manifest his salvation by the quality of his life, but keeping the Law did not save him. Eternal life for a Jew is contemplated as an inheritance (Isa. 55:3). At the resurrection of Israel some will be saved and some will be lost (Dan. 12:2), but the resurrection of righteous Israel will occur in connection with the second coming of Christ while the resurrection of the wicked in Israel will not be consummated until the end of the Millennium (Rev. 20:11-15).

Though in several passages Jews are said to inherit eternal life (Luke 10:25-29; 18:18-27; cf. Matt. 18:8-9), this inheritance must be understood as based on their new birth in this life. The New Testament reveals more clearly that Christians receive the gift of eternal life as a present possession (John 3:36; 5:24; 6:54; 20:31; 1 John 5:11-13). Likewise Christians have other confirming evidences that they have eternal life such as the fact that Christ indwells them (Col. 1:27) and that a new nature has been imparted to them (2 Peter 1:4).

e. THE COVENANT OF THE DAVIDIC KINGDOM. God gave David the promise that his throne and his kingdom would endure forever and that David's descendants would sit on the throne (2 Sam. 7:12-16). This will be fulfilled when Christ reigns on earth in His millennial kingdom. Also revealed in Scripture, however, is the fact of a spiritual kingdom in which all saints are citizens. This is called "the kingdom of God." Everyone who is born again belongs to this kingdom (John 3:3, 5; Col. 1:13).

In the Gospel of Matthew another term, "the kingdom of heaven," is used. This term, peculiar to Matthew, is held by many scholars to be identical to the kingdom of God, but certain differences appear in Matthew's Gospel. Though the two kingdoms have many identical aspects in that both contain those who have been born again, the kingdom of heaven seems to refer to a sphere of profession which includes those who profess salvation without reality as well as those who are saved. This is indicated in the Parable of the Wheat among the Weeds (Matt. 13:24-30, 36-43). The weeds appear in the early stages as similar to the wheat and cannot be separated from the wheat until the harvest, just as professing Christians form a part of the professing church but cannot be distinguished from the true church until the time of judgment. In the Parable of the Dragnet (vv. 47-50) a similar situation is contemplated where the kingdom of heaven is conceived as a net which has both good and bad fish in it, and the separation takes place at the end of the age. These parables are never used of the kingdom of God. The Parable of the Mustard Seed likewise indicates the extent of the professing church which includes unsaved people represented by birds perching in the branches.

Prophecy concerning the future of Israel and the church should be distinguished though in some events both are involved. The Old Testament prophesies a glorious future for Israel to be fulfilled in the millennial kingdom. For the Christian the blessed hope is the Rapture of the church. Israel's particular hope is the millennial kingdom. Both Christians and Israel will inhabit the New Jerusalem and the new earth in eternity.

THE CHURCH SPECIFICALLY CONSIDERED

The doctrine of the church considered in ecclesiology is naturally subdivided into three parts: (1) the Pauline revelation of a new order or class of humanity, namely, a redeemed company of both Jews and Gentiles which together with a resurrected Christ form a new creation which is also His body and His bride; (2) the outward or visible church, the assembly of those at any place who gather in the name of Christ; and (3) the walk and service of those who are saved.

The first main division of ecclesiology presents a body of truth of great importance. There can be no understanding of the distinction between the heavenly purpose of God for the church and the earthly purpose for Israel unless the peculiar character of the church in the present age is understood. The tendency in church history is to merge the program of God for the church with that of Israel. This has obscured the distinctions and special blessings which the church enjoys in time and eternity. This is seen in the relationship of the church to the three Persons of the Trinity.

The true church has a special relation to the first Person of the Godhead who is God the Father as indicated in the new birth. Passages such as 1 John speak of Christians as God's children.

Seven figures are used in the New Testament to describe the relationship of the church to Christ as the second Person: the Shepherd and the sheep, the Vine and the branches, the Cornerstone and the stones of the building, the High Priest and the kingdom of priests, the last Adam and the new creation, the Head and the body, and the Bridegroom and the bride. These will be considered at length later.

In relation to the Holy Spirit as the third Person of the Godhead, those in the church are born of the Spirit, indwelt by the Spirit, baptized by the Spirit, and sealed by the Spirit. These truths are distinct from what God has done for Israel in the Old Testament or what He contemplates to do in the future.

In addition to the relationship which the church has to the Triune God, other important relationships are revealed. These include the relationship to the kingdom of God, the kingdom of heaven, the angels, the world, saints of other dispensations, the nation Israel, service, and judgment.

The second division of ecclesiology concerns the outward organized or recognized assembly called the local church. In many theological systems this is considered the main aspect of ecclesiology. The New Testament gives instructions to the visible church and her organization and indicates those who are to exercise authority in the church. The New Testament also speaks of her ordinances, order, spiritual gifts, and ministries. These will be discussed later.

The third division of ecclesiology concerns the daily life and service of those who are saved. This element is often omitted in standard theologies dealing with ecclesiology. In ascertaining by what rule a Christian should live, recognition should be given to the peculiar character of the life of the church in the present age in contrast to the life of Israel in the Old Testament and the life of the saints in the future messianic kingdom. Each of these three major areas of revelation have their distinct characteristics. The present age is characterized as a grace system in contrast to the Mosaic Law which was a legal system. In the New Testament the provision of God for the supernatural life expected of a Christian is seen in the supernatural character of its requirements.

The third division of ecclesiology also includes recognition of the believer's position and possessions in Christ, his associations, life, contacts, deeds, witness, and warfare against the world, the flesh, and the devil. Ecclesiology has suffered in its presentation from neglect of the first and third divisions defined here. At least 24 far-reaching distinctions are to be observed between Israel and the church in contrast to 12 major features common to both. The fact that revelation concerning both Israel and the church includes truth about God, holiness, sin, and redemption by blood does not eliminate the contrasts between Israel and the church.

Generally speaking, Israel was appointed to live and serve under a meritorious, legal system in contrast to the church which serves under a gracious system. The main body of prophecy relating to Israel speaks of her citizenship now and of her future millennial destiny on the earth, followed by the new earth. By contrast Christians are described as citizens of heaven and do not share the earthly promises given to Israel.

The distinction between Israel and the church is seen in the covenants God made with Israel. Those covenants pertain to (1) a national entity (Jer. 31:36), (2) a land in perpetuity (Gen. 13:15), (3) a throne (2 Sam. 7:16; Ps. 89:36), (4) a King (Jer. 33:21), and (5) a kingdom (Dan. 7:14).

The church, composed of both Jews and Gentiles who put their trust in Christ, is a special body of people (Matt. 16:18) who share some things with Israel: (1) they are cosharers in the purpose of His incarnation, (2) the subjects of His ministry, (3) the objects of His death and resurrection, (4) the beneficiaries of His second advent, and (5) related to Him in His kingly reign. Contrasts between Israel and the church are seen in the distinctive revelations given of these two entities.

1. Two purposes. Two independent and wholly different purposes are seen in the Incarnation. As the Messiah and Israel's future King, Christ was born of a virgin and came into this human relationship with kingly rights so that He might fulfill the Davidic Covenant (2 Sam. 7:8-18; Ps. 89:20-37; Jer. 33:21-22, 25-26). The angel announced to the Virgin Mary, "You will be with Child and give birth to a Son, and you are to give Him the name Jesus. He will be great and will be called the Son of the Most High. The Lord God will give Him the throne of His father David, and He will reign over the

house of Jacob forever; His kingdom will never end" (Luke 1:31-33). As the rightful Heir through His human lineage, Christ will be the occupant of David's earthly throne and reign over the house of Jacob forever (Isa. 9:6-7; Luke 1:33). On the mediatorial and redemptive side through the Incarnation, Christ provided all the inexhaustible blessings through His redemption in dying on the cross for man's sins. Christ, in His life, death, and resurrection, accomplished the purposes relating to Israel as well as to the church.

2. Two lines of truth. Christ revealed two distinct lines of truth. In relation to Israel, Christ presented Himself as Israel's Messiah and called on the nation for repentance. He affirmed His distinctive purpose in the Incarnation when He said, "I was sent only to the lost sheep of Israel" (Matt. 15:24). In a similar way He sent His disciples to preach to Israel (10:5-6). When Israel's rejection became apparent, Christ began to speak of His departure and second advent and announced the previously unrevealed age which would intervene between the first and second comings of Christ. The disciples were no longer restricted to Israel alone but were commissioned to declare the Good News to every creature. His farewell message to Israel (Matt. 23:37–25:46) may be contrasted to His message concerning the future church (John 13–17).

3. Different objectives. In His death and resurrection the same wide and different objectives are discernible. To Israel Christ was a stumbling block (1 Cor. 1:23). Yet in His death He made possible the grace of God and the forgiveness of sins. Though the resurrection of Christ was anticipated by David (Ps. 16:10; Acts 2:25-31), His resurrection formed the great theological basis for the new creation in which the believer is in the resurrected Christ and the resurrected Christ is in the believer.

The unity between Christians and Christ is likened to the unity of the Persons of the Godhead (John 17:21-23). By the baptism of the Spirit, Christians are joined to the body of Christ and to Christ Himself (1 Cor. 6:17; 12:13; Gal. 3:27). Christians in union with the resurrected Christ are made partakers of His resurrection life (Col. 1:27) and are translated out of the power of darkness into the kingdom of the Son of His love (v. 13). In a Christian's unity with Christ he is crucified, dead, and buried with Christ and is now raised to walk in newness of life (Rom. 6:2-4; Col. 3:1). A Christian is now seated positionally with Christ in heaven (Eph. 2:6), is a citizen of heaven (Phil. 3:20), is forgiven all his sins (Col. 2:13), is justified

(Rom. 5:1), and is blessed with every spiritual blessing (Eph. 1:3). These tremendous truths which relate to Christians in the present age are a great advance over what Israel experienced spiritually in the Old Testament.

4. Rapture. The great events predicted for the close of the present age include the Rapture, when the church will be taken to be forever with the Lord (1 Cor. 15:35-53; 1 Thes. 4:13-17) and the Day of *Yahweh,* beginning at the Rapture and extending to the end of the Millennium which includes the regathering, judging, and restoration of Israel in fulfillment of her earthly covenants (Deut. 30:3-5; 2 Sam. 7:16; Ps. 89:34-37; Jer. 23:5-6; 31:35-37; 33:25-26).

5. Israel and the church. A distinction is made between Israel and the church in the coming kingdom. In the Millennium Israel and the church will be distinct entities with Israel occupying her ancient land and being the subjects of Christ's kingdom. But the church is said to coreign with Christ (Rev. 20:6).

Two revelations were given the Apostle Paul: (1) salvation for those who would put their faith in Christ, whether Jews or Gentiles, as provided in His death and resurrection (Gal. 1:11-12). The exercise of grace in the present age far surpasses anything experienced in the Old Testament (1 Peter 1:10-11). (2) The new divine purpose in the outcalling of the church (Eph. 3:6) is another New Testament revelation given to Paul. This new purpose is not merely that Gentiles are to be blessed, for the Old Testament predicted Gentile blessing, but that believing Jews and Gentiles are one in the church with no barrier between them (Gal. 3:28; Col. 3:11). The Apostle Paul distinguished between the Jews, the Gentiles, and the church of God (1 Cor. 10:32) as the three main elements of the divisions of humanity. The "Jews" and "Gentiles" refer to unbelievers in those racial groups today, and "the church of God" consists of all believers in the present Church Age, whether Jew or Gentile.

In the doctrine of the church it should also be evident that Judaism did not merge into Christianity. The church is an entirely new undertaking though both Jews and Gentiles are enjoying grace in the present age (Rom. 3:9; 10:12). Nicodemus, who was a religious Jew, was told by Christ that he must be born again (John 3:3, 5), and Paul prayed that the Israelites who had a zeal for God might be saved (Rom. 10:1-3).

Those who attempt to put the church and Israel together need to contemplate many important questions: Why the rent veil? Why

Pentecost? Why the distinctive message of the Epistles? Why the "better" things of the Book of Hebrews? Why the Jewish branches broken off and Gentile branches grafted in Romans 11:13-24? Why the present visitation of the Gentiles? Why the present indwelling by the Spirit of all who believe? Why the baptism of the Spirit, a unique work in the New Testament? Why two companies of the redeemed in the New Jerusalem? Why are earthly blessings given to Israel and heavenly blessings promised the church? Why the dramatic change from Law to grace? Why is Israel, though repudiated now, to be a restored wife of *Yahweh* whereas the church is the bride of Christ? Why the mysteries of the New Testament? Why the new creation? How could there be a church until the death of Christ, the resurrection of Christ, and the ascension of Christ, and the Day of Pentecost? How could the church, in which there is neither Jew nor Gentile, be any part of Israel in this or any other age?

Failure to understand the distinctive purpose of the church has been a serious fault of many studies in ecclesiology. As approached here, ecclesiology is considered in three divisions: (1) the church as an organism, (2) the organized church, and (3) the believer's rule of life.

THE CHURCH AS AN ORGANISM

CHAPTER • 22

GENERAL FEATURES OF THE DOCTRINE CONCERNING THE CHURCH

The first major division of ecclesiology has in view the church universal, that is, all the saved whether in heaven or in earth who belong to the church formed on the Day of Pentecost. Though in one sense an assembly, they are not geographically gathered in one place but are united by a supernatural relationship in the body of Christ and are an organism because they are in Christ.

Though the Protestant Reformation recovered many important truths such as the priesthood of the believer, justification by faith, and the truth that every individual is his own interpreter of the Bible assisted by the Holy Spirit, the great truths respecting the distinctive character of the church in the present age as taught in the early church were not fully discovered. Though theology recognizes the Pauline revelation of the church, the tendency is to merge what relates to the church and what relates to Israel. However, a careful study of the New Testament reveals that they are to a large degree independent and separable.

In the struggles of J.N. Darby to find his way in traditional theology, he came to understand that much light is thrown on God's present purpose if His purpose for Israel and the purpose of the church are distinguished. Though Darby has suffered caricature on the part of those who do not accept his teaching, he actually made a tremendous contribution, and the Brethren movement with which he was associated did much to turn individuals in the church back to a careful study of the Scriptures. Though Darby preferred to be known as an evangelist rather than as a theologian, his teachings have had a profound effect on evangelicalism to the present day.

In contemplating the church as the body of Christ in this division of ecclesiology a threefold approach will be observed: (1) general features of the doctrine concerning the church, (2) contrasts between Israel and the church, and (3) seven figures used of the church in relationship to Christ.

THE MEANING OF THE WORD "CHURCH"

The word "church" is a common word in the Greek language and was used originally for a political gathering constituting the government of a particular area. In the Old Testament the same word in the sense of "an assembly" was used to characterize Israel when she was assembled in one geographic location (Acts 7:38). In the New Testament, though the word was used occasionally for a geographic assembly as in a local church, sometimes it included the entire church (e.g., 9:31) whether in heaven or in earth (1 Cor. 10:32; Eph. 1:22; 5:23-25, 27, 29; Col. 1:18; Heb. 12:23). The concept of a church as a religious body without geographic location was a new use of the word in the New Testament and must be defined by the context.

In the Old Testament Greek translation (LXX), *ekklesia* is a translation of several Hebrew words, but in each case it refers to a geographic assembly of people and is never used in the theological sense of the body of Christ.

In the New Testament the church including all regenerated persons from Pentecost to the Rapture (1 Cor. 15:52) was united together and united to Christ by the baptism of the Spirit (12:12-13). Christ is the Head of the body (Eph. 1:22-23). The church is a holy temple for the habitation of God (2:21-22), and is one with Christ (5:30-32). The church is described as a chaste virgin waiting her husband (2 Cor. 11:2-4).

THE FACT OF A NEW DIVINE UNDERTAKING

The fact of a new divine undertaking in which Jews and Gentiles would share alike the spiritual blessings of salvation was a thought abhorrent to Jews steeped in their theology and traditions. Paul himself was an outstanding illustration of this before his salvation, and his conversion required a special revelation of Christ. Once Paul understood the new divine undertaking, however, he made the statement, "For there is no difference between Jew and Gentile—the same Lord is Lord of all and richly blesses all who call on Him" (Rom. 10:12; cf. 3:9).

The change from Jewish tradition to the new Christian revelation required the first church council to take up the question of whether Gentiles in the church had to follow Jewish religious laws (Acts 15:1). As recorded in verses 16-18, James affirmed that God had not forsaken His purpose to restore Israel but that in the present age Jews and Gentiles would be united in the church and this purpose would be consummated before Israel's restoration. "When they finished James spoke up: 'Brothers, listen to me. Simon has described to us how God at first showed His concern by taking from the Gentiles a people for Himself. The words of the prophets are in agreement with this, as it is written: "After this I will return and rebuild David's fallen tent. Its ruins I will rebuild, and I will restore it, that the remnant of men may seek the Lord, and all the Gentiles who bear My name, says the Lord, who does these things" that have been known for ages' " (Acts 15:13-18; cf. Amos 9:11-12). It is important to observe the time sequence in Acts 15:13-18. God was "first" taking Gentiles as a people to Himself in the present age and "after this" will restore Israel. This is the order of prophetic Scripture which makes the church the present purpose of God and the restoration of Israel an event which follows this Church Age and has its primary fulfillment in the millennial kingdom.

Based on this truth the decision was made that Gentiles were not required to observe the laws relating particularly to Israel in the Old Testament, but at the same time they were to avoid undue aggravation of Jews (vv. 19-21). The new divine undertaking was to include both Jews and Gentiles with their racial differences ignored (Eph. 2:14). Though it took time for some of the apostles to understand this, the council at Jerusalem recorded Peter's statement, "Brothers, you know that some time ago God made a choice among you that the Gentiles might hear from my lips the message of the Gospel and believe. God, who knows the heart, showed that He accepted them by giving the Holy Spirit to them, just as He did to us. He made no distinction between us and them, for He purified their hearts by faith. Now then, why do you try to test God by putting on the necks of the disciples a yoke that neither we nor our fathers have been able to bear? No! We believe it is through the grace of our Lord Jesus that we are saved, just as they are" (Acts 15:7-11).

This shows that God's purpose for the church was not His purpose for Israel and is a distinct purpose which is being fulfilled in the present age. For the present, the program of God for Israel as revealed in the Old Testament is suspended until after the Rapture of the church. Though the distinction between Israel and the church is made in the New Testament, throughout Scripture there are also some similarities, including salvation and the grace of God. The present age, however, was not foreseen by the prophets of the Old Testament (1 Peter 1:10-11).

VARIOUS TERMS EMPLOYED

Though the word "church" is often used as a technical term to apply to the saints of the present age, other terms likewise are used such as Christians, saints, believers, the elect, the body of Christ, brethren, witnesses, ambassadors, strangers, pilgrims, children of God.

Among the other designations applied to the true church, the declaration that she is a new creation is of high import (2 Cor. 5:17). The new creation incorporates Christ along with believers into one identity. In this respect the term "church" is somewhat different in that the church as a body may be contemplated apart from its Head just as the church may be contemplated as separate from though closely identified with Christ.

THE FIRST USE OF THE WORD "CHURCH"

In the New Testament the first use of the word "church" as the *ekklesia* is in Matthew 16:18 where Christ said, "And I tell you that you are Peter, and on this rock I will build My church, and the gates of hades will not overcome it." In referring to Peter as a rock (in keeping with the name "Peter," meaning a small rock) Christ used a play on words to declare that the church would be built on a rock, referring to Himself. Though there has been considerable discussion as to what this means, many hold that in making the statement Christ pointed to Himself as the Rock on which the church would build. This is in keeping with references to Christ as the foundation (1 Cor. 3:11) and Peter's description of the church as living stones built up on Christ (1 Peter 2:4-8).

Each of the five words, "I will build My church" has great doctrinal significance, and the phrase could be quoted each time emphasizing a different word.

In referring to Himself as "I," Christ stated that the building of the church is something He undertakes. It is Christ who is calling out, saving, and perfecting this specific company. The word "will" shows a prophetic aspect to Jesus' statement, and implies that the church was not in existence at that time and was not the work of Christ while He was on earth but would be realized in the future. This contradicts the thought that the church existed throughout the Old Testament. The word "build" suggests that this is a slow process continuing throughout the present age (Eph. 2:20; Heb. 3:6). Though God will use human instruments to proclaim the Gospel, the calling of the church to salvation and the forming of the church into the body of Christ is a work of God not of man. The expression "My church" points to the distinction between God's work for Israel and His work for the Gentile world. Though God loved Israel (Jer. 31:3), it does not complicate the fact that God also loved the church to an infinite degree (John 13:1; Eph. 5:25). This introductory word of Christ amplified in the Upper Room Discourse (John 13–17) points to the conclusion that the church was a future undertaking to be fulfilled in the present age.

THE CHURCH AS THE PRESENT DIVINE PURPOSE

When the Old Testament closed, no fulfillment of prophecies concerning the coming Messiah and King had yet taken place. The Incarnation had not been accomplished. Christ had not been crucified and resurrected, and the necessary preliminaries for establishing the church had not been accomplished. After Christ offered Himself as the Messiah to Israel as recorded in the early chapters of Matthew, the main body of the Jewish people rejected Christ (12:24). Christ then stated in seven parables the characteristics of the present age (Matt. 13). This revelation was necessary because the Old Testament did not present the truth of the period between the first and second comings of Christ.

In the parables of Matthew 13, dealing with the whole period between the first and second comings of Christ, three major features are presented: (1) that which is acceptable—the wheat (those saved), the pearl (the church), and the good fish (the saved); (2) that which represents blinded Israel, the "treasure hidden in a field" (v. 44); and (3) the presence of evil—the weeds, birds in the branches, leaven, and bad fish.

The truth as presented emphasizes the fact that the church is a mystery or a sacred secret hidden in the Old Testament and revealed in the New Testament in which the saved composed of both Jews and Gentiles are one body (Eph. 3:4-6). In this period Israel is blinded and will not have her eyes opened until the church is called out (Rom. 11:25; cf. Acts 15:13-18). The presence and character of evil throughout the age (2 Thes. 2:7) is indicated in the presence of the weeds, birds, leaven, and bad fish which will be judged by Christ at His second coming. At the Rapture the Holy Spirit indwelling the church will be taken away in the sense that He came at Pentecost though He will still be omnipresent and working in the world (John 14:17). This chapter demonstrates that God's purpose to fulfill His promises to Israel is not in the process of fulfillment until the church is taken out, though the promise of Israel's preservation is being honored (Jer. 31:35-37).

Though Matthew 13 deals with the entire interadvent age from Christ's incarnation to His second coming, most of this period is occupied by the church and God's fulfillment of His purposes for the church.

FOUR REASONS WHY THE CHURCH BEGAN AT PENTECOST

Though many theologians do not recognize the distinctive use of *ekklesia* for the body of Christ in the present age, good reasons are advanced in Scripture to indicate that the church began at Pentecost.

1. Christ's death. There could be no church in the world constituted as she is and distinctive in all her features until Christ's death (Acts 20:28; Rom. 3:24-26; Col. 1:13-14). The death of Christ is more than a mere anticipation, but the church, the body of Christ, is based wholly on His finished work, and she must be purified by His precious blood.

2. Christ's resurrection. There could be no church until Christ rose from the dead to provide her with a resurrection life

(Rom. 4:24; Col. 3:1-3). This is a new feature that had not been introduced before.

3. Christ's ascension. There could be no church until Christ ascended on high to become the Head of the church (Eph. 1:19-23; Heb. 7:25; 1 John 2:1). The church is a new creation with a new Head in the resurrected Christ. As such, He is also the Head of the body of Christ which is the church. The church in the present age could not survive if it were not for Christ's intercession and advocacy in heaven.

4. Holy Spirit's advent. There could be no church on earth until the advent of the Holy Spirit (Acts 1:5; 1 Cor. 12:13; Eph. 4:30). The coming of the Holy Spirit on the Day of Pentecost to indwell and seal the church made the church a temple or habitation of God. Saints had been regenerated before Pentecost but only at Pentecost was the church baptized by the Spirit into one body. Inasmuch as these important works essential to the character of the church did not occur before Pentecost, the church could not begin until that date. A church without the finished work on which to stand, a church without resurrection position or life, a church which is a new humanity but lacking a Head, a church without Pentecost or what Pentecost contributed is only a figment of theological fancy and is not the teaching of the New Testament.

THE CHURCH IN TYPE AND PROPHECY

Though the church was not in the Old Testament as a contemporary work of God and did not have a predicted future, in the Old Testament the church was anticipated in many types. Many of the sacrifices of the old order were foreshadowings of Christ's death. The same is true of the biblical offerings in which at least four of the seven feasts of *Yahweh* converge on the church. Some of the brides of the Old Testament are types of the church as a bride. Though the church appears in typology in the Old Testament, there were no specific prophecies concerning her until the New Testament revelation.

CHAPTER • 23

CONTRASTS BETWEEN ISRAEL AND THE CHURCH

Twenty-four contrasts between Israel and the church are presented here in outline. This presentation will be followed by a study of the important similarities as well.

THE EXTENT OF BIBLICAL REVELATION

Israel occupies nearly four fifths of the texts of the Bible, and the church in regard to primary application occupies slightly more than one fifth.

DIVINE PURPOSE

As previously mentioned, there are at least two major divine purposes, one for Israel and one for the church. These are distinct from God's purpose for the angels or for the Gentile world. God's purpose for Israel is related to her covenants, promises, and the provision for fulfillment in the earth. By contrast promises for the church relate to heavenly realities and her heavenly citizenship.

SEED OF ABRAHAM

Abraham was the progenitor of Israel as the nation of promise, and he is also the pattern of the Christian under grace. The promises of God to Abraham included personal promises and the promise that he would be progenitor of the nation Israel. In addition God promised that "all peoples on earth will be blessed through you" (Gen. 12:3). Taking the Abrahamic Covenant as a whole, it will be observed that there are three divisions of fulfillment: (1) the promises to all who descend from Abraham but especially promises to Israel as a race; (2) the promises to those in Israel who like Abraham exercise faith and will be declared righteous before God; (3) the promise to those who are the spiritual children of Abraham though not racially connected, but who like Abraham put their faith in God and fulfill the pledge of blessing to the entire world.

Only the descendants of Jacob will receive the fulfillment of the promise to be gathered in the Promised Land in the millennial kingdom. In addition to those who are racially and spiritually related to Abraham are those in the present age who are Gentiles but are called "children of Abraham" (Gal. 3:7) and are said to fulfill the promise to Abraham that, "All nations will be blessed through you" (v. 8; cf. Gen. 12:3). Though the church is here referred to as children of Abraham, it should be noted that the portion of the Abrahamic Covenant which they fulfill relates to the promise given to all Gentiles, not to Israel. Of great significance is the fact that the church is never called the seed of Jacob. The fact that the church is called the seed of Abraham should not lead to the confusion of Israel and the church. Some Israelites in the present age are not saved, as stated in Romans 9:6, and they are in contrast to "the Israel of God" (Gal. 6:16), which refers to Israelites in the present age who are saved.

BIRTH

An individual became an Israelite by being born to Israelite parents. By contrast Christians become what they are by spiritual birth and so are called the children of God who have an inheritance in Christ.

HEADSHIP

Abraham is the head of the Jewish race though not all the children of Abraham belong to Israel. Only the descendants of Jacob are properly considered Israelites. The descendants of Ishmael, Isaac's brother, and of Esau, Jacob's brother, and of other children born to Abraham after Sarah's death are not Israelites. Though individual

Gentiles in the church are called "Abraham's seed" (Gal. 3:29), and in a special sense God is their Father, they are also joined to Christ their resurrected Lord and new federal Head by the Holy Spirit.

COVENANTS

Israel enjoyed a special covenant relationship with God as revealed in the provisions of the Abrahamic Covenant, the Mosaic Covenant, the Davidic Covenant, and the New Covenant. The Abrahamic Covenant made special provisions for the descendants of Abraham and the nation Israel though it also included provision for Gentiles. The Mosaic Covenant related only to Israel. The Davidic Covenant was prophetic in that it promised that a descendant of David would sit on the throne of David forever, a prediction to be fulfilled in Christ's future kingdom. Israel also was included in the New Covenant, which will be fulfilled in the millennial kingdom and in eternity to come. All these covenants were unconditional except the Mosaic Covenant which is known as an ad interim covenant. It began with Moses and ended with Christ.

The other covenants given to Israel are unconditional in the sense that their fulfillment is absolutely certain even though human failure was involved. They are essentially gracious in their provisions. The church shares in the provisions of the Abrahamic and the New Covenants but not in the Mosaic and Davidic Covenants.

NATIONALITY

Israel belongs to the earth and to the world system; it is still in the world as one of the nations. In contrast the church is composed of individuals in all nations including Israel. The church has no biblical citizenship here, for believers are viewed as strangers and pilgrims.

DIVINE DEALING

In the Old Testament God dealt with the nations and Israel. The church is dealt with primarily as individuals without consideration of their political or racial background.

DISPENSATIONS

Of the various dispensations, Israel partakes of the Abrahamic, Mosaic, and millennial dispensations in a special way. The church has a partial relationship to the Abrahamic Covenant because it is included in the promised blessing to all nations. But the church has no relationship to the Mosaic Covenant. The dispensation of grace in the present age is the church's special economy or stewardship. And yet the church will share in the Millennium with the saved of Israel, for the church will reign with Christ, like Israel, and will enjoy the new heavens, the new earth, and the New Jerusalem. The distinction between Israel and the church, however, is maintained throughout the entire program of God.

MINISTRY

Israel was given no commission to send missionaries to the world or to proclaim a Gospel. Israelites had a relationship between themselves and God. By contrast the church was constituted a "foreign missionary society" from the time it was formed and was challenged to send the Gospel to the entire world.

THE DEATH OF CHRIST

The religious leaders of Israel demanded the death of Christ. Yet provision is made for their salvation on the basis of the sacrifice of Christ. The church on the other hand has a present and perfect salvation through the offering of Christ on the cross.

THE FATHER

God was known to Israel through His several titles, but individual Israelites did not view God as their Father. The Old Testament does reveal that God was Father to Israel in the sense of intimate relationship. Moses was instructed to perform miraculous wonders in his appearances before Pharaoh, "Then say to Pharaoh, 'This is what the LORD says: Israel is My firstborn son, and I told you, "Let My son go, so he may worship Me." But you refused to let him go; so I will kill your firstborn son' " (Ex. 4:22-23). In the Davidic Covenant God said concerning David, "I will be his Father, and he will be My son" (2 Sam. 7:14). God is compared to a father having compassion on his children (Ps. 103:13). In the case of Christians, however, God is especially their Father in the sense of having communicated His life to them in the new birth. Israelites were also born again in the Old Testament, but this truth was not clearly revealed or applied.

CHRIST

To Israelites Christ is Messiah, Emmanuel, and King with all that is implied in these titles. To the church Christ is Saviour, Lord, Bridegroom, and Head, which titles indicate a different relationship.

THE HOLY SPIRIT

The saints of the Old Testament were regenerated by the Holy Spirit. Apart from regeneration it would be difficult to explain the holy life of some of them. The indwelling of the Holy Spirit was rare and only sovereignly given for special purposes. There is no indication that the Holy Spirit sealed or baptized those who were saved. Also the filling of the Spirit, though sometimes experienced, does not compare to the filling of the Spirit available to Christians. In the present age believers are indwelt, sealed, and baptized, as well as regenerated, which gives them assurance of eternal salvation.

A GOVERNING PRINCIPLE

For 15 centuries the Law of Moses was Israel's rule of daily life. To experience God's love Israel needed to obey Him. "But from everlasting to everlasting the LORD's love is with those who fear Him, and His righteousness with their children's children—with those who keep His covenant and remember to obey His precepts" (Ps. 103:17-

18). Though Israel's blessings were conditional under the Mosaic Covenant, members of Christ's body, the church, are perfected in Christ, have already received many tokens of the grace of God, and are exhorted to serve on the basis of His grace.

DIVINE ENABLEMENT

The Law system provided no enabling power for its achievement. As individual saints who were not indwelt by the Spirit, they failed to obey the Law because of "the flesh" or the sin nature (Rom. 8:3). The church has also been given supernatural power, and it is possible for Christians not to fulfill the desires of the sin nature as they are under grace not under the Law (Rom. 6:14; 8:5-9).

TWO FAREWELL ADDRESSES

In the Olivet Discourse recorded in Matthew 23:37–25:46, Christ gave His farewell message to the nation Israel. In contrast to this, in John 13–17 Christ gave His parting message to the church as represented by the apostles.

THE PROMISE OF CHRIST'S RETURN

In keeping with promises to Israel in the Old and New Testaments, Christ promised to deliver Israel at His second coming. At that time Israel will be regathered to her own land (Deut. 30:1-8; Jer. 23:7-8; Matt. 24:31). However, Christ's promise to the church is in relation to the Rapture when He will come to take the church from earth to heaven (John 14:1-3; 1 Cor. 15:51-58; 1 Thes. 4:13-18). This promise of Christ for His church stands in sharp contrast to His second coming to rule over the earth and deliver Israel.

POSITION

Israel was in the position of being a servant (Isa. 41:8). By contrast believers in Christ in the church are called "friends" (John 15:15).

CHRIST'S EARTHLY REIGN

Though Israel will be prominent as the head of the nations in the millennial reign, the church will reign with Christ in the kingdom (2 Tim. 2:12). Though martyred Tribulation saints will also reign with Christ (Rev. 20:4), the church will have an exalted position as the wife and consort of Christ.

PRIESTHOOD

The nation Israel had a priesthood consisting of Aaron and his descendants. The church is a priesthood over which Christ is the High Priest (Heb. 5:4-6; 1 Peter 2:9).

MARRIAGE

The nation Israel is called the wife of *Yahweh*—a wife untrue and yet to be restored (Isa. 54:1-17; Jer. 3:1, 14, 20; Ezek. 16:1-59; Hosea 2:1-23; cf. Gal. 4:27). In contrast to this the church is considered now a virgin waiting for the coming of the Bridegroom and will be joined to Christ at the time of the Rapture (2 Cor. 11:2; Rev. 19:7-9).

JUDGMENTS

Israel is yet to be judged as a nation and as individuals (Ezek. 20:33-44; Matt. 25:1-13). On the other hand Christians will not come into judgment except at the Judgment Seat of Christ for their works (John 5:24; Rom. 8:1; 2 Cor. 5:10).

POSITION IN ETERNITY

In Hebrews 12:22-23 Old Testament saints including Israelites are referred to as "the spirits of righteous men made perfect" while the church is referred to as "the firstborn." Both will be in the New Jerusalem but their individual and corporate identity will be maintained.

In examining the contrasts between Israel and the church it is obvious there are similarities between them because they both are elect people. Each has his own peculiar relationship to God, to righteousness, to sin, to redemption, to salvation, to human responsibility, and to destiny. They are each witnesses to the Word of God; each may claim the same Shepherd; they have doctrines in common; the death of Christ is effective in its own way for each; they are alike loved with an everlasting love; and each will be glorified.

CHAPTER • 24

SEVEN FIGURES USED OF THE CHURCH IN HER RELATION TO CHRIST (I-V)

Though almost completely neglected in most theological works, the seven figures used of Christ's relationship to the church are the central revelation concerning God's purpose and plan for the church. Their importance justifies a careful study of each figure.

In addition to this grouping of seven figures depicting Christ in relation to the church are two other groups of seven, namely, the seven parables in Matthew 13 and the seven letters to the seven churches in Asia (Rev. 2–3). Brief consideration of these will be undertaken before examining the seven figures.

In the seven parables of Matthew 13 distinctive revelation is given of God's purpose in the present age, a subject not revealed in the Old Testament. In considering the mysteries of the kingdom of heaven it should be observed that they include the entire period from the first advent of Christ to His second advent. A major portion of this period chronologically is occupied by the church, the body of Christ. In verses 3-23 Christ characterized the present age to a harvest in which the farmer sows his seed. Four kinds of reception are given the seed, some falling on the hard, beaten path, some falling on rocky places or where there was little soil, some which fell on good ground but was choked by thorns, and still others that fell on good soil and brought forth good fruit. This illustrates the different receptions people give to the Gospel, as seen in the history of the church.

In the Parable of the Weeds among the Wheat (vv. 24-30, 36-43) Christ pictured the sphere of profession with the wheat and the weeds looking much alike in their early stages and inseparable until the time of judgment. This emphasizes the professing character of the kingdom of heaven or the professing church in the present age.

The Parable of the Mustard Seed (vv. 31-32) likens the kingdom of heaven to a rapidly growing tree coming from a very small seed and growing into a tree large enough for birds to lodge in the branches. The kingdom of heaven as a sphere of profession and the church as a sphere of profession have grown rapidly in the present age even though some like birds lodging in the branches have no real part in it.

The Parable of the Yeast or Leaven (v. 33) likens the Gospel to yeast fermenting in dough. Though some Bible teachers say yeast or leaven pictures the Gospel permeating the kingdom, ordinarily use of leaven or yeast in the Bible refers to evil. Israelites were forbidden to use leavened bread for certain sacrifices because the sacrifices were to be pure. Though it is true that the Gospel has permeated the professing church to some extent, it is also true that evil has permeated the church and has tended to puff it up and make it appear greater than it really is.

In the Parable of the Hidden Treasure (v. 44) some say that the treasure represents Christ and the man who found it represents individuals who put their trust in Christ. However, in salvation a person has nothing by which to purchase salvation, and in any case salvation is not secured by selling all a person has. A better interpretation is that the treasure represents Israel, which like a hidden treasure is often not acknowledged as a significant nation though it is a recognized entity in the world. Christ sold all He had in dying for Israel on the cross.

In the next parable, the Pearl of Great Value, though also sometimes identified as Christ, is better interpreted as the church for which Christ sold everything in dying for it on the cross. A pearl, coming from a wound in the oyster, speaks of the church as being related to Christ because of His wounds in His death on the cross.

The final Parable of the Dragnet pictures the kingdom of heaven as a net catching both good and bad fish which are not separated until the time of harvest. This is of course true of the sphere of profession which will have its final judgment at the second coming of Christ. It is also true of the church gathered at the Rapture which will be separated from those who are merely professing faith.

The kingdom in the present age incorporates both true believers and those merely professing faith. The King is absent and unseen but will return at the time of the Second Coming to establish His kingdom with power and great glory. Equating the present age to the millennial kingdom, as is commonly done in some forms of theology, ignores the dramatic difference between the present age in which the King is absent and the church is being formed and the millennial kingdom when Christ will reign on earth in visible power and glory and put down wickedness by immediate judgment. The end of the present age between the first and second comings of Christ is described in verses 49-50, "This is how it will be at the end of the age. The angels will come and separate the wicked from the righteous and throw them into the fiery furnace, where there will be weeping and gnashing of teeth."

In another group of seven are the seven letters to the churches of Asia recorded in Revelation 2–3. Each of these messages is important as a message from Christ to His church. It is deplorable that so little attention has been paid to these seven letters in contrast to the much greater attention given to other letters in the New Testament. Though addressed to seven churches actually located in Asia Minor, like the Epistles of Paul addressed to churches their message goes beyond their immediate destination to the church in the present age. The messages are delivered not only to the particular churches but to individuals who will hear and to any church existing today that corresponds to one of the churches. Together they form a picture of the professing church in its strengths and weaknesses.

The message to the church at Ephesus is a message to second-generation Christians who are exhorted not to forsake their love for Christ (2:4). The church at Smyrna under great persecution is exhorted to be faithful even to death (v. 10). To the church in Pergamum, infiltrated by worldliness and characterized by departure from God, the exhortation is to repent or experience the judgment of God (vv. 14-16). The church at Thyatira is pictured as deep in spiritual immorality and apostasy. They are promised judgment from God, and those true to the faith in the church are exhorted to be steadfast until Christ comes (vv. 20-26). The people in the spiritually dead church in Sardis are urged to repent or be judged by God (3:1-3). The church at Philadelphia for the most part kept the faith and served the Lord, and they are promised deliverance from the trial that will overtake the world after the Rapture. They are exhorted to hold fast until the Lord comes (vv. 10-11). The church at Laodicea, characterized as "neither cold nor hot," is declared to be rejected by Christ (vv. 15-16). In these churches some are found faithful and a promise of blessing is given to them. The final invitation in verses 19-21 is the invitation to welcome Christ and enter into fellowship with Him.

Of central importance are the seven figures of Christ in relationship to the church.

THE SHEPHERD AND THE SHEEP

The term "sheep" is often applied in the Bible to people. It pictures the utter helplessness of individuals to find their own way. The term is applied to Israel as well as the Gentiles who are judged at the second coming of Christ (Matt. 25:34). In general it relates to any people who are favored of God.

In the Old Testament, Christ was truly the Shepherd of Israel (Pss. 23:1; 74:1; 79:13; 95:7; 100:3; Jer. 23:1). In the discourse of Christ in John 10 under the figure of the Shepherd and the sheep, Christ is pictured first in His relationship to Israel and then in His relationship to the church. As Israel was to find salvation in Christ, so believers in the present age who are not of the same flock as Israel will form one flock with Israel in the present age. The "other sheep" mentioned in verse 16 are not Israel, the flock of sheep in the pen, but are present-age Gentile believers in Christ.

The figure of Christ as Shepherd and the church as the flock is part of the divine revelation concerning the nature of the church. The church had to come by Christ, the Gate, in the appointed way (v. 1). Christ is the true Shepherd who goes before His sheep, and they know His voice and follow Him (vv. 3-4). Christ Himself is the Door of the sheep, that is, through Him they go in and out and are protected from the dangers without (vv. 7-9, 28-29). The sheep receive salvation without merit on their part, and food for the new life is provided by the Shepherd. By comparison all other shepherds are hirelings at best and none have given nor could give their life for the sheep as the Good Shepherd has done (vv. 8, 10-14). Within the family of God there is a communion of understanding as the sheep know the Shepherd, as the Father knows the Son, and as the Son knows the Father (v. 15). Though the passage begins with Israel as the flock, the passage ends with Israel and the "other sheep" (v. 16) who will form one flock composed of both Jews and Gentiles in the present age.

Through Christ as their Shepherd believers receive life, liberty, and sustenance. The work of the Shepherd as Saviour is efficacious because He has laid down His life for His sheep, which makes possible a complete and eternal relationship established between the Shepherd and the sheep.

The doctrine of the shepherdhood of Christ introduced here is continued in His ceaseless intercession and advocacy at the right hand of the Father on behalf of His own (Heb. 7:25). Because of this, Christians can say with David, "The Lord is my Shepherd, I shall lack nothing" (Ps. 23:1).

THE VINE AND THE BRANCHES

The figure of the vine and the branches in John 15 is addressed to believers in the present age. As part of the Upper Room Discourse (John 13–17), the passage looks beyond the death, resurrection, and ascension of Christ, and beyond Pentecost. It is a revelation of the relationship of Christ to His church in the present age. In the Old Testament Israel was the vineyard of God (Isa. 5:1-7; Jer. 2:21; Hosea 10:1; Luke 20:9-16). When Christ introduced Himself as the "true Vine" (John 15:1), He was presenting Himself in contrast to the vine of Israel, which was fruitless. As the true Vine, He will be fruitful through the branches that draw their life from Him. This figure illustrates the truth of communion with Christ. This assumes union with Christ as indicated by the expression "every branch in Me" (v. 2). The union of a believer with Christ is never a human responsibility or accomplishment but is what God does in response to faith through His grace. The question of fruitfulness, not the question of salvation, is being discussed here. The figure presents Christ as pruning the vine, eliminating branches that bear no fruit in order to enhance the fruitfulness of the other branches. The disciples are said to be already pruned or "clean" (v. 3). The exhortation in this figure is to "remain in Me" or "abide in Me" in keeping with the promise of Christ that He will remain in the believer (v. 4). The point is that branches cannot bear fruit by themselves but must derive their life and fruitfulness from the vine (v. 4). Remaining in Christ or drawing fruit from Christ makes it possible for a believer to "bear much fruit" (v. 5). In verse 6 Christ changed the application to "anyone" who does not bear fruit. Christ did not say that the disciples were in danger of this judgment. In keeping with abiding or remaining in Christ they were urged to pray and were promised answers to prayer (v. 7).

The results of abiding or remaining in Christ include "pruning" (v. 2), effectual prayer (v. 7), heavenly joy (v. 11), and perpetual fruit (v. 16). Fruit is pictured here as the product of the vine working through the branches, a truth in harmony with the fruit of the Spirit (Gal. 5:22-23). In John 15, Christ spoke of degrees of fruitfulness, "fruit" (v. 2), "more fruitful" (v. 2), and "much fruit" (v. 8).

Few aspects of the Christian life are more vital than growth, improvement through discipline, measureless efficacy in prayer, and joy which comes from unbroken fellowship with Christ (1 John 1:3-4). Such fruit brings glory to God (John 15:8). God has given gifted members to the church so that they may bear much fruit. This purpose is stated in Ephesians 4:12-16, "To prepare God's people for works of service, so that the body of Christ may be built up until we all reach unity in the faith and in the knowledge of the Son of God and become mature, attaining to the whole measure of the fullness of Christ. Then we will no longer be infants, tossed back and forth by the waves, and blown here and there by every wind of teaching and by the cunning and craftiness of men in their deceitful scheming. Instead, speaking the truth in love, we will in all things grow up into Him who is the Head, that is, Christ. From Him the whole body, joined and held together by every supporting ligament, grows and builds itself up in love, as each part does its work."

The contribution which the figure of the vine and its branches makes to the doctrine of the church is to emphasize the provision of unbroken communion of the believer with the Lord, the enabling power of God resting on him both for his experience of joyous fellowship and for fruitfulness by prayer and testimony. The vine and the branches partake of one common life, that of Christ and the church.

THE CORNERSTONE AND THE STONES OF THE BUILDING

An obvious distinction between Israel and the church is that Israel *had* a temple (Ex. 25:8), and the church *is* a temple (Eph. 2:21). Just as God was present in the Old Testament temple, so He is present in the church indwelling those who are saved in the present age. By God's presence the temple is purified and made holy. This fact is stated in verses 19-22, "Consequently, you are no longer foreigners and aliens, but fellow citizens with God's people and members of God's household, built on the foundation of the apostles and prophets, with Christ Jesus Himself as the chief Cornerstone. In Him the whole building is joined together and rises to become a holy temple in the Lord. And in Him you too are being built together to become a dwelling in which God lives by His Spirit." Christ anticipated the present work of God for the church in His statement in Matthew 16:18, "On this rock I will build My church." References to the same concept are found in the New Testament (1 Cor. 3:9; Heb. 3:6; 1 Peter 2:5).

In relation to the Gentiles, Christ is the Smiting Stone in their final judgment. In relation to Israel, Christ's coming as the Servant rather than as the King became a Stumbling Block to the nation (Isa. 8:14-15; 1 Cor. 1:23; 1 Peter 2:8). In regard to the church Christ is the Foundation Stone (1 Cor. 3:11) and the Chief Cornerstone (Eph. 2:20-22; 1 Peter 2:4-5). Christ became the Chief Cornerstone through His resurrection even though the "builders"—Israel (Ps. 118:22-24)—opposed and rejected the Stone. Speaking of His resurrection, Peter wrote, "He is 'the Stone you builders rejected, which has become the Capstone' " (Acts 4:11). Quoting the same Old Testament passage, Christ forecast that the kingdom of God would be taken from them (the leaders of Israel) and given to a people, whether Jews or Gentiles, who would bring forth fruit (Matt. 21:43). This statement does not contradict the fact that Israel in the future will be restored spiritually and nationally. But it does anticipate that God's major purpose in the present age is building the church rather than advancing Israel.

In Matthew 21:42-44 Christ predicted that as the Stone He will destroy those who oppose Him. Other passages indicate that as the Stone He will destroy Gentile authority (cf. Ps. 2:7-9; Isa. 63:1-6; Rev. 19:15).

Viewing the church as a building points to three facts: each stone in the building is itself a living stone, that is, it partakes of the divine nature (1 Peter 2:5); its Chief Cornerstone, like its Foundation, is Christ (1 Cor. 3:11; Eph. 2:20-22; 1 Peter 2:6); and the whole structure is itself "a dwelling in which God lives by His Spirit" (Eph. 2:22).

The Apostle Paul reminded Gentile believers in Ephesus that they were "no longer foreigners and aliens, but fellow citizens with God's people and members of God's household" (v. 19). Paul added that the church is "built on the foundation of the apostles and prophets, with Christ Jesus Himself as the Chief Cornerstone. In Him the whole building is joined together and rises to become a holy temple in the Lord" (vv. 20-21).

The church is composed of individuals who are related to each other as stones are related in a building. In verses 19-21, however, Paul excluded the Old Testament saints and referred to New Testament saints as the building being erected on the foundation. Christians in the present age have a higher position of privilege than those in the Old Testament because they have received much more revelation of the grace of God and have also received much more of the supernatural work of God than the Old Testament saints.

Christians also are sanctified in a special sense (Heb. 10:10) and for this reason are called saints. In the Old Testament believers were not sanctified in the same sense. Though it is true that the word "saint" is applied to all who are saved regardless of the dispensation in which they live, this does not mean that they were equally recipients of the grace of God. The church in the present age is especially designed to manifest the grace of God, and this is the church's testimony in time as well as in eternity (Eph. 2:7).

The contribution which is made to the doctrine of the church by the figure of the Chief Cornerstone and the stones of the building is that each saved person is dependent on other saved persons. If one stone were taken from the structure, the whole building would be weakened, and this would deny the truth of the security of the believer. Christ Himself is constructing the building (Matt. 16:18). The church corporately as well as individual Christians are indwelt by the Spirit.

THE HIGH PRIEST AND THE KINGDOM OF PRIESTS

The fact that the church is "a royal priesthood" (1 Peter 2:9) is one of the most significant figures related to the church. Christ is said to be typified by the Old Testament high priest, Aaron, as well as by Melchizedek to whom Abraham paid tithes. As pointed out in Hebrews 5:1–8:6, Christ fulfilled the typology of both Aaron and Melchizedek. In His Aaronic ministry Christ offered a sacrifice to God, the sacrifice of Himself. In this undertaking He was both Sacrificer and Sacrifice. In this He went beyond the Aaronic pattern because an Aaronic priest could not be the sacrifice himself.

In a special sense Christ is also typified by Melchizedek because like Melchizedek He was not from the tribe of Levi nor descended from Aaron but was appointed a priest by God Himself. According to Psalm 110:4 Christ was made "a Priest forever, in the order of Melchizedek." Like Melchizedek His priesthood was not built on His parents or His genealogy. He was "without beginning of days or end of life" (Heb. 7:3). In contrast to the Aaronic priesthood Christ is a Priest forever. In this sense He is like Melchizedek whose death is not recorded in the Bible. Christ is the King as well as the Priest, and so Christians as priests under Christ are "a royal priesthood" (1 Peter 2:9). Though believers in the present age are priests under Christ, the Tribulation martyrs who are resurrected (Rev. 20:4) also "will be priests of God and of Christ and will reign with Him for a thousand years" (v. 6).

Present-age believers are to be committed to priestly service because of their relationship to Christ, their High Priest. This service to God includes sacrifice, worship, and intercession.

1. THE SERVICE OF SACRIFICE. Just as the Old Testament priest was sanctified and set apart by sacrifice and then having been inducted in the priest's office offered sacrifice for himself, so a believer in the present age is sanctified through the sacrifice of Christ. But as a believer he is also exhorted to sacrifice himself as stated in Romans 12:1, "Therefore, I urge you, brothers, in view of God's mercy, to offer your bodies as living sacrifices, holy and pleasing to God—which is your spiritual worship." Believers in the present age are "holy and pleasing to God" and are set apart for their priestly work just as Aaron and his sons were. When a person has been saved, he is indwelt by the Holy Spirit, is given eternal life, and is placed in the body of Christ by the baptism of the Holy Spirit. Therefore it is fitting and proper for a believer to present himself as a sacrifice to God. Apart from salvation he would not be qualified. A believer-priest may dedicate himself; but he does not consecrate himself for that is a work of God.

Christ's present work as the believer's High Priest in appointing, directing, and administering their service fulfills what was typified by the ministry of the Old Testament priests. Having been yielded to God and no longer conformed to the world, the believer-priest experiences a transforming life by the power of the indwelling Spirit and thus can "test and approve what God's will is—His good, pleasing, and perfect will" (v. 2).

When an Old Testament priest was consecrated for his sacred work, he was given a whole bath (Ex. 29:4). Afterward, though fully bathed, he was required to be cleansed by partial bathing by washing at the brazen laver to be prepared for his daily priestly service. Similarly New Testament believer-priests, though cleansed and forgiven at salvation, need to experience the constant cleansing that comes through confessing of sin, reading the Word of God, and being subject to the sanctifying work of the Holy Spirit (1 John 1:9). As the appointment of the Old Testament priests was for life, so the New Testament priests are priests before God forever.

2. The service of worship. Just as Old Testament saints were called to worship God, so priests in the present age also should worship the Lord. As the furnishings in the tabernacle and the temple spoke of Christ, so the believers' worship in the present age is by and through Christ alone. In keeping with this a believer worships by offering himself to God (Rom. 12:1). As stated in Hebrews 13:15, a believer's service involves the worship of praise: "Through Jesus, therefore, let us continually offer to God a sacrifice of praise—the fruit of lips that confess His name." In time as well as in eternity one of the prime functions of a believer is to offer praise to God. Old Testament sacrifices had to be offered in keeping with God's instructions (Ex. 30:9; Lev. 10:1). In the present age fleshly emotions or cold formality in worship should not be substituted for true devotion to Christ by the Spirit (1 Cor. 1:11-13; Col. 2:8, 16-19).

A New Testament priest should also offer devoted service and sacrificial gifts in his priestly function as stated in Hebrews 13:16, "And do not forget to do good and to share with others, for with such sacrifices God is pleased." The same expression is used of God's being "well pleased" with His Son (Matt. 3:17; 12:18; 17:5; Mark 1:11; Luke 3:22; 2 Peter 1:17). Included in the sacrifices are gifts given to God in which he shares with others. Some of the believer-priest's major responsibilities include offering himself, praise, faithful works, and gifts from his substance.

3. The service of intercession. As a prophet was God's representative sent to the people, so a priest was the people's representative to God. In the Old Testament, priests were not allowed in the most holy place of the tabernacle or temple except once a year when they were represented by the high priest who had previously offered sacrificial blood (Heb. 9:7). In the present priesthood of believers,

access into God's presence is immediate through Christ their High Priest, who is now in heaven interceding for them (Rom. 8:34; Heb. 4:14-16; 7:25; 9:24; 10:19-22). Because the veil in the temple was torn at the time of Christ's death, the way into God's presence is now open to every believer-priest on the ground of the shed blood of Christ (10:19-22). The intercessory work of a priest is one of His main responsibilities (Rom. 8:26-27; Col. 4:12; 1 Tim. 2:1; Heb. 10:19-22).

THE HEAD AND THE BODY WITH ITS MANY MEMBERS

In contrast to Israel which was a politically organized nation (Eph. 2:12), and in contrast to the visible church or the professing church which is a human organization, the true church is an organism, a living body of believers related to Christ as the Head. The figure of the head and the body with its many members is employed in Scripture more than any other to describe the relationship between believers and Christ. The Bible reveals certain features about the church as a body: (1) the church is a self-developing body, (2) the members of this body are appointed to specific service, and (3) the body is one though composed of many individuals.

1. The church is a self-developing body. The central text on the church as the body of Christ is Ephesians 4:11-16: "It was He who gave some to be apostles, some to be prophets, some to be evangelists, and some to be pastors and teachers, to prepare God's people for works of service, so that the body of Christ may be built up until we all reach unity in the faith and in the knowledge of the Son of God and become mature, attaining to the whole measure of the fullness of Christ. Then we will no longer be infants, tossed back and forth by the waves, and blown here and there by every wind of teaching and by the cunning and craftiness of men in their deceitful scheming. Instead, speaking the truth in love, we will in all things grow up into Him who is the Head, that is, Christ. From Him the whole body, joined and held together by every supporting ligament, grows and builds itself up in love, as each part does its work."

In the church as the body of Christ God has appointed some with special gifts as itemized in verse 11. The purpose of these gifts is to enable the laborers to prepare themselves and others for the work of serving the Lord. The goal of this service is to achieve unity in the faith, to have a full knowledge of Christ as the Son of God, to attain spiritual maturity, and to realize the measure of the fullness of Christ.

As believers experience this spiritual maturity, they are no longer children wavering between various teachings but instead speak spiritual truth in love, which causes the body to mature. Too much recognition cannot be given to uncounted multitudes of faithful witnesses who discharge their commission as Sunday School teachers, missionaries, personal soul-winners, and exponents of divine grace. Ministers in the church are not limited to those who are appointed as pastors. All members of the church are ministers, and their service is to minister on behalf of God according to their gifts. Though each individual believer is endowed with gifts with which to serve the Lord, obviously some are called to places of larger leadership. As such, pastors of churches need to be trained for this task. This involves schooling in college and seminary and growth in their personal lives to such maturity that they can be used of God in ministering to members of the church. As such, anyone who is a pastor, teacher, evangelist, or missionary should realize that he is not only a teacher but is also a role model. If a leader has no soul-winning passion, no missionary vision, and is inaccurate in his exposition of the Word of God, his lack in these respects will affect the people who follow him. Careful study of the Word of God requires scholarship on the part of the student. The concept that scholarship and spiritual passion cannot exist in the same person is a false idea as demonstrated in the case of Paul who on the one hand was a great scholar and on the other hand demonstrated faithful ministry in using his spiritual gifts.

The objective of the ministry is to help members of the body of Christ grow in their knowledge of Him, to become mature in their Christian faith, and be able to distinguish truth from error so they are not led astray by every new thought. Instead their ministry should be characterized by love and spiritual growth in relation to Christ as the Head of the body. Just as each part of the human body is held together by supporting ligaments so each member of the universal church is to do his part in the ministry.

2. The members of the body of Christ are appointed to specific service. Just as various parts of the human body are designed to function in special ways, so members of the body of Christ have differing gifts and yet function as a part of the whole. The

general truth that Christians should serve the Lord effectively is brought out in many passages of Scripture. The fact that Christians are members of the body of Christ and, like members of a human body, have special functions to perform is brought out in 1 Corinthians 12, which discusses the spiritual gifts to the church. The gifts regardless of their kind should be administered in love (1 Cor. 13) and in keeping with biblical instructions (1 Cor. 14). In Romans 12:3-8 the varied contributions of members of the body of Christ are mentioned. In 1 Peter 4:7-11 various aspects of ministry are revealed which take on even more significance in view of the fact that the Lord's coming may be near. The desired end is that God will be praised through Jesus Christ in everything that Christians do.

Though members are appointed to specific service, it is also true that the body is one with its many members. A number of verses speak of this fact, including those on the baptism of the Spirit (1 Cor. 12:13, 27; Gal. 3:27; Eph. 5:30).

The sovereignty of God in bestowing spiritual gifts is mentioned in 1 Corinthians 12:7-13. In all passages dealing with spiritual gifts the thought is that the gifts are given to believers by God who sovereignly determines what each believer should have.

3. The body of Christ is one. The extent of this theme is seen in the fact that the unity of the body is an essential element of the entire figure. Much that is important in theology is related to it (Eph. 1:22-23; 2:15-16; 3:6; 4:12-16; 5:30).

The argument relative to the one body in Christ is introduced in 1:22-23, "And God placed all things under His feet and appointed Him to be Head over everything for the church, which is His body, the fullness of Him who fills everything in every way."

In Ephesians 2 the fact of great differences between Jews and Gentiles is recognized, but in the one body Jews and Gentiles are united with no separation remaining. Because this has been a fact for the last 1,900 years, it is sometimes difficult for Christians to imagine the great gulf that existed between Jews and Gentiles before the beginning of the church.

Without releasing His power and sovereignty over the nations, God has declared His favor toward Israel as a special people. No other nation of people was chosen by God to occupy a place similar to Israel (Deut. 7:6-11). God pictures Himself as married to Israel (Jer. 3:14), and He distinguished and selected Israel out from other families of the earth (Amos 3:2). In keeping with this God has redeemed Israel from Egypt both by blood and by power (2 Sam. 7:23). According to Romans 9:4-5 Israel had a special place in God's plan and to Israel He gave special privileges: "Theirs is the adoption as sons; theirs the divine glory, the covenants, the receiving of the Law, the temple worship, and the promises. Theirs are the patriarchs, and from them is traced the human ancestry of Christ, who is God over all, forever praised! Amen."

The prejudice of Jew toward Gentile has often resulted in anti-Semitism. The Jews held that the Gentiles were contemptible; they did not normally welcome Gentiles into their houses. Peter was willing to enter the house of Cornelius only on direct, divine command (Acts 10:20). In Ephesians 2 the lost estate of the individual is disclosed in verses 1-3, and the position of Gentiles as a group is described in verse 12, "Remember that at that time you were separate from Christ, excluded from citizenship in Israel and foreigners to the covenants of the promise, without hope and without God in the world." Five disqualifying charges are related to the Gentiles; they are "separate from Christ," "excluded from citizenship in Israel," "foreigners to the covenants of the promise," and "without hope and without God in the world." These sweeping statements make it clear that Gentiles had no standing before God such as they have in the present age. In spite of the tremendous differences between Jews and Gentiles in the divine purpose, in the present age they are brought together in one body on the ground of the death and resurrection of Christ and the advent of the Holy Spirit. Each individual in the body of Christ is saved by the sovereign grace of God apart from human merit. Before their salvation, Jews and Gentiles "alike are all under sin" (Rom. 3:9). Though Gentiles as well as Israel have great future promises, the details of their hope differ.

The words "but now in Christ Jesus" (Eph. 2:13) indicate that Jews and Gentiles in the body of Christ have a new position in Christ and are brought into fellowship with God by the death of Christ. The possibility of Jews and Gentiles being at peace with one another is because "He Himself is our peace" (v. 14). In Christ both Jews and Gentiles are reconciled to God through the cross (v. 16). Peace is also God's message to the world, a peace with God and the peace of God (v. 17). The result is that the body of Christ is joined together and becomes the holy temple of the Lord (vv. 21-22).

In Ephesians 3 the church is said to be a "mystery" (v. 3), that is a sacred secret hitherto unrevealed truth in which the Gentiles are "heirs together" with believing Israelites (vv. 1-6). A mystery is a truth not revealed in the Old Testament but revealed in the New. In the Old Testament men were used to reveal God (2 Peter 1:21). So it is reasonable for members of the body of Christ to be channels of divine revelation to the world.

The fact that the church is a new purpose of God could not be more clearly stated than in Ephesians 3:3-9. The fact that the church is distinct from believers in the Old Testament makes unscriptural the point of view that Old Testament saints constituted a church. Though there are some similarities between Israel and the church, they are different; similarities do not prove identity. The fact that the church is a mystery, a new revelation in God's purposes (vv. 4-6) is amplified in verses 7-9. There Paul spoke of himself as an illustration of the difference between what was true in Judaism and what is true in the church. Though God manifested His grace to Israel, His primary purpose in dealing with Israel was to show His power, His wisdom, His holiness, and His faithfulness. In the church it is His purpose to manifest His grace (2:7).

In Ephesians 4 the fact of the unity of the body of Christ is enforced and with it is the exhortation for this unity to be observed in believers' relationships with each other. Paul stated that this unity is true because of "one body and one spirit . . . one hope . . . one Lord, one faith, one baptism, one God and Father of all, who is over all and through all and in all" (Eph. 4:4-6). This is the spiritual unity of the church about which Christ prayed in John 17:21.

CHAPTER • 25

SEVEN FIGURES USED OF THE CHURCH IN HER RELATION TO CHRIST (VI)

THE LAST ADAM AND THE NEW CREATION

An essential division of ecclesiology usually ignored in standard works is the revelation of the true church as the new creation with the resurrected Christ as its federal Head. This body of revelation is of supreme importance in understanding what God is undertaking in the present age.

At least four major themes are found in this doctrine: (1) the resurrected Christ, (2) the new creation, (3) the two creations requiring two commemorative days, and (4) the final transformation.

The new creation as a designation of the true church includes more than is comprehended in the idea that the church is Christ's body. In the new creation Christ is the all-important part whereas in the figure of the body the church is separate from and yet joined to the Head. The new creation is a unit that incorporates the resurrected Christ and that could not be what it is apart from Him.

THE RESURRECTED CHRIST

Most theological treatments of the resurrection of Christ view the subject from the standpoint of apologetics as a proof of the deity of Christ. The relationship of Christ's resurrection to the new creation is not mentioned. The Resurrection is far more than a reversal of His death. In His resurrection Christ became the pattern of glorified saints in heaven, and Christ's relationship to His church is different from anything that existed previously. If the church were in the Old Testament and the New Testament church is merely a continuation of it, differences are ignored. The resurrection of Christ, however, made possible an entirely new creation in contrast to the old creation of Adam.

The Resurrection is one of seven great, divine undertakings. These are: (1) the creation of angels; (2) the creation of material things, including man; (3) the Incarnation; (4) the death of Christ; (5) the resurrection of the Son of God; (6) the return of Christ to reign forever; and (7) the creation of the new heaven and the new earth. In this series of divine undertakings the resurrection of Christ is most important. A complete treatment of the resurrection of Christ includes not only His resurrection but also the resurrection of those who are in Him. The resurrection of Christ is the center of many important doctrines.

1. THE RESURRECTION OF CHRIST IS SUBJECT TO INDISPUTABLE PROOFS. It has been said that no event of history in the ancient world is more substantiated than the resurrection of Christ from the dead. Though, as an event, it is outside the range of the natural course of things and is supernatural in its origin, it is central in the concept of a supernatural world. The resurrection of Christ has solid proofs in Scripture.

a. THE TRUTHFULNESS OF CHRIST HIMSELF. The Saviour predicted His own resurrection before His death (cf. Matt. 12:38-40; 16:21; 17:9, 23; 20:19; 27:63; Mark 8:31; 9:9, 31; 10:34; 14:58; Luke 9:22; 18:33; John 2:19-21). Besides predicting His own resurrection, He also presented Himself as raised from the dead after the event occurred. The concept that He was self-deceived or an impostor is contradicted by His prophecy and its fulfillment.

b. THE EMPTY TOMB. Few would deny that the Saviour died on the cross or that He was buried, and many would accept the fact that the tomb was empty on the third day. Others, however, attempt to avoid the doctrine of the Resurrection by advancing the theory that He swooned and was resuscitated. This, however, is an impossible explanation on the basis of the known facts. Equally impossible is the notion that His followers removed His body, for three obstacles stood in the way of removing the body. There was the armed guard, the sealed stone, and the graveclothes which were left behind and which probably retained the form which they had when He occupied them. If the body of Christ had been taken away, the graveclothes would have been taken with Him.

On the Day of Pentecost the Jews believed Peter when he said that Christ rose from the dead. This suggests that when the report of His resurrection was circulated in Jerusalem, the Jews went out to the tomb and saw for themselves the eloquent evidence of the graveclothes which could be explained only by His resurrection. It is evident that no one stealing the body of Christ would have taken the time to remove the graveclothes while the body was still in the tomb, and apparently the graveclothes were in such form that it became clear to all observers that the body of Christ had slipped out of them without disturbing them. If the body had been stolen, it certainly would have been found by the Jews and the resurrection of Christ would have been refuted.

c. THE EXPERIENCE OF CHRIST'S FOLLOWERS. Christ's followers had natural emotions beginning with overwhelming sorrow and then overflowing joy when they recognized Christ after His resurrection. There is no indication that the disciples were credulous; at first they themselves could not believe that He had been resurrected. As they contemplated the facts, however, it was clear that this was the only logical explanation. This, of course, was confirmed by His appearances.

d. THE FACT OF THE CHURCH. The fact that the early followers of Jesus believed in the resurrection of Christ even to the point where they were willing to die rather than renounce their faith certainly points to solid proofs for the Resurrection. What greater proof could there be than the evidence in the tomb and the various appearances of Christ to the disciples? The fact that thousands believed in the resurrection of Christ indicates that it had a solid basis in fact.

e. THE EYEWITNESSES. Eyewitnesses at any event constitute solid proof that an event took place. In the case of the resurrection of Christ, the Scriptures record that the guards saw the angel roll the stone away from the tomb (Matt. 28:2-4), and in their terror they fled the scene. The chief priests (vv. 11-15) told the guards to say that someone stole the body while they slept. But that was obviously false because they could not have seen someone stealing the body while they were sleeping.

The first appearance of Christ was to Mary Magdalene (John 20:11-17; cf. Mark 16:9-11), who, though she was blinded by her tears, recognized His voice. The second appearance of Christ was to the other women who were returning to the tomb (Matt. 28:9-10). The third appearance was to Peter who was sought out by Christ because he needed restoration after having denied Christ (Luke

24:34; 1 Cor. 15:5). A fourth appearance was to two disciples on the road to Emmaus. The Scriptures indicate that the two were supernaturally hindered from recognizing Him until He broke bread, but they had the privilege of hearing Christ Himself expound the Old Testament concerning His death and resurrection (Mark 16:12-13; Luke 24:13-35). Christ appeared the fifth time to the 10 disciples (Mark 16:14; Luke 24:36-43; John 20:19-23) on the evening of the Resurrection Day when Thomas was absent. In this instance Christ affirmed the reality of His resurrection by referring to His body as having flesh and bone and by His being able to eat.

The sixth appearance was to the 11 disciples, this time with Thomas present (vv. 26-29). The seventh appearance (21:1-23) was to 7 disciples by the Sea of Galilee, which was introduced by the supernatural catch of fish. The eighth appearance was to 500, as revealed by Paul (1 Cor. 15:6). The ninth appearance was to James, the Lord's brother (v. 7). As a result of that appearance, James became a believer (Acts 1:14; Gal. 1:19). The tenth appearance was to the 11 disciples on the mountain in Galilee (Matt. 28:16-20). Another account of this is found in Mark 16:15-18 though it is not clear whether it is the same appearance or an earlier one. The eleventh appearance occurred at the time of His ascension from the Mount of Olives (Luke 24:44-53; Acts 1:3-9).

Subsequent appearances of Christ after He had been glorified in heaven are recorded in six instances. Stephen saw the resurrected Christ before his martyrdom (7:55-56). Christ appeared to Paul on the road to Damascus (9:3-6; cf. 22:6-11; 26:13-18), which resulted in Paul's conversion. Christ also appeared to Paul in Arabia (Gal. 1:17). This is implied in verse 12. Christ also appeared to Paul in the temple when Paul was told of his coming persecution (Acts 22:17-21; cf. 9:26-30). Christ also appeared to Paul when he was in prison in Caesarea and told him he would preach the Gospel in Rome (23:11). The final appearance of Christ was to the Apostle John in connection with the writing of the Book of Revelation (Rev. 1:12-20). In all, 17 appearances of Christ are clearly indicated. There may have been more that are not recorded in Scripture. How could there be more convincing proof of the resurrection of Christ than these various appearances to so many different people?

The attempts of unbelievers to dispute the fact of the empty tomb are built on the thesis that the supernatural, including the Resurrection, is impossible. The idea that the disciples had come to the wrong tomb is contradicted because the Roman guards witnessed the empty tomb, and the women obviously went to the tomb where the seal had been broken. The soldiers themselves bore testimony that the tomb was empty. Actually there are no alternative theories concerning the resurrection of Christ that have a scrap of evidence. If one accepts the concept of the supernatural on the basis of scriptural revelation, there is no proper motive for disputing the fact of the resurrection of Christ, and with the Resurrection comes the whole revelation of God found in the Scriptures and forming the basis of Christian theology.

f. THE DIRECT ASSERTIONS OF THE BIBLE. As indicated in the many accounts of His appearances and the record of what He said and did, the Bible clearly asserts the resurrection of Christ both as a historical fact and as a theological proof. In the Old Testament the resurrection of Christ was predicted. In the New Testament it is recorded, and the theology of the New Testament is built on the fact of the resurrection of Christ. Removing this fact from Christianity would cause the collapse of the whole of Christian theology.

g. THE RESURRECTION AND THE DIVINE PROGRAM. Obviously the resurrection of Christ was intrinsic and essential to God's program of redeeming man. Apart from the Resurrection there would be no certainty that the death of Christ provided forgiveness and salvation. Individuals who have come to the Bible with questions as to its validity have again and again been won to the Christian faith by the overwhelming evidence for the resurrection of Christ.

2. THE RESURRECTION OF CHRIST IS REASONABLE. Scripture is beyond reason inasmuch as it is a supernatural work of God who used human authors to write the Bible. If the concept of the supernatural is to be accepted there is no reasonable basis for denying the resurrection of Christ. The Resurrection is an essential part of biblical revelation viewed as prophecy in the Old Testament and presented as history in the New Testament.

In keeping with the doctrine of the Resurrection, Christ is the source of life. He had predicted, "I tell you the truth, a time is coming and has now come when the dead will hear the voice of the Son of God and those who hear will live. For as the Father has life in Himself, so He has granted the Son to have life in Himself" (John 5:25-26). He also said, "The thief comes only to steal and kill and destroy; I have come that they may have life, and have it to the full" (10:10). Christ also said, "No one takes it from Me, but I lay it down of My own accord. I have authority to lay it down and authority to take it up again. This command I received from My Father" (v. 18). So many passages refer to the resurrection of Christ that if this is removed from the Scriptures it makes impossible other doctrines revealed in connection with Christian theology. Christ was raised by the Father (Acts 2:24). In contrast to Adam who received life from God, Christ as the last Adam is the life-giving Spirit (1 Cor. 15:45). Adam brought death to the race, but the last Adam brought life (v. 22). Because of the deity of Christ, it was impossible for Him to remain dead physically (Acts 2:24).

3. The resurrection of Christ was prophesied. The Old Testament is specific about the fact of Christ's resurrection. In Psalm 16:8-10 David declared, "I have set the Lord always before me. Because He is at my right hand, I will not be shaken. Therefore my heart is glad and my tongue rejoices; my body also will rest secure, because You will not abandon me to the grave, nor will You let Your Holy One see decay." This Scripture is applied to Christ by Peter in Acts 2:30-31, "But he was a prophet and knew that God had promised him on oath that He would place one of his descendants on his throne. Seeing what was ahead, he spoke of the resurrection of the Christ, that He was not abandoned to the grave, nor did His body see decay." In Psalm 118:22-23 the psalmist declared, "The Stone the builders rejected has become the capstone; the Lord has done this, and it is marvelous in our eyes." Standing before the Sanhedrin, Paul gave a similar testimony about the death and resurrection of Christ. "Then know this, you and everyone else in Israel: It is by the name of Jesus Christ of Nazareth, whom you crucified but whom God raised from the dead, that this man stands before you completely healed. He is 'the Stone you builders rejected, which has become the capstone' " (Acts 4:10-11).

In the Gospel records it is clear that the disciples could not bring themselves to believe that He would either die or be raised from the dead. They apparently completely forgot His predictions of resurrection once they had seen Christ die on the cross. Only overwhelming evidence would have jarred them from their unbelief to complete faith in Christ.

4. The Scriptures give seven reasons for the Resurrection. Though the resurrection of Christ has been discussed in soteriology, at least seven reasons should be restated here in support of the doctrine of Resurrection.

a. BECAUSE OF WHO CHRIST IS. As the eternal God and as the One who has existed from eternity past and will exist into eternity future (Micah 5:2), He is called the Father of eternity (Isa. 9:6). His resurrection is a natural result of having the infinite attributes of Deity. The exceptional fact is not that Christ is Deity or that He was resurrected, but that as Deity He took on Himself a human body and went through the process of death requiring resurrection. The Scriptures give many evidences that Christ died, and He therefore had complete victory over death because of His resurrection (Rom. 6:9; Heb. 13:8). Because of who Christ is, it is obvious that death could not continue to possess His body (Acts 2:24).

b. TO FULFILL PROPHECY. Prophecies of the Old Testament such as Psalm 16:10—as well as His own prophecies given before His death—were fulfilled when He died on the cross and rose again. The prophecies of His work subsequent to His death and resurrection—such as the promise that He would sit on David's throne forever—make the Resurrection necessary (Isa. 9:6-7; Luke 1:31-33). David seems to be one of the few Old Testament characters who understood the fact that Christ had to die and be resurrected.

c. TO BECOME A BESTOWER OF LIFE. According to 1 Corinthians 15:45 Christ became "a life-giving Spirit," in contrast to Adam who "became a living being." In John 20:22 Christ breathed on the disciples and said, "Receive the Holy Spirit." Theologically, Christians are raised with Christ as far as their position is concerned (Col. 2:12). Christians are exhorted to live in keeping with the fact of Christ's resurrection (3:1-4). Believers in Christ who die are promised resurrection (1 Thes. 4:13-18).

d. TO IMPART POWER. In His last message recorded in Matthew, Christ said, "All authority in heaven and on earth has been given to Me" (Matt. 28:18). In Romans 6:3-4 the fact that the believers have been spiritually raised from the dead is presented as a demonstration of the power of Christ. In keeping with this Paul said in Philippians 4:13, "I can do everything through Him who gives me strength." Obviously the strength of a believer is derived from the power of Christ. In that power they can serve Christ acceptably (John 15:5).

e. TO BE HEAD OF HIS BODY, THE CHURCH. According to Ephesians 1:19-23 one of the purposes in raising Christ was to exalt Him into a place of supreme power. "That power is like the working of His mighty strength, which He exerted in Christ when He raised Him from the dead and seated Him at His right hand in the heavenly realms, far above all rule and authority, power and dominion, and every title that can be given, not only in the present age but also in the one to come. And God placed all things under His feet and appointed Him to be Head over everything for the church, which is His body, the fullness of Him who fills everything in every way." A similar truth is found in Philippians 2:9-11, "Therefore God exalted Him to the highest place and gave Him the name that is above every name, that at the name of Jesus every knee should bow, in heaven and on earth and under the earth, and every tongue confess that Jesus Christ is Lord, to the glory of God the Father." According to Ephesians 1:22-23, "God placed all things under His feet and appointed Him to be Head over everything for the church, which is His body, the fullness of Him who fills everything in every way."

f. RESURRECTION AND JUSTIFICATION. In Romans 4:25 the statement is made, "He was delivered over to death for our sins and was raised to life for our justification." The expression "for our justification" could also be translated "on account of our justification." Actually the death of Christ was sufficient to justify the believer, but the Resurrection demonstrated the value of His death and resurrection. According to 3:23-24, "For all have sinned and fall short of the glory of God, and are justified freely by His grace through the redemption that came by Christ Jesus." The Resurrection was the testimony of God to the fact that the ground for justification had been established in the death of Christ. If Christ had not been resurrected, believers would have no evidence that He had died for their justification.

g. CHRIST THE PATTERN OR FIRSTFRUITS. In view of the promised resurrection of all people, Christ is the pattern or example of this. Just as Jews brought to the priest a token of the coming harvest in a handful of grain—more than one stalk—so Christ is the Firstfruits and after Him will come the harvest of all those who have been saved in every age. According to Romans 8:29 the statement is made, "For those God foreknew He also predestined to be conformed to the likeness of His Son, that He might be the Firstborn among many brothers." Again in Philippians 3:20-21 Paul stated, "But our citizenship is in heaven. And we eagerly await a Saviour from there, the Lord Jesus Christ, who, by the power that enables Him to bring everything under His control, will transform our lowly bodies so that they will be like His glorious body." Christians are promised that they will be like Christ (1 John 3:2). According to 1 Corinthians

15:20, 23, "But Christ has indeed been raised from the dead, the Firstfruits of those who have fallen asleep. . . . But each in his own turn: Christ, the Firstfruits; then, when He comes, those who belong to Him."

5. THE RESURRECTION OF CHRIST IS ONE OF THREE STANDARDS OF POWER. In the three major dispensations revealed in Scripture each age includes a special demonstration of the power of God. For the Old Testament saints God demonstrated His power by their deliverance from Egypt. In the present age the resurrection of Christ is the standard of power. In the future age, the Millennium, the evidence of God's power will be in the regathering and restoration of Israel to their land.

According to Jeremiah 23:7-8 the same God who brought the Children of Israel out of Egypt will bring them back to their land, " 'So then, the days are coming,' declares the LORD, 'when people will no longer say, "As surely as the LORD lives, who brought the Israelites up out of Egypt," but they will say, "As surely as the LORD lives, who brought the descendants of Israel up out of the land of the north and out of all the countries where He had banished them." Then they will live in their own land.' "

Impressive as these proofs are of the power of God, the resurrection of Christ is even a greater evidence as stated in Ephesians 1:19-21, "That power is like the working of His mighty strength, which He exerted in Christ when He raised Him from the dead and seated Him at His right hand in the heavenly realms, far above all rule and authority, power and dominion, and every title that can be given, not only in the present age but also in the one to come." The power of Christ's resurrection is the power that is on behalf of the believer in the present age.

6. CHRIST'S RESURRECTION WAS AN ACTUAL RESURRECTION. As has been previously pointed out, all the theories that seek to explain away the resurrection of Christ have no evidence and are built on the false premise that the supernatural is impossible. The resurrection of Christ stands as a historical fact on which Christian theology can build.

7. THE RESURRECTION OF CHRIST IS UNTO A NEW ORDER. The resurrection of Christ introduced a new revelation of the grace of God. After the resurrection of Christ the Jews returned not to the Mosaic Law but turned instead to the new undertaking of God beginning on the Day of Pentecost which included the salvation of both

Jews and Gentiles to form the body of Christ. The resurrection of Christ is a supreme illustration of the believers' own resurrection bodies. Christians have the assurance that at the Rapture of the church they will receive new bodies like the body of Christ (1 Cor. 15:51-53). This is confirmed by the revelation recorded in 1 Thessalonians 4:13-18. According to Philippians 3:20-21 believers' bodies will be transformed and made like the glorious body of Christ. To those who may still be questioning the validity of the Christian faith, the doctrine of the Resurrection is a tremendous confirmation.

THE BELIEVER'S POSITION IN CHRIST

The dramatic difference between a person's position in Adam and a believer's position in Christ is stated in Colossians 1:13, "For He has rescued us from the dominion of darkness and brought us into the kingdom of the Son He loves." Though formerly spiritually dead and depraved, a Christian when he believes in Christ is born of God, becomes a member of the household and family of God, and occupies a place of an adult son. He is transferred from the fallen headship of the first Adam into the exalted and infinite headship of the last Adam. He is qualified through the imputed merit of Christ to be a partaker of the inheritance of the saints in light. Being in Christ he possesses every spiritual blessing and is made complete even to the satisfaction of God. He is justified forever. His citizenship is changed from earth to heaven. He will yet be delivered from the Adamic nature. He will receive a glorious body like Christ's resurrection body. Though personal identity continues, a Christian is totally changed when his glorification and sanctification are complete (cf. Eph. 5:27; 1 John 3:2; Jude 24).

The new creation incorporates two factors, the resurrected Christ and the entire company of believers who are identified as the true church.

1. The resurrected Christ. While Christ was on earth, His glory as the Son of God was veiled. But after His death, resurrection, and ascension, He became what He had been from all eternity, the glorified Christ. John, who in life had laid his head on Jesus' bosom, fell as dead at the feet of the glorified Christ (Rev. 1:17). Believers will share in the glory of Christ in heaven (Col. 3:4). All this is made possible by the redemption of Christ through His death and

partaking of His knowledge-surpassing exaltation in heaven.

2. The new humanity. Though works on systematic theology recognize that Christ was resurrected, they often fall short of expressing the glorious character of His humanity in heaven. These great truths are part of the new creation which is accomplished by regeneration and baptism of the Holy Spirit.

Seven great texts in the New Testament reveal the greatness of the new creation and the believer's part in it.

Second Corinthians 5:17-18, "Therefore, if anyone is in Christ, he is a new creation; the old has gone, the new has come! All this is from God, who reconciled us to Himself through Christ and gave us the ministry of reconciliation."

Galatians 3:27-28, "For all of you who were baptized into Christ have clothed yourselves with Christ. There is neither Jew nor Greek, slave nor free, male nor female, for you are all one in Christ Jesus."

Galatians 6:15, "Neither circumcision nor uncircumcision means anything; what counts is a new creation."

Ephesians 2:10, "For we are God's workmanship, created in Christ Jesus to do good works, which God prepared in advance for us to do."

Ephesians 2:15, "By abolishing in His flesh the Law with its commandments and regulations. His purpose was to create in Himself one new man out of the two, thus making peace."

Ephesians 4:21-24, "Surely you heard of Him and were taught in Him in accordance with the truth that is in Jesus. You were taught, with regard to your former way of life, to put off your old self, which is being corrupted by its deceitful desires; to be made new in the attitude of your minds; and to put on the new self, created to be like God in true righteousness and holiness."

Colossians 3:9-10, "Do not lie to each other, since you have taken off your old self with its practices and have put on the new self, which is being renewed in knowledge in the image of its Creator."

From these seven passages the truth is established that there is a new creation which is formed by the organic union of believers with Christ. Believers are now identified with Christ in His death, resurrection, and glorification (Rom. 6:2-4). Though the process of salvation is only partially completed in this life, it is obvious when believers stand in heaven complete, the full purpose of God in identifying them with the glorified Christ will be accomplished (Eph. 2:4-6). This is supported by Colossians 3:1-4 previously quoted. The 33 positions and possessions itemized in soteriology illustrate the tremendous extent of the work of Christ in salvation.

In the new creation the phrase "in Christ" is most important. This is a truth that is not mentioned in the Old Testament but appears in various ways in the New Testament about 130 times. The emphasis on this truth is often missing in current theological discussion. These many Scriptures combine to state the wonderful truth of a believer's present position and expectation of future glorification (Eph. 1:3-12, 15-23). In the new creation, Christians are united in the same sense that the Persons of the Trinity are united, and in a similar way all believers are united to each other as anticipated in the prayer of Christ (John 17:20-23). This truth involves the fact that the believer is in Christ and Christ is in the believer (14:20). So a believer who is in Christ has a position, possessions, safe-keeping, and association with Christ. It is also true that Christ in the believer gives life, character, and dynamic for life. All this is anticipated in the simple phrase in verse 20, "You are in Me, and I am in you."

THE TWO CREATIONS REQUIRE TWO COMMEMORATIVE DAYS

The New Testament clearly teaches that though the Sabbath Day was observed by Israel in keeping with the fourth commandment, Christians who accept the doctrine of the resurrection of Christ have a commemorative day on the first day of the week instead of the seventh. The deep-seated prejudices regarding the seventh-day Sabbath and the first-day celebration of the resurrection of Christ stem from a lack of comprehension of the tremendous gulf between the Mosaic Law and the present age of grace. The Mosaic Law and the Sabbath were part of the Old Testament order just as in the New Testament the observance of the first day of the week is significant of the present age as an age of grace. The failure to distinguish between God's command to the Jews and God's commands to Christians is at the root of this problem. The contrast between observing the seventh day of the week and the first day of the week is important for at least four reasons: (1) It determines an individual's conception of his blessing in grace. (2) It determines the character of the believer's conduct and the measure of comprehension of his scriptural obligation to God. (3) It is the central issue in the misleading teaching that confuses Israel and the church. (4) The enforcement of a day of rest on the first day of the week on a Christ-rejecting world has no scriptural support.

In considering the subject of the Jewish Sabbath in relation to the first day of the week observing the Resurrection, two major aspects of the subject need to be considered.

1. The biblical testimony regarding the Jewish Sabbath.

a. the period from Adam to Moses. Because God created the world in six days and rested on the seventh, some contend that the Sabbath was given to the entire human race beginning with Creation. There is no record, however, of any observance of the Sabbath until it was given in the fourth commandment to Moses and was applied only to the people of Israel. The attempt to apply the fourth commandment to Christians is based on the false idea that it is taught in the New Testament. Significantly, of the Ten Commandments nine are repeated in the New Testament, but the commandment concerning the Sabbath is not. The fact that there was no observance of the Sabbath before the Mosaic Law is supported by the fact that the heathen nations condemned for many things are not condemned for breaking the Sabbath. It would be incredible for a Sabbath to be observed for the many centuries before the Mosaic Law with no mention of it being recorded either in Scripture or in secular history.

Nehemiah 9:13-14 indicates that the observance of the Sabbath began with Moses. "You came down on Mount Sinai; You spoke to them from heaven. You gave them regulations and laws that are just and right, and decrees and commands that are good. You made known to them Your holy Sabbath and gave them commands, decrees and laws through Your servant Moses."

The Sabbath was given to Israel as a sign (Ex. 31:12-17) and was never addressed to the Gentiles in the Old Testament. The Sabbath, as part of the Law, did not begin to be enforced until Moses (Rom. 5:12-14). An important proof of the beginning of the Sabbath is also found in Ezekiel 20:10-12, "Therefore I led them out of Egypt and brought them into the desert. I gave them My decrees and made known to them My laws, for the man who obeys them will live by them. Also I gave them My Sabbaths as a sign between us, so they would know that I the Lord made them holy."

From the narrative of Israel's journeys in Exodus 16 it may be concluded that at that time they were not keeping the Sabbath, but verse 1 states that she journeyed between Elim and Sinai and the very next day was the first day of the week (the 15th day of the second month). This is brought out in the instructions God gave to Moses concerning the manna. From this it may be concluded that the Sabbath was imposed on Israel as a part of the Law as given by Moses. Before that it was not observed.

b. THE PERIOD FROM MOSES TO CHRIST. Exodus 31:12-17 concerns the instructions God gave Moses to deliver to the Children of Israel. They were instructed to keep the Sabbath by not doing any work therein. It was to be a perpetual sign to them of their special relationship to the Lord. The Sabbath was a part of Israel's Law which distinguished them from other peoples of the earth.

In addition to regular Sabbaths which were on the seventh day of each week, there were at least 15 additional Sabbaths on fixed days. In connection with the observance of Pentecost, a Sabbath was arbitrarily set on the 15th day of the month Abib. Obviously this date would not always fall on the seventh day of the week. If the crucifixion of Christ was on Friday, it appears from Mark 15:42 that the fixed Sabbath that week providentially fell on Saturday since preparations for it were on the 14th day of the month, the day before (Ex. 12:2, 6).

In a similar way the Feast of Firstfruits would not always have been on the seventh day because the day was appointed as a beginning of harvest (Deut. 16:9; cf. Lev. 23:15). By this it becomes evident that the sacred character of the day belonged to its relative place in a series of seven days and not to a particular day of the week.

From Moses to Christ the Sabbath was to be a day of physical rest, and the whole nation of Israel was bound to observe it at the penalty of death. No fire was to be kindled, no food prepared, no journey undertaken, no buying or selling permitted, and no burden to be borne. Even the land was to have its Sabbath (Ex. 31:12-17; 35:3; 16:22-26; Neh. 10:31; 13:15-21; Lev. 25:4; 2 Chron. 36:21). Because the Sabbath days and the Sabbath years were so poorly observed by Israel, they were carried off into captivity for 70 years to make up for what they had failed to do in observance of Sabbaths.

c. THE PERIOD REPRESENTED BY THE GOSPELS. Much confusion concerning the Sabbath has arisen because of the peculiar character of the period represented by the Gospels. Christ was living in the dispensation of the Law until His death. Christ recognized and enforced the Sabbath as an integral part of the whole Mosaic system.

He did insist, however, that the Mosaic system and the Sabbath in particular be delivered from the teachings of men which superimposed their type of observance on the Law of Moses.

Because He refused to accept these man-made additions to the Law, His teaching on the Sabbath was a major source of conflict with the Jews. In Mark 2:27 Christ said, "The Sabbath was made for man, not man for the Sabbath." He added, "So the Son of man is Lord even of the Sabbath" (v. 28). Attempts to make the Sabbath apply to all races is contradicted by the fact that the Sabbath is never, by any subsequent Scripture, applied to Gentiles. Also the word "man" is used in the Old Testament no less than 336 times when referring to Israel alone. Sometimes in the New Testament it referred only to Christians as in the statement, "The head of every man is Christ" (1 Cor. 11:3); and the statement, "If any man builds on this foundation" (3:12). So in stating that the Sabbath was made for man, Christ was referring specifically to Israel as Scripture nowhere imposes the Jewish Sabbath on either Gentiles or Christians.

d. THE PERIOD REPRESENTED BY THE ACTS AND THE EPISTLES. The fact that the Law had ceased as a rule of life is a frequent doctrine of the New Testament (John 1:16-17; Rom. 6:14; 7:1-6; 2 Cor. 3:1-18; Gal. 3:19-25; Eph. 2:15; Col. 2:14). The Law was terminated by the death of Christ (Rom. 7:7-14). The Law was "fading" (2 Cor. 3:7, 11, 13). "The veil" is "taken away" for those who are "in Christ" (v. 14). In verse 16, "Whenever anyone turns to the Lord, the veil is taken away." If the Law was imposed on the church it is incredible that early Christians are never recorded as having observed the Sabbath, and the necessity of recognizing the Sabbath was not incorporated in the new teachings in grace.

(1) The word "Sabbath" is used nine times in Acts in referring to the day to be observed; each time it is related only to unbelieving Jews. Paul took advantage of the fact that the Jews would be in the synagogues on the Sabbath and attempted to speak to them. It apparently was not his custom to go to the synagogues on the Sabbath apart from this purpose.

(2) In the Epistles no Christian is ever said to have observed the Sabbath Day. If early Christians observed the Sabbath, no such incident is mentioned in the Bible. No one was ever rebuked for not keeping the Sabbath. In Colossians 2:16-17 Paul wrote, "Therefore do not let anyone judge you by what you eat or drink, or with regard to a religious festival, a New Moon celebration or a Sabbath Day.

These are a shadow of the things that were to come; the reality, however, is found in Christ." Paul stated that the Sabbath and other special days were only shadows of the truth to be fulfilled in Christ Himself. According to verses 10-11 believers are given "fullness in Christ" and in Him have put off the old nature by a spiritual circumcision done by Christ. Christians in Christ share in His death and resurrection through the baptism of the Spirit (v. 12).

Since the Israelites failed to enter into rest under Joshua (Heb. 4:8), believers face the danger of not entering into the rest they have in Christ, which is not related to any one day of the week (vv. 9-10). Believers are urged to enter into the genuine rest they have in Christ, a rest that is not connected with the observance of a day and is related to grace rather than to keeping the Law.

It is most significant that in the Epistles observance of the Sabbath is specifically prohibited. The Galatians were rebuked for turning back to the observance of laws under which the Jews lived. Paul asked, "Do you wish to be enslaved by them all over again?" (Gal. 4:9) He pointed out that they were wrongly observing "special days and months and seasons and years" (v. 10). The reason for his objection was that they were departing from grace in observing the Law.

e. THE SABBATH IN PROPHECY. The Scriptures speak of the cessation of observing the Sabbath in the age of Israel's chastisement and its reestablishment after the present Church Age is finished. According to Hosea 2:11 Israel would come to a period when all her solemn feasts and Sabbaths would cease. This is fulfilled of course by the beginning of the present age on the Day of Pentecost. As also indicated, Israel's Sabbath will be reinstituted in the Great Tribulation and the millennial kingdom (Matt. 24:20; cf. Isa. 66:23). Also it is predicted that in the Millennium the Eastern Gate of Jerusalem will be shut through six working days but opened on the Sabbath and the New Moon (Ezek. 46:1).

f. THE EXACT DAY. Besides the weekly Sabbath Day, which fell on Saturday, there were fixed Sabbaths throughout the year without relationship to the seventh day. Each Sabbath was to begin at sunset and end with sunset, which is simple enough if it referred to Israel's land. But when applied to the whole day as observed in different time zones, obviously there could be no uniformity in observance.

2. THE BIBLICAL TESTIMONY CONCERNING THE LORD'S DAY. The New Testament does not instruct believers in Christ to observe the

Sabbath Day; instead it warns them against observing it. There are certain biblical reasons for this change.

a. THE MOSAIC SYSTEM HAS CEASED. The whole Mosaic system including its Sabbath Day has given way to the reign of grace. In spite of this some wanted to observe the seventh day by saying that the Ten Commandments were not part of the Law or by saying that in the early church the first day of the week was similar to the Jewish Sabbath. The argument that the Ten Commandments were not a part of the Law which was abolished is contradicted in the New Testament in Romans 7:7 where Paul referred to the tenth commandment as an example of the Law. The observance of the Sabbath was in recognition of the presence of *Yahweh* in the most holy place, and the altar, priesthood, and temple which were in Jerusalem. All these prerequisites no longer exist.

It is also inconsistent to try to make the first day have the character of the Sabbath. The first day of the week has an entirely different connotation. The first day of the week is not a part of the Sabbath Law, and no regulations are given in the Bible for its observance. Attempting to make the first day of the week a Sabbath mixes Law and grace. The concept of a Christian Sabbath is not supported by Scripture.

b. A NEW DAY IS DIVINELY APPOINTED UNDER GRACE. The new day according to Psalm 118:22-24 should be a day of rejoicing; no mention is made of resting. The Resurrection was appointed to take place on a certain day which the Lord had determined, and that day by divine intention was to be celebrated as the Scriptures indicate. The Lord's Day should not be confused with "the Day of the Lord." The Lord's Day is the first day of every week to be observed as the commemoration of the resurrection of Christ. The Day of the Lord refers to prophetic periods, the most important of which is still future, which relate to God's immediate judgment on sin as in the time of the Great Tribulation and the millennial kingdom which follows.

The first Lord's Day (the resurrection of Christ) was to be a pattern for Lord's Days that followed. It began early in the morning, continued with His precious fellowship, and closed with His benediction of peace. From that early morning to its close the day was a day of worship, activity, and joy. This is a day appointed for Christians to observe the resurrection of Christ. To move it to any other day would rob it of its symbolic meaning.

c. A NEW DAY IS INDICATED BY IMPORTANT EVENTS. Though it is true that keeping the Lord's Day was not made an explicit command in the New Testament, there was a command against the observance of the Sabbath Day. It is in keeping with grace that no specific commandments are given concerning its observance. The resurrection of Christ is vitally related to ages past, to the fulfillment of all prophecy, to the values of His death, to the church, to Israel, to Creation, to the purposes of God in grace which reach beyond ages to come, and to the eternal glory of God. The importance of the Resurrection and its observance is seen in the event itself which is absolutely essential to Christian faith and hope.

In the New Testament the Resurrection Day is designated as the first day of the week (Matt. 28:1; Mark 16:2; Luke 24:1; John 20:1, 19). The disciples met for worship and breaking of bread on the first day according to Acts 20:7. In 1 Corinthians 16:2 believers came together for fellowship on the first day of the week. No mention of observing the seventh day is found in Acts or the Epistles.

d. THE NEW DAY TYPIFIES THE NEW CREATION. In the Law the eighth day was the day of circumcision. Similarly the new day for a Christian indicates the fulfillment of the circumcision made without hands (Col. 2:11). It is a time of victory made possible by the resurrection and life of Christ. When the old creation was abolished, the Sabbath was abolished with it.

e. THE NEW DAY IS TYPICAL OF UNMERITED GRACE. In the Old Testament Israel rested from her labors on the seventh day. In the New Testament a believer observes the first day of the week in recognition that he has been delivered from legalism and observance of the Mosaic Law and his entrance into the position of being the object of God's abundant grace. A day of ceaseless worship and service belongs to a people who are related to God by the finished work of Christ. In contrast to the legalism of the seventh day the first day is characterized by the latitude and liberty belonging to grace.

f. THE NEW DAY BEGAN TO BE OBSERVED WITH THE RESURRECTION OF CHRIST. There is some evidence that the Sabbath will again be recognized in the future millennial kingdom (Isa. 66; Ezek. 45:17; 46:1-12).

In the New Testament there is no record of a Christian keeping a Sabbath Day even in error. On the other hand, as has been demonstrated, the first day of the week was observed in a manner consistent with its significance.

The testimony of the early fathers is also conclusive that the first day of the week, rather than the Sabbath, was observed.

Peter, Bishop of Alexandria (ca. A.D. 300), stated, "But the Lord's Day we celebrate as a day of joy, because on it He rose again, on which day we have received it for a custom not even to bow the knee" (Peter of Alexandria, Canon 15, *Ante-Nicene Fathers,* ed. Alexander Roberts and James Donaldson, 6:278).

Justin Martyr wrote, "And on the day called Sunday, all who live in cities or in the country gather together to one place, and the memoirs of the Apostles or the writings of the prophets are read as long as time permits; then, when the reader has ceased, the president [presiding official] verbally instructs, and exhorts to the imitation of these good things. Then we all rise together and pray, and, as we before said when our prayers ended, bread and wine and water are brought, and the president in like manner offers prayers and thanksgivings, according to his ability, and the people assent, saying 'Amen.' . . . but Sunday is the day on which we all hold our common assembly, because it is the first day on which God, having wrought a change in the darkness in matter, made the world; and Jesus Christ our Saviour on the same day rose from the dead" (Justin Martyr, "First Apology" 67, in *Ante-Nicene Fathers,* 1:185-86).

Ignatius, Bishop of Antioch (A.D. 110) wrote, "Let us therefore no longer keep the Sabbath after the Jewish manner, and rejoice in days of idleness; for 'he who does not work, let him not eat.' For say the [holy] oracles, 'From the sweat of thy face shalt thou eat thy bread.' But let everyone of you keep the Sabbath after a spiritual manner, rejoicing in meditation on the Law, not in relaxation of the body admiring the workmanship of God" (Ignatius, "To the Magnesians" 9, *Ante-Nicene Fathers,* 1:62-3).

Barnabas (A.D. 70) wrote, "Your present Sabbaths are not acceptable to me, but that is which I have made [namely this,], when, giving rest to all things, I shall make a new beginning of the eighth day, that is, a beginning of another world. Wherefore, also, we keep the eighth day with joyfulness, the day also in which Jesus rose again from the dead" ("Epistle of Barnabas," 15, 7, *Ante-Nicene Fathers,* 1:14).

In *The Teaching of the Twelve Apostles* the statement is made, "But every Lord's Day do ye gather yourselves together and break bread and give thanks after having confessed your transgressions, that your sacrifice may be pure" (*Didache* 14; *Ante-Nicene Fathers,* 7:381.)

From these quotations it is clear that the first day of the week was observed by the early church from the first century; and the Sabbath was considered a requirement of the Jewish Law.

g. THE NEW DAY HAS BEEN BLESSED OF GOD. In observing the history of the church it is clear that devout believers, martyrs, missionaries, and countless others for 2,000 years have recognized the first day of the week as a special day. The attempt to place Christians back under Jewish Law is not supported by the New Testament nor the practice of the early church.

THE FINAL TRANSFORMATION

Much that enters into the new creation is already an accomplished fact in and for the believer. Salvation in the present age is a distinct quality relating to the new order brought in by the incarnation, death, and resurrection of Christ. Several benefits of the new creation should be noted.

1. RELEASE FROM THE SIN NATURE. Though a Christian in this present world continues to have a sin nature, he has the prospect at the end of his earthly life of being released from this lifelong conflict with sin. The warfare between the flesh or sin nature and the Holy Spirit (Gal. 5:17) ends when a believer goes to heaven either by death or by the Rapture. As Paul stated, "For I am already being poured out like a drink offering, and the time has come for my departure. I have fought the good fight, I have finished the race, I have kept the faith. Now there is in store for me the crown of righteousness, which the Lord, the righteous Judge, will award to me on that day—and not only to me, but also to all who have longed for His appearing" (2 Tim. 4:6-8).

2. HEAVENLY CITIZENSHIP. The final transformation of a Christian includes his actual occupation of heavenly citizenship. In this transfer from earth to heaven a Christian exchanges his existence as a stranger and pilgrim to his place in glory in heaven which, though now not occupied, he holds by right and title from the moment of salvation through Christ. Words cannot describe the stupendous change of this transfer from earth to heaven, from part knowledge to whole knowledge, from seeing the glory of God in a "poor reflection" (1 Cor. 13:12) to seeing Christ face to face, from association with

fallen humanity to fellowship with glorified saints and angels, from a body doomed to death to a glorious, eternal body, from earthly dwelling places to what Christ has gone to prepare (John 14:2-3), to being "away from the body and at home with the Lord" (2 Cor. 5:8).

3. TRANSFORMED BODY. The third feature of salvation deferred to the end of this life is the possession of a transformed body which will make the Christian a new creation in every respect. Many Christians receive their new bodies through the process of death and resurrection. Others will receive their new bodies at the Rapture of the church (1 Cor. 15:51-53; Phil. 3:20-21). The transformation of a Christian's sinful body into a body suited for glory is an essential part of his hope (1 Cor. 15:20-23). As the present body is suited for earth, so the new body will be suited for heaven (vv. 35-57). Those who are saved will be resurrected in a series of resurrections: the resurrection of Christ Himself (Matt. 28:1-19; Mark 16:1-6; Luke 24:1-12; John 20:1-18), the resurrection which took place at the time of the resurrection of Christ (Matt. 27:51-53), the resurrection of the church (1 Cor. 15:51-53), the resurrection of the two witnesses (Rev. 11), the resurrection of the martyred saints of the Tribulation (20:4), the resurrection of Old Testament saints (Dan. 12:2-3), and the resurrection of the unsaved (Rev. 20:11-15).

Though the resurrection bodies of the unsaved will be bodies suited for eternal punishment, those of all ages who are saved will receive resurrection bodies similar to that of Christ. As Paul pointed out in 1 Corinthians 15:35-50, there are a variety of forms in bodies in God's creation. The bodies of the saved in heaven will be different from the bodies they have on earth.

Four contrasts are drawn: (a) a body that is sown or buried (vv. 42-44); (b) a body sown in dishonor and humiliation and raised in glory (v. 43); (c) a body sown in weakness is raised a powerful body (Phil. 3:21); and (d) a natural body adapted to this life which is raised a spiritual body, that is, a body capable of worship and spiritual ministry in heaven (1 Cor. 15:44).

Those living on earth at the time of the Rapture will have their bodies instantly changed to bodies like those resurrected at the time of Christ and like the resurrection body of Christ (vv. 50-53). Though Christ's body was not allowed to remain in the grave and see decay (Ps. 16:10; Acts 2:27-31), Christ's present body is the pattern of the believer's resurrection body. Before Christ rose from the dead there were restorations from death back to life in both the Old and

New Testaments (2 Kings 4:32-35; 13:21; Matt. 9:25; Luke 7:12-15; John 11:43; Acts 9:36-41; 14:19-20). These restorations occurring both before and after the resurrection of Christ were not resurrections in the sense that those receiving a body would last forever. Each died again and was buried (except the resurrection of Matt. 27:52-53).

The resurrection and translation of the church at the time of the Rapture, however, results in believers having bodies that will last forever and that are imperishable and immortal (1 Cor. 15:50-53). Sinfulness, which characterized their natural bodies (Eph. 2:1), will be removed. Christians throughout eternity will be special illustrations of the grace of God. The "redemption of our bodies" (Rom. 8:23) refers to the resurrection and translation of the saints when they will be given new and sinless bodies as an outgrowth of the victory that Christ accomplished in His redemption in dying on the cross. As Adam was related to the first creation which fell into sin, so Christ as the last Adam is related to the new creation which speaks of believers' perfection in heaven.

CHAPTER • 26

SEVEN FIGURES USED OF THE CHURCH IN HER RELATION TO CHRIST (VII)

THE BRIDEGROOM AND THE BRIDE

The Bridegroom and the bride—the last of the seven figures that speak of the relationship between Christ and the church—is distinctive in several respects. It is (1) a type in contrast with Israel, (2) a description of Christ's knowledge-surpassing love, (3) an assurance of Christ's authority, (4) a revelation of the Bride's distinctive position, (5) a surety of the bride's infinite glory, and (6) a fulfillment of the bride types. In contrast to the other figures used of the church, this is the eschatological anticipation of the future relationship of the Bridegroom and the bride.

CONTRASTED WITH ISRAEL

A common source of doctrinal error is the confusion of the church with Israel. Quite common in theological interpretation is the thought that the church is the successor of Israel, a concept that is not taught in Scripture.

It is true that Israel is sometimes related to God as the wife of *Yahweh* who has proved to be unfaithful (Hosea 2:2). In the future millennial reign of Christ, Israel, though an unfaithful wife, will be restored as pictured in verses 16-23. By contrast, the church is described as a virgin bride already espoused to one husband who will be claimed by Christ at the time of the Rapture (2 Cor. 11:1-2). In the revelation of this truth the distinction between Israel and the church, however, is maintained. Other passages bearing on this theme are found in both the Old and New Testaments (Isa. 54:5;

Jer. 3:1, 14, 20; Ezek. 16:1-59; Rom. 7:4; Eph. 5:25-33; Rev. 19:7-8; 21:1–22:7; cf. Heb. 12:22-24).

The relationship of the Bridegroom and the bride is also indicated in other Scriptures. In the Parable of the 10 Virgins (Matt. 25:1-13) Israel is related to the 10 virgins but not to the bride. While the figure of marriage is related to both Israel and the church, in general Israel is the unfaithful wife of *Yahweh* who will be restored in the Millennium while the church is pictured as the virgin bride awaiting the coming of the Bridegroom.

CHRIST'S KNOWLEDGE-SURPASSING LOVE

In Ephesians 3:17-21 the Apostle Paul prayed that the Ephesian Christians may know the infinite love of God, "And I pray that you, being rooted and established in love, may have power, together with all the saints, to grasp how wide and long and high and deep is the love of Christ, and to know this love that surpasses knowledge—that you may be filled to the measure of all the fullness of God. Now to Him who is able to do immeasurably more than all we ask or imagine, according to His power that is at work within us, to Him be glory in the church and in Christ Jesus throughout all generations, forever and ever! Amen."

In connection with the love of Christ for His church in 5:25, husbands are exhorted to love their wives as Christ loved the church. Many other contexts in Scripture reveal the love of Christ for His church (John 13:1; Rom. 8:38-39; 2 Cor. 5:14), a love that is true, faithful, and deep like that of a groom for his bride.

ASSURANCE OF THE BRIDE'S AUTHORITY

Though the church will be responsible to Christ, in describing the church as a bride or wife the church is given an elevated place of privilege above that of others. According to 2 Timothy 2:12 the church will reign with Christ. From Revelation 20:4-6 it may be learned that the Tribulation saints will reign with Christ but not in the role of the bride. In keeping with her standing as the bride and wife of Christ the church is described as a royal priesthood (1 Peter 2:9).

THE EXALTED POSITION OF THE BRIDE

The church as the bride of Christ is given an exalted position by virtue of His infinite majesty. In keeping with this, Christ announced that He was preparing a place for the bride (John 14:3). The church is also promised to be with Christ in His glory (17:24). As the wife of Christ, the church will share in the glory of Christ which exalts Him above any creature or power (Eph. 1:20-21).

THE PROMISE OF INFINITE GLORY

According to Romans 8:17 the church will share the glory of Christ. In keeping with this Christ referred to the glory He had with the Father in eternity past (John 17:5), the glory of His transfiguration (Matt. 17:1-8; Mark 9:2-13; Luke 9:28-36), and the glory He would have in His resurrection and in heaven (Rev. 1:13-18) and which would be revealed to the disciples when they too are with Christ in glory (John 17:24; Rom. 8:17; Col. 3:4). The believer in Christ is promised that his body will be made like the body of Christ in glory (1 Cor. 15:43; Phil. 3:21). As the bride of Christ, the church will be glorified by Christ Himself.

TYPES OF THE BRIDE

Whether or not they are specifically designated as types of the relationship of Christ to His church, several Old Testament women foreshadowed the exalted position of the bride of Christ.

1. EVE. Eve is related to Adam as the church is related to Christ. Adam was head of the old creation and Christ was head of the new (Rom. 5:12-21; 1 Cor. 15:21-22, 45-49).

Eve was formed from Adam's side (Gen. 2:21-22) which typically suggests that the church is made possible through the sacrifice and blood of Christ which flowed from His side in death.

In a similar way the pearl (Matt. 13:45-46) represents the church in the sense that a pearl is formed in darkness in the shell of the mollusk, and when brought into the light, shines with glory. Similarly the church, formed in the darkness of the world, will reflect the unsurpassing glory of Christ.

As Adam recognized that Eve was a part of himself (Gen. 2:23), so the church is in Christ and has no existence apart from Him.

2. Rebekah. Rebekah pictures the divine outcalling and consummation of the church as related to Christ, the Bridegroom. Isaac, Abraham's son, is unmistakably a type of Christ, God's only Son (Gen. 22:2; Heb. 11:17). As Isaac was obedient to his father's plan to put him to death, so Christ, loved by the Father, was obedient to death (John 3:16; Rom. 8:32; Phil. 2:8). Isaac's miraculous birth to Abraham and Sarah in their old age suggests Christ's resurrection from the dead (Heb. 11:19). Isaac is also a type of the spiritual children of Abraham (Gen. 15:5; Gal. 4:28-29).

As Abraham sent his servant to secure a bride for Isaac, so God the Father sends His Holy Spirit to secure a bride for Christ.

As the church is foreknown in election and is a bride chosen for Christ, so the servant of Abraham was directed to the young woman who was selected to be the bride of Isaac (Gen. 24:12-61). Rebekah's faith is seen in the fact that she willingly left her home to go with a servant she had not previously known and was willing to marry a man she had never seen. In a similar way the church loves Christ even though He has not yet been seen (1 Peter 1:8).

The many golden ornaments and jewels bestowed on Rebekah were a "foretaste" of the riches she would enjoy as the bride of Isaac. In a similar way the many blessings the church has now from God are tokens of the abundant care the church will enjoy in eternity (2 Cor. 1:22; Eph. 1:14). Rebekah's journey from her home to the home of Isaac illustrates the Christian's pilgrim walk. As the servant of Abraham revealed to Rebekah things about Isaac her future husband, so the Holy Spirit now reveals the teachings of Christ to the church (John 16:13-15; 1 Cor. 2:9-13).

As Isaac was walking in the field at the time Rebekah first met him, so the church will be lifted from her present pilgrim walk to be associated with Christ forever as His bride and wife (Gen. 24:62-67).

3. Boaz. Boaz the kinsman-redeemer who married Ruth is similar to Christ with a Gentile bride.

THE MEANING OF THE FIGURE OF THE BRIDE

In the symbolism of Christ as the Bridegroom and the church as His bride, there is abundant revelation of the unsurpassing love of

Christ, the unity between Christ and the church, and the authority and position to be accorded to the church in ages to come.

The figure of the bride and the Bridegroom supports the concept that there are three divisions in the human family during the present age: Gentiles, Jews, and Christians (1 Cor. 10:32). Redeemed Israelites living at the time of Christ's return to earth will share in His reign on earth. Believing Jews and Gentiles in the church will enjoy the privilege of being the heavenly bride of Christ.

"The Church's one Foundation
Is Jesus Christ her Lord;
She is His new creation
By water and the word:
From heaven He came and sought her
To be His holy Bride;
With His own blood He bought her,
And for her life He died.

Elect from every nation,
Yet one o'er all the earth,
Her charter of salvation
One Lord, one faith, one birth;
One holy Name she blesses,
Partakes one holy food,
And to one hope she presses,
With every grace endued.

Yet she on earth hath union
With God the Three in One,
And mystic sweet communion
With those whose rest is won:
O happy ones and holy!
Lord, give us grace that we,
Like them the meek and lowly,
On high may dwell with Thee."

THE ORGANIZED CHURCH

CHAPTER • 27

THE REVELATION OF THE ORGANIZED CHURCH

For the last 1,900 years Christians have associated with other Christians in church relationships, have endured persecution and conflicts, and have received the benefits of being a redeemed people.

By the fourth century of the Christian era many Christians dreamed of a conquered world ruled by the Messiah and of a political government operating under the authority of the church. To some extent this view has been perpetuated in Romanism.

In Protestantism after the Reformation the postmillennial theory was advocated which proposes that the church will gradually extend its power until the church rules the world and Christians have triumphed over the forces of evil. When this has come about Christ will return.

Events in the twentieth century have challenged this teaching; the concept that the church will ever rule the world seems farther from realization today than ever before.

Postmillennialism is not taught in Scripture for the Bible is clear that good and evil will coexist until the time of the second coming of Christ. The period before the Second Coming will be the worst period of rebellion against Christ the world has ever known.

Distinction should be made between the church as an organism, that is, true believers related to Christ through the baptism of the Spirit, and the organized church as seen in local churches or groups of churches that are united by some organizational features. Of necessity the organized church is restricted to living persons at a given time, bound together by whatever articles of agreement they accept. By contrast the universal church is an organism which includes all believers whether on earth or in heaven.

That organized churches are recognized in the New Testament is seen in Acts 11:22, which refers to "the church at Jerusalem" (cf. 15:22); in Paul's epistles to individual churches (in Rome, Corinth, Galatia, Ephesus, Philippi, Colossae, and Thessalonica); and in Christ's seven messages to seven churches of Asia (Rev. 2–3). The universal church is recognized in the New Testament by the several passages that speak of the church as the body of Christ (1 Cor. 12:12-13, 27; Eph. 1:22-23; 4:15-16; Col. 1:18; 2:19) and by Acts 9:31, which refers to "the church [sing.] throughout Judea, Galilee and Samaria."

The word "church" from the Greek *ekklesia* refers to a called-out assembly. In early Greek democracy citizens of a city-state were called to a central meeting place to carry on their civil business. In like manner Christians are called out from the world to form the body of Christ, and local congregations are formed from those who are called out in one locality. In local congregations, however, some who are associated outwardly with the church may not be genuine Christians. This fact, however, is never true of the church as the body of Christ.

In the early apostolic period churches were formed as a result of Paul's missionary journeys, and he remained an authority over these churches in their early stages. As they grew and matured the churches chose leaders from among their fellowships and gave them specific responsibilities.

In the early apostolic period there is no indication that there was more than one church in a locality. Even in connection with the churches to which Christ addressed His Word in Revelation 2–3, believers in churches who were wandering from God were not exhorted to leave and form a new local church. However, as more individuals came to Christ, it was only natural that more than one local church in a given locality would be formed.

In discussing the organized church three features can be distinguished: (a) the church as a local assembly, (b) a group of local churches, and (c) the visible church without reference to locality.

THE CHURCH AS A LOCAL ASSEMBLY

In the history of the church the local church or groups of churches were taken as the principal evidence of the work of Christ in the present age. Often attention is given to the organized church to the exclusion of the truth of the church as the body of Christ.

In its simplest concept the local church is an assembly of professed believers in one locality. It could be small and meet in a home (1 Cor. 16:19). Larger bodies might include many believers such as the church which was at Jerusalem (Acts 8:1). The fact of local churches is supported by many Scriptures (Matt. 18:17; Acts 8:1, 3; 11:22, 26; 12:1, 5; 14:23, 27; 15:3-4, 22; 18:22; 20:17, 28; Rom. 16:1, 5; 1 Cor. 1:2; 4:17; 6:4; 11:18, 22; 14:4-5, 12, 19, 23; 16:19; 2 Cor. 1:1; Gal. 1:2; Phil. 4:15; Col. 4:15-16; 1 Thes. 1:1; 2 Thes. 1:1; 1 Tim. 5:16; Phile. 2; James 5:14; 3 John 6, 9-10; Rev. 2:1, 8, 12, 18; 3:1, 7, 14).

When Constantine officially recognized the church as a legal entity in the fourth century, it soon expanded to a vast, super organization which later divided in the 11th century into the Roman Church and the Greek Church. With the rise of Protestant denominations thousands of individual churches have been formed with many of them being a part of a larger organization and others functioning as independent churches.

Five aspects of the local church should be considered: (1) the church and her doctrine, (2) the church and her service, (3) the church and her organization, (4) the church and her ordinances, and (5) the church and her order.

1. The church and her doctrine. Consideration of the church and her doctrine is an important aspect of church history. Following the apostolic period the church struggled to reach agreement on important central doctrines of the faith. First the question was considered whether anyone was empowered to add to the Bible, and the church rose up to deny that Scriptures could be supplemented by later writings. In the fourth century attempts were made to clarify the doctrine of the Trinity by stating the position of Christ in relation to the Father, and only later were doctrines of the Holy Spirit's person and work clarified. Following this there were the struggles to formulate a true doctrine of sin. For some centuries there was little progress as spiritual darkness rather than light characterized the organized church.

In the Protestant Reformation many churches withdrew from either the Greek Orthodox Church or the Roman Catholic Church and formed individual churches or groups of churches. Calvinists and Arminians debated the extent of the sovereignty of God. Division also occurred as to whether infant baptism and baptism by affusion were legitimate or whether immersion of believers was indicated in Scripture. Differences of opinion in these areas often led to the execution of those who differed. Doctrinal differences led to multiple divisions in the Protestant church. The emphasis on the church as an institution often overshadowed the scriptural truth of the church as the body of Christ. Though the contentions within the organized church could not divide the church as an organism, yet divisions in the church and departure from scriptural doctrine undoubtedly hindered the progress of evangelizing the world and sanctifying the people of God with the truth of Scripture.

2. The church and her service. The church and her service for God is often a major element of discussion in the organized church. Strictly speaking the organized church is not given a specific task, but rather individuals in the body of Christ are charged with the responsibility to proclaim the Gospel and to lead Christ-honoring lives. The concept of the church as an organism is clearly taught in Scripture (Eph. 4:11-16; Col. 2:19) and with it the commission is given to individuals in the church to evangelize the world (Matt. 28:16-20; Mark 16:14-16; Luke 24:47-48; Acts 1:8). As the Book of Acts illustrates, individual Christians were sent out to serve the Lord (8:5, 26-27, 39; 13:2; etc.). Many were called as separate individuals to accomplish the work of the Lord (vv. 1-3). The Scriptures do not seem to assign to the organized church as such the responsibilities that are directed to individuals.

3. The church and her organization. In the church's organization three general principles of government are followed: (1) the episcopal form of government, represented by Episcopalians and members of other denominations such as the Methodist Episcopal Church, in which bishops exercise rule over a number of churches ("episcopal" is from the Greek *episcopos* which means overseer or bishop); (2) the representative form of rule, represented by the Reformed churches which are governed by appointed boards; and (3) congregational government, which is followed by churches that are ruled directly by the congregation. This last class is represented by the Congregational, Christian, and Baptist churches. Each of these forms of government emphasizes that church government is a convenience which serves a limited purpose.

4. The church and the ordinance of baptism. In most Protestant churches two ordinances are practiced, the ordinance of baptism and the ordinance of the Lord's Supper. In the Roman Catholic

Church these are called sacraments and five additional sacraments are mentioned, namely, confirmation, penance, orders, matrimony, and extreme unction. The Roman Catholic sacraments are believed to be a visible sign of the invisible grace of God bestowed in the sacrament.

Literature bearing on the subject of baptism is so vast and differs so much in its theological statement that it is difficult to compress the results of these centuries of theological discussion since the early church fathers. Generally speaking the major divisions occur over whether baptism is a sacred rite or ceremony or whether it is an actual bestowal of grace, regeneration, or the Holy Spirit. Another division occurs over whether baptism is to be by immersion or by affusion, that is, by pouring or sprinkling water. Still another major division is whether baptism should be administered to infants or only to adult believers. Divisions also occur as to the precise meaning of both the ritual baptism and the real (Holy Spirit) baptism. The meaning and the mode of baptism is a major doctrine which separates various bodies of Christians. This is illustrated in the fact that many churches call themselves "Baptists" which signifies that they believe in baptism by immersion as an essential rite for admission into the local church. Because almost every view on baptism is controverted or opposed by some, it is difficult to find consensus that a majority of the church will receive.

a. BIBLICAL TERMS EMPLOYED. In the Septuagint, the Greek translation of the Old Testament, baptism is used for a variety of ceremonial washings for which a specific mode was not clearly indicated. In the New Testament the concept of baptism is used in various ways in addition to baptism as a rite or ceremony. The Greek words used for baptism are *baptizo*, generally defined as "to immerse" or "to dip"; *baptismos*, the noun form for the action; *bapto*, which is used three times in the New Testament for dipping (Luke 16:24; John 13:26; Rev. 19:13). Lexicographers tend to define the words in keeping with their doctrinal convictions and tend to ignore evidence to the contrary.

The word "baptism" in the New Testament is also complicated by the fact that it is frequently used of actions that have nothing to do with water baptism, such as baptism by fire (Matt. 3:9-12; Luke 3:16-17) which seems to refer to the judgments that will occur at the second coming of Christ. Nor does baptism in 1 Corinthians 10:1-2 refer to water: "For I do not want you to be ignorant of the fact, brothers, that our forefathers were all under the cloud and that they all passed through the sea. They were all baptized into Moses in the cloud and in the sea."

More important is the fact that the baptism of the Holy Spirit (12:13) is often ignored in supporting one view or the other on baptism. The baptism of the Holy Spirit refers to believers being placed into the body of Christ by the work of the Holy Spirit at the time of regeneration. As such, it is an initiation or placing, that is, a submersion into a new relationship without reference to the action of dipping, or removing.

b. THE BAPTISM BY JOHN. All four Gospels refer to John the Baptist's ministry of baptizing those who came to him in repentance of their sins (Matt. 3:1-12; Mark 1:1-8; Luke 3:1-20; John 1:6-8, 15-37). The baptism of John did not depict salvation but a change in the morality of the individual.

c. THE BAPTISM OF JESUS. All four Gospels refer to the fact that John baptized Jesus (Matt. 3:13-17; Mark 1:9-11; Luke 3:21-22; cf. John 1:31-34). Christ insisted that He be baptized saying, "Let it be so now; it is proper to do this to fulfill all righteousness" (Matt. 3:15). The baptism of Christ is distinct from all others and seems to have been a ritual to recognize that Christ was about to exercise His office of Prophet, Priest, and King. Similarities may be found in the rite of consecrating priests in the Old Testament who were washed, apparently by the application of water from a basin (Ex. 29:4; 40:12). It is obvious that Christ did not need a baptism of repentance since He is without sin. Therefore His baptism is unique.

d. THE BAPTISM OF JESUS' DISCIPLES. Though it is often assumed that Jesus' disciples were baptized by Him, there is no clear scriptural support for this conclusion. It is probable that at the beginning of Christ's public ministry, He may have baptized converts, but this work was soon delegated to His disciples (John 4:1-2). Christ's responsibility was eventually to baptize with the Holy Spirit (Matt. 3:11).

e. THE RITE OF CHRISTIAN BAPTISM. The command to administer baptism to Christians is clearly stated in the New Testament (28:19). The ritual is rejected, however, by Quakers and some who hold that it is a Jewish ordinance not perpetuated after the Apostolic Age. The fact that Christ commanded baptism in connection with His command to take the message of the Gospel to the whole world has led the great majority of Christians to recognize ritual baptism.

Just as circumcision as a sign and seal of the Mosaic Covenant sets apart individuals as belonging to God in the Old Testament, so baptism sets a Christian apart in a new relationship realized in salvation (Col. 2:9-12).

In the history of the controversy on the meaning of ritual baptism, the concept that it pictures—the baptism of the Holy Spirit—is almost totally ignored. The use of the word "baptism" for both the baptism of the Spirit and baptism by water signifies that water baptism refers to baptism by the Spirit or the joining of the Christian to Christ. Included in the concept of baptism is the fact that the rite is a symbol of purification, an outward sign that the individual is the object of divine grace, by which he has received regeneration and forgiveness of sin and has been set apart to a new life in Christ.

A major problem in discussions on baptism is the question of its mode. About one third of all Protestant churches hold that baptism is by immersion only and usually of adult believers only. A small number of churches practice "tri-baptism," in which the individual is immersed three times, in the name of each Person of the Trinity. About two thirds of the churches hold that the rite of baptism includes the application of water by other means such as sprinkling or pouring. Most who hold this view also recognize immersion as valid baptism. For many centuries the controversy has continued.

The controversy over the mode of baptism depends largely on the definition of the word *baptizo*. Those who hold to affusion point out that the Greek word *bapto*, which means "to dip," that is, to place into and remove, is never used of the ritual of baptism. So they hold that the rite of baptism indicates the placing in or initiation of a Christian in his new relationship to God and to his fellow believers. He is placed in this new relationship and not taken out of it again. Others who argue for immersion point out that when Jesus was baptized, He "went up out of the water" (Matt. 3:16) and that when the Ethiopian eunuch was baptized he "came up out of the water" (Acts 8:39).

Bible students differ on the meaning of Romans 6:1-10 and Colossians 2:11-13. Some hold that being placed in the water represents death and that being taken out of the water represents resurrection (Rom. 6:3-4). Affusionists hold that this is the result and not the process of baptism, that is, if an individual is placed in Christ then whatever Christ did, he does. So in Christ he died and in Christ he is made alive. Colossians 2:12 is interpreted in a similar way. Those who hold to immersion as the proper mode of baptism regard this as the primary meaning of the word *baptizo.* Those who hold to affusion believe that *baptizo* is used in a secondary sense of initiation or of being set apart by a cleansing rite as in Hebrews 9:10 where *baptismos* is translated "ceremonial washings."

Some refer also to the fact that various prepositions are used in connection with water baptism. Opposing views define the preposition in keeping with their theological understanding of the rite. In a number of instances the Jordan River is mentioned in connection with baptism. Immersionists say these references suggest baptism by immersion. Affusionists point out, however, that baptism by immersion is unlikely in some instances. In the case of the Philippian jailer and his family, "At that hour of the night the jailer . . . and all his family were baptized" (Acts 16:33). Affusionists point out that it was unlikely at that hour of the night that they would go to a body of water to be baptized by immersion. They suggest that pouring was more likely.

Because of the numerous arguments used both by affusionists and immersionists, it is difficult for anyone to attempt to solve this problem, and ultimately the choice has to be made as to which evidence is received and which is rejected. Controversy in the Christian church over the mode of baptism has been largely fruitless. It is more important to recognize the significance of the rite of baptism as related to the baptism of the Spirit and believers' initiation into their new life in Christ.

Another question about the rite of baptism is whether infants should be baptized. Many Protestant churches accept infant baptism, but many do not. The ultimate question is whether baptism by whatever mode should be administered only to adult believers or whether it should be administered to children.

Because circumcision was administered to infants in the Old Testament and water baptism is related to this in Colossians 2:11-12, infant baptism is held by some to replace circumcision as a rite for the church. Evidence for infant baptism is indecisive, though of the seven instances mentioned in the Book of Acts, five refer to households with the implication that this would include children. Infant baptism is ultimately an act of faith on the part of the parents that their children will respond to the teaching of the Gospel in due time and will accept Christ as Saviour. Some who hold to infant baptism regard it as no more than an act of dedication by the parents, whereas others believe that actual grace is bestowed. In the Lutheran Church it is commonly referred to as regeneration, but regeneration is redefined as meaning not salvation but merely the impartation of grace. The baptism of infants is also practiced by the Roman Catholic Church because of her view that apart from ritual baptism no one can go to heaven.

Taken as a whole the testimony for infant baptism is not explicit in the New Testament, and there is less basis for dispute than over the larger questions of the mode of water baptism and the meaning of baptism.

f. REAL BAPTISM. Complicating the subject of baptism is the fact that some churches teach that in the rite there is an actual transaction in which one is regenerated through water baptism. This is said to be true whether infants or adults are baptized. There is no basis in Scripture for this concept of baptismal regeneration though it was a common doctrine in the early church. Some who hold that water baptism is essential to regeneration redefine regeneration since not all children who were baptized as infants become believers in adulthood. Regeneration is properly defined as the new birth or bestowal of eternal life. It is an error to associate this with water baptism.

A practical approach to the problem is to recognize that there are differences of opinion in the Christian faith over the meaning and mode of baptism, but these should not normally be considered as divisive and making impossible the fellowship of Christians whose views differ on this matter. In Scripture the manifestation of love for fellow Christians is more definitive than what mode of baptism was employed (cf. John 13:34-35; 17:21-23).

5. THE CHURCH AND THE ORDINANCE OF THE LORD'S SUPPER. The Lord's Supper was instituted by Christ the night before His crucifixion as a part of the Passover celebration (Matt. 26:26-28; Mark 14:22-24; Luke 22:19-20). Various terms are used in the Scriptures to refer to the Lord's Supper such as "My body" and "My blood of the covenant" (Matt. 26:26, 28), "the breaking of bread" (Acts 2:42; 20:7), "a participation in the body of Christ" (1 Cor. 10:16), "the Lord's Supper" (11:20), "the bread" and "the cup of the Lord" (v. 27). Other designations, not given in the Bible, are the Eucharist, meaning "a ceremony of giving thanks," Communion, a memorial feast in commemoration of Jesus' death, and the presence of Christ.

Though scholars have debated the exact nature of the Lord's Supper, generally speaking they usually accept Paul's description of the Lord's Supper in verses 23-29. Paul wrote that this was received directly from the Lord. Christ took bread, gave thanks, broke it, and said, "This is My body, which is for you; do this in remembrance of Me" (v. 24). Paul continued, "In the same way, after supper He took the cup, saying, 'This cup is the New Covenant in My blood; do this, whenever you drink it, in remembrance of Me.' For whenever you eat this bread and drink this cup, you proclaim the Lord's death until He comes" (vv. 25-26). It is generally believed that the practice of the early church coincided with Paul's description and the accuracy of his account is assured by the doctrine of inspiration.

Paul warned that anyone who participates in the Lord's Supper "in an unworthy manner will be guilty of sinning against the body and blood of the Lord" (v. 27). Believers are urged to "examine" themselves, that is, to see if there are any shortcomings in their spiritual lives as a proper action preparatory for observance of the Lord's Supper (v. 28). Paul assured them, "For anyone who eats and drinks without recognizing the body of the Lord eats and drinks judgment on himself" (v. 29). Paul called attention to the fact that wrong observance of the Lord's Supper had caused some believers to be physically sick and others to die (v. 30). He said discipline would be applied to those who do not judge or discipline themselves (v. 32). As the Lord's Supper was sometimes observed in connection with a dinner meal, he urged them to avoid doing anything that would affect the sacredness of the Lord's Supper.

In general there is agreement that the bread represents the body of Christ and the cup represents His shed blood. In the history of the church various views have been offered of the meaning of these elements. The Roman Catholic Church defined the offering of the bread and the cup as a sacrifice to God in which the bread literally becomes the body of Christ and the cup literally becomes the blood of Christ. This is known as transubstantiation. Martin Luther rejected transubstantiation but held that the elements *contain* the body and blood of Christ in a spiritual sense. This view is known as consubstantiation. Calvin held that Christ was spiritually present in the elements, but not bodily. Zwingli taught that the Lord's Supper is a memorial to the death of Christ and that because His body was in heaven He could not be bodily present in the elements. Apart from the Roman Catholic and Lutheran churches, the majority of Protestantism holds to the Calvinistic or Zwinglian interpretations.

Most interpreters agree that the celebration of the Lord's Supper is a reminder of the death of Christ and an act whereby believers enjoy the benefits of salvation which He accomplished on the cross. The Lord's Supper, however, is more than a reminder of His death. It is also a call to holiness and self-judgment in order to be spiritually prepared for observing the communion and fellowship with Him which the Lord's Supper represents.

Various churches adopt their own regulations concerning the observance of the Lord's Supper including its frequency and specific character. In some Protestant churches those presiding at the Lord's table are limited to persons ordained to the ministry. In others this privilege is extended to any Christian believer. The Scriptures are silent on this and other details about the way the Lord's Supper is to be observed. Instead they concentrate on its spiritual meaning as a memorial and reminder of the death of Christ and a Christian's participation in His death by faith. In receiving the elements of the Lord's Supper Christians are recognizing the death of Christ as the only basis for their salvation.

6. THE CHURCH AND HER ORDER. The early church was a fellowship rather than an organization, and converts were numbered in the thousands before any clear church organization took place. The suggestion that the local church was organized after the model of the synagogue is not supported in Scripture. The inference that the church today must follow rigidly the customs of the early church is also subject to question. In reading the Acts and the Epistles, however, certain major factors emerge.

Undoubtedly the apostles provided leadership for the large church at Jerusalem, but as churches were established through the missionary work and evangelization of Paul and others, control was often in the hands of those who evangelized the church in the early stage. Only as the church matured were structures established. In Acts 6 seven men were set aside to assist the apostles in caring for the widows and similar needs in the early church (vv. 1-5). These men were set aside with prayer and laying on of hands by the apostles (v. 6). It is probable that these servants were later called deacons.

In Israel elders were a part of the government of Israel and are often referred to in the Old Testament. Elders were also appointed in the early church. The first mention of this is in 11:30. They were men of maturity and recognized leadership ability. In some cases they were appointed by the apostles, and in other cases they were apparently appointed either by common consent or by the vote of the local church. The Scriptures do not specify the method to be followed in electing elders and deacons. Elders (Gr., *presbyteros*) seem to be the same as bishops (Gr., *episkopos*). "Bishops" (KJV) or "overseers" (NIV) are referred to in Philippians 1:1; 1 Timothy 3:2; Titus 1:7; and 1 Peter 2:25. In Acts 14:23 Luke wrote, "Paul and Barnabas appointed elders for them in each church and, with prayer and fasting, committed them to the Lord in whom they had put their trust."

In Scripture there are frequent references to the apostles and elders as the church leaders responsible for maintaining order and discipline. Basic requirements for an elder or a bishop are stated in 1 Timothy 3:1-7, and qualifications for deacons are given in verses 8-13. Elders had to be above reproach morally and models of godly leadership in their own homes. Their Christian experience had to be mature, and they had to have a good reputation in the community. Deacons were to have similar requirements of maturity, morality, and ability (vv. 8-13).

Elders were to rule the local church (vv. 4-5; 5:17), to protect the local church from doctrinal error (Titus 1:9), and to serve the church with care as a shepherd serves his flock (John 21:16; Acts 20:28; Heb. 13:17; 1 Peter 5:2). In the early days of the church they were appointed by apostles but later were appointed or chosen by their congregations according to the elder's abilities and the guidance of the Holy Spirit.

The deacons were to be concerned with charity and caring for those with special needs as indicated by the original appointment in Acts 6:1-6 and later references (1 Tim. 3:8-13). These deacons and other leaders of the church were recognized by the laying on of hands of apostles (Acts 6:6; 13:3; 2 Tim. 1:6) or by elders (1 Tim. 4:14). The laying on of hands did not actually impart an assignment or ability; it visibly recognized the call of God of these leaders and demonstrated their support of them. Deacons might also have other spiritual gifts such as that of evangelism (Acts 21:8). These men were gifts to the church, in contrast to spiritual gifts given to men as in 1 Corinthians 12:7-11. Several gifts of ministry are also enumerated in Ephesians 4:11. No mention is made in the New Testament of ordination of leaders with spiritual gifts though gifts were recognized in setting apart elders and deacons for their ministry.

The New Testament makes no distinction between clergy and

laity though it does recognize that individual believers differ in their spiritual gifts and that some persons were set apart for leadership over others.

A GROUP OF LOCAL CHURCHES

In contrast to the church, the body of Christ is universal and is addressed as a single unit. Local churches consisted of professing believers in a locality who met for worship and service. Local churches are frequently mentioned in the New Testament (Acts 9:31; 15:41; 16:5; Rom. 16:4; 1 Cor. 11:16; 14:34; 16:1, 19; 2 Cor. 8:1, 18-19, 23-24; 12:13; Gal. 1:2, 22; 1 Thes. 2:14; Rev. 1:4, 11, 20; 2:7, 11, 17, 23; 3:6, 13, 22; 22:16). Though these churches recognized the leadership of apostles, there is no indication that the churches were organized into a denomination or some form of regional government. On the other hand the Scriptures do not forbid churches relating to each other in their common task.

THE VISIBLE CHURCH WITHOUT REFERENCE TO LOCALITY

In contrast to the church in the sense of the body of Christ which is universal whether in earth or heaven, the visible church which consists of professed believers in the world is often recognized without reference to locality (Acts 12:1; Rom. 16:16; 1 Cor. 4:17; 7:17; 11:16; 14:33-34; 15:9; 2 Cor. 11:28; 12:13; Gal. 1:13; Phil. 3:6; 2 Thes. 1:4). The visible church is also a subject of prophecy (2 Thes. 2:3; 1 Tim. 4:1-3; 2 Tim. 3:1-8; 4:3-4; 2 Peter 2:1–3:18; Rev. 2:1–3:22).

THE BELIEVER'S RULE OF LIFE

CHAPTER • 28

RULES OF LIFE IN THE OLD TESTAMENT PERIOD

Living a life which is well-pleasing to God is second in importance to the saving of the soul. Apart from a few theologians who dwell at length on the Ten Commandments as the standard for the Christian's walk, most theologies do not give any detailed instruction on the spiritual life. Any systematic theology that attempts to organize all that is found in the Scriptures should obviously include discussion of God's moral codes and instruction relating to them as contained in the Bible. Though God gave some instruction about human conduct even to Adam and Eve in the Garden of Eden, many of God's moral commands for man not only are stated in explicit regulations in the Scriptures but also are illustrated in the Bible in the lives of individuals.

In Scripture it is evident that in successive periods of time the required moral code differs in many respects. Before Moses the Bible includes only fragmentary references to the explicit moral codes which preceded the Mosaic Law. This is because the period of time from Creation to Moses was already history. The tremendous change brought about by the Mosaic Law is recorded frequently in Scripture. For instance Nehemiah 9:13-14 states, "You came down on Mount Sinai; You spoke to them from heaven. You gave them regulations and laws that are just and right, and decrees and commands that are good. You made known to them Your holy Sabbath and gave them commands, decrees, and laws through Your servant Moses." In Ezekiel 20:10-12 God said, "Therefore I led them [Israel] out of Egypt and brought them into the desert. I gave them My decrees and made known to them My laws, for the man who obeys them will live by them. Also I gave them My Sabbaths as a sign between us, so they would know that I the Lord made them holy."

In the New Testament one is confronted immediately by the fact that a new relationship is revealed with a different and higher requirement for daily living (John 1:16-17; Rom. 6:14; 7:2-6; 2 Cor. 3:1-18; Gal. 3:19-25; Eph. 2:15; Col. 2:14). The prophetic Scriptures anticipate that after the second coming of Christ there will be still another rule of life which will continue throughout the millennial reign of Christ on earth. Though there are similarities in all dispensations, because God is the same God and basic morality does not change, the particular requirements in each dispensation were measured by the divine revelation given concerning it.

The present age is especially complex as it is built on the principle of grace that is less obvious in other dispensations. Though legal regulations in the Mosaic period as well as in the future Millennium set forth the righteous demands of God, in the present dispensation of grace the Bible emphasizes that works are not a means of attaining favor with God either in the matter of salvation or in the matter of sanctification. Regulations in the present age are supernatural requirements dependent on the indwelling Spirit for power to attain them. In "covenant theology" the attempt is made to minimize the distinctions between different dispensations and to magnify their similarities. Covenant theology, though related to other theologies, has its primary source in Cocceius (1603-1669). He postulated a so-called covenant of works before the Fall, which covenant of course was broken, and a covenant of grace was instituted thereafter.

There is little or no evidence of a covenant of works in the Bible except that obviously Adam and Eve suffered as a result of their disobeying God in regard to the tree of the knowledge of good and evil. It is also clear that Adam and Eve became the recipients of the grace of God and were saved on that basis. Covenant theology generally fails to recognize distinct rules of life and the sharp distinction between the works principle as a rule of life (not as a way of salvation) in the Mosaic Covenant and the grace principle as a rule of life in the present age.

There are spiritual laws in every dispensation and also grace in every dispensation. But the distinctions revealed for the present age are too often placed under the legal requirement of obedience to the Law as a means of attaining God's blessings. In every dispensation believers in Christ are saved by grace apart from human merit. But for believers in the Mosaic era the enjoyment of God's blessings depended on their human attainments in following the Mosaic code.

On the other hand many of the blessings God showers on believers in the Church Age are not conditioned on human attainments. For the purpose of studying rules of life in Scripture it will be sufficient to examine four major economies—the pre-Mosaic, the Mosaic, the future millennial kingdom, and the Church Age—and the distinctions which may be observed between them.

THE PRE-MOSAIC ECONOMY

In the pre-Mosaic economy, largely revealed in the Book of Genesis, four divine dispensations were evident. These were (1) the dispensation of innocence, before the Fall; (2) the dispensation of conscience, in which conscience was the dominant factor requiring choice between good and evil; (3) the dispensation of government, an age of obligation to human government which to some extent continued in later dispensations; and (4) the dispensation of promise, in which God chose Abraham and his descendants and promised that they would be the special channel of divine blessing.

Because these four dispensations were already past by the time the first Scripture was written, only brief mention is made of the history of them and God's relationship to people in those economies.

Several passages in Genesis bring this out. For instance, God told Adam and Eve, "You must not eat from the tree of the knowledge of good and evil, for when you eat of it you will surely die" (2:17). Eve added, "You must not touch it" (3:3). This points to moral obligation on their part, the necessity of obedience, and the penalty for disobeying the moral command.

God told Cain that his offering was not accepted because he had not done "what is right" (4:7). Apparently God had revealed to Adam, Eve, Cain, and Abel the importance of blood sacrifice (vv. 2-4; cf. 3:21). After Cain's murder of Abel, God said, "If anyone kills Cain, he will suffer vengeance seven times over" (4:15). This revealed God's moral standard that one murder did not justify another.

Later God said the following regarding Abraham: "For I have chosen him, so that he will direct his children and his household after him to keep the way of the LORD by doing what is right and just, so that the LORD will bring about for Abraham what He has promised him" (18:19). This reveals that before the Law there was some understanding of the mind and the will of God and an awareness that God is righteous and requires human obedience. Genesis 26:5 adds, "Because Abraham obeyed Me and kept My requirements, My commands, My decrees and My laws." The obedience of Abraham was part of his walk of faith with the Lord though there was no distinct revelation of the details of the rule of life in that period.

In Romans 5:13 Paul wrote, "For before the Law was given, sin was in the world. But sin is not taken into account when there is no law." This states the important principle that obligation to obey God is related to the extent of revelation. For this reason there could be no transgression of the Mosaic Law before it was instituted. Furthermore the Mosaic Law was limited to the people of Israel and was not extended to nor required of the Gentile world. This does not mean that there were no moral requirements before Moses, but rather that the requirements are not spelled out in Scripture. No doubt there was direct revelation from God to godly men in this period which is not recorded in the Bible.

THE MOSAIC ECONOMY

With the coming of Moses and growth of the nation Israel, the Mosaic Law was given. It included more than 600 detailed laws including rituals which Israel was required as a nation to observe. The purpose of the Law was to reveal sin (Rom. 5:20; 7:7; Gal. 3:19) and to demonstrate man's need of Christ (v. 24). The Law of Moses included God's instructions for Israel's civil, religious, and moral life. Two truths should be emphasized in relation to the Mosaic Law: (1) it was never addressed to Gentiles except those who became Israelites as proselytes, and (2) it was not a way of salvation.

Salvation is not given in response to obeying commands. It is given to those in every age who place their trust in God for forgiveness of sin. The Mosaic sacrificial system was given as a means of restoring fellowship with God for believers who fell into sin. The sacrifices were to be offered by Israelites who had placed their faith in *Yahweh.* Apart from this faith, the sacrifices were meaningless rituals. The sacrifices anticipated the future sacrifice of Christ which was not understood by Old Testament saints. A standard for confession and forgiveness, without animal sacrifices, was established for Christians in need of cleansing from daily sin (1 John 1:9).

The nation Israel descended physically from Abraham, Isaac, and Jacob. As a nation and race, they received special promises from God both for their present and the future and were given privileges that do not extend to the Gentile world.

Israelites were promised blessing in return for obedience to the Law, and were told that God would discipline them if they failed to keep the Law. This is illustrated in Deuteronomy 28. The first 14 verses promised blessing to those who keep His commandments, and verses 15-68 are a declaration of curses and judgments that would fall on the nation if she disobeyed. Subsequently both the blessings and the curses were fulfilled.

It is clear in Old Testament predictions that Israel as a nation would depart from God (4:26-28). The spiritual life of Israel was not on an even plane. In one period they were disobedient and God disciplined them, and in another they were generally obedient and enjoyed God's blessings. The Old Testament did not anticipate the present day of grace but did look forward to the future kingdom when Israel would possess her land on earth. Many Scriptures speak of this period (cf. Ezek. 20:33-44; Mal. 3:1-6; Matt. 24:37–25:30). In the kingdom both reward and judgment will be experienced by Israel (Dan. 12:2; Matt. 7:13-14; Luke 10:25-28; 18:18-21).

Even the Old Testament made clear that righteousness could be received only by faith and not by works (Gen. 15:6; cf. Hab. 2:4).

In the Bible the word "law" does not always refer to the Mosaic system or to any part of it. Certain facts about law, however, may be observed. (1) The Ten Commandments are God's Law (cf. Luke 10:25-28; Rom. 7:7-14). (2) The entire governing code for Israel as recorded in Exodus and Leviticus is the Law. (3) The rule of life yet to be applied in the coming messianic kingdom is law but not the Mosaic Law. (4) Any rule of conduct prescribed by men may be referred to as law (1 Tim. 1:8-9; 2 Tim. 2:5; cf. Matt. 20:15; Luke 20:22). (5) Any recognized principle of action is a law and sometimes is equivalent to power (Rom. 7:21; 8:2). (6) The entire will of God reaching to every detail of an individual believer's life is the law of God but should be distinguished from the Mosaic Law (7:22; 8:4). (7) The will of Christ for the believer in the present age is "the law of Christ" (cf. John 13:34; 15:10; 1 Cor. 9:21; Gal. 6:2). In the Mosaic period there was grace along with law just as in the present dispensation there is law with grace. The dominating factor in the present age is that God is dealing with believers on a gracious basis rather than on a meritorious basis as indicated in the Mosaic period.

In the Mosaic dispensation the will of God for individual Israelites as well as for the nation as a whole consisted of three parts: (1) the Commandments, which regulated moral issues (Ex. 20), (2) the judgments, which regulated the civic issues (21:1–24:11), and (3) the ordinances, which regulated the religious issues (24:12–31:18). It is generally agreed that both the judgments and the ordinances of the Mosaic Law ceased with the crucifixion of Christ. Continued misunderstanding, however, exists in relation to the Ten Commandments. Many people teach that these are continued in the present age of grace. The fact is that nine of the Ten Commandments are repeated in the New Testament and with higher standards, but the fourth commandment concerning the Sabbath is not found in the New Testament revelation concerning the age of grace. The moral code for believers in the Church Age includes the nine commandments but it goes far beyond them to include much more.

In attempting to understand the Mosaic system two features of its truth are important: (1) the relation the Mosaic Law sustained to the time of its reign and (2) the application of the Mosaic system.

1. The Mosaic Law was temporary. The Mosaic Law was given as a temporary, not an eternal, rule of life. Before the Mosaic Law was given those laws did not apply, and after the Mosaic Law was concluded the Law was no longer a basic moral code for Christians in the present age.

In view of the temporal character of the Law of Moses the question is raised as to why this revelation was given. The answer to this question is in Galatians 3:19, "What, then, was the purpose of the Law? It was added because of transgressions until the Seed to whom the promise referred had come." Any transgression of the Law of God or anything out of harmony with the holiness of God is sin in any dispensation and requires the grace of God for forgiveness. Even Adam and Eve were told not to disobey. The introduction of the Law did not change the fact of the sin nature and consequent spiritual death (Rom. 5:12-14). The Law changed the character of personal wrongdoing by making it a violation of the Law. It made sin rebellion against specific commands of God with corresponding punishment that comes from a broken law.

The Law was given Israel not to create an obedient people but rather to prove their utter sinfulness and helplessness. This is indicated in Paul's own experience in 7:8, "But sin, seizing the opportunity afforded by the commandment, produced in me every kind of covetous desire. For apart from Law, sin is dead." That the Law was holy and righteous is obvious as stated by Paul in verses 12-13, "So then, the Law is holy, and the commandment is holy, righteous, and good. Did that which is good, then, become death to me? By no means! But in order that sin might be recognized as sin, it produced death in me through what was good, so that through the commandment sin might become utterly sinful." Apart from Christ there has been universal failure to keep such laws as God has revealed.

The Law was never given as a means for salvation or justification (3:20; cf. Gal. 3:11, 24). The Law therefore became a curse to Israel (v. 10) bringing them condemnation (2 Cor. 3:9) and death (Rom. 7:10-11). A beneficial effect of the Law was to drive Israel to Christ as the only Saviour and Mediator.

a. THE LAW BEGAN ITS REIGN AT MOUNT SINAI. Before the Law was given, no one was responsible to keep it. With the introduction of the Law Israel was required to obey it as stated in Deuteronomy 5:1-3, "Moses summoned all Israel and said: Hear, O Israel, the decrees and laws I declare in your hearing today. Learn them and be sure to follow them. The LORD our God made a covenant with us at Horeb. It was not with our fathers that the LORD made this covenant, but with us, with all of us who are alive here today."

The people voluntarily pledged their obedience to the Law without recognizing their inability to keep it. This is stated in Exodus 19:3-8, "Then Moses went up to God, and the LORD called to him from the mountain and said, 'This is what you are to say to the house of Jacob and what you are to tell the people of Israel: "You yourselves have seen what I did to Egypt, and how I carried you on eagles' wings and brought you to Myself. Now if you obey Me fully and keep My covenant, then out of all nations you will be My treasured possession. Although the whole earth is Mine, you will be for Me a kingdom of priests and a holy nation." These are the words you are to speak to the Israelites.' So Moses went back and summoned the elders of the people and set before them all the words the LORD had commanded him to speak. The people all responded together, 'We will do everything the LORD has said.' So Moses brought their answer back to the LORD."

Once the Children of Israel had accepted the Law, it became immediately evident that they were dealing with the unapproachable and holy character of God as stated in verses 18-21, "Mount Sinai was covered with smoke, because the LORD descended on it in fire. The smoke billowed up from it like smoke from a furnace, the whole mountain trembled violently, and the sound of the trumpet grew louder and louder. Then Moses spoke and the voice of God answered him. The LORD descended to the top of Mount Sinai and called Moses to the top of the mountain. So Moses went up and the LORD said to him, 'Go down and warn the people so they do not force their way through to see the LORD and many of them perish.' " The same thought is expressed in Hebrews 12:18-21.

b. THE REIGN OF THE LAW WAS TERMINATED WITH THE DEATH OF CHRIST. Previous dispensations to some extent continued after they came to a formal close, but the Law came to an abrupt end at the time of the death of Christ.

The Law was given only until "the Seed to whom the promise referred had come" (Gal. 3:19). It resulted in those under the Law coming clearly under condemnation with salvation only available to them through faith in Christ.

Paul in Galatians came to the conclusion, "Before this faith came, we were held prisoners by the Law, locked up until faith should be revealed. So the Law was put in charge to lead us to Christ that we might be justified by faith. Now that faith has come, we are no longer under the supervision of the Law" (vv. 23-25).

2. THE APPLICATION OF THE LAW. The Mosaic Law was given only to the Children of Israel as a way of life. Though others could read the Mosaic code and be instructed concerning the righteousness of God, those who were not Israelites were not under its provisions. This is seen for instance in the Law of the Sabbath which was never applied to Gentiles in the Old Testament. This fact is stated clearly by Moses in Deuteronomy 5:1-3, "Moses summoned all Israel and said: Hear, O Israel, the decrees and laws I declare in your hearing today. Learn them and be sure to follow them. The LORD our God made a covenant with us at Horeb. It was not with our fathers that the LORD made this covenant, but with us, with all of us who are alive here today." The ultimate Law was summarized in the Ten Commandments which were not made applicable to people other than Israel even though it coincided with general principles of law which exist in all dispensations such as the law against idolatry, murder, adultery, dishonesty, and coveting.

In summarizing Israel's place of blessing Paul stated in Romans 9:4-5, "Theirs is the adoption as sons; theirs the divine glory, the covenants, the receiving of the Law, the temple worship, and the promises. Theirs are the patriarchs, and from them is traced the human ancestry of Christ, who is God over all, forever praised! Amen." By contrast Gentiles were on the outside as stated in Ephesians 2:11-12, "Therefore, remember that formerly you who are Gentiles by birth and called 'uncircumcised' by those who call themselves 'the circumcision' (that done in the body by the hands of men)— remember that at that time you were separate from Christ, excluded from citizenship in Israel and foreigners to the covenants of the promise, without hope and without God in the world." Gentiles are said not to be under the Mosaic code as in Romans 2:14, "Indeed, when Gentiles, who do not have the Law, do by nature things required by the Law, they are a law for themselves, even though they do not have the Law."

The Law which was given by Moses was a covenant of works, that was "added" after centuries of human history; its reign was terminated by the death of Christ; it was given to Israel only; and since it was never given to Gentiles, the only relationship that Gentiles can sustain to it is to impose it on themselves but this is obviously not the intent of Scripture.

CHAPTER • 29

THE FUTURE KINGDOM ECONOMY

Before considering the distinctives of the present grace economy as a rule of life for the church it is necessary to consider not only the economy or rule of life under the Mosaic Covenant which is already past but also the future kingdom economy or the rule of life in the millennial kingdom. Even among conservative expositors of the Bible who recognize the inspiration of Scripture, there are differences of opinion as to how the present age relates to the Mosaic economy and how it relates to the future economy of the kingdom following the second coming of Christ. This is brought out in clear detail by contrasting the premillennial view of the second coming of Christ with the postmillennial view and the amillennial view. Even within these major systems of interpretation, there are subdivisions which further complicate the theological problem.

THE PREMILLENNIAL VIEW OF THE FUTURE KINGDOM ECONOMY

According to premillennial interpreters, the second coming of Christ will be followed by a reign of Christ on earth for 1,000 years. The Second Advent will introduce an economy or dispensation distinct from the Mosaic economy and from the economy of grace in the present age. This will be treated more in detail in the study of eschatology, but certain important distinctions should be observed before attempting to define the present economy under grace. The premillennial view is based on the Davidic Covenant in which God promised David's descendants that his kingdom would endure forever. "When your days are over and you rest with your fathers, I will raise up your offspring to succeed you, who will come from your own body, and I will establish his kingdom. He is the one who will build a house for My Name, and I will establish the throne of his kingdom forever. I will be his Father, and he will be My son. When he does wrong, I will punish him with the rod of men, with floggings inflicted by men. But My love will never be taken away from him, as I took it away from Saul, whom I removed from before you. Your house and your kingdom will endure forever before Me; your throne will be established forever" (2 Sam. 7:12-16).

This covenant with David is interpreted by premillenarians as a literal promise of a political government over which one of David's descendants would reign forever, that is, as long as the earth is in existence. Though a descendant of David has not sat on a throne in Israel continuously without interruption, the Davidic Covenant does affirm that a descendant would reign from time to time until the end of the earth, that is, till the end of the Millennium. Twenty descendants of David beginning with Solomon (1 Kings 1:28-30, 43) and continuing through Zedekiah (2 Chron. 36:11-14) ruled in Jerusalem until the Babylonian Exile (vv. 15-21). The next Descendant will be the Messiah, Jesus Christ, who will reign from Jerusalem for 1,000 years in the millennial kingdom. Jesus Christ is qualified to sit on the throne of David forever (Luke 1:32; Rev. 1:5-7), and this is what repeated promises in the Old Testament affirm.

This concept is supported by Psalm 72, written by David to Solomon (KJV) or by Solomon (NIV), which promised a future kingdom of justice under the reign of Christ (vv. 1-4). The everlasting character of the kingdom under God's "royal Son" is said to endure forever. "He will endure as long as the sun, as long as the moon, through all generations. He will be like rain falling on a mown field, like showers watering the earth. In His days the righteous will flourish; prosperity will abound till the moon is no more" (vv. 5-7).

The future kingdom anticipated in this psalm will include the entire world, "He will rule from sea to sea and from the [Euphrates] River to the ends of the earth. The desert tribes will bow before Him and His enemies will lick the dust. The kings of Tarshish and of distant shores will bring tribute to Him; the kings of Sheba and Seba will present Him gifts. All kings will bow down to Him and all nations will serve Him" (vv. 8-11). This King will endure as long as the sun endures and will bring blessing to the entire world, "May His name endure forever; may it continue as long as the sun. All nations will be blessed through Him, and they will call Him blessed. Praise be to the LORD God, the God of Israel, who alone does marvelous deeds. Praise be to His glorious name forever; may the whole earth be filled with His glory. Amen and Amen" (vv. 17-19).

The same truth is stated in Psalm 89, which affirms that David's Descendant will reign. "I will also appoint Him My Firstborn, the most exalted of the kings of the earth. I will maintain My love to Him forever, and My covenant with Him will never fail. I will establish His line forever, His throne as long as the heavens endure" (vv. 27-29).

The promise to establish this kingdom depends on God's faithfulness rather than man's, and even though David's royal descendants departed from God, the promise will ultimately have its fulfillment. This is stated clearly in verses 30-37. "If his sons forsake My law and do not follow My statutes, if they violate My decrees and fail to keep My commands, I will punish their sin with the rod, their iniquity with flogging; but I will not take My love from him, nor will I ever betray My faithfulness. I will not violate My covenant or alter what My lips have uttered. Once for all, I have sworn by My holiness—and I will not lie to David—that his line will continue forever and his throne endure before Me like the sun; it will be established forever like the moon, the faithful witness in the sky" (vv. 30-37). This psalm affirms that God will discipline His people who depart from Him in the period before the ultimate fulfillment, but their departure from the will of God will not change God's ultimate purpose to have a descendant of David sit on the Davidic throne forever.

The teaching of these portions of Scripture is confirmed in Isaiah 9:6-7, "For to us a Child is born, to us a Son is given, and the government will be on His shoulders. And He will be called Wonderful Counselor, Mighty God, Everlasting Father, Prince of Peace. Of the increase of His government and peace there will be no end."

This future kingdom will be characterized by righteousness and peace as brought out in 2:2-4, "In the last days the mountain of the LORD's temple will be established as chief among the mountains; it will be raised above the hills, and all nations will stream to it. Many peoples will come and say, 'Come, let us go up to the mountain of the LORD, to the house of the God of Jacob. He will teach us His ways, so that we may walk in His paths.' The Law will go out from Zion, the word of the LORD from Jerusalem. He will judge between the nations and will settle disputes for many peoples. They will beat their swords into plowshares and their spears into pruning hooks. Nation will not take up sword against nation, nor will they train for war anymore."

The righteous and peaceful character of the kingdom is brought out in 11:1-9. Along with the Messiah's exercise of universal justice (vv. 3-5), animals will no longer be ferocious (vv. 7-9). Also, "The earth will be full of the knowledge of the LORD as the waters cover the sea" (v. 9).

Jeremiah described this period as the time when Israel will be regathered and ruled by the Lord. " 'The days are coming,' declares the LORD, 'when I will raise up to David a righteous Branch, a King who will reign wisely and do what is just and right in the land. In His days Judah will be saved and Israel will live in safety. This is the name by which He will be called: The LORD Our Righteousness. So then, the days are coming,' declares the LORD, 'when people will no longer say, "As surely as the LORD lives, who brought the Israelites up out of Egypt," but they will say, "As surely as the LORD lives, who brought the descendants of Israel up out of the land of the north and out of all the countries where He had banished them." Then they will live in their own land' " (Jer. 23:5-8).

Hosea 3:4-5 points up the fact that there will be many years in which no king would sit on David's throne before its final fulfillment in the last days. "For the Israelites will live many days without king or prince, without sacrifice or sacred stones, without ephod or idol. Afterward the Israelites will return and seek the LORD their God and David their king. They will come trembling to the LORD and to His blessings in the last days."

Other passages which confirm these prophecies are numerous (Isa. 4:2-6; 14:1-8; 35:1-10; 52:1-12; 59:20–60:22; 62:1-12; 66:1-24; Jer. 31:36-37; 33:1-26; Joel 3:17-21; Amos 9:11-15; Zeph. 3:14-20; Zech. 14:16-21).

Even the Old Testament anticipated a New Covenant that would replace the Mosaic Covenant (Jer. 31:31-34). The gracious promises of God which stem from the fact that Christ died on the cross for the sins of the whole world are applied to the church in the present age, but the same gracious principles will be applied to Israel in the Millennium. At that time according to verses 31-32 it will replace the Mosaic Covenant, and the Law of God will be written on their hearts instead of tables of stone. The proclamation of the truth about the Lord will no longer be necessary because " 'they will all know Me, from the least of them to the greatest' declares the LORD" (v. 34). This promise is said to be as certain as the decree of the moon and the stars, and as long as they remain, Israel will continue as a nation (vv. 35-36).

The premillennial interpretation of Scripture considered here will be presented in more detail in the study of eschatology.

THE POSTMILLENNIAL VIEW OF THE PRESENT AGE

The postmillennial view has largely vanished from the current scene though there are present attempts to revive it. At the present time there is no large body of Christians or a theological school dedicated to its presentation though a form of postmillennialism has some vocal advocates. Postmillennialism, however, was a prominant interpretation of Scripture in the 19th century and before World War I.

In general the concept of postmillennialism is that the Gospel will eventually dominate the world scene and extend the application of biblical laws and truth to the entire globe. Most theologies written with this point of view anticipate a future time when there will be almost universal recognition of Jesus Christ as God and Saviour.

In the latter part of the 19th century this point of view was linked by liberal thinkers with the concept of evolution as a form in which the world would be progressing to a better situation.

The awesome events of World War I and World War II and numerous other wars have made untenable the claim that the world is getting better and is gradually surrendering to the precepts of the Gospel. The fact is that the Scriptures clearly state that the world as it progresses to its climax will grow worse and worse spiritually and theologically, as stated in 2 Timothy 3:1-9 and 2 Peter. In the future Tribulation that will precede the second coming of Christ the spiritual and theological condition of the world will be deplorable and at its lowest point (Rev. 6–18).

THE AMILLENNIAL VIEW OF THE PRESENT AGE

As will be brought out in the detailed study of eschatology, the majority view of conservative Christians since the fourth century is what has been known as amillennialism. This view denies a literal kingdom and reign of Christ on earth in the sense of the millennial kingdom. It generally views the fulfillment of kingdom promises in the present age in a spiritual way as fulfilled before the second coming of Christ.

The amillennial view is usually traced to Augustine, a Roman Catholic bishop of Hippo (354-430). Previous to Augustine, the Alexandrian school of theology in Alexandria, Egypt had attempted to combine biblical eschatology with the idealism of Plato. In order to accomplish this, however, they had to spiritualize and interpret much of the Scriptures in a nonliteral sense. All theologians today recognize that the Alexandrian school was heretical in its biblical teachings.

To some extent Augustine remedied the situation by holding that Scripture as a whole should be interpreted in its grammatical, historical, and literal sense except for prophecies of the future. In the amillennial view expressed by later Roman Catholic theologians and also the Protestant Reformers, the Bible as a whole and even eschatology were treated literally with the exception that prophecies concerning the future Great Tribulation and Christ's millennial rule were spiritualized. Conservative amillenarians usually agree with premillenarians on the literal character of the second coming of Christ, the literal character of heaven and hell, and many other areas of scriptural truth.

In the history of amillennial interpretation various views have been offered, each of which denies the premillennial interpretation of a future kingdom on earth. Augustine viewed the Millennium as being fulfilled now in a spiritual sense as God rules in the hearts of Christians. Obviously this does not fulfill literally the many passages relating to the future kingdom, but as Calvin later expressed it, amillenarians held that the Bible was not intended to be taken literally in these kingdom promises. The Augustinian view, also embraced by the Protestant Reformers, continues to be the mainline amillennial interpretation.

Other views, however, have been advanced, all of which deny a literal future millennial kingdom. In about 1860 the view arose in Germany that the millennial promises will be fulfilled in man's intermediate state, that is, in the rule of God in heaven between the time a saint dies and the time all saints are resurrected. Some theologians combined this with the concept that the Millennium is being fulfilled on earth, and they related some passages to earth and some passages to heaven.

Another form of amillennialism views the promises of the kingdom as being conditional and unfulfilled because of the failures of men. Premillenarians feel that this is refuted by passages that affirm God's intention to fulfill the promise even if men failed.

Still another approach is that the future kingdom passages will be fulfilled in the eternal state in the new heavens and the new earth (Rev. 21–22). This point of view usually avoids passages that teach that in the Millennium there will be sin, death, birth, and many other factors that indicate that people will still be in their natural bodies and in natural situations. All amillenarians unite in denying the premillennial view though they are not in agreement among themselves as to how passages that appear to teach this should be interpreted.

THE TEACHINGS OF CHRIST ON THE FUTURE KINGDOM

As presented particularly in the Synoptics, Christ is introduced as the King who will sit on David's throne. This concept is introduced early in Matthew where the lineage of Christ through Joseph is traced back to David because David was the legal progenitor of Christ. And in Luke 3:23-38 the genealogy of Mary is traced back to David to show that Christ had a physical link with David and the tribe of Judah. In connection with the birth of Christ, Mary was informed by the angel that her Son was to be named Jesus and that "He will be great and will be called the Son of the Most High. The Lord God will give Him the throne of His father David, and He will reign over the house of Jacob forever; His kingdom will never end" (1:32-33). It should be obvious that Mary understood this as a literal fulfillment of the promise given to David that he would have a Son who would reign over the house of Jacob forever.

The fact that Jesus was born King of the Jews is confirmed by the coming of the Magi (Matt. 2:1-6). Jesus is declared to be the One who fulfills the Old Testament promises of the coming King and Messiah.

As the public life of Christ unfolded, His message was summarized in the words, "Repent, for the kingdom of heaven is near" (Matt. 4:17). In the Sermon on the Mount (Matt. 5–7) moral principles relating to the kingdom are detailed with some application to the present.

In a series of parables in Matthew 13 Christ presented the distinctive character of the present age of the grace economy which was not revealed in the Old Testament. Throughout the Gospels Christ is consistently presented as the King who will fulfill the Old Testament promises.

Matthew, after presenting His credentials evidenced by Christ's miracles (Matt. 8–12) pointed out that He was rejected by His own people (13:53-58). As His ministry led to the time of the Crucifixion, He repeatedly warned His disciples that He was to be crucified and would rise from the dead.

It is clear from many Scriptures that the disciples did not understand the difference between the first and second comings of Christ. They assumed that He would fulfill the promises related to His second coming, that is, that He would reign over the earth as King of kings and Lord of lords and would rescue His people from their oppressors. Even at the time of His ascension into heaven His disciples were still asking questions as to when the promises of His second coming were to be fulfilled (Acts 1:6-8).

CONCEPTS OF THE KINGDOM

In both the Old and New Testaments the concept of the kingdom rule of God is presented in various ways. As it relates to the eschatological program of God, it is primarily a concept in which Christ would reign politically with Jerusalem as His capital in the period after His second coming.

The Scriptures also present the concept of a kingdom now in which Christ rules over the hearts of the saints who acknowledge Him as Lord and Saviour. This kind of kingdom has always been present in the world and is fulfilled by individuals who recognize Christ as their King and Ruler.

In referring to the doctrine of the kingdom, Matthew often used the term "kingdom of heaven" in contrast to the term "kingdom of God," as used in the rest of the New Testament and a few times by Matthew himself. Most scholars hold that these two concepts are one and the same as a rule of God over human beings on earth. However in Matthew the "kingdom of heaven" refers to the kingdom as a sphere of profession in which there are both wheat and weeds that look like wheat (13:4-30, 36-43). The kingdom of heaven is also compared to a net full of good and bad fish which will be separated at the end of the age (vv. 47-50). By contrast the kingdom of God is always represented as including only those who have been redeemed by salvation and holy angels. This contrasts with the kingdom of heaven which never includes angels but does include those who are professing Christians but are not saved. Though most scholars ignore this distinction, it does give added light on the character of the future kingdom on earth as including not only the saved but also some who outwardly appear to be saved but are not.

If the premillennial view is correct, the future kingdom will have a different rule of life than the present age, and the present age is distinct from either the Mosaic era or the future kingdom. If the amillennial and postmillennial views are correct, this distinction will be blurred, and a legalistic quality to the present age will be introduced, an emphasis that contradicts the gracious rule of life presented in the New Testament.

CHAPTER • 30

THE PRESENT GRACE ECONOMY

GENERAL FEATURES OF THE GRACE ECONOMY

The grace economy and the economies of the future kingdom and the Mosaic Covenant are distinct dispensations or rules of life that characterize their respective periods. Though the various economies have several features in common each economy is also different in some notable respects.

In the present age salvation of those who believe in Christ places the saved one in the position of a son of God, a citizen of heaven, and a member of the family and household of God. Such a position demands a corresponding manner of life. Grace in the present age not only provides a perfect salvation and eternal keeping for one who believes in Christ, but grace provides more divine enablement than in previous economies for the daily life of the one who is saved. This is accomplished through the indwelling Holy Spirit, the completed Word of God, and Christ's intercession in heaven.

Though there is a measure of grace in every dispensation, as salvation is always by grace, the rule of life under the present Church Age or age of grace contrasts sharply with that required in the Old Testament or with what will be required in the future kingdom. The Bible as a Book from God for all people of all ages reveals the will of God concerning the manner of life in various dispensations in keeping with their particular covenants with God. The daily life of those who are saved by grace in this dispensation is in effect from the time of the death of Christ to the second coming of Christ. The gracious rule of life in the teachings of grace is more complete than other dispensations.

The classification of the present age as the age of grace does not imply that divine grace has not been exercised in past ages. It is rather that in the present age not only the grace of God in salvation is revealed in additional detail, but also that grace was introduced as a dominant factor in the present rule of life. This is summarized in John 1:17, "For the Law was given through Moses; grace and truth came through Jesus Christ."

The present age is distinguished from other ages by the fact that there is revelation of grace in the calling out of the church from both Jews and Gentiles. Old Testament saints are not revealed as being in the new federal headship of the resurrected Christ nor were their lives "hidden with Christ in God" (Col. 3:3). The present age is contrasted to the Mosaic Age in Galatians 3:23-25, "Before this faith came, we were held prisoners by the Law, locked up until faith should be revealed. So the Law was put in charge to lead us to Christ that we might be justified by faith. Now that faith has come, we are no longer under the supervision of the Law."

Jews in the Mosaic dispensation were born into a covenant relationship with God, and sacrifices were provided for a righteous restoration to their covenant privileges if they sinned. This was God's gracious provision for them. An individual Jew might fail in his conduct, neglect the sacrifices, and eventually be cast out without salvation (Gen. 17:14; Deut. 28:58-61; Matt. 10:32-33; 24:50-51; 25:11-12, 29-30). The Law was not a condition of salvation. One who was saved under the Mosaic dispensation would obviously attempt to keep the Law, and one who rejected the Law would reveal his lack of faith in God.

At the time of Christ's second coming there will be a separation of the saved and the unsaved according to Ezekiel 20:34-38, and all Israelites will be rescued from their persecutors at the time of the Second Coming (Rom. 11:26-27). The fact that grace is extended to Israel in the future is brought out in passages such as Isaiah 60:1–62:12. The distinction between the Mosaic dispensation and the dispensation of grace, however, is that the Mosaic system was a legal rule of life whereas the present age of grace is a gracious rule of life. Though there is grace in law and law in grace, the two systems stand in contrast to each other.

Of the church it is declared in Ephesians 2:6-7, "And God raised us up with Christ and seated us with Him in the heavenly realms in Christ Jesus, in order that in the coming ages He might show the incomparable riches of His grace, expressed in His kindness to us in

Christ Jesus." By contrast, Israel's contribution will be to demonstrate God's faithfulness and righteousness.

The general facts about grace are presented in Titus 2:11-14, "For the grace of God that brings salvation has appeared to all men. It teaches us to say 'No' to ungodliness and worldly passions, and to live self-controlled, upright, and godly lives in this present age, while we wait for the blessed hope—the glorious appearing of our great God and Saviour, Jesus Christ, who gave Himself for us to redeem us from all wickedness and to purify for Himself a people that are His very own, eager to do what is good."

In this passage the statement is made that the grace of God has appeared to all men, whether Jew or Gentile. The same revelation of grace which brings salvation also teaches that those who receive the grace of God should live as the objects of God's grace. This gracious rule of life is not imposed on non-Christians. Until an unsaved person receives Christ, God's gift in grace, no other issue needs to be raised. The teachings of grace are found in Acts and the Epistles and certain portions of the Gospels. The grace economy presents a supernatural ideal in keeping with the Christian's heavenly citizenship and also provides supernatural power by the indwelling Holy Spirit so that the rule of life may be fulfilled.

Under grace there is a price to pay for those believers who do not walk in keeping with their standing in grace before God. They will lose communion and fellowship with God, will experience loss of power in life and service, and will fail to produce the spiritual fruit they should. In spite of human failure the believer's exalted position in Christ through faith alone is in itself an appeal for a walk that corresponds to that exalted position. A general analysis of grace teachings includes three specific features as well as revealing new relationships in grace.

THREE SPECIFIC FEATURES OF THE GRACE ECONOMY

Three specific features that characterize a believer's walk in the present age include the independent and uncomplicated character of grace teachings, their exalted requirements, and the divine enablement given to believers to help them to live as the recipients of God's grace.

1. The independent and uncomplicated character of grace

TEACHINGS. The governing principles that belong to this age are by their nature to be distinguished from the legal systems of the Mosaic Law as well as the kingdom economy. In the present age emphasis is on the foundational truths that Christ has died, is risen, is ascended, and that the Spirit is now resident in the hearts of all who believe. These great truths create an entirely new relationship between God and those who are saved.

2. THE EXALTED REQUIREMENTS OF THE GRACE ECONOMY. What is expected of a believer in this age of grace is immeasurably more difficult than the prescribed Law of Moses or the standards of the kingdom. In keeping with them the divine enablement provided under grace is nothing less than the infinite power of the indwelling Holy Spirit. The teachings of grace as a rule of life are addressed to those who are born of and indwelt by the Spirit. Positionally the believer is already in a heavenly relationship to Christ and his citizenship has been transferred from earth to heaven. Accordingly the supernatural life required of believers should be in keeping with their heavenly citizenship.

The high standard of living under grace is brought out in 2 Corinthians 10:5, "We demolish arguments and every pretension that sets itself up against the knowledge of God, and we take captive every thought to make it obedient to Christ." In Ephesians 5:20 Christians are exhorted to be "always giving thanks to God the Father for everything, in the name of our Lord Jesus Christ." In 4:1 Christians are urged to "live a life worthy of the calling you have received." In 5:2 Christians are instructed to "live a life of love, just as Christ loved us and gave Himself up for us as a fragrant offering and sacrifice to God." Christians are exhorted in Galatians 5:16 to "live by the Spirit, and you will not gratify the desires of the sinful nature." According to Ephesians 4:30 Christians are exhorted, "Do not grieve the Holy Spirit of God, with whom you were sealed for the day of redemption."

A series of exhortations is found in 1 Thessalonians 5:14-22, "And we urge you, brothers, warn those who are idle, encourage the timid, help the weak, be patient with everyone. Make sure that nobody pays back wrong for wrong, but always try to be kind to each other and to everyone else. Be joyful always; pray continually; give thanks in all circumstances, for this is God's will for you in Christ Jesus. Do not put out the Spirit's fire; do not treat prophecies with contempt. Test everything. Hold on to the good. Avoid every kind of evil."

In 1 John 1:7 Christians are exhorted to "walk in the light, as He is in the light" with the result that "we have fellowship one with another, and the blood of Jesus, His Son, purifies us from all sin." A higher standard of conduct exceeds that revealed in the Mosaic Law as it demands a superhuman manner of life of which these passages are a sample.

In contrast to the requirement of the Mosaic Law to love one's neighbor as himself, Christ stated in John 13:34-35, "A new command I give you: Love one another. As I have loved you, so you must love one another. All men will know that you are My disciples if you love one another." In Matthew 5:43-46 the requirements that were greater than the Law of Moses are stated, "You have heard that it was said, 'Love your neighbor and hate your enemy.' But I tell you: Love your enemies and pray for those who persecute you, that you may be sons of your Father in heaven. He causes His sun to rise on the evil and the good, and sends rain on the righteous and the unrighteous. If you love those who love you, what reward will you get? Are not even the tax collectors doing that?"

Love under grace is a "fruit of the Spirit" (Gal. 5:22), a work of the Spirit which enables Christians to love others as God loves them. Scripture declares, "God has poured out His love into our hearts by the Holy Spirit, whom He has given us" (Rom. 5:5). Love under grace is especially revealed as the dynamic for winning souls. Paul's statements in 9:1-3 are typical of this point. "I speak the truth in Christ—I am not lying, my conscience confirms it in the Holy Spirit—I have great sorrow and unceasing anguish in my heart. For I could wish that I myself were cursed and cut off from Christ for the sake of my brothers, those of my own race." Though in the Mosaic Law as well as in the future kingdom, evangelization is not required, Israel was to be a light to Gentiles (Isa. 42:6).

3. The divine enablement. Godly living is made possible by the supernatural power provided for the execution of the superhuman rule of life under grace. The enablement of the indwelling Holy Spirit given to every saved person is mentioned repeatedly in Scripture (John 7:37-39; Rom. 5:5; 8:9; 1 Cor. 2:12; 6:19; Gal. 3:2; 1 Thes. 4:8; 1 John 3:24; 4:13). These superhuman requirements are addressed to all who have experienced the grace of God in salvation in the present age. But the gracious character of God's provision of the indwelling Holy Spirit is revealed in such passages as 1 Corinthians 6:19-20 where the appeal is not to establish merit in order to

be indwelt but rather to lead a holy life because of the grace of God.

In the Old Testament order the Spirit could be given to some and also be taken away as illustrated in the case of Saul. Under grace the Spirit indwells every believer and never withdraws, as illustrated in John 14:16 and 1 John 2:27.

The new enabling power of the Spirit characterizes this age in contrast to "the old way of the written code" (Rom. 7:6). Under the Law circumcision was of the flesh. Under grace circumcision is of the heart (2:29). The challenge in the age of grace is for believers to adjust their hearts to the holy presence of the Spirit and to live in an unbroken attitude of dependence on Him. In a believer's struggle between the sin nature and the new nature he can be victorious only as the Spirit of God gives grace. Many Scripture passages speak of the special character of the present grace economy (John 7:37-39; Acts 1:8; Rom. 6:14; 8:4; 1 Cor. 12:4-7; 2 Cor. 10:3-5; Gal. 5:16; Eph. 6:10-11; Phil. 2:13; Col. 2:6).

Taken as a whole the grace economy can be summed up in two great doctrines of the New Testament: (1) the supernatural manner of life is to be Christlike (1 Cor. 9:21; Phil. 1:21; 2:5; 1 Peter 2:21; 1 John 4:17); (2) the supreme purpose of the indwelling Spirit is to reproduce Christlikeness in the believer, as stated in Galatians 5:22-23, "But the fruit of the Spirit is love, joy, peace, patience, kindness, goodness, faithfulness, gentleness, and self-control. Against such things there is no law."

Divine grace imparted by the indwelling Holy Spirit issues in a manifestation of the graciousness of God in the heart of the believer. It is not an imitation of God's graciousness but is produced by the indwelling Spirit in the life and service of a believer. This is an extensive doctrine in the New Testament (Rom. 12:3-6; 15:15; 1 Cor. 1:4; 3:10; 15:10; 2 Cor. 1:12; 4:15; 6:1-3; 8:1, 6-7, 9; 9:8, 14; 12:9; Gal. 2:9; Eph. 3:2-8; 4:7, 29; Phil. 1:7; Col. 3:16; 4:6; 2 Thes. 1:12; 2 Tim. 2:1; Heb. 4:16; 12:15; James 4:6; 2 Peter 3:18).

THE GRACE RELATIONSHIPS

The Christian's daily life is one of adjusting to certain important relationships. The distinctive features of the grace order are based on the threefold truth that the believer is appointed to uphold (1) relationships to the Persons of the Godhead; (2) a relationship to the world system; and (3) relationships to other Christians who are fellow members in the body of Christ. These major relationships are supported by many exhortations in the New Testament.

1. Relationships to the Persons of the Godhead. The supreme obligation which rests on the Christian pertains to his relationships to the Persons of the Godhead. This includes the entire sphere of moral and spiritual responsibility, fellowship with the Persons of the Godhead, the exercise of praise and prayer, and obedience to the mind and the will of God.

2. In relationship to the world system. As Christ stated in His High Priestly Prayer a Christian has only a limited relationship to the world system (John 17:14, 16). A believer is a citizen of heaven, and therefore in the present world he is an ambassador, a stranger, a pilgrim, and a witness against the evils of the cosmos and Satan. A Christian is given instructions for his conflict with Satan and the world system. A believer's world relationship can be presented in four areas:

a. to Satan and his emissaries. This relationship is one of enmity and conflict in which the Christian must rely on the grace of God. Instructions given in Ephesians 6:10-12 indicate how a Christian needs to appropriate what God has provided. In 1 John 4:4 emphasis is placed on the fact that God is greater than the believer's enemy, Satan.

b. the world system. A believer is told not to love the world (1 John 2:15-17) nor to have any fellowship with the works of darkness (Eph. 5:11). In relation to those outside the church, Christians are exhorted, "Be wise in the way you act toward outsiders; make the most of every opportunity. Let your conversation be always full of grace, seasoned with salt, so that you may know how to answer everyone" (Col. 4:5-6).

c. to human governments. Though directed to wage war against the world system, Christians are also directed to maintain allegiance to world governments even though Satan controls them (Matt. 4:8-9; Luke 4:5-7; 21:24). In Romans 13:1-7 a detailed account is given of the believer's relationship and subjection to world government. In general Christians are instructed to submit to the human government unless this would be contrary to the will of God (1 Peter 2:13-17).

d. to the unsaved as individuals. A Christian should have

compassion for and the love of Christ toward the unsaved and should endeavor to bring them to the Lord for salvation (2 Cor. 5:14-16).

3. THE RELATIONSHIP TO THE BODY OF CHRIST. The basis for fellowship and kinship with the company of the redeemed is revealed in the New Testament along with exhortations for a corresponding conduct toward fellow believers.

a. CHRISTIANS IN RELATION TO OTHER CHRISTIANS IN GENERAL. Love is revealed as the underlying principle of this relationship (John 13:34-35). The same truth is emphasized in other passages (1 Cor. 12:26; Eph. 5:2; Heb. 13:1; 1 John 4:7, 11). The transformed human character should be especially evident in their relationship to fellow Christians (Rom. 12:9-16). In Colossians 3:12-13 this is summarized, "Therefore, as God's chosen people, holy and dearly loved, clothe yourselves with compassion, kindness, humility, gentleness, and patience. Bear with each other and forgive whatever grievances you may have against one another. Forgive as the Lord forgave you." To this can be added the exhortation of Peter, "Finally, all of you, live in harmony with one another; be sympathetic, love as brothers, be compassionate and humble. Do not repay evil with evil or insult with insult, but with blessing, because to this you were called so that you may inherit a blessing" (1 Peter 3:8-9).

Many other exhortations in Scripture deal with Christian kindness, love of the brethren, and the avoiding of strife (Eph. 4:31-32; 5:21; Phil. 2:3-4; 1 Thes. 4:6, 9; James 4:11; 1 Peter 5:5).

Christians are exhorted to do good to all but especially to those who are also believers (Gal. 6:10; 1 John 3:17). Prayer is an indispensable part of their lives and testimony (Eph. 6:18; James 5:16).

b. A CHRISTIAN'S RELATIONSHIP TO THOSE WHO ARE IN AUTHORITY IN THE ASSEMBLY OF BELIEVERS. The Word of God deals explicitly with the necessity of recognizing authority in the local church (1 Thes. 5:12-13; Heb. 13:7, 17).

c. THE RELATIONSHIP OF CHRISTIAN HUSBANDS AND WIVES. This explicitly includes husbands loving their wives and wives submitting to their husbands (Eph. 5:21-33; Col. 3:18-19; 1 Peter 3:1-7).

d. THE RELATIONSHIP OF CHRISTIAN PARENTS AND CHILDREN. Children are to obey their parents, and fathers are to bring up their children in the knowledge of Scripture and not provoke them to wrath (Eph. 6:1, 4; Col. 3:20-21; 2 Tim. 3:2).

e. THE RELATIONSHIP OF CHRISTIAN MASTERS AND SERVANTS. Servants are to obey their masters giving them good service, and masters are to be kind and just to their servants (Col. 3:22–4:1; cf. Eph. 6:5-9).

f. A CHRISTIAN'S OBLIGATION TO AN ERRING BROTHER. A number of passages indicate that Christians have a special responsibility to treat an erring brother properly. They should approach him with a spirit of meekness (Gal. 6:1), with appropriate warning for the unruly, and special support of those who are weak (1 Thes. 5:14). Christians should not participate with unruly brethren who create dissension (2 Thes. 3:6, 11-15), with disorderly believers who are busybodies, with those who shirk honest toil, nor with those who are careless in their Christian conduct. A sincere believer, however, may disagree with another in matters of biblical interpretation without necessarily causing a problem. Believers should not be separated over minor questions of doctrine but should separate themselves from those who are teaching wrong doctrine in major areas (2 John 9-11).

The goal in dealing with an erring brother is restoration. However, those who are needlessly contentious should be avoided (Rom. 16:17-18).

g. A CHRISTIAN'S OBLIGATION TO A WEAK BROTHER. Christians should consider not only their own consciences but also the consciences of others. In relation to a weak brother they should not put a stumbling block in his way by their own exercise of freedom. Exhortations to Christians in this situation are found in Romans 14:1-4, 15-23.

CHAPTER • 31

CONTRASTS BETWEEN LAW AND GRACE

It is important to consider the wide differences between the principle of Law and the principle of grace as they relate to the divine government of man. The three major systems of the divine government are the dispensations of Law, grace, and kingdom. Though there is some similarity, these systems cannot be comingled. A number of important issues are involved including revelation concerning God, prophecy and its fulfillment, the union between type and antitype, the revelation concerning Satan and evil, the doctrine of man and his sin, the requirement of holiness in the conduct of saints, and the continuity of purpose in the program of the ages. On the one hand the Scriptures demonstrate an amazing unity derived from the unchanging character of God, and on the other hand the Scriptures display the differences in rules of life that are applied to different periods.

Three particulars emerge: (1) The three major dispensations present independent, sufficient, and complete systems of the divine rule in the earth. (2) In these systems the order varies with respect to the sequence of the divine blessing and the human obligation. (3) These systems differ according to the degree of divine enablement provided.

THE THREE COMPLETE SYSTEMS OF DIVINE RULE IN THE EARTH

Though dispensations with varying rules of life existed before Moses, they were not given extensive revelation because these dispensations were already past when the Mosaic Law was written by Moses. The

Scriptures give major attention to the systems of Law, grace, and kingdom.

1. THE TEACHINGS OF THE LAW OF MOSES. This was revealed by God to Moses in the wilderness and accepted by Israel at Sinai. It was addressed only to Israel and not to other races or governments. The nation of Israel under the Law occupies most of the Old Testament and a major part of the Gospels up to the time of the death of Christ. Additional light is given in the New Testament as it contrasts the Law with grace.

The Law of Moses was complete within itself. It was sufficient to regulate the conduct of Israelites under every circumstance that might arise. In her relationship to God the nation remained for 1,500 years under the Law of Moses.

2. THE TEACHINGS OF GRACE. Like the teachings of the Law of Moses which were addressed to Israel alone, the teachings of grace are not applied to men outside the present age. The standards in the present age are addressed particularly to believers in Christ and not to the world as a whole. The instructions under grace indicate what Christians should be expected to do in relationship to God, man, and human governments.

Until Christ died and was resurrected the full teachings of grace could not be disclosed and so they are found only in limited portions of the Gospels before being given in full in the rest of the New Testament.

In the present age which is considered as primarily for the Gentiles, the covenants with Israel are not fulfilled, though Israel's continuance as a nation in the present age is part of God's covenant purpose (Jer. 31:35-37).

The present age is characterized by a unique emphasis on the individual and God's provision for personal salvation, personal indwelling of the Spirit, personal gifts for service, and personal transformation into the image of Christ.

3. THE TEACHINGS OF THE KINGDOM ARE YET FUTURE. They anticipate the binding of Satan, a purified earth, the restoration of Israel, and the person of Christ as the King. So the revelation of the standards for the millennial kingdom were addressed to Israel and to nations that will enter the kingdom. Obviously under the peculiar circumstances of the millennial kingdom a special rule of life will be required.

The return of Christ to rule in His millennial kingdom is a sudden event which will destroy Gentile world powers, bind Satan, and cast the world ruler and the false prophet into the lake of fire (Rev. 19:11–20:6). For the millennial kingdom no rule of life is indicated for the church because the church will have been rendered perfect in its sanctification and glorification.

In the present age there are three major classifications of the human family (1 Cor. 10:32). Before the time of Abraham the entire human race was considered Gentile. Beginning with Abraham, Isaac, and Jacob a special people, Israel, were separated from the world's population. With the Day of Pentecost the church began as the body of Christ constituting a group composed of both Jews and Gentiles who put their trust in Christ.

a. THE SIMILARITY AND DISSIMILARITY BETWEEN THE TEACHINGS OF THE LAW OF MOSES AND THE TEACHINGS OF GRACE. Many interpreters of Scripture attempt to impose the moral commandments of the Ten Commandments on the church. All of the commandments except the rule of the Sabbath are repeated in the New Testament and are accepted as a part of the rule of grace. However, these commandments appear under the different approach of grace as a rule of life instead of Law. The Ten Commandments as recorded in Exodus 20:3-17 can be compared to similar statements in the New Testament.

1. "You shall have no other gods before Me."	1. "We are . . . telling you to turn from these worthless things to the living God" (Acts 14:15).
2. "You shall not make for yourself an idol. . . . You shall not bow down to them or worship them."	2. "Dear children, keep yourselves from idols" (1 John 5:21).
3. "You shall not misuse the name of the LORD your God."	3. "Above all, my brothers, do not swear—not by heaven or by earth or by anything else" (James 5:12).
4. "Remember the Sabbath Day by keeping it holy."	4. No such command is found in the teachings of grace.

5. "Honor your father and your mother."	5. "Children, obey your parents in the Lord, for this is right" (Eph. 6:1).
6. "You shall not murder."	6. "Anyone who hates his brother is a murderer, and you know that no murderer has eternal life in him" (1 John 3:15).
7. "You shall not commit adultery."	7. "Neither the sexually immoral nor idolators nor adulterers . . . will inherit the kingdom of God" (1 Cor. 6:9-10).
8. "You shall not steal."	8. "Steal no longer" (Eph. 4:28).
9. "You shall not give false testimony."	9. "Do not lie" (Col. 3:9).
10. "You shall not covet."	10. "But among you there must not be even a hint of sexual immorality . . . or of greed [KJV, covetousness], because they are improper for God's holy people" (Eph. 5:3).

The similarity between the Ten Commandments and commandments under grace stem from the fact that God does not change. The difference in the command concerning the Sabbath illustrates the difference between these two rules of life that have a different dispensational background. Characteristically in the Old Testament, blessings were promised for obedience whereas in the New Testament, blessings are promised on the basis of the grace of God.

It is significant, however, that under the teachings of grace the appeal of the first commandment is repeated no less than 50 times, the second 12 times, the third 4 times, the fourth not at all, the fifth 6 times, the sixth 6 times, the seventh 12 times, the eighth 6 times, the ninth 4 times, and the tenth 9 times.

Under grace, commands are given in far greater detail than in the

Ten Commandments because the Ten Commandments require no life of prayer, no Christian service, no evangelism, no missionary effort, no Gospel preaching, no life and walk in the Spirit, no union with Christ, no fellowship with saints. In the present age of grace there is much more demand on a Christian to conform to the moral will of God than in the Old Testament. Christians are not obligated to obey the hundreds of commands given to Israel beyond the Ten Commandments.

b. THE SIMILARITY AND DISSIMILARITY BETWEEN THE TEACHINGS OF THE LAW OF MOSES AND THE TEACHINGS OF THE KINGDOM. Though the Law of Moses and the kingdom economy are both basically legal, they have similarities and dissimilarities.

(1) In the Mosaic Covenant as well as the kingdom economy blessing is promised on the basis of obedience. Emphasis is on good works which are recognized by God with rewards. In the Law of Moses blessings are promised for obedience (Ex. 20:12; 19:8; Deut. 28:1-68).

(2) Though the two economies have similarities, the kingdom economy is more strict than the Mosaic (Matt. 5:17-28; cf. vv. 31-48; 6:1-18, 24-34; 7:12). Though some of the exhortations of Matthew 5–7 have general application to all dispensations, others cannot have full application until the future kingdom economy.

(3) In the future kingdom economy additions are made to the truth involved in the Mosaic revelation. New commands were issued by Christ concerning marriage and divorce, the taking of an oath, and the personal obligation to others. Instead of demanding retribution for offenses, the other cheek is to be turned, the second mile is to be traveled, appeals are made for sincerity in almsgiving, in prayer, and in fasting. Though there is application for the present age, complete fulfillment will be in the kingdom.

c. THE SIMILARITY AND DISSIMILARITY BETWEEN THE TEACHINGS OF GRACE AND THE TEACHINGS OF THE KINGDOM. Contrasts between Law and grace are extensive as illustrated in Matthew 5–7. Though some of the concepts of the Sermon on the Mount are applicable to all dispensations, others clearly cannot be applied literally until the Kingdom Age begins.

The preaching of John the Baptist was something new and involved moral preparation for the coming kingdom. John included in his message, however, the change that would be brought about by the death of Christ in pointing to Christ as the Lamb of God who would take away the sin of the world (John 1:29).

In Luke 3:7-14 John the Baptist demanded a high standard of obedience including sharing of goods and food with the needy. Tax collectors were exhorted to be honest, and soldiers were told not to do violence to anyone. The preaching of John the Baptist was something new for it extended beyond the Mosaic Law and anticipated the future rule of the King in the Millennium.

At least three major distinctions are seen when the teachings of grace are contrasted with the teachings of the kingdom.

First, the kingdom message of hope is extended beyond the present age into the future economy. By contrast the teachings of grace relate primarily to heaven rather than to an earthly dispensation.

Second, the two lines of teaching may be identified by the use of words such as "righteousness" and "peace" that relate to the kingdom, in contrast to the words "believe" and "grace" that relate to the church.

Third, the kingdom teaching in the Gospels is based on obedience in contrast to grace which is related to faith.

It is sometimes assumed that the millennial reign of the Messiah will be a period of sinlessness on earth. Though the economy of the kingdom will be basically legal, and it will be unusual in that Satan will be bound, there will be immediate judgment for sin, and its moral requirements will be higher than the Mosaic Law. On the other hand it should be clear that in the millennial kingdom there will be evil to judge, and some will fail because they do not do the will of the King.

(1) Though the Sermon on the Mount should not be considered as completely eschatological, it obviously anticipates the moral situations of the millennial kingdom in some of its exhortations.

(a) In the Beatitudes blessing is promised to the faithful child of God who is obedient. Though this is possible to some extent in the present age, the ultimate fulfillment will be in the kingdom period. Contrasting exhortations can be found in the Old Testament in Isaiah 57:15 and in the present age in Colossians 3:12.

(b) Those who mourn are promised comfort, which promise will have its ultimate fulfillment in the kingdom. Though in mourning today because of their many problems, Israel is promised blessing when the Lord comes (Isa. 61:2-3).

(c) The promise is given to the meek that they will inherit the earth (Matt. 5:5) which is not true in the present age but will be true in the kingdom.

(d) Those who thirst for righteousness will be fully satisfied in the kingdom period (v. 6).

(e) The showing of mercy is promised to those who are merciful, which places mercy somewhat on a legal basis. By contrast Christians are exhorted to be merciful on the basis of the fact that they have received mercy (Eph. 2:4-5; Titus 3:5). Under a legal approach mercy is given to those who are merciful (Pss. 18:24-26; 103:17-18).

(f) The pure in heart will see God, which contrasts with the present promise to believers under grace that God has already revealed Himself to them (2 Cor. 4:6; Heb. 2:9). Under the Mosaic Law the Israelites were told to have clean hands and a pure heart and then they would be able to see God (Ps. 24:3-4).

(g) Peacemakers are declared to be "sons of God" (Matt. 5:9). Peace is one of the two great words in the kingdom, the other word being "righteousness" (cf. Ps. 72:3, 7). Under grace one is a child of God through faith in Christ (Gal. 3:26).

(h) Blessing is promised to the persecuted (Matt. 5:10). A Christian who suffers with Christ receives his reward in heaven (Phil. 1:29; 2 Tim. 3:12). In the millennial kingdom blessing is promised to those who have experienced persecution and they are promised a place in the kingdom. However, even those in the kingdom are promised "reward in heaven" (Matt. 5–12) in addition to reward on earth.

In general the Beatitudes speak of blessing coming from obedience, and though it may have an oblique reference to Christians, its primary reference is to the future millennial kingdom. Everything that is demanded in the kingdom as a condition of blessing is freely given under grace (cf. Gal. 5:22-23).

(2) The similitudes of the righteous in the kingdom. In Matthew 5:13-16 the children of the kingdom are likened to salt and light. On the other hand Christians are exhorted to walk as children of light (Eph. 5:8) and are declared to be the children of the light and the children of the day (1 Thes. 5:5). In various passages of the Old Testament, Gentiles are promised light in the future kingdom (Isa. 42:6; 49:6; 58:8; 60:3, 20).

(3) Christ interpreted the Law in its relationship to the kingdom. Law in the kingdom is more intensified than the Law of Moses. By contrast, a Christian is not under the Law and has no altar other than Christ (Heb. 13:10). While Christians are exhorted to live

peaceably (Rom. 12:17-21), the child of the kingdom is warned that he will be cast into prison unless he lives peaceably (Matt. 5:25-26). In this connection the extreme legal penalty for wrongdoing is imposed (vv. 20-22, 29-30). By contrast the child of God under grace is promised no condemnation even though chastisement may be his experience if he walks contrary to the will of God (John 5:24; 10:28; Rom. 8:1; 1 Cor. 11:30-31).

(4) Mere externalism is rebuked (Matt. 6:1-7, 16-18; 7:21-29). By contrast a Christian at the Judgment Seat of Christ will receive rewards for proper service but will not be condemned for sins.

(5) Prayer for the kingdom and in the kingdom. What is commonly called "the Lord's Prayer" is in reality the prayer that Christ taught His disciples when they were anticipating the kingdom (Matt. 6:8-15; 7:7-11). However, the principles in the Lord's Prayer have a wider application than the Kingdom Age. Though it is wrong for Christians not to forgive each other, their basis of forgiving one another is the fact that Christ has forgiven them (Eph. 4:32; Col. 3:13; cf. 1 John 1:9). Under grace Christians are exhorted to believe (Eph. 4:32) and are forgiven on the basis of confession (1 John 1:9). These words do not represent meritorious work, but they do represent a simple adjustment of the heart to what is provided in the grace of God.

(6) The law governing riches in the kingdom. The right use of riches (Matt. 6:19-24) will be rewarded in heaven both for the Christian and for the child of the kingdom. For both it is true that no one can "serve both God and money" (v. 24).

(7) The Father's care over the children of the kingdom is presented in 6:25-34 and is a precious reminder that God cares for His own in every dispensation. In the age of grace, however, believers are to cast their care on the Lord because He has promised to care for them (Phil. 4:6; 1 Peter 5:7). Under the Law believers were to cast their burden on the Lord and then they would be sustained (Ps. 55:22).

(8) Warning against the judgment of others. Under the kingdom they were sternly warned not to judge others or they would be judged. Under grace, judgment is forbidden because Christ will be the Judge (Rom. 14:10-13). But even under grace a believer who disobeys is chastened by the Father (1 Cor. 11:27-32).

(9) Warning against false prophets. Both in the kingdom and under grace there is warning against false prophets (Matt. 7:15-20; 2 Peter 2:1; 2 John 1:7-11). In the present age Satan can appear as

an angel of light (2 Cor. 11:13-15) while in the kingdom he will be bound.

(10) Three determining statements concerning the kingdom.

(a) According to Matthew 5:20 righteousness better than that of the scribes and the Pharisees is necessary to enter the kingdom. Under grace it is made clear that man's righteousness is never enough, for man can be saved only by the mercy of God (Titus 3:5).

(b) The so-called "Golden Rule," that one should do to others as he wishes others would do to him (Matt. 7:12), is related to the Law and the Prophets. Under grace Christians are commanded to do good because they are children of grace.

(c) According to verses 13-14 the gate to salvation is narrow and the gate to destruction is wide. Under grace the typical exhortation is to anyone who will believe. Even in grace the gate to salvation is narrow in the sense that only Christ can save.

The teachings of Law, grace, and kingdom offer many contrasts even though there is similarity in each and the contrasts are not absolute.

THE SEQUENCE OF DIVINE BLESSING AND THE HUMAN OBLIGATION

The second major distinction between the teachings of Law and the teachings of grace is seen in the varying order between the divine blessing and the human obligation. Under the Law of Moses blessing in this life is promised for obedience. Under grace obedience is exhorted on the basis that the Christian has already received grace. Though in every dispensation people are saved only by grace, in both the Mosaic Law and the coming kingdom period emphasis is on obedience to various commands as evidence of faith.

The covenant made with Abraham 400 years before the Law is a gracious covenant, and its gracious promises continue in their application to the present and the future. The reign of Law given through Moses ceased with the death of Christ. The faith principle introduced in the Abrahamic Covenant is now continued in the present age of grace and will have its ultimate fulfillment in the Kingdom Age and in eternity. As Abraham was justified by faith (Gen. 15:6), Christians in the present age are justified by faith. By contrast the Law is not of faith (Gal. 3:9-12) which is emphasized in Paul's dealing with the problem of legalism in the Galatian church (4:21-31). Though works are not the ground of salvation in any dispensation, it is obvious that in the Mosaic period as well as in the future kingdom works are much more prominent as evidence of faith than in the present age.

DIFFERENT DEGREES OF DIFFICULTY AND DIFFERENT DEGREES OF DIVINE ENABLEMENT

As previously discussed, a believer in the present age has received divine enablement in the Person of the indwelling Holy Spirit, the intercession of Christ in heaven, and the blessing of associating with other believers. Under the Law this was not the universal pattern. Christians have a much higher standard of conduct than those under the Law and in keeping with this they have available more enablement from God.

CHAPTER • 32

THE LAW SYSTEMS AND JUDAISM DONE AWAY

In contrast to other biblical covenants the Mosaic Law was given only for a time. It began with Moses and it ended with Christ. The written instructions of the teaching of Moses are not applicable to the present age. The Law, which conditioned blessing on the ground of personal merit, is done away. The Law principle of dependence on the energy of the flesh has been abolished.

UNDER GRACE THE LAW OF MOSES IS DONE AWAY

Though in the kingdom economy a legal system will again appear, the laws of the Mosaic Covenant were done away completely by the death of Christ.

1. THE PASSING OF THE LAW OF MOSES IS TAUGHT EXPLICITLY IN THE NEW TESTAMENT. In Romans 4:13-24, contrasts between the promises to Abraham and the promises to Moses are clearly stated. The promise to Abraham was of faith and by grace. The Law came later and imposed a rule of Law on the people of Israel. But salvation did not come through the Law but rather from the promises given to Abraham as stated in verse 16, "Therefore, the promise comes by faith, so that it may be by grace and may be guaranteed to all Abraham's offspring—not only to those who are of the Law but also to those who are of the faith of Abraham." The Law was given in the Old Testament until the Messiah would come (Gal. 3:19). Though all are under the condemnation of sin, the gracious promise of God in the Gospel is given to those who believe (v. 22). In the present age the divine blessing is now centered in Christ as the sole object of faith (Acts 4:12).

It should be observed that the Law was given only to Israel (Rom. 9:4). Gentiles are never judged on the basis of the Mosaic Law but on such revelation as God had given before the Mosaic Law was written.

With the death of Christ both Jews and Gentiles are related to grace alone as a rule of life. The Gospel of grace is therefore the remedy both for those who sinned without the Law and those who sinned under the Law. Though Gentiles are under some moral laws which bring them to the point of guilt before God, remedy for them as well as for Jews is by salvation in Christ.

Three major aspects of the Law should be considered in connection with the abolishing of the Law.

First, both the commandments and requirements of the Mosaic system and the commandments and requirements of the kingdom are holy and legal in character, and both are set aside during the present reign of grace.

Second, every human work which is wrought with the view of meriting acceptance with God is legal in character. Only through the finished work of Christ is acceptance with God perfectly secured. That acceptance can be experienced only through faith which turns from dependence on merit and rests entirely on Christ as the sufficient Saviour.

Third, any manner of life which is lived in dependence on the flesh rather than dependence on the Spirit is legal in character and is not applicable to the present age of grace. As Galatians 5:18 expresses it, "But if you are led by the Spirit, you are not under Law."

A number of important passages relate to the question of the passing of the Law. In Galatians 3:23 the statement is made, "Before this faith came, we were held prisoners by the Law, locked up until faith should be revealed." This is not the present experience of the unsaved, but the apostle was speaking of Jews who lived under both the dispensation of Moses and the dispensation of grace. By the death of Christ all humanity is delivered from the obligation of meritorious works, as brought out in Romans 8:3-4 and Galatians 3:10, 13.

In Romans 4:14 Paul wrote, "For if those who live by Law are heirs, faith has no value and the promise is worthless." This is true of all humanity when the larger aspects of the Law are in view. It is stated here that if those under the Law are heirs with Christians, then faith would be rendered void.

In 3:31 the statement is made, "Do we, then, nullify the Law by this faith? Not at all! Rather, we uphold the Law." The point is that the ultimate law of righteousness is fulfilled by Christ dying on the cross.

The Law, though completely superseded by grace, may be self-imposed by putting Christians under the legal code of Moses or the laws of the future kingdom. A return to the Mosaic Law, however, is contrary to the will of God and the standards of experience of the unsaved before they accept Christ. The apostle was speaking as a Jew who had lived under the dispensation of Moses and was now under the dispensation of grace. By the death of Christ, however, obligation of meritorious works on the part of both Jew and Gentile is abolished. Those who attempt to keep the works of the Law are condemned by it (Rom. 8:3-4; Gal. 3:10). In Romans 4:14 the point is made that if salvation is by the Law then faith is made void. The fact is no one can inherit salvation by the Law.

In Romans 2:13 Paul wrote, "For it is not those who hear the Law who are righteous in God's sight, but it is those who obey the Law who will be declared righteous." This is a restatement of the inherent principle of the Law that hearing is not enough, and doing is required. Yet it is also true that no one is justified by keeping the Law (Rom. 3:20; Gal. 3:11).

In the extended argument of Paul in Romans 7:15–8:13 the Law is said to be good, but this is in reference to the wider sphere of the whole will of God rather than the limited commandments of Moses.

The fact that the Mosaic Law has been superseded by grace is brought out in John 1:16-17. "From the fullness of His grace we have all received one blessing after another. For the Law was given through Moses; grace and truth came through Jesus Christ."

In Galatians 3:19-25 the point is made that the Law was a schoolmaster to bring Jews to Christ by demonstrating the impossibility of their keeping the Law and in this way opening their hearts to receive the grace of God by faith.

According to Romans 6:14 Christians are not under the Law but under grace. Romans 7:2-6 points out that by the death of Christ believers are dead to the Law and that it has no more dominion over them. So they should serve in newness of life under grace.

In 2 Corinthians 3:7-13 the fact that the Law was gracious and is now done away obviously infers that the present administration of the Holy Spirit is even more glorious.

The striking contrast represented in this entire context can be arranged in parallel columns.

The Teachings of the Law	The Teachings of Grace
1. Written with ink.	1. Written with the Spirit of the living God.
2. In tables of stone.	2. In fleshy tables of the heart.
3. The letter kills.	3. The Spirit gives life.
4. The ministration of death.	4. The ministration of the Spirit.
5. Was glorious.	5. Is rather glorious.
6. Is done away.	6. Remains.
7. Is abolished.	7. Believers have hope.

In Galatians 5:18 the fact that Christians are led by the Spirit proves that they are not under the Law. In Ephesians 2:15 the enmity of the Law and its requirements were declared to be abolished. In Colossians 2:14 Christ, being nailed to the cross, abolished the Law.

The written Law of Moses was not intended to be the rule of the believer's life under grace, but nevertheless the abiding principles of the Law which are adaptable with grace are carried forward and restated under the teachings of grace not as law but reformed to the mold of infinite grace.

2. The error of comingling the Law of the kingdom and the teachings of grace. The future millennial kingdom will obviously bring in many situations which are not true in the present age. For this reason it is not possible to apply literally the principles of the kingdom now before it is established. As a legal system, the laws of the kingdom cannot be applied literally to the Christian's rule of life in the present age.

a. the two systems cannot coexist. Because of the contrasts between the present age and the kingdom, it is wrong to take passages out of context by applying something intended for the future to the present situation. The principles for the kingdom are obviously related to future kingdom conditions when the earth will be under the power and presence of Christ as King of kings, when Satan will be bound, when creation will be delivered, and when all will know the Lord from the least to the greatest. An attempt to impose the kingdom rules on the present age is accordingly inappropriate.

UNDER GRACE THE LAW OF WORKS IS DONE AWAY

Though the Law of Moses may reflect the righteousness of God and the certainty of judgment on sin, if the Law is applied in the present age as a basis for merit with God it is a complete contradiction of the principles of grace. Under the Law Jews were blessed if they obeyed. Under grace the appeal is to obey because one has received the grace of God.

Though it is true that rewards will be bestowed for faithful service of saints in the present age, their works do not become a ground for acceptance by God.

UNDER GRACE THE LAW PRINCIPLE OF DEPENDENCE ON THE ENERGY OF THE FLESH IS DONE AWAY

Under the Law believers were not given spiritual enablement for keeping the Law, and they were dependent on the flesh.

Under grace God has provided the transforming power of the indwelling Holy Spirit, the full revelation of the written Word of God, the intercession of Christ at the right hand of the Father, and many other aspects that characterize the present age of grace. In the present age the New Testament clearly teaches that Christians should not rely on the energy of sinful flesh to accomplish righteousness before God but rather should depend on the Holy Spirit of God to enable them to lead the kind of lives that are pleasing to God.

UNDER GRACE THE MOSAIC RELIGION IS DONE AWAY

With the passing of the Law of Moses, the Mosaic religion observed by Jews is also abolished. In the present age Jews and Gentiles approach God on the same basis of grace and faith in Christ.

When seen as one of the three major economies, the dispensation of the Mosaic Law has clearly been ended, and the dispensation of grace is now God's present economy. The Scriptures predict a revival of Israel and a restoration of their national existence at the time of the second coming of Christ. Though the kingdom economy is not a revival of Mosaic Law, it does provide new religious rites for the Jew. In attempting to contrast the present age of grace with the future age of the kingdom it is most important to observe that in the present age Jew and Gentile are alike. In the Kingdom Age the Jew and Gentile will receive separate treatment once again, and Israel will be a favored people occupying the land promised to Abraham.

As pointed out earlier, in the Protestant Reformation the great Pauline revelation of justification by faith alone as taught in the Scriptures was restored to the theology of the church. Unfortunately, however, theologians were unprepared to receive the added truth of the second Pauline revelation of the doctrine of grace and the church which is Christ's body. This was due to a misguided concept that the church as an institution was the successor or fulfillment of Judaism. Only by observing Pauline revelation concerning the church can proper distinctions be maintained both for the present and for the future.

In the eternal purpose of God, a heavenly people are now being called out for specific heavenly glory made possible by the death, resurrection, and ascension of Christ and by the advent of the Holy Spirit. This divine purpose in no sense is a realization of the promises and covenants made to Israel even though it is also true that every promise will yet be fulfilled.

The fact that the church is a mystery was not revealed in the Old Testament. The truth that the church is the body of Christ as well as the bride of Christ reveals the distinctive character of the present age and of the church. The benediction of the Apostle Paul is appropriate in expressing these facts, "Now to Him who is able to establish you by my Gospel and the proclamation of Jesus Christ, according to the revelation of the mystery hidden for long ages past, but now revealed and made known through the prophetic writings by the command of the eternal God, so that all nations might believe and obey Him—to the only wise God be glory forever through Jesus Christ! Amen" (Rom. 16:25-27).

PART • SEVEN

ESCHATOLOGY

CHAPTER • 33

INTRODUCTION TO ESCHATOLOGY

The last major division of systematic theology is called eschatology from the Greek *eschatos* meaning "last" or "farthest." Eschatology is the science of last things. As revealed in the Bible, eschatology must include all that was prophetic when written though probably half the prophecies have been literally fulfilled. A true eschatology not only gives predictions as to how world history will be consummated but it also casts light on the present meaning of life and events as they move toward their climax.

ESCHATOLOGY GENERALLY NEGLECTED

Of all the fields of theology eschatology has been the most neglected. Even capable theologians such as Charles Hodge confess that prophecy is not within their area of study and that prophetic interpretation involves scholarship that specializes in this doctrine.

In discussing the Second Advent Hodge stated:

> This is a very comprehensive and very difficult subject. It is intimately allied with all the other great doctrines which fall under the head of eschatology. It has excited so much interest in all ages of the church, that books written upon it would of themselves make a library. The subject cannot be adequately discussed without taking a survey of all the prophetic teachings of the Scriptures both of the Old Testament and of the New. This task cannot be satisfactorily challenged by any one who has not made the study of prophecies a specialty. The author, knowing that he has no such qualifications for the work, proposes to

> confine himself in great measure to a historical survey of the different schemes of interpreting scriptural prophecies relating to this subject (*Systematic Theology*. New York: Charles Scribner's Sons, 1892, III, p. 790).

Not only do theologians tend to avoid eschatology, but also courses of instruction in theological seminaries often include little instruction on eschatology. This is in spite of the fact that Christianity does not make logical sense if it does not have a future for all eternity.

Among conservative theologians a literal second coming of Christ is usually affirmed, followed by the judgment of all men and heaven and hell. Disagreements arise principally from the doctrine of the Millennium in the Old and the New Testaments (see previous discussion of the kingdom economy in ecclesiology).

The neglect of prophecy has no reasonable basis. Approximately one fourth of the Bible was prophetic when it was written and about one half of these prophecies have already been literally fulfilled. A fair induction would be that unfulfilled prophecies will be fulfilled in the same literal way as prophecy was fulfilled in the past.

Because prophecy is an integral part of scriptural revelation from Genesis to Revelation, a neglect of this important theme leaves one with an incomplete theology as well as an incomplete philosophy of life. Christianity by its nature is eschatological in its anticipation of the glorious future. Without a future climax to history, Christianity is left without a reasonable explanation of life.

In view of the fact that many of the major writers of Scripture specialize in prophecy and that Jesus Christ Himself included prophecy throughout His ministry, it may be concluded that this neglect of prophecy is a major omission in the scholarly study of theology. No one can be a competent expositor of the Bible without determining what fulfillment of prophecy involves. Even if there is disagreement on details, some agreements can be reached which would give life and faith an intelligent end.

Christ Himself not only recognized prophecy as being fulfilled but also declared that one of the ministries of the Holy Spirit was to declare future things (John 16:12-15).

In Paul's ministry at Thessalonica, which was only three or four weeks in duration, he nevertheless included major elements of prophecy including the fact that the Lord was coming soon. Each chapter of 1 and 2 Thessalonians includes prophecy. It is obvious that Paul did not consider prophecy an obscure and unimportant subject but made it one of the major aspects of revealed truth.

As pointed out in the study of the kingdom economy, three major approaches to prophecy are followed by conservative scholars with each of their theories being related to a literal second coming of Christ.

THE MILLENNIUM IN ESCHATOLOGY

The premillennial interpretation considers prophecy as revealing a literal 1,000-year reign of Christ on earth following His second coming. Accordingly it is properly labeled premillennial. In the early history of the church it was called chiliasm from the Greek word *chilias* meaning "one thousand."

One of the two other major views of the Millennium is amillennialism, which denies a literal political kingdom of Christ on earth. Amillenarians interpret Scriptures relating to the future kingdom as (1) applying to the present age, (2) applying to the believer's intermediate state in heaven, (3) as finding fulfillment in present earth or heaven, or (4) as finding fulfillment in the new heavens and new earth in eternity. Each of the various approaches to amillennialism are negative or contradictory to premillennialism. Even though each view differs greatly from the others, they unite in denying a literal millennial reign of Christ on earth after His second coming.

The postmillennial view is similar to some forms of amillennialism in that it holds that the millennial kingdom will occur before the Second Coming, and the Second Coming therefore will be after the Millennium. Postmillennialism became a leading interpretation in the 18th and 19th centuries and embraces the idea that the Gospel would be so effective that the entire world would be Christianized, resulting in a thousand years of a golden age in which Christ would be honored and Christianity would be the dominant theory of society. Because no such age has actually begun, postmillenarians usually hold that the Millennium is still future but about to begin at any time. In the 19th century postmillennial views were combined with organic evolution as a major means of bringing about the golden age. All conservative theologians oppose evolution. Great prophecy conferences were held in the last quarter of the 19th century and the opening of the 20th century as a means of combating postmillennial evolution. These conferences which earlier included all three conservative millennial views gradually became limited to those who upheld the premillennial interpretation.

As will be demonstrated later, premillennialism was the dominant view of the church in the first two centuries of the Christian era. As a method of interpretation it was largely discarded by the Roman Catholic Church and was not adopted by the Protestant Reformers. In Bible study movements of various kinds that arose in the 18th and 19th centuries and continuing in the 20th century, premillennialism became a live option for eschatology. Though no major denomination embraced it as its official doctrine until the 20th century, the Bible institute movement which later became the Bible college movement was almost entirely premillennial. The Bible conference movement in America also was almost entirely premillennial, and many lay people were convinced of its truth even though they remained in church relationships where no particular stand for eschatology was adopted. Though some argued that a particular view of eschatology should be avoided because it is divisive, the historic fact is that this argument is without an adequate foundation. In the history of the church differences in eschatology did not cause divisions. Important divisions in the church usually arose from such areas as inspiration of the Bible, the ordinances of baptism and the Lord's Supper, and sometimes were caused by politics. Various views on the Millennium were usually held to some degree within a denomination.

The Bible college movement was largely premillennial because this offered a sensible and consistent interpretation of the entire Bible. Premillennialism was not adopted by theological seminaries or denominations until the 20th century. Neglect of prophecy has led to neglect of the Bible as a whole and has often opened the way for liberal theological concepts which are destructive of historic Christian theology.

The importance of the study of prophecy is stated by George N.H. Peters:

> The history of the human race is, as able theologians have remarked, the history of God's dealings with man. It is a fulfilling of revelation; yea, more: it is an unfolding of the ways of God, a comprehensive confirmation of, and an appointed aid in inter-

> preting the plan of redemption. Hence, God Himself appeals to it, not merely as the evidence of the truth declared, but as the mode by which we alone can obtain a full and complete view of the divine purpose relating to salvation. To do this we must, however, regard *past, present, and future* history. The latter must be received as predicted, for we may rest assured, from the past and present fulfillment of the Word of God, thus changed into historical reality, that the predictions and promises relating to the future will also in their turn become veritable history. It is *this faith,* which grasps the future as already present, that can form a decided and unmistakable unity (*The Theocratic Kingdom.* Grand Rapids: Kregel Publications, 1952, I, p. 13).

Having spoken of the importance of biblical interpretation in giving language its reasonable grammatic meaning, Peters goes on to say:

> On a proposition which has brought forth many volumes in its discussion, we desire simply to announce our position, and assign a few reasons in its behalf. Its import is of such weight; the consequences of its adoption are of such moment; the tendency it possesses of leading to the truth and of vindicating Scripture is of such value, that we cannot pass it by without some explanations and reflections. We unhesitatingly plant ourselves upon the famous maxim (*Eccl. Polity,* B. 2.) of the able Hooker: "I hold for a most infallible rule in expositions of the Sacred Scriptures, that where a literal construction will stand, the furthest from the letter is commonly the worst. There is nothing more dangerous than this licentious and deluding art, which changes the meaning of words, as alchemy doth, or would do, the substance of metals, making of anything what it pleases, and bringing in the end all truth to nothing." The primitive church occupied this position, and Irenaeus (*Adv. Haer.* 2, C. 27) gives us the general sentiment when (in the language of Neander, *Hist. Dogmas,* p. 77) "he says of the Holy Scriptures: that what the understanding can daily make use of, what it can easily know, is that which lies before our eyes, unambiguously, literally, and clearly in Holy Writ." However much this principle of interpretation was subverted, as history attests, by succeeding centuries (not without protests), yet at the Reformation it was again revived. Thus

> Luther (*Table Talk*, "On God's Word," 11) remarks: "I have grounded my preaching upon the literal Word; he that pleases may follow me, he that will not may stay." In confirmation of such a course, it may be said: if God has really intended to make known His will to man, it follows that to secure knowledge on our part, He must convey His truth to us *in accordance* with the well-known rules of language. He must *adapt Himself to our mode* of communicating thought and ideas. If His words were given to be understood, it follows that He must have employed language to convey the sense intended, agreeably to the laws grammatically expressed, controlling all language; and that, instead of seeking a sense which the words in themselves do not contain, we are primarily to obtain the sense that the words obviously embrace, making due allowance for the existence of figures of speech when indicated by the context, scope, or construction of the passage. By "literal," we mean the grammatical interpretation of Scripture (*Ibid.*, p. 47).

Understanding prophecy is necessary to understanding the Scriptures. For instance there is no proper approach to the Gospels without seeing in them fulfillment of Old Testament predictions respecting the Messiah. In like manner the Book of Revelation is a terminal where great lines of prophetic truth combine like railroad lines running into a union station. Prophecy is therefore the capstone of theological truth presented in the entire Scriptures. One who does not have a clear grasp of prophecy is not able to express in any cogent way the ultimate end of biblical faith.

Knowledge of biblical prophecy qualifies all Christian life and service. In prophecy one comes to know the faithfulness of God by His Word. When men of faith like Daniel believe implicitly in the accuracy and literalness of the Word of God (cf. Dan. 9), it should lead to the same conclusion on the part of those who study the Bible today. Prophecy is intended to be illuminating, comforting (1 Thes. 4:18), and sanctifying (John 17:17) in presenting the wonderful expectation of Christ's promised return.

Though there is much divergence of interpretation in prophecy, it is obvious that the Scriptures present only one system of truth. The Bible does not lend itself to the support of amillennial, postmillennial, and premillennial schemes of interpretation at the same time. It is important for a scholar to weigh the claims of each point of view in relation to biblical statements and arrive at a definite position. The present tendency toward a form of agnosticism in which scholars claim themselves unable to interpret the Bible eschatologically is an unnecessary conclusion. The major facts of eschatology can be known.

Eschatology is studied in the following divisions: (1) general features, (2) the seven major highways of prophecy, (3) major themes of Old Testament prophecy, (4) major themes of New Testament prophecy, (5) predicted events in their order, (6) the judgments, and (7) the eternal state.

GENERAL FEATURES OF ESCHATOLOGY

CHAPTER • 34

A BRIEF HISTORY OF CHILIASM

Chiliasm is the historical word referring to the concept of a Kingdom Age of 1,000 years which will follow the second coming of Christ. Compared with other views, the distinctive feature of this doctrine is that Christ will return *before* the 1,000 years. During this 1,000 years He will be personally present on the earth, exercising His rightful authority as King and securing and sustaining all the blessings on earth ascribed to that period.

In modern discussion the term "chiliasm" has been replaced by the designation "premillennialism," which is distinguished from postmillennialism and amillennialism. The doctrine is supported by a series of resurrections of all the righteous beginning with the resurrection of Christ and concluding with the resurrection mentioned in Revelation 20:4. All of these resurrections precede the 1,000-year kingdom according to verses 4-6. In 1 Corinthians 15:23-26, which discusses the order of the resurrections, Christ is named as the Firstfruits, to be followed by the resurrection of those who are His when He returns. The end of human history will be revealed after the judgment of all the wicked men and angels. As Paul expressed it in this passage, "For as in Adam all die, so in Christ all will be made alive. But each in his own turn: Christ, the Firstfruits; then, when He comes, those who belong to Him. Then the end will come, when He hands over the kingdom to God the Father after He has destroyed all dominion, authority, and power. For He must reign until He has put all His enemies under His feet. The last enemy to be destroyed is death. For He 'has put everything under His feet' " (vv. 22-27). The premillennial teaching of a future kingdom on earth following the second coming of Christ permits a literal interpretation of many Old Testament and New Testament passages that describe such a period as a time of peace, justice, and general blessing on society.

The history of premillennialism as a doctrine may be approached under seven time periods.

THE PERIOD AS REVEALED IN THE OLD TESTAMENT

The future millennial kingdom is important for it is the fulfillment of many promises given to Israel—a glorious period of righteousness and peace when her Messiah will come. During the kingdom Christ will sit on David's throne in Jerusalem and rule over Israel as well as over the entire world (Ps. 89:19-37; Jer. 23:5-6). In the discussion to follow, additional revelation will be considered on the important doctrine of the future kingdom.

THE MESSIANIC KINGDOM OFFERED TO ISRAEL AT CHRIST'S FIRST ADVENT

When Christ began His public ministry, it was commonly believed by the people of Israel that the Messiah would deliver them from their enemies and bring in a literal kingdom on earth in which they would be honored. No one seems to have understood the difference between the first and second comings of Christ until after His ascension into heaven.

In presenting Himself to the people of Israel Jesus clearly claimed to be the Christ and to be the One who fulfilled Old Testament prophecies. In offering Himself He presented to them the kingdom as being at hand.

THE KINGDOM REJECTED AND POSTPONED

The Gospel records clearly testify that Christ was rejected by the religious leaders of His day as well as by many of the common people, though some were His loyal followers. Some contention has arisen over the idea that if Christ offered to bring in the future kingdom this would make unnecessary His death and resurrection. Such criticism fails to distinguish that what is offered in a genuine way was also rejected. This was part of God's plan from eternity past.

The Children of Israel went through a similar experience at Kadesh Barnea when on their journey from Egypt to the Promised Land they failed to trust God and rejected the leadership of Moses. The result was that they spent 40 years wandering in the wilderness before the promise was realistically fulfilled. Yet the offer of God to bring them into the land flowing with milk and honey was genuine even though in the sovereign plan of God the offer would be rejected.

In like manner Christ made a genuine offer of Himself as the King of Israel and stated the moral principles of His kingdom in the Sermon on the Mount (Matt. 5–7). The argument that by this act He was making His death unnecessary does not take into proper consideration the difference between the divine and the human viewpoints. God can make a genuine offer of salvation to an unsaved person even though God knows that he is not elect to salvation.

Nothing is clearer in both Testaments than the importance and essential character of the death of Christ on the cross for the sins of the whole world to be followed by His bodily resurrection. Christ stated that He had come for this purpose (20:28; Mark 10:45). After rejection of the miracles which were performed in Matthew 8–12 and other indications of rejection of Christ's message, it was revealed that the kingdom would not be brought in immediately because of this rejection. Christ stated the facts relating to the period between His first and second comings in Matthew 13. In other statements He predicted His death and resurrection (12:39-40; 16:21; 17:22-23).

The night before His crucifixion Christ outlined the major doctrinal features of the present age (John 13–17). Before His ascension He prophesied the coming of the Holy Spirit and the future witness to the entire earth (Acts 1:8). Just as the prophecies of His death and resurrection and the present age between the first and second advents were literally fulfilled, so the promise of the period after His second coming demands the same factual and literal interpretation.

CHILIASTIC BELIEFS HELD BY THE EARLY CHURCH

Premillenarians believe that their interpretation of the Scriptures is a self-consistent, justifiable conclusion from interpreting prophecies of the future in a literal way. As the early church tended to do this, the evidence supports the fact that the early church was premillennial. Some internal evidences from the Scriptures confirm that the early church followed the premillennial interpretation of prophecy.

In the church council held in Jerusalem (Acts 15) the problem raised was whether Gentile believers had to be circumcised. The record of the meeting not only presents the problem but also the solution as recorded in verses 5-11, "Then some of the believers who belonged to the party of the Pharisees stood up and said, 'The Gentiles must be circumcised and required to obey the Law of Moses.' The apostles and elders met to consider this question. After much discussion, Peter got up and addressed them: 'Brothers, you know that some time ago God made a choice among you that the Gentiles might hear from my lips the message of the Gospel and believe. God, who knows the heart, showed that He accepted them by giving the Holy Spirit to them, just as He did to us. He made no distinction between us and them, for He purified their hearts by faith. Now then, why do you try to test God by putting on the necks of the disciples a yoke that neither we nor our fathers have been able to bear? No! We believe it is through the grace of our Lord Jesus that we are saved, just as they are.' "

The solution to the problem was to recognize that Gentiles in the present age are being blessed of God. They came to the conclusion that the ultimate time for Israel's blessing would be in the future kingdom period. In the present time God does not make a distinction between saved Jews and Gentiles in the church but gives them the same spiritual blessings and the same salvation.

This is confirmed when James gave his point of view, "When they finished, James spoke up: 'Brothers, listen to me. Simon has described to us how God at first showed His concern by taking from the Gentiles a people for Himself. The words of the prophets are in agreement with this, as it is written: "After this I will return and rebuild David's fallen tent. Its ruins I will rebuild, and I will restore it, that the remnant of men may seek the Lord, and all the Gentiles who bear My name, says the Lord, who does these things" that have been known for ages' " (vv. 13-18). In brief, the present age is a time for Gentile blessing. After this present age David's kingdom will be restored, and it will be a final blessing for the Jews as well as for the Gentiles. As stated in verse 14, God will first take "from the Gentiles a people for Himself." Verse 16 states that after the Gentile period of blessing "David's fallen tent," referring to his kingdom, will be restored with Christ sitting on the throne of David and David ruling under Christ as a prince (Ezek. 34:23-24; 37:24-25; Amos

9:11-12). Properly interpreted Acts 15 is a clear statement that the present age is a time of special Gentile blessing and that the future age after the Second Coming will be a time of special blessing for Israel.

Another major passage supporting the premillennial view is Romans 9–11. These chapters face the same problem of how Israel is related to the present age and to the future age. In these chapters the present age is described as a time of Gentile blessing when Gentiles are grafted into the olive tree, the place of blessing in keeping with the Abrahamic Covenant (11:17). Again in the passage the chronological order of blessing is that the Jews will be blessed after the period of Gentile blessing. The passage predicts that Israel will be grafted back into the olive tree (vv. 23-24). As the period of Gentile blessing closes with the Rapture of the church, it necessarily involves that Israel will be blessed after the second coming of Christ, in keeping with premillennial interpretation.

This is confirmed by the prophecy in verses 25-26. During the present age Jews generally have difficulty accepting the Gospel of salvation; many of them have rejected Christ as their Messiah. When the Rapture occurs their hardening will be removed, and many Jews will realize that Christ fulfilled the prophecies of their Messiah and will turn to Him in faith. Again the major line of demarcation is the second coming of Christ before which Gentiles are blessed and after which Jews are blessed. (In the period between the Rapture and the Second Coming both Jews and Gentiles suffer.) This would realistically require a millennial kingdom to fulfill the promise of special blessing on Jews.

THE CHILIASTIC EXPECTATION CONTINUED UNTIL THE ROMAN APOSTASY

In the years that followed the apostolic period there were many centuries in which spiritual darkness characterized the world. The Middle Ages are often called the "Dark Ages." In the period immediately following the Apostolic Age, however, there is clear evidence of premillennial faith as the normal orthodox position of the church.

This is presented by George N.H. Peters' comments on Justin Martyr, who along with others held to the premillennial second coming of Christ.

> Our doctrine is traced *continuously* from the Apostles themselves, seeing that (Prop. 72, Obs. 3, note 1) the first Fathers, who present millenarian views, saw and conversed either with the Apostles or the elders following them. So extensively, so generally was chiliasm perpetuated, that Justin Martyr *positively asserts that all the orthodox* adopted and upheld it. Justin's language is explicit (*Dial. with Trypho*, sec. 2); for after stating the chiliastic doctrine, he asserts: "it is to be *thoroughly proved* that it will come to pass. But I have also signified unto thee, on the other hand, that many—even those of that race of Christians *who follow not godly and pure doctrine—do not acknowledge it.* For I have demonstrated to thee, that these are indeed *called* Christians; but are atheists and impious heretics, because that in all things they teach what is blasphemous, and ungodly, and unsound," etc. He adds: "But I and whatsoever Christians *are orthodox in all things* do know that there will be a resurrection of the flesh, and a thousand years in the city of Jerusalem, built, adorned, and enlarged, according as Ezekiel, Isaiah, and other prophets have promised. For Isaiah saith of this thousand years (ch. 65:17) 'Behold, I create new heavens and a new earth: and the former shall not be remembered, nor come into mind; but be ye glad and rejoice in those which I create: for, behold, I create Jerusalem to triumph, and my people to rejoice,' etc. Moreover, a certain man among us, whose name is *John, being one of the twelve Apostles of Christ,* in that revelation which was shown to him prophesied, that those who believe in our Christ shall fulfill a thousand years at Jerusalem; and *after that* the general, and, in a word, the everlasting resurrection, and last judgment of all together. Whereof also *our Lord spake* when He said, that therein they shall neither marry, nor be given in marriage, but shall be equal with the angels, being made the sons of the resurrection of God" (*The Theocratic Kingdom.* Grand Rapids: Kregel Publications, 1952, I, p. 480).

As Justin Martyr testified, there have always been those who rejected the second coming of Christ and the millennial kingdom to follow, but they were not considered orthodox. In the modern world these denials have appeared in three areas. (1) Liberalism tends to belittle the Scriptures bearing on the theme, considering the subject of the Millennium itself as unworthy of scholarly investigation.

(2) The scholarship of those who defend the premillennial interpretation is attacked. (3) Even in relatively conservative scholarship there seems to be a tendency today to belittle the evidence for premillennialism in the early centuries.

The evidence from the early church is set forth by Peters: "Since many of our opponents, in order to make an erroneous impression on those unacquainted with Eccles. History, *purposely mingle the later* Fathers with *the earlier* (as if they were *contemporary*), it will be proper to give the Fathers *in chronological* order, so that the ordinary reader can see *for himself* when they lived, and *form his own judgment* respecting their position in history. This decides the question *of priority,* and also that of *the later* introduction of opposing influences. We will, therefore, mention those that are *expressly named* by both ancients and moderns" (*Ibid.*, p. 494).

Peters lists as advocates of premillennialism in the first century the following among the twelve Apostles: Andrew, Peter, Philip, Thomas, James, John and Matthew. Besides others such as Aristio and John the Presbyter these are all cited by Papias. This evidence from Papias is cited by Irenaeus (*Ibid.*, p. 494).

Others who are mentioned by Peters are Clement of Rome, Barnabas, Hermas, Ignatius, Polycarp, and Papias (*Ibid.*, pp. 494-95).

The conclusions of Peters have of course been attacked because some of his evidence is not entirely conclusive. But the general strength of the position is sustained, and no one apparently is able to cite solid evidence of an amillenarian in the first century or the first 90 years of the second century.

Advocates of premillennialism in the second century include the following according to Peters: Pothinus, Justin Martyr, Melito, Hegisippus, Tatian, Irenaeus, Tertullian, Hippolytus, and Apollinaris (*Ibid.*, pp. 495-96).

No opposition to premillennialism can be cited in the second century except in the last 10 years when the Alexandrian School of Theology in Egypt began to promote its heresies.

Peters also cites advocates of premillennialism in the third century including Cyprian, Commodian, Nepos, Coracion, Victorinus, Methodius, and Lactantius. Practically all scholars agree that at the closing of the second century and beginning in the third century there was opposition to premillennialism which originated in the School of Theology in Alexandria, Egypt.

Though some of the conclusions of Peters have been debated, the weight of the numerous names cited with no names offered by rebuttal until the third century is overwhelming proof that the early church was premillennial.

The School of Theology at Alexandria attempted to combine Christian theology with the philosophy of Plato, a pure idealist. The viewpoint of Plato was so contrary to Scripture that the only way any resemblance could be noted would be by taking the Scripture in a nonliteral sense. The result was that most of the important doctrines of the faith were subverted and with it the premillennial teaching. Scholars of every viewpoint of eschatology agree that leaders of the School of Alexandria were heretics and that their viewpoint has never been accepted as orthodox. The first amillenarians from the School of Alexandria were Gaius (or Caius), a third-century theologian; Clement, who taught in Alexandria from 193 to 220; his pupil Origen (185-254), who was an outstanding advocate of amillennialism; and Dionysius (190-265). The teachings of Clement and Origen are well established as in opposition to premillennialism.

Even amillenarians like W.H. Rutgers admit that the Alexandrian school was heretical: "Clement, engrossed and charmed by Greek philosophy, applied this erroneous allegorical method to Holy Writ. It was a one-sided emphasis: opposed to the real, the visible, phenomenal, spatial, and temporal. A platonic idealistic philosophy could not countenance carnalistic, sensualistic conceptions of the future as that advanced by chiliasm. It shook the very foundation on which chiliasm rested" (*Premillennialism in America.* Goes, Holland: Oosterbaan Le Contre, p. 64).

As the amillennial interpretation of the Alexandrian school penetrated the church, it first overcame the opposition of Nepos an ardent premillenarian who effectively refuted the doctrine with many churches in North Africa withdrawing in protest against the spiritualization of Origen. Nepos, however, died in the middle of the controversy and his successors were not able to overcome the tide of opposition to premillennialism. As a result North Africa became a desert for Christian churches in the many centuries that followed.

In summary, the first two centuries were almost without disputation centuries in which premillennialism was the orthodox doctrine. With the close of the second and third centuries the Alexandrian School of Theology became an effective foe to premillennialism, spiritualizing Scripture instead of using literal interpretation. This devastated the theology of the church not only in regard to premillennialism but also in other areas of doctrine. Support for amillennialism is almost completely absent in the first and second centuries, and in the third century the Alexandrian form of amillennialism was labeled by all orthodox theologians as heretical and destructive.

In the fourth and fifth centuries Augustine in his theological writings attempted to restore proper biblical interpretation of Scripture. As a whole he upheld the grammatical, historical, and literal interpretation. He believed, however, that eschatology required a special nonliteral hermeneutic in its interpretation with the result that he refused the millennial teaching. In his amillennial interpretation, however, he tended to take literally the prophecies of the future in regard to the second coming of Christ, the final judgments, the resurrection of the righteous and the wicked, and other aspects of eschatology. The principal fatality of his nonliteral interpretation was the millennial kingdom. This point of view has continued to the present day.

Though many interpreted the kingdom as a literal thousand years, most amillenarians held that the Millennium began in the first century, and that the present age, as seen by Augustine, is the Millennium. Satan is now bound, and when the second coming of Christ occurs the Millennium will end and eternity will begin. Augustinian amillennialism continues to be the mainline of amillennial teaching, though variations of the view have arisen in the last few centuries.

The establishing of a different hermeneutic for eschatology from the method used in interpreting other Scriptures is questionable especially when the nonliteral interpretation arbitrarily selects the millennial kingdom as the doctrine to be spiritualized while holding that other prophecies are literal. It is obvious that rejection of the Millennium was based not so much on lack of evidence in the Bible as resistance to the doctrine itself.

CHILIASM BEGAN TO BE RESTORED IN THE REFORMATION

The period between Augustine and the Protestant Reformation was largely a time of spiritual darkness. Though a few bright lights appeared as devoted souls who believed the Scriptures, for the most part the rank and file of those in the church as well as out of the church had limited comprehension of scriptural doctrine. Opponents of premillennialism often revealed ignorance of the doctrine itself even though there were competent scholars in other areas. It was not until the Protestant Reformation when the principle of every man being his own interpreter of the Bible as led by the Holy Spirit was established that the groundwork was laid for individual study of the Scriptures leading to the premillennial view.

The main leaders of the Protestant Reformation such as Martin Luther and John Calvin were amillennial and interpreted prophecy concerning endtime events as being fulfilled. They viewed the Roman Catholic Church as the beast of Revelation 13 and the apostasy of the Roman Church as fulfilling the prophecies of apostasy in the endtime. Even though not premillennial, Luther and Calvin anticipated the possibility that Christ might return in their lifetimes.

CHILIASM SINCE THE REFORMATION

Because most historical scholars since the Reformation have not believed in premillennialism, their writings have not given much space to this doctrine. In the 19th century within orthodox Christianity postmillennialism was the prevailing point of view, as illustrated in Charles Hodge. There were, however, some premillenarians including outstanding American scholars such as Cotton Mather (1663-1728), son of Increase Mather (1639-1723), and grandson of Richard Mather (1596-1669). They were Congregational clergymen in New England and were relatively well informed on premillennialism. Increase Mather was the sixth president of Harvard University. There is clear evidence that Cotton Mather was premillennial (Peters, *The Theocratic Kingdom.* I, pp. 541-42).

Since the Protestant Reformation three major views of the Millennium, as mentioned earlier, surfaced and may be further described.

1. The theory of Whitby. Daniel Whitby (1638-1725) was an English theologian who contended that the Millennium was yet future and would result from preaching the Gospel and Christianizing of the world. His view of postmillennialism, though anticipated in some earlier writers, became the standard of postmillennial theology in the years that followed. Generally speaking, those who embraced his view regarded the millennial kingdom as a result of the triumph of the Gospel. In the 20th century liberal theologians adopted the postmillennial view as confirming their evolutionary conclusions that

the world was getting increasingly better.

2. Amillennialism. As previously indicated, amillennialism characterized the theology of the early church beginning with the close of the second century and was eventually adopted by the Roman Church which followed Augustine. Many scholars in the 19th and 20th centuries classified themselves as either amillennial or postmillennial. Their interpretations of Scripture passages that teach a millennial kingdom were based on taking the prophecies as nonliteral and for the most part as being fulfilled in the present age. Their views differed widely but were united on the denial of a literal Millennium after the second coming of Christ.

As previously mentioned, amillennialism for the most part followed Augustine, who held that the present age between the first and second comings of Christ is the Millennium. Later, scholars in the 19th and 20th centuries adopted the idea that the Millennium was the intermediate state between the death and resurrection of Christians. A more recent point of view is that the Millennium will be fulfilled in the new heavens, the new earth, and the New Jerusalem.

3. Premillennialism. Peters lists outstanding clergymen who are premillenarians. In the United States from more than 11 denominations Peters named 360 of America's most honored expositors, editors, and preachers as premillenarians. Similarly 470 widely known ministers and writers of Europe are mentioned by name, among whom are such scholars as Bengel, Olshausen, Gill, Stier, Alford, Lange, Meyer, Starke, Fausset, Jones, and Mast. Others who have written extensively are Keach, Bonar, Tait, Ryle, Seiss, Cumming, Fry, MacIntosh, Wells, Demarast, Delitzsch, Ebrard, Mede, Goodwin, Elliott, Cunningham, Darby, and his associates (*The Theocratic Kingdom.* I, p. 524).

After Peters' work was written, the 20th century continued to produce premillennial scholars who have written extensively. Also in the 20th century for the first time denominations and independent church fellowships appeared that were committed to premillennial interpretation.

CHAPTER • 35

THE BIBLICAL CONCEPT OF PROPHECY

Only God knows the future; therefore human writers of Scripture were enabled to write prophecy through God's supernatural guidance and revelation. Though the Bible does not give all the details of endtime events, what is revealed helps make life meaningful.

Under these circumstances it is amazing how many neglect prophetic Scriptures almost entirely. Though requiring careful study to decide what the Scriptures teach on the subject of prophecy, even a simplistic approach to Christianity provides a basis for faith in important future major events.

In studying the biblical concept of prophecy six general subjects will be examined: (1) the prophet, (2) the prophet's message, (3) the prophet's power, (4) the selection of prophets, (5) the fulfillment of prophecy, and (6) the history of prophecy.

THE PROPHET

In general, prophets in Scripture were those who spoke for God. A prophet was God's voice to the people in contrast to the priest who represented the people in approaching God. In Christ both activities unite for He is both the Prophet and the Priest.

Prophecy does not necessarily always concern the future, for prophets often delivered a message for a contemporary situation. Prophecy is both forthtelling and foretelling.

Often in the Old Testament a prophet would deliver a message with the introduction, "Thus saith the LORD." Prophets did more than just speak for God. Sometimes they were also considered seers, those who see things that others do not. In addition a prophet was often a patriot, reformer, and revivalist in the midst of God's people. A prophet's ministry became especially necessary in times of spiritual declension, and many of the great prophecies were given at a time when the people of God needed encouragement as well as challenge.

The Scriptures reveal a variety of divine methods of revealing the mind and will of God to a prophet. Often God enhanced their ability to see truth embodied in the word "seer." Sometimes they heard messages that other men did not. Prophets often "saw" truth concerning Judah and Jerusalem (Isa. 2:1). Prophets would freely say that their message was not their own but was a message from God (cf. Jer. 23:16; Ezek. 13:2). Often the burden to present the truth of God was like a burning fire within (cf. Jer. 20:9; Ezek. 3:1-27). There was also a personal element in prophecy (cf. Jer. 15:16; 20:7; Ezek. 3:3).

In the New Testament, prophets had a different role. They had less of the role of patriot, reformer, and revivalist and more the role of communicating truth from God. In 1 Corinthians 14:3 it is stated, "Everyone who prophesies speaks to men for their strengthening, encouragement, and comfort." The gift of prophecy is included as a ministry gift (Eph. 4:11). Some who had the gift of prophecy, that is, having the gift of foretelling events or bringing a communication from God, were not always fully recognized as prophets who executed this office regularly, such as Paul, Peter, and others.

THE PROPHET'S MESSAGE

In Scripture all truth is prophecy in the sense that it came from God, but many prophecies were predictive in their character. This is true of the great biblical covenants such as the Abrahamic, Palestinian, Davidic, and New Covenants. Prophecies related to various peoples including Israel. Prophecies about Gentiles were presented by Nahum, Obadiah, and Jonah though that was not their main burden of revelation. The greatest treatment of prophecy pertaining to the Gentiles is seen in Daniel chapters 2, 7–8, which spoke of the great empires of the future from Daniel's perspective.

From the standpoint of spiritual progress, the future of Israel became a major element of predictive prophecy. It included her obedience and disobedience, her revivals and apostasies, her worldwide dispersions and regatherings, her repentance and return from sin, her regathering, and the establishing of her kingdom after the second coming of Christ.

A central subject of prophecy is the two advents of the Messiah, including His suffering (Gen. 3:15; Acts 1:9) and His coming to reign (Deut. 30:3; Acts 1:9-11). The Day of the Lord occupies a large place in both the Old and New Testaments as a time when God deals directly with the world in judgment (Isa. 2:10-22; Rev. 19:11-21). The doctrine of the kingdom also is a large subject in the Old Testament (Gen. 1:26-28; Zech. 12:8; cf. Luke 1:31-33; 1 Cor. 15:28). Great chapters on prophecy include the predictions of Moses concerning the future of Israel (Deut. 28–30). In Psalm 2 the second coming of Christ is predicted, and Daniel 2 and 7 mention the four great world empires. It is obvious that prophecy of future events as well as proclamation of present truth characterize Scripture.

THE PROPHET'S POWER

In the Old Testament, prophets were often seen as equal to or greater than kings, though humanly speaking, kings had the power to kill prophets. On the other hand prophets would often dictate to kings, and divine protection would be given them. A number of Scriptures support this concept (Num. 11:25, 29; 24:2; 2 Kings 2:15; 3:15; 1 Chron. 12:18; 2 Chron. 24:27; Isa. 11:2; 42:1; 61:1; Ezek. 1:3; 3:14, 22; 11:5; Joel 2:28-29).

THE SELECTION OF PROPHETS

The prophets who were chosen by God carried the authority of being His choice. The prophets were not always in sympathy with their message as illustrated by Saul (1 Sam. 10:11; 19:24), Balaam (Num. 23:5-10), and Caiaphas (John 11:52). The prophetic office in the Old Testament seems to have existed for a lifetime.

THE FULFILLMENT OF PROPHECY

As a divine test of a prophet's authenticity as appointed by God, prophecies had to be fulfilled (Deut. 18:21-22). In the New Testament frequent reference is made to fulfilled events as spoken by the Lord through a prophet, which emphasizes the character of true prophecy in all Scripture.

Prophecies in the Bible are so specific and numerous that skeptics can hardly account for prophecies as mere conjecture by man. It would be impossible, apart from divine revelation, for a prophet to be right consistently in his predictions. An outstanding illustration is Daniel 11:1-35 in which there are approximately 135 prophecies, all of which have been literally fulfilled.

THE HISTORY OF PROPHECY

The prophetic story of prophecy especially as it relates to the Old Testament largely revolves around the Abrahamic, Palestinian, and Davidic Covenants. These prophecies center on Israel and are in contrast to the church, which has a heavenly purpose and will be consummated in heaven according to Hebrews 2:10.

In the fulfillment of Old and New Testament prophecies the principle is illustrated again and again that the natural, literal, and grammatical meaning is what is intended. Little support is given for the notion that prophecy should not be interpreted in a literal way. It is unreasonable to suppose that predictions yet unfulfilled will be realized in some spiritualized manner when prophetic events now already fulfilled have been completed literally.

1. FOUR PROPHETS IN SCRIPTURE SERVE AS MILESTONES. Though there were many prophets in the course of history, obviously some brought messages of great importance and should be singled out as outstanding.

a. ABRAHAM. God gave Abraham a tremendous sweep of prophecy in the Abrahamic Covenant recorded in Genesis 12:1-3. Many of the promises of the Abrahamic Covenant have already been fulfilled, including the fact that Abraham was a great man, that he was the father of a great people, that his people would bring blessing to the entire world, and that those who bless Israel would be blessed, and those who curse Israel would be cursed. Though some prophecies related to the Abrahamic Covenant still await future fulfillment, the amazing literalness of the fulfillments to date illustrates that the future promises yet to be fulfilled for Israel and for the church will be fulfilled literally. In addition to the Abrahamic Covenant itself,

Abraham was told that his people would go to a strange land for hundreds of years and eventually would come out with great wealth (15:13-14). This was fulfilled as recorded in Exodus. The importance of Abraham is demonstrated by the fact that Genesis 12–50 is devoted to the history of Abraham, Isaac, Jacob, and Jacob's sons.

b. MOSES. One of the greatest Old Testament prophets was Moses (Deut. 34:10-12). He was not only the great lawgiver and the writer of the Pentateuch but also he saw the program of God for Israel continuing into the future. This included her occupation of the Promised Land, her dispersion into captivities, her regatherings, and her ultimate blessing from God. Moses did not foresee the church, and his viewpoint was similar to that of Daniel in its expansive character.

c. DANIEL. Daniel was given the two great prophetic programs pertaining to the future of Israel and to the future of Gentile power. On the basis of his prophecy in Daniel 9:24-27, 490 years were described as a basic unit of prophetic fulfillment for Israel. Of these, 483 years were fulfilled before Messiah was cut off and crucified (v. 26). The last 7 years await future fulfillment, and will be fulfilled literally just as the preceding years were fulfilled literally. What Daniel revealed is expanded in the New Testament especially in the Book of Revelation. Daniel's prophecies about the Gentiles outlined the future of Babylon, Medo-Persia, Greece, and Rome to be followed by the kingdom from heaven—the Millennium.

d. CHRIST. Of all the prophets Christ is the greatest. His message was most complete and pertinent to understanding the future. A complete theology can be developed from the teaching ministry of Christ with contributions in all the great fields of bibliology, theology proper, angelology, anthropology, hamartiology, soteriology, ecclesiology, and eschatology. In His major discourses He dealt with extensive subjects such as the ethical character of the kingdom (Matt. 5–7), the major features of the present age between the first and second advents of Christ (Matt. 13), a truth not revealed in the Old Testament, and prophecies of endtime events with the prediction of His own second coming (Matt. 24–25). Christ introduced the subject of the Rapture of the church (John 14:1-3) and the moral decline and unprecedented Tribulation of the endtimes (Matt. 24:21-22). He predicted the coming of the future world ruler who would desecrate the temple (v. 15). He described His own glorious appearing when He will return to the earth (v. 27). He predicted the regathering of Israel (v. 31) and God's judgment on Israel (24:37–25:30). The judgments of the nations concluded His Olivet Discourse as recorded in verses 31-46.

2. John the Baptist. In the New Testament the introductory prophet was John the Baptist. As the forerunner of Christ, he fulfilled the promise of the voice in the wilderness as predicted by Isaiah 40:3-5. His message was a call to repentance as a spiritual preparation for the coming of Christ. His introduction of Christ was no doubt his major contribution.

John the Baptist became a problem to those who opposed his ministry. His introduction of Christ as the coming King brought astonishment to the religious world in Jerusalem and upset the political authorities. He was filled with the Spirit from birth (Luke 1:15). His conception was miraculous (vv. 18, 36-37). He was sent as a light to the world in preparing the way of the Messiah (John 1:6-7). Christ declared him the greatest of the prophets who had preceded Christ, and at the same time Christ exalted the work of future prophets who would reveal New Testament truth (Matt. 11:11-15).

In many respects John's ministry was a consummation of the Old Testament order of priests (v. 13). Just as Christ was rejected so was John the Baptist rejected, ending with his execution. No doubt John as well as the Apostles had inaccurate anticipations of what Christ would do in His first coming because they did not recognize the difference between the First and Second Comings. John and the Apostles were disappointed that Christ did not lead Israel out of her captivity and submission to the Roman Empire and establish His glorious rule predicted by the prophets. They did not understand that this was reserved for Christ's second coming.

The importance of John's prophetic message was to announce that the kingdom was at hand in the sense that the King was now present. His exhortation was that they should prepare spiritually for the coming of the Lord.

3. False prophets. False prophets are also mentioned in the Bible as existing throughout Scripture but especially in the last days. Mention of this is found in numerous passages (Matt. 7:15; 24:11, 24; Mark 13:22; Acts 16:16; 1 Cor. 14:29; 2 Peter 2:1; 1 John 4:1; Rev. 16:13; 19:20; 20:10). The satanic purpose of raising false prophets was to confuse the people of God and reduce confidence in those who brought true prophecies.

4. Classification of Old Testament prophecies. Classifying

the Old Testament written prophecies helps to distinguish the movement of prophecy in the Old Testament (dates are approximate).

a. BEFORE THE EXILE.

(1) To Nineveh, Jonah—862 B.C.

(2) To the Ten Tribes, Amos—787 B.C.; Hosea—785-725 B.C.; Obadiah—887 B.C.; Joel—800 B.C.

(3) To Judah, Isaiah—760-698 B.C.; Micah—750-710 B.C.; Nahum—713 B.C.; Habakkuk—626 B.C.; Zephaniah—630 B.C.; Jeremiah—629-588 B.C.

b. PROPHETS OF THE EXILE. Ezekiel—595-574 B.C.; Daniel—607-534 B.C.

c. POSTEXILIC PROPHETS. Haggai—520 B.C.; Zechariah—520-487 B.C.; Malachi—397 B.C.

CHAPTER • 36

MAJOR THEMES OF OLD TESTAMENT PROPHECY

Before turning to the major "highways" of prophecy a survey of Old Testament prophecy is helpful. The many subjects of Old Testament prophecy can be summarized in seven major themes: (1) prophecies regarding the Gentiles, (2) prophecies regarding Israel's early history, (3) prophecies regarding the nation Israel, (4) prophecies regarding the dispersions and regatherings of Israel, (5) prophecies regarding the advent of the Messiah, (6) prophecies regarding the Great Tribulation, and (7) prophecies regarding the Day of *Yahweh* and the messianic kingdom. Special attention will be directed later to the themes of judgments in Scripture and of the eternal state.

PROPHECIES REGARDING THE GENTILES

From Adam to Abraham mankind is presented as Gentile. After Abraham mankind is divided into two major divisions consisting of (a) Jacob, his 12 sons, and their descendants, and (b) the rest of mankind. This division of Jew and Gentile was continued until the New Testament when a third element was introduced—those who are included in the church. At least seven major aspects of Gentile prophecy are revealed in the Old Testament.

1. Earliest predictions. Though there were general predictions concerning the coming of the Messiah as early as Genesis 3:15 when it was predicted that an offspring of Eve would crush Satan, there were also predictions that the ground would be cursed and man would labor to produce his food (vv. 17-19). In 9:25-27 God predicted that the three sons of Noah would be the progenitors of the entire human race. Details which itemize the descendants of the three sons

of Noah are given in Genesis 10.

2. Judgments on nations. The judgments on nations adjacent to Israel are found throughout the Old Testament. Among the important predictions are those concerning Babylon and Chaldea (Isa. 13:1-22; 14:18-23; Jer. 50:1–51:64), Assyria (Isa. 14:24-27), Moab (15:1–16:14), Damascus (17:1-14; Jer. 49:23-27), Egypt (Isa. 19:1-25; Jer. 46:2-28), Philistia and Tyre (Isa. 23:1-18; Jer. 47:1-7), Edom (49:7-22), Ammon (vv. 1-6), and Elam (vv. 34-39).

3. The times of the Gentiles. This term, found in the New Testament in Luke 21:24, is a period of extensive predictions in the Old Testament especially in relationship to Israel. The times of the Gentiles is defined as the period in which Jerusalem will be under the general rulership of Gentiles. This began with the fall of Jerusalem to Nebuchadnezzar and his armies in 605 B.C. and will continue until the second coming of Christ. This period, which is not defined as to the extent of years, includes the period in the Old Testament from 605 B.C. and continues through the present age to the end of the Great Tribulation and up to the second coming of Christ. This period is interrupted by a parenthetical time period devoted to the calling out of the church from the Day of Pentecost to the Rapture. During this period Israel temporarily had possession of Jerusalem for brief periods of time as is true today, but even in these circumstances her possession was not secure, and as is true at the present time it was only possible by the help of Gentile nations such as the United States. Prophecy indicates Israel will lose control of Jerusalem especially in the period of the Great Tribulation preceding the Second Coming.

4. Monarchies. The succession of monarchies in the times of the Gentiles was a major prediction in the Old Testament. According to Daniel 2, 7–8, four world empires would be prominent in the times of the Gentiles beginning with the empire of Babylon, followed by the empire of the Medes and the Persians beginning in 539 B.C., to be followed in the fourth century B.C. by the conquest of Alexander the Great and the empire of Greece. The empire of Rome gradually developed in the second and first centuries B.C. Daniel mentioned by name the empires of Babylon, Medo-Persia, and Greece, but the great empire which followed Greece, though unnamed, was obviously that of Rome, the greatest of all world empires in its geographic extent as well as in its duration.

The times of the Gentiles are being interrupted by the present

Church Age from Pentecost to the Rapture, and the times of the Gentiles will be resumed with the seven years mentioned in Daniel 9:27 climaxing in the second coming of Christ when Gentile rule will be destroyed (Rev. 19). If the earlier empires of Egypt and Assyria are added to the four that Daniel predicted there will be six major world empires. The sixth empire of Rome in such a series will have its final consummation in the world empire preceding the second coming of Christ. The seventh great empire would then be the millennial kingdom which will occupy the entire world. Though these empires are called world empires, it is obvious that the first five empires did not cover the entire globe. The last three and one half years of the Roman Empire which is yet future will be worldwide and will be brought to its close by the second coming of Christ.

5. The judgment of Gentile nations. This is a major theme of Old Testament prophecy with much Scripture dealing with it. Some of these judgments have already taken place, but the final judgment will come at the second coming of Christ (Ps. 2:1-10; Isa. 63:1-6; Joel 3:2-16; Zeph. 3:8; Zech. 14:1-3).

6. The Gentile nations and everlasting judgment. Though the Old Testament predicts the destruction of Gentile power, the New Testament makes it more specific in the description of judgment of the nations in Matthew 25:31-46. At the time of the Second Coming, Christ will judge the entire Gentile world, and those who are "goats" or unsaved will be cast into everlasting fire (v. 41). Gentiles who have been born again through faith in Christ in the Great Tribulation and who are on earth at the time of the Second Coming are called "sheep" and will be ushered into the millennial kingdom in their natural bodies and will inhabit the earth along with believing Israelites and resurrected and translated saints.

7. The Gentile nations and the kingdom. Though the millennial kingdom features Israel as its main element with Jesus Christ and David resurrected and presiding over Israel in Jerusalem (Ezek. 34:23-24; 37:24), the millennial kingdom will also bring blessing to the Gentiles who are saved during the Great Tribulation and are still alive, as well as Gentiles who will be resurrected at the time when the millennial kingdom begins (Dan. 12:1-2). Many Old Testament passages predict that Gentiles will share in the blessings of the millennial kingdom (Isa. 11:10; 42:1-6; 49:6-22; 60; 62–63). Millennial Israel will be exalted as a people favored by the Lord with Gentiles operating in lesser capacities (14:1-2; 60:12; 61:5). The sheep of

Matthew 25:31-46 will constitute the righteous remnant of the Gentiles who will enter the millennial kingdom and will be the forerunners of the many Gentiles who will be born in the millennial kingdom.

PROPHECIES REGARDING ISRAEL'S EARLY HISTORY

The early history of Israel beginning with the call of Abraham and the subsequent birth of Isaac and Jacob and his 12 sons is presented in Genesis as the beginnings of the nation Israel. Many of these prophecies have already been fulfilled, but others, such as Israel's ultimate possession of the land (Gen. 12:7), await the second coming of Christ for their complete fulfillment. In addition to the role of Abraham, Isaac, and Jacob, the Scriptures speak of Israel's Egyptian bondage and release (15:13-14), the character and destiny of Jacob's sons (49:1-28), Israel's conquest of Palestine following the Egyptian bondage (Deut. 28:1-67; cf. Lev. 26:3-46; Deut. 30:1-3; Ps. 106:1-48; Jer. 9:16; 18:15-17; Ezek. 12:14-15; 20:23; 22:15; Neh. 1:8; James 1:1). It is evident in tracing the history of Israel that they are a chosen people selected sovereignly by God to be a channel of blessing to the world.

PROPHECIES REGARDING THE NATION ISRAEL

Beginning with the Abrahamic Covenant (Gen. 12:1-3; 13:14-17; 15:1-7, 18-21; 17:1-8) and continuing throughout the Old Testament many predictions were made concerning Israel. These promises include a national entity (Jer. 31:36), a land (Gen. 12:7; 13:15), a throne (2 Sam. 7:16; Ps. 89:36), a king (Jer. 33:21), and a kingdom (Dan. 7:14). Though other dispensations followed the dispensation of Abraham, the divine blessings promised in the Abrahamic Covenant continue throughout human history. The Scriptures predicted, however, that the blessings of the covenant may be suspended from time to time if the people do not respond and walk with God. But such interruptions are only temporary and constitute a chastisement of the nation Israel. Their sins, however, do not abrogate the eternal promises of the Abrahamic Covenant. The many references to her possession of the land that characterize the Old Testament revelation concerning the future of Israel whether in times of revival or apostasy make clear that the ultimate fulfillment of the promise of the land is yet to take place at the second coming of Christ.

PROPHECIES REGARDING THE DISPERSIONS AND REGATHERINGS OF ISRAEL

Three dispersions of Israel and three returns to the land were predicted in the Old Testament. The first of these was fulfilled when Israel went down to Egypt at the time of Jacob to escape the famine in Palestine. Their return from Egypt constituted the first return to the land. Their second dispersion occurred in the eighth, seventh, and sixth centuries B.C. during the Assyrian captivity of the 10 tribes and the later Captivity of the two remaining tribes in Babylon. Extensive prophecies are given in Scripture for these events (Gen. 15:13-14; Lev. 26:32-39; Deut. 28:63-68; Neh. 1:8; Ps. 44:11; Jer. 9:16; 18:15-17; 29:10; Ezek. 12:14-15; 20:23; 22:15; James 1:1).

Even though Israel suffered centuries of dispersions among the Gentiles, their continuance as a nation is assured in Scripture (Jer. 31:36; Matt. 24:34; James 1:1; Rev. 7:4-8; 14:2-5).

In the first advent of Christ Israel as a nation rejected her Messiah (Matt. 23:37-39). As a result, her national chastisement will continue until Christ comes again. In a similar way Israel at Kadesh Barnea rejected God's promise of the land, and her wilderness experience was extended for 38 years. Though the deliverance of Israel in both cases was delayed, the ultimate fulfillment of the promises was assured. When Christ comes again He will complete the regathering of the godly remnant of His people into their own land and cause them to enter into the glory and blessedness of every covenant promise God made concerning them (Deut. 30:1-10; Isa. 11:11-12; Jer. 23:3-8; Ezek. 37:21-25; Matt. 24:31).

PROPHECIES REGARDING THE ADVENT OF MESSIAH

From 1 Peter 1:10-11 it is clear that the prophets of the Old Testament were unable to distinguish the two advents of their Messiah. There does not seem to be anyone who distinguished the first and second comings of Christ with an age between until after His ascension into heaven following His first advent. Even the disciples, who were closely associated with Him for more than three years, could not understand the death and resurrection of Christ and His ascension into heaven for they were expecting that somehow He would bring in the glorious Kingdom Age predicted in the Old Testament.

Part of the difficulty was that in the Old Testament often the first and second comings of Christ were mentioned together in the same verses as in Isaiah 61:1-2. When Christ read this passage in the synagogue of Nazareth, He ceased abruptly when He had read the record of those features that were predicted for His first advent (Luke 4:18-21). In like manner the angel Gabriel in announcing the ministry of Christ combined the first and second advents (1:31-33). Old Testament prophecies that described Christ as the sacrificial, unresisting Lamb (Isa. 53:1-12) also portrayed Him as the conquering and glorious Lion of the tribe of Judah (Isa. 11:1-12; Jer. 23:5-6).

Prophecy concerning the coming of the Messiah stated that He would come from the tribe of Judah (Gen. 49:10); He would be a descendant of David (Isa. 11:1; Jer. 33:21); He would be born of a virgin (Isa. 7:14) in Bethlehem of Judea (Micah 5:2); He would die a sacrificial death (Isa. 53:1-12) by crucifixion (Ps. 22:1-21); He would rise from the dead (16:8-11); and He would come to earth a second time (Deut. 30:3) in the clouds of heaven (Dan. 7:13). Every prophecy relating to His first coming was fulfilled literally, and the same expectation is justified for the promises concerning His second coming.

PROPHECIES REGARDING THE GREAT TRIBULATION

Throughout the Old Testament there is anticipation that there would be unprecedented Tribulation before the second coming of Christ (Deut. 4:29-30; 12:1; Ps. 2:5; Isa. 26:16-20; Jer. 30:4-7). The New Testament adds many additional prophecies about that awesome time period. Because the Rapture will occur before the endtime events, after the Rapture and before the Second Coming mankind will include only Jews and Gentiles and not the church, the body of Christ. The endtime prophecies that will be fulfilled after the church is raptured will complete the time of the Gentiles as well as the last seven years of Daniel 9:24-27. When Christ returns there will be complete destruction of Gentile power and institutions (Rev. 17–18;

19:17-21). In the Great Tribulation the Gentiles will be judged, and Israel will experience her final hour of affliction (Ezek. 20:33-44; Matt. 24:37–25:30).

PROPHECIES REGARDING THE DAY OF YAHWEH *AND THE MESSIANIC KINGDOM*

The extended period of the Day of *Yahweh* beginning with the Rapture includes the endtime events preceding the Second Coming as well as the 1,000-year kingdom which will follow the Second Advent. In keeping with the use of this term throughout the Old and New Testaments the Day of *Yahweh* is a period that deals with direct judgment on human sin. Various periods of judgment in the Old Testament were also called the Day of *Yahweh,* but many prophecies spoke specifically of that which will precede the second coming of Christ.

With respect to the amount of Scripture involved there is no theme of Old Testament prophecy comparable to that of the messianic kingdom. Many major sections of Old Testament prophecy deal with this subject which is only briefly summarized in Revelation 20 in the New Testament. The major passages with prophecies to be fulfilled in the 1,000-year reign of Christ include extensive sections from all the Major Prophets and several of the Minor Prophets (Isa. 11:1-16; 12:1-6; 24:22–27:13; 35:1-10; 52:1-12; 54:1–55:13; 59:20–66:24; Jer. 23:3-8; 31:1-40; 32:37-41; 33:1-26; Ezek. 34:11-31; 36:32-38; 37:1-28; 40:1–48:35; Dan. 2:44-45; 7:14; Hosea 3:4-5; 13:9–14:9; Joel 2:28–3:21; Amos 9:11-15; Zeph. 3:14-20; Zech. 8:1-23; 14:9-21).

The erroneous concept that the idea of a millennial kingdom after the second coming of Christ is introduced only in Revelation 20 provides no adequate explanation for these many major passages in the Old Testament.

CHAPTER • 37

MAJOR THEMES OF NEW TESTAMENT PROPHECY

The Old Testament closed without the many prophecies of the coming Messiah being fulfilled. For 400 years before the birth of Christ there seems to have been no prophetic witness. However, the expectation of Israel that her Messiah would come continued. The sensational character of the announcement of Christ's birth by the heavenly hosts introduced the tremendous scope of revelation that would be realized during the lifetime of Christ.

The Gospel of Matthew opens by introducing the genealogy of Christ (Matt. 1:1). The record of His birth in 2:1-2 as well as Luke's description of the background of His birth and His birth itself set the stage for the dramatic events to follow (Luke 1:1–2:20). In New Testament revelation additional information is given including a number of New Testament themes: (1) the new age, (2) the new divine purpose, (3) the nation Israel, (4) the Gentiles, (5) the Great Tribulation, (6) Satan and the forces of evil, (7) the second coming of Christ, (8) the messianic kingdom, and (9) the eternal state.

THE NEW AGE

The New Testament introduced a new dispensation not anticipated in Old Testament prophecy. Its major features described as mysteries in Matthew 13 introduced the revelation of the many new features that characterize the age between the first and second comings of Christ. In the Bible a mystery is a truth hidden in the Old Testament but revealed in the New (Rom. 11:25; 1 Cor. 15:51; Eph. 3:1-6; 5:25-32; Col. 1:27; 2 Thes. 2:7).

In describing the present age Matthew used the expression "the kingdom of heaven" which described a rule of God on earth including both those who are genuinely saved and those who profess salvation. This rule continues through the present age and also in the Millennium.

Though many scholars make the kingdom of heaven equivalent to the kingdom of God, in its usage in the New Testament the kingdom of God includes only those who are saved and also includes the holy angels. The kingdom of God does not have any weeds (Matt. 13:25) nor bad fish (v. 48). The kingdom of heaven includes both the saved and professing Christians, but not angels. The aspects of the kingdom of heaven and the kingdom of God fulfilled in the present age are called mysteries because they were not formerly revealed. Matthew 13 states in seven parables the features of the new age between the first and second comings of Christ. In the age relating to the church, Israel is seen as a "treasure" hidden in the field (v. 44). The church is indicated by the pearl which the merchant, referring to Christ, purchased with "everything he had" (vv. 45-46).

The present age is characterized by the dual development of both good and evil (vv. 24-30, 36-43). As the age progresses, evil also matures, as mentioned frequently in the New Testament (2 Thes. 2:1-12; 1 Tim. 4:1-3; 2 Tim. 3:1-5; James 5:1-10; 2 Peter 2:1–3:8; Jude 1-23; Rev. 3:14-22; 4–18). In contrast to the postmillennial anticipation of a gradually improving world the Scriptures instead predict that things will get worse and worse as the age progresses, and in no sense will a converted world await Christ on His return (Matt. 13:1-50; 24:38-39; 2 Tim. 3:13).

THE NEW DIVINE PURPOSE

The New Testament introduces the church as a new classification of humanity in addition to the Jews and the Gentiles (1 Cor. 10:32). The word "church," first used in Matthew 16:18, refers to all who are born again in this age. By being baptized by the Holy Spirit they are in Christ, and form with Christ the new creation including both Jews and Gentiles (Eph. 3:1-6).

Seven figures are used to speak of the church's relationship to Christ. These include His sheep (John 10:6-16), branches in the vine (15:1-6), stones in the building (Eph. 2:19-22), a holy priesthood (1 Peter 2:5; cf. Heb. 8:1), the new creation (2 Cor. 5:17),

His body (Eph. 1:22-23; 3:6), and His bride in heaven (Rev. 19:7-8).

When the divine purpose of calling out the church has been completed, Christ will receive His own (John 14:1-3; 1 Thes. 4:13-17). Christians who have died will be raised (1 Cor. 15:23, 52; 1 Thes. 4:13-17), and Christians who are living will be translated, that is, their bodies will be instantly changed to bodies suited for heaven (1 Cor. 15:51; 1 Thes. 4:13-17). All Christians whether transformed by resurrection or translation shall receive a new body like His glorious body (Phil. 3:21). When Christ returns to reign on earth for 1,000 years, the church will return with Him (Rev. 19:14; 20:6).

THE NATION ISRAEL

The New Testament resumes the history of Israel where the Old Testament left them, a disorganized and scattered people, some of whom were dwelling in the land but not possessing it. In the present dispensation Israel nationally is set aside and there is no progress politically. But as individuals they are on the same plane before God as Gentiles (Rom. 3:9; 10:12). During the present age Jews have the same offer of salvation by grace alone as Gentiles, their former exalted position above Gentiles in the Old Testament is mentioned by Paul in Romans 9:4-5.

During the present age Israel as a nation is hidden (Matt. 13:44); hardened or spiritually blinded (Rom. 11:25); broken off (v. 17); without her national center Jerusalem (Luke 21:24); and scattered (James 1:1). In the coming Great Tribulation the Jews will be hated and persecuted (Matt. 24:9), and in the kingdom they will be regathered (v. 31; cf. Ezek. 39:25-28) and delivered from her enemies (Rom. 11:26).

Christ predicted that the wrath of God would fall on them and that their beloved city Jerusalem would be destroyed (Luke 21:20-24). The city was destroyed in A.D. 70, but Israel still awaits the future sorrows of her time of Tribulation (Matt. 24:9-26). The nation will experience sifting judgments before her entrance into kingdom glory (24:37–25:30; cf. Ezek. 20:38).

At His second coming Christ will occupy the throne of David (Matt. 25:31; cf. 2 Sam. 7:16; 1 Chron. 17:12; Luke 1:31-33; Acts

15:16-17). The Apostle Paul prophesied Israel's spiritual and national restoration (Rom. 11:22-31). In the coming time of Tribulation preceding the Second Coming 144,000 Israelites will be kept alive through the period (Rev. 7:3-8; 14:1-5), but many others will by martyred (7:9-17; cf. Zech. 13:8-9). The godly remnant of Israel will enter the millennial kingdom including those who survived the Tribulation as well as those Old Testament saints and Tribulation saints who will be resurrected from the dead (Rev. 12:13-17; 20:4-6; cf. Dan. 12:2).

THE GENTILES

The Old Testament contains many references to the future of the Gentiles. From the standpoint of the New Testament the times of the Gentiles (Luke 21:24) which began with the Babylonian Captivity in 605 B.C., will continue until the second coming of Christ (Dan. 2:44-45).

The progress of the times of the Gentiles is interrupted by the Church Age during which the Roman Empire gradually faded from history. When the Church Age is ended, Gentile history is resumed with the revived Roman Empire in the form of 10 nations banded together as a political unit (Rev. 13:1; 17:16; cf. Dan. 7:7, 20, 24). The Gentiles will be judged at the second coming of Christ (Matt. 25:31-46; Rev. 19:15-21).

THE GREAT TRIBULATION

The future period of the Great Tribulation prophesied by Christ (Matt. 24:9-28) is described by the Apostle Paul (1 Thes. 5:1-9; 2 Thes. 2:1-12); and John recorded at length the details of the tremendous divine program leading up to the second coming of Christ (Rev. 3:10; 6:1–19:6). The entire period between the Rapture and the Second Coming is a time of Tribulation, but the last three and one half years are called "the Great Tribulation" (Matt. 24:21-27; cf. Dan. 12:1). When Christ returns, the times of the Gentiles will cease with God's judgments on Gentile political power. Steps will be taken to assure the absolute reign of Christ on earth for the 1,000 years.

SATAN AND THE FORCES OF EVIL

Prophecy concerning Satan began in the Old Testament (Isa. 14:12-17; Ezek. 28:11-19). Satan will be expelled from heaven and will be restricted to earth (Rev. 12:7-12) three and one half years before the Second Coming. At Christ's second coming Satan will be bound and confined to the Abyss (20:1-3). At the end of the Millennium Satan will be allowed to lead a final revolt against God (vv. 7-9) and then will begin his eternal doom in the lake of fire (v. 10). Along with the revelation of the power of Satan is the fact that this power is communicated to the future world ruler (13:2-4) and will empower the world ruler as "the man of lawlessness" (2 Thes. 2:3; cf. Dan. 7:8; 9:24-27; 11:36-45). The final world ruler is described by the Apostle Paul as desecrating the restored temple, declaring himself to be God, and then being destroyed at the glorious appearing of Christ (2 Thes. 2:1-12). The Apostle John predicted the world ruler's governmental power and final doom (Rev. 13:1-10; 19:20; 20:10).

THE SECOND COMING OF CHRIST

The second coming of Christ is one of the great themes in Scripture and was the subject of the first prediction by man (Jude 14-15) and the last message of the Bible (Rev. 22:20). The Second Coming is related to the many passages in the Old Testament concerning the Day of *Yahweh* and the glorious kingdom on earth over which Christ will reign in the Millennium. Likewise in the New Testament many predictions refer to His future second coming (Matt. 23:37–25:46; Mark 13:1-37; Luke 21:5-38). The Second Coming was also emphasized by the Apostle Paul (Rom. 11:26; 1 Thes. 3:13; 5:1-4; 2 Thes. 1:7–2:12), James (James 5:1-8), Peter (2 Peter 2:1–3:18), Jude (Jude 14-15), and John (Rev.).

THE MESSIANIC KINGDOM

The messianic kingdom of Christ on earth following His second coming is a major subject of Old Testament prophecy. In the Synoptic Gospels Christ announced that the kingdom was at hand, and He displayed the credentials predicted in the Old Testament for the

Messiah. In His Sermon on the Mount (Matt. 5–7), Christ revealed the ethical principles that would characterize the future kingdom, along with some present applications. When His message was rejected, Christ introduced the mystery form of the kingdom to be realized in the present age (Matt. 13) and announced the future church (16:18). In the Olivet Discourse (Matt. 24–25) the events leading up to His second coming and the judgments related to it were revealed. In His crucifixion He died as the King of Israel. In His resurrection Christ became qualified to reign on the throne of David forever. As the Apostle John revealed in Revelation 19–20, Christ in His second coming will subdue the world, judge the enemies of God, rescue the righteous, and carry on His kingdom on earth for 1,000 years before the eternal state.

THE ETERNAL STATE

Though the eternal state is anticipated in the prediction of the everlasting kingdom (Dan. 7:14, 26), a detailed picture of the eternal state is given in Revelation 21–22. Central in the revelation is the heavenly city, the New Jerusalem which will be the place of the residence of God, the holy angels, and the saints of all ages throughout eternity to come. The eternal destiny of the lost is also described in 20:11-15.

The major themes of both Old Testament and New Testament prophecy will be approached from the standpoint of the major highways of prophecy running from Genesis to Revelation, disclosing God's plans for salvation, for the great nations of the world, for Israel, for the church, and the climax of human history in eternity to come.

MAJOR HIGHWAYS OF PROPHECY

CHAPTER • 38

PROPHECY CONCERNING THE LORD JESUS CHRIST

The Bible, opening with the words, "In the beginning God" (Gen. 1:1), and closing with reference to "the Lord Jesus" (Rev. 22:20-21), is preeminently a revelation of Jesus Christ. Though the Bible obviously treats many subjects—including the history of man, the existence of angels, the revelation of God's purposes for the nations, Israel, and the church, and includes in its revelation facts from eternity past to eternity future—Jesus Christ is revealed as the Center. He is presented as the Creator, the Messiah of Israel, the Saviour of the saints, the Head of the church, and King of kings over all creation. As the theme of divine revelation, the person and work of Jesus Christ threads its way from the first to the last book of the Bible.

In the major works of Christ, the Father and the Holy Spirit participate, but early in Scripture the focus of divine revelation is on Jesus Christ. In the fall of Adam and Eve from their pristine purity in their partaking disobediently of the tree of the knowledge of good and evil, Jesus Christ is introduced as the Offspring of the woman who would crush the head of the serpent (Gen. 3:15). This is the first intimation of God's plan for a redeemed people who would share the blessings of eternity with the Triune God. Early in the history of the race Abel's offering of the firstborn of the flock introduced the theme of blood redemption which runs as a scarlet thread from Genesis to Revelation. The depravity of the race that was revealed in Cain's murder of Abel and the continued downward course of depravity in the Cainite civilization required the blotting out of the entire human race except for Noah and his family.

The human race continued its downward course leading to the Tower of Babel. It was then that God turned to His special purpose for Abraham, Isaac, Jacob, and the 12 sons of Jacob. Through their line would come the promised Saviour and the people of Israel through whom God would speak by means of their prophets, the writers of Scripture, the 12 Apostles, and preeminently, Jesus Christ, thus fulfilling the promise to Abraham that his descendants would bring blessing on all peoples of the earth (Gen. 12:1-3).

THE SEED

As recorded in 3:15, God declared that the Offspring of Eve would conquer Satan who was portrayed as a serpent. The fulfillment of this promise is a major theme of Scripture. The promise given originally to Abraham (12:1-3) was narrowed to his son Isaac (26:2-4), then further narrowed to Jacob and his sons (28:13-15). Other sons of Abraham were eliminated as inheritors of the promise as was Esau, Jacob's older twin. The Old Testament is primarily a history of the sons of Jacob in their relationship to each other, to the Gentile world, and to God. The promise of the coming Deliverer would be fulfilled by a descendant of Judah who would hold the divine scepter as King (49:10).

It was in this prophetic foreview that David was appointed king of Israel. To David was given the Davidic Covenant. Through Nathan God declared that David's descendants and David's throne would endure forever (2 Sam. 7:12-16; cf. 1 Chron. 17:3-15).

The descendants of David occupied the throne of David until the time of the Babylonian Captivity. In the reign of Jehoiakim, the king of Judah who destroyed the scroll containing Jeremiah's prophecies, God stated, "Therefore, this is what the LORD says about Jehoiakim king of Judah: He will have no one to sit on the throne of David; his body will be thrown out and exposed to the heat by day and the frost by night. I will punish him and his children and his attendants for their wickedness; I will bring on them and those living in Jerusalem and the people of Judah every disaster I pronounced against them, because they have not listened" (Jer. 36:30-31).

The New Testament genealogies of Jesus were written in fulfillment of this curse on the line of Jehoiakim. In Matthew 1:1-16 the line of Jehoiakim is traced to Joseph (the husband of Mary), who was the legal heir of the throne and was in the cursed genealogy from Jehoiakim which had descended from David through Solomon. By contrast the genealogy of Mary the mother of Jesus in Luke 3:23-38 is traced to David through Nathan another son of David other than Solomon, thereby confirming the curse on Jehoiakim. Though legally Christ received the title of a Son of David through Joseph, the physical connection was through Nathan, a line other than that of Solomon and Jehoiakim. The genealogies confirm the necessity of the Virgin Birth and the impossibility of Joseph being the father of the Messiah. The fact that Jesus Christ was the literal Son of David is confirmed by many Scriptures (e.g., Ps. 89:20-37; Jer. 23:5-6; 33:17; Matt. 21:9; 22:42; Mark 10:47; Acts 2:30; 13:23; Rom. 1:3). The promises given to the descendants of Abraham and the descendants of David as they relate to Jesus Christ have been and will be literally fulfilled.

A PROPHET

Moses predicted that the coming Messiah would be the greatest of the prophets, "The LORD your God will raise up for you a Prophet like me from among your own brothers. You must listen to Him. . . . 'I will put My words in His mouth, and He will tell them everything I command Him. If anyone does not listen to My words that the Prophet speaks in My name, I Myself will call him to account' " (Deut. 18:15, 18-19). Knowledge of this prophecy was widespread in Israel at the time of Christ. Because they revered Moses as their great prophet, his prediction of another prophet was easily linked to their expectation of the Messiah. To this expectation Philip referred as recorded in John 1:45: "Philip found Nathanael and told him, 'We have found the One Moses wrote about in the Law, and about whom the prophets also wrote—Jesus of Nazareth, the son of Joseph.' " Peter quoted the same prophecy in his sermon (Acts 3:22-23). In Stephen's address before his martyrdom he also quoted this prophecy. "This is that Moses who told the Israelites, 'God will send you a Prophet like me from your own people' " (7:37).

Jesus Christ in His public ministry assumed the role of a prophet. He said He was delivering a message from God (John 7:16) and that what He said was given to Him by God the Father. "When he looks at Me, he sees the One who sent Me. I have come into the world as a light, so that no one who believes in Me should stay in darkness.

As for the person who hears My words but does not keep them, I do not judge him. For I did not come to judge the world, but to save it. There is a judge for the one who rejects Me and does not accept My words; that very word which I spoke will condemn him at the last day. For I did not speak of My own accord, but the Father who sent Me commanded Me what to say and how to say it. I know that His command leads to eternal life. So whatever I say is just what the Father has told Me to say" (12:45-50). Christ again and again referred to His message as a message from God the Father (14:24; 17:8).

In His earthly ministry Christ was not a prophet simply as a foreteller of future events but also a prophet in the sense of One who forthtold what God had delivered to Him. The extensive nature of His teachings included facts about the Bible, God, angels, sin, salvation, the coming church, and prophecies of the end of the age including His second coming. Especially important were His predictions of His own death, burial, resurrection, ascension, the coming of the Holy Spirit, and His own second coming. He spoke of the beginning, character, course, and end of the present age; He predicted the church, her beginning, character, safety, Rapture, and destiny; He described the Great Tribulation, the man of sin, the coming of false christs, and the future judgments, and He announced His messianic kingdom and the eternal state of both the saved and the lost. A comprehensive systematic theology could be written based entirely on the prophetic ministry of Christ.

PRIEST

Though the Old Testament predicted the coming of Christ as a Priest (Ps. 110:1-4), most of the references to Christ in His future priestly work are seen in the types of the priesthoods in the Old Testament. Generally speaking, before the Mosaic Law was given, the head of the family was the priest for that family. With the coming of the Mosaic Law Aaron and his descendants were made into a special priesthood. Unique among the Old Testament references to priesthood was Melchizedek to whom Abraham brought tithes. "Then Melchizedek king of Salem brought out bread and wine. He was priest of God Most High, and he blessed Abram, saying, 'Blessed be Abram by God Most High, Creator of heaven and earth. And blessed be God Most High, who delivered your enemies into your hand.' Then Abram gave him a tenth of everything" (Gen. 14:18-20). In Psalm 110:4 the psalmist wrote of Christ, "You are a Priest forever, in the order of Melchizedek." From the Old Testament itself it is obvious that Christ fulfilled the qualifications both of Melchizedek and his priesthood and the Aaronic priesthood which was an integral part of the Mosaic Covenant.

In Hebrews the office of Christ as Priest fulfilling the requirements of the order of Melchizedek is discussed at length (Heb. 5:4-10). Like Melchizedek Christ was appointed Priest by an act of God. The discussion of Melchizedek as a type of Christ in His priesthood is continued in 7:1-28. His priesthood is superior to that of Aaron because the Melchizedek priesthood had no predecessors and no successors. This is illustrated in Christ's eternal priesthood.

The Aaronic priesthood, however, does illustrate some of the works of Christ as Priest (8:1-5). Not only in His office was Christ perpetually a Priest, but also His one offering was sufficient for all time in contrast to the Aaronic offerings which were constantly repeated (9:23-28). The intercession of Christ as our High Priest continues forever (John 17:1-26; Rom. 8:34; Heb. 7:25). Because as God all of Christ's attributes are infinite, as the believer's High Priest He can give His full attention to the needs of one believer while at the same time giving His full attention to the needs of all other believers. His intercession is such that when a Christian prays he in effect joins a prayer meeting already in session in heaven. Believers in Christ, who also constitute a priesthood (1 Peter 2:9) serve as priests under Jesus Christ as their High Priest.

KING

As early as Genesis 17:16, God predicted concerning Sarah, "I will bless her and will surely give you a son by her. I will bless her so that she will be the mother of nations; kings of peoples will come from her." It was not until the final years of Samuel as judge that the elders of Israel came to Samuel and said, "You are old, and your sons do not walk in your ways; now appoint a king to lead us, such as all the other nations have" (1 Sam. 8:4). Though warned that a king would not meet their needs, God appointed Saul as recorded in 9:17, "When Samuel caught sight of Saul, the LORD said to him, 'This is the man I spoke to you about; He will govern My people.' "

Saul, though he had a good beginning as king, soon proved to be disobedient to the Lord, and Samuel was informed that Saul would be replaced as king. Samuel was divinely directed to David and anointed him as king (16:1-13). After David killed Goliath and became a hero in Israel, Saul attempted to kill him suspecting that David might be his successor. Years of testing followed for David before Saul died and David began ruling over the 12 tribes of Israel.

In the context of David's reign as king God announced through Nathan the prophet His plan that the kingdom of David would continue forever and a descendant of David would sit on the throne. Nathan told David, "When your days are over and you rest with your fathers, I will raise up your offspring to succeed you, who will come from your own body, and I will establish his kingdom. He is the one who will build a house for My Name, and I will establish the throne of his kingdom forever. I will be his Father, and he will be My son. When he does wrong, I will punish him with the rod of men, with floggings inflicted by men. But My love will never be taken away from him, as I took it away from Saul, whom I removed from before you. Your house and your kingdom will endure forever before Me; your throne will be established forever" (2 Sam. 7:12-16; cf. 1 Chron. 17:3-15). The Davidic Covenant takes its place with the Abrahamic Covenant as a declaration of God's purpose to have Christ sit on the throne of David forever, a prediction to be fulfilled in the millennial kingdom.

This prediction to David is important because it forms the background for the millennial kingdom which will follow the second coming of Christ. Because amillenarians and postmillenarians deny that this prophecy will be fulfilled literally with a kingdom on earth, the promise to David becomes an important feature of eschatology. Just as those who have attempted to deny a future millennial kingdom tend to spiritualize the promise of the land to Abraham, so they also spiritualize the Davidic Covenant and consider David's throne the same as the throne of God in heaven and the rule of the seed of David as being fulfilled spiritually and not in a literal political manner. Yet it should be obvious that David's throne was never the Father's throne in heaven, and ruling from a throne in heaven is not the equivalent to ruling on David's throne on earth.

Before Jesus was born Mary was informed, "You will be with child and give birth to a Son, and you are to give Him the name Jesus. He will be great and will be called the Son of the Most High. The Lord God will give Him the throne of His father David, and He will reign over the house of Jacob forever; his kingdom will never end" (Luke 1:31-33). Mary understood this as referring to an earthly rule of the son of David, and this was the common belief of the nation of Israel. If a literal interpretation of the Davidic Covenant were in error, it is unexplainable why the angel would have given this prediction to Mary, thus perpetuating what the amillenarians considered to be an erroneous interpretation.

The fulfillment of the Davidic Covenant is the theme of Psalm 89. The entire psalm anticipates David's Descendant sitting on the throne. "I will also appoint him [David] My firstborn, the most exalted of the kings of the earth. I will maintain My love to him forever, and My covenant with him will never fail. I will establish his line forever, his throne as long as the heavens endure. If his sons forsake My law and do not follow My statutes, if they violate My decrees and fail to keep My commands, I will punish their sin with the rod, their iniquity with flogging; but I will not take My love from him nor will ever betray My faithfulness. I will not violate My covenant or alter what My lips have uttered. Once for all, I have sworn by My holiness—and I will not lie to David—that his line will continue forever and his throne endure before Me like the sun; it will be established forever like the moon, the faithful witness in the sky" (vv. 27-37).

In His earthly ministry Christ repeatedly affirmed that He is the King of Israel, and only after His rejection did He reveal the character of the present age (Matt. 13) and announce the fact that He was to be crucified. The disciples who followed Christ for more than three years did so with the anticipation that He was the King who would sit on the throne of David and redeem Israel. They did not understand until after His ascension into heaven that there would be a time period between the first and second comings of Christ and that the promise of the earthly reign would not be fulfilled until Christ returned the second time.

Christ, however, assured the disciples of the certainty of the future kingdom. He said to them, "I tell you the truth, at the renewal of all things, when the Son of man sits on His glorious throne, you who have followed Me will also sit on 12 thrones, judging the 12 tribes of Israel" (19:28). When the mother of Zebedee's sons came to Jesus requesting that her sons sit on His right and left in His kingdom

(20:20-21), Christ did not tell her she was mistaken about an expectation of an earthly political kingdom. Instead He said, "These places belong to those for whom they have been prepared by My Father" (v. 23).

In His triumphal approach to Jerusalem when He was hailed as the Son of David (21:9) Christ did not rebuke them but accepted the title.

When Christ returns to earth, "He will sit on His throne in heavenly glory" (25:31). It would reflect unduly on the integrity of Christ if these prophecies were not taken in their literal sense. According to 1 Corinthians 15:24-28 Christ will first destroy all dominion, authority, and power and put all enemies under His feet. When this has been accomplished He will hand over the kingdom to God the Father. This final victory can only come after He has reigned for 1,000 years and vanquished Satan and those who follow him in the rebellion in Revelation 20, after He has judged all the wicked in the judgment of the Great White Throne, and then has established the new heavens, the new earth, and the New Jerusalem. In this sense Christ will continue to rule even as God the Father does, but its mediatorial government will have been brought to its conclusion with literal fulfillment of all the promises.

THE TWO ADVENTS

All conservative interpreters of Scripture agree that the Bible predicts two advents of Christ. In His first advent He was born in Bethlehem, lived among men, died on the cross, rose again, and ascended into heaven. These events pertaining to His first coming were the fulfillment of many predictions in Scripture.

The Scriptures predict the second coming of Christ and a literal return to the earth in fulfillment of the promises which He Himself made. In Matthew 24:27 He said, "For as lightning comes from the east and flashes to the west, so will be the coming of the Son of man." Christ added, "At that time the sign of the Son of man will appear in the sky, and all the nations of the earth will mourn. They will see the Son of man coming on the clouds of the sky, with power and great glory" (v. 30). When Christ ascended, the promise of His second coming was confirmed by the angels who addressed the disciples, " 'Men of Galilee,' they said, 'why do you stand here looking into the sky? This same Jesus, who has been taken from you into heaven, will come back in the same way you have seen Him go into heaven' " (Acts 1:11).

In the Old Testament, predictions of the coming of Christ included both His sufferings and His glorious reign. The mystery of how both would be included was solved when it was realized that there would be two comings, His first and second advents, with a long period of time between. The fact of such a long time period between His first and second comings was not revealed in the Old Testament. The interadvent period was explained by Christ Himself (Matt. 13:3-52; cf. Eph. 3:1-6).

The mingled prediction of suffering and glory to follow is frequently featured in Old Testament prophecy. In Isaiah 61:1-3 it was predicted, "The Spirit of the Sovereign LORD is on me, because the LORD has anointed me to preach good news to the poor. He has sent me to bind up the brokenhearted, to proclaim freedom for the captives and release for the prisoners, to proclaim the year of the LORD's favor and the day of vengeance of our God, to comfort all who mourn, and provide for those who grieve in Zion—to bestow on them a crown of beauty instead of ashes, the oil of gladness instead of mourning, and a garment of praise instead of a spirit of despair. They will be called oaks of righteousness, a planting of the LORD for the display of His splendor."

When Christ quoted from this passage in the synagogue at Nazareth (Luke 4:18-19), He read only the first aspect of the promise referring to His first coming and stopped. When Christ said, "Today this Scripture is fulfilled in your hearing" (v. 21), He was referring to that aspect of the prophecy that related to His first advent.

A similar prophecy is found in Malachi 3:1, "See, I will send My messenger, who will prepare the way before Me. Then suddenly the Lord you are seeking will come to His temple; the Messenger of the covenant, whom you desire, will come." The first part of this verse refers to the coming of John the Baptist and is related to the First Advent (Matt. 11:10; Mark 1:2; Luke 7:27). But the rest of the passage continuing to Malachi 3:6 relates to the second advent of Christ.

Another important text already quoted is that of Luke 1:30-33 in which the first coming of Jesus was announced. The prediction goes right on, however, to predict His occupancy of the throne of His father David and His eternal reign which will be fulfilled in connection with His second coming.

Both the first and second advents of Christ are major doctrines of the Scriptures and need to be considered separately.

1. The First Advent. Anticipating the physical birth of Christ at His first advent Isaiah predicted that a virgin would bear a son who would be called "Immanuel" (Isa. 7:14). Isaiah 9:6-7 adds, "For to us a Child is born, to us a Son is given, and the government will be on His shoulders. And He will be called Wonderful Counselor, Mighty God, Everlasting Father, Prince of Peace. Of the increase of His government and peace there will be no end. He will reign on David's throne and over his kingdom, establishing and upholding it with justice and righteousness from that time on and forever. The zeal of the Lord Almighty will accomplish this." Again the mingled picture of His first and second advents is revealed. The Christ Child would be born in Bethlehem (Micah 5:2). His first coming would be one of suffering and death as revealed in every Old Testament sacrifice in which an animal was slain. Many passages speak particularly of His death (Gen. 3:15; Ps. 22:1-21; Isa. 52:13–53:12), and of His resurrection after His crucifixion (Pss. 16:1-11; 22:22-31; 118:22-24). As many as 300 separate prophecies may be identified as belonging to the First Advent and have been fulfilled literally. It is reasonable therefore to conclude that the Second Advent will also be literal, and the events preceding and following will be literally fulfilled. A highway of the First Advent can be traced to many Scriptures (Gen. 3:15; 12:3; 17:19; 24:60; 28:14; 49:10; 2 Sam. 7:16; Pss. 2:2; 16:10; 22:1-18; Isa. 7:13-14; 9:6; 28:16; 42:1-7; 49:1-6; 50:4-7; 52:13–53:12; 61:1; Dan. 9:25-26; Hosea 2:23; Micah 5:2; Hag. 2:7; Zech. 9:9; 11:11-13; 13:7; Mal. 3:1-2; Matt. 1:1, 23; 2:1-6; 4:15-16; 12:18-21; 21:1-5, 42; 26:31; 27:9-10, 34-35, 50; 28:5-6; Acts 1:9).

2. The Second Advent. Though not distinguished from the First Advent in the Old Testament, the Second Advent is in itself a major revelation of prophecy. The distinction between the first and second comings of Christ was perplexing to the prophets. For those living now between the two Advents the problem of interpreting which passages refer to the First Advent and which refer to the Second Advent is simple because of the characteristics revealed concerning them.

The two Advents are implied in the Abrahamic and Davidic Covenants. In both there is the promise of a lineage and of a birth of a son. In the case of Abraham the birth of a son is to the end that there may be a seed both physical (Gen. 13:16) and spiritual (15:5), the latter having been made possible by the death of Christ in His first advent. To David the birth of a son was to the end that there would be a descendant of his on David's throne forever (Jer. 33:17).

The Bible teaches that the Lord Jesus Christ will return to this earth (Zech. 14:4) personally (Matt. 25:31; Rev. 19:11-16) and in the clouds (Matt. 24:30; Acts 1:11; Rev. 1:7). There is no more difficulty in believing in the second coming of Christ to the earth than there is in the First Coming.

The second coming of Christ has the distinction of being the first prophecy recorded as uttered by man (Jude 14-15). It was also the last message from the ascended Christ as well as the last word of the Bible (Rev. 22:20-21). The second coming of Christ is unique because it occupies more Scriptures than almost any other doctrine and is an outstanding theme of both the Old and New Testaments. All other prophecies of Scripture to some extent cluster around either the first advent or the second advent of Christ.

In the highway of prophecy concerning the Second Advent there are at least 44 major predictions, beginning with the first direct mention of it in Deuteronomy 30:3 and continuing to the last promise of the Bible. In addition to this large volume of Scripture are also many other passages that refer to the Rapture of the church which is distinguished in the New Testament from the formal second coming of Christ.

At least seven distinct achievements are consummated in the Second Advent:

(1) Christ Himself will return as He went, in the clouds of heaven and with power and great glory.

(2) Christ will sit on the throne of His father David, which is the throne of His glory, and reign forever.

(3) Christ will come, not to a converted world, but to the earth in rebellion against God and His Messiah, and will conquer it by His own infinite power.

(4) At Christ's coming, judgment will fall on Israel, the nations, Satan, and the lawless one.

(5) Christ's coming will be accompanied with the convulsion of nature which will be released from the curse.

(6) Christ's coming will provoke Israel's long-predicted repentance and bring her to salvation.

(7) At His coming Christ will establish His kingdom of righteous-

ness and peace, with converted Israel regathered to her own land, united and blessed under her King, and with Gentiles, as a subordinate people, sharing in that kingdom.

The extent of this subject in Scripture can only partially be indicated in the following list of major passages (Deut. 30:3; Pss. 2:1-9; 24:1-10; 50:1-5; 96:10-13; 110:1; Isa. 9:7; 11:10-12; 63:1-6; Jer. 23:5-6; Ezek. 37:21-22; Dan. 2:44-45; 7:13-14; Hosea 3:4-5; Amos 9:11-15; Micah 4:7; Zech. 2:10-12; 6:12-13; 12:10; 13:6; 14:1-9; Matt. 19:28; 23:39; 24:17-31; 25:6, 31-46; Mark 13:24-27; Luke 12:35-40; 17:24-37; 18:8; 21:25-28; 24:25-26; Acts 1:10-11; 15:16-18; Rom. 11:25-27; 2 Thes. 2:8; 1 Tim. 6:14-15; James 5:7-8; 2 Peter 3:3-4; Jude 14-15; Rev. 1:7-8; 2:25-28; 16:15; 19:11-21; 20:4-6; 22:20). In consideration of the two Advents a number of items need to be noted: (1) In His first advent Christ came as the Redeemer from sin, which purpose demanded His death, His resurrection, and His present ministry in heaven; In His second advent Christ comes to to rescue Israel from her persecutors and restore her as a nation (Rom. 11:26-27). (2) In His first advent Christ came "gentle and riding on a donkey" (Zech. 9:9) and on earth was born, lived, and died; in His second advent He comes with power and great glory (Rev. 19:11-16). (3) In His first coming He was rejected of men; but in His second coming He comes as King of kings and Lord of lords and is the Judge and Ruler of men (v. 16). (4) In His first coming Christ provided salvation for individual Jews and Gentiles; in His second coming He comes to judge both Jews and Gentiles (Ezek. 20:34-38; Matt. 25:31-46). (5) In His first coming Christ merely judged and resisted Satan (Col. 2:15); but in His second advent He binds Satan and conquers the forces of evil (Rev. 20:1-3). Any study of the first and second advents of Christ can only review partially all that the Scripture reveals and the tremendous implications of this doctrine to all other doctrines of Scripture.

The coming of Christ for His church, an important prophecy concerning Him, will be treated in connection with prophecy concerning the church.

CHAPTER • 39

PROPHECY CONCERNING ISRAEL'S COVENANTS

In the study of prophecy Israel's covenants have often been neglected and misinterpreted. Because these covenants extend not only to Israel but also are related to many other aspects of prophecy, unless the promises made to Israel in their covenants are clearly understood, prophecy of future events will remain in a state of confusion.

Beginning with the covenant with Abraham, prophecy concerning Israel and her covenants becomes a dominant factor in the interpretation of prophecy. In the Old Testament Israel is said to be a special people with a special place in God's larger purpose for creation and with a special future.

Moses said, "For you are a people holy to the LORD your God. The LORD your God has chosen you out of all the peoples on the face of the earth to be His people, His treasured possession. The LORD did not set His affection on you and choose you because you were more numerous than other peoples, for you were the fewest of all peoples. But it was because the LORD loved you and kept the oath He swore to your forefathers that He brought you out with a mighty hand and redeemed you from the land of slavery, from the power of Pharaoh king of Egypt" (Deut. 7:6-8). The special place of Israel is also stated in 14:2, "For you are a people holy to the LORD your God. Out of all the peoples on the face of the earth, the LORD has chosen you to be His treasured possession." In discussing the promise of future blessing on Israel at the time of the second coming of Christ Paul wrote, "For God's gifts and His call are irrevocable" (Rom. 11:29).

Once it is understood that God has an eternal plan for Israel distinct from His plan for the Gentiles and the church, prophecy takes on a new character of accuracy and literal fulfillment. The mass of humanity was considered Gentiles until the time of Abraham. With the birth of Isaac and Jacob and his 12 sons Israel was regarded as a people separate from the Gentiles. With the advent of the church on the Day of Pentecost humanity was divided into three major divisions, Jews, Gentiles, and the church of God (1 Cor. 10:32).

The people of Israel derived their name from the title given Jacob (Gen. 32:28). They were also designated "Jews," which is derived from the name of Judah, one of the principal tribes of Israel and the one through whom Christ came in His Incarnation. After the Divided Kingdom the 10 tribes were often designated by the name Israel and the 2 remaining tribes were known as Judah. In their future restoration the 10 tribes and the 2 tribes will be restored (Isa. 11:11-13; Jer. 23:5-8; Ezek. 37:11-24).

Sometimes in Scripture the term "Israel" refers to the godly remnant as opposed to others who are descendants of Jacob but are not walking with God (Rom. 9:6-8). The fact that the Bible recognized an "Israel" within the nation itself has been a basis for the teaching that the church is the true Israel of the Old Testament. However, this is not sustained in the study of the hundreds of instances in the Bible where the term "Israel" is used. The one or two instances where there could be some confusion should be interpreted on the basis of the hundreds of other instances of Israel that refer to the sons of Jacob.

Gentiles are called the children of Abraham in the sense that they are born of God in a way similar to Abraham's faith (Gen. 15:6; Rom. 4:12). The part the Gentiles share in the Abrahamic Covenant is designated as stemming from the blessing given to the nations, "Consider Abraham: 'He believed God, and it was credited to him as righteousness.' Understand, then, that those who believe are children of Abraham. The Scripture foresaw that God would justify the Gentiles by faith, and announced the Gospel in advance to Abraham: 'All nations will be blessed through you.' So those who have faith are blessed along with Abraham, the man of faith" (Gal. 3:6-9). In other words, Christians are children of God like Abraham but do not inherit the promises given to Israel, Abraham's physical descendants.

Four major covenants made by God with Israel are revealed in Scripture: (1) the covenant made with Abraham, (2) the covenant given through Moses, (3) the covenant made with David, and (4) the New Covenant. Their contents form the structure of prophecy relating to the nation Israel.

THE ABRAHAMIC COVENANT

The Abrahamic Covenant introduced in Genesis 12:1-3 is confirmed and amplified in later revelation (13:14-17; 15:4-21; 17:1-8; 22:17-18). In every case it is presented as an unconditional gracious covenant depending on God's faithfulness for its fulfillment.

The covenant originally given to Abraham is narrowed to some and not all of his descendants, and is restated to Isaac (26:3-5) and to Jacob (28:13-15; 35:9-12). Unlike the Mosaic Covenant, which was given only for a specific time, the Abrahamic Covenant reaches from the time of its initiation into eternity to come.

Major features of the covenant include the following:

(1) "I will make you into a great nation" (12:2). This prediction was fulfilled not only through Isaac and Jacob but also through Ishmael, Esau, and the children of Abraham through Keturah, his wife after Sarah's death (v. 2; 17:20-21; 25:1-4; 26:4; 27:38-40; 36:10-19).

(2) "I will bless you" (12:2). This prophecy has been fulfilled and is being fulfilled in both the earthly and heavenly blessings afforded Abraham and his descendants.

(3) "I will make your name great" (v. 2). This promise is fulfilled not only in the fact that Abraham is considered great in Judaism and in the Christian faith but also in the fact that Muslims regard Abraham as a prophet.

(4) "You will be a blessing" (v. 2). This prophecy was fulfilled especially through Isaac and Jacob and extends to Gentile believers (Gal. 3:13-14).

(5) "I will bless those who bless you, and whoever curses you I will curse" (Gen. 12:3). This promise is fulfilled in history in that the nations that were kind to Israel were blessed of God, and the nations that cursed Israel experienced God's judgment as illustrated in Egypt, Assyria, Babylon, Medo-Persia, Greece, Rome, Spain, modern Germany, modern Russia, and the United States (Deut. 30:7; Isa. 14:1-2; Zech. 14:1-3; Matt. 25:31-46).

(6) "All peoples on earth will be blessed through you" (Gen. 12:3). Fulfillment of this promise is recorded in both the Old and New Testaments. From Israel came the prophets of the Old Testa-

ment, the writers of the Old Testament, the writers of the New Testament, the 12 Apostles, and preeminently Jesus Christ, who was born of the tribe of Judah and was in the line of David.

(7) "To your offspring [Abraham's physical descendants] I will give this land" (v. 7). This promise of the land is reiterated in countless passages in the Old Testament, and its fulfillment is an essential part of the history of Israel as well as a prophecy of its future. The exact boundaries of the land are described in 15:18-21 as extending from the River Egypt to the River Euphrates. The Abrahamic Covenant is the foundational promise on which the other covenants depend.

THE MOSAIC COVENANT

The Mosaic Law was given to Israel by Moses (Ex. 20:1–31:18; John 1:17) and governed three major areas of her life: (1) the commandments dealing with God's moral law (Ex. 20:1-26); (2) the judgments, which governed the social life of Israel (21:1–24:11); and (3) the ordinances, which instructed them concerning their religious life (24:12–31:18).

The promises of the Mosaic Law were conditional, depending on Israel's obedience. Moses told the children of Israel that if they obeyed the Law they would be blessed of God and if they did not they would be cursed and disciplined (Deut. 28:1-68).

The Law was not a way of salvation but was a rule of life. Its application was limited to Israel. The Mosaic Law terminated at the time of the death of Christ.

By indicating conduct that was sinful in God's sight the Mosaic Law was a preparatory provision for Israel which would lead them to Christ.

In Galatians 3:19 Paul raised a question about the purpose of the Law. He stated, "What, then, was the purpose of the Law? It was added because of transgressions until the Seed to whom the promise referred had come. The Law was put into effect through angels by a mediator." The Law characterized sin as transgression, but before the Law came the sin was not attributed to them (Rom. 5:13). The purpose of the Law was not only to prove that the sins forbidden were sinful but also to prove the sinfulness of man (7:11-13). From Galatians 3:19 it is clear that the Law was an *ad interim* provision. Because the Law could only condemn and not save, it was a means to bring people to recognize the necessity of Christ as their Sin Bearer. The Law was intended to be a discipline leading people to holy lives. This goal could only be fulfilled by becoming a disciple of Christ (Matt. 11:29; John 17:6-8; Titus 2:11-13). In Galatians, Paul pointed out that the Law was not a means to salvation and that it was not a means to sanctification. Both salvation and sanctification are to be found only in Jesus Christ and are obtained through grace, not Law.

The Mosaic Law was limited to those who were in covenant relationship to God by physical birth as descendants of Jacob. With the coming of Christ, grace as a rule of life superseded Law as a rule of life (John 1:17).

THE DAVIDIC COVENANT

The covenant God made with David (2 Sam. 7:11-16) is like the gracious covenant He made with Abraham; both are unconditional and everlasting in their duration. The Davidic Covenant guaranteed that a descendant of David would sit on his throne forever. The details of the covenant in 2 Samuel 7 include the fact that David was to have a child not yet born who would succeed him on the throne. This son who was Solomon would build the temple that David desired to build. The throne of Solomon's kingdom would continue forever, and it would not be taken away from him even if he sinned. The covenant included the fact that David's posterity, his throne, and his kingdom would be established forever.

Though the throne of Solomon would continue forever, it is not promised that Solomon's posterity would sit on the throne. Later in the genealogies of the New Testament it becomes clear that Christ's physical lineage from David would go through David's son Nathan rather than Solomon and would terminate in Mary the physical mother of Christ in contrast to Joseph, who is in the physical lineage of Solomon which had been cursed.

There are many confirmations of this covenant in the Old Testament, and the unconditional character of the covenant is especially supported in Psalm 89:3-4, 28-29, 32-37. All conservative scholars agree that the Davidic Covenant was fulfilled in Christ, but those who oppose the concept of a millennial kingdom on earth attempt to equate the throne of David with the throne of God in heaven.

However, David's throne was never a heavenly throne; it was related to the earth and to political government over the land of Israel. This is the way it was interpreted in Israel at the time Christ was on earth, and it was supported by the message of the angel to Mary that Christ would inherit the Davidic throne (Luke 1:31-33).

Christ is not fulfilling this covenant in heaven at the right hand of the Father. Fulfillment requires that Christ will return and establish His kingdom on earth as predicted in many Old Testament passages and in Revelation 20. The language of the Old Testament is so specific that only a literal fulfillment in harmony with many other Old Testament promises will satisfy these promises.

An analysis of the covenant as it is stated and confirmed in the Old Testament indicates that David, Solomon, and Mary understood the covenant to be literal (2 Sam. 7:18-29; 2 Chron. 6:14-16; Luke 1:31-33). A literal fulfillment was universally expected by the Jews. One of the reasons Christ was born as a Descendant of David was to qualify Him for this throne. The Scriptures teach that Christ's present throne is not the throne of David and that He is anticipating that in the future millennial kingdom, when the foes of God are put down, He will reign on the Davidic throne (cf. Ps. 110). David's kingly line, throne, and kingdom will be fulfilled primarily in the Millennium but it will merge with the kingdom of God in eternity.

THE NEW COVENANT

Because the Mosaic Covenant was intended to be a temporary covenant the Old Testament promised that it would be superseded by a new covenant, " 'The time is coming,' declares the LORD, 'when I will make a new covenant with the house of Israel and with the house of Judah. It will not be like the covenant I made with their forefathers when I took them by the hand to lead them out of Egypt, because they broke My covenant, though I was a husband to them,' declares the LORD. 'This is the covenant I will make with the house of Israel after that time,' declares the LORD. 'I will put My law in their minds and write it on their hearts. I will be their God, and they will be My people. No longer will a man teach his neighbor, or a man his brother, saying, "Know the LORD," because they will all know Me, from the least of them to the greatest,' declares the LORD. 'For I will forgive their wickedness and will remember their sins no more' " (Jer. 31:31-34).

The fact of a New Covenant is recognized by all conservative scholars. The coming of Christ brought in a new order (John 1:17) which is supported by the designation Old and New Testaments in which the Scriptures are divided. Interpretation of the New Covenant has varied according to whether the millennial view of the interpreter is postmillennial, amillennial, or premillennial.

Conservative postmillenarians regard the promise of the New Covenant as fulfilled in the glory of the last 1,000 years of the present age in which the Gospel will be triumphant and the world will become Christianized.

The amillennial interpretation views the promises of the New Covenant as being fulfilled in the church. Those adhering to this point of view of course ignore the particulars of the covenant such as the prediction that everyone will know the Lord as well as the many details that describe the Millennium as a golden age in which Satan will be bound and when universal peace on earth will be present.

Premillenarians have varied somewhat in their interpretation of the New Covenant. Some say it was given to Israel and has application to the church. Others hold that there are two New Covenants, one for Israel (Jer. 31) to be fulfilled in the Millennium and the other for the church being fulfilled in the present age. Still another plausible point of view is that the New Covenant is a covenant of grace brought in by the death of Christ which had application to any people with whom God is dealing graciously. In the case of Israel the New Covenant will be fulfilled in the millennial kingdom, and in the case of the church it is being fulfilled in the present age. The ultimate gracious promises of God will be fulfilled in the New Jerusalem to all who are saved.

The New Covenant is confirmed in two other Old Testament passages, Isaiah 61:8-9 and Ezekiel 37:21-28. In these passages the New Covenant in relation to Israel includes promises of the everlasting character of the covenant, Israel's regathering, the rejoining of the 10 tribes of the kingdom of Israel and the 2 tribes of the kingdom of Judah who will be ruled by one King, their spiritual revival, their living in the land forever, God's presence with them, and their having a testimony that they are a nation blessed by God. If the promises and provisions of the covenant are taken in the normal, literal sense, they require a millennial kingdom (in addition to the present age) to allow for a literal fulfillment.

The New Covenant as it relates to the church is mentioned in the New Testament in connection with the Lord's Supper where the elements are declared to be a memorial of the New Covenant (Matt. 26:28; Mark 14:24; Luke 22:20). And believers today are called "ministers of a New Covenant" (2 Cor. 3:6). In Hebrews 8:1-13 the point is made that even the Old Testament by prophesying a New Covenant indicated that the Mosaic Covenant would be terminated. It is most significant, however, that the writer of Hebrews did not claim that the New Covenant with Israel is being fulfilled today. He was simply emphasizing the word "new" to prove that the Mosaic Law has terminated. The rest of the revelation given in Jeremiah 31 will have its fulfillment in the future millennial kingdom, not in the present age. The essential character of the New Covenant as a gracious provision of God is further supported in Hebrews 10:16-17, " 'This is the covenant I will make with them after that time, says the Lord. I will put My laws in their hearts, and I will write them on their minds.' Then he adds: 'Their sins and lawless acts I will remember no more.' "

When the covenants with Israel are examined as a whole, they embody seven major features: (1) a nation forever, (2) a land forever, (3) a King forever, (4) a throne forever, (5) a kingdom forever, (6) a New Covenant, and (7) abiding blessings.

SEVEN MAJOR FEATURES OF ISRAEL'S COVENANTS

The importance of a literal interpretation of prophecy becomes evident in the study of Israel's covenants and her future fulfillment. Those who attempt to take this in a nonliteral sense end up in total confusion with many different interpretations. Far more plausible and in keeping with the way the Scriptures present these covenants is the expectation that God will fulfill literally all His promises to Israel and that future fulfillment of the Abrahamic Covenant, the Davidic Covenant, and the New Covenant may be expected. As such they form a central feature of eschatology. When terms are taken literally, Israel is not the church and the millennial kingdom is not the church; Zion is Jerusalem not heaven; and the throne of David is an earthly throne which has never been nor ever will be in heaven. A study of the main features of the covenants will support this.

1. A NATION FOREVER. This is stated explicitly in Jeremiah 31:31-37 in which God declares Israel will continue as long as the sun, moon, and stars continue. Even in her time of apostasy and sin, Jeremiah wrote, God will never reject Israel.

Just as the promise of the land is everlasting, so the people must be everlasting to inherit and inhabit the new earth (Isa. 65:17; 66:22; Heb. 1:10-12; 2 Peter 3:4-14; Rev. 20:11; 21:1). The everlasting character of His promise to the nation is supported in Genesis 17:7-8. According to Isaiah 66:22 Israel will remain as a people even when there are a new heavens and a new earth.

Romans 11 is devoted to proofs that Israel will never be cast off but rather will be restored to covenanted blessings. This is supported by the fact that Paul was saved. He represented the godly remnant. Though national unbelief was foreseen and Israel was cut off from the olive tree of blessing, she will be grafted in again at the second coming of Christ (vv. 23-24) and Israel will be delivered from her persecutors in the Great Tribulation (vv. 25-29). Though Christians are properly related to Abraham as a spiritual seed (Gen. 15:5-6; Gal. 3:29) and partake of the spiritual blessings promised through the Abrahamic and New Covenants, Israel has her own place and is yet to be exalted as the earthly people of God.

The distinctive place of Israel as a nation is stated in Deuteronomy 7:6-8, "For you are a people holy to the LORD your God. The LORD your God has chosen you out of all the peoples on the face of the earth to be His people, His treasured possession. The LORD did not set His affection on you and choose you because you were more numerous than other peoples, for you were the fewest of all peoples." God declared that His everlasting love for Israel will be the basis of her restoration (Jer. 31:3-4).

2. A LAND FOREVER. The promise of the land given to Abraham (Gen. 15:18) is related to what is known as the Palestinian Covenant. Though the promise of the possession of the land ultimately is secure, the possession during the history of Israel was conditioned on her obedience to the Law. Accordingly they were warned that failure to keep the Law would result in her dispossession of the land.

a. THE REMOVAL OF THE NATION FROM THE LAND BECAUSE OF HER UNFAITHFULNESS. Scripture records three distinct dispossessions of or dispersions from the land: (1) the sojourn of Israel in Egypt, (2) the Babylonian and Assyrian captivities, and (3) Israel's ultimate scattering over all the world (Gen. 15:13-14, 16; Jer. 25:11-12; Deut.

28:63-68; cf. 30:1-3). Along with the three dispossessions are three restorations; the return from Egypt, the return from the Babylonian Captivity, and the future restoration of Israel from all over the world (Gen. 15:14; cf. Josh. 1:2-7; Dan. 9:2; cf. Jer. 23:5-8; 25:11-12; Ezek. 37:21-25; Acts 15:14-17).

History has recorded the three dispossessions from the land of Israel and the 20th century has witnessed the beginning of the third and final restoration.

b. A FUTURE REPENTANCE OF ISRAEL. Along with the predictions of Israel's apostasies are prophecies of her future repentance with the emergence of a godly remnant who will recognize the Messiah on His return (cf. Isa. 61:2-3; Zech. 12:10; Matt. 5:4; 24:30). A future remnant of Israel will turn to the Lord at the time of the second coming of Christ (Zech. 12:10-14).

c. THE RETURN OF THE MESSIAH. The final possession of the land will occur at the time of the second coming of Christ, "Then the LORD your God will restore your fortunes and have compassion on you and gather you again from all the nations where He scattered you. Even if you have been banished to the most distant land under the heavens, from there the LORD your God will gather you and bring you back. He will bring you to the land that belonged to your fathers, and you will take possession of it. He will make you more prosperous and numerous than your fathers. The LORD your God will circumcise your hearts and the hearts of your descendants, so that you may love Him with all your heart and with all your soul, and live" (Deut. 30:3-6). According to Amos 9:9-15 the Davidic government will be restored, the cities of Israel will be rebuilt, and the Children of Israel will be restored to the land. This restoration is fulfilled only in part today but will have complete fulfillment after the return of Christ.

d. ISRAEL'S RESTORATION TO THE LAND. Many prophecies speak of Israel's return to the land such as Isaiah 11:11-12, "In that day the Lord will reach out His hand a second time to reclaim the remnant that is left of His people from Assyria, from Lower Egypt, from Upper Egypt, from Cush, from Elam, from Babylonia, from Hamath, and from the islands of the sea. He will raise a banner for the nations and gather the exiles of Israel; He will assemble the scattered people of Judah from the four quarters of the earth."

A detailed prediction of their return is given in Jeremiah 23:5-8, " 'The days are coming,' declares the LORD, 'when I will raise up to

David a righteous Branch, a King who will reign wisely and do what is just and right in the land. In His days Judah will be saved and Israel will live in safety. This is the name by which He will be called: The LORD Our Righteousness. So then, the days are coming,' declares the LORD, 'when people will no longer say, "As surely as the LORD lives, who brought the Israelites up out of Egypt," but they will say, "As surely as the LORD lives, who brought the descendants of Israel up out of the land of the north and out of all the countries where He had banished them." Then they will live in their own land.' "

The New Testament also records the gathering of the saved of Israel (Matt. 24:29-31). Some say this passage refers to the gathering of the elect among the Gentiles as well as the elect Jews at the beginning of the millennial kingdom.

The boundaries of the land to which Israel will be restored are clearly stated in Genesis 15:18-21. The attempt of amillenarians to see this as a description of heaven is contrary to its meaning. The promise of the land is repeated so often in the Old Testament that it should be clear that God intended it to be taken literally. Though the fulfillment of the promise is to those who survive the Tribulation at the time of the Second Coming and are still in their natural bodies, resurrected Israel of course will also be in the millennial kingdom.

e. ISRAEL'S CONVERSION AS A NATION. Many Scriptures point to the fact that before the Second Coming there will be a revival of Israel and that many will constitute the godly remnant. Though all will not be saved, the godly remnant will be rescued by Christ at His second coming and installed in their Promised Land. Israel's judgments at the time of the Second Coming will purge out unbelievers (Ezek. 20:33-44; Mal. 3:1-6; Matt. 24:37–25:30).

Israel's future conversion stems from their deliverance from their persecutors as mentioned in Romans 11:26-27. Other passages add additional light on her spiritual conversion (Deut. 30:4-8; Ps. 80:3, 7, 17-19; Isa. 66:8; Jer. 23:5-6; 31:31-34; Ezek. 11:19-20).

f. THE JUDGMENT OF ISRAEL'S OPPRESSORS. The Abrahamic Covenant promised that God will curse those who curse Abraham's seed. This has been fulfilled in history and will also be fulfilled in the future in the judgment of the nations (Matt. 25:31-46). In the Great Tribulation Satan will launch a worldwide effort to exterminate the Jewish people. A Gentile who befriends a Jew at that time would do so only because of his faith in Christ and his belief in the Scriptures. Such a Gentile is one of the "sheep" mentioned in verses 31-46.

g. THE NATIONS WILL BE BLESSED. Though Israel is in the center of blessing in the millennial kingdom, the Gentile world will be blessed along with Israel (Ps. 72:1-20; Isa. 60:1-22; 62:1-12; 65:17-25; 66:10-14; Ezek. 37:21-28).

3. A KING FOREVER. As provided in the Davidic Covenant, David's posterity will provide a suitable Person to occupy the throne forever. This is assured by the fact that Jesus Christ died and rose again and is thus qualified to sit on the throne forever. His reign will have no end (2 Sam. 7:16; Ps. 89:36; Jer. 33:17).

4. A THRONE FOREVER. As implied in the eternity of the kingdom, so the throne of David will continue as stated in Psalm 89:36-37, "That his line will continue forever and his throne endure before Me like the sun; it will be established forever like the moon, the faithful witness in the sky." The same thought is confirmed in Isaiah 9:6-7, "For to us a Child is born, to us a Son is given, and the government will be on His shoulders. And He will be called Wonderful Counselor, Mighty God, Everlasting Father, Prince of Peace. Of the increase of His government and peace there will be no end. He will reign on David's throne and over His kingdom, establishing and upholding it with justice and righteousness from that time on and forever. The zeal of the LORD Almighty will accomplish this." The promise to Mary likewise confirms that Christ will sit on the throne (Luke 1:31-33). Since David's throne is related to the millennial kingdom and will be an earthly throne, it must not be confused with the throne of God in heaven.

5. A KINGDOM FOREVER. In the scriptural description of the future kingdom, the King, His throne, and His kingdom are inseparable, and all of them will continue forever. The reigning King will be the Incarnate Christ (Isa. 7:14), the Son of God (Micah 5:2). He will be the rightful Heir to David's throne (Isa. 11:1-5; Jer. 23:5; Ezek. 34:23; Hosea 3:4-5). As predicted in Daniel 7, the kingdom will come from heaven but will exert its power on the earth (Isa. 2:4; 11:4-5; Jer. 33:14-17; Hosea 2:18). The kingdom will be on earth (Ps. 2:8; Isa. 11:9; 42:4; Jer. 23:5; Zech. 14:9), and the capital of the kingdom will be Jerusalem (Isa. 2:1-3; 62:1-7; Zech. 8:20-23; Luke 21:24). The King will rule over Israel (Deut. 30:3-6; Isa 11:11-12; 14:1-3; 60:1-22; Jer. 23:6-8; Micah 4:6-8), and over Gentiles (Pss. 72:11, 17; 86:9; Isa. 45:6; Dan. 7:13-14; Micah 4:2; Zech. 8:22;

Amos 9:12). This kingdom on earth will be established at the second coming of Christ (Deut. 30:3; Pss. 50:3-5; 96:13; Zech. 2:10-12; Mal. 3:1-4; Rev. 19:5-6).

6. A New Covenant. As previously indicated, Israel will be the object of a new gracious covenant from God. As promised in the Old Testament (Jer. 31:31-34), its particular application is to Israel in the millennial kingdom. Like the other unconditional covenants, the Abrahamic, the Palestinian, and the Davidic, the fulfillment rests on the faithfulness of God and not on the worthiness of men. Though the blessings of the Mosaic Covenant were conditioned on obedience to the Law, the ultimate fulfillment of the unconditional covenants will be on the basis of God's grace and faithfulness.

7. Abiding blessings. Many blessings are promised in the covenants. The abundant blessings of the New Covenant will be realized in the millennial kingdom. "Then will the eyes of the blind be opened and the ears of the deaf unstopped. Then will the lame leap like a deer, and the tongue of the dumb shout for joy. Water will gush forth in the wilderness and streams in the desert. The burning sand will become a pool, the thirsty ground bubbling springs. In the haunts where jackals once lay, grass and reeds and papyrus will grow. And a highway will be there; it will be called the Way of Holiness. The unclean will not journey on it; it will be for those who walk in that Way; wicked fools will not go about on it. No lion will be there, nor will any ferocious beast get up on it; they will not be found there. But only the redeemed will walk there, and the ransomed of the Lord will return. They will enter Zion with singing; everlasting joy will crown their heads. Gladness and joy will overtake them, and sorrow and sighing will flee away" (Isa. 35:5-10).

God will be Israel's God and they will be His people (Jer. 31:33; Ezek. 37:27; Zech. 8:8; Rev. 21:3). These promises will be fulfilled in the millennial kingdom as well as in eternity in the New Jerusalem.

It is important to observe that the great covenants of God, which continue forever and which provide blessing in the millennial kingdom as well as in the eternal state, are all based on His gracious provision through Jesus Christ by His sacrifice on the cross. He is able to end the Mosaic Law and introduce the New Covenant of grace in which God gives those who trust Him blessings they do not deserve in time and in eternity.

CHAPTER • 40

ISRAEL'S 490 PROPHETIC YEARS

The ninth chapter of Daniel is one of the most important prophetic sections in the Old Testament. The great variety of interpretations is in itself a testimony to the importance of this chapter.

THE SEVENTY YEARS OF JERUSALEM'S DESOLATIONS

The opening verses of Daniel 9 recording the first year of the Medo-Persian rule of Babylon (539 B.C.) describe Daniel's excitement at finding in the writings of Jeremiah 29:10 the prophecy that the desolations of Jerusalem would continue for only 70 years. As approximately 67 years had already elapsed since Jerusalem fell to Nebuchadnezzar (605 B.C.), he pleaded with God to restore His people, the city of Jerusalem, and the sanctuary in keeping with the prophecy (Dan. 9:4-19). The answer to Daniel's prayer is found in the Book of Ezra when 50,000 returned to the land of Israel.

This introduction to the important prophecy of Daniel 9:24-27 is most significant for it reveals that Daniel interpreted the prophecy of the 70 years literally, and Daniel was on good ground in praying that God would fulfill His promise. As Daniel continued his petition to the Lord, the Angel Gabriel came to him with a special message from God (vv. 20-23).

THE SEVENTY SEVENS

Gabriel announced to Daniel, "Seventy 'sevens' are decreed for your people and your holy city to finish transgression, to put an end to sin, to atone for wickedness, to bring in everlasting righteousness, to seal up vision and prophecy and to anoint the most holy" (v. 24). Because the literal meaning of the 70 years of Jerusalem's desolation is indicated in verse 2, most expositors recognize that the figure of 70 "sevens," or 490 are units of years rather than days and that they describe the extended period of Israel's future history.

In verse 24 the period of 490 years includes the completion of six major prophecies: (1) "to finish transgression," (2) "to put an end to sin," (3) "to atone for wickedness," (4) "to bring in everlasting righteousness," (5) "to seal up vision and prophecy," and (6) "to anoint the most holy." Before dealing with the chronological problems of the 70 sevens, attention should be given to these six predictions of prophecy. A great variety of explanations have been given depending on the expositor's premises and theological point of view.

The first three predictions—finishing transgression, putting an end to sin, and atoning for wickedness—indicate God's intention to bring an end to Israel's apostasy and sin. The reference to providing atonement for wickedness clearly speaks of the atoning work of Christ on the cross.

The fourth prophecy, "to bring in everlasting righteousness," seems to refer not only to the death of Christ but also to the righteousness which will be brought to earth in the millennial kingdom as prophesied in Jeremiah 23:5-6, " 'The days are coming,' declares the LORD, 'when I will raise up to David a righteous Branch, a King who will reign wisely and do what is just and right in the land. In His days Judah will be saved and Israel will live in safety. This is the name by which He will be called: The LORD Our Righteousness.' "

The fifth prophecy, "to seal up vision and prophecy," predicts the cessation of prophetic activity. After the second coming of Christ prophets other than Jesus Christ Himself are unnecessary.

The sixth prediction, "to anoint the most holy," is perhaps the most difficult to explain. Some have taken this to refer to the sacred temple built by Zerubbabel 70 years earlier, while others say it refers to the New Jerusalem (Rev. 21:1-27). Some premillennial scholars suggest that it could refer to the holy temple of the millennial kingdom.

After summarizing the major events of the entire period, Daniel 9:25-27 divides the 490 years into three segments, "Know and understand this: From the issuing of the decree to restore and rebuild Jerusalem until the Anointed One, the Ruler, comes, there will be seven 'sevens,' and sixty-two 'sevens.' It will be rebuilt with streets and a trench, but in times of trouble. After the sixty-two 'sevens,' the Anointed One will be cut off and will have nothing. The people of the ruler who will come will destroy the city and the sanctuary. The end will come like a flood: War will continue until the end, and desolations have been decreed. He will confirm a covenant with many for one 'seven.' In the middle of the 'seven' he will put an end to sacrifice and offering. And on a wing of the temple he will set up an abomination that causes desolation, until the end that is decreed is poured out on him."

The first of the three time divisions is described as "7 'sevens' " or 49 years. The second segment is designated as "62 'sevens' " or 434 years, in which the prophecy will be fulfilled that the streets and trench will be rebuilt in a time of trouble, referring to the rebuilding of Jerusalem. A great variety of explanations are given; the most cogent seems to be that a 49-year period marked the time necessary to rebuild Jerusalem after the wall was completed by Nehemiah. The 434 years describe the period that immediately follows and that leads up to the prophecy of verse 26. After 49 years plus 434, or a total of 483 years, two other events are prophesied: "the Anointed One will be cut off and will have nothing" and "the city and the sanctuary" referring to Jerusalem and the temple, will be destroyed by "the people of the ruler who will come." Also to be fulfilled is the war that "will continue until the end" and the occurrence of the "desolations" that "have been decreed." The final seven years (v. 27), often called "Daniel's 70th Week," will begin with a covenant intended to extend for seven years. The seven years are divided into two halves and at the middle of the seven years action will be taken which "will put an end to sacrifice and offering."

The interpretation of these verses is difficult because of the great varieties of opinions among both Christological and non-Christological interpreters.

NON-CHRISTOLOGICAL INTERPRETATIONS

The non-Christological interpretations attempt to explain this passage in a way that does not refer to Jesus Christ. One of these is to attempt to find fulfillment of the 70 sevens in the persecutions of Antiochus IV, commonly known as Antiochus Epiphanes. Antiochus defiled the temple of Israel attempting to stamp out Judaism and stop the sacrifices. This precipitated the Maccabean revolt. Antiochus who reigned over Syria (175-164 B.C.) put down the revolt with great cruelty, killing tens of thousands of men, women, and children but eventually he had to give up and allow the reconsecration of the temple.

Among other non-Christological interpretations is the attempt to begin the 70 sevens at the same time as the beginning of the 70 years of desolations of Jerusalem, namely, 605 B.C. However, this does not give a satisfactory interpretation of the first 49 years of the prophecy. Others begin the period when Jerusalem was destroyed in 586 B.C. This would make the first 49 years terminate approximately in 538 B.C. when a substantial group of Jews were allowed to return to Israel. This view says the desecration mentioned in Daniel 9:26 was fulfilled in the desecration of the temple of Antiochus (168 B.C.). This view is flawed, however, by the fact that the beginning of the 70 sevens does not relate to the prophecy in Jeremiah 25:11; 29:10, and the terminus of the 70 weeks would be fulfilled not in 168 B.C. but in 96 B.C. Some interpreters, however, who follow this view try to solve this problem by saying that the Book of Daniel is mistaken. This non-Christological view does not give serious consideration to the literal interpretation of prophecy and is built on the assumption that both Jeremiah and Daniel were wrong in their chronology.

Among the Jews the common interpretation is that the prediction of the desecration of the temple was fulfilled at the time of the destruction of Jerusalem in A.D. 70. This does not of course provide for any literal fulfillment of the chronology.

CHRISTOLOGIAL INTERPRETATIONS

Most Christological interpreters agree that the prophecy relates to Jesus Christ though a variety of explanations are given regarding the combination of the 69 sevens at the time of Christ's public ministry and death. The problem is complicated by the fact that there is no general agreement as to the beginning of the 490 years. Four decrees were given relative to the rebuilding of Jerusalem: (1) the decree of Cyrus to rebuild the temple (2 Chron. 36:22-23; Ezra 1:1-4; 6:1-5); (2) the decree of Darius, which confirmed the decree of Cyrus (vv. 6-12); (3) the decree of Artaxerxes (7:11-26); and (4) the decree of Artaxerxes given to Nehemiah relating to the rebuilding of the city (Neh. 2:1-8). Though various facts can be presented in support of each of these interpretations, the fact is that the wall of Jerusalem was not built until approximately 444 B.C. when Nehemiah returned to Jerusalem. The beginning of the 70 sevens is most easily understood as the year 444 B.C.

Using 444 B.C. as the starting point of the 70 sevens, and computing the first 69 sevens or 483 years as composed of 12 months or 360 days (as is normal in the Old Testament), this prophecy allows for the time of Christ's birth and life on earth, and the 483 years can be seen as terminating before the death of Christ. The current trend of scholarship to date the death of Christ in A.D. 28 or 29 allows ample time for the prophecies to be fulfilled literally.

The main problem in the interpretation of Daniel 9:24-27 is how the last seven years should be interpreted. At least five theories may be considered.

THE LAST SEVEN YEARS OF ISRAEL'S PROPHECY

The two non-Christological interpretations, already discussed, obviously failed to find any literal fulfillment of the last seven years of the prophecy.

Three Christological views have been advanced by conservative scholars. One view is that the last seven years of Daniel's prophecy is an indefinite period which does not have its fulfillment until the consummation of human history. However, if the first 483 years are interpreted literally there is no justification for turning to a completely nonliteral interpretation of the last seven years. As a matter of fact, nothing has happened in history to correspond to what was predicted in Daniel 9:27.

A second Christological view, however, which attempts literal fulfillment of the seven years, computes the 483 years as being completed at the time of the baptism of Christ. From this interpretation the first half of the seven years is fulfilled in Christ's ministry before the cross. Those holding this view say that the prediction that sacrifice and offering will cease at the middle of the seven-year period was fulfilled in Christ's crucifixion. Having come to this point in literal fulfillment, however, they are at a loss to explain literally the final three and one half years.

Though agreement of interpretation even among conservative scholars seems to be impossible, the interpretation that provides the most literal and accurate interpretation of the last seven years regards the entire seven-year period as yet future. If the 70 years of the desolations of Jerusalem were literal and the 483 years leading up to the final seven years were literal, it is reasonable to assume that the last seven years will likewise have literal fulfillment. When Christ died on the cross, the sacrifices and offerings did not cease. They continued until A.D. 70 when Jerusalem was destroyed. The cutting off of the "Anointed One" (v. 26), Christ's death, occurred not in the middle of the seven years but after the 483rd year, that is, before the last seven years, which have not yet begun.

Daniel wrote that two events will occur after the 483 years but they are not said to be part of the last 7 years. This is strong support for the view that there is a period of time between the end of year 483 and the beginning of the last 7 years. In addition to the prediction that the Messiah will be cut off, the prophecy is made, "The people of the ruler who will come will destroy the city and the sanctuary" (v. 26). The most plausible explanation of this destruction is that it refers to the destruction of Jerusalem which occurred at least 35 years after the death of Christ in A.D. 70. Both of these events are described as being after the 69th week but are not included in the 70th week.

Objection is sometimes raised that Scripture does not allow for an interruption of a period of time within the 490 years. Such an interval, however, is supported by the fact that Old Testament prophecy allows for a parenthesis between the first and second comings of Christ, which interval has now extended for more than 1,900 years. The interpolation of these 1,900 years between Christ's first and second comings is evident in Daniel 2. In the image there is a time gap between the empires suggested by an interval between the legs and the feet. Also in Daniel 7:1-27 the fulfillment of the last Gentile empire is still future. Other time intervals occur as, for example, between Hosea 3:4 and Hosea 3:5. The separation of Daniel's final years from the preceding 483 years permits a literal interpretation of the seven years, and it coincides with the prophecies of a future period of years leading up to the second coming of Christ as indicated in the Book of Revelation.

"The ruler who will come" is related to "the people" who destroyed Jerusalem in A.D. 70, but the ruler himself is yet future and probably refers to the final world ruler. He will make a seven-year covenant with Israel. Though amillenarians resist the concept of the interval between the 69 sevens and the 70th seven, the premillennial interpretation provides for the most literal interpretation and is superior in explaining all the prophecies relative to this important period in Israel's history, the last seven years before the Second Advent.

In view of the prophecy of Daniel 9:24-27 it is evident that Daniel was given the remarkable assignment of not only defining the period of Israel's history including her last seven years before the second coming of Christ but also the massive revelation of the four major empires beginning with Babylon which would culminate at the second coming of Christ and be followed by the kingdom from heaven. Daniel's prophecies continue to be the important key to understanding the prophetic future as well as the fulfillment of prophecy in the past.

CHAPTER • 41

PROPHECY CONCERNING THE GENTILES

Prophecies which were given before the revelation of the Abrahamic Covenant were general prophecies concerning the Gentiles or the entire human race. Genesis 3:14-19 contains the promises predicting the effect of sin on the human race. These promises have been fulfilled and will continue to be fulfilled until the end of the millennial kingdom.

After Cain's murder of his brother Abel, judgment on Cain and his descendants was prophesied (4:10-12). In Genesis 6 God declared His purpose to wipe out the human race except for Noah and his family by a great Flood. These predictions about the Flood have been completely fulfilled (7:1–8:18). After the Flood God declared, "Never again will I curse the ground because of man, even though every inclination of his heart is evil from childhood. And never again will I destroy all living creatures, as I have done. As long as the earth endures, seedtime and harvest, cold and heat, summer and winter, day and night will never cease" (8:21-22).

In Genesis 9 God blessed Noah and made a covenant with him in which He promised that animals, birds, and fish were given into Noah's hands (v. 2). Also He gave Noah green plants for food and for the first time authorized the eating of meat (vv. 3-5). For the first time He gave the law that if man sheds the blood of another person, his own blood should be shed (v. 6). God also promised that never again would life on earth be destroyed by a flood (vv. 11-17).

Following Noah's drunkenness, predictions were given about his three sons and their descendants. Noah pronounced a curse on Canaan the son of Ham and Canaan's descendants because of Ham's disrespect for his father (vv. 24-25). Noah declared that Canaan would be Shem's slave (v. 26) and that Japheth would have extended territory on earth and that Canaan would also be Japheth's slave (v. 27). These prophecies are being fulfilled throughout the period of the human race on earth.

PROPHECIES CONCERNING THE EMPIRES OF EGYPT AND ASSYRIA

Though there is comparatively little mention of Egypt in the early chapters of Genesis, 3,000 years before Christ Egypt was one of the first great empires of the Middle East. With the discoveries of archeologists in the last century the history of Egypt is now well known from about 3000 B.C. and evidence points to the fact that it was one of the great nations of the past.

Before later empires of Assyria and Babylon were formed Egypt was already an advanced nation nourished by the rich Nile Valley. Egypt already had an advanced culture, its own literature, and a history that extended over hundreds of years. It was to Egypt that Jacob and his sons went for relief from famine in Canaan when Joseph was a major administrator of the Egyptian nation.

Egypt already was a nation of the past when Moses wrote the Pentateuch. The first mention of Egypt in Scripture is in Genesis 10:6 where Mizraim is another name for Egypt (v. 13). Some believe that the modern title of Egypt came from a king by the name of Egyptus who lived about 1485 B.C. The Egyptians called their own land Kemmet, meaning "The Black Land," and Egypt was also mentioned as "the land of Ham" referring to the fact that Egyptians were descendants of Ham the son of Noah.

Abraham went to Egypt because of famine in Canaan (12:10). He was clearly out of the will of God in going to Egypt. But God delivered him from his deception that Sarah was his sister. This was a half truth as she was his half-sister as well as his wife. From this trip to Egypt, Hagar the handmaid was taken back to the Promised Land where she ultimately became the mother of Ishmael (16:1-6). In 26:2 Isaac was told not to go to the land of Egypt as Abraham had done. But Hagar took a wife for Ishmael from Egypt (21:21).

When Jacob and his family went to Egypt, their trip fulfilled the prophecy given to Abraham that his descendants would go to a land where they were strangers. Israel became a great nation in Egypt though they were enslaved and mistreated. When they went to the

Promised Land, they left with great possessions (15:13-14). The River of Egypt, the boundary between Egypt and Canaan, was also the predicted boundary of the land promised to Abraham.

There are more than 700 references to Egypt in the Old Testament but less than 30 in the New Testament. Most of the latter refer to Israel coming out of Egypt as a fulfillment of God's promise.

At the time of Solomon there was considerable commerce between Israel and Egypt, and Pharaoh's daughter was made the wife of Solomon (1 Kings 3:1). Solomon imported horses from Egypt (10:28) and apparently purchased chariots made in Egypt (vv. 26, 29). The commerce with Egypt in Solomon's day was contrary to God's standards (Deut. 17:16).

The Scriptures predicted that Israel would continue to have relationships with Egypt throughout the Old Testament period and even predicted future relationships (Isa. 18–20). God's future dealings with Egypt are revealed in 19:16-25. Egypt was also mentioned in Jeremiah 42–43; 46. God promised protection for Israel so that she need not be afraid of Egypt (46:27-28).

Egypt was mentioned in Ezekiel 29–32, and the Book of Daniel also has a few scattered prophecies concerning Egypt, identified as "the king of the South" (9:15; 11:5-6, 9, 11, 14-15, 25, 29, 40). These prophecies have already been fulfilled. In verses 36-45 reference is made to the king of the South invading Israel, an event that will be part of the war immediately preceding the second coming of Christ. The Minor Prophets also spoke of Egypt (Hosea 7:11-16; 8:13; 9:3, 6; 11:1, 5). Joel predicted the future desolation of Egypt (3:19), and Micah 7:12 predicted the regathering of Israel from Assyria and Egypt. Zechariah added that Israel will be brought out of Egypt when Israel is regathered (10:10). The final Old Testament reference to Egypt is 14:18-19, which speaks of Egypt in the millennial kingdom.

In Scripture, Egypt has a prominent place among the nations of the world. She was the first great empire of history and a land that nurtured the children of Israel during a period of their growth from a family of 70 to a nation of probably 2½ million people. Later Egypt provided a place of safety for Jesus when Mary and Joseph fled from the wrath of Herod (Matt. 2:13-15).

Assyria is important in biblical prophecy primarily as the nation that carried out God's judgment on the 10 tribes of Israel. Assyria first exacted tribute from Israel (2 Kings 15:19-20). When the Assyrians carried off the 10 northern tribes of Israel into captivity (vv. 29-30), this fulfilled Moses' prediction of one of God's judgments on Israel for her sin (Deut. 28:15-68). The account of Assyria's dealings with Israel is detailed in 2 Kings 15:19–19:36 and 2 Chronicles 28:16–33:11. Isaiah recorded the attempt of Assyria to conquer the two remaining tribes of Judah and Benjamin and God's deliverance of them (Isa. 36:1–37:37; 38:6). Though Judah successfully avoided surrender to Assyria, more than a century later Nebuchadnezzar attacked Jerusalem in 605, 597, and 586 B.C. and took Judah into the Babylonian Captivity.

Assyria was probably included in future prophecies about the kingdom of the north in the final world war that will precede the second coming of Christ (Dan. 11:40), and Scripture also mentions that a highway will be built between Egypt and Assyria in the millennial kingdom. In this future period Assyria, Israel, and Egypt will all worship God (Isa. 19:23-25).

PROPHECY CONCERNING BABYLON

Though Babylon is mentioned only a few times in the New Testament, over 600 references to Babylon are found in the Old Testament. The importance of Babylon stems from the fact that the two remaining tribes of Judah and Benjamin were carried into Captivity by the Babylonians. In the revelations given to Daniel Babylon was the first of four empires that are described prophetically. Daniel's prophecies in chapters 2, 7, 8, and 11 form the basis for world history from Daniel's time until the second coming of Christ.

Another factor that makes Babylon important is that the times of the Gentiles began with the fall of Jerusalem in 605 B.C., a period interrupted by the Church Age from Pentecost to the Rapture but not ending until the second coming of Christ (Luke 21:24; Rev. 19).

Another important factor is the prophecy given through Daniel concerning Israel's history, beginning with her return to their land after Babylon was conquered by the Medes and Persians in 539 B.C. Later the reconstruction of Jerusalem was begun in 444 B.C. as described in the Book of Nehemiah. Daniel prophesied the background of Israel's history beginning with the fall of Jerusalem to Babylon in 605 B.C. and climaxing with the end of the times of the Gentiles at the second coming of Christ (Dan. 7:11-13, 26-27; Rev. 19:11-21).

The historic background for the prophecies concerning Babylon include the first reference in connection with the Tower of Babel (Gen. 10:10) and the many historic references in Kings and Chronicles (2 Kings 17–25; 2 Chron. 32–36; Ezra 1–8; Neh. 7:6; 13:6; Isa. 13–14; 21:9; 39; 43:14; 47–48; Jer. 20–52; Ezek. 17; 19:9; 21; 24:2; 26:7; 29:18; 30:25; 32:11). Hundreds of references emphasize the importance of Babylon in the history of Israel and of the Gentiles.

In the providence of God Daniel, while still in his late teens, became the ruler of Babylon under Nebuchadnezzar and served Nebuchadnezzar for the remainder of his 40-year reign. In three major visions amplified by lesser visions Daniel foresaw the times of the Gentiles as beginning with Babylon. The prominence of Gentiles from 605 B.C. to the second coming of Christ raises questions concerning Israel's program. But God also selected Daniel to prophesy about Israel's program (Dan. 9:24-27), which coincides with a portion of the Gentile program.

In all three major visions (Dan. 2; 7–8) Daniel saw Gentile times running from the time of Babylon to the consummation of the second coming of Christ. He also prophesied the death of Christ (9:26). Daniel did not predict the period between the first and second comings of Christ though such a period is partially intimated in verse 26, which depicts the two events of the death of Christ and the destruction of Jerusalem. Daniel had no information about the formation of the church as the body of Christ in the important period from Pentecost to the Rapture.

When Daniel interpreted Nebuchadnezzar's vision of the statue, the prophet-statesman said to the king, "You are that head of gold" (2:36). Nebuchadnezzar later attempted to blot out the idea that there would be any empires following his. He sought to do this by making an image all of gold, which occasioned Daniel's three companions being thrown into a furnace and miraculously preserved (Dan. 3).

In Daniel 7, which records the first of Daniel's four visions which occurred more than 40 years after the events in Daniel 2, the Babylonian Empire is seen as a lion, the first of the four great beasts that came up out of the sea (7:4). Though the vision does not expressly state that the lion is Babylon, this is clear from the fact that the second and third beasts are named Medo-Persia and Greece (8:20-22). The lion is the fit symbol of the kingdom of Babylon as the most grand of great beasts. In a similar way the head of gold in

Daniel 2 represented the glory of Babylon for gold is more valuable than the other materials seen in the image of Daniel 2. Also gold has a higher specific gravity than the other materials of the image, and this made the image of Daniel top-heavy which contributed to its destruction.

Babylon was the greatest of the world empires up to that time. Also Babylon was significant as the captor of the two tribes of Benjamin and Judah and as the nation that destroyed the city of Jerusalem and its beautiful temple. Jerusalem lay in waste from its destruction in 586 B.C. until the construction of the wall in 444 B.C. This represented God's judgment on Israel and also indicated that Babylon, because of its hatred for *Yahweh,* was subject to ultimate destruction.

In the New Testament Babylon is mentioned principally in the Book of Revelation in connection with the judgment of God on Gentile power at the time of the second coming of Christ. In 14:8 the destruction of Babylon the Great is prophesied. In 16:19 Babylon as a great city is pictured as being destroyed. In Revelation 17 the world religion symbolized by the woman on the scarlet-colored beast has on her forehead the words, "MYSTERY BABYLON THE GREAT THE MOTHER OF PROSTITUTES AND OF THE ABOMINATIONS OF THE EARTH" (v. 5). In 18:2, 10, and 21 Babylon is represented as a great city that will be destroyed just before the second coming of Christ.

The New Testament references to Babylon present three major facts about the nation: (1) Babylon will be a city, (2) Babylon will be a political power, and (3) Babylon will be a false religion.

Some believe that the city of Babylon will be the capital of the world government during the three and one half years of Great Tribulation preceding the second coming of Christ. This would require that Babylon be rebuilt on its ancient site. Others believe that Babylon as the city refers to Rome as a possible center of political and religious power in the endtime.

Religiously Babylon represents many of the pagan doctrines and customs that were incorporated in the Roman Catholic Church. These will be supremely manifested in the false religions of the endtime and the future world church. The religious aspect of Babylon and its destruction are described in Revelation 17.

Though the final world government will consist of a revived Roman Empire, its political power and opposition to God are indicated by the world power of the endtime being described as Babylon. In a sense Babylon began the times of the Gentiles. And the destruction of Gentile power at the end of the Tribulation by the second coming of Christ is presented as a destruction of political Babylon.

Though scholars have various opinions on Revelation 18, the destruction of the great city may be one of the results of the earthquake described in 16:19-21, a passage which mentions Babylon.

Taken as a whole, Babylon combines all the elements of anti-God movements in the world, both in the political and religious powers of the ancient world and in the final endtime form of world religion.

PROPHECY CONCERNING THE MEDES AND THE PERSIANS

When Babylon fell in 539 B.C., the period of Medo-Persian power began. It continued for about 200 years. The Old Testament mentions either the Medes or the Persians about 50 times. The importance of these 200 years is primarily how they relate to Israel's restoration to her land.

The Medes had appeared earlier in history in connection with the downfall of Assyria. As early as 614 B.C. the Medes captured Asshur, the capital of Assyria, and two years later the Medes joined the Chaldeans in bringing about the complete downfall of the Assyrian Empire. After the downfall of Assyria, Babylon came into power, and in various situations the Medes served as an ally of Babylon. Toward the end of the Babylonian Empire the Persians rose up as a political and military force. Under Cyrus II the Persians conquered Media in 549 B.C. and thereafter the two countries were combined in the Medo-Persian Empire. They were able to conquer Babylon in 539 B.C. and they continued in power until the rise of Alexander the Great of Greece in 334 B.C.

In Scripture the Medes were mentioned as attacking Babylon (Isa. 13:17). In verse 19 the fall of Babylon was prophesied. It is not clear whether this was fulfilled in 539 B.C. or whether it refers to the fall of Babylon prophesied in Revelation 18. Jeremiah pointed out that the Medes, as a persecutor of the people of Israel, would be punished along with other nations (Jer. 25:25). Jeremiah also prophesied that the Medes would conquer Babylon (51:11, 28).

The Prophet Daniel, however, gave the most information about the role of the Medes and the Persians in their control of the Middle

East for more than 200 years. In the image seen by Nebuchadnezzar in Daniel 2 the Medes and the Persians were represented by the upper part of the body made of silver, a metal inferior to gold which represented Babylon and which prompted Daniel to say, "After you [Babylon], another kingdom will rise, inferior to yours" (v. 39). In Daniel's vision of the four great beasts in Daniel 7, Medo-Persia is represented as a bear with three ribs in its mouth (v. 5). A bear, though inferior to a lion, which symbolized Babylon, was seen by Daniel as a great and powerful beast. Various interpretations are given to the three ribs, but one possible explanation is that they represented the Medes, the Persians, and the Babylonians (v. 5). In Daniel 8 the kings of Media and Persia were described as the "two-horned ram" designated as "the kings of Media and Persia" (v. 20). The power of Media and Persia was described in verses 3-4. One horn was said to be larger than the other (v. 3), indicating that Persia was more powerful than Media. The ram, referring to Medo-Persia, was pictured as having the ability to overcome all that contended against it (vv. 3-4). The power of the Medo-Persian Empire was described also in 11:2-3.

Under the Medo-Persian reign Israel was allowed to go back to her land, build her temple, and eventually the walls of Jerusalem and the city itself in the period between 538 B.C. and 400 B.C. The rulers of Medo-Persia were kinder to the Jews than any of the other world empires.

The Prophet Daniel witnessed the fulfillment of the prophecy that Babylon would be succeeded by the Medes and the Persians, and Daniel himself served as an important official in Babylon under the Medes and Persians even though he was of advanced age. The incident of the lions' den tells much about Daniel's personal prayer life as well as his skill and integrity (Dan. 6). Daniel may have been influential in securing the permission of Cyrus to permit Israel to return to her land (2 Chron. 36:22-23; Ezra 1:1-4).

Before Cyrus was born Isaiah made the remarkable prediction that in the rebuilding of the temple and the city of Jerusalem (Isa. 44:28) Cyrus would be involved. On the question of who gave the first permission to rebuild Jerusalem various opinions have been advanced. Because Daniel 9:25 begins the 490 years of Israel's future with the command to restore Jerusalem, scholars have differed as to the exact date to which this verse refers. Though the matter is complicated, probably the best conclusion is that the 490 years of

Israel's prophecy began in 444 B.C. when Nehemiah motivated the Jews to rebuild the wall of Jerusalem.

With the rise of Alexander the Great, king of Macedonia, the third empire of Daniel's vision in Daniel 7 appeared. In the image of Daniel 2 the lower part of the body, which was made of bronze, represented Greece. In the vision of Daniel 7 the empire of Greece was portrayed by the leopard with four wings and four heads (v. 6). The leopard, a beast with incredible speed, accurately described the lightning-speed conquest of Alexander in which he took his armies all the way to India. The four heads and the four wings represented the fact that after Alexander died in Babylon (in 323 B.C.) his empire would be divided among four of his successors.

In Daniel 8 a more detailed prophecy was given concerning both Medo-Persia and Greece. In verses 1-4 the conquests of Medo-Persia were prophesied and Daniel identified the ram as "the kings of Media and Persia." In verses 5-8 the ram was destroyed by a goat with one prominent horn. According to verse 21 "the shaggy goat is the king of Greece, and the large horn between his eyes is the first king," i.e., Alexander. The rapid conquest of Greece was described in verse 5, "As I was thinking about this, suddenly a goat with a prominent horn between his eyes came from the west, crossing the whole earth without touching the ground." The fact that the goat did not touch the ground indicated the speed of Alexander's conquest.

The death of Alexander the Great was predicted in verse 8, ("the large horn was broken off"), and his successors, who divided his empire into four parts, were represented by the "four prominent horns" (v. 8). The horns were said to be "four kingdoms that will emerge from his nation but will not have the same power" (v. 22). According to secular history the four rulers who headed up the division of the Grecian Empire were Ptolemy who was given Egypt; Seleucus who was given Syria, Israel, and the East; Lysimachus who was given Thrace and parts of Asia Minor; and Cassander who was given Macedonia and Greece.

Later the kingdom was divided in a different way. Macedonia and Thrace were joined, and eventually the three major kingdoms which continued the Grecian power were Macedonia, Syria, and Egypt. They were finally conquered by the Roman Empire.

One of the important factors related to the Grecian Empire was the rise of Antiochus Epiphanes, known in secular history as Antiochus IV who reigned over Syria 175-163 B.C. Daniel described him prophetically in Daniel 11:21-35 (cf. 1 and 2 Maccabees). Antiochus desecrated the temple of Israel by offering a sow on the altar and stopping the sacrifices. This precipitated the Maccabean revolt, to which Antiochus responded by killing thousands of the Jews who opposed him. In addition to the prophecies of Daniel 11 about Antiochus, he was described as a little horn that would desecrate the holy temple (8:9-14). This desecration by Antiochus IV is now fulfilled prophecy. Yet in a similar way the final world ruler during the three and one half years preceding the second coming of Christ will also desecrate the temple (9:27; Matt. 24:15-22; 2 Thes. 2:3-4; Rev. 13:14-15). Like Antiochus, the final ruler of Gentile power before Christ's second coming will persecute the people of Israel, desecrate their temple, and set himself up as God.

Daniel 11:3-35 gives a detailed prophetic revelation of the various political movements of the kingdom of Greece after Alexander's death. In this amazing section more than 100 prophecies are made, all of which have been literally fulfilled, including those that refer to Antiochus Epiphanes. These prophecies are so detailed that many scholars who deny the possibility of accurate prophetic revelation advance the theory that the Book of Daniel was a forgery written after the events had happened. Many conservative scholars have supported the authenticity of Daniel's prophecies as written by Daniel in the sixth century B.C. and regard them as authentic prophecies of future events.

PROPHECY CONCERNING THE EMPIRE OF ROME

While the prophecies relating to the empire of Greece were being fulfilled, including the prophecies of Antiochus Epiphanes, the fourth empire revealed to Daniel was gaining power. After conquering all of Italy, Rome then defeated Sicily in 242 B.C., thus demonstrating her rising power. Roman conquests were then directed at Spain and Carthage, which came under complete Roman control and eventually were destroyed in 146 B.C. The Mediterranean Sea was already being surrounded by countries conquered by Rome as early as the beginning of the second century B.C.

In Daniel's first revelation of the fourth world empire (2:40-43) he referred to Rome by saying, "As iron breaks things to pieces, so it will crush and break all the others" (v. 40). Though Daniel did not identify Rome by name, history makes it plain that the great empire of Rome which followed that of Greece was anticipated in these prophecies.

In 7:7 Rome as the fourth beast was described as "terrifying and frightening and very powerful. It had large iron teeth; it crushed and devoured its victims and trampled underfoot whatever was left."

The description of the Roman Empire in Daniel 2 and 7 was dramatically fulfilled in history. As Rome continued its conquests to the east, eventually going all the way to the Euphrates River, each nation as it was conquered was brutally treated, with its manpower carried off as slaves. Roman power was supported by contingents of Roman soldiers. The great contribution of Rome in architecture and roads were all built by slave labor, which included 150,000 Jews who were in Egypt as slaves during the lifetime of Christ.

Though some have attempted to deny that the fourth empire is Rome, there is no plausible explanation of the fourth empire other than to identify it as Rome. Since the empire of Greece, Rome was the only world empire that emerged and it continued for almost 1,000 years, leaving an influence on culture, government, architecture, and literature that was unprecedented by any previous empire. Only those who refuse to acknowledge the accuracy of literal prophecy can avoid the conclusion that the fourth empire was Rome.

A problem that remains is to identify the fulfillment of the last stage of the Roman Empire defined in Daniel 2 as having "feet partly of iron and partly of baked clay" (v. 33) and as the beast with 10 horns (7:7).

Many attempts have been made to find this final stage of the Roman Empire in history, but no explanation has been advanced that in any way approaches the literal fulfillment of the final phases of the empire as portrayed in Daniel. The Roman Empire never had a 10-nation composition as implied in the 10 horns (v. 7), and explained as "10 kings who will come from this kingdom" (v. 24). The fulfillment of prophecies about the Roman Empire seems to have come to a complete halt with the first coming of Christ. Its final prophecies will not be fulfilled until after the Rapture.

In keeping with the Old Testament approach to prophecy, the present age from Pentecost to the Rapture is not included in the prophetic visions of the Old Testament. The first and second comings of Christ are often considered in the same passage as one event (e.g., Isa. 61:1-2). Though the final seven years of the prophetic future culminating in the second coming of Christ are given extensive prophetic revelation in both the Old and New Testaments, the peculiar character of the present age, in which Jews and Gentiles are baptized into one body (1 Cor. 12:13) and in which Christ and the Holy Spirit indwells believers (John 14:20; 1 Cor. 6:19-20), was not revealed. The present Church Age is distinguished from all other dispensations. The baptism of the Spirit was never mentioned in any other dispensation. The universal indwelling of the Holy Spirit in believers was not known in the Old Testament, but is an essential feature of the present dispensation. In the millennial kingdom the indwelling of the Holy Spirit will again be universal in believers, but not the baptism of the Spirit. The distinctive feature of the present age referred to by Christ in His statement, "You are in Me, and I am in you" (John 14:20) is completely unknown in Old Testament history and prophecy.

As has often been pointed out, the Old Testament views the first and second comings of Christ as two distant mountains which seemingly are side by side. When one arrives at the first mountain, however, he discovers there is a great valley between the two mountains. The valley is hidden from distant sight but becomes apparent once the first mountain is reached. The present age is like that valley, hidden from sight in the Old Testament. Attempts to evade the doctrine that the present Church Age is distinctive from anything in the past or in the future can only be supported either by denying the clear revelation of Scripture or by spiritualizing its plain statements and making them teach something other than their literal meaning. The only way, therefore, the prophecies of the Old Testament regarding the final state of the Roman Empire can be literally interpreted is to predict a future revival of the Roman Empire after the present age and its ultimate destruction at the second coming of Christ (Rev. 19). As far as history is concerned the Roman Empire which first showed its power in the first century B.C. was never completely destroyed as a political entity until its final king was killed in A.D. 1453 by Mohammed II. Though continuing in name as the Holy Roman Empire, even this aspect has disappeared from contemporary history.

The revival of the Roman Empire will be in three stages. The first stage will be the emergence of the 10 kingdoms once controlled by the ancient Roman Empire. The 10 horns of Daniel 7:7 and Revelation 13:1 are said to be 10 simultaneous kingdoms banded together in a political union (Dan. 7:24). Their names are not given in Scripture, but presumably they were once controlled by the ancient Roman Empire. They may refer to the major countries surrounding the Mediterranean Sea including Spain, France, Italy, Greece, possibly Syria in western Asia, and Egypt and Libya in northern Africa, and others.

The second stage of the revival of the Roman Empire will be the emergence of a man revealed in verse 8 as "another horn, a little one, which came up among them," with the result that "three of the first horns were uprooted before it." This little horn will be a king, as described in verse 24. "Another king will arise, different from the earlier ones; he will subdue three kings." He apparently will soon conquer the seven remaining kingdoms for they are regarded as part of his political power from then on (Rev. 17:16). The second stage then will be a consolidation of 10 countries into one political unit dominated by a dictator.

The third stage of the revival of the Roman Empire will be an expansion of its power to the entire world, beginning in the middle of the last seven years of Daniel's prophecy for Israel (Dan. 9:27) and continuing for three and one half years or 42 months (Rev. 13:5). This world government will include the entire globe (Dan. 7:23; Rev. 13:7).

As a world emperor, who will be Satan's masterpiece of substitution for Jesus Christ as God and King of kings, the final world ruler will be the little horn of Daniel 7:8, the king who "will exalt and magnify himself above every god" (11:36), the one who will be the "man of lawlessness" (2 Thes. 2:3), a head of the beast coming out of the sea (Rev. 13:2-3), and the beast who will be destroyed by Christ and cast into the lake of fire at His second coming (19:20). According to Daniel 9:26 the "people of the [world] ruler . . . will come [and] will destroy the city and the sanctuary" and "will confirm a covenant with many for one 'seven' " (v. 27). His world empire will begin at the middle of the last seven years leading up to the second coming of Christ. This will be the beginning of 42 months or three and one half years of world domination (Rev. 13:5).

The first half of the final seven years will feature a world church, symbolized by the "great prostitute" of Revelation 17. It will be succeeded by a world religion consisting of the worship of the world dictator and of Satan (13:4), which will continue for the last 42 months preceding the second coming of Christ. The power of this world dictator will extend to the control of the total economy of the world so that no one can buy or sell except by his authority (v. 17).

The final form of world religion will actually be Satan's masterpiece of substitution for the worship of Jesus Christ. The future world ruler will claim to be God and will abolish all religions including the worship of Christ (Dan. 11:36-37). The only powers he will recognize will be the power of Satan and military power (vv. 38-39).

Though the final world empire before the second coming of Christ will continue for 42 months, its final stage will be disrupted by the great catastrophes described in Revelation 6–18. Simultaneously, a world war, with the land of Israel as the battlefield, will feature great armies from the north, east, and south engaged in brutal battle (Dan. 11:40-45; Rev. 16:13-16). The end of the Roman Empire and of Gentile times will occur at the second coming of Christ (Rev. 19:11-21).

The final world war will be at the instigation of Satan himself (16:13-16). At first glance this seems to be a paradox. The world government was put in place in Revelation 13 with the help of satanic power. Less than three and one half years later Satan will instigate the gathering of the armies of the world to fight against the leader of the world government. The reason behind this paradox is that Satan knows that Christ is coming again with the armies from heaven, and he is gathering all the military forces of the world to the land of Israel to combat the army from heaven (19:11-16). Though Satan knows he cannot win, he will be driven nevertheless by his own evil nature to oppose God in every possible way. The result will be that he will be cast into the Abyss and rendered inactive during the millennial kingdom (20:1-3).

At the end of the 1,000 years Satan will be released and he will incite a rebellion against God (vv. 7-9). But God will destroy those who surround Satan and support his cause. Satan will then be cast into the lake of fire, where the world ruler and false prophet were cast, 1,000 years before. All three "will be tormented day and night forever and ever" (v. 10), dramatic proof of eternal punishment. The fact that the beast and the false prophet will still be in the lake of fire refutes the idea of annihilation. As Gentile power will come to its end at the time of the Second Coming, so all satanic power will come to its end with Satan and the demon world judged at the beginning of the eternal state (Rev. 21–22).

CHAPTER • 42

PROPHECY CONCERNING SATAN, EVIL, AND THE MAN OF LAWLESSNESS

In human philosophies the problem of evil in the world is usually considered an unsolvable problem. However, the Bible provides the only satisfactory answer. Scripture reveals that sin began with the fall of Satan and the angels who fell with him. Through Satan's temptations, evil extended to the human race in the sin of Adam and Eve. As these doctrines were discussed in the section on angelology, only a summary is necessary here to deal with the final judgments of Satan, of evil, and of the man of lawlessness, the person who symbolizes all evil and will be the world dictator reigning before the second coming of Christ.

Scripture describes not only the origin of evil but also its final disposition by a righteous God. The Scriptures make clear that evil did not begin with man and will not be solved by man. History and prophecy testify to the all-sufficiency of God in power and wisdom to permit evil to the extent that it is good and wise in God's judgment and to bring it to final judgment and disposition in His time. The answer of biblical theologians to the great problem of evil is that God has permitted it as a means to display His own infinite perfections and glory. God did not create evil; He is permitting it for a time.

In judgment on sin God demonstrates His righteousness and power. By His introduction of grace into the human situation (where men can be saved by grace through faith in Christ in keeping with His righteousness), God demonstrates as well His wisdom, love, and goodness. Though it is beyond man's understanding how God could tolerate evil in the world—evil that resulted in the death of His own Son on a cross—the only plausible answer is that this ultimately will display God's infinite perfections.

SATAN

Satan was originally created as a holy angel and given a high place of authority over the angelic world. Long before man was created, Satan's desire to be like God resulted in his being judged. The angels who supported and sinned with him were also judged, and they became the demon world. Some were bound and are awaiting judgment (Jude 6). Others like Satan were allowed some freedom in keeping with God's providential purposes (1 Peter 5:8).

After Adam and Eve were created in the Garden of Eden, Satan led them into disobedience which plunged the entire human race into sin (Rom. 5:12). At the same time God predicted, "I will put enmity between you and the woman, and between your offspring and hers; He will crush your head, and you will strike His heel" (Gen. 3:15). In this brief promise God anticipated the cross of Christ in which Christ would be wounded and die but would ultimately crush the power of Satan by casting him into the lake of fire (John 16:11; Col. 2:14-15; Rev. 20:10).

The order of God's execution of judgment on Satan is as follows: (1) Satan was judged at the Cross. (2) He will be cast out of heaven when defeated in the angelic war which is yet to come (12:7-12). (3) He will be cast into the Abyss which will be sealed for 1,000 years (20:1-3). (4) He will be loosed for a short time for his wickedness to reach its consummation (vv. 3, 7-9). (5) He will be cast into the lake of burning sulfur (v. 10). The first of these events as sovereignly decreed by God has been fulfilled. The others are yet to be fulfilled. Christians can to some extent be afflicted by Satan as illustrated in the case of Job. The ultimate defeat of Satan and God's righteous judgment on him is assured, and those who put their trust in Christ are on the side that will win.

EVIL

Scripture reveals that evil will also follow a predetermined program. Rather than evil being gradually overcome by human effort, it can be conquered only by God. The essential features of God's dealing with evil are these: (1) Israel's transgressions will be finished when her Messiah returns and she enters into the kingdom (Dan. 9:24; Rom. 11:26-27). (2) Whatever evil will exist in the Millennium will be judged instantly by the King (Isa. 11:3-4). Though mere profession of faith that does not openly challenge Christ as King of kings will be permitted, unbelievers will be judged at the end of the Millennium. (3) Evil will be banished forever from the new heaven and the new earth and righteousness will dwell in eternity (2 Peter 3:13; Rev. 21:27).

THE MAN OF LAWLESSNESS

The prophetic Scriptures anticipate the coming of an antichrist, a superman who will be Satan's counterfeit of Jesus Christ as King of kings and Lord of lords. According to John's epistles there have been many antichrists (1 John 2:18, 22; 4:3; 2 John 7). The coming superman will be a world ruler in the period preceding Christ's second coming. He is never actually called "antichrist," but he fulfills the meaning of the name inasmuch as "anti" means "against" as well as "instead of." For this reason many address this coming world leader as the Antichrist, the one who will fulfill all the qualities of preceding antichrists.

In Daniel's vision of the four great empires, the fourth empire identified as Rome was described as having 10 horns in its later stage (Dan. 7:7). An eleventh little horn is spoken of in verse 8. He will uproot 3 of the 10 kings represented by the horns and will eventually gain control of all 10 kingdoms which the horns represent (vv. 8, 11, 20-21, 23-24). This ruler will receive his power from Satan (Rev. 13:2; Luke 4:5-7). Though expositors differ in their identification of this man in biblical prophecy, a plausible conclusion is that this little horn is a superman who will gain control of the 10 kingdoms revealed in Daniel 7. He is first identified as the one who gains control of 3 of the kingdoms (v. 8), but it is implied that he gains control of all 10. As such he can be identified more than seven years before the second coming of Christ.

When this ruler gains power over the 10 kingdoms, he will impose a peace treaty on Israel (9:27) for seven years which will enable people to identify him. In the middle of the seven years he will become a world ruler (7:23, Rev. 13:7). Christ referred to him as "standing in the holy place" and desecrating the temple by " 'the abomination that causes desolation,' spoken of through the Prophet Daniel" (Matt. 24:15). In a future temple yet to be built, orthodox

Jews will offer the sacrifices of the Mosaic Law, and this world ruler will desecrate the temple and stand in the temple to be worshiped (2 Thes. 2:4). An idol representing him will also be erected in the temple and made the object of worship (Rev. 13:14-15). He will receive "a fatal wound" but will be "healed" (v. 3) and will be associated with "the false prophet" (19:20). This false prophet will perform miracles that will cause people to worship the world ruler (13:11-18).

The ruler of verse 7 will be a king who "will do as he pleases" and who "will exalt and magnify himself above every god" (Dan. 11:36). Some consider him as having been personified by the "ruler of Tyre" (Ezek. 28:1-10), with Satan being identified with the king of Tyre in verses 11-19. The man of lawlessness will be the final ruler of the times of the Gentiles (Luke 21:24) and will be judged by Christ in His second coming when the world ruler as well as the false prophet associated with him will be thrown into the lake of burning sulfur (Rev. 19:20).

The man of lawlessness is the ultimate substitute for Jesus Christ as King of kings and Lord of lords. This ruler will be empowered by Satan to dominate the whole world in the 42 months preceding the second coming of Christ (13:5).

A most significant reference to this lawless leader is found in Daniel 9:24-27, where he is referred to as "the ruler" (v. 26). He will make a covenant with Israel for the last seven years leading up to the second coming of Christ. According to verse 27, "He will confirm a covenant with many for one 'seven,' " but "in the middle of that 'seven' he will put an end to sacrifice and offering. And one who causes desolation will place abominations on a wing of the temple until the end that is decreed is poured out on him." Opinions differ on the identification of this person who will make the covenant.

Generally speaking amillenarians, who find this entire passage fulfilled in the first century, regard "he" in verse 27 as Christ.

In verse 25 Christ is called "the Anointed One, the ruler" and in verse 26 "the Anointed One" who "will be cut off and will have nothing."

In contrast to these references to Christ will be another "ruler" who is said to be related to "the people . . . who . . . will destroy the city and the sanctuary." Taking "he" in verse 27 as referring back to its nearest antecedent, premillenarians hold that the ruler mentioned here is related to the people who destroyed Jerusalem in A.D. 70. He is not said to have anything to do with the destruction of Jerusalem in A.D. 70, but he is said to be of the same people (i.e., the Romans). As the head of the revived Roman Empire he will be related politically to the people who in the first century destroyed Jerusalem.

The problem in trying to see the predictions in verse 27 as already fulfilled is that this does not conform to any series of facts which would constitute a legitimate fulfillment. Though it is true that Christ inaugurated the New Covenant of grace through His death on the cross, this does not introduce a covenant for only seven years, and it was not introduced at the beginning of His public ministry but by His death on the cross. Amillenarians, however, hold that the first half of the seven years is the time of His public ministry and that at His death, which they place in the middle of the last seven years, an end was made of sacrifices and offerings. However, the facts are that Jewish offerings continued until A.D. 70 and were not discontinued by the death of Christ. Also the New Covenant was brought in by His death. This was before the seven years, not in the middle of them. The explanation of amillenarians also leaves unexplained how the three and one half years which conclude the 70 sevens of Daniel is fulfilled in any realistic way.

Premillenarians believe that the fulfillment of the last seven of the 70 sevens of Daniel's prophecy will be in the future because no literal fulfillment has yet occurred. Support for this comes from the fact that in verse 26 two events are said to occur after the 69th seven but are not a part of the 70th seven. One of these events is that "the Anointed One," Christ, will be crucified. The second event is the destruction of Jerusalem, which was at least 35 years after Christ's crucifixion. There is no possibility of finding a past fulfillment of the last seven years in view of the fact that the period between the 69th and the 70th seven is much longer than seven years. That is, the 70th did not occur immediately after the 69th. Though Jews say that the 70th week was fulfilled in connection with the destruction of Jerusalem in A.D. 70, a preferable view is to consider the entire age since the death of Christ and the destruction of Jerusalem as occurring in the period between the 69th and the 70th seven, which in turn means that the literal fulfillment of the 70th seven is yet future.

The possibility for such literal fulfillment is supported by yet unfulfilled prophecies of the coming 10-nation kingdom (7:7). A future ruler not yet seen on the pages of world history will fulfill 9:27 by imposing a peace treaty on Israel intended to last for seven years. The first half of this will bring peace to Israel and is the reason for the statement in 1 Thessalonians 5:3 that a period of peace will precede the Great Tribulation. The last half of the 70th seven will be a period of 42 months, a prophecy written by John in Revelation 13:5 and unfulfilled late in the first century long after the crucifixion of Christ. All these facts combine to require a time period between the 69th seven and the beginning of the 70th seven.

This interpretation allows for complete future fulfillment of the catastrophes of Revelation 6–18 and many other passages such as Daniel 11:40-44 which speak of the endtime conflict as being terminated by the second coming of Christ. A literal interpretation of prophecy strongly suggests that a future seven-year period prior to the second coming of Christ is by far the best way to explain these prophecies.

Other substantial prophecies support the concept of a future fulfillment of Daniel's last seven years before the second coming of Christ.

In 2 Thessalonians 2:1-10 an extended revelation is given concerning the activities of the lawless one:

> Concerning the coming of our Lord Jesus Christ and our being gathered to Him, we ask you, brothers, not to become easily unsettled or alarmed by some prophecy, report, or letter supposed to have come from us, saying that the Day of the Lord has already come. Don't let anyone deceive you in any way, for that day will not come until the rebellion occurs and the man of lawlessness is revealed, the man doomed to destruction. He opposes and exalts himself over everything that is called God or is worshiped, and even sets himself up in God's temple, proclaiming himself to be God. Don't you remember that when I was with you I used to tell you these things? And now you know what is holding him back, so that he may be revealed at the proper time. For the secret power of lawlessness is already at work; but the One who now holds it back will continue to do so till He is taken out of the way. And then the lawless one will be revealed, whom the Lord Jesus will overthrow with the breath of His mouth and destroy by the splendor of His coming. The coming of the lawless one will be in accordance with the work of Satan displayed in all kinds of counterfeit miracles, signs, and wonders, and in every sort of evil that deceives those who are

perishing. They perish because they refused to love the truth and so be saved.

Here Paul was correcting the false teachings the Thessalonians had received from certain Bible teachers that they were already in the Day of the Lord, the time of trouble. Paul points out that the Day of the Lord had not begun because the major events of the day had not been fulfilled.

The "Day of the Lord" or "the Day of *Yahweh*" is an expression frequently found in Scripture to refer to a day of trouble or day of judgment (Isa. 13:6, 9; 14:3; Ezek. 7:19; 13:5; 30:3; Joel 1:15; 2:1, 11, 31; 3:14; Amos 5:18, 20; Obad. 15; Zeph. 1:7-8, 14, 18; 2:2; Zech. 12:8; 14:1). The times of judgments predicted in the Old Testament are described by terms other than "the Day of the Lord" such as "that day" or a day in which destruction and judgment is promised. It is a common doctrine in the Old Testament.

Second Thessalonians 2 refers to a future time of judgment which includes the whole period beginning at the Rapture of the church and extending to the end of the millennial kingdom. The significant factor that sets it aside as the Day of the Lord is that it is a time of immediate divine judgment on sin (2 Peter 3:10).

Other terms found in Scripture such as "the day of Jesus Christ" or similar expressions seem to refer to the Rapture specifically rather than to a time of judgment (1 Cor. 1:8; 2 Cor. 1:14; Phil. 1:6, 10; 2:16). Likewise the expression "the day of God" (2 Peter 3:12) probably refers to the period of time after the Day of the Lord and refers to eternity future.

Seven facts may be observed in the teaching of 2 Thessalonians 2:1-10. (1) The Day of the Lord is a period beginning immediately at the Rapture of the church (1 Thes. 5:1-2). (2) In the Day of the Lord the lawless one will claim to be God (2 Thes. 2:4). (3) He will sit in the temple (v. 4), a reference to a Jewish temple yet to be built. (4) He will be revealed in God's appointed time after the Rapture (v. 6). (5) After the church indwelt by the Holy Spirit is removed by the Rapture the lawless one will be destroyed by Christ in His second coming and cast into the lake of burning sulfur (Rev. 19:20). (6) He will exercise satanic power (2 Thes. 2:9). (7) He will deceive non-Christians, who are described as those who do not "love the truth" (v. 10).

The extended description of his activities revealed in Revelation

13:1-8 as well as other passages of Revelation speak of his world government during the last 42 months immediately before the second coming of Christ. He will blaspheme God, persecute all who will not worship him, exercise great power, claim to be God, control the financial transactions of the world, and exercise satanic power such as the world has never seen before. Though he has great power, he will come to his end at the time of the second coming of Christ.

The lawless one will be revealed after the Rapture of the church and will increase his power until he is finally a world ruler for the last 42 months preceding the second coming of Christ. He will be part of Satan's imitation of the Trinity in which Satan takes the place of God the Father, the lawless one takes the place of Christ, and the false prophet takes the place of the Holy Spirit.

C H A P T E R • 4 3

PROPHECY CONCERNING THE COURSE AND END OF APOSTATE CHRISTENDOM

Just as Scripture distinguishes Christians who are genuinely born again and baptized into the body of Christ from professing Christians who are not saved, so contrasts can be made of the church as the body of Christ and Christendom as a whole. Much can be learned from this contrast which helps one to understand the movements of history, the present age, and the prophetic future. In prophecy the true church, the body of Christ, has a different course than apostate Christendom in both its beginning and its climax.

The concept of a professing church is presented in Matthew 13 as the kingdom of heaven. In seven parables the religious character of the Interadvent Age, that is, the age from the first coming of Christ to the second coming of Christ, is predicted. This age is longer than the period of the true church, the body of Christ, which runs from Pentecost to the Rapture. The professing body pictured in Matthew 13 begins with Christ's public ministry and continues after the Rapture until His second coming.

According to Matthew 13 three particular features are prominent throughout the present age: (1) what is good is represented by the wheat, the meal, the pearl of great value, and the good fish; (2) Israel is represented by the treasure hidden in the field, or hidden in the world; (3) what is evil is represented by the weeds, the birds in the mustard tree, the leaven in the dough, and the bad fish which are thrown away.

Matthew 13 reveals that there will be a mixture of good and bad throughout the entire period with divine activity seen in the sowing of the good seed of the Gospel. The wheat represents those who respond to the sowing of the Gospel and are saved, and the weeds represent those who profess faith without reality. As the professing church increased throughout history, many are represented by the wheat but likewise many are represented by the weeds. In the Middle Ages, when there were so few true Christians, the professing church almost engulfed the body of true believers.

Instead of the present age being one of growing triumph and victory over an evil world as suggested by postmillennialism, both good and evil grow and as the age progresses the professing church is becoming increasingly corrupt, as indicated in many New Testament passages (1 Tim. 4:1; 2 Tim. 3:1-13; 4:3-4; 2 Peter 2–3; Jude 3-19; Rev. 6–18). Christ at His second coming will judge the world that has increasingly rejected the Gospel and whose rejection will climax in Satan's world political system, the ultimate in apostate religion. The proclamation of the Gospel has failed to reach the great majority of the world and because of their exceeding sinfulness Christ will come on them in judgment.

This downward course of evil is illustrated in the image of Daniel 2 which begins with gold and ends with iron mixed with clay. It is reflected also in the four beasts of Daniel 7 with the final empire being the worst by far in cruelty and unbelief. The fourth empire of Daniel 7 ends in a world government dominated by a Satan-empowered world ruler who is utterly evil (Rev. 13).

In Matthew 13 the leaven working in the meal symbolizes the permeating power of certain forms of evil within the church itself. The leaven was forbidden in some of the sacrifices of Israel because leaven symbolized corruption. In Matthew 13 it suggests that corruption works subtly. Though some have said leaven represents the Gospel penetrating the world, the view that it represents evil is far more in keeping with its usage in Scripture where it means formality (Matt. 23:14, 16, 23-28), unbelief (22:23-29), and worldliness (22:16-21; Mark 3:6; 1 Cor. 5:6-8).

The final apostasy is revealed in 2 Thessalonians 2:3 as being brought in by the lawless one who will become the world emperor and the object of worship. The final form of satanic world religions will capture everything evil in all preceding false religions and will be completely blasphemous. The second coming of Christ will be a fitting end to this response to the revelation which God has given in the Bible.

In Scripture Babylon is often used as the ultimate in apostate religion. Babylon of course refers to the empire that conquered Jerusalem in 605 B.C. The final form of religion in the world is also referred to as Babylon in Revelation 17 even though the political power in the end is designated in Daniel 7 as the consummation of the fourth empire, namely, Rome.

In Revelation 17 the great prostitute who is astride the scarlet beast has long been recognized as the symbol of apostate religion. In the Protestant Reformation it was considered a symbol of the Roman Catholic Church in its corruption, a view which has continued until the 20th century. With the rise of the World Council of Churches, which represents a world religion, some evidence leads to the conclusion that the woman represents the future world church rather than specifically the Roman Catholic Church. This world church will apparently include all forms of Christendom, namely the Roman Catholic Church, the Greek Orthodox Church, and Protestantism. As portrayed in Revelation 17 it describes the world church movement as it will appear after the Rapture of the true church. Though in the world church movement today undoubtedly there are some genuine Christians who have been misled into thinking that the goal of Christianity is to achieve a single organization embracing all Christendom, once the Rapture of the church occurs all these beneficial influences will be removed, and those remaining will only be those who are professing Christians but are outside the body of Christ.

The scarlet beast (v. 3) refers to the political power described in Revelation 13. The prophetic period leading up to the second coming of Christ, the seven-year period described in Daniel 9:27, is divided into two halves. The woman representing the professing church in Revelation 17 will be active in the first half of this seven-year period. The world church will cooperate with the political power of the 10 kingdoms to achieve world domination. The woman is dressed in the garb of religion, with purple and scarlet, gold and precious stones and pearls—features that are all too prominent in false religions. Her character is represented in the title written on her forehead, "MYSTERY BABYLON THE GREAT THE MOTHER OF PROSTITUTES AND OF THE ABOMINATIONS OF THE EARTH" (v. 5).

The evil character of the woman is seen in the fact that she will be "drunk with the blood of the saints, the blood of those who bore testimony to Jesus" (v. 6). The scarlet beast is described in verse 8 as "the beast, which you saw, once was, now is not, and will come up out of the Abyss and go to his destruction." The Roman Empire as the beast has ceased to exist as far as the pages of history are concerned but will be revived in the last time to fulfill its role as the political power of the endtime.

Apostate Christendom, represented by the woman, will be destroyed by the 10 kings, the revived Roman Empire, in order to make way for the final form of world religion which will be in power for the last 42 months preceding the second coming of Christ. According to verse 16 the woman is destroyed, and the purpose is "to give the beast their power to rule, until God's words are fulfilled" (v. 17). The woman is further described as "the great city that rules over the kings of the earth" (v. 18).

The apostate religion represented by the beast also permeates Babylon as a city, as described in Revelation 18. Scholars have differed as to whether the reference to Babylon in Revelation 18 refers to false religion symbolically presented as a great city which will be destroyed or whether it represents a literal city which will be made the capital of the world government in the 42 months preceding the second coming of Christ.

In some passages such as Isaiah 13:6-13 Babylon is described as being suddenly destroyed without remedy. Because this was never actually fulfilled in history as a catastrophic event, the conclusion has been reached that Babylon will be rebuilt.

An alternative view is that it refers to Rome which some scholars believe will be the capital city of the final world government. This seems to be supported by the statement that the wicked woman will sit on "seven hills" (Rev. 17:9). However, the text also states that the seven hills represent the seven heads of the beast which refer to seven rulers.

Because there is some uncertainty as to whether the seven hills represent Rome, the concept of Babylon as the capital city has some support. Actually Rome had 10 hills and in the course of its history, though known as the city of seven hills, the same seven hills have not always been in view.

The great earthquake of 16:17-21 will destroy the cities of the Gentiles, and "God remembered Babylon the Great and gave her the cup filled with the wine of the fury of His wrath" (v. 19). This may mean that the great city of Revelation 18 will be destroyed by an earthquake, as part of the final judgment that precedes the second coming of Christ. So, the distinction is sometimes made that Revelation 17 represents Babylon ecclesiastically or religiously and Revelation 18 represents Babylon politically. Though the woman will be destroyed in the middle of that last seven-year period, the city of Babylon represented in Revelation 18 will be destroyed at the end of the seven-year period preceding the second coming of Christ.

Though the significance of the symbolism involved may be debated, the Scriptures are clear that God will judge religion which is mere profession and political power that blasphemously opposes God. The victory will come with the second coming of Christ and the judgment of evil on the earth.

The concept of apostate Christendom beginning before Pentecost and continuing after the Rapture casts light on the characteristics of the interadvent period. While the true church will be raptured before the climax of the judgments preceding the second coming of Christ, the apostate church composed entirely of unbelievers will continue into the endtime and be destroyed just before the Great Tribulation. The final form of apostate religion will be the worship of the world ruler and of Satan in the 42 months preceding the second coming of Christ. Then Babylon in both its political and religious aspects will be judged and destroyed, and the way will be paved for the 1,000-year reign of Christ on earth, a period characterized as one of righteousness and peace.

CHAPTER • 44

PROPHECY CONCERNING THE GREAT TRIBULATION

THE DOCTRINE OF TRIBULATION IN GENERAL

Reference has been made previously to the final time of Tribulation leading up to the second coming of Christ. The seven-year period between the Rapture and the second coming of Christ is often called the Tribulation, but Scripture never uses this precise terminology. In John 16:33 Christ warned His disciples, "In this world you will have trouble [KJV, tribulation]. But take heart! I have overcome the world." Throughout Scripture the people of God have had trouble as illustrated in many chapters in the Old Testament that refer to Israel's troubles. Prophecy indicates there is still trouble ahead for Israel (Jer. 30:7) as well as the church and the world.

In the period between the Rapture and the second coming of Christ three specific time periods can be observed: (1) a time of preparation between the Rapture and the emergence of the ruler of the 10 kingdoms; (2) 42 months of peace for Israel, the first half of the last seven years (Dan. 9:27); (3) the Great Tribulation, the time of unprecedented trouble which will be fulfilled in the 42 months leading up to the second coming of Christ, the last half of the seven-year period marked off by the treaty with Israel. Only the last 42 months of trouble before the Second Coming are called "the Great Tribulation" (Rev. 7:14). Christ referred to this period as the major sign of the second coming of Christ when He predicted, "For then there will be great distress, unequaled from the beginning of the world until now—and never to be equaled again. If those days had not been cut short, no one would survive, but for the sake of the elect those days will be shortened" (Matt. 24:21-22). Daniel also referred to this period as the time of unprecedented distress when he predicted, "There will be a time of distress such as has not happened from the beginning of nations until then" (Dan. 12:1). The Great Tribulation is distinguished from other times of trouble as being without precedent in the extent of its sufferings.

After the Rapture of the church a 10-nation kingdom will emerge. In Daniel 7 these nations are symbolically represented as 10 horns of the fourth beast. Later in the chapter an interpretation of them is given, "The ten horns are ten kings who will come from this kingdom" (v. 24). The 10-horned beast of Revelation 13 is prophetic of the same future alliance of nations. According to Daniel 7:8 another horn will come up among the 10 horns and uproot 3 of the 10. The little horn is later identified as "another king" who will "subdue three kings" (v. 24).

After gaining control of the 10 kingdoms, composed of 10 countries forming a revival of the ancient Roman Empire, the king will attempt to solve the problem of Israel in relation to the other countries of the Middle East. He will impose a peace treaty on Israel (9:27), which will be hailed as a great step forward toward peace (1 Thes. 5:3). Though Scripture does not describe the details of the peace treaty, it obviously is an imposed peace, not a negotiated one; undoubtedly it will fix the boundaries of Israel; it will provide them protection from attack; and it will restore normal trading relations with Israel's neighbors. The period of peace will continue for 42 months.

Scholars differ as to what will cause the abrupt change from the time of peace to the period that follows, but a plausible explanation is that the prophecies of Ezekiel 38–39 will be fulfilled at that time. This unusual prophecy predicts an invasion of Israel from the north by a small group of nations joining with a great army from the "far north" of the Holy Land (38:6). This reference could be to no country other than Russia because this is the only nation that is to the "far north" of Israel.

The prophecy describes a strange war in which there will be no opposing army, but God Himself will interpose with a series of catastrophes including a great earthquake, a plague, a torrent of rain including hailstones, and the showering of the invaders with burning sulfur (vv. 19-22). The result will be that the entire invading force will be wiped out (39:1-4). After the battle it will take Israel seven months just to bury the dead (v. 12).

The destruction of Russia and her supporting countries will undoubtedly bring an imbalance of power in the world. Apparently in that future day there will be a balance between the power of Russia and anti-Russian forces of the world similar to what exists today with neither side able to defeat the other. Then with Russia at least temporarily disabled and its army destroyed, the ruler of the 10 kingdoms, who apparently will rise as leader of the world's anti-Russian forces, will proclaim himself dictator over the whole world. Apparently no one will be strong enough to contend against him, and he will gain control of the entire world without a war (Rev. 13:4). This emergence of a world government will bring an end to the first period of three and one half years and begin the final 42 months leading up to the second coming of Christ (v. 5).

As the dictator of the entire world, the ruler of the 10 kingdoms will assume all the power of his position, ruling over every group of people (v. 7) and demanding that all worship him as god or be killed (vv. 8, 15). He will be supported by another person referred to as "another beast, coming out of the earth" (v. 11). In order to buy or sell everyone will be forced to receive a mark on their right hand or forehead indicating they are worshipers of the beast (vv. 16-17). Because the ruler will persecute anyone who will not worship him, the great catastrophes pictured in Revelation 6–18 will follow.

Many expositors believe that the catastrophes described as seven seals, seven trumpets of angels, and seven bowls of wrath (6:1–8:1; 8:2–9:21; 11:15-19; 16:1-21) will be spread over the entire last seven years before the second coming of Christ. Though this is a common position, there are indications that the Great Tribulation, the second half of the seven-year period, will begin with the opening of the seals. In the first seal a ruler who will conquer the world without a fight is pictured (6:1). In the fourth seal a fourth part of the earth will be killed (vv. 7-8). If any question remains as to whether the world government beginning 42 months before the second coming of Christ was indicated in verse 1 it should be certain that the killing of one fourth of the population (vv. 7-8) will introduce the period commonly described as without precedent. With the present population of the world, this would represent the death of more than 1 billion people.

Even if questions remain concerning the meanings of the symbols in the great catastrophes pictured in Revelation 6–18 obviously great catastrophes will occur on earth including one fourth of the earth killed in 6:8 and one third of the earth remaining in 9:18. Other catastrophes, such as the final great earthquake described in 16:18-21, also will cause great loss of life. This is described as an earthquake so great that the great city, probably a reference to Babylon in Revelation 18, will be "split into three parts" and "the cities of the nations collapsed." This refers to the entire globe except for the nation Israel. The extent of the earthquake is described in 16:20, "Every island fled away and the mountains could not be found." In addition to the earthquake which apparently will shake to pieces all the buildings of the world except those in Israel, there will be a supernatural hailstorm with hailstones weighing "a hundred pounds each" (v. 21). In these terrible disasters 80 to 90 percent of the population of the world will be destroyed before the second coming of Christ.

In addition to the great catastrophes inflicted as judgments of God will be the massacre of those who will not worship the world ruler as god. Only the limitation of the period to 42 months will make it impossible for him to carry out his program completely. Gentile and Jewish survivors will be on earth when Christ returns.

In addition to the detailed prophecies of Revelation the final time of Tribulation is described in many passages of Scripture (Ps. 2; Isa. 24; Jer. 30:7-9; Dan. 9:27; 11:40–12:1, 11; Matt. 24:21-30; Mark 13:24; 1 Thes. 5:1-8; 2 Thes. 2:4; Rev. 3:10).

Other features of the Great Tribulation are also discussed in Scripture. The role of Israel in the Great Tribulation is described in 12:1-6 as a time of trouble from which she should flee. In answering the questions of the disciples about the end of the age, Christ exhorted the Children of Israel to flee to the mountains (Matt. 24:16) when their temple will be desecrated at the beginning of the Great Tribulation. Christ described the Great Tribulation as a time of such distress that if He did not come back in the Second Coming the entire human race would be wiped out (v. 22).

The extent of suffering and death in the Great Tribulation makes the teaching of a posttribulational Rapture untenable because only a few will survive the whole period. The possibility of going through the Great Tribulation and being raptured at the end hardly fulfills the description given in Titus 2:13 of "the blessed hope." The views pertaining to the church in relation to the Great Tribulation will be considered in the next chapter.

CHAPTER • 45

PROPHECY CONCERNING THE CHURCH

The prophetic picture of the church the body of Christ must be distinguished from the future of apostate Christendom. As previously explained, Christendom is seen in Matthew 13 as the entire period between the first coming of Christ and the second coming of Christ. The church on the other hand began on the Day of Pentecost and will be taken to heaven on the day of the Rapture.

Christ predicted the formation of the church in Matthew 16:18, "And I tell you that you are Peter, and on this rock I will build My church, and the gates of hades will not overcome it." In this declaration Christ implied not only that His church was not then in existence but also that He by His own power would construct her and that the gates of hell would never prevail against her. Though assailed by Satan, God's ultimate purpose of presenting the church in perfection and glory will be achieved.

The course of the true church on earth is traced through the Acts and the Epistles and the climax is found in Revelation 2–3 where messages to seven churches in Asia Minor are recorded. The church is not seen in Revelation 4–18 because the church is in heaven during this period. At the second coming of Christ the church will return to earth with Christ to share in the millennial kingdom.

At least seven major features form the theme of prophecy concerning the future experiences of the church. These seven events include (1) the last days of the church in the world, (2) the Rapture of the church including the resurrection of the dead in Christ and the translation of living saints, (3) the Judgment Seat of Christ, (4) the marriage of the Lamb, (5) the return of the church with Christ at His second coming, (6) the reign of the church with Christ in the Millennium, and (7) the church in the New Jerusalem in the eternal state.

THE LAST DAYS OF THE CHURCH IN THE WORLD

The last days of the church in the world relate to the final period of the present age before the Rapture. These should be contrasted to the last days for Israel which refers to the last days of her entire history from Jacob to the end of the Millennium (Num. 24:14; Deut. 31:29; Isa. 2:2; Jer. 23:20; 30:24; 49:39; Ezek. 38:16; Dan. 2:28; 10:14; Hosea 3:5; Micah 4:1). The last days for the church are prophesied in the New Testament (1 Tim. 4:1; 2 Tim. 3:1-8; Heb. 1:1-2; James 5:3; 1 Peter 1:5, 20; 2 Peter 3:1-9; 1 John 2:18; Jude 18). The last days for the church are days of evil and apostasy (2 Tim. 3:1-5), days in which people will depart from true faith (1 Tim. 4:1-2). Apostasy is the main theme of 2 Peter 2–3. Leaders in the apostasy are those who claim to be Christians but actually are unbelievers proclaiming a false gospel. Nothing is more foreign to the prophetic details of the endtime than the postmillennial teaching that the world will get better as a result of preaching the Gospel.

Another expression in contrast to the last days of the church and the last days of Israel is "the time of the end" (Dan. 12:4). This period refers expressly to the last three and one half years leading to the second coming of Christ, the time of the Great Tribulation as referred to by expressions similar to "the time of the end" (8:17-19; 9:26; 11:35, 40, 45; 12:4, 6, 9). The time of the end will begin with the desecration of the temple (Matt. 24:15) and will conclude with the destruction of Gentile power at the time of the second coming of Christ (2 Thes. 2:8; Rev. 19:19-20).

THE DOCTRINE OF RESURRECTION

The Bible includes references to seven people who were restored to life such as the son of the widow (1 Kings 17:22), the son of the Shunammite (2 Kings 4:35), the dead man restored by Elisha (13:21), the resurrection of Jairus' daughter (Matt. 9:25; Mark 5:42), the son of the widow of Nain (Luke 7:15), Lazarus of Bethany (John 11:44), and Dorcas (Acts 9:40). It may be presumed that all these, when raised from the dead, were restored to their former lives and eventually died the second time. An exception to this rule of death and resurrection are Enoch and Elijah (Gen. 5:24; 2 Kings 2:11; Heb. 11:5), who were caught up to heaven without dying.

The Scriptures are clear that all men continue to exist forever whether removed from this life by death or the Rapture (Dan. 12:2; John 5:28-29; Acts 24:15).

One of the erroneous concepts is the teaching that all people will be raised at the same time and then be judged. The Scriptures are clear that while all will be raised, each will be raised in his own order with the various resurrections differing in time and circumstance as well as result. At least seven resurrections to an immortal body are recorded in Scripture.

The first Person to receive a resurrection body that will never die is Jesus Christ. This is referred to frequently in Scripture. The resurrection of Christ is a subject of prophecy (Ps. 16:10; Matt. 16:21; 26:32; Mark 9:9; John 2:19; Acts 26:22-23). His resurrection was announced by angels (Matt. 28:6; Mark 16:6; Luke 24:6), and was accompanied by evidences of its reality (Matt. 27:66; Luke 24:39; John 20:20; Acts 1:3). The Book of Acts presents the resurrection of Christ as a major teaching of the Apostles (2:23-24; 3:14-15; 4:33; 10:39-41; 17:2-3), and in the Epistles the resurrection of Christ is a central theme (Rom. 4:25; 10:9; 1 Cor. 15:4; Eph. 1:20; 1 Thes. 4:14; 2 Tim. 2:8; 1 Peter 1:3, 21).

The many appearances of Christ after His resurrection confirmed the announcement of the angels. Christ appeared to Mary Magdalene (Mark 16:9; John 20:11-18), to other women (Matt. 28:9), to Peter (1 Cor. 15:5), to the two disciples on the road to Emmaus (Luke 24:15), to "the eleven" disciples—only 10 were actually present as Thomas was absent—(Luke 24:36; John 20:19), to the 11 disciples (v. 26), to the disciples at the Sea of Galilee (21:1), to the 500 believers (1 Cor. 15:6), to the 11 disciples in Galilee (Matt. 28:17), to James (1 Cor. 15:7), to His disciples at the time of His ascension (Luke 24:50; Acts 1:3-11), to Stephen (7:55), to Paul (9:5; 1 Cor. 15:8).

Christ was resurrected with a new body that would be immortal, that is, that would never die (Mark 16:14; Luke 24:33-49; John 20:19-23). As such the body of Christ in His resurrection is the pattern that will be followed by all the saved at the time of their resurrections (1 John 3:2).

At the time of the death of Christ an earthquake broke open the tombs of many and the curtain of the temple tore from top to bottom (Matt. 27:51-52). After the resurrection of Christ some in the tombs came out and appeared to many people (vv. 52-53). No other explanation of this resurrection is given. Possibly this was the fulfillment of the type of the firstfruits (Lev. 23:9-14). At the beginning of the harvest season the Israelites took to the priest a sheaf of grain consisting of several stalks in anticipation of the coming full harvest. In harmony with this practice was the fact that when Christ was raised, a token resurrection occurred which anticipated a later harvest of resurrection. The resurrection of Christ and the resurrection of the few saints on the day of His resurrection are two resurrections in the past.

The third resurrection will occur at the Rapture of the church (1 Cor. 15:52; 1 Thes. 4:16). The resurrection of the "dead in Christ" (v. 16) seems to limit this resurrection to those who have been baptized into the body of Christ by the Holy Spirit at the time they became a part of the church (1 Cor. 12:13). Though Old Testament saints were in Christ representatively, they were not a part of His body, the church, and apparently their resurrection will occur later.

In Revelation 11, prior to the seventh trumpet, two witnesses will have three and one half years of prophetic ministry (vv. 3-13). They will be kept alive supernaturally and will prophesy for 1,260 days. At the end of this period God will permit their enemies to kill them, and their bodies will lie in the streets of Jerusalem for three and one half days. They will then be raised from the dead and ascend to heaven (vv. 7-12). It may be debated whether their three and one half year period of prophecy is the first half or the second half of the last seven years leading up to the second coming of Christ, but the context seems to point to the Great Tribulation before the seven bowls of the wrath of God (Rev. 16) will be poured out in rapid succession immediately before the second coming of Christ.

These first four resurrections will be followed by two resurrections of the righteous. According to 20:4 the believers who will be martyred in the Tribulation will be given a special resurrection, "And I saw the souls of those who had been beheaded because of their testimony for Jesus and because of the word of God. They had not worshiped the beast or his image and had not received his mark on their foreheads or their hands. They came to life and reigned with Christ a thousand years." The fact that this resurrection will be limited to those who came out of the Tribulation is another indirect confirmation that the church will have already been raptured prior to the endtime.

Though it has been commonly believed that Old Testament saints will be resurrected at the Rapture, there is indication that instead their resurrection will occur at the time of the second coming either immediately before or immediately after the resurrection of the Tribulation saints. According to Isaiah 26:19 the resurrection of the Old Testament saints will occur after the time of Tribulation, "But your dead will live; their bodies will rise. You who dwell in the dust, wake up and shout for joy. Your dew is like the dew of the morning; the earth will give birth to her dead." The verses immediately before that verse (vv. 16-18) are among the few references to the resurrection of the dead in the Old Testament. Daniel declared, "Multitudes who sleep in the dust of the earth will awake: some to everlasting life, others to shame and everlasting contempt" (12:2). The context preceding this reference in 11:36-45 deals with the Great Tribulation, and 12:1 indicates that the resurrection will be the close of that time period.

Though verse 2 speaks of the resurrection of both the saints and the unsaved, Daniel made a clear distinction between the two resurrections—a resurrection of "some to everlasting life" and a resurrection of "others to shame and everlasting contempt." Revelation 20:4-6 places the millennial kingdom between the resurrection of the Old Testament and the Tribulation saints and the resurrection of the wicked dead. Thus the resurrection of the wicked 1,000 years after the Second Coming is another indication that the millennial kingdom will follow the second coming of Christ.

The seventh and final resurrection is detailed by John in verses 11-15. The resurrection of the wicked will occur 1,000 years after the second coming of Christ and will include all those whose names are not written in "the Book of Life" (v. 15). The awful fact is that the resurrection of the wicked will result in their receiving a body that is still wicked and subject to existing forever in the lake of burning sulfur. The beast and the false prophet, who will be cast into the lake of burning sulfur at the beginning of the Millennium (19:20), will still be there 1,000 years later when the devil and the fallen angels join them (20:10).

These seven resurrections, beginning with the resurrection of Christ and ending with the resurrection of the wicked, repudiate the concept that all will be raised and judged at the same time. Though all will be judged, as the Scriptures state (Heb. 9:27), the judgments will occur at different times and under different circumstances according to those being judged.

THE TIME OF THE RAPTURE OF THE CHURCH

A very important item in the prophetic future is the question of when the Rapture of the church will take place. Liberal theologians have omitted this doctrine almost entirely by their rejection of some of the literal aspects of resurrection and judgment. Among premillenarians, however, at least four views have been advanced: (1) the pretribulation Rapture, (2) the midtribulation Rapture, (3) the partial Rapture, and (4) the posttribulation Rapture. The problem of determining which is the correct interpretation of Scripture involves a comprehensive review of the doctrine of the church as a distinct body of saints and the consideration of various New Testament Scriptures. In the 20th century a number of comprehensive treatments of the pretribulational Rapture and of the posttribulational Rapture have been written.

The posttribulational Rapture has been the view of the majority of the professing church. Included among its advocates are those who are amillennial, that is, those who deny a literal 1,000 year reign of Christ on earth, and postmillenarians who merge the Rapture and the second coming of Christ into one event at the end of the millennial kingdom. Some premillenarians have adopted the midtribulational view that the church is raptured in the middle of the last seven years before the second coming of Christ. A few have advocated the partial Rapture view that saints will be raptured at various times before the Second Coming according to their spiritual preparation. All liberal interpretations of Scripture and some premillenarians support one of the three views other than pretribulationalism.

The pretribulational Rapture as a doctrine of Scripture is held only by premillenarians. Because premillenarianism is in itself a minority view of the church and belief in the pretribulational Rapture is held only by some who are premillennial, it becomes clear that the doctrine of the pretribulation Rapture is also a minority view. Under these circumstances the question can be raised whether there is biblical support for this view.

Arguments for pretribulationalism are based on two important premises: (1) definition of the church as a group of saints distinct from the saints either before or after the present age; (2) the doctrine of a literal period of unprecedented trouble in the world between the Rapture and the second coming of Christ, a period of more than seven years, closing with the three and one half years of the Great Tribulation. Attention to these premises has already been given in the discussion of ecclesiology and of prophecies concerning the Great Tribulation.

Until A.D. 190 the early church fathers were almost unanimous in holding to the premillennial interpretation of Scripture. They were confused by the fact that the Bible affirms that major events will take place before the Second Coming such as the appearance of the Antichrist and a single worldwide government. On the other hand they recognized the teaching of the Scriptures that the coming of Christ for the church is imminent. The early church fathers accordingly were confused and often they spoke of the Rapture as imminent and then later affirmed that some event must take place first which would deny its imminency. The doctrine of the Rapture as a separate teaching was not clarified in the early centuries of the church and was obscured completely as the amillennial view became dominant in the second, third, and fourth centuries and became the majority view of the church. In a climate where premillennialism itself was being attacked and discredited there was no proper basis for considering such a doctrine as the pretribulation Rapture.

With the Protestant Reformation building its eschatology largely on Augustine, who embraced a nonliteral interpretation of prophecy, little attention was paid then to the doctrine of the Rapture. However, one of the central doctrines of the Reformation that every believer may be his own interpreter of Scripture provided a basis for future Bible study which eventually reconsidered the whole question of the Millennium, the Rapture, and the second coming of Christ.

Church doctrine for many centuries also confused Israel and the church. Under these conditions there were insufficient grounds for reconsideration of a pretribulation Rapture as Israel is plainly mentioned in the Bible as existing in the Great Tribulation. With the rise of the Bible study movement, especially as it related to the Plymouth Brethren who separated the program of God for the church from that for Israel, clarification of the issues resulted in reconsideration of the place of the Rapture in the prophetic program of God.

Like many other major doctrines of Scripture which took centuries to clarify, the doctrine of pretribulationism has slowly been clarified. For the last century prophecy has been an area of concentrated study with the result that the issues involved have been greatly clarified.

The events of the 20th century have tended to support a more literal interpretation of prophecy. Postmillennialism, with its vain hope of a future kingdom on earth before the second coming of Christ, was crushed by World Wars I and II. Though there are current attempts to revive this doctrine, there is no theological school or Protestant denomination that embraces this concept. Accordingly the study is reduced to the question of whether the Bible teaches that the Rapture will occur before a literal Tribulation period or whether it teaches that the Rapture will be merged with the second coming of Christ.

The major arguments in the controversy between pretribulationalism and posttribulationalism involve a number of important issues.

Prominent in the discussions by posttribulationalists is the argument that posttribulationalism is an old doctrine extending from the first century until now. However, Paul labeled posttribulationalism a false doctrine in 2 Thessalonians 2. The Thessalonians had been informed by false teachers that they were already in the Day of the Lord or in the Tribulation. But Paul stated that they were not in the time of Tribulation and that in fact they would not enter this period.

In 1 Thessalonians 5:9 Paul had written, "For God did not appoint us to suffer wrath but to receive salvation through our Lord Jesus Christ." In 2 Thessalonians 2:7 he wrote that the coming of the man of lawlessness will not occur until after what is holding back or restraining sin "is taken out of the way." Though scholars differ on the identity of the restrainer, the major restraining force in the world today is the church indwelt by the Holy Spirit. The removal of what is restraining could only be accomplished by the Rapture. Though it is true that posttribulationalism is ancient, it is also true that Scripture labels it a false teaching.

The principles of interpretation or hermeneutics play an important part in the doctrine of the pretribulational Rapture. Those who spiritualize prophecy including the time of Tribulation have assumed a point of view that makes impossible a pretribulation Rapture. Only those who are willing to accept prophecy as literal and who distinguish God's program for Israel from His program for the church are in a position to consider a pretribulational Rapture.

The nature of the Tribulation period is an important facet in pretribulationalism. In the last 25 years there has been a remarkable turn to a more literal view of the Tribulation period which is the entire period of more than seven years between the Rapture and Christ's second coming. Whereas a generation ago practically all posttribulationalists spiritualized the Tribulation as a long period of time being fulfilled by the church in the present age, some now hold that the Tribulation will be a literal period of seven years in length preceding the Second Coming. By this change they have moved closer to the pretribulational point of view in their premises and have made their own task more difficult. If the church has to go through the Great Tribulation and be decimated by the catastrophes and judgments that occur, with only a fraction of the world's population surviving, it is difficult to support the concept that the believer's hope of the Rapture at the end of the Tribulation is a "blessed hope" (Titus 2:13). The hope of survival through the Great Tribulation is hardly a comforting hope or one that is imminent. Such a view makes Paul's comforting message to the Thessalonians (1 Thes. 4:13-18) incredible because they would not see their loved ones until after the Tribulation. If the Tribulation is literal the pretribulationalists have by far the better explanation of the blessed hope extended to the church.

As previously stated, the concept of the church as a program separate from God's program for Israel is another factor essential to the pretribulational view. So long as the church and Israel are not kept distinct, it is impossible to establish a pretribulational Rapture for the church because Israel will clearly be in the Great Tribulation (Rev. 7). However, not all who are opposed to pretribulationalism confuse Israel and the church because such a view occasions the serious problems of applying both the Old Testament curses on Israel and the promises of blessings to the church. Of the hundreds of occurrences of the word "Israel" in Scripture only a few are even in doubt as to the intention of the title. Increasingly scholars who are amillennial or posttribulational recognize that the church and Israel are not synonymous.

The doctrine of imminency is another area of discussion related to the Rapture question. Every passage referring to the Rapture speaks of it as an imminent event, an event that could occur at any moment, in contrast to the passages referring to the Second Coming which speak of numerous events that will precede it (Matt. 24:15-30;

Rev. 6–18). Exhortations relating to the Rapture lose most of their significance if the Rapture is not imminent.

As previously mentioned, the presence of the Holy Spirit indwelling the church beginning on the Day of Pentecost is another important area of study relative to the pretribulation Rapture. If what is restraining sin (2 Thes. 2:7) is the church indwelt by the Holy Spirit and this has to be removed before the events of the Day of the Lord can take place, then a pretribulational Rapture must occur before the man of lawlessness will be revealed (vv. 7-8).

Various other Scriptures indicate that an interval will occur between the Rapture and the Second Coming. The Judgment Seat of Christ (2 Cor. 5:10) seems to take place in heaven rather than on earth and is not related to any of the events that will occur at the time of the Second Coming. Though several judgments are indicated at the time of the Second Coming, no reference is made to the church being judged at that time.

If the 24 elders of Revelation 4–5 represent the church as judged and glorified, a pretribulational Rapture is required because these two chapters relate to the period before the Second Coming. The elders' crowns will be crowns of reward. The wedding feast announced in Revelation 19:7-10 implies that the Groom has already come for His bride, because the feast is the final stage in the oriental order of marriage.

Survivors of the Tribulation will be in their natural bodies and in the Millennium will carry on normal activities (Isa. 65:20-25). If all the Tribulation saints were raptured at the time of the Second Coming, there would be no one to occupy the earth and fulfill these prophecies in the Millennium.

Another significant passage is Matthew 25:31-46, which describes a judgment following Christ's second coming and the establishing of His throne on earth. At that time the sheep, representing the saved, will be separated from the goats, representing the unsaved. If a Rapture had taken place in connection with Christ's coming from heaven to earth, this separation of believers from unbelievers would have already taken place before Christ arrived on earth and this judgment of the Gentiles would be unnecessary. Also the judgment of Israel (Ezek. 20:34-38), to occur soon after the Second Coming, will be unnecessary if the saved in Israel were already separated from the unsaved by the Rapture of the church.

Many contrasts exist between the Rapture and the Second Coming. At the Rapture, saints will meet Christ in the air. At the Second Coming, Christ will meet the Tribulation saints on earth. At the time of the Rapture the Mount of Olives will remain unchanged. When the second coming of Christ occurs a valley will appear between the north and south sections of the mount (Zech. 14:4-5). There is no record of any saints being translated and given immortal bodies at the time of the second coming of Christ. It would be amazing if such a major event as the Rapture would not be included in the detailed account of the Second Coming of Revelation 19. The Rapture is a movement of saints from earth to heaven as Christ promised (John 14:2-3). At the Second Coming the movement of saints will be from heaven to earth in a grand procession totally different from that of the Rapture (Rev. 19:11-21).

At the Rapture the world will not be judged, but at the Second Coming all mankind will be judged. The Rapture by its nature is an imminent event that occurs quickly (1 Cor. 15:51-53) in contrast to the Second Coming which will involve a series of events that will take many hours (Rev. 19). The Rapture concerns only the saved, in contrast to the Second Coming which will involve the judgment of both the saved and the lost. Scripture does not indicate that any change in Satan occurs at the Rapture, but at the Second Coming Satan will be bound for 1,000 years.

Many signs of the Second Coming are yet to be fulfilled, but none of these signs relate to the Rapture. Significantly in many passages dealing with the resurrection of saints the only one in which living saints will be translated is the Rapture of the church. Though the many reasons for a pretribulational Rapture require a separate treatment of greater length, a summary of major arguments indicates that there is a sound scriptural basis for the doctrine.

In refuting pretribulationalism, posttribulationalists almost universally refer to Matthew 24:40-41, which clearly relates to the second coming of Christ. At that time according to these verses, "Two men will be in the field; one will be taken and the other left. Two women will be grinding with a hand mill; one will be taken and the other left." Posttribulationists agree that this refers to the Rapture at the second coming of Christ.

As this is the only positive text posttribulationists offer it assumes major interest. In the context, however, the illustration of Noah and the ark is mentioned, and those outside the ark "knew nothing about what would happen until the Flood came and took them all away.

That is how it will be at the coming of the Son of man" (Matt. 24:39). Posttribulationalists hold that the one taken away is raptured. The problem for posttribulationalists is that in the Flood the ones taken away were the unsaved who were drowned. The fact is the one not taken away is saved just as it was in the time of Noah, and there is no rapture of the saved in Matthew.

If there is any doubt on this, the parallel passage in Luke 17:34-37 makes it clear. Luke states that one will be taken and the other will be left. When the disciples asked, "Where Lord?" He replied, "Where there is a dead body, there the vultures will gather." In other words the one who will be taken will be dead and his body will be eaten by the vultures. So the only text advanced by posttribulationalism as directly teaching the concept of a posttribulational Rapture actually states exactly the opposite point of view. This leads to the conclusion that there is no passage in Scripture that specifically states that the Rapture will occur after the Tribulation in connection with the second coming of Christ to the earth.

THE JUDGMENT SEAT OF CHRIST

In keeping with the fact that judgment follows resurrection, the Scriptures indicate that the church will experience a special judgment in heaven following the Rapture. The central passage on this doctrine is 2 Corinthians 5:10, "For we must all appear before the Judgment Seat of Christ, that each one may receive what is due him for the things done while in the body, whether good or bad."

Is this a judgment on sin? The Roman Catholic Church teaches the doctrine of purgatory, the necessity of further cleansing from sin after death before one can enter heaven. Protestants have generally held to the doctrine of justification by faith, the teaching that all who are saved are completely justified and declared righteous by God. The present position of the church before God is seen as being in the person and work of Christ. Believers are therefore perfect positionally in contrast to their spiritual state in which they still experience sin and temptation.

At the Judgment Seat of Christ sin will not be the subject of consideration. At that time believers will be perfect, with no sin nature, and will never sin again in thought, word, or deed. Therefore any concept of discipline because of previous sins is unnecessary and would be unfruitful. The question of their righteousness before God was settled when they were justified by faith. The Judgment Seat of Christ deals with works, not with sin. Believers will be judged on whether their works were good (worth something) or whether they were bad (worthless), as stated in verse 10.

Paul used several illustrations in speaking of the believers' judgment at the Judgment Seat of Christ. In 1 Corinthians 3:11-16 he wrote about constructing a building with Christ as the foundation and believers using either gold, silver, and costly stones, or wood, hay, and straw. The "building" will be tested by fire and the wood, hay, and straw—worthless works—will be reduced to ashes whereas the gold, silver, and costly stones—worthy works—will remain. Gold may be typical of anything that glorifies God. Silver seems to represent redemption and may speak of soul-winning. Costly stones represent all the other things that believers can do, even simple and humble tasks that may reflect the glory of God. According to 4:5 every Christian will apparently receive some reward, "Therefore judge nothing before the appointed time; wait till the Lord comes. He will bring to light what is hidden in darkness and will expose the motives of men's hearts. At that time each will receive his praise from God."

A second illustration is found in 9:24-27. Here Paul used the figure of a race. Believers are urged to run the race of life and lay aside anything that would hinder their receiving "a crown that will last forever" (v. 25).

A third illustration, found in Romans 14:10-12, pertains to a trusteeship or stewardship. Christians are exhorted not to belittle or judge their fellow Christians because the matter of evaluation of their lives is God's doing. The fact is each Christian will give account of himself to God as stated in verse 12, "So then, each of us will give an account of himself to God." This judgment is not a comparative one in which one Christian will be compared to another. It relates instead to the gifts and opportunities God has given each Christian. Every Christian has equal opportunity for reward for the judgment will be based not on what others have done but on what he himself has done as God's steward. It is most encouraging for those who labor obscurely and in minor roles in the church to know that their opportunity for service and reward is the same as those who are prominent and successful. Every Christian at the Judgment Seat of Christ will be saved (1 Cor. 3:15), but his reward will be determined on the quality of his life.

THE MARRIAGE OF THE LAMB

Marriage is used in Scripture to depict the relationship between Christ and the church. According to 2 Corinthians 11:2 the church is a bride waiting for the coming of Christ, her Bridegroom.

In Bible times a wedding had three steps. The first stage was reached when the parents of the bridegroom gave a dowry to the bride's parents. The second stage would usually follow a year later, when the groom and his male friends went in procession at midnight from his home to the bride's home. The bride would be waiting there with her friends and then they would join the procession, returning to the home of the groom. The third stage was the wedding feast illustrated at the wedding of Cana in John 2:1-11. The feast might extend for days, depending on the wealth of the people involved.

The church is already married to Christ. From the time when a person is saved, Christ Himself paid the "dowry" in His sacrifice on the cross. The coming of the Bridegroom for His bride will occur at the Rapture of the church, and the wedding feast will follow. When used as an illustration in Scripture weddings normally are seen as occurring on earth as in Matthew 22:1-14. In Revelation 19:9 the wedding feast is announced in connection with the second coming of Christ. This may suggest that the feast had not yet occurred. Though not stated explicitly in Scripture, the wedding feast may be fulfilled in the early years of the millennial reign of Christ in which millions of saints will attend Christ and the church as His bride. Though the first two stages of the marriage are relatively literal, it is obvious that the marriage feast embracing millions of people has to be taken in a more symbolic way. The distinction between the church and angels and the saints of other ages is preserved in this illustration.

THE RETURN OF THE CHURCH WITH CHRIST

The church, which will be caught up in the Rapture to heaven, will return with Christ in His second coming to the earth when He will establish His millennial kingdom. Paul wrote of the church in Colossians 3:4, "When Christ, who is your life, appears, then you also will appear with Him in glory." The church, having been glorified at the Rapture, will appear at the Second Coming as glorified saints accompanying the glorified Saviour. Reference to this event is found in other passages also (1 Thes. 3:13; Jude 14; Rev. 19:8, 14). The church will be a part of that grand procession which may require many hours for all church believers to come from heaven to the earth (vv. 11-21) with the destination being the Mount of Olives for all church believers (Zech. 14:4). Following this return stupendous events of judgment and reward will occur. Members of the church will experience the promise given in 2 Timothy 2:12 that they will "reign with Him." As the bride and wife of Christ, the church will be fittingly honored in the millennial kingdom and throughout eternity.

The figure of marriage is also used, however, of Israel which is regarded as an unfaithful wife who will be restored to her husband (Hosea 2:14-23). The Tribulation saints who are resurrected at the time of the Second Coming will likewise reign with Christ (Rev. 20:4-6). The distinctions between these groups of individuals will continue for all eternity. And yet all will be the people of God, including all those who are redeemed by faith in Him. Though there is similarity in the rewards of various groups of saints, the recipients will still be distinct. The church will be like a bride claimed by her bridegroom. Israel will be like the estranged wife of the Lord who will be restored. The Tribulation saints will share with the church the role of priesthood in which Christ will be their High Priest (v. 6).

THE CHURCH IN THE NEW JERUSALEM

Just as the church will be with Christ throughout His millennial reign, so the church will also have her place in the New Jerusalem in the eternal state. The saints of all ages will be there along with the holy angels and the glorious presence of God Himself. In the New Jerusalem, however, the individuality of individuals and groups will again be observed with Israel being treated as Israel, the church as the church, and others as "the spirits of righteous men made perfect" (Heb. 12:23). The presence of Israel in the New Jerusalem is seen in the fact that the names of the 12 tribes are inscribed on the 12 gates (Rev. 21:12). The fact that the church is in the New Jerusalem is indicated in Hebrews 12:23 where "the church of the firstborn" is said to be in the heavenly city. When prophecy is taken as a whole, it presents a marvelous picture of God's plans for the future in which every child of God will participate. This great sequence of events will begin for the church when in the Rapture Christ comes for His own.

CHAPTER • 46

PREDICTED EVENTS IN THEIR ORDER

Because the details of prophecy are somewhat complicated, a statement of predicted events in their order provides an organizing principle that can cast light on biblical prophecy.

THE PREDICTION OF DEATH FOR DISOBEDIENCE

The first prophecy in Scripture relates to the warning God gave to Adam and Eve concerning the tree of the knowledge of good and evil.

God declared, "You must not eat from the tree of the knowledge of good and evil, for when you eat of it you will surely die" (Gen. 2:17). This prophecy was tragically fulfilled when Adam and Eve partook of the tree of the knowledge of good and evil and experienced spiritual death, and the beginning of physical death.

THE PROPHECIES OF THE RESULTS OF SIN

Prophecies of the results of Adam and Eve's sin include physical death for them and the curse of sin in relation to them and the serpent (Gen. 3:14-19).

To Adam and Eve the promise of coming salvation in Christ was given in the statement to the serpent, "He will crush your head, and you will strike His heel" (v. 15). This is the first announcement of the death of Christ that would provide salvation and victory over Satan. It would be a fatal blow to Satan, but in return the Saviour would be crucified and saints would be saved.

THE CURSE ON CAIN

Because Cain murdered his brother Abel, God pronounced a curse on the ground and predicted that Cain would be a wanderer though God would protect him from physical death (4:8-16). Cain murdered Abel because God accepted Abel's sacrifice, and not Cain's.

THE PREDICTION OF THE FLOOD

Because of the wickedness of men, God determined to wipe out the human race except for Noah and his family (6:5-7). This prophecy was fulfilled 120 years after it was given (v. 3).

THE PREDICTION THAT THE FLOOD WILL NEVER BE REPEATED

The promise of God never again to destroy the earth by water (8:21) has been kept. The final judgment will destroy the earth by fire (2 Peter 3:5-7).

NOAH'S PREDICTION ABOUT HIS SONS

In the prediction concerning Noah's sons, Canaan was cursed, Japheth was promised a large number of descendants, and Shem was given a special blessing from God (Gen. 9:24-27).

THE ABRAHAMIC COVENANT

In the Abrahamic Covenant God promised that Abram's name would be great, that a great nation would come from him under God's blessing, and that Abraham in turn would be a blessing to all peoples of the earth (12:1-3). Those who bless Abram's posterity will be blessed, and those who curse Abram's posterity will be cursed. The promise was confirmed and enlarged in verse 7 when Abram's descendants were given title to the Promised Land. Abraham's descendants have not yet taken possession of their land.

ISRAEL'S BONDAGE IN EGYPT

In connection with the confirmation of the Abrahamic Covenant, Abraham was told that his descendants would to go a strange land, be enslaved and mistreated, and after hundreds of years come back with great possessions (15:13-16).

THE ABRAHAMIC PROMISE GIVEN TO JACOB AND HIS SONS AND NOT TO ESAU

As Jacob was traveling to Paddan Aram to secure a wife, God revealed that the Abrahamic promise would be fulfilled through his descendants and not through Esau (28:10-15) or Ishmael (26:2-6). The details of the covenant were reiterated, namely, that he would have many descendants, that God would give them the holy land, that all people on earth would be blessed through him and his offspring, and that God would watch over him and bring him back to the land.

THE PROMISE OF THE LAND TO ISRAEL

As anticipated in the promise given to Abraham (15:13-14), the people of Israel returned to the land as recorded in Exodus and for the first time possessed a substantial portion of it (Deut. 4:14-24; 31:19-23; Josh. 1:2-5; 21:43). Though the statement is made that "the LORD gave Israel all the land He had sworn to give their forefathers, and they took possession of it and settled there" (v. 43), actually they were given only the land that they claimed, that is, "every place where you set your foot" (1:3). The possession of all the land is still future as indicated in 23:5, 13. This is an important factor because Israel has never possessed the total land and will not do so until after the second coming of Christ.

ISRAEL'S CAPTIVITIES

Three dispossessions of the land were foretold for Israel: (a) the Egyptian bondage (Gen. 15:13-14), (b) the Assyrian and Babylonian captivities (Jer. 25:11-12), and (c) the final scattering among the nations (Deut. 28:63-68; cf. 30:1-3; Lev. 26:3-46; Neh. 1:8; Ps. 106:1-48; Jer. 9:16; 18:15-17; Ezek. 12:14-15; 20:23; 22:15; James 1:1).

JUDGMENTS TO FALL ON THE NATIONS SURROUNDING ISRAEL

Along with the prophecies about Israel in the Old Testament are the prophecies about the Gentile nations whom God would use to chastise Israel because of her sins. According to Luke 21:24, "Jerusalem will be trampled on by the Gentiles until the times of the Gentiles are fulfilled." From 605 B.C., when Jerusalem fell to Nebuchadnezzar, to the second coming of Christ the times of the Gentiles will dominate history. Though Israel has possessed Jerusalem temporarily at various times during this period, they will not be free from Gentile oppression until the second coming of Christ.

Many judgments are prophesied to fall on the nations: (a) Babylon (Isa. 13; 14:18-27; Jer. 50–51); (b) Moab (Isa. 15–16; Jer. 48); (c) Damascus (Isa. 17; Jer. 49:23-27); (d) Egypt (Isa. 19; Jer. 46:2-28); (e) Tyre (Isa. 23; Ezek. 27); (f) Ammon (Jer. 49:1-6); (g) Edom (Isa. 21:11-12; Jer. 49:7-22; Ezek. 35; Obad. 1-16); (h) Elam (Jer. 49:34-39). Though God used these nations to discipline Israel, His judgment always fell on them for their wickedness.

ISRAEL'S RETURN TO THE LAND AFTER THE CAPTIVITIES

Though only a portion of Israel returned to the land after the captivities, they did not possess all the land as described in Ezra and Nehemiah. Her third and final restoration will not come until after Israel is scattered all over the world (Deut. 28:63-68; Jer. 23:5-8).

THE MINISTRY OF JOHN THE BAPTIST

To John the Baptist was given the great privilege of being the forerunner of Jesus Christ. His message and ministry prepared the way for the coming of Israel's Messiah. Though Christ was crucified and

John himself was executed, John's ministry was unique and one of high privilege (Isa. 40:3-5; Mal. 4:5-6; cf. Luke 1:5-25, 57-66).

THE BIRTH OF CHRIST

Many predictions of the coming of Christ are those that relate to His birth (Gen. 3:15; Isa. 7:14; 9:6; Micah 5:2; Luke 1:31-35).

THE OFFICES OF CHRIST

Old Testament prophecies anticipate Christ's offices.

1. As a Prophet. His coming as a Prophet is anticipated in Deuteronomy 18:15-19. His prophetic ministry included both forth-telling, or delivering a message from God, as well as foretelling, or issuing prophetic statements (cf. John 1:1-2, 21, 45; 6:14; 7:16; 8:28; 12:49-50; 14:10, 24; 17:8; Acts 3:22-23; 7:37). Most major discourses are prophecies concerning the future (Matt. 5–7; 13; 24–25; Mark 4:1-20; 13:1-2; Luke 6:20-49; 8:4-15; 21:5-6; John 13–17).
2. As a Priest. Christ fulfilled what was anticipated in both the priesthood of Aaron and the priesthood of Melchizedek (Ps. 110:4; Zech. 6:12-13; Heb. 5:1-10; 7; 8:1-5; 9:11-28; 10:1-18; 13:20).
3. As a King. Christ fulfilled the promises given to David about a Descendant who would reign on his throne forever (2 Sam. 7:16; Pss. 2:6-10; 72:1-19; Isa. 9:6-7; Zech. 9:9; Matt. 21:1-9; 27:11; Luke 1:32-33).

THE MINISTRIES OF CHRIST ON EARTH

In addition to the ministries performed through the three offices of Christ, the Old Testament also predicted the miracles of Christ and His many ministries to those in need (Isa. 35:5-6; 49:1-7; 61:1-3).

THE DEATH OF CHRIST

The offerings performed by the priests under the Law of Moses anticipated in type the death of Christ as the sacrifice for the whole world. The death of Christ was directly predicted in the Old Testament (Ps. 22:1-21; Isa. 52:13–53:12). Christ Himself prophesied His own death (Matt. 16:21; Mark 8:31; Luke 9:22; 18:31-34; John 12:32-33).

THE BURIAL OF CHRIST

The burial of Christ was predicted (Isa. 53:9; cf. Matt. 27:57-60). In the offering of the scapegoat (Lev. 16:10) the burial of Christ was foreshadowed. As an emphasis on the finished work of Christ, His burial is mentioned in the New Testament as part of the Gospel (1 Cor. 15:1-4) and as essential for the sanctification of the believer (Rom. 6:1-10).

THE RESURRECTION OF CHRIST

The resurrection of Christ was anticipated in every prophecy of His ministry following His death and especially in His reigning on earth in the future kingdom. Many types and predictions anticipated the resurrection of Christ (cf. Lev. 14:4-7; Ps. 16:8-11 [cf. Acts 2:25-31]; Ps. 22:22 [cf. Heb. 2:12]; Ps. 118:22-24 [cf. Acts 4:10-11]). Christ prophesied His own resurrection frequently in the Gospels (Matt. 12:38-40; 16:21; 17:9, 23; 27:63; Mark 8:31; 9:9, 31; 10:34; 14:58; Luke 9:22; 18:33; John 2:19-22).

THE ASCENSION OF CHRIST

Christ referred to His own ascension in talking to Mary Magdalene (John 20:17). His ascension is implied in Psalm 24. In offering the wave sheaf offering (Lev. 23:9-12) both His resurrection and ascension were anticipated. Resurrected and ascended into heaven, Christ is the Firstfruits of all believers who will be resurrected and like Him will appear in heaven in glorified bodies. The waving of the representative sheaf of grain was "on the day after the Sabbath" (v. 11), that is, the Resurrection Day or the first day of the week. Often in the Gospel of John, Jesus said He came from the Father and would return to Him.

THE INTERADVENT AGE

Though in general the present age, in which God is calling out the church, is not the subject of Old Testament prophecy, there are some anticipations of the longer period that extends from the first coming of Christ to His second coming. In the Old Testament, prophecies about this period of time relate primarily to events preceding the Second Coming, including the last seven years leading up to the second coming of Christ (Dan. 9:27), the time of peace related to the first half of the last seven years (Ezek. 38:11, 14; 1 Thes. 5:3), and the Great Tribulation which will close the Interadvent Age (Dan. 9:27; 11:40-45; 12:1, 7, 11-12).

The present age is prophesied in detail in Matthew 13 as a period in which good and evil mature side by side (vv. 1-9, 18-23, 24-30). The sphere of profession will be greatly expanded in the professing church (vv. 31-33). The separation of the good and evil is prophesied as occurring at the second coming of Christ (vv. 37-43). During the present age Israel will be hidden as a treasure in a field (v. 44), and the true church, represented by the pearl of great value, is a central feature of the period (v. 45). The sphere of profession will come into judgment at the second coming of Christ as illustrated in the net with good and bad fish (vv. 47-51).

Further details are given concerning the present age in 24:4-27; Galatians 1:4; and 2 Timothy 4:10. The Interadvent Age will be especially significant to Jews (Matt. 23:37-39; Rom. 11:20; James 1:1), Gentiles (Luke 21:24), and the church (Matt. 16:18; Acts 15:13-14; Rom. 11:25). The Upper Room Discourse (John 13–17) specifically dealt with the Church Age from Pentecost to the Rapture. The Interadvent Age is the period from before the introduction of the church on the Day of Pentecost to the second coming of Christ.

THE DAY OF PENTECOST

Pentecost is anticipated typically in the wave loaves of Leviticus 23:15-21. Two loaves were presented by the priest as a wave offering to the Lord 50 days after the offering of the wave sheaf in the firstfruits offering (23:9-14). This corresponds to the precise period of time from the resurrection of Christ, the Firstfruits (1 Cor. 15:20), to the Day of Pentecost.

Jewish and Gentile believers, represented by the two loaves, are united into one body by the baptism of the Holy Spirit (12:13). The leaven which was included in the loaves speaks of the imperfection of believers who form the body of Christ.

THE CHURCH

Many details about the church, including her beginning, character, course, and final days on the earth are given in the New Testament. Christ's specific prophecy about the beginning of the church is recorded in Matthew 16:18, "And I tell you that you are Peter, and on this rock I will build My church, and the gates of hades will not overcome it."

The Upper Room Discourse (John 13–17) anticipates many details relating to the unusual character of the church. These include her Rapture (14:3), her new privileges in prayer (vv. 13-14), the promise of the indwelling Holy Spirit (vv. 15-17), the indwelling of the church in Christ and Christ's indwelling in them (v. 20), the Holy Spirit teaching them the truth (vv. 25-26), Christ's bestowal of peace (v. 27), the church as the branch of the vine (15:1-14), Christ's appointment to them to bear fruit with assurance of answered prayer (vv. 15-16), the command for Christians to love each other (v. 17), the warning about coming persecution of believers (vv. 18-25; 16:1-4), the prediction of the Spirit's work in convicting sinners of sin, righteousness, and judgment (vv. 7-11), the additional promise that the Spirit of Truth would guide believers into all truth (vv. 12-14). Christ's Upper Room Discourse also includes His prediction of their abandonment of Him when He was arrested (v. 32), and His High Priestly Prayer for His disciples, their protection in the world, and their sanctification, prayer for those who are yet to believe, the prayer for unity of believers, and the prayer that they be with Christ in glory.

THE DESTRUCTION OF JERUSALEM

Christ predicted the destruction of Jerusalem, which was fulfilled in A.D. 70 (Matt. 24:2; Mark 13:1-2; Luke 21:20-24).

THE LAST DAYS FOR THE CHURCH

The last days for the church are to be distinguished from the last days of Israel because they relate to the church in the period leading up to the Rapture (1 Tim. 4:1-3; 2 Tim. 3:1-5; James 5:1-10; 2 Peter 2:1-22; 3:3-10; Jude 1-25; Rev. 3:14-20).

The last days for the church, the body of Christ, will culminate in the Rapture which will begin the Day of the Lord. The professing church composed of those not saved at the time of the Rapture will continue into the seven-year period that will precede the second coming of Christ.

THE RESURRECTIONS

Though a number of restorations to life of those who had died are found in the Old and New Testaments, the first to receive an immortal body was Jesus Christ in His resurrection. On the day of His resurrection there also was a token resurrection of a few saints in Jerusalem (Matt. 27:52-53).

The resurrection of the church will be fulfilled at the end of the Church Age at the time of the Rapture (1 Cor. 15:51-58; 1 Thes. 4:13-18). The resurrection of the two witnesses in Revelation 11 will come at the close of their 42-month ministry and will result in their being caught up to heaven.

At the time of the second coming of Christ those who will have been martyred in the Great Tribulation will be resurrected (20:4). This is described as "the first resurrection" (v. 5) not in the sense that it was the first of all resurrections but that it was first or before the resurrection of the wicked, which will occur 1,000 years later (v. 6). Probably at the time of the resurrection of Tribulation saints Old Testament saints will be raised (Dan. 12:1-3; cf. Isa. 26:19).

The resurrection of the wicked will occur at the end of the Millennium (Rev. 20:11-15). Though not revealed in Scripture, there will necessarily be a Rapture of living millennial saints and a resurrection of saints who will die in the Millennium.

This will occur at the end of the Millennium when the present earth and heavens are destroyed. All mankind who are considered righteous will be resurrected in their order and live in the New Jerusalem and the new earth (21:2-27).

THE RAPTURE OF LIVING SAINTS

At the time of the Rapture of the church the dead in Christ will be resurrected (1 Cor. 15:51-53; 1 Thes. 4:13-18), and living saints will be raptured and given bodies like those raised from the dead in preparation for their eternal presence with Christ.

The doctrine of the Rapture was a truth said to be a mystery, that is, not revealed in the Old Testament (1 Cor. 15:51). In the Rapture the bodies of all Christians living on the earth at that time will be transformed into bodies suited for heaven. After meeting the Lord in the air they will be caught up to heaven (John 14:1-3; 2 Thes. 2:1; Heb. 9:28).

THE CHURCH IN HEAVEN

During the period between the Rapture and the second coming of Christ the church will be in heaven, delivered from the time of trouble on earth including the Great Tribulation. The 24 elders in heaven probably refer to the church rewarded and crowned after the Rapture but before the Second Coming (Rev. 5:9-10). The Marriage Supper of the Lamb may take place in heaven before the Second Coming or, perhaps more likely, on the millennial earth immediately after the Second Coming since it is announced in connection with the second coming of Christ (Rev. 19:7-9).

THE BELIEVERS' REWARDS AT THE JUDGMENT SEAT OF CHRIST

One of the major features in the period immediately after the Rapture is the rewarding of believers for their ministry on earth on behalf of Christ (Rom. 14:10-12; 1 Cor. 3:11-15; 9:16-27; 2 Cor. 5:9-11; Rev. 3:11; 22:12).

THE APPEARING OF THE MAN OF LAWLESSNESS

Immediately after the Rapture the man of lawlessness will appear in connection with the prophesied formation of a 10-nation confederacy consisting of the revival of the Roman Empire (Dan. 7:7-8, 15-26; Rev. 13:1-9). Additional references to the man of lawlessness are found in several other Scriptures (Ezek. 28:1-10; Dan. 9:27; 11:36-45; Matt. 24:15; John 5:43; 2 Thes. 2:1-12; Rev. 6:2; 19:19-20; 20:10). He will make a seven-year covenant with Israel leading up to the second coming of Christ (Dan. 9:27) and will become a world dictator three and one half years before the second coming of Christ (7:23; Rev. 13:7).

The man of lawlessness will be Satan's substitute for Christ and is considered by many to fulfill the description of the Antichrist of the end of the age. He will be Satan's substitute for Christ as King of kings, and will be empowered by Satan himself (v. 2). He will be cast in the lake of fire at the time of the second coming of Christ (19:20).

THE DESTRUCTION OF ECCLESIASTICAL BABYLON

The world church movement, which was organized in 1948 as the World Council of Churches, will play a major role in the first half of the last seven years leading up to the second coming of Christ. In Revelation 17 the world church composed of those unsaved at the Rapture is described as "the great prostitute" (v. 1), and she is pictured sitting on a scarlet beast, which pictures world government. This beast may be identified with the beast of 13:1-8. The woman riding the beast represents world religion having worldwide political power in the first half of the last seven years before the second coming of Christ (17:7). Her title is given in verse 5, "MYSTERY BABYLON THE GREAT THE MOTHER OF PROSTITUTES AND OF THE ABOMINATIONS OF THE EARTH." She will be responsible for the martyrdom of many saints in the Tribulation, for she is the woman who was "drunk with the blood of the saints" (v. 6).

At the midpoint of the last seven years before the second coming of Christ the 10 horns, symbolic of the 10 kingdoms that will constitute a revived form of the Roman Empire, will destroy the woman and burn her with fire (v. 16).

The purpose of this is to prepare the way for the final form of world religion which will be atheism centering in the world dictator empowered by Satan (13:2-8).

THE GREAT TRIBULATION

The last three and one half years leading up to the second coming of Christ is designated the end of the age and the Great Tribulation (Deut. 4:29-30; Ps. 2:5; Jer. 30:4-7; Dan. 11:40-45; 12:1; Matt. 24:15-28; 1 Thes. 5:1-11; 2 Thes. 2:8-12; Rev. 3:10; 7:13-14). Some believe the entire seven years are indicated in Revelation 6–18, whereas others hold that this passage describes only the second half of the seven-year period. If the first view is correct, then the judgments described as the breaking of the seals, the sounding of the trumpets, and the pouring out of the bowls of wrath on the world extend over the seven years. If the latter view is correct, then the three series of judgments will occur in the last three and one half years.

The Great Tribulation will be a time of unprecedented trouble for the world as a whole because of the awesome, catastrophic judgments poured out on the earth. It will be a special time of judgment for Israel (Jer. 30:4-7) and a time of martyrdom for many of those who turn to Christ (Rev. 7:13-14). In the Great Tribulation most of the world's population will be destroyed.

The climax of the Tribulation with the outpouring of the seventh bowl will result in an earthquake that will cause the cities of the Gentiles to collapse (16:19), and a great hailstorm with hailstones weighing 100 pounds each (v. 21). This will be a time of trouble far greater than anything in the past or anything that will follow (Matt. 24:21-22).

ISRAEL'S FINAL SUFFERINGS

In prophecies concerning Israel's future she is described as enduring great sufferings preceding the second coming of Christ (Deut. 28:63-68; Jer. 30:4; Matt. 24:21-27). In keeping with Satan's purpose to destroy Israel by extermination, world anti-Semitism will result in the people of Israel being severely tried and reduced in number during this period. According to Zechariah 13:8-9, "Two thirds will be struck down and perish; yet one third will be left in it. This third I will bring into the fire; I will refine them like silver and test them like gold. They will call on My name and I will answer them; I will say, 'They are My people,' and they will say, 'The LORD is our

God.' " The prophecy of Israel's trouble (Jer. 30:4-7) predicts the time of her suffering (it will be "a time of trouble for Jacob"), but also her deliverance (Jacob "will be saved out of it"). The deliverance of Israel will come at the second coming of Christ.

THE BATTLE OF ARMAGEDDON

The final great war which will be waged in the Holy Land immediately before the second coming of Christ is commonly called "the battle of Armageddon." In Revelation 16:13-14 John wrote, "I saw three evil spirits that looked like frogs; they came out of the mouth of the dragon, out of the mouth of the beast and out of the mouth of the false prophet. They are spirits of demons performing miraculous signs, and they go out to the kings of the whole world, to gather them for the battle on the great day of God Almighty."

These verses seem to present a paradox in that a worldwide government will be formed at the midpoint of the last seven years by the deceptive work of Satan (13:2-8), but then approximately three years later Satan will send out demons to deceive the world into engaging in a world war, in which the world will contend with the world ruler for his power. How can this apparent battle of a kingdom against itself be explained?

The answer is found in Revelation 19. Satan, knowing that the second coming of Christ is near, will marshal all the military power of the world in the Holy Land to contend with the procession of the army from heaven which will feature the second coming of Christ. When Christ appears in His second coming the armies on both sides of the conflict will unite to battle with the army from heaven but to no avail. Christ will simply speak the word, represented by a sharp sword coming from His mouth (v. 15), and the armies and their horses will be slain.

The world war which precedes the second coming of Christ is referred to as the battle of Armageddon because the center of the conflict is in a place called Armageddon, that is, the Mount of Megiddo in northern Israel. From other Scriptures it is apparent that the war extends to the whole area as much as 200 miles north and south and east all the way to the Euphrates River (Dan. 11:40-44; Rev. 16:12). The valley of Armageddon extending from Mount Megiddo eastward is a large area but too small to contain the great armies of this conflict in the end time.

On the day of the second coming of Christ (Zech. 12:1-9; 14:1-3) the destruction of the armies of the world will fulfill that anticipated in the destruction of the image by a rock "cut out, but not by human hands" (Dan. 2:31-35) and the destruction of the world empire of the beast (7:26-27).

The world ruler and the false prophet will be cast into the lake of fire (Rev. 19:20).

THE DESTRUCTION OF POLITICAL AND COMMERCIAL BABYLON

While ecclesiastical Babylon will be destroyed three and one half years before the second coming of Christ (Rev. 17:16), the destruction of the world empire pictured as political and commercial Babylon will occur at the time of the second coming of Christ.

In Revelation 18 this is pictured as a great city destroyed by earthquake and fire. Some identify this as Rome and others as rebuilt Babylon. It will serve as the capital of the world empire during the Great Tribulation.

THE MARRIAGE OF THE LAMB

Announced in Revelation 19:7-9 is the "Wedding Supper of the Lamb." In keeping with the traditional marriage with its three parts, the final step is the wedding supper held for several days after the bridegroom has claimed his bride.

Because the announcement of the wedding supper is placed immediately before the Second Coming, the question had been raised as to whether this will occur in heaven during the time of trouble on earth or whether it will be fulfilled soon after the beginning of the millennial kingdom.

It is probable that this will be fulfilled in the early part of the millennial kingdom. In any case it is not a physical feast with millions of people being involved but rather a symbolic picture of the joyous fellowship of the church as the bride and wife of Christ along with saints of other dispensations who will all enjoy Christ's presence.

THE SECOND COMING OF CHRIST

Many of these endtime events will occur in rapid succession and will climax in the second coming of Christ. The glorious coming of Christ will include a great procession of saints and angels coming triumphantly to the earth with Christ to put down evil and to establish the millennial kingdom (Rev. 19:11-16).

The second coming of Christ is anticipated by Daniel, "In my vision at night I looked, and there before me was one like a son of man, coming with the clouds of heaven. He approached the Ancient of Days and was led into His presence. He was given authority, glory, and sovereign power; all peoples, nations, and men of every language worshiped Him. His dominion is an everlasting dominion that will not pass away, and His kingdom is one that will never be destroyed" (Dan. 7:13-14).

Christ predicted His return in Matthew 24:27. He said, "As the lightning comes from the east and flashes to the west, so will be the coming of the Son of man." Christ added, "At that time the sign of the Son of man will appear in the sky, and all the nations of the earth will mourn. They will see the Son of man coming on the clouds of the sky, with power and great glory. And He will send His angels with a loud trumpet call, and they will gather His elect from the four winds, from one end of the heavens to the other" (vv. 30-31).

In connection with His second coming Christ will judge Israel (Ezek. 20:33-44) and the Gentile world (Matt. 25:31-46). He will come as the Saviour of Israel (Isa. 63:1, 4; Rom. 11:26-27), and He will destroy Gentile powers (Pss. 2:7-9; 96:13; 98:9; Isa. 63:1-6; Dan. 2:44-45; Matt. 24:29-30; 2 Thes. 1:7-10; Rev. 19:11-16). The second coming of Christ will mark the deliverance of persecuted Christians whether Jews or Gentiles, and the judgment of the world. The Second Coming also is the prelude for the millennial kingdom which will follow.

THE BINDING AND CONFINING OF SATAN

In the sequence of events that follow the second coming of Christ a prominent prediction is the binding and confining of Satan (Rev. 20:1-3). This prophecy is given in the context of the destruction of the world's armies and the casting of the beast and the false prophet into the lake of fire which follows the second coming of Christ. It is followed by the announcement of the resurrection of those who were beheaded because of their faith in Christ and refusal to worship the beast (vv. 4-6).

In this context it is unwarranted to lift out the section on the binding of Satan and make it refer to the first coming of Christ as is often done by amillenarians. The New Testament clearly teaches that Satan is not bound and is active in the present age as indicated in 1 Peter 5:8-9, "Your enemy the devil prowls around like a roaring lion looking for someone to devour. Resist him, standing firm in the faith, because you know that your brothers throughout the world are undergoing the same kind of sufferings." Instead of being bound and inactive, Satan is especially active during the present age and will reach a new height of activity in the Great Tribulation preceding the second coming of Christ.

In his binding in Revelation 20:1-3 Satan and the demon world will be rendered totally inactive throughout the millennial kingdom. Except for the sinful nature of man, only forces of good will be active. No one will be able to blame Satan for their sinfulness in the millennial kingdom, and the failure of man even in these ideal circumstances makes clear that salvation is available only by the grace of God and on the basis of the death of Christ.

The description of Satan's binding is explicit. He will be bound, then thrown into the Abyss, the home of the demon world, and then the door to the Abyss will be locked and sealed. This is all part of the vision given to John. In addition to the vision, however, is added the revelation of the purpose of the binding of Satan, "to keep him from deceiving the nations anymore until the thousand years were ended. After that, he must be set free for a short time" (v. 3). The Scriptures could not be more explicit that the timing of this binding is before the 1,000 years, but his loosing is at the end of the 1,000 years and that between those two events he will be kept completely out of activity in the world. There is no justification for the amillennial interpretation which makes this almost a nonliteral event.

The Millennium will demonstrate that even when Satan is bound the inherent evil in man's sin nature will manifest itself in unbelief on the part of those at the end of that era who will rebel against God when Satan is loosed.

THE REGATHERING AND JUDGMENT OF SORROWING ISRAEL

Many passages in the Old Testament record the prophecies of Israel's ultimate restoration. At the second coming of Christ Israel will be regathered (Jer. 23:7-8) and restored as a nation (Ezek. 37:21-28). As indicated in 20:33-44, the unbelievers in Israel will be purged out and only the godly remnant of Israel will be restored to their ancient land to enjoy the millennial reign of Christ. Resurrected Israelites (Dan. 12:1-3) will join those Israelites who will survive the Tribulation and still be in their natural bodies. The judgments on Israel were included as an essential part of the Olivet Discourse (Matt. 24:37–25:30). The promise given to Daniel is typical of the promises given to the Israelites who were saved in the Old Testament, "As for you, go your way till the end. You will rest, and then at the end of the days you will rise to receive your allotted inheritance" (Dan. 12:13). The subject of the resurrection of Israel and her restoration as a nation is so prevalent in the Old Testament that the only reasonable conclusion is that Israel will experience these promises literally (Deut. 30:1-8; Isa. 11:1-16; Jer. 23:5-8; 30:4-11; 31:7-17, 23-37; Amos 9:11-15).

THE JUDGMENT OF THE GENTILES

The Gentile world will be judged by Christ after His second coming. This judgment described in Matthew 25:31-46 relates to Gentiles racially, not to political entities or countries. This judgment will be in contrast to the special judgment on Israel predicted in Ezekiel 20:33-44. The judgment in Matthew refers to living Gentiles on the earth at the time of the Second Coming.

Expositors who try to make this a general judgment of all men do so only at the expense of ignoring the details of the passage. In this concluding portion of the Olivet Discourse there is no mention of anyone being resurrected, there is no mention of Israel, and there is no mention of the church. The judgment of the Gentiles is a special judgment relating to those who survive the Tribulation and will be on earth at the time of the second coming of Christ.

The judgment is described as the separation of sheep from goats, which in the passage clearly indicates the separation of those who are saved, the sheep, from those who are lost, the goats. Some expositors have had difficulty with this passage because it does not mention the ground of salvation but only the works of the sheep and the goats. However, a careful study of this passage reveals that the actions of the "sheep" are not the basis of salvation but the evidence of it.

In the Great Tribulation when the world is in the grip of satanic anti-Semitism, for a Gentile to befriend a Jew, designated "brothers," will be unmistakable evidence that such Gentiles will be believers and will have accepted the biblical status of the Jews as a special people. Those Gentiles will not be saved because they performed these acts of mercy, but they will do them because they are saved. It is a simple illustration of Jesus' statement that a tree is known by its fruit (Matt. 7:20). The sheep, representing saved Gentiles, will enter the millennial kingdom with eternal life, and the goats, representing unsaved Gentiles in the Tribulation, will be cast into eternal punishment (25:36-46).

Though the prophecy refers to the particular judgment of living Gentiles at the time of the second coming of Christ, the principles of kindness, befriending the homeless, helping the helpless, feeding the hungry, and having compassion on those in trouble should in every dispensation be the evidence of the transforming salvation which a believer has in Christ. The judgment of the nations is also significant as the final chapter in the divine judgment of Gentiles in their relation to Israel (Gen. 12:1-3; Pss. 96:13; 98:9; Joel 3:2-16).

LIFE IN THE MILLENNIUM

Life in the millennial kingdom is a frequent topic of prophecy in Scripture and is a major theme of Old Testament revelation. It will be the time of Israel's glory and exaltation as well as a time of Gentile blessing (Isa. 11:10; 14:1-2; 60:12; 61:5; Ezek. 37:22; Matt. 25:34). Life will be tranquil (Isa. 11:6-9; 65:18-25; Jer. 31:31-33). It will be a period when Christ will reign in righteousness in Jerusalem, the capital of the entire world (Ps. 72:1-19; Isa. 11:1-5; Matt. 5:1–7:29). The curse will be at least partially lifted from the earth, and the earth again will be fruitful as it was during the time of blessedness in the Garden of Eden (Rom. 8:18-23).

Christ will be gloriously present in the Millennium, reigning in

Jerusalem and fulfilling His role as King of kings and Lord of lords (Isa. 2:1-4; Rev. 19:11-16). The earth will be renovated (Isa. 40:4-5). In keeping with Solomon's prayer the earth will be filled with the glory of God (Ps. 72:19). This glory will be somewhat veiled because those still in the flesh will not be able to view Christ in His heavenly glory.

Some of the aspects of the glory of God are indicated in Christ's glorious rule (Pss. 2:8-9; 72:19; Isa. 9:6-7; 11:4; Heb. 2:8-9). The Promised Land will be possessed by the Jews (Gen. 15:7; 17:8; Dan. 8:9; 11:16, 41). Christ will exercise His office as a glorious Prophet and Lawgiver (Deut. 18:18-19; Isa. 2:2-4; 33:21-22; 42:4; Acts 3:22). The millennial reign of Christ will fulfill the Davidic Covenant (2 Sam. 7:12-16; Isa. 9:6-7; Matt. 25:31; Luke 1:31-33). In every respect the rule of Christ in the millennial kingdom will be glorious (Ps. 72; Isa. 9:7; 11:10; Jer. 23:6).

In the millennial kingdom there will be a new level of spirituality common in life on earth. This will be because all people will have knowledge of God (Isa. 11:9). God promised also to plant His Law in the hearts of believers (Jer. 31:33-34). Righteousness will characterize life on earth (Ps. 72:7), and Christ will judge with complete righteousness (Isa. 11:3-5). There will be peace among nations (2:4). Life in the millennial kingdom will be a time of great joy for the people of God (12:3-4; 61:3, 7). The power of the Holy Spirit will be evident in the millennial kingdom, and believers will be indwelt by the Spirit (32:15; 44:3; Ezek. 39:29; Joel 2:28-29).

The center of worship will be the millennial temple (Ezek. 40–46). Various explanations have been given of this millennial temple and its sacrificial system. The only interpretation that does justice to the passage is that a literal temple will be built according to the specifications given to Ezekiel, and that literal sacrifices will be offered as a memorial to the death of Christ. In the ideal situation of the Millennium people will apparently need this reminder of the awfulness of sin and the sacrifice of Christ which was necessary for believers to be saved. Peace and justice will also characterize the millennial kingdom as described in Psalm 72 and Isaiah 11. Probably the majority of mankind will be saved, but there will still be sin and death and divine judgment on any open sin.

The earth will enjoy fruitfulness never before known since the Garden of Eden (Isa. 35:1-2). There will be abundant rainfall (30:23; 35:7), and there will be plenty of food for all (30:23-24). In contrast to the present age in which prosperity is realized only by a portion of the race, the millennial kingdom will be one of general prosperity and blessing (Jer. 31:12; Ezek. 34:25-27; Joel 2:21-27; Amos 9:13-14).

Apparently there will be longer life and a better state of health in the Millennium than in previous dispensations. Though Christ healed many in His life on earth, in the millennial kingdom there will be a more universal experience of physical health (Isa. 29:18; 61:1-3; 65:20). Apparently the human race will greatly increase in numbers throughout the millennial kingdom as life will be lengthened and death will be less common (v. 20). Jerusalem as the capital of the world will apparently be elevated above the land which surrounds it (Zech. 14:10).

THE LOOSING OF SATAN AND THE LAST REVOLT

After being confined in the abyss for the 1,000 years of the millennial kingdom Satan will be freed and will lose no time gathering followers who will be professing Christians but not genuinely saved, and he will surround Jerusalem the capital city of the world. His freedom will be brief because fire will come down from heaven and devour the rebels (Rev. 20:7-9). He will be "thrown into the lake of burning sulfur, where the beast and the false prophet had been thrown. They will be tormented day and night forever and ever" (v. 10). The revelation that the beast and the false prophet are still in the lake of fire after 1,000 years makes clear that eternal punishment lasts forever. Satan who was judged by the Cross (John 16:11) and who was banished from heaven at the beginning of the Great Tribulation (Rev. 12:7-12) and who spent 1,000 years in the Abyss (20:1-3), will come to his final doom.

THE PASSING AWAY OF THE PRESENT HEAVENS AND EARTH

At the end of the millennial kingdom the present earth and the heavens (the starry universe, not the abode of God) will be destroyed. According to Revelation 20:11, "Earth and sky fled from His presence, and there was no place for them." According to 21:1,

"The first heaven and the first earth had passed away, and there was no longer any sea." According to 2 Peter 3:12 at the beginning of eternity the heavens will be destroyed by fire and the elements will melt in heat. Though some have postulated that the earth and the heavens will be renovated, it is more in keeping with the Scriptures to understand that the present earth and heavens are destroyed and an entirely new situation created for eternity (cf. Isa. 65:17; 66:22; Heb. 1:10-12).

THE DESTINY OF THE WICKED

At the end of the Millennium and after the destruction of the earth the final judgment of the wicked is described in Revelation 20:11-15. The remaining dead, apparently consisting of only unsaved, will be taken out of their temporary place of punishment described as hades and will be cast into the lake of fire because their names are not recorded in the Book of Life.

This is called "the second death" (v. 14), meaning eternal separation from God and eternal punishment in hell for their sin and unbelief.

THE CREATION OF THE NEW HEAVENS AND THE NEW EARTH

A new heavens and a new earth will be created. These will differ dramatically from the present heavens and earth. On the new earth there will be no more sea or ocean (21:1), and in the heavens there will be no sun or moon (v. 23). Central to the picture of eternity is the New Jerusalem described in detail in Revelation 21–22. It will be a city of tremendous size, 1,500 miles square and 1,500 miles high. It will consist of translucent materials like gems in every color of the rainbow. Even the gold will have a translucent character and will look like glass.

The glory and light of the city will be the presence of God (21:23-25). Apparently there will be no stars in heaven as the continuous presence of God in the heavenly city will not allow darkness which would enable one to see the stars. In the city will be the saved of all ages (Heb. 12:22-24).

THE DESTINY OF THE SAVED

The Scriptures are clear that the saved of all ages will dwell in the heavenly city, which will rest on the new earth (Isa. 66:22; Rev. 21:3-4). The saved, however, will continue to have separate corporate identities, such as the church, Israel, and saints of other ages. The unending bliss of the saved will be in contrast to the brevity of human life and will continue to be a means by which the grace of God will be manifested to those to whom He has given salvation.

The Day of the Lord in 2 Peter 3 is said to climax with the destruction of the present earth through fire (v. 10). The same event which closes the Day of the Lord, which began at the Rapture, will begin the Day of God (v. 12), a unique expression which apparently refers to eternity future (cf. v. 12; 1 Cor. 15:28).

The major events in their order and as revealed in the Word of God provide an outline of the divine program which culminates in eternity.

CHAPTER • 47

THE JUDGMENTS

Of the eight judgments pronounced in the Bible one is past, two relate to the present, and five are future. The five yet-future judgments are themes of unfulfilled prophecy. Instead of one final judgment, the Scriptures reveal that there are a series of judgments differing in respect to time, theme, subject, and circumstances. The body of truth relating to the judgments gives important insights into God's program.

THE DIVINE JUDGMENTS THROUGH THE CROSS

As indicated in the discussion of soteriology, three features of divine judgment are related to Christ's death on the cross: (1) the judgment of the sin of the world, (2) the judgment of the believer's sin nature, and (3) the judgment of Satan.

1. JUDGMENT OF SIN IN THE WORLD. The divine judgment on the sin of the world in the cross of Christ reveals on the one hand the infinite extent of the problem of sin and on the other hand the complete answer that God provides in the cross of Christ. Though some theologians hold that Christ died only for the elect, the Scriptures are plain in affirming that Christ died for the sins of the whole world (Isa. 53:6; John 1:29; 3:16-19; 2 Cor. 5:14-19; Heb. 2:9; 2 Peter 2:1; 1 John 2:2). Though it is true that Christ died with the view to saving the elect, the purpose of His death related to the whole world in that the infinite value of His death was sufficient for all and made the entire world savable even though it is applied only to those who believe (John 10:11; Eph. 5:25-27; 1 John 2:2). No human being goes to eternal punishment because Christ has not died

for him but rather because he as an unbeliever has not availed himself of what Christ has done for him in dying on the cross.

2. THE JUDGMENT OF THE BELIEVER. The judgment of the believer's sin nature was also accomplished by Christ on the cross. This judgment is related only to those who are saved but is far reaching in its significance (Rom. 6:1-10). Though the death of Christ does not obliterate the power of the sin nature, it provides for divine forgiveness for the fact of the sin nature and provides power for victory over it. This power is not available to the unsaved (Jude 19). In dying on the cross Christ provided a divine remedy for the believer's sin nature in the form of divine judgment on Christ (Rom. 6:1-10; Gal. 5:24; Eph. 4:22-24; Col. 3:9-10).

3. SATAN'S JUDGMENT. The judgment of Satan was also accomplished through Christ's death on the cross. Though Scripture does not reveal all the details about the relationship of angels to God, various instances of conflict with Satan and the fallen angels reveal God's superior power. In the protevangelium of Genesis 3:15 the superior power of God is indicated. Again in Christ's temptation in the wilderness (Luke 4:1-14) the superior power of Christ the Son of God over Satan is revealed. In the war in heaven Satan will be cast out in the middle of the last seven years leading up to the second coming of Christ (Rev. 12:7-12), and at Christ's second coming Satan and the demon world will be rendered powerless (1 Cor. 15:25-26; Rev. 20:1-3). The judgment of Satan by Christ as He died on the cross is also mentioned frequently in Scripture (John 12:31; 14:30; 16:11; Col. 2:14-15).

THE SELF-JUDGMENT OF THE BELIEVER

Though believers are saved and justified by faith in Christ as the crucified Saviour, the Scriptures assume that Christians will battle with sin and will not always be victorious. So it is necessary for believers to judge their own sins in the light of Scripture. Extended revelation of this truth is given in Hebrews 12:3-15. In this passage it is revealed that every son in the Father's household is subject to chastisement when sin intrudes on his Christian life. In verse 6 believers are said to be both chastised and scourged. Scourging seems to reflect a once-for-all conquering of human will. Chastisement on the other hand may be repeated many times in dealing with lesser problems of the believer in his spiritual life. In John 15:2 Christ said that the branches of the vine had to be pruned in order to bring forth more fruit. This pruning refers to discipline. Those who do not judge their own sins partake of the Lord's Supper unworthily (1 Cor. 11:30). Also revealed is the truth that "if we judged ourselves, we would not come under judgment." When we are judged by the Lord, we are disciplined so that we will not be condemned with the world (1 Cor. 11:31-32).

THE CHASTENING JUDGMENTS OF GOD

As indicated in the passage dealing with self-judgment, a Christian who does not judge his own sin requires God's chastening to bring him back in fellowship with God and to identify him as a child of God in contrast to the unsaved in the world. If a believer judges himself, he will not need this chastening judgment. And if he does not judge himself he will experience God's discipline (1 John 1:9).

THE JUDGMENT OF THE BELIEVERS' WORKS

Though believers are under no condemnation in respect to their sins, having been justified by faith (John 3:18; 5:24; Rom. 8:1, 13-17), they are subject to judgment at the Judgment Seat of Christ in relation to their works. At the Judgment Seat of Christ believers' works will be evaluated to demonstrate whether they were good or bad, and rewards will be conferred (2 Cor. 5:10; cf. Rom. 14:10-12; 1 Cor. 3:9-15; 9:24-27). The goal of the Christian in his life is to be pleasing to God whether in time or eternity. The Judgment Seat of Christ is not related to salvation but to the bestowal of rewards, and every Christian is assured that he will receive some reward (1 Cor. 4:5; cf. Eph. 6:8; 2 Tim. 4:8; Rev. 22:12).

THE JUDGMENT OF ISRAEL

At the second coming of Christ Israel will be judged. The saved who have died will be resurrected, and those who are living will be judged relative to their salvation and their works. The practical application of the second coming of Christ to Israel is seen in Matthew 24:32–25:30. The unsaved in Israel who will be living on earth at the time of the Second Coming will be purged out, according to Ezekiel 20:33-44. The righteous will be resurrected and rewarded (Dan. 12:2-3). This is in keeping with the fact that all the righteous, regardless of the dispensation in which they lived and whether resurrected or living in mortal bodies, will participate in the millennial kingdom and will be rewarded in a similar way as the church will be rewarded at the Judgment Seat of Christ (Mal. 3:16-18). The coming of Christ will occasion sanctification which will be complete for those who are resurrected but will extend to some extent to Israelites living at the time of the Second Coming. On the one hand the fact that all are saved by grace in every dispensation is upheld; on the other hand the importance of works on the part of those who are saved is specifically taught and relates to Israel and the saved Gentiles of the Old Testament as well as to the church.

THE JUDGMENT OF THE GENTILES

As previously pointed out, Scripture reveals that God will judge the Gentiles for their sins and in particular will judge Gentiles living at the time of the second coming of Christ. At the judgment of the Gentiles Christ will separate the sheep, representing the saved, from the goats, representing the lost (Matt. 25:31-46). Though salvation is by grace and through faith, the saved who come out of the Great Tribulation will be identified by their works in befriending their Jewish brothers. In the universal anti-Semitism of the Great Tribulation one who befriends Jews will by this evidence manifest his salvation.

Throughout history there have been judgments of the nations as revealed in the Old Testament, and the unsaved in all nations will be judged at the Great White Throne Judgment at the end of the Millennium (Rev. 20:11-15).

THE JUDGMENT OF ANGELS

Though there has been ceaseless warfare between the holy angels and Satan and the demon world, God manifests His power in subduing the power of evil angels in various ways. In the millennial kingdom Satan and the demon world will be rendered inactive. At the end of the Millennium Satan and the demonic world will once again be released (Rev. 20:7-10). When Satan and the fallen angels are cast into the lake of fire (v. 10), the final judgment on sin in the angelic world will take place (2 Peter 2:4; Jude 6). Then all opposing forces of God will be dealt with in judgment as indicated in 1 Corinthians 15:24-26, "Then the end will come, when He hands over the kingdom to God the Father after He has destroyed all dominion, authority, and power. For He must reign until He has put all His enemies under His feet. The last enemy to be destroyed is death."

THE JUDGMENT OF THE GREAT WHITE THRONE

As previously considered, the Judgment of the Great White Throne which will occur before the eternal state begins is the final judgment on the wicked. All whose names are not written in the Book of Life will be cast into the lake of fire. The tragedy of this judgment is that Christ died even for these unsaved people, but they did not avail themselves of God's gift of grace and therefore will eternally experience God's righteous judgment on them (Rev. 20:11-15).

The itemization of the judgments of God, some of which are past, some present, and some future, makes clear that the concept that there is only one general final judgment is not supported in Scripture. Though it is true that everyone will be judged, angels and men will not be judged at the same time, at the same place, or on the same basis.

CHAPTER • 48

THE ETERNAL STATE

Truth concerning the eternal state is revealed in Scripture and may be considered under a number of general divisions: (1) the intermediate state, (2) angels and men who enter the eternal state, (3) various spheres of existence, (4) theories relating to a future state, (5) hell, (6) the new earth, and (7) heaven.

THE INTERMEDIATE STATE

As used in theology, the term "intermediate state" refers to the state of human souls in the interval between their death and resurrection. Those who will be translated at the Rapture of the church will not enter the intermediate state, but apart from them the order of death, an intermediate state, and resurrection are universal. The Scriptures are clear that death is not an unconscious condition for either the saved or the unsaved. Several aspects of this important teaching are revealed in Scripture.

1. Two important words of location. The Old Testament word *sheol* and the New Testament word *hades* are identical in meaning, referring to the place where those who die go. In some passages they refer to the grave in which the body is placed and in others to the place where the souls are waiting for the resurrection of the body as indicated in the intermediate state. Neither of these terms is ever used for the eternal destiny of men. Both the saved and the unsaved at death have bodies that are subject to burial. The intermediate state of the unsaved is one of torment and suffering (cf. Isa. 14:9-11; Ezek. 32:21; Jonah 2:2). In contrast, the intermediate state of the righteous is one of bliss and peace (cf. 2 Sam. 22:6; Pss. 18:5;

116:3). The rich man in hades was fully possessed of all his faculties and was in suffering, in contrast to Lazarus who was in a state of bliss (Luke 16:19-31).

The separation of the unsaved who have died from the saved is eternal, and no change of their situation is indicated until the Judgment of the Great White Throne. The state of the saved is represented as being in paradise (23:43) or being with Abraham (16:22).

Some believe that paradise before the resurrection of Christ was a place distinct from heaven though it was a place of joy and peace. Beginning with the resurrection of Christ the Scriptures are clear that the saved are in heaven itself in the presence of God. The change in situations for the saved is believed to be revealed in Ephesians 4:7-10, "But to each one of us grace has been given as Christ apportioned it. This is why it says: 'When He ascended on high, He led captives in His train and gave gifts to men.' (What does 'He ascended' mean except that He also descended to the lower, earthly regions? He who descended is the very One who ascended higher than all the heavens, in order to fill the whole universe.)"

Others on the basis of Daniel 7:9-10 believe that paradise is identical to heaven even in the Old Testament. The New Testament is clear that at least since the ascension of Christ those who are saved go immediately to heaven at death, and when the resurrection of the dead in Christ and the Rapture of the living church is consummated, they will go immediately into the presence of Christ (1 Thes. 4:17) in bodies suited for eternity.

2. THE DOCTRINE OF SLEEP. The believer's death is referred to in Scripture as being like sleep (John 11:11-13; 1 Cor. 15:51; 1 Thes. 4:14). Some have confused the fact that the body sleeps in the grave with the concept that the soul sleeps. The Scriptures are clear that the soul of a Christian at death goes immediately into the presence of God. As Paul expressed it, while in this life "we are at home in the body," but after death we are "away from it" (2 Cor. 5:9). Christ on the cross assured the thief who accepted Him as Saviour, "Today you will be with Me in paradise" (Luke 23:43). Paul in Philippians 1:23 stated that at death the soul departs to be with Christ. From these verses it is clear that there is no loss of consciousness in death and that both the saved and the unsaved are in a conscious existence in their intermediate state.

3. AN INTERMEDIATE BODY. The concept of an intermediate body between death and resurrection is discussed in 2 Corinthians 5:1-5.

At the present time believers are in an "earthly tent" (v. 1), but they long for their "heavenly dwelling" (v. 2). References to believers after death but before resurrection all seem to suggest that they have a body, as in the case of Lazarus (Luke 16:19-25). When Moses and Elijah met with Christ on the Mount of Transfiguration, they were represented as having bodies (Matt. 17:1-3; Mark 9:4; Luke 9:30). In Revelation 6:9-11 the martyred dead are seen in heaven and robes will be given to them, which indicates they will have bodies. The martyred dead in 7:13-17 are represented as wearing robes and being before the throne of God. Though full revelation was not given in Scripture concerning the exact characteristics of these bodies, apparently they will not be suited for eternity for they will be replaced by resurrection bodies.

ANGELS AND MEN WHO ENTER THE ETERNAL STATE

Created beings are subject to a fourfold classification—angels, Gentiles, Jews, and Christians. These can be further divided into 12 subdivisions or classes: (1) unfallen angels, (2) fallen angels, (3) saved Gentiles, (4) unsaved Gentiles, (5) Gentiles of the kingdom, (6) Gentiles barred from the kingdom, (7) Jews in the kingdom, (8) Jews excluded from the kingdom, (9) Jews saved by entry into the church, (10) Jews condemned for rejecting the Gospel, (11) the unsaved as a whole, and (12) Christians.

1. Unfallen angels. The unfallen angels are those who have maintained their holy estate. Though tempted at the same time as Satan and the fallen angels, when they resisted this temptation they apparently were rendered secure for all eternity and no further departure from God has occurred among the angels.

2. Fallen angels. These angels are those who were created holy but when Satan sinned they fell with him (Rev. 12:9). As fallen angels they are identified with Satan in his work opposing God. Their destiny is sealed, and with Satan they will be forever in the lake of burning sulfur (Matt. 24:41; Rev. 20:10).

3. Saved Gentiles. In the Old Testament saved Gentiles include believers who were not Jews such as Adam, Enoch, Noah, Job, and Melchizedek. They will share eternity with others who are saved in later dispensations.

4. Unsaved Gentiles. Most Gentiles in the Old Testament were

unsaved. They will be resurrected at the Great White Throne Judgment and cast into the lake of fire (Rev. 20:14-15).

5. Gentiles in the kingdom. Gentiles in the kingdom refer to those who will live during the time of the millennial kingdom and will be saved by faith in Christ. After the Millennium those Gentiles will walk by the light of the eternal city and will have part in the New Jerusalem with the saints of all ages in the eternal state.

6. Gentiles barred from the kingdom. Gentiles who will be barred from entering the millennial kingdom are those who are lost and who will ultimately be subject to eternal punishment (Matt. 25:41-46).

7. Jews in the kingdom. Jews in the millennial kingdom are those who in Israel will put their trust in Christ and be saved. Some of these will have come out of the Tribulation time, and others will be born in the kingdom. They will share the New Jerusalem with others who are saved. They are distinguished from those in Israel who do not put their trust in Christ and will be subject to eternal judgment (Dan. 12:2-3; Ezek. 20:33-44; Matt. 24:37–25:30).

8. Jews excluded from the kingdom. This includes those who are not saved at the time of the second coming of Christ and so will not be allowed to participate in the kingdom period. Other references to unsaved Jews are found in Matthew 24:50-51; 25:10-12.

9. Jews saved by entry into the church. Jews saved in the church between the time of Pentecost and the Rapture are baptized into the body of Christ and have equal place with Gentiles who are saved. Though the church was largely Jewish in its early years, in the centuries since then Gentiles have become dominant in number. But Jews and Gentiles alike share the blessed promises in grace for those who are saved in the present Church Age.

10. Condemned Jews. Jews who are condemned for rejecting the Gospel are unsaved just as Gentiles are unsaved (John 3:18; 8:24).

11. The unsaved as a whole. This group is also treated in Scripture as one category and without recognition of the various classes otherwise indicated. Even though Christ died for them they are lost and excluded from the glory of the redeemed.

12. "Christians." This refers to both Jews and Gentiles who are saved in Christ in the present dispensation. They form the one body of Christ, are branches of the Vine, and share the eternal blessings of God as pronounced on the church. In the church Jews and Gentiles have equality and are exhorted to maintain in their experience the

same unity that is true of their position in Christ (John 17:21-23; Eph. 4:1-4).

VARIOUS SPHERES OF EXISTENCE

In general Scripture recognizes two classes of humanity, those who are saved and those who are unsaved. For them there are two spheres of existence in eternity, heaven and the lake of fire.

In many Bible passages, there is distinction between the millennial kingdom and the new earth and the new heavens. Though in one sense Christ will deliver the kingdom up to God at the end of the Millennium (1 Cor. 15:24-28), there is also a sense in which His rule as the Son of David will continue forever (Isa. 9:6-7; Dan. 7:14; Luke 1:31-33; Rev. 11:15). In the eternal state those who dwell in the heavenly city, the New Jerusalem, will include all the saved of every dispensation (Heb. 12:22-24). In the New Jerusalem, however, they will retain their individual as well as their corporate identities in accord with the dispensation in which they lived and in keeping with the promises God has given them.

Though the saved will live in the New Jerusalem, nothing is said concerning their relationship to the new heavens except that the New Jerusalem is said to come down from God out of heaven (Rev. 3:12; 21:2, 10). The eternal existence of the saved is in contrast to the tragic eternal punishment of the lost (Matt. 25:41, 46; Rev. 20:15; 21:8, 27; 22:11, 15).

THEORIES RELATING TO A FUTURE STATE

Human speculation on life after death is as old as the human race. Many ignore divine revelation and engage in speculation which is without supporting facts. As many as seven theories have been advanced.

1. Cessation of existence. Some believe in death as the cessation of existence, a view known as mortalism. In other words man is only an animal, and life ceases at death. This point of view is in keeping with atheism, which denies the supernatural and the existence of God.

2. Transmigration of the soul. This view has been advanced

by a number of religions, including Hinduism, Buddhism, and Jainism. The idea is that the soul passes from one incarnation to another. There is no ground for this belief and it arises from pure speculation.

3. Conditional immortality. Because of the natural aversion in human thought to the concept of eternal punishment, conditional immortality is widely held by liberals who do not accept the truth of the Bible about life after death. The thought is that those who are worthy of life after death may be resurrected, but all others who die will never be resurrected. A variation of this view is the concept that the unsaved will be resurrected, judged, and then annihilated, and that this is the meaning assigned to the second death (Rev. 20:14-15; 21:8). This is sometimes called annihilationism.

4. Universalism. This is the concept that all men will be resurrected and will live forever in heaven. This view has arisen in part in objection to the concept of limited redemption, the teaching that Christ died only for the elect. The truth is ignored that the Scriptures clearly indicate that salvation is not universally applied, though it is universally provided for by the death of Christ. Though some who are universalists recognize an element of retribution for those who have been sinful, they believe in the final salvation of all.

5. Restitutionalism or reconciliation. This is another variation of universalism. This concept is that all created beings will be reconciled to God including even the fallen angels and Satan. This view is drawn from Philippians 2:10-11, "That at the name of Jesus every knee should bow, in heaven and on earth and under the earth, and every tongue confess that Jesus Christ is Lord, to the glory of God the Father." This passage does not teach restitutionalism, however, but rather that Christ's authority will be acknowledged by all. Their forced confession that Jesus Christ is Lord will come too late for their salvation. The unsaved will continue in their rebellion and anarchy even though they will experience divine judgment. Though Scripture predicts that Jesus Christ will "bring everything under His control" (3:21), it does not indicate that all will be saved. This point of view builds on human sentiment and reason rather than on the Word of God.

6. Purgatory. The concept of purgatory is held by the Roman Catholic Church. This advances the idea that Christ's death was a satisfaction for sins committed before baptism, but those who sin after baptism must atone for those sins in purgatory unless they are

cared for in life. Because no one can confess all his sins, everyone must pass through this experience of purgation. On this theory prayers for the dead and contributions to the church for offering up prayers are offered as the remedy. In effect this view denies the fact that Christ is the propitiation for the believer's sin (1 John 2:2) and it denies the truth of justification by faith (Rom. 5:1).

7. Nirvana. Nirvana refers to the condition in which a human life is extinguished like a lamp being blown out and is the belief of Buddhists. This belief is built on the concept that the immaterial part of man is absorbed into the divine and that this may begin even in this life by the renunciation of all personal desires. In contrast the Bible teaches eternal punishment, as will be considered in the following section on the doctrine of hell.

THE DOCTRINE OF HELL

Though the doctrine of eternal punishment is a teaching that many question or deny, the doctrine does not originate in human reason nor is it a product of human sympathy. It is taught in the Bible and therefore is to be accepted as part of God's revelation to man. It is difficult for man to realize the awfulness of sin and the infinite holiness of God and to face objectively the fact that an infinitely holy God must require infinite punishment for sin. In this doctrine as in many others God has not revealed everything (Deut. 29:29).

God's permission of sin in the universe, in which He is sovereign and in which He as the holy God hates sin, is difficult for one to understand. The Scriptures state that sin has done much damage to multitudes of beings including both angels and men. The Scriptures also affirm that human sin demanded of God the greatest sacrifice He could make in giving His Son to be crucified for the sins of the whole world. It was necessary for Christ as a man to enter into the awful experience on the cross as He quoted Psalm 22:1, "My God, My God, why have You forsaken Me?"

To understand the doctrine of evil in the universe one must understand three facts: (1) Evil caused God to will the doom of multitudes of men and angels, which is an essential feature in the final solution of the problem. (2) By faith man must accept the revelation of Scripture that God's answer to the problem of sin is the best that the infinite God devised and that God was wholly free from any wrong motive in the condemnation of the wicked. (3) In keeping with scriptural revelation man must believe that God has done everything in perfect righteousness and that His punishment of sin is justified and in fact demonstrates His holiness and infinite glory. In the end those who believe the Bible must accept the doctrine of eternal punishment with the same finality as they accept the doctrine of eternal heaven as being in keeping with a God who is at the same time a God of infinite love and righteousness.

Though the Scriptures refer to God as "a God of retribution" and as One who "will repay in full" (Jer. 51:56), this is spoken in connection with the sins of nations who are repaid for blaspheming God and being cruel to the people of Israel. God does not punish the wicked with emotional vindictiveness but rather in sad recognition that there is no other righteous way to deal with infinite sin on the part of those who do not avail themselves of God's gift of salvation. If God can judge the angels who fell into sin on the basis of their one transgression, it should be obvious that His righteousness would require infinite suffering for those who did not avail themselves of salvation and grace made possible by the death of Christ.

The state of the lost is described in detail in Romans 1:18-32. In Ephesians 2:12 the lost are said to be "separate from Christ, excluded from citizenship in Israel and foreigners to the covenants of the promise, without hope and without God in the world." As the Scriptures reveal the truth of God's grace, the concept that remains difficult to understand is not the eternal punishment of the lost but the fact that God can forgive and justify sinners who come to Christ by faith.

Just as heaven is viewed as both a place and a relationship to Christ so the eternal state of the lost is referred to as a place and separation from God.

In Scripture a distinction must be observed between the temporary place of the lost before the Judgment of the Great White Throne and the eternal place of their condemnation. In the Old Testament the word "sheol" is used almost equally in reference to the grave where the body is placed and to the place to which the soul goes at death (Deut. 32:22; 2 Sam. 22:6; Job 17:13; 26:6; Pss. 16:10; 30:3; 49:15; 86:13; 139:8; Prov. 5:5; 27:20; Ezek. 32:21; Amos 9:2; Jonah 2:2; Hab. 2:5). In Psalm 16:10, sheol seems to refer to the grave where Christ's body was placed, whereas in Deuteronomy 32:22 sheol refers to the place of the soul.

In the New Testament the word corresponding to sheol is hades (Matt. 11:23; 16:18; Luke 10:15; 16:23; Rev. 1:8; 20:13-14). A graphic picture of hades is given in Luke 16 in the contrast between the state of Lazarus the poor beggar and the state of the rich man. Both apparently had bodies, both were conscious, and the rich man had memory of his life on earth and was concerned for the unsaved state of his brothers. The place of the rich man and that of Lazarus were separated by a great distance (v. 23), and there was "a great chasm" between the two (v. 26). Though some have considered this a parable and do not take it literally, in no case in Scripture does an illustration or a symbolic presentation include a named person such as Lazarus. Christ is referring here to a historical situation. Though hades is a present place of conscious torment for the unsaved, it is not their permanent lot. They will remain in hades until their final judgment (Rev. 20:13-15). Though hades is usually used in reference to the state of man after death, like sheol it is sometimes used of the grave (1 Cor. 15:55).

Some believe that before the resurrection of Christ hades also included the saved, an inference from Luke 16:19-31. Christ on the cross assured the thief who trusted Him that they would both be in paradise (23:43).

Paul, in recounting his experience recorded in 2 Corinthians 12:2-4, referred to himself as being "caught up to paradise" (v. 4). In Revelation 2:7 the tree of life is said to be in the paradise of God, and those who overcome will be able to eat of it. It is debatable whether paradise was distinct from heaven before the resurrection of Christ, but after the resurrection of Christ it is clearly synonymous with heaven itself.

In the New Testament the common word used for eternal punishment is "gehenna." In Hebrew, gehenna means the Valley of Hinnom and refers to the valley south of Jerusalem, where human sacrifices were sometimes made (2 Chron. 33:6; Jer. 7:31). At the time of Christ it was a place where rubbish was burned continuously and accordingly became a synonym for judgment. Christ used the word frequently to refer to eternal punishment (Matt. 5:22, 29-30; 10:28; 18:9; 23:15, 33; Mark 9:43, 45, 47; Luke 12:5). The same word is used in James 3:6 in reference to constant fire.

As these references indicate, gehenna is equivalent to the "lake of fire" and in Mark 9:48 it is described as a place where "their worm does not die, and the fire is not quenched."

The lake of fire or the lake of burning sulfur is equivalent to gehenna (Rev. 14:10; 19:20; 20:10, 14-15; 21:8). Revelation 14:11 states that "the smoke of their torment rises forever and ever." In 19:20 the beast and the false prophet, who will be thrown into the lake of burning sulfur before the Millennium, will still be there in conscious torment at the end of the Millennium. "And the devil, who deceived them, was thrown into the lake of burning sulfur, where the beast and the false prophet had been thrown. They will be tormented day and night forever and ever" (20:10). The pronoun "they" refers to the beast and the false prophet who were cast into the lake of burning sulfur at the beginning of the Millennium as well as the devil who is cast into the lake of fire at the end of the Millennium. In verse 14 the lake of fire is made equivalent to "the second death." In Matthew 25:46 the goats representing the unsaved who will be living at the second coming of Christ will be cast into "eternal punishment," or "eternal fire" (v. 41).

Because the wicked dead, aside from the beast and the false prophet, will not be cast into the lake of fire until after the Millennium, some believe that this reference to everlasting fire refers to the fact that they are forever in the state of being in fire whether in hades or in the lake of fire. Others believe it speaks specifically of the lake of fire which they will begin to share at that time with the beast and the false prophet.

Though many have attempted to soften the revelation of Scripture concerning eternal punishment, a study of all passages relating to eternal punishment reveals that the lake of fire is just as everlasting as heaven. In relation to the judgment on angels, when some of them sinned against God they were confined to "Tartarus" (rendered "hell" in 2 Peter 2:4) awaiting eternal judgment. This is a place of "darkness," where angels are "bound with everlasting chains for judgment on the great Day" (Jude 6). It is not clear whether this is the exact equivalent of either hades or gehenna.

Attempts to avoid the doctrine of eternal punishment often emphasize God's attribute of love while ignoring His attributes of holiness, righteousness, and justice. Though in the wisdom of natural man this would be a desirable conclusion, the Scriptures are clear on the subject of eternal punishment. This doctrine remains a motivation for evangelism ("Knowing therefore the terror of the Lord, we persuade men," 2 Cor. 5:11, KJV) and for responding to the Gospel in faith.

THE NEW EARTH

In Isaiah 65:17 a prophecy is given concerning the new heavens and the new earth, "Behold, I will create new heavens and a new earth. The former things will not be remembered, nor will they come to mind." Though this pronouncement is given in a context that refers to the Millennium, it is clear from Revelation 21–22 that the new heavens and new earth will not be created until after the old earth is destroyed. According to 2 Peter 3:10, "But the Day of the Lord will come like a thief. The heavens will disappear with a roar; the elements will be destroyed by fire, and the earth and everything in it will be laid bare." In verse 12 the statement is made, "That day will bring about the destruction of the heavens by fire, and the elements will melt in the heat." Since the present earth and heavens will be destroyed, believers "are looking forward to a new heaven and a new earth, the home of righteousness" (v. 13).

The creation of the new heavens and new earth will follow the destruction of the present heavens and earth. "Then I saw a new heaven and a new earth, for the first heaven and the first earth had passed away, and there was no longer any sea" (Rev. 21:1).

The few references to the new earth do not give much information except that it will not have any oceans. Because directions on the new earth are said to be north, south, east, and west in reference to the gates of the city of Jerusalem, it may be inferred that the new earth will be round as the only other alternative would be a flat earth which is out of keeping with anything known in the physical world today. Life on the new earth, however, was described in detail in verses 3-4, "And I heard a loud voice from the throne saying, 'Now the dwelling of God is with men, and He will live with them. They will be His people, and God Himself will be with them and be their God. He will wipe every tear from their eyes. There will be no more death or mourning or crying or pain, for the old order of things has passed away.' " The new earth will be the dwelling place of the saints of all ages who will have their home in the New Jerusalem.

THE DOCTRINE OF HEAVEN

Three distinct heavens are identified in Scripture. The first is that of the atmosphere about the earth in which are the birds and the clouds of heaven. The second is the world of planets and stars which is the abode of the angels. The third is the celestial realm where God abides in supreme glory. In the eternal state nothing is revealed about the new heavens except that no sun or moon will be there (Rev. 21:23). As the earth will be bathed in the glory of God and there will be no night, it would be useless to place stars in the heavens which could not be seen. As far as scriptural revelation is concerned, the glory of God will be seen supremely in the New Jerusalem.

The fact of heaven is supported by the testimony of Christ Himself who frequently spoke of it as the residence of God (Matt. 5:16, 34, 45; 6:1, 9-10, 20; 7:11, 21; 10:32-33; 11:25; 12:50; 16:17, 19; 18:10, 14, 18-19; 21:25; 23:9, 22; 24:35-36; 28:2, 18). The other Gospels and the epistles of Paul also refer to heaven as the dwelling place of God. In Revelation 4–5 John saw a revelation of heaven itself which may be compared to the revelation given in Daniel 7. In His ascension Christ returned to heaven (Acts 1:11).

Paul also confirmed the fact of heaven in 2 Corinthians 12:1-9 where he recorded his experience of being caught up into heaven which he equated with paradise (v. 4). Some believe this experience occurred when Paul was stoned at Lystra and was left for dead (Acts 14:19). Paul referred to being in heaven as being away from the body and being with the Lord (2 Cor. 5:8). Paul stated again that being in heaven is far better than being on earth (Phil. 1:23). Though he was not permitted to state what he saw in heaven (2 Cor. 12:4), he was nevertheless an experienced witness who could testify to the reality of heaven.

Additional testimony is given by the Apostle John who in Revelation 4 and 5 was translated to heaven either bodily or in a vision. He was permitted to record his experience in full in Revelation 4–5 as part of God's revelation of what will yet come to pass.

The Scriptures clearly reveal that heaven is far better than earth (2 Cor. 5:8; Phil. 1:23). In heaven the child of God will be made sinless and will be given a body similar to that of Christ's body (Rom. 8:29; Phil. 3:20-21; 1 John 3:1-3). Those who are saved in the present age form the new creation (2 Cor. 5:17) and as such are removed from their former racial significance of being either Jews or Gentiles and are made one in the body of Christ. When they will be in heaven their bodies will be transformed, their whole being will be conformed to Christ (1 John 3:2), and they will be forever with

Christ in glory (Col. 3:4; 1 Thes. 4:17).

Heaven is a suitable abode of God and His people. Though the present location of heaven will be changed when the New Jerusalem descends on the new earth, the people of God and the holy angels will all be with the Lord in the heavenly city of the New Jerusalem, which will be heaven because it is the place of God's abode.

Essential features are mentioned concerning heaven. It will be a place of abundant godly life (1 Tim. 4:8), and a place of rest (Rev. 14:13). In heaven believers will have increased knowledge (1 Cor. 13:8-10, 12), and all the saints will be holy as God is holy (Rev. 21:27). In heaven they will enjoy fulfillment by serving the Lord (22:3). An important part of the ministry of all created beings in heaven will be to give glory to God and worship Him (19:1). In comparison to believers' earthly existence their heavenly situation will be far more glorious (2 Cor. 4:17; Col. 3:4). The destiny of saints in heaven is based on their faith in God and Christ and their having partaken of the water of life (Rev. 22:17).

The presence of God is referred to as the third heaven in 2 Corinthians 12:2 in contrast to the atmospheric heaven and the starry heavens (Matt. 8:20; 13:32; 24:30; 26:64; Rev. 6:13).

The location of the third heaven, the home of the Triune God, is not specified in Scripture, but in eternity it will be the same as the New Jerusalem on the new earth. When believers die they go at once to be with Christ (2 Cor. 5:8; Phil. 1:23). At the end of the Millennium they will be with Him in the New Jerusalem.

The panorama of biblical truth revealed in prophecy is greater than can be comprehended by man in his present estate. The glory of the future world overshadows the glory of the present life. As heaven is above earth, the believer in Christ, rejoicing in the blessings which he now has in serving the Lord, can look forward with great anticipation to the blessed hope of Christ's return at the Rapture for His church and to the glorious events that will follow and eventually end with the New Jerusalem as the eternal home of the saints of all ages.

A believer in Scripture can only exclaim in keeping with the words of Paul the greatness of the revelation that God has given, "Oh, the depth of the riches of the wisdom and knowledge of God! How unsearchable His judgments, and His paths beyond tracing out! 'Who has known the mind of the Lord? Or who has been His counselor? Who has ever given to God, that God should repay him?'

For from Him and through Him and to Him are all things. To Him be the glory forever! Amen" (Rom. 11:33-36).

BIBLICAL INDEX

◆ **Genesis**

♦ Proverbs

♦ Isaiah

♦ Daniel

♦ Hosea

♦ Joel

♦ John

♦ Acts

♦ Romans

◆ 1 Corinthians

♦ 2 Corinthians

♦ **Galatians**

♦ **Ephesians**

♦ Philippians

♦ Colossians

♦ James

♦ 1 Peter

♦ 2 Peter

♦ 1 John

BIBLIOGRAPHY

Editors' Note: Inclusion of a systematic theology or other works in the Bibliography does not necessarily indicate approval of the contents by the editors, the publishers, or Dallas Theological Seminary. Works are included that are representative of various theological positions.

SELECTED READINGS IN SOTERIOLOGY

Aulen, Gustaf. *Christus Victor.* New York: Macmillan Co., 1951. Propounds the "dramatic" view of the Atonement.

Barth, Karl. *Church Dogmatics.* 5 vols. in 14. Edinburgh: T. & T. Clark, 1936-77. 4:1:3:3-156, 514-642. Neoorthodox.

Berkhouwer, G.C. *The Work of Christ.* Grand Rapids: Wm. B. Eerdmans Publishing Co., 1965. Modern Reformed.

_____. *Divine Election.* Grand Rapids: Wm. B. Eerdmans Publishing Co., 1960. Modern Reformed.

_____. *Faith and Perseverance.* Grand Rapids: Wm. B. Eerdmans Publishing Co., 1958. Modern Reformed.

Bloesch, Donald G. *Essentials of Evangelical Theology.* 2 vols. New York: Harper and Row, 1978-79. 1:148-252; 2:6-30. Neoevangelical.

Brunner, Emil. *Dogmatics.* 3 vols. Philadelphia: Westminster Press, 1950-62. 3:134-289. Neoorthodox.

Buis, H. *The Doctrine of Eternal Punishment.* Philadelphia: Presbyterian and Reformed Publishing Co., 1957. Conservative.

Buswell, J. Oliver. *A Systematic Theology of the Christian Religion.* 2 vols. Grand Rapids: Zondervan Publishing House, 1962-63. 2:70-215. Conservative, premillennial, covenant, Reformed.

Carter, Charles W., ed. *A Contemporary Wesleyan Theology.* 2 vols. Grand Rapids: Zondervan Publishing House, 1983. 1:473-520. Various conservative essays.

Chafer, Lewis Sperry. *Grace.* Wheaton, IL: VanKampen Press, 1922. Calvinistic, conservative, premillennial.

———. *Salvation.* Grand Rapids: Zondervan Publishing House, 1978. Calvinistic, conservative, premillennial.

Cobb, John. *Process Theology as Political Theology.* Philadelphia: Westminster Press, 1982. Process theology.

Cone, James H. *God of the Oppressed.* Minneapolis, MN: Seabury, 1975. pp. 138-62, 226-77. Black liberation.

Culpepper, Robert H. *Interpreting the Atonement.* Grand Rapids: Wm. B. Eerdmans Publishing Co., 1966. Conservative.

Douty, Norman. *The Death of Christ.* Swengel, PA: Reiner, 1972. Calvinist.

Ebeling, Gerhard. *The Nature of Faith.* Philadelphia: Fortress, 1962. Liberal.

Erickson, Millard J. *Christian Theology.* 3 vols. Grand Rapids: Baker Book House, 1983-85. 2:761-842 and 3:887-1024. Conservative, nondispensational, premillennial.

———, ed. *The New Life.* Grand Rapids: Baker Book House, 1979. pp. 15-158. Conservative, nondispensational, premillennial.

Green, Michael B. *The Meaning of Salvation.* Philadelphia: Westminster Press, 1965. Conservative.

Gromacki, Robert G. *Salvation Is Forever.* Chicago: Moody, 1973. Conservative.

Guitierrez, Gustavo. *A Theology of Liberation.* Maryknoll, NY: Orbis, 1973. pp. 145-88. Liberation theology.

Hodge, Charles. *Systematic Theology.* 2:313-34, 455-732. Reformed, postmillennial, conservative.

Hodges, Zane. *The Gospel under Siege.* Dallas, TX: Redencion Viva, 1981. Faith without works for assurance, premillennial, dispensational.

———. *Grace in Eclipse.* Dallas, TX: Redencion Viva, 1985. Premillennial, dispensational.

Hodgson, Leonard. *The Doctrine of the Atonement.* London: Nisbet, 1951. Conservative.

Horne, Charles M. *Doctrine of Salvation.* Chicago: Moody Press, 1984. Conservative.

Jones, E. Stanley. *Conversion.* New York: Abingdon Press, 1959. Psychology.

Kevan, Ernest F. *Salvation.* Grand Rapids: Wm. B. Eerdmans Publishing Co., 1963. Conservative.

Knox, John. *The Death of Christ.* New York: Abingdon Press, 1958. Liberal.

Kung, Hans. *Justification: The Doctrine of Karl Barth and a Catholic Reflection.* New York: Nelson, 1964. Modern Catholic.

Lightner, Robert. *The Death Christ Died: A Case for Unlimited Atonement.* Des Plaines, IL: Regular Baptist Press, 1967. Conservative, premillennial, dispensational.

____. *Heaven for Those Who Can't Believe.* Schaumburg, IL: Regular Baptist Press, 1977. On infants and the mentally ill. Conservative, premillennial, dispensational.

____. *Evangelical Theology.* pp. 185-215. Conservative, premillennial, dispensational.

McDonald, H.D. *The Atonement in the Death of Christ.* Grand Rapids: Baker Book House, 1985. Conservative.

____. *Salvation.* Westchester, IL: Crossway Books, 1982. Conservative.

Marshall, I. Howard. *Kept by the Power of God.* Minneapolis: Bethany Fellowship, 1969. Arminian, moderate conservative.

Morey, Robert A. *Death and the Afterlife.* Minneapolis: Bethany Fellowship, 1984. Conservative.

Morris, Leon. *The Apostolic Preaching of the Cross.* 3rd ed. Grand Rapids: Wm. B. Eerdmans Publishing Co., 1965. Conservative, amillennial.

____. *The Cross in the New Testament.* Grand Rapids: Wm. B. Eerdmans Publishing Co., 1965. Conservative, amillennial.

Murray, John. *Redemption Accomplished and Applied.* Grand Rapids: Wm. B. Eerdmans Publishing Co., 1955. Classical Reformed position.

Ogden, Schubert M. *On Theology.* San Francisco: Harper and Row, 1986. pp. 134-50. Process theology.

Packer, J.I. *Evangelism and the Sovereignty of God.* London: InterVarsity Press, 1961. Calvinist, conservative.

Pinnock, Clark, ed. *Grace Unlimited.* Minneapolis: Bethany Fellowship, 1975. Arminian, Conservative.

Pieper, Franz A.C. *Christian Dogmatics.* 4 vols. Saint Louis: Concordia Publishing, 1950-57. 2:397-557, 3:473-506. Traditional Lutheran, neo-orthodox.

Piper, John. *The Justification of God: An Exegetical and Theological Study of Romans 9:1-23.* Grand Rapids: Baker Book House, 1983. Calvinist.

Rahner, Karl. *Foundations of Christian Faith.* New York: Crossroad, 1982. pp. 116-37. Modern Catholic.

Ryrie, Charles C. *Basic Theology.* Wheaton, IL: Victor Books, 1986. pp. 275-342. Conservative, premillennial, dispensational.

_____. *The Grace of God.* Chicago: Moody Press, 1963. Conservative, premillennial, dispensational.

Seymour, R.A. *All About Repentance.* Hollywood, FL: Harvest House, 1974. Conservative.

Shank, R. *Elect in the Son.* Springfield, MO: Westcott Press, 1970. Arminian, conservative.

_____. *Life in the Son.* Springfield, MO: Westcott Press, 1960. Arminian, conservative.

Shedd, William G.T. *Dogmatic Theology.* 2:353-587, 3:401-70. Conservative, Calvinistic.

Steele, David N., and Curtis C. Thomas. *The Five Points of Calvinism.* Grand Rapids, Baker Book House, 1963. Conservative, Calvinistic.

Tillich, Paul. *Systematic Theology.* 3 vols. Chicago: University of Chicago, 1951-63. 2:118-82. Liberal.

Wallace, Ronald S. *The Atoning Death of Christ.* Westchester, IL: Crossway Books, 1981. Conservative.

Wells, David. *The Search for Salvation.* Downers Grove, IL: InterVarsity Press, 1978. Conservative.

Whale, J.S. *Victor and Victim.* London: Cambridge, 1960. Liberal.

Woodson, Leslie H. *Hell and Salvation.* Old Tappan, NJ: Fleming H. Revell Co., 1973. Conservative.

Ziesler, J.A. *The Meaning of Righteousness in Paul.* Cambridge: Cambridge University Press, 1972. Technical support of forensic justification.

SELECTED READINGS IN ECCLESIOLOGY

Barth, Karl. *Dogmatics.* 4:3:2, 4:4 also 4:1, sec. 62; 4:2, sec. 67. Neoorthodox.

Beasely-Murray, G.R. *Baptism in the New Testament.* Grand Rapids: Wm. B. Eerdmans Publishing Co., 1962. Traditional Baptist.

Berkhouwer, G.C. *The Church.* Grand Rapids: Wm. B. Eerdmans Publishing Co., 1976. Modern Reformed, neoorthodox.

____. *Faith and Sanctification.* Grand Rapids: Wm. B. Eerdmans Publishing Co., 1952. Modern Reformed, neoorthodox.

____. *The Sacraments.* Grand Rapids: Wm. B. Eerdmans Publishing Co., 1969. Modern Reformed, neoorthodox.

Bloesch, Donald G. *Theology.* 2:104-54. Neoevangelical.

Bridge, Donald, and David Phypers. *The Water That Divides.* Downers Grove, IL: InterVarsity Press, 1977. Two viewpoints, conservative.

Bromiley, Geoffrey. *Children of Promise.* Grand Rapids: Wm. B. Eerdmans Publishing Co., 1979. Infant baptism, conservative.

Brown, Harold O.J. *The Protest of a Troubled Protestant.* Grand Rapids: Zondervan Publishing House, 1970. Anti-ecumenical.

Brown, Robert McAffee. *The Ecumenical Revolution: an Interpretation of the Catholic-Protestant Dialogue.* New York: Doubleday, 1967. Protestant friendly to Roman Catholicism.

Brunner, Heinrich Emil. *Dogmatics.* 3:3-133. Neoorthodox.

Buswell, J. Oliver. *Systematic Theology* 2:216-84. Conservative, premillennial, covenant, Reformed.

Carter, Charles W., ed. *A Contemporary Wesleyan Theology.* 2:571-628.

Various conservative essays.

Cooke, Bernard. *Ministry to Word and Sacraments.* Philadelphia: Fortress, 1976. Modern Catholic.

Congar, Yves. *The Mystery of the Church.* 2nd rev. ed. Baltimore: Helicon Press, 1965. Catholic.

Dieter, Melvin R., *et al. Five Views on Sanctification.* Grand Rapids: Academic Books, 1987. Conservative options.

Douglas, J.D., ed. *Let the Earth Hear His Voice.* Minneapolis: World Wide Publications, 1975. Conservative missions response to ecumenism.

Dulles, Avery. *Models of the Church.* New York: Doubleday, 1974. Liberal.

Eliade, Mircea. *The Sacred and the Profane.* New York: Harcourt, Brace & World, 1959. Liberal.

Erickson, Millard J. *Christian Theology.* 3:1025-148. Conservative, nondispensational, premillennial.

____, ed. *The New Life.* Grand Rapids: Baker Book House, 1979. pp. 253-412. Conservative, premillennial.

Farley, Edward, *Ecclesial Man: A Social Phenomenology of Faith and Reality.* Philadelphia: Fortress, 1975. Liberal/sociological.

Fletcher, Joseph. *Situation Ethics.* Philadelphia: Westminster, 1966. Liberal.

Frankena, William. *Ethics.* 2nd ed. Englewood Cliffs, NJ: Prentice-Hall, 1973. Secular philosophy.

Geisler, Norman. *Options in Contemporary Christian Ethics.* Grand Rapids: Baker Book House, 1981. Conservative.

Getz, Gene A. *Measure of a Church.* Glendale, CA: G/L Regal Books, 1975. Conservative church renewal, premillennial.

____. *Sharpening the Focus of the Church.* Wheaton, IL: Victor Books, 1984. Conservative options.

Guitierrez, Gustavo. *A Theology of Liberation.* pp. 251-86. Liberation theology.

Henry, Carl F.H. *Christian Personal Ethics.* Grand Rapids: Baker Book House, 1977. Conservative, premillennial.

Jackson, Paul Rainey. *Doctrine and Administration of the Church.* Rev. ed. Schaumburg, IL: Regular Baptist Press, 1980. Traditional Baptist.

Jay, Eric. G. *The Church: Its Changing Image through Twenty Centuries.* 2 vols. London: SPCK, 1977-78. Historical survey.

Jewett, Paul K. *Infant Baptism and the Covenant of Grace.* Grand Rapids: Wm. B. Eerdmans Publishing Co., 1978. Pro-infant baptism, neo-orthodox.

Kavanagh, Aidan. *The Shape of Baptism: The Rite of Christian Initiation.* New York: Pueblo, 1978. Catholic.

Knox, John. *The Ethics of Jesus in the Teaching of the Church.* New York: Abingdon, 1961. Liberal.

Kung, Hans. *The Church.* New York: Sheed and Ward, 1968. Modern Catholic.

Lightner, Robert. *Church Union.* Des Plaines, IL: Regular Baptist Press, 1971. Anti-ecumenism.

Lutzer, Erwin. *The Necessity of Ethical Absolutes.* Grand Rapids: Zondervan Publishing House, 1981. Conservative, premillennial.

MacGregor, Geddes. *Corpus Christi: The Nature of the Church according to the Reformed Tradition.* Philadelphia: Westminster Press, 1958. Reformed.

McIntire, Carl. *Servants of Apostasy.* Haddenfield, NJ: Christian Beacon Press, 1955. Anti-ecumenical, conservative.

Marshall, I. Howard. *Last Supper and Lord's Supper.* Grand Rapids: Wm. B. Eerdmans Publishing Co., 1980. Amillennial.

Moltmann, Jurgen. *The Church in the Power of the Spirit.* London: SCM Press, 1977. Liberal.

Montgomery, John Warwick. *Ecumenicity, Evangelicals and Rome.* Grand Rapids: Zondervan Publishing House, 1969. Anti-ecumenical, conservative.

Moody, Dale. *The Word of Truth.* Grand Rapids: Wm. B. Eerdmans Publishing Co., 1981. pp. 427-80. Baptist, neoorthodox.

Mooneyham, W. Stanley, ed. *The Dynamics of Christian Unity.* Grand Rapids: Zondervan Publishing House, 1963. NAE essays.

Moule, Charles F.D. *Worship in the New Testament.* London: Lutterworth, 1961. Moderating.

Needham, David C. *Birthright.* Portland, OR: Multnomah Press, 1979. Conservative, new approach to sanctification.

Niebuhr, H.R. *Christ and Culture.* New York: Harper & Row, 1951. Neoorthodox.

Neuner, J. and J. Dupuis, eds. *The Christian Faith in the Doctrinal Documents of the Catholic Church.* pp. 213-72, 335-522. Roman Catholic.

Pieper, Franz. *Christian Dogmatics.* 3:104-472. Traditional Lutheran, neoorthodox.

Radmacher, Earl D. *What the Church Is All About.* Chicago: Moody Press, 1972. Conservative, premillennial, dispensational.

Rahner, Karl. *Foundations of Christian Faith.* New York: Crossroad, 1982. pp. 322-430. Modern Catholic.

Rentorff, Fritz. *Church and Theology.* Philadelphia: Westminster, 1971. Neoorthodox.

Richards, Larry. *New Face for the Church.* Grand Rapids: Zondervan Publishing House, 1970. Church renewal, conservative.

Rusch, William. *Ecumenism: A Movement toward Church Unity.* Philadelphia: Fortress, 1985. Pro-ecumenism.

Ryrie, Charles C. *Balancing the Christian Life.* Chicago: Moody Press, 1969. Conservative, premillennial, dispensational.

———. *Basic Theology.* pp. 391-438. Conservative, premillennial, dispensational.

Saucy, Robert. *The Church in God's Program.* Chicago: Moody Press, 1972. Dispensational, premillennial.

Schaeffer, Francis. *Church at the End of the Twentieth Century.* Downers Grove, IL: InterVarsity Press, 1970. Conservative, premillennial.

Schlink, Edmund. *The Doctrine of Baptism.* St. Louis: Concordia Publishing House, 1972. Lutheran, amillennial.

Schweizer, Eduard. *The Church as the Body of Christ.* Atlanta: John Knox, 1964. Moderating.

____. *Church Order in the New Testament.* Naperville, IL: Allenson, 1961. Moderating.

Thielicke, Helmut. *The Evangelical Faith.* 2:199-300. Modern Lutheran.

Webber, R.E. *The Church in the World.* Grand Rapids: Zondervan Publishing House, 1986. Conservative.

Welch, Claude. *The Reality of the Church.* New York: Charles Scribner's Sons, 1958. Liberal.

White, Jerry. *The Church and the Parachurch: An Uneasy Marriage.* Portland, OR: Multnomah Press, 1983. Conservative.

SELECTED READINGS IN ESCHATOLOGY

Adams, Jay. *The Time Is at Hand.* Nutley, NJ: Presbyterian and Reformed Publishing Co., 1973. Amillennial, conservative.

Alves, Rubem. *A Theology of Human Hope.* Washington, D.C.: Corpus Books, 1969. Liberation theology.

Archer, Gleason; Paul Feinberg; Douglas Moo; Richard Reiter. *The Rapture: Pre-, Mid- or Post-tribulational?* Grand Rapids: Wm. B. Eerdmans Publishing Co., 1984. Premillennial, conservative.

Barth, Karl. *Church Dogmatics.* 4:3:2:902-42. Neoorthodox.

Beasley-Murray, George. *Jesus and the Kingdom of God.* Grand Rapids: Wm. B. Eerdmans Publishing Co., 1985. Conservative amillennial refutation of liberal ideas.

Beechick, Allen. *The Pre-Tribulational Rapture.* Denver: Accent Books, 1980. Pretribulational.

Berkouwer, G.C. *The Return of Christ.* Grand Rapids: Wm. B. Eerdmans Publishing Co., 1972. Modern Reformed.

Blackstone, W.E. *Jesus Is Coming.* New York: Fleming H. Revell Co., 1898. Pretribulational, premillennial.

Bloesch, Donald G. *Evangelical Theology.* 2:174-234. Neoevangelical.

Boettner, Lorraine. *The Millennium.* Philadelphia: Presbyterian and Reformed Publishing Co., 1957. Postmillennial, conservative.

Braaten, Carl E. *Eschatology and Ethics.* Minneapolis: Augsburg, 1974. Modern Lutheran.

Bright, John. *The Kingdom of God.* New York: Abingdon, 1953. Neoorthodox.

Brunner, Emil. *Dogmatics.* 3:339-445. Neoorthodox.

Buis, Harry. *The Doctrine of Eternal Punishment.* Philadelphia: Presbyterian and Reformed Publishing Co., 1957. Reformed.

Bultmann, Rudolf. *History and Eschatology.* New York: Harper, 1957. Liberal.

Buswell, J. Oliver. *Systematic Theology.* 2:295-553. Conservative, premillennial, covenant, Reformed.

Carter, Charles W., ed. *A Contemporary Wesleyan Theology.* 2:1099-140. Various conservative essays.

Chilton, David. *Paradise Restored.* Tyler, TX: Reconstruction Press, 1985. Postmillennial.

Clouse, Robert, ed. *The Meaning of the Millennium.* Downers Grove, IL: InterVarsity Press, 1977. Conservative options.

Cobb, John. *Process Theology as Political Theology.* Philadelphia: Westminster Press, 1982. pp. 65-82. Process theology.

Cox, William E. *Amillennialism Today.* Philadelphia: Presbyterian and Reformed Publishing Co., 1966. Amillennial.

Cullman, Oscar. *Christ and Time.* rev. ed. Philadelphia: Westminster Press, 1964. Liberal.

Eliade, Mircea. *Cosmos and History: The Myth of Eternal Return.* New York: Harper and Brothers, 1959. Liberal.

Erickson, Millard J. *Christian Theology.* 3:1149-242. Conservative, nondispensational, premillennial.

———. *Contemporary Options in Eschatology.* Grand Rapids: Baker Book House, 1977. Survey, conservative, nondispensational, premillennial.

———, ed. *The New Life.* pp. 413-524. Conservative, nondispensational, premillennial.

Froom, Leroy Edwin. *The Prophetic Faith of Our Fathers.* 4 vols. Washington, D.C.: Review and Herald, 1950-54. Seventh-Day Adventist, amillennial.

Fuller, Daniel. *Gospel and Law: Contrast or Continuum? The Hermeneutics of Dispensationalism and Covenant Theology.* Grand Rapids: Wm. B. Eerdmans Publishing Co., 1980. Anti-dispensational, anti-covenant theology, amillennial.

Gromacki, Robert. *Are These the Last Days?* Old Tappan, NJ: Fleming H. Revell Co., 1970. Premillennial.

Gundry, Robert H. *The Church and the Tribulation.* Grand Rapids: Zondervan Publishing House, 1973. Posttribulational, premillennial.

Guitierrez, Gustavo. *A Theology of Liberation.* pp. 213-50. Liberation theology.

Harris, Murray. *Raised Immortal: Resurrection and Immortality in the New Testament.* Grand Rapids: Wm. B. Eerdmans Publishing Co., 1983. Conservative.

Hick, John. *Death and Eternal Life.* New York: Harper and Row, 1976. Liberal.

Hoekema, Anthony. *The Bible and the Future.* Grand Rapids: Wm. B. Eerdmans Publishing Co., 1979. Reformed amillennial.

Hoyt, Herman A. *The End Times.* Chicago: Moody Press, 1969. Premillennial.

LaRondelle, Hans K. *Israel of God in Prophecy.* Berrien Springs, Mich.: Andrews, 1983. Anti-dispensational, Seventh-Day Adventist.

Kik, Marcellus. *Revelation 20.* Philadelphia: Presbyterian and Reformed Publishing Co., 1955. Postmillennial, conservative.

Kummel, W.G. *Promise and Fulfillment.* Naperville, IL: Allenson, 1957. Liberal.

Ladd, George. *The Blessed Hope.* Grand Rapids: Wm. B. Eerdmans Publishing Co., 1956. Posttribulational, premillennial.

____. *Jesus and the Kingdom.* New York: Harper and Row, 1964. Posttribulational, premillennial.

Lightner, Robert. *Evangelical Theology.* Conservative, premillennial, dispensational.

Lundstrom, Gosta. *The Kingdom of God in the Teaching of Jesus.* Richmond: Knox, 1963. Liberal survey.

McClain, Alva J. *The Greatness of the Kingdom.* Grand Rapids: Zondervan Publishing House, 1959. Premillennial, dispensational.

Martin, James. *The Last Judgment in Protestant Theology from Orthodoxy to Ritschl.* Grand Rapids: Wm. B. Eerdmans Publishing Co., 1963. Critical of systematic theology.

Mason, Clarence E. *Prophetic Problems.* Chicago: Moody Press, 1973. Premillennial, dispensational.

Moltmann, Jurgen. *Theology of Hope.* New York: Harper and Row, 1967. Liberal.

Moore, A.L. *The Parousia in the New Testament.* Leiden: E.J. Brill, 1966. Conservative.

Pannenberg, Wolfhart. *Theology and the Kingdom of God.* Philadelphia: Westminster, 1969. Moderating to liberal.

Payne, J. Barton. *The Imminent Appearing of Christ.* Grand Rapids: Wm. B. Eerdmans Publishing Co., 1962. Posttribulational, premillennial.

Pentecost, J. Dwight. *Things to Come.* Findlay, OH: Dunham Books, 1958. Premillennial, dispensational.

Perrin, Norman. *The Kingdom of God in the Teaching of Jesus.* London: SCM, 1963. Liberal.

Peters, George N.H. *Theocratic Kingdom.* 3 vols. Grand Rapids: Kregel Publications, 1952. Premillennial.

Pieper, Francis. *Christian Dogmatics.* 3:507-55. Traditional Lutheran.

Rahner, Karl. *Foundations of Christian Faith.* pp. 431-47. Modern Roman Catholic.

Ribberbos, Herman. *The Coming of the Kingdom.* Philadelphia: Presbyterian and Reformed Publishing Co., 1962. Postmillennial, conservative.

Ryrie, Charles C. *Basic Theology.* pp. 437-522. Conservative, premillennial, dispensational.

——. *Dispensationalism Today.* Chicago: Moody Press, 1965. Dispensational, premillennial.

____. *The Basis of the Premillennial Truth.* New York: Loizeaux Brothers, 1953. Dispensational, premillennial.

____. *The Final Countdown.* Wheaton, IL: Victor Books, 1982. Dispensational, premillennial.

____. *What You Should Know about the Rapture.* Chicago: Moody Press, 1981. Dispensational, premillennial.

Schnackenburg, Rudolf. *God's Rule and Kingdom.* New York: Herder and Herder, 1963. Modern Catholic.

Shedd, William G.T. *Dogmatic Theology.* 2:591-754, 3:471-528. Calvinistic, postmillennial, conservative.

Smith, Wilbur M. *The Biblical Outline of Heaven.* Chicago: Moody Press, 1968. Premillennial, conservative.

Stendahl, Krister, ed. *Immortality and Resurrection.* New York: Macmillan, 1965. Four liberal essays.

Tan, Paul Lee. *The Interpretation of Prophecy.* Winona Lake, IN: BHB Books, 1974. Conservative, premillennial.

Thielicke, Helmut. *The Evangelical Faith.* 2:377-466. Modern Lutheran.

Tillich, Paul. *Systematic Theology.* 3:297-426. Liberal, neoorthodox.

Travis, Stephen H. *Christian Hope and the Future.* Downers Grove, IL: InterVarsity Press, 1980. Amillennial, conservative.

Walvoord, John F. *The Blessed Hope and the Tribulation.* Grand Rapids: Zondervan Publishing House, 1976. Pretribulational refutation of Gundry.

____. *The Millennial Kingdom.* Findlay, OH: Dunham Books, 1959. Moderate Calvinist, premillennial, dispensational.

____. *The Rapture Question.* Revised and enlarged ed. Grand Rapids: Zondervan Publishing House, 1979. Moderate Calvinist, premillennial, dispensational.

Wood, Leon. *The Bible and Future Events.* Grand Rapids: Zondervan Publishing House, 1973. Premillennial.